the
UNDERSIDE
of American History: Other Readings

THIRD EDITION

VOLUME II: since 1865

Edited by
THOMAS R. FRAZIER
The Bernard M. Baruch College of The City University of New York

Under the General Editorship of
JOHN MORTON BLUM
Yale University

HARCOURT BRACE JOVANOVICH, INC.
New York   San Diego   Chicago   San Francisco   Atlanta

To the
Stewart A. Newman family

ISBN: 0-15-592848-1

Library of Congress Catalog Card Number: 77-91913

Printed in the United States of America

Page 388 constitutes a continuation of the copyright page.

Preface

The past two decades have seen a rising tide of protest from segments of American society that have felt themselves excluded from the American dream. Neither the protest nor the exclusion is new, however. From the beginning of New World settlement, the benefits reaped from development have been unequally distributed. Historians of America, for the most part, have only recently begun to deal in any satisfactory manner with the causes and consequences of this inequity. Traditional history textbooks have tended to smooth out the past to give a picture of gradual but steady change, suggesting that Americans are a single people with a clear common goal that they are progressively achieving. The protest of the 1960s, however, shattered that consensus, as the untold history—the "underside" of American life—emerged to challenge and disturb the nation.

The Underside of American History, Third Edition, presents a selection of nontraditional readings in American history and is intended to supplement existing textbooks. The first two editions dealt with a variety of groups in American society, among them American Indians, blacks, women, East Asian immigrants, poor whites, Mexican-Americans, children, and industrial workers. This third edition, in which over half of the selections are new, continues the concerns of the first two editions, adding such topics as the elderly, working-class culture, ecological disaster, migrant farm workers, and frontier violence. This collection points out that many of the problems of America today have existed since the nation's beginning, and it suggests that until some creative resolutions of the inequities of American life are found, conflict, stress, and repression will continue to characterize much of American society.

The articles in this collection are arranged in roughly chronological order: Volume I begins with the colonial period and continues through Reconstruction, and Volume II covers mainly the period between Reconstruction and the present. Each volume contains a general introduction presenting the major themes to be taken up in the readings. In addition, each selection is introduced by a brief headnote that places the

selection in historical context and explains its significance. Annotated
bibliographies, with books available in paperback marked by an asterisk,
close each of the collection's major sections. And for the instructor's
convenience, a test booklet on the two volumes is also available.

I gratefully acknowledge the advice and assistance of the following
historians: Carol Ruth Berkin of Baruch College of the City University of
New York, Stanley Buder of Baruch College of the City University of
New York, Mary Beth Norton of Cornell University, Paula Fass of the
University of California at Berkeley, Laurence Veysey of the University
of California at Santa Cruz, Daniel Walkowitz of Rutgers University, and
Gary Nash of the University of California at Los Angeles.

THOMAS R. FRAZIER

Contents

The Early Twentieth Century 2 *104*

Depression 3 and War *200*

Contents

Postwar 4 America

Introduction

To introduce the following readings, it may be helpful to provide a brief sketch of the aspects of post–Civil War American history with which they deal. As in Volume I of *The Underside of American History*, Third Edition, the selections printed here seek to redress an imbalance that is found in many textbooks and books of readings. The emphasis here is on material either left out or treated insufficiently in the standard works. The purpose is not to present a balanced view of the past but to fill in some of the gaps. Therefore, the readings found here must be considered in a larger context to avoid excessive distortion. They do, however, present an essential part of the whole, and must be considered in any attempt to gain a comprehensive picture of the American past.

In the Northern view, the Civil War was a struggle not only to secure the Union but also to abolish slavery permanently. With Northern victory over the rebellious Southerners, the United States government won an opportunity to reorganize American political and economic life so that the egalitarian ideas expressed in the Declaration of Independence would extend to the lives of blacks as well as whites. And, indeed, federal legislation in the decade after 1865 held out considerable promise for the future of the democracy: the Thirteenth Amendment ended slavery or involuntary servitude within the United States; the Freedmen's Bureau was created to provide Southern blacks with services of various types; universal male suffrage was established; and federal authority was used in attempts to nullify the various "black codes" by which Southern states sought to restrict the lives of the freedmen as they had restricted the lives of the slaves. However, federal concern for the civil rights of the freedmen soon gave way to growing public sentiment for conciliation of the South. Reaction to the deprivation of the war years and to the unprecedented federal intervention in states' affairs during the Reconstruction period worked again to deprive Southern blacks of federal protection, leaving them at the mercy of political opportunists and deeply embittered Southern whites. By 1877, when the last of the Reconstruction governments collapsed, control over the South had passed back into the hands of local officials. National unity had been restored, but only at the cost of

1

forcing the freed blacks back into positions of political and economic dependence. For the most part, sharecroppers replaced slaves, and ownership of the large plantations shifted from the planters of the old aristocracy to the prospering businessmen in the cities and towns.

In the last quarter of the nineteenth century, the moral fiber of the nation appeared to disintegrate completely. Fraud and corruption characterized the post-Reconstruction governments in the South, and the politics of the boss-controlled Northern cities were no better. The nation as a whole embarked on a course of unabashed materialism that was to earn the postwar decades the label "the Gilded Age," a term supplied by Mark Twain. As industrial capitalism took root in the United States, the world of business defined a new elite and a new ethic, and private interests assumed a large measure of control over public policy. "Laissez faire," or "let alone"—the very opposite of the philosophy that had prevailed during the brief Reconstruction period—became the watchword of the age, with disastrous results for the traditionally oppressed groups of Americans—the freedmen, Indians, laborers, and immigrants—for the sprawling cities, and for the land itself, which was heedlessly exploited. Laissez faire philosophy was written into new state constitutions, reviving the doctrine of states' rights. And rigid segregation as well as systematic disfranchisement proceeded apace in the South. The convict-lease system, by which law enforcement authorities hired out prisoners to plantation owners, and laws governing contract labor and "vagrancy" operated in the interest of the powerful Southern whites, with the result that most blacks were reduced to virtual serfdom by the end of the century.

In the postwar years, the theory of social Darwinism, an application of the theory of evolution to society, provided a new rationale for the idea of white supremacy. Adherents to this philosophy held that certain natural laws operated to destroy the elements of society that were least fit for survival. Thus, in the view of the social Darwinists, the best means of improving society was to let nature take its course—to allow competitive struggle to purify civilization in the slow process of social evolution. Running parallel to social Darwinism and based on equally dubious historical and scientific research were new racial theories asserting the superiority of the Anglo-Saxon and his institutions. The term "Anglo-Saxon" replaced the term "Protestant English" as the designation of the self-conscious racial elite in the United States, and a cult of Anglo-Saxon (or Teutonic, or Aryan, or Nordic) supremacy developed among the upper classes of the East as well as among whites of the South. Antiblack racism, which had existed for centuries in the New World (as well as in the Old World), was now provided with "scientific" underpinnings, as was prejudice against the Irish, Central and Southern Europeans (who were mostly Catholics or Jews), East Asians, and all other ethnic, racial, or religious groups who could not easily be assimilated into white Protestant culture.

Late in the nineteenth century, the new racism was put to the service of imperialism. The "white man's burden" was seen as the need to extend his civilization over all the world, and the old doctrine of Manifest Destiny was revived to justify the new interest in extraterritorial expansion. "Scientific" racism increased sentiment for the restriction of immigration until, in the first decade of the twentieth century, Congress effectively ended Chinese and Japanese immigration to this country. Furthermore, the racist ideology fueled antiblack feeling to the point that both rural and urban blacks across the country faced the constant threat of personal violence. As racist concepts fermented in both the North and the South, the first years of the twentieth century were perhaps the worst since the Civil War for American blacks. Between 1889 and 1918, more than two thousand blacks were murdered by white lynch mobs. So pervasive was the climate of violence in those years that white mobs lynched over seven hundred whites as well.

The Gilded Age was also a dark period in the history of American labor. The last two decades of the nineteenth century brought rapid economic expansion and increasing mechanization. Yet as industrialization progressed, the plight of urban laborers worsened. Child and convict labor were exploited, employers commonly used wage cuts and layoffs to increase profits, working weeks grew longer, and working conditions became ever harsher and more dangerous. The few national trade unions that had existed since the Civil War largely excluded blacks and immigrants; in any case, they protected only skilled craftsmen. Moreover, there was no federal legislation to protect factory workers. When in desperation these workers attempted to organize to improve their position, they met concerted resistance from factory owners, who sometimes hired private armies to thwart attempts at unionization. Especially during depressions, disputes between labor and capital tended to erupt into violence, and the number of strikes and lockouts soared. By the end of the century, the American Federation of Labor, stressing practical, economic goals rather than the moral or political aims of its predecessors, had successfully united the more conservative craft unions in a national body. Industrial unionism, however, was not really successful until the Second World War, after a concerted campaign for organization in the mass-production industries finally won management recognition of the unions' right to bargain on behalf of their members.

Throughout the Gilded Age, powerful forces—including Protestantism and capitalism—fought to maintain the status quo. Yet there were strong dissident elements in American society, continuing the domestic tradition of social and political radicalism first expressed by the authors of the Declaration of Independence. As refugees from the failed republican and socialist revolutions of mid-nineteenth-century Europe came to the United States in search of a more receptive climate for their doctrines of social change, they reinforced the ranks of dissidents. Toward the end of the nineteenth century, socialists, communists, anarchists, and radicals of various convictions played leading roles in a variety of new movements and political parties that challenged the ideas and policies of the dominant groups in American life. Indeed, from colonial times to the present, radical ideas have given many Americans a vision of a more humane world than that produced by the uncontrolled competition of capitalism.

Populism, one protest movement of the turbulent 1890s, marked an important attempt to draw the groups most urgently in need of social and governmental reform—especially black and white farm laborers and industrial workers—into a single movement. Though the movement in itself made no significant gains, it paved the way for a new era of reform that opened with the twentieth century.

Progressivism, the new reform movement, grew out of a widespread recognition of the need to reassess and adjust American economic and political institutions. Spearheaded by President Theodore Roosevelt, the new movement reflected the energy of renewed prosperity and apparent stability. Generally, the Progressives' goal in politics was to return the government at its various levels to the people. This called for breaking up the political machines that dominated municipal, state, and national government. In economics, the Progressives called for breaking up the large industrial and financial combines—trusts, cartels, and other business coalitions—that had a stranglehold on the American economy and virtually owned the United States Senate.

Though in theory this movement was a reassertion of traditional democratic principles, it failed to take any real steps toward bringing the ethnic and religious minorities in America into the mainstream of American life. Indeed, the progressive movement was based squarely on America's comfortable and growing white urban middle class, and progressive ideas reflected the self-interest and the biases of this acknowledged elite. The white middle class tended to link the corruption of the cities with blacks and immigrants, especially after the large movement of Catholic and Jewish immigrants into Northern cities in the first decade of the twentieth century. Not incidentally, some of the political machines attacked by the Progressives were made up of immigrant groups that had formed voting blocs in an attempt to secure a voice in American government after normal routes to political power were closed to them.

In fact, the years in which Progressive ideas met their greatest triumphs were also years of some of the most violent social disruptions and the most oppressive governmental activity of this century. The administration of President Woodrow Wilson reversed a long-standing national policy against racial segregation of federal office workers. The Ku Klux Klan, which had originated in the South immediately after the Civil War, was revived in 1915 and was active for over a decade not only in the South but in Northern cities, where it attacked blacks, Catholics, Jews, and "aliens" generally. Violent race riots exploded in the North and the South, culminating in the bloody summer of 1919. Both laborers and immigrants were increasingly suspected of radicalism, and radicalism was increasingly associated with the "red menace." Government suppression of assumed radicals reached mammoth proportions at the end of the First World War, when, during the Red Scare of 1919 and 1920, thousands of people were arrested on dubious charges of subversion and sedition and many innocent immigrants were deported. Fear and resentment of immigrants reached such heights that in the 1920s Congress halted virtually all immigration from countries outside Western Europe. The much contested, unenforceable Prohibition Amendment of 1919 was perhaps indicative of the Progressives' rather naive faith in moral legislation as the solution to social ills.

On the positive side, the Progressives undertook several significant and useful reforms that moved state and city governments closer to the ideal of representative government. Also, they generally supported the goals of organized labor, thereby bringing about industrial labor reforms that were long overdue.

Perhaps more dramatically, the Progressives provided influential support for the women's suffrage movement, which had made little headway since the first women's rights convention in 1848. Ironically, by the time the feminists won the vote with the Nineteenth Amendment of 1920, the women's movement had split into so many factions that the new vote had little effect on existing social, economic, or political policy. Rather, most of the feminists came from the white middle class and voted in the interest of that group, reflecting the bias of the Progressives in general.

The 1920s were years of regression, as Americans, wearied by the First World War and disappointed with the results of the reform efforts of the preceding two decades, focused again on private interests. The government went a step beyond laissez faire to adopt a protective attitude toward business, and there was a resurgence of elitism among white Protestant Americans. Continued prosperity seemed to confirm the conviction of middle-class America that business was an agent of the general good. Yet the 1920s rivaled the Gilded Age as a period of corrupt political and financial operations. During these years, even the gains made by labor since the beginning of the century were all but nullified, as public opinion, political power, and even the United States courts sided with management in labor disputes arising from the disparity between wage increases and rising profits and the rising cost of living.

Throughout the 1920s' return to "normalcy," most of the structural problems of society were either ignored or expected to disappear with increasing affluence. What went largely unnoticed beyond the nation's farms was the fact that a serious agricultural depression was in progress, and that the slogans of good health and prosperity would mean nothing when the bubble of economic stability burst. Burst it did. With the crash of 1929, not only the United States but the entire Western world was plunged into the deepest and most far-reaching depression of modern times.

The Depression affected almost everyone in the country. Despite federal attempts to protect banks and industry, the bottom fell out of the American stock market. Thousands fell from prosperity as a result of their own financial speculations. As investment and private spending dropped, many businesses were forced to shut down, causing widespread unemployment among both white-collar and industrial workers. Urban America was hard hit, but the nation's agricultural workers, whose position in the economy had been declining since the early twenties, suffered most from the economic collapse.

In the South most farm laborers, black and white, still worked as tenant farmers or sharecroppers, and foreclosures began adding to the numbers of tenants and migrants. These workers had virtually no economic or political power, though they often constituted a majority in their political jurisdictions. As farm prices went down and the federal government launched no positive program for control, agricultural laborers found themselves increasingly helpless, and violence flared up in rural America. Desperate workers attempted to organize to force aid from the landlords and the local political establishments, who were usually the same people. On the West Coast, migrant workers, many of foreign origin, also sought to protect themselves by banding together. However, most attempts at organization faltered before the joint opposition of landowners and law enforcement authorities. To this day, farm laborers—largely unorganized—remain one of the most depressed segments of the American working class. And, since the closing years of the Depression, federal attempts to aid agriculture have consisted primarily of granting government subsidies to the landlords without requiring that a just portion be passed along to the workers—a pattern that only reinforces the existing inequities.

The coming of the Second World War finally enabled the United States to recover from the Depression. The decision of the Roosevelt administration to supply war materiel for the Allies gave a spurt to American industry, and, with America's entry into the war in 1941, most of the nation's unemployment problems temporarily disappeared because of the demands of a wartime economy.

At the same time, the coming of war led to one of the most repressive acts in the history of American government—the arbitrary arrest and imprisonment of over 100,000 resident aliens and American citizens of Japanese ancestry. For several years these prisoners were kept in concentration camps in the nation's interior, while their property was confiscated without due process of law. The fact that German-Americans were not subjected to the same kind of treatment, even though many of them had openly supported the Nazi regime during the early years of the European war, testifies to the continued tendency of the dominant powers in America to discriminate against nonwhite minorities.

Probably never before or never since have the American people been as unified as they were during the Second World War. The pressures of the war economy brought industrial unions increased recognition and bargaining power, yet labor-management conflicts were few. Once the war was well under way, most Americans closed ranks in order to win it. In 1945, the atom bomb finally brought the war to a close, and those who had supported the Allied struggle for freedom abroad expected to share in the fruits of victory at home. Members of all minority groups had participated in the war, many nonwhites in segregated military units. Back in civilian life, they were unwilling to settle again for the second-class citizenship that had been forced upon them before the war. Especially in Northern cities, renewed racial unrest began to signal the presence of the volcano that was to erupt so visibly in the 1960s.

During and after the Second World War, American blacks won a series of minor victories in the area of civil rights. Under President Roosevelt, racial discrimination in the civil service and in the defense industry was curtailed somewhat, and in 1948 President Truman issued an executive order that officially ended segregation in the armed forces. Action in federal courts brought gains in the areas of voting rights and property ownership. With respect to public facilities, federal courts still upheld the "separate but equal" principle enunciated by the Supreme Court in 1896, but they at last seemed determined to see that separate facilities were truly equal.

Finally, in 1954, the civil rights movement won a major victory with a Supreme Court decision reversing the "separate but equal" doctrine by declaring segregated public schools inherently unequal. Although the federal government did little to implement the ruling—indeed, President Eisenhower opposed forced desegregation—minority groups in America began to feel renewed confidence in the regular political processes of the nation. Blacks of North and South as well as liberal whites joined in direct-action campaigns aimed at securing full citizenship rights for the minority groups of America, and leaders such as Martin Luther King emerged to champion nonviolent resistance to discrimination of all types.

The optimism of the late 1950s and early 1960s was shortlived, however, and by 1964 most nonwhite groups in America had ceased looking to Washington, to the courts, or even to sympathetic whites for assistance in their struggle. Legal victories had proved hollow for the masses of nonwhites, who were still virtually powerless economically and politically, and racism still pervaded white society. Now new leaders such as Malcolm X urged nonwhites to free themselves from white domination by any means possible—by revolution, if necessary. Oppressed groups of Americans increasingly repudiated the philosophy of nonviolent coercion, and a new string of uprisings exploded in urban ghettos. In a literal sense, the decade of the 1960s was marked by the revolt of the victims of American history.

Borrowing the metaphors of colonialism and stressing unity with the colonized peoples around the world who were seeking to throw off foreign domination, America's nonwhite minorities began to explore ways to achieve some degree of power and the right to self-determination in American society. The watchword of the revolution of the 1960s was "Black Power," a slogan first injected into the public consciousness in 1966 by young blacks of the Student Nonviolent Coordinating Committee (later renamed the Student National Coordinating Committee in keeping with its newly militant commitment). Other groups seeking similar freedoms adapted the slogan to their own use and took its lesson to heart. And so the cries of "Brown Power" were raised by chicanos, "Red Power" by American Indians, and "Woman Power" by feminists. Likewise other groups are beginning to seek a degree of self-determination. Students, hospital patients, prisoners, and juveniles wanted to share in the decision making in their respective institutions.

As the 1970s began, it became clear that the repressive policies of the federal government, in reaction to the rising tide of revolt, would succeed in reducing the influence of the movements for social change. By the mid-seventies little of the organized protest of the sixties remained. Even government opposition, however, was unable to turn back all of the gains of the previous decade. As the seventies come to a close, one can see quiet advances continuing to be made on many levels and among many of the previously oppressed groups. Yet it is unclear whether these gains can be considered permanent. There is a growing reaction among the more comfortable segments of the society to the progressive changes taking place, and unless considerable pressure can be maintained, the recent crusade for human rights in America may come to a halt.

1

Reconstruction and the Gilded Age

Race Relations: Attitudes, Irritation, and Violence

JOEL WILLIAMSON

Revisionist history is history written in order to "revise" the generally held interpretation of a period, movement, idea, or person. The reason such a revision is possible, or even necessary, may be newly found information, new methodology, a changed perspective on national or international political events, or most commonly, a changed political, social or intellectual environment. The writing of the history of Reconstruction carefully follows the changing social environment of race relations in the United States for the past one hundred years.

Shortly after the end of Reconstruction historians wrote about the period as though it were a noble but failed experiment. By the end of the nineteenth century the era following the Civil War was increasingly looked upon as a tragically misguided and fortunately unsuccessful attempt to force a racially equal political and social society on the defeated South. This point of view found its definitive statement in the 1929 book, **The Tragic Era,** by historian-journalist Claude Bowers. The influence of the brilliant film **The Birth of a Nation** in reinforcing in the popular mind the ideas expressed by the historians during this period cannot be overestimated. Reconstruction was seen as a time when corrupt carpetbaggers from the North joined with the traitorous scalawags and the primitive and ignorant freed slaves to dominate the prostrate but still proud white South. At stake was the future of a traditionally aristocratic and genteel society which was thought to have flourished so brilliantly in the ante-bellum years.

In his book, **The Era of Reconstruction 1865–1877,** published in 1965, historian Kenneth Stampp demolishes what he calls "the tragic legend" of Reconstruction and ushers in a new period of revisionist writing on the period. What some have called the Second Reconstruction—the 1950s and 1960s—has seen a thorough rewriting of the history of the first Reconstruction. It has become clear that one's attitude toward the events of Reconstruction depends largely on one's attitude toward the idea of equality for Afro-Americans. During the years when the tragic legend held sway, there was widespread agreement among intellectuals and the public at large that black people were inherently inferior to whites. A major factor in the revisionist history of the 1950s and 1960s, influenced by the civil rights move- ment and black assertiveness, was the insistence by the historians engaged in this enterprise that any apparent black inferiority was a result of deprivation and discrimination and was by no means inherent.

Although the tragic legend has few if any defenders in the American intellectual community today, the popular understanding of Reconstruction still contains many myths created by this earlier ver- sion of the period. The corrupt carpetbagger and his ignorant dupe, the freedman, still hold sway in the minds of many in spite of the thoroughgoing academic revision. It might be assumed that this myth fills a felt need on the part of many who continue to believe in it in the face of so much evidence to the contrary.

Joel Williamson, of the University of North Carolina, has pro- vided us with what is perhaps the best revisionist study of a single state during Reconstruction. His description and analysis of events in the crucial state of South Carolina set a standard against which other studies have to be measured. In the chapter from this work reprinted below, Williamson provides insight into the ideology of racism which became so important for the future of race relations in the South. Important in countering some of the continuing myths of Reconstruc- tion is his analysis of the place of violence during the period, par- ticularly the role of self-defense and outright aggression in the lives of the freedmen.

Until the nightmare of racial antipathy in America ends, if ever, Reconstruction historiography will continue to reflect the chang- ing concerns of the present as the past is enlisted in an ongoing struggle for racial liberation or oppression.

The white community largely determined the nature of relationships be- tween the races in post-bellum South Carolina. The basic assumption un- derlying the attitudes of the whites was that the Negro race was inher- ently and immutably inferior to their own. The argument supporting this assumption and, hence, the white man's attitudes toward the Negro, had been developed well before emancipation. In essence, it was conceived as

"Race Relations: Attitudes, Irritation, and Violence." From Joel Williamson, *After Slavery: The Negro in South Carolina During Reconstruction, 1861–1877* (Chapel Hill, N.C.: The University of North Carolina Press, 1965), pp. 240–73. Reprinted by permission of the University of North Carolina Press.

a rationalization of slavery, but both the argument and the attitudes which it generated lived long after slavery had died.

Like the society which gave it birth, the proslavery position was capable of both mercurial evolution and rigid staticism. Generally the argument passed through two grand phases. During the colonial period and far into the Jeffersonian years, Southerners argued that slavery was justified, primarily, as a means of civilizing the Negro. Taking their cue from their European cousins, early Southerners looked upon Negroes as their cultural inferiors. Rising with the ground swell of scientificism and rationalism, seeing an unfolding physical and moral universe which they were rapidly mastering, it was not strange that Southern whites saw cultural difference as cultural inferiority and discriminated against Negroes and Indians, both slave and free, upon these grounds. Incipient masters as they were, the discrimination was not at first well defined, but by the end of the first century of colonization the color line was clearly and unmistakably drawn.

Yet the very system which damned the Negro in this way also held out to him the promise of eventual redemption. The assumption was that association with the white man would civilize the Negro, and there was nothing in the system which ruled that Negroes could not attain a cultural parity with their white neighbors. In this view, slavery was but a school for the Negro, an institution which would die of atrophy when the period of tutelage had passed. The belief that total liberation lay somewhere in the future was given the semblance of reality by the partial acculturation of the great mass of slaves, by the freeing of a few, and by the emergence of a host of emancipation societies in the Southern states.

In the third and fourth decades of the nineteenth century, a profound change occurred in the Southern interpretation of slavery. This shift in thought coincided with a rising conviction among Southerners that they could not, or would not, exist in a society without this form of human bondage. With rather frightening precipitancy Southerners turned away from arguing that slavery was merely a temporary aberration, a short but necessary interval on the path from Africa to the West. Now it became a touchstone peculiarly their own, a talisman which would guide them in the construction of a society of transcendent excellence. As their thinking about slavery altered, so too did their attitudes toward the Negro. Southerners now argued that Negro inferiority was not merely cultural but natural, a permanent, inbred, incurable affliction which uniquely fitted that race to perpetual slavery.

Virtually every field of creative intellectual activity in the South turned its energies to buttressing the new faith. Ministers were in the vanguard. Assiduously they searched their Bibles anew for words to sanctify the eternal enslavement of the Negro. They found them in abundance. Natural scientists, eminent scholars such as Henry W. Ravenel, argued that the races had been separately created, that the Negro and the white were not the fruit of a common genealogical tree. The Negro, they asserted, was biologically unique, an intermediate species suspended somewhere between the animal and human worlds. Economists contended that slavery was not only necessary to Southern prosperity, but essential to the Negro's very existence, that without the guidance of the whites the childlike, improvident Negro would perish. Early-day sociologists maintained that perpetual Negro slavery was a social "mudsill," a foundation upon which the South would erect a superior civilization. Medical men concluded that Negroes possessed strange immunities and weird physical adaptations which fitted them to labor in the fields as white men never could. William Gilmore Simms, Henry Timrod, Sidney Lanier, and other Southern writers turned their whole creative efforts to works which established a convenient color code, damning black as forever inferior (and, indeed, evil) and praising white as good and true. Simultaneously, Southerners at large argued that the Negro was happy in slavery; it was the one social estate congenial to his nature; it was, in short, a positive good.

Having passed through three decades of repetition and refinement, the new proslavery persuasion evolved an elaborate and rigid ritual well before the Civil War began. It had developed a unique vocabulary, an intellectual shorthand of ideas and assumptions, and a facile jargon, all of which were intelligible only to the initiated. In the mind of the South, the educated South, the new argument approached a complicated and well-integrated synthesis of all knowledge justifying perpetual slavery.

Inevitably the question arises: Against whom were the Southerners contending? Unburdened by the immediate moral problem of slave ownership in their midst, many and perhaps most Northerners accepted Negro inferiority as a postulate. Slavery might seem wrong to some Northerners, but it did not necessarily follow that even those devotees of antislavery regarded the Negro as the equal of the white. Most Northerners who cared hardly understood the language of pro-slavery apologists, and the few who did seldom bothered to answer. Furthermore, most Northern intellectuals were much too busy constructing arguments to convince themselves that slavery was wrong to heed seriously the polemics of the opposition. Nor was the proslavery plea addressed to articulate critics within the South, for these did not exist. Ultimately, the argument was the South's answer to itself, each man's reply to his own conscience, to his unspoken criticism of the peculiar institution.

Spawned to justify slavery, the argument asserting the Negro's inherent inferiority did not die with emancipation. After a generation of self-indoctrination, for such it was, Southerners could hardly be expected to concede that emancipation by the sword invalidated their argument or altered the basic nature of the Negro. Reconstruction correspondence is replete with restatements of the argument. Occasionally, its tenets were adapted to shifts in scientific theory. "The work goes far to strengthen my own views as to the difference in the origin of the two races," wrote former Governor Francis Pickens to former Governor A. G. Magrath in 1867 concerning a borrowed book. "I see Agassiz has come out on the same side lately, & says he would have come out before, but he feared people might suppose he was for slavery." Agassiz, Pickens explained, had recently conducted an experiment which indicated that "the clean footed

[bird] was higher in progressive procreation" than the web-footed. "So too of the negro, no full blooded negro can open his fingers as clean as a white man, between his fingers there is a ligament of skin at the root which looks partly like webb. So in like manner there is a skin or webb between the toes of an old full blooded negro. And the inference is that he is lower in progressive procreation than the white man."[1] Most often, however, the argument was repeated in a language essentially unchanged. "The African has been, in all ages, a savage or a slave," declared B. F. Perry in 1866. "God created him inferior to the white man in form, color and intellect, and no legislation or culture can make him his equal . . . His color is black; his head covered with wool instead of hair, his form and features will not compete with the caucasian race, and it is in vain to think of elevating him to the dignity of the white man. God created differences between the two races, and nothing can make him equal."[2] After 1867, many comprehensive reproductions of the argument in book form circulated in the state. Interestingly, one of these was written by Hinton Rowan Helper, the North Carolinian whose denunciation of slavery had caused such a furor in the late 1850s. Dedicating his work to the ideal of bringing the nation "under the Exclusive Occupancy and Control of the Heaven-descended and Incomparably Superior White Races of Mankind," Helper hoped that after the Fourth of July, 1876, "No Slave nor Would be Slave, No Negro nor Mulatto, No Chinaman nor unnative Indians, No Black nor Bi-colored Individual of whatever Name or Nationality, shall ever again find Domicile anywhere Within the Boundaries of the United States of America . . ."[3]

Precisely as before the war, Northerners could scarcely translate the jargon of the proslavery profession. A Bureau officer in Greenville was astounded by the effectiveness of Perry's use of the old arguments to fight Negro suffrage; but he was also amused at "the Confusion of certain Radical pundits, who did not know what the governor is (or was) talking about."[4] Scarcely a Southerner raised a critical voice against either slavery or the persisting assumption of innate Negro inferiority. Those few who did so seem usually to have had strong affiliations abroad. For instance, A. L. Taveau, who in 1865 concluded that the ideal of the happy slave was a "delusion," had been educated primarily in France by his *émigré* father.[5] Joseph E. Holmes, a Laurens county native who lived in London in the early postwar years, put both Negroes and whites into the framework of a neatly preserved Jeffersonian universe. "I know well how hard it is for men to give up preconceived notions or opinions or make allowances for the effects of education & circumstances on others," he lectured

[1] F. W. Pickens to A. G. Magrath, February 19, 1867, F. W. Pickens Papers.

[2] *New York Times*, October 7, 1866, p. 2.

[3] Hinton Rowan Helper, *Nojoque; a Question for a Continent* (New York, 1867). See also: Hinton Rowan Helper, *The Negroes in Negroland; the Negroes in America; and Negroes Generally* (New York, 1868).

[4] James H. Croushore and David M. Potter (eds.), *John William De Forest, A Union Officer in the Reconstruction* (New Haven, 1948), p. 192.

[5] A. L. Taveau to William Aiken, April 24, 1865, A. L. Taveau Papers.

his young nephew from the South, then a student at Edinburgh. "You I suppose think the negro by nature an inferior race & that he should be made to keep that lower position. I believe his origin as good as my own & I claim nothing of natural rights for myself that I am not ready to concede to him." A year later, he continued in the same rare vein:

> The government must educate the negro & treat him in all respects as it does other men & white people must recognize the same civil rights for him as they claim for themselves, or else it will ever be a war of races & life & property in the south will be precarious enough, and the sooner the whites kill off the whole race of darkies hip & thigh the better, unless they conclude to leave the country & live apart from the negro or conclude that a perfect acknowledgment of the equality of rights & duties is the true policy . . . For your own good. For the blessing of your home & neighborhood I hope you will go home to pacify & conciliate the discordant elements. If however you like war better than peace, strife & hatred better than love & good will, it is easy to be pleased on that score. We can any of us get up a row at any time by impudence & insolence, by hard words & frowning looks, by saying to any of our fellow creatures stand aside for I am your superior.[6]

Few Southern whites could be so objective, and even fewer were openly so. Nevertheless, native whites continued as before the war to rehearse to one another the same hackneyed phrases arguing the Negro's incorrigible inferiority, suggesting that it was still themselves against whom they were contending.

Applied to the hard realities of Reconstruction times, the persisting assumptions of the proslavery argument generated in the white community a clear, complex, and, within its own context, logical pattern of attitudes toward the freedman.

A central theme of native white thought was that Negroes should be subordinated to whites whenever and wherever contact between the races occurred. Emancipation hardly altered this attitude. The subordination of the freedmen had obvious economic advantages for whites of all stations, but in the minds of the dominant group it also had higher purposes. Most important, it was God's way. Dr. John Bachman, a New York Lutheran clergyman transplanted to South Carolina soil during the ante-bellum period and closely identified with the low-country aristocracy, wrote to a friend in September, 1865, that he hoped for the most stringent regulations for the freedman, that "the negro be placed in the situation for which God intended him—the inferior of the white man."[7] Negro subordination was also natural law. "The resistance to social equality is a law

---

[6] Joseph E. Holmes to Nickels J. Holmes, August 29, 1866; November 24, 1867, N. J. Holmes Papers.
[7] John Bachman to E. Elliott, September 11, 1865, Habersham Elliott Papers.

of race—a law of nature," argued a Columbian in December, 1868, "and has existed in all ages and in all places. It exists to-day in New York and in New England, as well as here, and always will."[8] Without conceding that Negroes could be made the equals of whites, many whites continued to believe that slavery had been God's plan for civilizing the Negro. "What is to happen to the negro and white?" asked a young Columbian in her diary in March, 1865, as the prospect of freeing the slaves loomed before her. "Has God taken this means of making the negroes suffer bodily as did the Israelites, placing them in bondage to a superior people, in order to force intelligence and civilization upon them?"[9] Many of her contemporaries would have answered in the affirmative, and some would have added that emancipation was another step forward in a divinely in-spired process. To rice planter Robert A. Pringle it seemed "as if Provi-dence has forced upon us the civilization of the negro & now that that has been accomplished we are forced to submit to having them freed in our midst and the work of making him an intelligent free laborer capable of providing for himself given us to do."[10] In freedom, as in slavery, subor-dination was thus necessary to the cultural elevation of the Negro, just as the student is below the master. Finally, subordination was essential to the Negro's very existence. "The negro is the most inferior of the human race, far beneath the Indian or Hindu, and how can it be expected that they will be the white Man's equal," asked Grace Elmore. "It will be with them as with the Indian whereever [sic] the white has found foot hold, the negro will disappear except where he is kept in subjection, and con-sequently where it will be in the interest of the master to promote the welfare of the body and soul."[11]

For most native whites, verbalization and elaborate rationalizations were unnecessary. Slavery itself had offered sufficient prima facie evidence of the inferiority of the Negro, his subordination was in the natural order of things, and the practical income from the system was obvious and de-sirable. The determination of the masses to keep the freedman in subjec-tion was expressed by their actions rather than their words.

Native whites also commonly believed that the co-existence of the two races was impossible, that nature had made them incompatible. Grace Elmore, observing the state of relations between Negroes and whites in June, 1865, caught the flavor of this feeling. "Both parties are very in-different and the most that is felt is polite and gentle interest in the affairs of each other," she noted. "In most instances there is I think a bitter feel-ing & a sharp antagonism between the two races. I almost believe they are natural enemies and that only their relative positions [in slavery] bound them in affection as well as law together."[12] The failure of the Black Code and the continuing "misbehavior" of the Negro in an unstable political and social order confirmed native whites in their belief that the two races

[8] New York Times, December 25, 1868, p. 2.
[9] Grace B. Elmore MS Diary, entry for March 4, 1865.
[10] R. A. Pringle to W. R. Johnson, August 19, 1865, R. A. Pringle Papers.
[11] Grace B. Elmore MS Diary, entry for March 4, 1865.
[12] Ibid., entry for June 25, 1865.

could not live together in peace. Complaining of larceny by Negroes during the summer of 1866, a Laurens woman wrote: "I believe they will have to leave the country or the white people will leave them for they will kill and destroy so much that we cannot flourish together."[13] After the inauguration of Congressional Reconstruction, many native whites believed that the issue had been irrevocably drawn. "The negro & the white (Southern) man cannot fraternize," concluded a Laurens native in 1868. "They are compelled to be distinct and I may also say hostile classes. One or the other will rule."[14]

Directly reflecting the general belief in inherent Negro inferiority was the expectation that the race was soon to disappear entirely from the Southern scene, by a common analogy, just as the Indian had gone. He would die primarily because the Yankee had deprived him of the protection previously afforded by his master and could offer no viable substitute. Thus bereft, the Negro himself would be incapable of wrestling a subsistence from the forces of nature. Seeing the beginning of the end as Sherman entered the state in January, 1865, Henry Ravenel confided to a friend that he refused to grieve over the death of Tom, "a faithful servant," because, as he explained, "deep & dark as is the ruin approaching for all of us, the woe impending over this hapless race seems infinitely greater. What is to become of these luckless wretches when crushed upon the nether millstone of Yankee pity?"[15] In June, 1865, Mary Chesnut saw in the destruction of the economic aristocracy of the South the destruction also of the Negro. "Better teach the Negroes to stand alone," she admonished Andrew Johnson and the North, "before they break up all they leaned on."[16] Several months later, in Abbeville District, a late slaveholder concurred: "They will perish by hunger and disease and melt away as snow before the rising sun."[17]

Many native whites believed that competition with the superior white race would hasten the demise of the Negro. A Northern reporter in Orangeburg in July, 1865, thought that the Southern people were "nearly unanimous" in this opinion.[18] Three years later, a native white correspondent of the *Times* was "solemnly impressed with the conviction that the colored race in the South is destined to die out under the operation of natural causes," and that, like the Indian, "the darker and inferior race must go to the wall," driven to this end by "being in contact and competition with a superior race."[19]

During the early years of freedom, a high rate of mortality among Negroes and the emigration of many from the state lent an appearance of validity to the theory that the black race was destined to vanish. How-

---

[13] "Mother" to Nickels J. Holmes, July 25, 1866, N. J. Holmes Papers.

[14] J. D. Young to his sister, May 1, 1868, W. D. Simpson Papers.

[15] H. W. Ravenel to R. H. Gourdin, January 21, 1865, R. H. Gourdin Papers.

[16] Mary Boykin Chesnut, *A Diary from Dixie*, ed. Ben Ames Williams (Cambridge, 1949), p. 539.

[17] William Hill to his brother, September 8, 1865, William Hill Papers.

[18] *The Nation*, I, No. 4 (July 27, 1865), 107.

[19] *New York Times*, June 1, 1868, p. 5; see also January 15, 1869, p. 2.

ever, federal and state censuses soon showed the Negro population as actually increasing. Under such evidence "the vanish theory" rapidly ceased to be a part of the Southerner's thinking. It was supplanted in part by the expectation that the rate of increase among whites would outstrip that of the Negroes and eventually reduce the latter to an insignificant proportion of the total population.

Many whites, perhaps most of those in the middle and lower districts, believed that the incompatibility of the two races would lead to an open "war of the races" in which the Negro would meet his sudden demise.

This attitude, too, was a logical concomitant of a continuing current of ante-bellum Southern thought. Whatever else it might have been, slavery was also a system for keeping Negroes in subjection. Force was more than a convenient element for control; the very real danger of insurrection made it necessary. In South Carolina itself, within the memory of many whites still living during Reconstruction, two widespread conspiracies had been discovered. On July 4, 1816, a score of Negroes in Camden had plotted to seize the state arsenal in that town and thus give arms to a mass of insurrectionists. Six years later, in Charleston, the Denmark Vesey conspiracy was discovered and proved to be even more formidable as a threat to the sense of security of the white community. In addition, Carolinians had constantly before them the horrible examples of actual slave insurrections in other places. They were particularly frightened by a successful revolt of the Negroes of Santo Domingo in the 1790s and by the sanguinary Nat Turner rising in Virginia in 1831. During the 1830s, even as they lavished their intellectual energies upon the elaboration of the proslavery argument, South Carolinians turned their organizational energies toward perfecting a system of slave control unprecedented in severity. The slave code was revamped, repressive legislation for the better regulation of both the free Negro and slave populations enacted, and the traditional method of enforcing the system, the patrol, revitalized.

Ultimately, slavery rested upon force, an overriding, all-pervasive force employed not solely by the relatively few Southerners who owned slaves, but by the white community as a whole. (In a sense, the patrol institutionalized the white community's interest in slavery, in the control of the Negro.) In South Carolina, the patrol was formally begun in the early eighteenth century and, though nominally separate, existed in close conjunction with the militia. Every able, adult white male was constrained to join both groups. For service in the patrol no compensation was given, indicating the spirit of public necessity which lay behind it. Significantly, each district (county) in the state was divided into regiments and each regiment into "beats." The same men who made up the militia company in a beat were organized into several patrols which took turns in maintaining a moving, and, usually, mounted watch on the activities of the Negroes. This group was authorized by law to exercise an immediate discipline over Negroes, both slave and free, which was in many ways more harsh than that which the slaveholder himself was legally granted. Moreover, the slaveholder could not interfere with the patrol as it performed its duties upon his slaves. So central was the patrol to the political and social fabric of South Carolina that its area of responsibility, the beat, became the local area of governmental organization, and the term remained in use until it was changed to "township" by the Republicans in 1868. In its first century of existence, the patrol occasionally lost its alertness. After 1816, however, it was active almost continually, realerted again and again by insurrections, by the discovery of insurrectionary plots, and by rumors of both. Throughout the three decades preceding the war, while the proslavery argument was developing to a crescendo of intensity, and particularly after John Brown's raid, the patrol maintained a feverish activity which abated only slightly after the military situation had attained some stability early in the war. After a century and a half of such surveillance, it is small wonder that Negro folklore produced a song which advised the sable brother, "Run, nigger, run, or the patrol'll get you."[20]

Having lived all their lives under such tension, most whites, particularly those in the heavily Negro districts of the lowcountry, believed that the inevitable result of emancipation and the removal of the restraints previously exercised on the Negro would be racial violence. Significantly, they most often spoke of the expected war of races as if it were a mass insurrection of slaves, as they termed it, a "rising." The mistress of a plantation near Columbia subsequently recalled those first anxious days: "Opposite, in a settlement of our houses left on the lot, the negroes were packed and sang as only they could sing in these times, the nights through, keeping our spirits alive and awake to expectation of a horde pouring into our houses to cut our throats and dance like fiends over our remains."[21] Having passed through the lower and middle districts in the summer of 1865, a Northern traveler found this fear "almost universal."[22]

As the summer passed without any widespread insurrection occurring, native whites began to look forward to the Christmas season as the time of rebellion. The Fourth of July (Independence Day!) and Christmas or New Year's Day had marked a large number of insurrections and planned insurrections. Ironically, in South Carolina during the ante-bellum period, it became almost traditional for whites to anticipate these occasions with anxiety rather than pleasure. After emancipation, far from abating, these apprehensions were greatly increased by the deliberate agitation of some Union officials, army officers, and troops (particularly Negro troops), by the failure of others to present a stern face to the Negro, and by the rising dissatisfaction of Negro laborers with the results of their economic arrangements during the first year of freedom. Hearing in October of a thwarted conspiracy among the Negroes to rebel near Winnsboro, a young Columbia woman fearfully predicted: "They will be tried by a military court in Winnsboro and will not be hung, so that the whole countryside will be unsafe. Dr. Sims stated that the Yankee troops had encouraged their belief that land would be given them and

---

[20] Thomas J. Kirkland and Robert M. Kennedy, *Historic Camden*, Part 2 (Columbia, 1926), p. 193.
[21] Sally Elmore Taylor MS Memoir.
[22] *The Nation*, I, No. 4 (July 27, 1865), 107; I, No. 11 (September 14, 1865), 331.

when the higher officers denied this, the negroes became desperate. The negroes are organizing and drilling and will certainly rise."[23] As Christmas approached tension increased. In Abbeville District, a young woman whose husband would be absent during the holidays was invited by Judge Wardlaw, one of the authors of the Black Code, to stay with his family "as there is fear that the negros [*sic*] on the plantations will rise in rebellion about that time."[24] Early in December, near Fort Motte in Orangeburg District, a young planter was warned by his stockman that his Negro laborers would attack the barns near the end of the month when "hungary came." The thoughts which passed through that young man's mind during the next few weeks were perhaps shared by many white Carolinians. "Adger you have seen nothing over your way of the freedman as [he] really is," he cautioned his brother. "If they are already planning for an attack on barns &c. what are we to look for? I confess I am very anxious. I am trying to do my best here, am out early & late, but meet with sour looks, & uncivil words." A week later, the planter, a battle-tested veteran of the Confederate Army, was even more timorous. Denouncing the improvidence of the Negro in a letter to his mother, he added:

> . . . And then when to their animal nature, ready for anything like riot or robbery is applied the teachings & drillings, which those negro troops that have infest our country have been so eager to inculcate, when from the ignorant he rises into the bloodthirsty & revengeful brute, eager to possess all he sees, unable to look beyond the present but merely acting under the direction of blind & maddened impulse, of animal desires & passions. Mother I shuddered yesterday, when I was having some hogs killed, to see the fiendish eagerness in some of them to stab & kill, the delight in the suffering of others![25]

Native whites moved to meet the imagined menace with the same spirit, language, and action with which threats of insurrection had been met during the slave period. Governor Perry, in October, 1865, asked the legislature to restore the militia to full strength to guard against "insurrection and domestic violence."[26] The legislature responded with alacrity. The patrol laws were rewritten much as if the Negro were still a slave and candidly looked to the suppression of Negro revolts. By joint resolution the governor was "authorized to employ, as far as may be necessary, the militia and volunteer police forces of this State for the purpose of enforcing the Patrol Laws of the State, so far as they are applicable to the changed condition of society under the new Constitution, and of pre-

[23] Grace B. Elmore MS Diary, entry for October 1, 1865.
[24] Rebecca S. Cheves to J. R. Cheves, November 19, 1865, R. S. Cheves Papers.
[25] A. T. Smythe to John Smythe, December 5, 1865; A. T. Smythe to his mother, December 12, 1865, A. T. Smythe Letters. For indications of the prevalence of such thinking, see: *The Nation*, I, No. 21 (November 23, 1865), 651.
[26] *Intelligencer* (Anderson), November 2, 1865.

serving law and order in the State."[27] The volunteer police force was, of course, the patrol. The new governor, James L. Orr, vetoed the modified patrol law on the ground that any patrol was incompatible with the Negro's freedom. Thereafter, organization of the "volunteer police" as a sort of posse proceeded only slowly despite the circulation of a rumor that a widespread plot had been discovered among the free but oppressed Negroes of Jamaica to rebel on Christmas Eve, burn Kingston, and massacre its citizens.[28] However, early in 1866, the militia was reestablished in its traditional form. For instance, General Order Number One for the Ninth Brigade prescribed the same "beat" boundaries which had existed before the war.[29]

The failure of the Negroes to rise in mass rebellion during the winter of 1865–1866 relieved the anxieties of the whites only temporarily. Again, in the following winter, white citizens were gravely concerned over "threats of insurrection" among the Negroes.[30] During the months in which Negro voters were rising to political power, many whites still feared a war of races. A Charleston physician, writing to his brother in February, 1868, anticipated a rebellion in the North against the Radicals, "and we will have to guard ourselves against the negroes while they are fighting it out there."[31] The spectre of Negro insurrection and interracial war would mark the mind of the South for many years to come.

At least some whites looked eagerly forward to the vanishing of the Negro race, either by violence or otherwise. Contemporaries believed that such an attitude was particularly prevalent among the less affluent elements of the white community. A Northern traveler in the sand hills southwest of Columbia in December, 1865, lodged a night in the home of a "low white" widow. She had lost a son at Petersburg, but she "niver knowed" why the rich folks brought on the war. "They's lost all their niggers, and she was mighty glad of it. She wished them and the niggers had been at the bottom o' the sea."[32] Such anti-Negro attitudes were hardly less prevalent among late slaveholders. "I am utterly disgusted with the race," wrote one aristocrat, "and trust that I may some day be in a land that is purged of them."[33]

The attitudes evinced by freedmen toward native whites were largely responses to attitudes manifested by whites themselves. In freedom the Negro obviously resented having been held in slavery. But resentment seldom passed into hatred, either against their late masters or against the

[27] Reports and Resolutions (1865), pp. 195–96.

[28] Intelligencer (Anderson), November 30, December 7, 14, 1865.

[29] MS General Order No. 1, 9th Brigade, January 5, 1866, South Carolina Militia Papers.

[30] W. J. B. Cooper to a friend, December 11, 1866; S. W. Maurice and others to James L. Orr, December 11, 1866, Freedmen File; J. A. Mitchell to his sister, December 5, 1866, J. A. Mitchell Papers.

[31] J. B. Elliott to Habersham Elliott, February 2, 1866, Habersham Elliott Papers.

[32] The Nation, II, No. 28 (January 11, 1866), 47.

[33] H. W. Ravenel to A. L. Taveau, June 27, 1865, A. L. Taveau Papers.

whites generally, and the desire for revenge was certainly an alien emotion. Even among the fevered agitations of war, Thomas Wentworth Higginson was struck by "the absence of affection and the absence of revenge" in the feelings of his Negro troops toward their former owners. "It was not the individual, but the ownership, of which they complained," he interpreted.[34]

Negroes were nonplused by white anxiety. "What for we rise?" scoffed a Charleston Negro in the summer of 1865, "we have our freedom now."[35] The inevitable "war of races" was also discounted by the Negro leadership. "Have you any fear of a war of races here, in this State?" asked a Northerner of Beverly Nash in 1867. "Oh, no!" Nash answered. "I hope not. I don't see why we should not all live peaceably together."[36]

Even though Negroes were not liable to engage in any general armed rebellion against the whites, they nevertheless resented the assumptions of the proslavery argument and the subordinate status in society which these assumptions assigned to them. In slavery they had resisted subjection by rebellion, flight, sabotage, incendiarism, insolence, and a thousand and one minor defiances. In freedom the Negro resented attempts at his subordination as he had resented slavery, and he expressed his resentment by the same means. As he gained political power, he added new forms of resistance, and the feelings of the race found voice in an articulate, burgeoning leadership. He asserted the equality of his race with others; or, rather, he declared the cultural meaninglessness of race. "All bloods are one," cried the Reverend Henry Turner, a Carolina-born Negro who had recruited colored troops in Washington during the war, to a mass meeting of Negroes in Columbia in April, 1867. "The difference of race is nothing," he continued, arguing that it was simply the result of climatic variations. What he wanted was "universally equal rights—white, negro, Indian—all, without reference to the flatness of his nose or the length of his heel."[37] The Negro also argued that his intelligence, his integrity, and his capacity fitted him for participation in the ordinary affairs of society. Once in power, he moved to achieve this goal, and he saw no halfway house in freedom.

Negroes, collectively, were suspicious of the intentions of the white community as a group. They frequently assumed that the whites were plotting to damage them in their posture as free men; and the plot, they believed, often included violence. A case in point occurred in the village of Anderson in July, 1868. Mary, a Negro girl of "notorious" reputation, suddenly disappeared from the village. The Negroes, convinced that she had been killed by the whites and her body thrown into a nearby river, "drug" the stream in search of the corpse. After much agitation within the Negro community, a white man reported having seen Mary in

---

34 Thomas Wentworth Higginson, *Army Life in a Black Regiment* (Boston, 1890), pp. 249–50.
35 *The Nation*, I, No. 11 (September 14, 1865), 331–32.
36 *New York Times*, August 9, 1867, p. 2.
37 *Ibid.*, May 5, 1867, p. 1.

Walhalla, a village some forty miles distant by rail. The Negroes distrusted the testimony of the white man, saying that it was a trick conceived by the whites to halt their investigation. The Negro community then sent an agent to Walhalla, where he found and interviewed Mary. He returned to Anderson and reported his conversation with the girl in detail. Still, most of the Negroes refused to believe the girl had not been murdered by the whites, saying that the whites had bribed their emissary to tell this story.[38]

The attitudes thus assumed by each race toward the other made friction between them inevitable. Frequently, the conflict ended with a feeling of irritation; often it flared into open violence, and occasionally the violence assumed a horrendous magnitude.

Irritation between the races was a continuing occurrence, correlated in large measure with the assertiveness of Negroes. In the early postwar months, many whites were offended by the mere freedom of their slaves. Many directed their irritation not at the liberators but toward the freedmen themselves. In July, 1865, for instance, a Cooper River rice planter complained that the freedmen were disgustingly presumptuous and revealingly confessed that many Negroes he had liked best as slaves he now disliked most.[39] Difficulties in adjusting to a new economic order often gave positive substance to irritation, but as Negroes gained political power occasions for racial friction multiplied. That the Negro had become a voter was a thorn in the side of many native whites. In the presidential election of 1868, one ancient aristocrat regretted that he could not support Chase because "he goes for Negro suffrage, which is so horrible to us."[40] Several months later, the best advice which a dying man could give to his body servant was: "Miles, serve your God, and let politics alone."[41] The presumption of the Negro in seeking public office still further exasperated the whites. Noting that a mulatto had been nominated for secretary of state by the Republicans in 1868, a Charleston physician pronounced South Carolina "a miserable land to live in."[42] Seeing Negroes actually in office heightened the outrage. As the big guns noisily saluted the inauguration of South Carolina's first Republican governor in July, 1868, the widow of an old planter sat in her house near the campus of the University writing to her daughter in Charleston, struggling to find words sufficiently vitriolic to describe the "crow-congress," the "monkey-show," the "menagerie" which was the legislature and the "Yankee-nigger government programe" which was the constitution.[43]

Native whites were not always able to abstain from contact with Negro officials, and they seldom came away from such encounters without a feeling of having been degraded. "We are being made, however,

[38] *Intelligencer* (Anderson), July 29, 1868.
[39] [—.—.] Deas to his daughter, July 1, 1865, [—.—.] Deas Papers.
[40] William Heyward to James Gregorie, June 15, 1868, Gregorie–Elliott Papers.
[41] Anonymous to Mrs. Cicero Adams, February 11, 1869, N. A. Nicholson Papers.
[42] J. B. Elliott to Habersham Elliott, February 2, 1868, Habersham Elliott Papers.
[43] Louisa S. McCord to her daughter, July 9, 1868, A. T. Smythe Letters.

day by day, to realize the equalities of all things," complained a Charleston lady, "and brings to my mind the scenes I have read of during the Revolution in France of the hundred days, when the Nobility were so terribly treated. Surely our humiliation has been great when a Black Postmaster is established here at Headquarters and our *Gentlemen's Sons* to work under his biddings."[44] Neither was the native white lawyer in a commanding position when pleading before a Negro judge or Negro jurors. A lawyer who had left the state chided one who had remained, suggesting a typical reaction: "Well, Dick, you have a charming Supreme Court in S. C. now—a contemptible scallawag occupying the seat once adorned by O'Neal and Dunkin, and two carpet baggers (& one of them a *negro*) in the seats once graced by Wardlaw & Withers. How do you feel before such a Bench? When you address such creatures as 'your Honors,' dont the blood boil or grow chill in your veins? and how can you say 'Gentlemen of the Jury' to a panel of loathsome, leather-headed negroes?"[45] After appearing before this Supreme Court, another lawyer pronounced it "a damnable farce!"[46] Occasionally, however, whites found themselves totally under the thumb of Negro authorities. A native white inmate of the insane asylum wrote to a friend in the ministry asking his help in securing his discharge. The minister advised him to read his Bible. The patient replied with more than paranoic emotion that "if the stupid Negroes who act as Regents of this Institution had read the Bible as much or as long as either my Wife or I have done, they would not need when sitting as a board on Such Cases as mine, to ask the Stupid and insulting questions that some of them now do when exercising their brief authority While I appear before them."[47]

Irritations might have remained merely irritations had there not been individuals on both sides who were prone, almost eager, to do violence to members of the other race.

To an extent, a readiness for violence was a part of the social order of the white community and was not pointed directly at Negroes. On occasion, the "code of honor" might demand that the most refined white citizen commit mayhem upon his fellows. One Bureau officer thought that poor whites sometimes murdered "black 'uns" not because of their color, "but simply kill them in the exercise of their ordinary pugnacity."[48] Nevertheless, even in slavery the Negro had been a special object of violence by the militant element in the white community, a violence from which a slave's pecuniary value did not always exempt him. Physical force and the threat of bodily harm was, traditionally, the ultimate means of controlling the Negro. Such was the case in slavery, and it did not cease to be so afterward.

[44] Eliza T. Holmes to Mary Boykin Chesnut, April 8, 1873, Williams–Chesnut–Manning Papers.
[45] A. W. Dozier to Richard Dozier, March 21, 1870, R. W. Dozier Papers.
[46] B. W. Rutledge to G. W. Spencer, February 6, 1870, G. W. Spencer Papers.
[47] J. H. Cathcart to W. H. Hemphill, January 4, 1875, Hemphill Papers.
[48] Croushore and Potter, *A Union Officer*, p. 153.

The Negro was well aware, and doubtless the whites intended that he should be, that aggressiveness on his part would draw down upon him sudden, overwhelming, and awful violence. Particularly in periods of political turmoil, the threat became general and darkly menacing. In the heat of the campaign of 1876, an Abbeville farmer wrote to his cousin in North Carolina: "The Negroes here are more uneasy than they have ever before been, and not without very good reasons either, for there is a great many whites will hurt them with just the least provocation."[49]

Readiness for violence was not the exclusive monopoly of the white man. Yet, as with the whites, not all of the violent propensities of Negroes were directed against whites for racial reasons. Negroes subscribed in full to the "code" idolized by the whites, and, while the Negro's rationales may not have been as elaborately matured, the results were equally bloody. As Negroes organized politically, their potential for violence was more often turned against the whites as a race. It was, after all, but a short step from fighting to gain one's freedom to fighting to preserve it. During the campaign of 1876, R. H. Cain was reported to have written in the *Missionary Record* and repeated to a large gathering of Negroes in Charleston: "There are 80,000 black men in the State who can use Winchesters and 200,000 black women who can light a torch and use a knife." During the same period, Negro women were reported to be "carrying axes or hatchets in their hands hanging down at their sides, their aprons or dresses half-concealing the weapons."[50]

There were numerous incidents, of course, in which individual whites assaulted Negroes for reasons in some degree attributable to racial differences. In the summer of 1865, William Lemons, a hotel clerk in Newberry, attacked and beat Burrel Mayes, a mulatto, for asking Lemons to hold his carpetbag. Interestingly, Mayes was nearly white and had served as a Confederate soldier, enlisting in Columbia, it was said, under the name of John Brown.[51] Contrary to tradition, Negroes also instigated and won violent encounters with whites. In the spring of 1870, an Abbeville planter wrote to a friend in Virginia that, "One negro has with the assistance of others whipped and beat three white men at Abbeville Court-House one of them was John Turner from Buck Level. This negro I expect will be the next Sheriff. He speaks of running for the office. If he runs he will be sure to be elected and we will be in a worse fix than now."[52] Similarly, in 1876, a medical student in Charleston related the experience of a young friend who "was walking with the young ladies and a negro run against them, when they were near home, after Turner got them home he went back and went for the 'nig' and was giving him 'fits' when two other negroes came up and doubled on him, and one of them struck him in the head with a brick bat, which laid him out for a while. Then they ran off."[53]

[49] J. L. Harris to J. W. Holland, July 11, 1876, J. W. Holland Papers.
[50] Myrta Lockett Avary, *Dixie after the War* (New York, 1906), p. 362.
[51] *Intelligencer* (Anderson), July 27, 1865.
[52] A. W. Moore to E. H. Dabbs, April 30, 1870, A. L. Burt Papers.
[53] J. E. Renwick to his brother, January 5, 1876, W. W. Renwick Papers.

More indicative of racial antagonisms were recurrent conflicts involving more or less organized groups of whites and Negroes. In such encounters individuals frequently were not personally acquainted with their opponents and recognized the enemy solely by the color of his skin. Here, obviously, the color line was distinctly drawn. During Reconstruction, violence of this nature fell into four rather distinct, nonsuccessive phases. The first phase followed immediately after the war and continued for approximately a year. It was characterized by riots almost devoid of political content. The second phase, beginning with the political elevation of the Negro and terminating with the end of the elections of 1868, produced violence which arose from altered political conditions. In the third period, from October, 1870, through the summer of 1871, the so-called Ku Klux Klan disturbances reached their height. Violence in the final and most fevered period coincided with the campaign of 1876.

Between July, 1865, and November, 1866, there were three major race riots in South Carolina. Two of these were between white Union soldiers and Negroes. After a shooting skirmish in the Market Place in Charleston on Saturday, July 8, organized groups of a New York Zouave regiment kept up a running fight with Negro soldiers of the Twenty-first United States Colored Troops (formerly the Third South Carolina) well into the following week. The riot was stopped only by exiling the Zouaves to Morris Island.[54] In Marion, in the spring of 1866, a gang of soldiers went on a spree which ended with the burning of the house of "courtesan" Kate Lewis (color unknown) and the building used as a school for the freed people, "several of whom were beaten quite severely."[55] More accurately suggestive of things to come was a riot which occurred between native whites and Negro Charlestonians in June, 1866. A scene typical of this and later riots was staged on Sunday, June 24, at 8:00 in the evening. At that time, a mob of about twenty-five Negroes turned into Tradd Street from King and halted in the front yard of a house where a young man, George F. Ahrens, stood on the portico watching them. Presently, a white man, Richard M. Brantford, happened to turn into Tradd from Orange Street at the opposite end of the block. Perceiving the militant disposition of the Negroes, he tried to run away. With cries of "Charge" and "Fire" by several of the Negroes, they hurled a shower of bricks on the fleeing Brantford. The first missile thrown hit the fugitive in the back. Then one of many struck his head and he fell to

[54] *New York Times*, July 16, p. 3; 24, p. 2, 1865.
[55] *Intelligencer* (Anderson), April 19, 1866, quoting the Marion *Star*. Antagonism between Northern white troops and Southern Negroes was, of course, not unusual. Higginson had seen it in the islands during the war. Higginson, *Black Regiment*, pp. 16, 251. Native whites were alert to record a continuation of this attitude among the occupation forces. A young student in Columbia in October, 1868, wrote that the men of the garrison "are itching to get a shot at the negroes and the officers too if they try to take the nigger side, for they are radical mostly." Edward R. Crosland to his mother, October 31, 1868, Edward Crosland Papers. For the existence of the same spirit during the Ku Klux riots, see J. M. Dennis to J. Y. Harris, July 6, 1871, J. Y. Harris Papers.

the pavement. Scipio Fraser, one of the rioters, shouted "Kill the rebel son of a bitch." "Then the crowd gathered around him, as he lay on the ground," Ahrens testified, "kicked him and struck him with brick bats. They then left him and I saw two colored men come up Tradd Street, picked up Brantford and carried him home. . . . The same evening . . . Scipio Fraser came into my yard and was talking about the riot. He said: 'I, and no one else, killed the rebel son of a bitch, and he is not the first, nor he will not be the last I will kill.' "[56] A week later, Charleston was still racked by sporadic fighting.[57]

In the interior during this period, violence of the mass sort was characterized by the assaults of roving bands of outlaws upon hapless Negroes who came their way. In addition, more or less respectable groups of white citizens organized as "home police," or vigilantes, or militia attempted to keep the Negro population under control. In Orangeburg District, in November, 1866, the first clear case of lynching occurred when a mob of whites summarily dispatched two Negro men who had, allegedly, "waylaid" on the road and "killed with axes" a widow and her eight-year-old daughter.[58]

A second wave of violence coincided with the rise of the Negro to political power. During this period, Negroes were as often the aggressors as were the whites. In the fall of 1867, the Union League Club of Hunnicutt's Crossing in Pickens District, after killing a young man in a fight with the white membership of a local debating club, assumed control of the neighborhood. For several days, they marched about in a military fashion, bearing arms, arresting and imprisoning whites whom they accused of participating in the riot.[59] Several months later, in Orangeburg District, "a military company of negroes" surrounded the house of a Mr. Hane who, supposedly, had shot a Negro. They held the white man as a prisoner "with the avowed intention of hanging him in case the wounded negro should die." Hane was later delivered to a magistrate, but the whites learned that the lynch rope in Orangeburg was racially impartial.[60] As the Republicans progressed to political dominance, Negroes became increasingly restless. In several areas incendiarism was rampant, and in Williamsburg District and on John's Island large groups of Negroes were said to be organizing militarily, in the latter case "to patrol the island and keep down the white people."[61]

Anxious elements within the white community retaliated in kind, particularly in the upcountry counties where the Negro population was not in an overwhelming majority. In its most violent form, white retaliation was an irregular campaign of terrorism against Radical leaders. In-

---

[56] *House Journal* (Special Session, 1868), pp. 169–73.

[57] *New York Times*, July 10, 1866, p. 5.

[58] David Gavin MS Diary, II, 404; *New York Times*, November 20, 1867, p. 5.

[59] *Report of the Secretary of War* (1867), I, 370–467.

[60] *New York Times*, January 10, 1868, p. 8.

[61] MS petition of several citizens of Kingstree to Governor James L. Orr, July 26, 1868, Freedmen File; *New York Times*, September 28, 1868, p. 5.

terestingly, the whites reacted violently only after the state elections of 1868 had been lost, and there was no hint at the time (though this certainly came later) that any such organization as the Ku Klux Klan lay behind it. On June 1, 1868, Solomon George Washington Dill, senator-elect from Kershaw District, was assassinated in his home.[62] When the legislature convened several weeks later, members were mysteriously warned that if they dared return to their homes after the session they would be killed. As a Northern-born Negro member later declared, on the eve of adjournment each member asked himself, "Will it be I?"[63] Shortly after the close of the session, James Martin, an Irish immigrant who had become a Radical member from Abbeville, was "pursued by a gang of ruffians" from Abbeville Courthouse and killed.[64] In mid-October, B. F. Randolph, a Northern-born Negro Methodist clergyman, was shot dead by unknown parties at Donaldsville, while on a speaking tour.[65] Several days after Randolph's demise, the president of the Union League Club in Newberry, a Negro named Lee Nance, was assassinated in his front yard by a band of mounted whites.[66]

The organization of the Negro militia was the specific Radical answer to these offerings of violence by the whites. When the legislature reconvened during the winter of 1869, it hastened to pass the law necessary to organize the militia fully. It also authorized the governor to buy 2,000 stand of arms "of the most approved pattern."[67] However, even as the legislature acted, violent outbursts became less frequent and by late spring had virtually ceased. Politicians promptly pre-empted the higher ranks in the militia and the paper organization was completed, but only a few local units were actually established.

During the spring of 1870, the situation changed drastically when incumbent Governor Scott deliberately revitalized the militia and transformed it into a giant political machine for use in combatting his enemies within and outside of the Republican party. Legally, white men could have joined the militia as enlisted men; indeed, technically, they were required to join. In reality, however, whites simply refused to serve in militia companies in which Negroes were their equals or, occasionally, their superiors, and the governor refused to accept all-white companies. Therefore, whites were effectively excluded. But there was no dearth of Negro volunteers. Few young men could resist the attractions of militia

---

[62] Kirkland and Kennedy, *Historic Camden*, p. 201.

[63] *New York Times*, October 22, 1868, p. 5; *House Journal* (1868–1869), p. 46.

[64] *House Journal* (1868–1869), p. 27.

[65] *Intelligencer* (Anderson), October 21, 1868; *New York Times*, October 19, p. 1; 28, p. 5, 1868. Interestingly, the assailants in each of these cases were never satisfactorily identified. A white man of doubtful sanity confessed to killing Randolph for money, but before he identified his employer or employers the supposed assassin was, himself, killed by persons unknown. *Journal* (Bennettsville), December 24, 1868; *Southern Enterprise* (Greenville), December 8, 1869.

[66] *Intelligencer* (Anderson), October 28, 1868, quoting the Newberry *Herald*, October 21, 1868.

[67] *House Journal* (1868–1869), p. 131; *New York Times*, April 21, 1869, p. 2.

service: dashing, varicolored uniforms, shining arms and clattering accoutrements, the roll of the drum, the intricate and endless ritual of the drill, and the incomparable comaraderie of fellows under arms. On the eve of the election of 1870, the militia rolls had swelled to include more than ninety thousand men. The highest ranks were of course, held by Scott's friends; but the key officers were actually the captains of local companies. Almost invariably, they were strong characters in the Negro community, sometimes noted for their prudence, often for their bellicosity. Demanding and, frequently, enjoying the complete loyalty of their men, they often failed to accord the same measure of loyalty to their nominal commanders. Some of them used their men badly, deliberately maneuvering them in ways menacing to the whites or calling out their companies to settle personal grudges.

Ultimately, the so-called Ku Klux riots of 1870–1871 occurred not because Negroes were organized in militia companies, but because the Negro militia was, in certain areas, heavily and effectively armed. From the Southern white's point of view, a well-armed Negro militia was precisely what John Brown had sought to achieve at Harper's Ferry in 1859. It was, in short, an insurrection with a high potential for disaster. The Ku Klux riots, it is true, did have a political flavor; but the flavor was of frustration, not hope. It is highly significant that the first outbreak on October 19, 1870, occurred only after the election was over. Having lost the state elections, native whites were bitter, but no white leader seemed to think that any amount of violence would recall the results of the election or improve the political prospectus for 1872. Quite clearly, the Ku Klux riots were also influenced by any number of local and personal enmities, but these were merely ancillary to the main body. Whites were also irritated and alarmed by the very existence of the Negro militia, but irritation and fear led to action only when and where the militia was armed.

This conclusion is supported by the fact that the counties which suffered most from violence were also the counties in which the Negro militia was most heavily and effectively armed. Since Scott had arms enough for barely a tenth of his force, he chose to issue the bulk of those in counties where the normal Republican majority was jeopardized by white intimidation. To the Laurens militia, he sent 620 breech-loading, rifled muskets, 50 Winchester rifles, and 18,000 rounds of ammunition, that is, roughly 10 percent of the total distributed. It was in Laurens that the first and bloodiest of the riots took place. Comparably large quantities of arms and ammunition were dispatched to the militia in Spartanburg, Newberry, Union, Chester, York, Fairfield, Kershaw, and Edgefield counties. Each of these was also a center for large-scale violence. On the other hand, no arms were issued in the heavily white counties of Oconee, Pickens, and Greenville, and only 96 muskets were sent to Anderson and Abbeville counties together. In each of these areas, there were no significant outbreaks. The same pattern generally prevailed in the lowcountry where the Negro population was heavy. In the Fifth Regiment, centering in Marion and Georgetown, only ninety muskets were given the militia and no riots occurred. The only exceptions were Charleston and Beaufort counties where the militia was both well organized and well armed. Here, however, the primary purpose was probably exhibitory rather than militant.[68]

The signal importance of arming the militia in precipitating the Ku Klux disturbances was also revealed in the unerring, almost instinctive accuracy with which even the least organized white mobs focused as if by careful concensus upon the seizure 'of the arsenals of the militia as their goal. This was dramatically evident in the Laurens riot. Since early September, 1870, whites had been aware that a large quantity of arms and ammunition had been received by the local militia and stored by them in their armory on main street and in the fortresslike barn behind the house of their colonel. Beginning with a fist-fight between a native white and a carpetbagger on the town square, within a few minutes and apparently spontaneously the struggle grew into a shooting attack on the militia's armory. During the next few hours, the "volunteer police" managed, quite legally, to seize all of the guns in both the armory and the barn and deposit them in the courthouse. Within a day after the militia was disarmed, violence ceased.[69] In Newberry, York, Chester, and Union counties confrontations and running battles between the Negro militia and white "citizen's committees" produced the same result.[70] In Spartanburg, the same pattern developed over a period of several months. On September 23, 1870, in Columbia, 192 breech-loading, rifled muskets were drawn for the Spartanburg militia.[71] On the following day, whites in Spartanburg were greatly agitated by a rumor that twenty-four boxes of Winchesters and seven boxes of ammunition had arrived for the militia and were stored in the county jail. On November 17, some twenty to fifty men, "fantasticly attired," unsuccessfully assaulted the jail. Thereafter, the arms were secreted by the authorities. During the ensuing four months a rash of Ku Klux visitations broke the peace of the county. A number of those visited were militiamen, whose houses were searched for arms. On March 22, 1871, the last large-scale raid was made on the house of a man whose son was the local militia brigadier. It was suspected that the arms had been hidden there. In Spartanburg, as elsewhere, peace was restored only after the arms were withdrawn.[72]

To label these riots the result of a Ku Klux "conspiracy" is inaccurate and misleading. These affrays were largely spontaneous. There was no conspiracy above the very local level, and often none existed there. There were local organizations of Klansmen in South Carolina in 1870 and 1871, but it is highly doubtful that any of these were organized before this

---

[68] *Reports and Resolutions* (1870–1871), pp. 521–611.

[69] The complete story of the Laurens riot is provided by an eye-witness, Mary Motte, in a series of letters to her son in Missouri. Mary Motte to Robert Motte, September 3, 1866, and following, J. R. and Mary Motte Papers.

[70] *New York Times,* March 13, p. 3; April 28, p. 1, 1871; *Ku Klux Conspiracy,* Vols. III, IV, V.

[71] *Reports and Resolutions* (1870–1871), p. 593.

[72] *A History of Spartanburg County,* pp. 150, 153–54, 156; *Ku Klux Conspiracy,* Vols. III, IV, V.

time and it is a virtual certainty that no statewide or even widespread organization of the order ever existed. In the Laurens riot, the most murderous of the sequence, white participants made no attempt to disguise themselves in the fashion of the Klan and were not members of that society. Yet, the racial and social objects of the Klan were in perfect harmony with the objects of the white community, and it was hardly necessary for white males to swear solemn oaths, perform rituals, and wear costumes to pursue the same ends. There was a unity of feeling and action in the white community, which rendered forms unimportant. Actually, all those more or less impromptu organizations which the Radicals chose to call Klans were only up-dated versions of the patrol, revitalized to meet still another "rising" by the Negroes. This was probably what the editor of the *Nation* meant when he very astutely observed that "the South before the war was one vast Ku-Klux Klan."[73]

The published record suggests that all responsible leaders of the white community deprecated the lawlessness of the rioters. However, private correspondence indicates that the great mass of white Carolinians were pleased by the results of a terrorist program. "It may seem very disloyal & Ku Kluxish in me, but I am exceedingly delighted at the Union & York 'outrages (?),'" wrote a Georgetown druggist in February, 1871, concluding that such events "will teach the misguided African to stand in the subordinate position nature intended."[74] In Chester County, planter Robert Hemphill noted that one of his Negro neighbors was visited by the Klan for "having guns in store, & . . . acting the Big man & fool generally," and another was threatened by the Klan for having, in his capacity as overseer of a public road, "ordered out his hands, & among them some white men which gave offence." Declared Hemphill, "The K. K.s are an excellent institution if kept in proper bounds. They have been of immense benefit in our county."[75] In Spartanburg, a small farmer hoped that the Klan would so frighten Negro legislators that they would resign and prevent his being "sold out for taxes in a year or to more." He explained: "There is a new sort of beings got up called KKs that has made a powerful show. These KKs whip and kill as they pleas."[76] One group of Klansmen fleeing across Edgefield county in November, 1871, en route to political asylum in Georgia probably never discovered that the band of mounted men pursuing them were not irate federals but local citizens fervently attempting to congratulate them upon their work.[77] When alleged Klansmen were arrested, virtually the entire white community leaped to their defense.[78] After several were convicted, the white com-

[73] *The Nation*, VII, No. 167 (September 10, 1868), 204.

[74] T. P. Bailey to R. H. McKie, February 20, 1871, R. H. McKie Papers.

[75] R. N. Hemphill to W. R. Hemphill, April 20, May 9, 1871, Hemphill Papers.

[76] Edward Lipscomb to Smith Lipscomb, April 11, 1871, Edward Lipscomb Papers.

[77] Anonymous to Dr. James Renwick, November 14, 1871, W. W. Renwick Papers.

[78] Wade Hampton was a leading organizer in a statewide movement to raise money and engage lawyers to defend supposed Klansmen. Wade Hampton to A. L. Burt, October 22, November 25, 1871, A. L. Burt Papers.

munity negotiated for their freedom much as if they were soldiers taken as prisoners of war. Quite obviously, the mass of native whites felt that a little Klanning was a good thing.

As an instrument for disarming the Negro militia, violence was a success. As a political tool promising ultimate victory, however, terrorism was a failure. Negroes were indeed frightened, but they were neither scared into the Democracy nor away from Republicanism. Moreover, violence simply provided more excellent grist for the Radical mill, allowing Northern Republicans to profit electorally at home by waving the freshly bloodied shirt and Southern Republicans to invoke the aid of the federal military. Finally, Negroes themselves might be driven to meet violence with violence, and in the lowcountry this could only mean disaster for the whites. Rather deliberately, the white leadership weighed the consequences of further violence and, during the winter and spring of 1871, moved to halt it. On March 13, a native white delegation waited on Governor Scott and secured his promise to recall the arms of the militia, since, as Scott asserted, "their arms provoked assaults and violence that otherwise would not have arisen."[79] In the following month, Scott kept his promise. Responding, the white leadership took to the stump and by mid-summer, 1871, had squelched the riotous elements as decisively as if the mobs had been under their military command. Ironically, in Spartanburg, where a series of public meetings were held for this purpose, one of the speakers was a legislator who had been a local Klan leader.[80]

The fear of some white leaders that Klan violence might lead to retaliation by Negroes was well grounded in fact. In the middle and lower portions of the state, indignation within the Negro community was marked. Late in March, 1871, a resident of Georgetown reported that the "negroes here of late have become quite outrageous in the town. . . ."[81] On July 1, 1871, in Barnwell County a group of twenty-five armed Negroes attacked the house of a white man who had reputedly wronged one of their number. They wounded the owner, his wife, and his mother and killed a white man who happened to be visiting the owner at the time of the raid.[82] In Camden, three days later (on the fifty-fifth anniversary of a major insurrectionary threat), the Negro militia attempted to rescue one of their number from the town marshal by whom he had been arrested. A riot was narrowly averted only by the intervention of cooler heads which prevented "the street from flowing with blood."[83]

During the summer, the white community itself put a stop to further Ku Klux outbreaks; nevertheless, in October, Scott persuaded Grant to suspend the operation of the writ of *habeas corpus* in nine counties, some of which had been the scene of only minor disturbances. The military moved in and hundreds of arrests were made. The proceedings were long

[79] *New York Times*, March 22, 1871, p. 2.
[80] *A History of Spartanburg County*, pp. 153–54.
[81] T. P. Bailey to R. H. McKie, March 27, 1871, R. H. McKie Papers.
[82] *New York Times*, July 4, 1871, p. 1.
[83] Kirkland and Kennedy, *Historic Camden*, pp. 208–09.

drawn out. In hearings before federal commissioners, presentments of grand juries, and finally on trial before federal district courts in Columbia and Charleston, stories of Ku Klux atrocities were repeated in all their brutal and gory detail again and again. Even some conservative native whites were revolted by the awful exhibition.[84] However, the great mass of native whites learned only one lesson: that a show of force in areas where they were numerically strong brought about similar displays in areas where Negroes were safely in the majority, and that the continued use of violence ultimately produced a crushing imposition of federal power. Under the circumstances, force was seen to be an instrument of restricted usefulness. For some five years after the summer of 1871, with only sporadic and scattered interruptions, the white community sought to gain its ends through persuasion rather than force.

By 1876, political prospects had changed. Only three Southern states remained under Radical control. The last to free itself had been Mississippi which, in 1875, had combined the careful, controlled use of force with the threat of unlimited violence to overwhelm its Negro majority. During the Redemption struggle in Mississippi, the Grant administration had shown itself unwilling to intervene as it had, say, in South Carolina in 1871. South Carolina consciously and deliberately took its cue from Mississippi.

The instrument which a major element of the Redeemer leadership forged to do violence upon and to threaten the Negro voter was the "Rifle" and "Sabre" Clubs. The forging began in Edgefield, Barnwell, and Aiken counties during the campaign of 1874 when the Negro militia of Edgefield was again supplied with state arms. The whites reacted by organizing themselves into rifle and sabre clubs, many of which had existed in previous times as social clubs more or less devoted to the cultivation of the military arts. In this instance, conflict was averted by the timely arrival of United States troops. Presumably peace was restored by Governor Chamberlain's withdrawal of the arms of the militia and ordering the dissolution of all military organizations, both Negro and white, within the county.[85] However, far from dissolving, the white clubs remained active and, indeed, proliferated throughout the state. By the summer of 1875, the captain of a club in Abbeville had the temerity to ask the governor to supply his men with arms.[86] As the more violent element in the Redeemer leadership became increasingly strong after the fall of 1875, these military clubs emerged as a primary political tool.

The first and highly successful use of force was made by the whites of Edgefield, Barnwell, and Aiken counties, a stronghold of the militant "straightout" Democracy. Early in the spring of 1876, the Negro population in this area grew restive. Doubtless they heard the false rumor that

---

[84] A. M. Seibels to John Fox, December 24, 1871, John Fox Papers.

[85] *New York Times*, September 1, p. 5; 27, p. 1; 28, p. 1; October 6, p. 1; 7, p. 1; December 1, p. 1, 1874; January 22, p. 6; 27, p. 6; 30, p. 4, 1875.

[86] R. R. Hemphill to D. H. Chamberlain, August 25, 1875, Hemphill Papers.

several Negroes had been lynched in Edgefield for the murder of a white couple. Meanwhile, a displaced Negro politician from Georgia named Doc Adams was allowed to re-organize and re-arm a Negro militia company in Hamburg. A village of some five-hundred people, Hamburg was unique. Lying directly across the Savannah River from Augusta, it had been a major depot on the route connecting Charleston with the up-country. After a railroad bridge was built between Hamburg and Augusta, the village declined rapidly. By 1876, it had become partly a ghost city, inhabited almost exclusively by Negroes and governed completely by Negro officers. Its most important citizen was Prince Rivers, recently the first sergeant of the First South Carolina Regiment of Volunteers and, for several years, a leading member in the legislature. In the summer of 1876, Rivers was both the trial justice for the Hamburg area and a major general of militia. He had originally organized Hamburg's militia company in 1870 as a part of the Scott campaign. Since that time the unit hardly existed other than on paper. Under Adams, however, the company included about eighty men who drilled frequently in the streets of Hamburg and were armed with the best Winchester rifles. The sequel is worthy of close scrutiny because it indicates the manner and spirit in which white Democrats used force in the campaign of 1876.

On July 4, 1876, Adams was drilling his company on a deserted street in Hamburg when two young white men approached in a buggy. Finding the militia obstructing their advance, the whites demanded the right of way. After a hostile exchange, both parties retired. Later, the father of one of the young men retained Matthew C. Butler to press charges against Adams and other officers of the company for obstructing the highways. Butler, recently a major-general of Confederate cavalry and a prominent Reform politician, was a leading lawyer of Edgefield, and most importantly, a leader if not the commander of the Edgefield County rifle and sabre clubs.

On Saturday morning, July 8, General Butler called on Rivers and demanded that he investigate, in his capacity as trial justice, Adams's conduct in the incident. In the negotiations which ensued, Adams declined to accede to Butler's demands, first, that his militia surrender their arms and, second, that the captain apologize personally to the young men. Finally, the militia refused the advice of Rivers that they give up their rifles and withdrew to their armory, a large brick structure standing alone near the bank of the Savannah.

The primary object of the whites in pressing the issue, apparently, was the disarming of the Hamburg militia. One of the militiamen had been told by a white friend on the day before the riot that their arms were to be taken by force if necessary. Also, a white citizen of Hamburg subsequently testified that he had overheard General Butler tell another man Saturday afternoon before the riot that "they wanted those guns and were bound to have them." Yet the circumstances suggest that the whites preferred taking the arms by force rather than having them surrendered. In adding his demand for a personal apology to terms which were already unacceptable to the Negroes, Butler probably hoped to push the issue to a forceful settlement. Furthermore, the whites were obviously prepared for a fight. Immediately after the militia retired to its armory, several rifle and saber clubs from remote parts of the county appeared on the scene and must have been in the saddle well before this impasse was reached. Militant Redeemers were set to provide the Negro voter with a horrible example of the awful force which lay behind the white man's threats.

The whites quickly surrounded the armory. At 7:30, filling the still summer air with rebel yells, they opened fire. The militia answered in kind. Thirty minutes later, the Negroes drew first blood. McKie Meriwether, aged nineteen, was killed instantly when struck in the head by a Minie ball. The whites then wheeled in a cannon from Augusta and fired two rounds of grape and two of scrap into the armory, driving the defenders into the cellar. About ten o'clock, the Negro marshal of Hamburg was cut down by rifle fire as he attempted to escape across a fence at the rear of the armory. The first lieutenant of the militia company was captured as he fled and was shot down in the midst of his captors while General Butler was questioning him. At eleven o'clock, the armory was stormed and by midnight the town had been thoroughly sacked and twenty-nine Negroes captured, not all of whom belonged to the militia. Doc Adams was one of those who escaped.

At one o'clock Sunday morning, Butler departed, ordering a detail of twenty-five men to escort the prisoners to the county jail in Aiken. Enroute the guard separated four of the most prominent Negro leaders from the rest, took them aside and ordered them to run. As they ran, three of the guards shot them down. Several other Negro leaders were saved from the same fate by a party of Georgians in the guard who, after much pleading, were allowed to take them to Augusta. The main body of prisoners were then ordered to run and the guards fired into them with undetermined effect.[87]

The reaction of the native whites to the Hamburg riot was much the same as the response evoked by the Ku Klux raids. The Conservative press generally deplored such outrages, but, as Chamberlain observed, these disturbances were seen to have practical advantages for the whites which induced them "to overlook the naked brutality of the occurrence, and seek to find some excuse or explanation of conduct which ought to receive only unqualified abhorrence and condemnation . . ."[88] The re-

---

[87] There are numerous contemporary accounts of the Hamburg Riot, each having a pronounced political bias. The most informative reports are contained in: *South Carolina in 1876. Testimony as to the Denial of the Elective Franchise in South Carolina at the Election of 1875 and 1876*, Sen. Misc. Doc. No. 48 (3 vols.), 44th Cong., 2nd Sess. (Cited hereinafter as *South Carolina in 1876*); *Recent Election in South Carolina, Testimony Taken by the Select Committee on the Recent Election in South Carolina*, House Misc. Doc. No. 31 (3 parts), 44th Cong., 2nd Sess. (Cited hereinafter as *Recent Election in South Carolina*). Not entirely accurate but relatively impartial accounts appeared in the *New York Times*, July 10, p. 1; 12, p. 5; 14, p. 1; 18, p. 2; 19, p. 5; August 3, p. 1, 1876.

[88] D. H. Chamberlain to U. S. Grant, July 22, 1876, quoted in the *New York Times*, August 7, p. 5, 1876.

sponse of the Reverend Cornish substantiated Chamberlain's analysis. Even after attending the hearing in which Butler and some seventy or eighty other rioters were arraigned, Cornish refused to believe that the affair was anything but a Radical ruse. "Taking the negro testimony only on both sides," he concluded "it would appear that the Hamburg riot was gotten up designedly by the Radicals for political purposes." Further, he felt that the state's case against the white rioters was "gotten up" for the purpose of political persecution.[89]

Politically, the Hamburg riot abruptly ended Chamberlain's alliance with Conservatives of the fusionist persuasion. It also brought about a temporary reversal in Grant's policy of not interfering militarily in the internal policies of the Southern states. Responding to pleas from Chamberlain and Senator T. J. Robertson, the President ordered the army into the state to maintain order. Garrisons all along the Atlantic seaboard were soon stripped of troops for the purpose. By election day, there were more federal soldiers in South Carolina than at any time since the close of the war.[90] The result was a curtailment in the actual use of force by the militant Democracy. Nevertheless, in mid-September, rifle and sabre clubs in the Edgefield, Aiken, and Barnwell area again precipitated a riot in which two whites and an estimated fifteen Negroes were killed. Even greater disaster was prevented, however, when a small detachment of United States infantry arrived in time to halt an attack by some eight hundred white men on an entrenched force of one hundred Negroes near Silverton.[91] A month later, a skirmish in which a white man was killed and a white person and two Negroes were wounded occasioned a similar confrontation. But, again, a small contingent of federal troops arrived to force the whites to desist.[92] In other places and, after mid-October, in those three most agitated districts, the militant wing of the Democracy was constrained to rely more on the threat of violence than its actual implementation in attempting to frighten Negroes away from the polls.

Among Negroes indignation rose to the danger point. In Columbia,

---

[89] J. H. Cornish MS Diary, entry for August 10, 1876.

[90] Nevertheless, there were never enough federal troops to afford Negroes adequate protection. This was partly because of Custer's defeat at the Little Big Horn on June 25, 1876, after which the army depleted its eastern posts and recruited vigorously to fight the Sioux War. When the political and racial situation in the South became critical, the army had to strain its resources to the maximum by channeling men recruited for the Sioux War into the South and by reducing eastern garrisons to the care taker level to create an inadequate force of some 2,500 soldiers for Southern duty. These few had to move either by foot or rail and major elements were shifted between Columbia, Tallahassee, and New Orleans so that their effectiveness was severely limited. There is reason to doubt that the administration could have smothered violence under a military blanket even had it chosen to make the attempt. *Use of the Army in Certain of the Southern States,* House Ex. Doc. No. 30, 44th Cong., 2nd Sess., pp. 13 ff.

[91] *New York Times,* October 16, p. 1; 24, p. 1, 1876; J. H. Cornish MS Diary, entries for September 5, 19, 20, 1876; *South Carolina in 1876.*

[92] Alvin Hart to D. A. Tompkins, October 24, 1876, D. A. Tompkins Papers; *New York Times,* October 20, 1876, p. 1.

on July 20, R. B. Elliott called a convention of leading Negroes to protest the Hamburg murders and consider a course of action. Particularly
in Charleston did tempers flare. On July 10, a mass meeting of Negroes
declared that, "The late unwarrantable slaughter of our brethren at
Hamburg, by the order of Gen. M. C. Butler, of Edgefield County, was
an unmitigated and foul murder, premeditated and predetermined, and a
sought-for opportunity by a band of lawless men in the county known
as Regulators, who are the enemies of the colored race in that county,
composed of ex-Confederate soldiers, banded together for the purpose of
intimidating the colored laborers and voters at elections, and keeping the
'negroes in their place,' as they say."[93] A week later, another such meeting
indicated that the Negroes would fight if another such outrage occurred.
The assembly resolved to ask Chamberlain to bring Butler and his followers to justice. One speaker declared that he "hoped the Republican
party would show them that a colored man's life was as good as a white
man's," and a voice in the crowd cried, "Put Chamberlain out if he don't
stand by us." Meanwhile, a large crowd of Negroes, unable to press into
the meeting hall, filled the sidewalks and the streets near the entrance.
They refused to move to allow the street car to pass and when a policeman arrested one of the immovables the crowd freed him by force.[94]

Thereafter, the situation became increasingly explosive. In the lowcountry, where the Negro population outnumbered the white by more
than three to one, roles were reversed. Here, Negroes were menacing
and whites were fearful. Early in September, the Combahee rice workers
threatened mass violence, and even though this disturbance was almost
entirely economic in its origin the whites interpreted it as another Negro
"rising." During the evening of September 6, rioting broke out in Charleston when a Negro mob assaulted a group of Democrats. In the fight
which followed one of the whites was killed and several wounded. "The
rioters held King Street, the main thoroughfare, from midnight until sun-
rise," a *Times* correspondent reported, "breaking windows, robbing stores,
and attacking and beating indiscriminately every white man who showed
his face."[95] Elderly Charlestonians later recalled hearing cries in the night
of "Kill them! Kill them all! Dis town is ours!" On the following day,
Negro rioters retired to the back streets where they continued their attacks for several days, defiant of whites and authorities alike. Terrified,
whites stuck to their houses, shutters closed and shades drawn.[96] Hamburg
was strikingly reversed as whites were terrorized by roving bands of rioting, looting Negroes. "When the riot took place in Charleston," wrote a
Carolinian a decade afterward, "Wade Hampton *told* me he shed tears
when he heard of the cowardice of his fellow townsmen."[97] Six weeks

[93] The Address of the meeting, reprinted in the *New York Times*, July 24, 1876,
p. 6.

[94] *Ibid.*, July 21, 1876, p. 2, quoting the Charleston *News and Courier*, July 18,
1876. See also: *New York Times*, July 24, 1876, p. 6.

[95] *Ibid.*, September 8, p. 5; 11, p. 8, 1876.

[96] Avary, *Dixie after the War*, p. 362.

[97] C. W. Moise to F. W. Dawson, September 15, 1885, F. W. Dawson Papers.

later, a political meeting at Cainhoy, a village ten miles up-river from Charleston, ended in a shooting riot in which one Negro and four whites were killed.[98] Again in Charleston, on the day following the election, a street brawl over election returns produced a general melee between the races in which one white and one Negro were killed.[99] For the whites of the lowcountry, violence was obviously no solution to the political problem.

Long after the election was over, an atmosphere of fear hung over both Negroes and whites in South Carolina. A totally unfounded rumor that the rifle and sabre clubs were ravaging the Negro population of Abbeville County and that several captured Negroes had been horribly poisoned in the Anderson jail gained wide currency during December, 1876. In February, 1877, in Charleston, an old resident found the Negroes "far from quiet or civil," and "much disposed to unprovoked annoyance." Many of the young white men, he added, had "resumed their pistols lest they be again caught unprepared."[100]

Once in office, the Redeemers hastened to reduce the military poten- tial of the Negro community to a point where it posed no serious threat to white domination. Rifle and sabre clubs quickly gained legal status by being mustered into the militia under the Hampton government. The transition was only thinly veiled. In reply to a request by the captain of the Brunson Mounted Rifles that his unit be commissioned, Hampton's secretary relayed the governor's approval. "Of course it must not be a *Rifle Club*," he cautioned.[101] Strangely, some elements of the Negro militia were retained and continued active into the twentieth century. However, the Negro militia was distinctly separated from the white, its numbers comparatively small, and its displays were always ornamental and never militant.[102] On July 6, 1877, the state's adjutant and inspector general ordered local units to collect arms and ammunition "now in the hands of members of disbanded companies or of private persons . . ."[103] With the execution of this order the balance of military power shifted definitely in favor of the white community. Thereafter, no white person in South Carolina need fear more than an isolated and temporary threat of injury at the hands of Negroes. On the other side, any Negro could expect a show of aggressiveness on his part to be met by galloping, crushing, mer- ciless violence from the white community.

---

[98] *New York Times*, October 17, p. 4; 18, p. 4; 21, p. 3; 31, p. 2, 1876; Avary, *Dixie after the War*, p. 362.

[99] *New York Times*, November 9, p. 1; 16, p. 1, 1876.

[100] *Ibid.*, December 11, p. 1, 1876; Anonymous to "Belle," February 23, 1877, W. H. and W. G. De Saussure Papers.

[101] B. A. Williams to Wade Hampton, February 19, 1877; Wade Hampton to B. A. Williams, February 23, 1877, B. A. Williams Papers.

[102] George Brown Tindall, *South Carolina Negroes, 1877–1900* (Columbia, 1952), pp. 286–88.

[103] E. W. Moise to B. A. Williams, July 6, 1877, B. A. Williams Papers.

Children

at

Work

JEREMY P. FELT

The factory system, which was developing rapidly in mid-nineteenth century America, had one feature that many found appealing: the possibility of employment for the tens of thousands of vagrant children who roamed the streets of America's cities. The problem of what to do with poor children had been present since the early Colonial period when hundreds of children were shipped from England to help alleviate the labor shortage in Virginia. Many indentured children were apprenticed, but most became common laborers. These latter often caused problems for their masters, both by being difficult at work and by running away.

In the early nineteenth century "reform schools" came into existence to help make sober, hard-working citizens out of the footloose young. These largely failed, and when the factories began to hire large numbers of children between the ages of five and fifteen, it seemed that inroads would be made into the problem. As it turned out, many of the children who ended up working were not homeless wanderers, but children whose wages added to the meager incomes of their families.

Although public education was well established, at least in the cities of the Northeast, there were not enough places in the schools for all of the children, even if all had wished to attend. Compulsory attendance at school was only implemented after the Civil War; in many cases children were discouraged from attending.

Although a growing body of literature suggested that childhood was a special time of life with its own social and psychological needs, most people looked on children as small adults and expected them to fulfill adult economic roles at the earliest possible moment. Thus, if there was a job in a factory that could be done by a five-year-old, one should be hired to do it.

In the introductory chapter to his book on child labor reform, Jeremy P. Felt, of the University of Vermont, describes some of the conditions under which children worked in industry in the mid-nineteenth century. He notes the importance of the work ethic to the managers of the society and their belief that hard work at an early age was appropriate for many children. We see the beginnings of the movement to reform those conditions as people became aware of the physical and psychological damage done to the children by their horrendous working environment.

Only later, with a wider dissemination of the ideas of developmental psychology and educational reform, did the notion of childhood as a special period in life take hold. Today, with a change in the structures of industry and commerce leading to greater unemployment and the breakdown of public education, we again face the problem of thousands of children wandering the streets with nothing to do and no place to go.

Any system of labor which results in such injury to the physical nature and an ignorance so deplorable as found among these children . . . is not only a disgrace, but will . . . prove dangerous to the prosperity and stability of our free institutions.

—CHARLES F. PECK, *Commissioner of Statistics of Labor, State of New York, 1884*

At the turn of the last century New York was the leading industrial state in the nation. With garment centers, flour mills, carpet plants, foundries, machine shops, cotton mills, and shoe factories sprawling from Brooklyn to Buffalo, the Empire State held first place in thirty-six of the country's ninety-nine principal industries.[1] Children helped New York attain this preeminence, though in the course of their labors some fell down elevator shafts, burned to death, were mangled by machinery, worked standing in several inches of water, delivered messages to houses of prostitution, stood on their feet for twelve hours a day, sold newspapers at two o'clock in the morning, or froze to death in delivery wagons. In 1880 the highly conservative *Tenth Census* reported over 60,000 children between the ages of ten and fifteen at work in the state at occupations ranging from agriculture to mining and from manufacturing to

[1] New York State Department of Labor, *Report on the Growth of Industry in New York* (Albany: Argus Co., 1904), 5–6.

"Origins of the Problem (1830–86)" (Editor's title: "Children at Work"). Chapter 1 of *Hostages of Fortune: Child Labor Reform in New York State* by Jeremy P. Felt (Syracuse, N.Y.: Syracuse University Press, 1965), pp. 1–16. Copyright © 1965 by Syracuse University Press. Reprinted by permission of the publisher.

personal services. Yet, at the same time, Charles Loring Brace of the Children's Aid Society told the *New York Times* that at least 100,000 children between the ages of eight and sixteen worked in New York City alone. Moreover, only about 35 per cent of the state's youngsters between the ages of five and twenty-one attended public school.[2] Most of the remainder worked.

Of course New York was not the only state with a child labor problem after the Civil War. In 1880, an estimated 6 percent of the entire nation's children between the ages of ten and fifteen worked in some kind of industry. All of the New England states passed child labor laws in the 1840s, and by 1880 seven states had established a minimum age for employment and twelve had set maximum hours for child workers. Southern states in the 1880s were on the verge of a threefold increase in their cotton mill working force, 25 per cent of whom would be children under sixteen.[3] Because New York had a serious child labor problem yet eventually developed one of the country's most effective labor codes, its struggle to achieve this reform is of particular interest, especially since it reflected so many features of the battles against child labor as carried on in other states.

Between the end of the Civil War and the passage of the state's first factory act in 1886, some of the charitable societies, the state labor organizations, and a few politicians began to realize that New York had a sizable child labor problem. The actions taken by these groups to curb child labor proved ineffective since the number of child workers increased steadily throughout the period. Extremely rapid industrialization occurred in an atmosphere heavily conditioned by puritanical ideas of the virtue of hard work and the vice of idleness. The prevailing social ethic still resembled the idea expressed by the framers of a Virginia statute of 1646 who believed in work "for the better educating of youth in honest and profitable trades and manufactures, as also to avoid sloath and idlenesse wherewith such young children are easily corrupted."[4] The common law regarded the child as a miniature adult. Blackstone's *Commentaries*, for example, contains no chapter on infancy. The child was, in the

---

[2] U.S., Department of the Interior, Census Office, *Statistics of the Population of the United States at the Tenth Census* (Washington, D.C.: U.S. Government Printing Office, 1883), pp. 705, 722, 839, 892; *New York Times*, December 26, 1882; State of New York, Bureau of Labor Statistics, *II Report* (1884), pp. 296–98. The population of New York City in 1880 was 1,206,299, an increase of 28 percent over 1870.

[3] Elizabeth S. Johnson, "Child Labor Legislation," in John R. Commons, *History of Labour in the United States* (4 vols., New York: Macmillan Co., 1918–35), III, 403–04. The states with a minimum age for employment were Massachusetts, New Hampshire, New Jersey, Pennsylvania, Rhode Island, Vermont, and Wisconsin. Those setting maximum hours were Connecticut, Indiana, Maine, Maryland, Massachusetts, Minnesota, Ohio, Pennsylvania, Rhode Island, South Dakota, Vermont, and Wisconsin. For the southern figures see *ibid.*, 405, and Elizabeth H. Davidson, *Child Labor Legislation in the Southern Textile States* (Chapel Hill: University of North Carolina Press, 1939).

[4] W. W. Henning (ed.), *The Statutes at Large, Being a Collection of All the Laws of Virginia (1619–1792)* (13 vols., Richmond, 1809–23), II, 336.

words of Florence Kelley, "an incidental phenomenon." Pauper children had been apprenticed since at least the time of the Elizabethan Poor Law of 1598, and New York State sanctioned the practice in a law of 1826. Alexander Hamilton's argument that one of the advantages of a manufacturing system would be the opportunity for early employment of children is well known. Less well known is the fact that Hamilton's opponents, in attacking the need for manufacturing, did not reproach him for advocating child labor but sought only to prove that manufacturing was not necessary to provide employment for children.[5] As the Gilded Age began, the puritan ethic reappeared in the Gospel of Wealth with the emphasis shifted to the moral duty of the individual to acquire property and wealth through industry and thrift.[6] It is not surprising that although the 1880s were a time of growing awareness of child labor, the solutions offered were fumbling and naive.

While the puritan heritage enjoined man to work hard and save, it also stressed the importance of education. To some Americans the rise of a large industrial working class, both immigrant and native, in the mid-nineteenth century was cause for uneasiness and alarm. The new urban proletariat had missed the beneficent puritan influences available in small towns. They were uneducated, unassimilated, and to the older middle and upper classes in the Northeast they seemed a frightening incarnation of Hamilton's "Great Beast." Education of the youngest laborers seemed to be the answer and, faced with a practical reason for implementing the puritan injunction, several states passed compulsory education laws.[7] The education laws failed to accomplish their purpose. The very group they were supposed to help—the poverty-stricken lower classes—benefited least. Some poor children were dragooned into school, but school probably influenced them far less than the labor they engaged in after school. In many instances school authorities accepted poverty as a valid excuse for nonattendance. School systems were not anxious to increase their enrollment and their costs by hunting for poor children. Hence already weak laws were often destroyed by lax enforcement on the part of the schools.

An 1853 action of the New York State Senate illustrates the ambiguity, hypocrisy, and confused thinking behind many of the early education laws. Defeating a bill to prohibit children under ten from working in factories, the legislators immediately passed one regulating truancy because they believed it "the imperative duty of the State to enforce, by

---

[5] Florence Kelley, "On Some Changes in the Legal Status of the Child Since Blackstone," *International Review*, XIII (August, 1882), 83–98; Edith Abbott, "A Study of the Early History of Child Labor in America," *American Journal of Sociology*, XIV (July, 1908), 17; New York, *Laws of 1826*, ch. 254; Elizabeth L. Otey, "The Beginnings of Child Labor Legislation in Certain States," in U.S., Senate, *Report on Condition of Women and Child Wage-Earners in the United States* (Senate Document 645, 19 vols., Washington: U.S. Government Printing Office, 1910–13), VI, 27–29 (hereafter cited as Senate Document 645).

[6] For a full discussion of this point see Ralph H. Gabriel, *The Course of American Democratic Thought* (New York: The Ronald Press Co., 1940), chapter 18.

[7] This point is developed by Rush Welter in his *Popular Education and Democratic Thought in America* (New York: Columbia University Press, 1962), pp. 103–05.

legal enactment, the proper care, training, and education of its children."[8]

The conviction that education and friendly interest would solve the problems of New York's laboring children found active expression in the work of Charles Loring Brace, founder of the Children's Aid Society of New York City. Alarmed that 4,000 of the 11,000 children between the ages of five and sixteen in the city's tenement-packed Eleventh Ward were not attending school, Brace worked to establish lodging houses, reading rooms, and industrial schools. At first he thought that sending children into the country would be the best solution for homeless and wandering delinquents. He hoped "to be the means of draining the city of these children, by communicating with farmers, manufacturers, or families in the country who have need of them for employment." During 1868 Brace actually placed almost 2,000 children in country homes and provided rooms for over 11,000 more in his five metropolitan lodging houses. By 1871 he estimated that about 2,000 children under fifteen were working in the New York City paper collar industry alone, although the 1870 Federal Census claimed that only 4,269 children under fifteen worked in manufacturing of all kinds in the metropolitan area. Brace saw four-year-olds working in a Manhattan tobacco factory for three dollars a week and was appalled by the twenty to thirty thousand child vagrants he believed were present in the city. Concluding that "the evil is already vast . . . and must be checked" and that it "can only be restrained by legislation," Brace asked Charles E. Whitehead, the legal counsel for the Children's Aid Society, to draft a child labor bill.[9]

The proposed statute, for which the society lobbied unsuccessfully in four legislative sessions (1871–76), would have prohibited children under ten from work in manufacturing. In addition it required that children up to twelve show that they could read "intelligibly" before going to work, and it limited children under sixteen to a sixty-hour week. Every factory worker under sixteen was to file a teacher's certificate with his employer, indicating that he had attended school for at least three months during the year preceding the start of employment. The bill also requested funds for one factory inspector. Although it failed to become law, the Children's Aid Society bill of 1872 foreshadowed later legislation such as the Factory Act of 1886. Clearly visible in the early bill were some potential legislative loopholes: the loose educational standard implied in the

[8] *Senate Journal*, 1853, pp. 898, 924; *Assembly Documents*, 1853, vol. IV, no. 94; *Assembly Journal*, 1853, p. 961; *Laws of 1853*, ch. 185. During the entire period up to the Civil War, New York passed only three laws which might conceivably apply to child labor: one in 1831 requiring the education of child paupers; one in 1850 providing for the payment of a child's wages directly to him if the parents did not request otherwise; and one in 1853 establishing a ten-hour day on public works. (*Laws of 1831*, ch. 277; *Laws of 1850*, ch. 266; *Laws of 1853*, ch. 641.)

[9] Charles L. Brace, *The Dangerous Classes of New York and Twenty Years Work Among Them* (New York: Wynkoop and Hallenbeck Co., 1872), pp. 31, 90–93, 356–57; *New York Times*, December 25, 1868, January 26, 1873; U.S., Department of the Interior, Census Office, *The Statistics of the Population of the United States*, IX Census (1870) (3 vols., Washington: U.S. Government Printing Office, 1872), I, 793.

word "intelligibly"; the absence of a valid requirement for proof of age; the acceptance of a teacher's certificate, readily obtained in overcrowded schools; and the request for only one factory inspector to cover the entire state. Even the Children's Aid Society approved an exception to the educational requirement stating that it did not apply to any family that had more than one child between twelve and sixteen if the commissioners of the poor certified that the family needed the child's earnings.[10]

The Children's Aid Society was not the only organization groping its way toward a solution for the city's social problems. In the 1860s the Citizen's Association, an anti-Tweed group led by Peter Cooper, August Belmont, William B. Astor, and other prominent New Yorkers, investigated metropolitan health conditions. Under the direction of Dr. Stephen Smith, later Commissioner of the Metropolitan Board of Health, the association's physicians found that the death rate in New York City for the period 1861–66 averaged thirty-eight per thousand, compared to the national rate of sixteen per thousand.[11] Since over half the city's population of 800,000 was jammed into 15,000 tenements in 1864, this high death rate is not surprising. Child labor was only one product of life in overcrowded tenements where garbage and slops oozed down stairwells and children urinated on the walls: disease, death, sweatshop labor, prostitution, drunkenness, and poverty contributed to the general decay.

Investigating "Ragpicker's Court," a tenement near Mulberry Street and the Bowery, writers for *Harper's Weekly* were shocked. It was horrifying that "right in the very rooms where their food is cooked and eaten, where their children are born and reared, where they sleep at night—God knows how!— . . . these scavengers of the streets dump the filthy refuse of the city, and assort it for the buyers of such rubbish."[12] Few children were seen, most of them "being away on begging tours, or engaged as boot-blacks or street musicians."[13] In "Gotham Court" on Cherry Street lived Danny Burke, "the youngest newsboy in New York," not quite four years old, who upon being coaxed by a bystander gleefully shouted "Even' Teldram, two cents!"[14] Moving on to "Bottle Alley," near Five Points, the journalists observed a bachelor quarters occupied by five Italians: a carpenter, a shoemaker, and three streetsweepers. "The floor is destitute of carpet, is sunken in one corner, and is covered with grease and dirt," reported one investigator. "The ceiling and walls are more like those of a smoke-house than of a dwelling." In this case, Italian cooking failed to whet the appetite; the food was "gathered principally from the garbage boxes on the streets or from the offal of the markets" and boiled in a pot once a week. Adults might digest garbage, but the children "with their little pinched faces and shivering forms" would hardly thrive on it.[15]

[10] Brace, *Dangerous Classes*, pp. 362–65.

[11] Stephen Smith, *The City That Was* (New York: Frank Allaben Co., 1911), pp. 20, 40.

[12] *Harper's Weekly*, March 29, 1879, p. 246.

[13] *Ibid.*, April 5, 1879, p. 266.

[14] *Ibid.*

[15] *Ibid.*, March 22, 29, 1879, pp. 246, 227.

The Citizen's Association was asking a question whose answer was too complicated for the times when it tried to discover why the city government had done nothing and why the City Inspector's department was a "gigantic imposture," most of whose health wardens were "grossly ignorant" liquor dealers.[16] Many reformers were to ask how such things could be. Like the blind men describing an elephant, each saw the solution in the particular part of the problem he happened to be observing. To the Citizen's Association the answer was better health administration and better housing; to C. L. Brace it had been lodging houses and fresh air; to the charitable societies it was piecemeal handouts; and to Elbridge Gerry, the future president of the Society for the Prevention of Cruelty to Children, humane treatment of children. That child labor, slums, crime, poverty, and vice were the results of society's failure to cope with its industrial revolution and not of individual depravity was a concept that rarely penetrated to the working level of reform. Hence the solutions were superficial, the results negligible and short-lived. Like the other community improvement organizations of the era (the State Charities Aid Association, the New York Association for Improving the Condition of the Poor, the New York Charities Organization Society, the Y.M.C.A., and the Children's Aid Society), the Citizen's Association struck the edge of the child labor problem and glanced off into other endeavors. The children remained and their numbers increased. In 1869 the *New York Times* warned that "a great multitude of the youth of the City are . . . growing up, stunted in body, and with not even the rudiments of school training, a prey to the insatiable requirements of industry and capital."[17]

In 1874 Brace and the Children's Aid Society took advantage of a wave of anti-Tweed sentiment and obtained New York's first compulsory education law. Believing that he had achieved all that was necessary, Brace abandoned his effort to secure a factory law. "If we could train the children of the streets to habits of industry," he wrote, "and give them the rudiments of moral and mental education, we need not trouble ourselves with anything more. A child in any degree educated and disciplined can easily make an honest living in this country."[18]

The reformers were going to have to "trouble themselves more." At the time the Compulsory Education Law of 1874 was passed, New York was in the midst of a tremendous expansion of her men's clothing industry, the leading enterprise in the state between 1880 and 1909 with an annual output worth over $81,000,000.[19] The largest part of this thriving industry, which employed German, Jewish, and Italian immigrants, was carried on in New York City tenements, which by the late 1860s

---

[16] Smith, *City That Was*, pp. 145, 166–67.

[17] *New York Times*, October 6, 1869.

[18] Brace, *Dangerous Classes*, p. 96; Henry F. May, *The Protestant Churches and Industrial America* (New York: Harper and Bros., 1949), p. 112. Brace later modified his view; by 1882 he had come out for a more equitable distribution of wealth.

[19] Louis M. Hacker, Abraham Venitsky, and Dora Sandorowitz, "The Beginnings of Industrial Enterprise after the Civil War," Alexander C. Flick (ed.), *History of the State of New York* (10 vols., New York: Columbia University Press, 1933–37), X, 13–14.

numbered over 18,000 and housed half a million persons.[20] A large number of children worked in the clothing industry. About 25 percent of the ready-made clothing was manufactured by tenement family homeworkers.[21] It was common for an entire family to be engaged in the operation with the younger children sewing, pulling bastings, or carrying clothing in and out of the building. The children faded in and out of the tenement working force like guerrilla troops. One minute they were working and the next, when an inspector arrived, they were at play or "just there." As late as 1911, Florence Kelley of the National Consumers' League said that the only way to find the number of children in industrial homework was to have two inspectors to check each tenement in the city, one by day and one by night.[22]

The tenement grapevine was remarkably efficient and often fooled investigators. In 1897 W. J. Neely, a factory inspector, complained that the tenement workers "place in charge a janitor paid to lie and deceive by the sweaters, so as to fool the inspectors both of the health board and the factory department, giving warning from front house to back, and floor to floor, to clear out the children." A factory inspector, he added, "must have the abilities of the fabled French detectives in the popular novels."[23] The warning system was good enough to deceive a trained university investigator who observed the city at about the same time as Inspector Neely. Jesse E. Pope reported that he had "visited during the last six years, scores of [clothing] shops of all classes in all parts of New York City." He had not "recorded one instance of flagrant abuse of children." Pope said that he had seen only a few cases of child labor in all that time, yet he commented that while "many children were employed in carrying garments to and from the warehouse . . . clothing is bulky rather than heavy, and the bundles . . . therefore, would not in general weigh enough to overtax the strength of the child."

While Pope was asserting that "the number of children employed has been greatly overestimated by sympathetic visitors, who [have] . . . seen a few children engaged in pulling bastings,"[24] New York City granted

[20] Roy Lubove, *The Progressives and the Slums: Tenement House Reform in New York City 1890–1917* (University of Pittsburgh Press, 1962), pp. 12–20; Senate Document 645, II, 500–02.

[21] There were two main classes of tenement labor: the tenement "sweat shop," which was, in effect, a factory in a tenement which employed workers from more than one family, and the tenement "homeworkers," usually from one family, who labored in their own tenement flat. Together, the two classes produced about one-half of the city's ready-made clothing.

[22] Florence Kelley, "Report of the Committee on Child Labor," XII New York State Conference of Charities and Correction, *Proceedings*, in *Annual Report of the State Board of Charities for the Year 1911* (3 vols., Albany: Argus Co., 1912) I, 88.

[23] *XII Annual Report of the Factory Inspector* (1897), p. 760. (All factory inspection reports, bureau of labor statistics reports, and labor department reports are from the state of New York unless otherwise identified.)

[24] Jesse E. Pope, *The Clothing Industry in New York* (University of Missouri Studies, Social Science Series, Columbia [Mo.], 1905), pp. 30, 58.

9,644 licenses for tenement house manufacturing, the "vast majority" for the garment trade. Investigating tenement homework in 1910, federal agents concluded that "all children of a household where home work is done are drafted into this work with more or less regularity, after school, at night, and on Sunday."[25] The New York Bureau of Labor Statistics warned in 1902 that in estimating the number of child tenement workers it was "advisable to ascertain the total number of children, for even those who attend school regularly do more or less work at home."[26] In 1874 a ratio of *one* employed child to each of New York City's tenements would have meant about twenty thousand children. Would they be guaranteed "the rudiments of moral and mental education" by the new compulsory education law?

Concern over an uneducated working class prompted twenty-eight states to pass compulsory education laws during the post-Civil War period; New York patterned hers upon an earlier Massachusetts statute of 1852.[27] The 1874 law required children between the ages of eight and fourteen to attend school fourteen weeks a year, of which at least eight must be consecutive. No such child might work in any business without a certificate showing that he had attended school for fourteen weeks in the year preceding employment, and the employer had to keep a list of all these children as well as their school attendance certificates. This act was doomed by both its failure to require adequate proof of age and its ridiculous enforcement provisions. A child of eleven found working without a school certificate could easily claim, with parental backing, to be fifteen. Moreover, the enforcement burden was placed upon local school officials, who were expected to visit factories. Since there were no funds to pay the expenses of school authorities,[28] the alacrity and enthusiasm with which they enforced the compulsory education laws can be imagined. This attempt to use already overburdened school officials as unpaid factory inspectors reveals at best the naivete and at worst the calculated hypocrisy of the legislators.

Some educators did not believe in compulsory education and would have agreed with B. B. Snow, the Auburn Superintendent of Schools, that "the compulsory attendance of the element attempted to be reached by the law would be detrimental to the well-being of any respectable school."[29] In 1882 while some of the reformers complained about the metropolitan area's 100,000 "little toilers," C. L. Brace found that the New York City Board of Education had issued only 688 school attendance certificates in compliance with the compulsory education law.[30] The public did not care; it agreed with Superintendent Snow that "while every community would approve the compulsory attendance, in a suitable

---

[25] Senate Document 645, II, 218, 230.

[26] *XX Report Bureau of Labor Statistics* (1902), p. 70.

[27] Commons, *History of Labor*, III, 411.

[28] *Laws of 1874*, ch. 421; *Laws of 1876*, ch. 372.

[29] *II Report Bureau of Labor Statistics* (1884), pp. 304–05.

[30] Infra, p. 17; *New York Times*, December 26, 1882; *Tenth Census* (1880), pp. 705, 722, 839, 892.

school, of idle and vagrant boys, there would be little sympathy in the project of taking children from work when the proceeds of their labor are needed for the support of indigent and infirm parents."[31]

In 1882, Elbridge Gerry, President of the Society for the Prevention of Cruelty to Children, and Dr. Abraham Jacobi, President of the New York State Medical Association, tried a frontal assault on the problem. The two were alarmed not only by the number of children employed in the manufacture of artificial feathers, in the tobacco factories, and in the paper collar industry, but by the health hazards to which they were exposed. While tobacco presented the most immediate physical danger, both feathers and paper collars required excessive hours of work. It was not unusual for eight-year-olds to work ten hours a day cutting, steaming, curling, and packing feathers from cock tails or for a child of twelve to count and box twenty thousand paper collars in a single day.[32] Moreover, the manufacture of paper collars involved the use of dangerous aniline dyes. One of the first medical attacks on child labor occurred in 1879 when Dr. Roger S. Tracy published an article in *Buck's Hygiene* sharply criticizing the "inexorable discipline of the factory" and its effect upon the physical condition of growing children.[33]

Gerry and Dr. Jacobi now proposed a child labor bill that was much more sweeping than Brace's effort of ten years before. Many of its provisions anticipated modern statutes. It required every prospective child worker to be examined by a physician and barred all factory work for those under fourteen. The bill established a ten-hour day for children over fourteen and prohibited them from operating dangerous machinery or working in hazardous industries such as glass, mercury, lead, arsenic, iron, bricks, and matches. It also banned work in the home manufacture of cigars.

It was a tribute to the growing strength of the movement for child labor reform and to the increasing political leverage of labor that political leaders permitted this bill to pass the state Senate unanimously.[34] It was then killed by the time-honored device of placing it so late on the Assembly calendar that it could not be considered before the legislature ad-

---

[31] *II Report Bureau of Labor Statistics* (1884), p. 305.

[32] *New York Times*, February 16, 1882; Helen Campbell, *Darkness and Daylight, or Lights and Shadows of New York Life* (Hartford, Conn.: A. D. Worthington Co., 1892), p. 141.

[33] Roger S. Tracy, M.D., "Hygiene of Occupation," *Buck's Hygiene*, vol. II, reprinted in *II Report Bureau of Labor Statistics* (1884), (pp. 197–265), p. 201.

[34] Fred R. Fairchild, *The Factory Legislation of the State of New York* ("Publications of the American Economic Association," 3rd Series, Vol. VII, No. 4, New York: Macmillan Co., 1905), p. 40; *Senate Journal*, 1882, pp. 871–72. One of the legislative techniques used by the New York Legislature for disposing of measures which the leadership does not want enacted, but for which enough public sentiment or lobby pressure has been aroused so that the proposal cannot be ignored, is to have one house pass the bill with the understanding that the other house will reject it. Each house does a certain amount of the other's "dirty work" in this fashion. This enables members of, say, the Assembly, to face their constituents, or the lobbyists, and "blame" the bill's failure on the Senate.

journed.[35] In the same session, however, another Gerry-sponsored bill to prohibit the "hiring out" of children in houses of refuge and reformatories was passed. This system had two advantages: it enabled employers to obtain cheap labor from the poorhouses and it saved the state money because the child's earnings were used to pay his living expenses. After hearing Richard M. Hoe, manager of the house of refuge in New York City, state that the bill would add $40,000 a year to the cost of running the house, Governor Alonzo B. Cornell vetoed it. "It will hardly be questioned," he asserted, "that some regular system of industry is in the highest degree desirable, not only to make the institution as little burdensome to the public treasury as possible, but especially to accustom the children to industrious habits."[36]

The charitable organizations failed to pass their bills because they had been unable to mobilize public opinion against child labor. Most people, if they thought about it at all, believed that a comparatively small number of children were working to support needy parents. The average New Yorker in the 1880s was as opposed to state interference in the family as he was to state meddling in the market place. The state legislature was composed, for the most part, of blocs or groups whose votes were controlled by powerful economic interests. Only one force could outbid the business group: an aroused public threatening recalcitrant legislators with political extinction. The public was apathetic, but another large pressure group with the power to inflict political penalties was coming into existence: organized labor.

Drawing its strength from the hundred trade unions in New York City and from others in upstate cities, the New York labor movement included such strong craft unions as the typographers, hod-hoisters, lathers, cabinetmakers, bricklayers, and plumbers. Since 1865, New York labor had maintained a lobby, The Workingmen's Assembly, to work for favorable legislation; by 1880 labor was powerful enough to elect twenty supporters to the legislature.[37] Under the leadership of George Blair, an enthusiastic Knight of Labor from New York City, the Workingmen's Assembly had opposed child labor since 1877, at least for the record. Labor was not, however, primarily concerned with the abolition of child labor. Of much greater importance were its demands for changes in the system of contract prison labor, for establishment of a board of arbitration and mediation, and for creation of a bureau of labor statistics.[38] While legislation passed in response to pressure from labor might benefit working children, these benefits were not the main reason for labor's interest. Two examples are the Cigar Law of 1883 and the Bureau of Labor Statistics Law of 1884. Both were steps in the fight against child labor, but neither was intended primarily as a child labor bill.

[35] *Assembly Journal*, 1882, vol. II, 1126.
[36] *New York Tribune*, April 12, 1882.
[37] Howard L. Hurwitz, *Theodore Roosevelt and Labor in New York State, 1880–1900* (Columbia University *Studies in History, Economics and Public Law*, No. 500, 1943), pp. 20–26.
[38] Fairchild, *Factory Legislation*, pp. 31–35.

For several years the Cigarmakers' International Union had been aware that a large number of children were employed in the home manufacture of cigars, a practice that was having a disastrous effect on the wage level of union cigar makers. The homeworkers could not be organized, their low wages threatened nontenement manufacturers and frustrated the attempts of the Cigarmakers' Union to control the trade. According to statistics compiled by Samuel Gompers in 1881, the manufacture of cigars in tenements accounted for almost one-half of the city's cigar production. About ten thousand persons were engaged in the trade, including several thousand young children.[39] The working conditions were appalling. A typical tenement sweatshop jammed two hundred persons into "a space 14 × 40 feet, five stories and more, toppling skyward."[40] Knowing that they would be turned out of their homes by their tenement landlord-employers if production lagged, entire immigrant families worked fourteen to twenty hours a day. Clare de Graffenried found a five-year-old girl busily stripping out the midrib of tobacco leaves. The tobacco was everywhere. "Children delve in it," De Graffenried wrote, "roll in it, sleep beside it. The dust seasons their food and befouls the water they drink, and the hands of the mother are seldom washed when she leaves the cigar table to prepare meals or nurse her babe."[41] Under these circumstances health deteriorated. Describing the appearance of the little tobacco workers, a New York cigar maker likened it to "that which we would find in some of the pauper schools that Dickens describes in England."[42] In 1879 Dr. Roger S. Tracy declared that "sexual development is decidedly retarded in young girls who enter the factories before sexual evolution has begun." Whether it was retardation or simply frequent miscarriages, Dr. Tracy found that as a class cigar makers had far fewer children than did other tenement residents. The infant death rate in cigar tenements was about 20 per cent higher

[39] Samuel Gompers, *Seventy Years of Life and Labour* (2 vols., London: Hurst and Blackett, Ltd., 1925), I, 189. There is disagreement on the number of persons employed in tenement cigar manufacture in New York City during the 1880s. Edith Abbott cites a Cigarmakers' Union circular giving 3,600 as the number (*Women in Industry*, New York: D. Appleton Co., 1913), p. 201; Howard Hurwitz gives a figure of 8,000 to 10,000 (*Theodore Roosevelt and Labor*, p. 79); the *New York Times* gave a figure of about 8,000 for 1884 (January 30, 1884); the Federal Census of 1880 reported 14,476 persons engaged in tobacco, cigars, and cigarette production, tenement and nontenement, in New York City (U.S., Department of the Interior, Census Office, *Report on the Manufactures of the United States at the Tenth Census*, Washington: Government Printing Office, 1883), p. 418. To complicate matters further, Hurwitz asserts that some 70,000 persons (tenement and nontenement) were working in cigars at the time. If Hurwitz' figures, based on Cigarmakers' Union sources, are accurate, it means that about one-seventh of the cigar labor force (those in tenements) produced just under one-half the total product.
[40] Clare de Graffenried, "Child Labor," *Publications of the American Economic Association*, Vol. V (1890), 98–99.
[41] *Ibid.*, p. 99.
[42] *II Report Bureau of Labor Statistics* (1884), p. 146.

than in tenements generally.[43] "Day after day, year after year," De Graffenried reported, "children are born into this poisoned air, take it in with mother's milk, wilt and die in it, or live through puny, wailing infancy into abnormal childhood, predestined to nervous excitation, disease and depravity."[44]

The New York City Board of Health did not agree. In 1883 when the New York labor movement successfully sponsored a bill to prohibit cigar making in tenements, the Board of Health opposed it, claiming that no one's health was endangered by tenement manufacture. The Health Department knew better, of course, but was alarmed at the prospect of having to enforce the proposed law.[45] And what of the compulsory education law? Could not the Health Department and the Board of Education combine to eliminate child labor in the tenements during school hours? When a New York City cigar maker was asked this in 1883, he replied that

> Occasionally . . . the board of education wake up and for about ten to thirty days at a time they send out inspectors to pick up children on the streets who do not attend school, and then they lapse into this stupor again and that's the last of it; as far as having any effect on the moral condition of these children, the board of education does absolutely nothing.[46]

Piloting the cigar bill of 1883 through the legislature, its sponsors encountered the same problems that were to impede the efforts of later reformers. Attempts were made to delay the progress of the measure. On one occasion the bill was called up for consideration in the Senate at the end of a session and the clerk was unable to find the official copy; on another, Assemblyman Lucas Van Allen of New York City tried to cripple the bill with an amendment stating that it would go into effect only when the New York City Board of Health certified that the tenement trade was injurious to health.[47] Another problem stemmed from the labor union's tendency to view tenement manufacture as the concern solely of organized labor. The union made only halfhearted attempts to interest charitable organizations in the fight and thus had to work alone. Labor's main motive in proposing the law was to secure control of the cigar trade; exposure of tenement conditions and the education of the public were secondary considerations. Success finally came when the cigar bill passed in 1883 with the support of "silk stocking" representatives like Theodore Roosevelt, trade union legislators such as David Healy and Godfrey Ernst, and Tammany men led by Senator Thomas F. Grady.[48]

---

[43] *Ibid.*, pp. 236–37; Hurwitz, *Theodore Roosevelt and Labor*, p. 80.

[44] De Graffenried, "Child Labor," pp. 99–100.

[45] Resolution of the New York City Board of Health, January 29, 1883, cited in Fairchild, *Factory Legislation*, p. 17; *Assembly Journal*, 1883, p. 167.

[46] *II Report Bureau of Labor Statistics* (1884), p. 151.

[47] Gompers, *Life and Labour*, I, 192; *Assembly Journal*, 1883, p. 167.

[48] Gompers, *Life and Labour*, I, 192–94.

Limited to New York City, the bill prohibited the manufacture of cigars or the preparation of tobacco in rooms used as dwellings.[49]

Not realizing that they would make more money by using large factory rooms and better machinery for cigar making, the tenement manufacturers hastily obtained signatures from their dependent workers on petitions asserting the joys of tenement living. Thus armed, they descended upon Albany in force to defend their liberty at a hearing before Governor Grover Cleveland on March 8, 1883. In presenting their case the tenement manufacturers used two arguments that were to become standard among opponents of child labor regulation: they pleaded that the proposed statute would throw needy families out of work and predicted that its passage would drive industry out of the state.[50] Representing the Cigarmakers' Union at the hearing was a young assemblyman, Theodore Roosevelt, whom Gompers had recently shown through several tenements. Roosevelt assured Cleveland that while he usually opposed trade union proposals, the horrible conditions he had seen in the tenements made this an exceptional case. Later Roosevelt reported that although the conservative Cleveland had had reservations about the cigar bill, the facts had convinced the governor.[51] He signed the bill on March 12, 1883.

The tenement manufacturers lost no time in arranging a court test. Determined to find some constitutional flaw in the law, the New York Court of Appeals discovered that it embraced more than one subject ("tenements" and "all dwellings"), thus violating the state constitution's requirement that local or private bills deal with one subject only. The section of the law prohibiting the manufacture of cigars in all dwellings was therefore declared unconstitutional in January, 1884.[52] Ironically, the court did not pass upon the constitutionality of another section of the act, which prohibited anyone from living in a room in which cigars were manufactured. This section was left on the statute books, and conceivably might have been used to control the tenement trade although it would have presented immense problems of interpretation and enforcement.

In May, 1884, the legislature passed a second cigar bill. Prohibiting the manufacture of cigars on any floor of a tenement house if the floor was also used as a home or residence, the 1884 bill eliminated the confusion over the definitions of "tenement houses" and "dwellings" that had proved fatal to the first law, but it applied only to cities of the "first class" with more than 500,000 population (New York and Brooklyn). Mistakenly believing that the need for reform was related to the size of a community, the drafters left cigar homework in upstate cities like Troy unregulated.[53]

The second cigar law was struck down by the same court that had rejected the first on the grounds that it permitted unconstitutional inter-

[49] *Laws of 1883*, ch. 93.
[50] *New York Times*, March 14, 1883.
[51] Hurwitz, *Theodore Roosevelt and Labor*, p. 88.
[52] Fairchild, *Factory Legislation*, p. 19; Gompers, *Life and Labour*, I, 196.
[53] *Laws of 1884*, ch. 272.

ference with personal freedom and private property. The court maintained further that the act did not concern public health and hence could not be justified as a proper use of the police power. "What possible relation can cigar-making in any building have to the health of the general public?" the court asked. The judges found it difficult to see "how the cigar-maker is to be improved in his health or his morals by forcing him from his home and its hallowed associations and beneficent influences, to ply his trade elsewhere."[54] The statute was also found to impair the obligation of contracts. The courts were a perennial obstacle in the path of labor legislation. As Samuel Gompers put it years later: "One of the most difficult problems which the labor movement has had to meet has been the inability of the average judge to understand that industrial justice is not an abstract matter, but must be shaped to meet working relations and the needs of workers for a better life."[55] Eventually the Cigarmakers' Union succeeded in putting an end to tenement manufacture. By 1900 its agitation and, more importantly, the development of better cigar-making machinery requiring large factories, effected a sharp reduction in the number of tenement cigar workrooms.[56]

Before 1886, the most significant legislative gain for the cause of child labor reform was the organization of a state bureau of labor statistics in 1883. In demanding such a bureau, the New York labor movement anticipated one of the fundamental principles of successful reform—the accumulation and mastery of data. Because of public apathy, those who opposed change had always been able to assert that a proposed reform was unnecessary. The reformers had to marshal overwhelming evidence. In later years the Rev. Charles H. Parkhurst would preach against Tammany with a fat envelope of affidavits at his elbow, and Florence Kelley would rise in a public hearing to answer manufacturers' objections by telling each factory owner of the specific abuses in his own plant. Labor in the 1880s needed data to support its legislative demands.[57]

Since there were no accurate labor statistics for New York, the new bureau was to "collect, assort, systematize and present" data on "all departments of labor in the State, especially in relation to the commercial, industrial, social and sanitary condition of workingmen." It was high time; ten other states had already established such bureaus, beginning with Massachusetts in 1869.[58] But from the outset the bureau was severely

---

[54] *In re Jacobs*, 98. N.Y. 98 (1885). Adolph Strasser of the Cigarmakers' Union retained Roscoe Conkling as attorney for the union in this case. Conkling failed to appear in court, and pocketed his fee of $1,000, refusing to refund it. Gompers and Strasser both reported that Conkling had tried unsuccessfully to get a postponement of the case because he had another case in Hartford, Connecticut, at the same time.

[55] Gompers, *Life and Labour*, I, 197.

[56] Edith Abbott reported only 775 persons authorized to manufacture cigars in tenements in 1901. (*Women in Industry*, p. 201.)

[57] C. H. Parkhurst, *My Forty Years in New York* (New York: Macmillan Co., 1923), p. 126; Josephine Goldmark, *Impatient Crusader: Florence Kelley's Life Story* (Urbana: University of Illinois Press, 1953), pp. 72–73.

[58] As William F. Willoughby, of the United States Department of Labor put it in

hampered by lack of personnel, funds, and power. The legislature regarded the new organization as an offhand concession to labor and did not intend, at least initially, to take it seriously. The staff of the new bureau consisted of Charles F. Peck, the Commissioner of Statistics of Labor and a personal friend of Lieutenant Governor David B. Hill; and David Healy, the Chief Clerk. These two men were to examine the entire state. Attempting to buttress his staff by using trade union members as investigators, Peck dispatched a union cigar maker to check on one of the tenement cigar companies. Upon entering the premises, the cigar maker was thrown out. His assailant was arrested and brought to trial, but the case was dismissed by a police justice who said the investigator had no right to be in the factory without the owner's permission. In 1884 the state attorney general warned Peck that his bureau could not "safely undertake to compel owners . . . of manufacturing establishments to open them to . . . examination and visitation." He reminded the new commissioner that the right of citizens to be secure in their property "against unnecessary searches and inquisitorial examinations is sacredly regarded."[59]

Perhaps this climate of opinion was responsible for the rather meager statistical results of the bureau's child labor survey—the first official inquiry into New York's child labor problem. Conducted in 1883–84 at the request of the Workingmen's Assembly, the study revealed that of the 15,928 persons employed in the 151 factories visited by Peck's investigators, only 261 were under the age of fourteen. This was a lower percentage of child employment than that reported for New York by the conservative Federal Census of 1880. In 1886 the New York factory inspector was to discover that the Harmony Cotton Mills in Cohoes alone employed two hundred children under thirteen.[60]

There are several reasons why this first official study was worthless as a statistical measure of New York's child labor problem. In the first place, Peck was justifiably doubtful about the legality of his surveying activities, and in many cases his investigators accepted the word of the

---

1901: "the same difficulty [in evaluating the work of state bureaus of labor statistics] is here met with as in the effort to show the good resulting from the work of a university. We know, nevertheless, that . . . [such bureaus] have accomplished a great deal of good." ("State Activities in Relation to Labor in the United States," *Johns Hopkins University Studies in Historical and Political Science*, XIX [1900], 11). Fairchild's judgment was that the New York bureau "furnish[ed] a certain official mouthpiece for the organized labor of the state." (*Factory Legislation*, p. 26.)

[59] *Laws of 1883*, ch. 356; *I Report Bureau of Labor Statistics* (1883), p. 4; *II Report Bureau of Labor Statistics* (1884), pp. 20, 60. The police justice who affirmed the right of manufacturers to keep out state investigators later gave out the opinion that picketing was a form of assault. (Gompers, *Life and Labour*, I, 311.) By 1896 the bureau's annual appropriation had risen to over $25,000, as much as the federal Children's Bureau received in the first year of its operation.

[60] *II Report Bureau of Labor Statistics* (1884), pp. 22–25; *First Annual Report of the Factory Inspectors of the State of New York* (1886) (Albany: Argus Co., 1887), p. 13.

employer as proof of the ages of his child workers. Furthermore, the commissioner was no Florence Kelley; he lacked the fire, determination, and analytical power of that remarkable woman. Miss Kelley, soon to be appointed Chief Factory Inspector of Illinois, always assumed that employers were guilty until proven innocent; Peck was less suspicious. While the commissioner did develop (and express) some social convictions as he saw how work affected children, his studies, largely conducted by trade unionists, inevitably reflected the rather pedestrian attitude of organized labor toward the problem of working children. Labor was against child labor because children depressed wages and could not be unionized, but the unions had so many irons in the fire that they could not attack the problem with the single-minded crusading zeal of the philanthropic and social-work reform groups. And it was not only that labor had many other interests. Some trade unionists believed that child labor regulation was an interference with family rights; indeed, some of their own children worked. In an age when some union men opposed the minimum wage because it violated the right of employer and employee to free negotiation, one could not expect to find effective opposition to child labor.

However paltry the statistics produced by his study, Commissioner Peck became aware that the state did have a child labor problem and was the first official to suggest a concrete solution. An investigation of the Harmony Cotton Mills in Cohoes, a few miles from Albany, was his introduction to child labor. Standing in the street one cold day in 1883 he saw "hundreds of thin and scantily clad girls and boys ranging from eight to fifteen years of age, hurrying home with dinner pail in hand." Peck observed that "their sallow, parchment-like complexion, dwarfed bodies, pinched and care-worn faces spoke more eloquently than words," and he expressed doubts about the stability of American institutions under such a system of labor.

This investigation had started with one of the worst offenders. In 1886, the Harmony Mills were found to employ 3,200 workers, 1,200 of them under sixteen and 200 under thirteen. According to the Cohoes Police Sergeant, Matthew Smith, a majority of the children supported shiftless parents "in idleness and beer." Peck found some of the children ignorant beyond belief, unable to name the state in which they lived, the county, the state capital, or the president of the United States. The Compulsory Education Law of 1874 was on the statute books, but the mayor of Cohoes told Peck that he was still deciding whether or not to enforce it. After all, parents were out of work and starving. Why compound their misery by taking away their children's jobs? Some felt that the education of mill children was a waste of time. In a moment of public dedication the Cohoes fire chief started a night school, but found to his amazement that the children were restive after a day in the mills. Nine out of ten of them went to the school "out of pure deviltry; we have been compelled to call officers to restrain them," he complained.

The argument that children's earnings were necessary for parental survival was reiterated through the years as an answer to demands for reform. Many parents joined eagerly in the destruction of their own standard of living; by allowing their children to work, these people were keeping their own wages down. An overseer at the Harmony Mills reported that he had found it necessary to tell some parents who "bring their little children here, that if we took them in they would have to bring their cradles with them." While it was true that in some cases the earnings of children were essential to the home, in many other instances the parents were deliberately avoiding work or the children were taking home only a small fraction of their pay. The police chief of Little Falls believed that most of the children's money was spent on cigarettes and crap games. In any case, the times clearly demanded that some question be raised about the validity of a system under which honest and well-intentioned adults were forced to rely upon the wages of their children.

The prevailing ethic shied away from such questioning. Business executives like Stephen Sanford of the Sanford & Sons carpet firm in Amsterdam were concerned lest enforcement of the compulsory education law lead to "prying" and "interfering with family rights." He need not have worried. In 1880 the school attendance figures for Albany showed that of the 35,500 children of school age only 13,914 were attending school, and the Albany superintendent believed that "compared with other localities in this state, this is a favorable exhibit." Some of the missing children were, of course, in parochial and private schools but State Superintendent Ruggles simply did not know where "many" of them were. Besides, work never hurt anyone. "There are worse calamities that may befall the children of the poor than being put at regular employment," Calvin Patterson, the Brooklyn Superintendent of Schools, asserted. The only alternative to child labor was the "reconstruction of the whole social fabric, upon a new basis." That was unthinkable. "The most we can do," said Patterson, "is to temper the conditions of child labor with humanity."

Commissioner Peck believed that more could be done. His investigation of child labor had convinced him of two things: that New York had a serious child labor problem and that the compulsory education law was "to all intent and purpose, a dead letter." In his 1884 report, he strongly urged that New York pass a factory act and provide a force of factory inspectors.[61] Even this modest proposal is sufficient to mark Peck as one of the most perceptive and radical state officials of his day. Because of the political climate of the mid-eighties his plan was destined to succeed.

[61] All data and quotes from Peck's investigation are in *II Report Bureau of Labor Statistics* (1884), pp. 65, 67, 73, 77, 94, 98, 266–67, 277, 300, 302, 355–56.

Industrial Workers
Struggle for Power

HERBERT G. GUTMAN

Too often the history of the workingman in the United States has been depicted as the slow, inexorable growth of the craft union and, until the Second World War, the spectacular failures of industrial unionism. This is only a partial view of the American worker, however, for at no time in the history of our country have a majority of the workers been enrolled in unions.

Labor organizations were not widespread before the end of the Civil War, and with the possible exception of the labor movement during the Jacksonian period, they rarely had either a consistent program or sufficient power to carry out any projects they began. Even the Jacksonian labor movement died in the Panic of 1837 and the ensuing waves of unemployment, which—along with an influx of poor white immigrants—placed power in the hands of the owners of industry. Craft workers, since they remained in relatively short supply, were able to sell their skills individually and had little to gain from collective bargaining. The unskilled and semiskilled workers of factories and mines, however, were put at a great disadvantage by increased competition for jobs, for their work required little training and they were easily replaceable. Ironically, it was the craft unions that attained the earliest successes, and the skilled workers were those protected by the first permanent national labor organization, the American Federation of Labor (the AFL), which was founded in 1881.

After the Civil War, industrial development in the United States took place at a rate perhaps unprecedented in the history of the world. The great wealth of natural resources, the abundant—indeed, superabundant—supply of labor, and fifty years of peace (the ten-week Spanish-American War of 1898 being only a minor diversion in American life) favored the United States in its competition with European industrial powers.

During this period of rapid industrial advance, each new wave of immigrants, chiefly from Eastern and Southern Europe, stiffened the competition for unskilled jobs. Profiting from the oversupply of labor, the owners of many industries drove wages down and thus increased profits at the expense of the workers. In the contest for jobs and profits, various groups of workers were often pitted against one another, thus exacerbating existing hostilities among different religious and ethnic groups. Antiblack sentiment, in particular, received an ominous boost as blacks were increasingly used to fill positions vacated by strikers. In fact, the use of black workers as strikebreakers and as a threat to would-be labor organizers continued in industrial work at least until the formation of the Congress of Industrial Organizations (the CIO) in 1936, and to this day it continues in the Southern textile industry, which is perhaps the most under-organized in America. Many blacks have sometimes found it impossible to get jobs except as a result of labor-management strife.

Herbert G. Gutman, of the City College of the City University of New York, has written extensively on the life of the ordinary working-man during the Gilded Age. He has pointed out how traditional labor historians distort the image of the American workingman by focusing on the most dramatic or the most successful episodes in his struggles. In the essay reprinted here, Gutman examines industrial workers' attempts to organize in the face of a growing alliance between industrial capitalists and state and national governments. In the process, he arrives at some surprising conclusions.

Until very recent times, the worker never seemed as glamorous or important as the entrepreneur. This is especially true of the Gilded Age, where attention focuses more readily upon Jim Fisk, Commodore Vanderbilt, or John D. Rockefeller than on the men whose labor built their fortunes. Most studies have devoted too much attention to too little. Excessive interest in the Haymarket riot, the "Molly Maguires," the great strikes of 1877, the Homestead lockout, and the Pullman strike has obscured the more important currents of which these things were only symptoms. Close attention has also focused on the small craft unions, the Knights of Labor, and the early socialists, excluding the great mass of workers who belonged to none of these groups and creating an uneven picture of labor in the Gilded Age.[1]

Labor history had little to do with those matters scholars tradition-

[1] See John R. Commons *et al.*, eds., *A Documentary History of American Industrial Society* (New York: Russell and Russell, 1958), IX, pp. i–viii.

"Industrial Workers Struggle for Power" (orig. chap. 3, "The Workers' Search for Power") by Herbert G. Gutman. From *The Gilded Age*, revised and enlarged edition, edited by H. Wayne Morgan (Syracuse, N.Y.: Syracuse University Press, 1970), pp. 31–53. Copyright © 1970 by Syracuse University Press. Reprinted by permission of the publisher.

ally and excessively emphasize. Too few workers belonged to trade unions to make the unions important. There was a fundamental distinction between wage earners as a social class and the small minority of the working population that belonged to labor organizations. The full story of the wage earner is much more than the tale of struggling craft unions and the exhortations of committed trade unionists and assorted reformers and radicals. A national perspective often misrepresented those issues important to large segments of the postbellum working population and to other economic and social groups who had contact with the wage earners.[2] Most of the available literature about labor in the Gilded Age is thin, and there are huge gaps in our knowledge of the entire period.[3] Little was written about the workers themselves, their communities, and the day-to-day occurrences that shaped their outlook. Excessive concern with craft workers has meant the serious neglect of the impact of industrial capitalism—a new way of life—upon large segments of the population.

A rather stereotyped conception of labor and of industrial relations in the Gilded Age has gained widespread credence, and final and conclusive generalizations about labor abound: "During the depression from 1873 to 1879, employers sought to eliminate trade unions by a *systematic* policy of lock-outs, blacklists, labor espionage, and legal prosecution. The *widespread* use of blacklists and Pinkerton labor spies caused labor to organize *more or less* secretly and *undoubtedly* helped bring on the violence that *characterized* labor strife during this period."[4] One historian asserts: "Employers *everywhere* seemed determined to rid themselves of 'restrictions upon free enterprise' by smashing unions."[5] The "*typical* [labor] organization during the seventies," writes another scholar, "was secret for protection against intrusion by outsiders."[6] Such seemingly final judgments are questionable: How *systematic* were lockouts, black-

[2] See Thomas C. Cochran, "The Social Sciences and the Problem of Historical Synthesis," in Fritz Stern, ed., *The Varieties of History* (New York: Meridian Books, 1956), pp. 352–56; Frank Tannenbaum, *A Philosophy of Labor* (New York: Knopf, 1951), p. 68; John Hall, "The Knights of St. Crispin in Massachusetts, 1869–1878," *Journal of Economic History*, 17 (June, 1958), 174–75.

[3] The literature is voluminous, if not always accurate or comprehensive; see Harold Williamson, ed., *The Growth of the American Economy* (New York: Prentice-Hall, 1951), p. 462; Anthony Bimba, *The Molly Maguires* (New York: International Pubs., 1932); J. Walter Coleman, *The Molly Maguire Riots* (Richmond, Va.: Garrett and Massie, 1936); George McNeil, ed., *The Labor Movement* (New York, 1892), pp. 241–67; Andrew Roy, *A History of the Coal Miners of the United States* (Columbus: J. L. Trauger, 1903); John R. Commons *et al.*, *History of Labor in the United States* (New York: Macmillan, 1918), II, pp. 179–80; McAlister Coleman, *Men and Coal* (New York: Farrar & Rinehart, 1943), pp. 42–44; Arthur Suffern, *Conciliation and Arbitration in the Coal Industry of America* (Boston: Houghton Mifflin, 1915), pp. 7–17.

[4] Richard Lester, *Economics of Labor* (New York: Macmillan, 1947), p. 545; emphasis added.

[5] Herbert Harris, *American Labor* (New Haven: Yale University Press, 1938), p. 75.

[6] Selig Perlman, "Upheaval and Reorganization Since 1876," in Commons *et al.*, *History of Labor*, II, p. 196.

lists, and legal prosecutions? How *widespread* was the use of labor spies and private detectives? Was the secret union the *typical* form of labor organization? Did violence *characterize* industrial relations?

It is widely believed that the industrialist exercised a great deal of power and had almost unlimited freedom of choice when dealing with his workers after the Civil War. Part of this belief reflects the weakness or absence of trade unions. Another justification for this interpretation, however, is more shaky—the assumption that industrialism generated new kinds of economic power which immediately affected the social structure and ideology. The supposition that "interests" rapidly reshaped "ideas" is misleading. "The social pyramid," Joseph Schumpeter pointed out, "is never made of a single substance, is never seamless." The economic interpretation of history "would at once become untenable and unrealistic . . . if its formulation failed to consider that the manner in which production shapes social life is essentially influenced by the fact that human protagonists have always been shaped by past situations."[7]

In postbellum America, the relationship between "interest" and "ideology" was very complex and subtle. Industrial capitalism was a new way of life and was not fully institutionalized. Much of the history of industrialism is the story of the painful process by which an old way of life was discarded for a new one so that a central issue was the rejection or modification of a set of "rules" and "commands" that no longer fitted the new industrial context. Since so much was new, traditional stereotypes about the popular sanctioning of the rules and values of industrial society either demand severe qualification or entirely fall by the wayside. Among questionable commonly held generalizations are those that insist that the worker was isolated from the rest of society; that the employer had an easy time and a relatively free hand in imposing the new disciplines; that the spirit of the times, the ethic of the Gilded Age, worked to the advantage of the owner of industrial property; that workers found little if any sympathy from nonworkers; that the quest for wealth obliterated nonpecuniary values; and that industrialists swept aside countless obstacles with great ease.

The new way of life was more popular and more quickly sanctioned in large cities than in small one- or two-industry towns. Put another way, the social environment in the large American city after the Civil War was more often hostile toward workers than that in smaller industrial towns. Employers in large cities had more freedom of choice than counterparts in small towns, where local conditions often hampered the employer's decision-making power. The ideology of many nonworkers in these small towns was not entirely hospitable toward industrial, as opposed to traditional, business enterprise. Strikes and lockouts in large cities seldom lasted as long as similar disputes outside of urban centers. In the large city, there was almost no sympathy for the city worker among the middle and upper classes. A good deal of pro-labor and anti-industrial sentiment flowed from similar occupational groups in the small towns. Small-town

[7] J. A. Schumpeter, "The Problem of Classes," in Reinhard Bendix and Seymour Lipset, eds., *Class, Status and Power* (Glencoe: Free Press, 1953), p. 79.

employers of factory labor often reached out of the local environment for aid in solving industrial disputes, but diverse elements in the social structure and ideology shaped such decisions.

The direct economic relationships in large cities and in small towns and outlying industrial regions were similar, but the social structures differed profoundly. Private enterprise was central to the economy of both the small industrial town and the large metropolitan city, but functioned in a different social environment. The social structure and ideology of a given time are not derived only from economic institutions.[8] In a time of rapid economic and social transformation, when industrial capitalism was relatively new, parts of an ideology alien to industrialism retained a powerful hold on many who lived outside large cities.

Men and their thoughts were different in the large cities. "The modern town," John Hobson wrote of the large nineteenth-century cities, "is a result of the desire to produce and distribute most economically the largest aggregate of material goods: economy of work, not convenience of life, is the object." In such an environment, "anti-social feelings" were exhibited "at every point by the competition of workers with one another, the antagonism between employer and employed, between sellers and buyers, factory and factory, shop and shop."[9] Persons dealt with each other less as human beings and more as objects. The *Chicago Times*, for example, argued that "political economy" was "in reality the autocrat of the age" and occupied "the position once held by the Caesars and the Popes."[10] According to the *New York Times*, the "antagonistic . . . position between employers and the employed on the subject of work and wages" was "unavoidable. . . . The object of trade is to get as much as you may and give as little as you can."[11] The *Chicago Tribune* celebrated the coming of the centennial in 1876: "Suddenly acquired wealth, decked in all the colors of the rainbow, flaunts its robe before the eyes of Labor, and laughs with contempt at honest poverty." The country, "great in all the material powers of a vast empire," was entering "upon the second century weak and poor in social morality as compared with one hundred years ago."[12]

Much more than economic considerations shaped the status of the urban working population, for the social structure in large cities unavoidably widened the distance between social and economic classes. Home and job often were far apart. A man's fellow workers were not necessarily his friends and neighbors. Face-to-face relationships became less meaningful as the city grew larger and production became more diverse and specialized. "It has always been difficult for well-to-do people of the upper and middle classes," wrote Samuel Lane Loomis, a Protestant minister, in the 1880s, "to sympathize with and to understand the needs of

---

[8] *Loc. cit.*

[9] Adna Weber, *The Growth of Cities in the Nineteenth Century* (New York: Macmillan, 1899), pp. 433–34.

[10] *Chicago Times*, May 22, 1876.

[11] *New York Times*, Nov. 20, 1876.

[12] *Chicago Tribune*, July 4, 1876.

their poorer neighbors." The large city, both impersonal and confining, made it even harder. Loomis was convinced that "a great and growing gulf" lay "between the working-class and those above them."[13] A Massachusetts clergyman saw a similar void between the social classes and complained: "I once knew a wealthy manufacturer who personally visited and looked after the comforts of his invalid operatives. I know of no such case now."[14] The fabric of human relationships was cloaked in a kind of shadowed anonymity that became more and more characteristic of urban life.[15]

Social contact was more direct in the smaller post–Civil War industrial towns and regions. *Cooper's New Monthly*, a reform trade union journal, insisted that while "money" was the "sole measure of gentility and respectability" in large cities, "a more democratic feeling" prevailed in small towns.[16] "The most happy and contented workingmen in the country," wrote the *Iron Molder's Journal*, "are those residing in small towns and villages. . . . We want more towns and villages and less cities."[17] Except for certain parts of New England and the mid-Atlantic states, the post–Civil War industrial towns and regions were relatively new to that kind of enterprise. Men and women who lived and worked in these areas usually had known another way of life, and they contrasted the present with the past.

The nineteenth-century notion of enterprise came quickly to these regions after the Civil War, but the social distance between the various economic classes that characterized the large city came much more slowly and hardly paralleled industrial developments. In the midst of the new industrial enterprise with its new set of commands, men often clung to older "agrarian" attitudes, and they judged the economic and social behavior of local industrialists by these values.

The social structure of the large city differed from that of the small industrial town because of the more direct human relationships among the residents of the smaller towns. Although many persons were not personally involved in the industrial process, they felt its presence. Life was more difficult and less cosmopolitan in small towns, but it was also less complicated. This life was not romantic, since it frequently meant company-owned houses and stores and conflicts between workers and employers over rights taken for granted in agricultural communities and large cities.[18] Yet the nonurban industrial environment had in it a kind

[13] Samuel Lane Loomis, *Modern Cities and Their Religious Problems* (New York: Baker and Taylor, 1887), pp. 60–61, 63–66.

[14] Massachusetts Bureau of Labor Statistics, *Second Annual Report 1870–1871* (Boston, 1871), p. 475.

[15] See, e.g., Louis Wirth, "Urbanism as a Way of Life," in Paul Hatt and Albert Reiss, Jr., eds., *Cities and Society* (Glencoe: Free Press, 1957), pp. 36–63; Bert F. Hoselitz, "The City, the Factory, and Economic Growth," *American Economic Review*, 45 (May, 1955), 166–84.

[16] "The Distribution of Wealth," *Cooper's New Monthly*, 1 (July, 1874), 7–9.

[17] *Iron Molder's Journal*, Jan., 1874, 204.

[18] See Ohio Bureau of Labor Statistics, *First Annual Report 1877* (Columbus, 1878), pp. 156–92.

of compelling simplicity. There the inhabitants lived and worked together, and a certain sense of community threaded their everyday lives.

The first year of the 1873 depression sharply suggested the differences between the large urban center and the small industrial town. There
was no question about the severity of the economic crisis. Its consequences were felt throughout the entire industrial sector, and production,
employment, and income fell sharply everywhere.[19] The dollar value
of business failures in 1873 was greater than in any other single year between 1857 and 1893.[20] Deflation in the iron and steel industry was especially severe: 266 of the nation's 666 iron furnaces were out of blast by
January 1, 1874, and more than 50 percent of the rail mills were silent.[21]
A New York philanthropic organization figured that 25 percent of the
city's workers—nearly 100,000 persons—were unemployed in the winter
months of 1873–74.[22]

"The simple fact is that a great many laboring men are out of work,"
wrote the New York Graphic. "It is not the fault of merchants and manufacturers that they refuse to employ four men when they can pay but one,
and decline to pay four dollars for work which they can buy for two and
a half."[23] Gloom and pessimism settled over the entire country, and the
most optimistic predicted only that the panic would end in the late spring
months of 1873.[24] James Swank, the secretary of the American Iron and
Steel Association, found the country suffering "from a calamity which
may be likened to a famine or a flood."[25]

A number of serious labor difficulties occurred in small industrial
towns and outlying industrial regions during the first year of the depression, revealing much about the social structure of these areas. Although
each had its own unique character, a common set of problems shaped
them all. Demand fell away and industrialists cut production and costs
to sell off accumulated inventory and retain shrinking markets. This general contraction caused harsh industrial conflict in many parts of the
country. "No sooner does a depression in trade set in," observed David
A. Harris, the conservative head of the Sons of Vulcan, a national craft

---

[19] A. Ross Eckler, "A Measure of the Severity of Depression, 1873–1932," Review of
Economic Statistics, 15 (May, 1933), 75–81; O. V. Wells, "The Depression of
1873–1879," Agricultural History, 11 (July, 1937), 237–49; Rendigs Fels, "American
Business Cycles, 1865–1879," American Economic Review, 41 (Sept., 1951), 325–49;
Alvin Hansen, Business Cycles and National Income (New York: Norton, 1951),
pp. 24–26, 39–41.

[20] T. E. Burton, Financial Crises and Periods of Industrial and Commercial Depression (New York: Appleton, 1902), p. 344.

[21] Annual Report of the Secretary of the American Iron and Steel Association of
the Year 1874 (Philadelphia, 1875), pp. 4–5.

[22] New York Association for Improving the Condition of the Poor, Thirty-first
Annual Report (New York, 1874), p. 28.

[23] New York Graphic, Jan. 14, 1874.

[24] American Manufacturer, Oct. 30, 1873.

[25] Annual Report of the Secretary of the American Iron and Steel Association for
the Year 1874, pp. 12, 81–82.

union for puddlers and boilermen, "than all expressions of friendship to the toiler are forgotten."[26]

The *New York Times* insisted that the depression would "bring wages down for all time," and advised employers to dismiss workers who struck against wage reductions. This was not the time for the "insane imitations of the miserable class warfare and jealousy of Europe."[27] The *Chicago Times* stated that strikers were "idiots" and "criminals." Its sister newspaper, the *Chicago Evening Journal*, said the crisis was not "an unmixed evil," since labor would finally learn "the folly and danger of trade organizations, strikes, and combinations . . . against capital."[28] *Iron Age* was similarly sanguine. "We are sorry for those who suffer," it explained, "but if the power of the trade unions for mischief is weakened . . . the country will have gained far more than it loses from the partial depression of industry." Perhaps "simple workingmen" would learn they were misled by "demagogues and unprincipled agitators." Trade unions "crippled that productive power of capital" and retarded the operation of "beneficent natural laws of progress and development."[29] James Swank was somewhat more generous. Prices had fallen, and it was "neither right nor practicable for all the loss to be borne by the employers." "Some of it," he explained, "must be shared by the workingmen. . . . We must hereafter be contented with lower wages for our labor and be more thankful for the opportunity to labor at all."[30]

In cutting costs in 1873 and 1874, many employers found that certain aspects of the social structure and ideology in small industrial towns hindered their freedom of action. It was easy to announce a wage cut or refuse to negotiate with a local trade union, but it was difficult to enforce such decisions. In instance after instance, and for reasons that varied from region to region, employers reached outside of their environment to help assert their authority.

Industrialists used various methods to strengthen their local positions with workers. The state militia brought order to a town or region swept by industrial conflict. Troops were used in railroad strikes in Indiana, Ohio, and Pennsylvania; in a dispute involving iron heaters and rollers in Newport, Kentucky; in a strike of Colorado ore diggers; in two strikes of Illinois coal miners; and in a strike of Michigan ore workers.[31]

Other employers aggravated racial and nationality problems among workers by introducing new ethnic groups to end strikes, forcing men to work under new contracts, and destroying local trade unions. Negroes

[26] *Vulcan Record*, 1 (Sept., 1874), 12–14.

[27] *New York Times*, Oct. 27, Nov. 2, 15, 1873.

[28] *Chicago Times*, Oct. 3, Nov. 3, 1873.

[29] *Iron Molder's Journal*, 1 (Dec., 1873), 161; *Iron Age*, May 26, 1874, 14.

[30] *Annual Report of the Secretary of the American Iron and Steel Association for the Year 1874*, pp. 81–82.

[31] See Herbert G. Gutman, "Trouble on the Railroads in 1873–1874: Prelude to the 1877 Crisis," *Labor History*, 2 (Spring, 1962), 215–35; *Cincinnati Enquirer*, Feb.–March, 1874; *Chicago Times*, Nov. 12, 1873; *Chicago Tribune*, Nov. 10–20, 1874.

were used in coal disputes.[32] Danish, Norwegian, and Swedish immigrants went into mines in Illinois, and into the Shenango Valley and the northern anthracite region of Pennsylvania. Germans went to coal mines in northern Ohio along with Italian workers. Some Italians also were used in western Pennsylvania as coal miners, and in western and northern New York as railroad workers.[33] A number of employers imposed their authority in other ways. Regional, not local, blacklists were tried in the Illinois coal fields, on certain railroads, in the Ohio Valley iron towns, and in the iron mills of eastern Pennsylvania.[34] Mine operators in Pennsylvania's Shenango Valley and Tioga coal region used state laws to evict discontented workers from company-owned houses in midwinter.[35]

The social structure in these small towns and the ideology of many of their residents, who were neither workers nor employers, shaped the behavior of those employers who reached outside local environments to win industrial disputes. The story was different for every town, but had certain similarities. The strikes and lockouts had little meaning in and of themselves, but the incidents shed light on the distribution of power in these towns, on important social and economic relationships which shaped the attitudes and actions of workers and employers.

One neglected aspect of the small industrial town after the Civil War is its political structure. Because workers made up a large proportion of the electorate and often participated actively in local politics, they influenced local and regional affairs more than wage earners in the larger cities. In 1874, few workers held elected or appointed offices in large cities. In that year, however, the postmaster of Whistler, Alabama, was a member of the Iron Molder's International Union.[36] George Kinghorn, a leading trade unionist in the southern Illinois coal fields, was postmaster of West Belleville, Illinois.[37] A local labor party swept an election in Evansville, Indiana.[38] Joliet, Illinois, had three workers on its city council.[39] A prominent official of the local union of iron heaters and rollers sat on the city council in Newport, Kentucky.[40] Coal and ore miners ran for the state legislature in Carthage, Missouri, in Clay County, Indiana, and in Belleville, Illinois.[41] The residents of Virginia City, a town famous in western mythology, sent the president of the local miners' union to Con-

[32] *Workingman's Advocate*, March 28, June 27–July 4, 1874; John James, "The Miners' Strike in the Hocking Valley," *Cooper's New Monthly*, 1 (July, 1874), 4.

[33] *Chicago Tribune*, April 23, 1874; *Workingman's Advocate*, July 11–18, 1874; *New York World*, July 23, 1874.

[34] *Workingman's Advocate*, March 28, 1874; *Chicago Times*, Nov. 7–9, 1874; *Cincinnati Commercial*, Feb. 11, 1874; *Iron Age*, Aug. 13, 1874, 14.

[35] See Herbert G. Gutman, "Two Lockouts in Pennsylvania, 1873–1874," *The Pennsylvania Magazine of History and Biography*, 83 (July, 1959), 317–18, 322–26.

[36] *Iron Molder's Journal*, Dec., 1874, 138.

[37] *Chicago Tribune*, Nov. 19, 1874.

[38] *Workingman's Advocate*, April 14, 1874.

[39] *Ibid.*

[40] *Cincinnati Commercial*, Jan. 18, 1874.

[41] *Workingman's Advocate*, Sept. 5–12, Nov. 7, 28, 1874.

gress.[42] In other instances, town officials and other officeholders who were not wage earners sympathized with the problems and difficulties of local workers or displayed an unusual degree of objectivity during local industrial disputes.

Many local newspapers criticized the industrial entrepreneur, and editorials defended *local* workers and demanded redress for their grievances. Certain of these newspapers were entirely independent; others warmly endorsed local trade union activities.

The small businessmen and shopkeepers, lawyers and professional people, and other nonindustrial members of the middle class were a small but vital element in these industrial towns. Unlike the urban middle class they had direct and everyday contact with the new industrialism and with the problems and outlook of workers and employers. Many had risen from a lower station in life and knew the meaning of hardship and toil, and could judge the troubles of both workers and employers by personal experience. While they invariably accepted the concepts of private property and free entrepreneurship, their judgments about the *social* behavior of industrialists often drew upon noneconomic considerations and values. Some saw no necessary contradiction between private enterprise and gain and decent, humane social relations between workers and employers.

In a number of industrial conflicts, segments of the local middle class sided with workers. A Maryland weekly newspaper complained in 1876: "In the changes of the last thirty years not the least unfortunate is the separation of personal relations between employers and employees."[43] While most metropolitan newspapers sang paeans of joy for the industrial entrepreneur and the new way of life, the *Youngstown Miner and Manufacturer* thought it completely wrong that the "Vanderbilts, Stewarts, and Astors bear, in proportion to their resources, infinitely less of the burden incident to society than the poorest worker."[44] The *Ironton Register* defended dismissed iron strikers as "upright and esteemed . . . citizens" who had been sacrificed "to the cold demands on business."[45] The *Portsmouth Times* boasted: "We have very little of the codfish aristocracy, and industrious laborers are looked upon here with as much respect as any class of people."[46]

In 1873 when the depression called a temporary halt to the expansion of the Illinois mining industry, Braidwood, Illinois, was less than a dozen years old.[47] Coal mining and Braidwood had grown together, and by 1873, 6,000 persons lived in the town. Except for the supervisors and the small businessmen and shopkeepers, most residents were coal miners. Braidwood had no "agricultural neighborhood to give it support," and

[42] *Iron Molder's Journal*, Dec., 1874, 138.

[43] *Frostburg Mining Journal*, Nov. 25, 1876.

[44] *Cooper's New Monthly*, 1 (Jan., 1874), 16.

[45] *Iron Age*, March 5, 1874; *Cincinnati Commercial*, Jan. 29, Feb. 3, 1874.

[46] *Portsmouth Times*, Feb. 7, 1874.

[47] See Herbert G. Gutman, "The Braidwood Lockout of 1874," *Journal of the Illinois State Historical Society*, 53 (Spring, 1960), 5–28.

"without its coal-shafts" it would have had "no reasonable apology for existing." The town had three coal companies, but the Chicago, Wilmington and Vermillion Coal Company was by far the largest, and its president, James Monroe Walker, also headed the Chicago, Burlington and Quincy Railroad. This firm operated five shafts and employed 900 men—more than half the resident miners. Most of the owners did not live in the town. The miners were a mixed lot, and unlike most other small industrial towns in this era Braidwood had an ethnically diverse population. About half the miners came from Ireland. Another 25 percent were English, Welsh, and Scotch. A smaller number were Swedes, Italians, and Germans, and still others came from France and Belgium and even from Poland and Russia. There were also native-born miners. "The town of Braidwood," a contemporary noted, "is . . . nearly akin to Babel as regards the confusion of tongues." Although they came from diverse backgrounds, they were a surprisingly cohesive social community. A trade union started in 1872 was strong enough to extract a reasonable wage agreement from the three coal firms. A hostile observer complained that nearly all the voters were miners and that a majority of the aldermen and justices of the peace "are or have been miners."

The depression cut the demand for coal and created serious problems for the operators. By March, 1874, at least 25 percent of the miners were unemployed, and the town was "dull beyond all precedent." In late May the operators, led by the Chicago, Wilmington and Vermillion firm, cut the rate for digging coal from $1.25 to $1.10 a ton and cut the price for "pushing" coal from the work wall to the shaft nearly in half. They announced that the mines would close on June 1 unless the men accepted the new contract for a full year. The miners' efforts to compromise and suggestions of arbitration were summarily rejected, and the mines closed.

The Chicago, Wilmington and Vermillion company approached private labor contracting agencies in Chicago and recruited a large number of unskilled laborers, most of whom were Scandinavian immigrants and were not miners. Three days after the strike began, sixty-five Chicago workers arrived. More came two weeks later, and a few arrived daily until the end of July, when the number increased sharply. At the same time, anticipating trouble in putting the new men to work, the operators brought special armed Chicago Pinkerton police to the town.

Difficulties plagued the operators from the start. The miners realized they had to check the owners' strategy in order to gain a victory. As soon as new workers arrived, committees of miners explained the difficulty to them. "We ask the skilled miners not to work," the leader of the strikers explained. "As to green hands, we are glad to see them go to work for we know they are . . . a positive detriment to the company." All but three of the first sixty-five new workers decided to return to Chicago and, since they lacked funds, the miners and other local residents paid their rail fare and cheered them as they boarded a Chicago-bound train. By mid-July one shaft that usually employed two hundred men had no more than ten workers. At the end of July, only 102 men worked in the mines, and not one of them was a resident miner. The disaffected miners also met the challenge of the Pinkerton men. The miners appointed a seventy-two-man committee to prevent violence and to protect company property. The mayor and the sheriff swore in twelve of these men as special deputies, and, with one exception—when the wives of certain miners chased and struck the son of famed detective Allan Pinkerton—the miners behaved in a quiet and orderly manner.

Braidwood's tiny middle class "all back[ed] the miners." They denied complaints by the owners that the miners were irresponsible and violent. One citizen condemned the coal companies for creating "excitement so as to crush the miners" and declared that "public sympathy" was "entirely" with the workers. The operators wanted Pinkerton and his men appointed "special deputies" and made "merchant police" with power to arrest persons trespassing on company properties, but the mayor and the sheriff turned them down and deputized the strikers. Mayor Goodrich forbade parading in the streets by the Pinkerton men, and the sheriff ordered them to surrender their rifles and muskets. He did not want "a lot of strangers dragooning a quiet town with deadly weapons in their hands," and feared the miners "a good deal less than . . . the Chicago watchmen."

The operators faced other troubles. Local judges and police officials enforced the law more rigorously against them and their men than against the resident miners. Two new workers who got into a fight one Sunday were arrested for violating the Sabbath law and fined fifty dollars and court costs. Unable to pay the fine, they were put to work on the town streets. Another, jailed for hitting an elderly woman with a club, was fined one-hundred dollars and court costs. A company watchman was arrested four times, twice for "insulting townspeople."

Frustrated in these and other ways by the miners and the townspeople, the operators finally turned for help to the state government, and E. L. Higgins, the adjutant general and head of the state militia, went to Braidwood to see if troops were needed. Higgins openly supported the mine owners. He tried to prevent union men from talking with new workers, and although he asked the mayor to meet him in the office of the Chicago, Wilmington and Vermillion firm, he "never went to see the officers of the city . . . to gain an unprejudiced account of the strike." "If this is what the military forces and officers are kept for," one miner observed, "it is high time . . . such men [were] struck off the State Government payroll and placed where they belong." Mayor Goodrich reminded Higgins that neither the Braidwood nor the Will County authorities had asked for state interference. In a bitter letter to the Chicago Times, Goodrich wondered whether Higgins had come "in his official capacity or as an agent of the coal company," and firmly insisted that "the citizens of this city were not aware that martial law had been proclaimed or an embargo placed upon their speech."

Unable fully to exercise their authority in the town and worried about the possibility of losing the fall trade, the operators surrendered to the strikers fourteen weeks after the struggle began. The final agreement pleased the miners. They were especially amused when the Chicago, Wilmington and Vermillion company agreed to send all the new workers back to Chicago. A spokesman for the operators, however, bitterly as-

sailed the Braidwood mayor and other public officials for their failure
to understand the meaning of "peace, order, and freedom." Surely the
operators had further cause for complaint in 1877 when Daniel Mc-
Laughlin, the president of the miners' union, was elected mayor of Braidwood, other miners were chosen aldermen, and one became police magistrate.

Manufacturers in the small industrial iron towns of the Ohio Valley
such as Ironton and Portsmouth, Ohio, and Newport and Covington,
Kentucky, had similar troubles.[48] Several thousand men and fifteen iron
mills were involved in a dispute over wages that lasted for several months.
The mill owners who belonged to the Ohio Valley Iron Association cut
the wages of skilled iron heaters and roller men 20 percent on December
1, 1873. After the workers complained that the manufacturers were taking "undue advantage" of them "owing to the present financial trouble,"
their wages were cut another 10 percent. The valley mill owners worked
out a common policy; they decided to close all the mills for a month or so
in December and then reopen them under the new scale. Hard times
would bring new workers.

Although the mill owners in large cities such as St. Louis, Indianapolis, and Cincinnati found it easy to bring in new workers from the outside, it was another story in the small towns. They could hire new hands
in Pittsburgh, Philadelphia, and other eastern cities, but the social environment in Covington, Portsmouth, Newport, and Ironton made it
difficult to keep these men. Fellow townspeople sympathized with the
locked-out workers. In such an environment they were a relatively
homogeneous group and made up a large part of the total population of
the town. When workers agitated in small towns, paraded the streets, or
engaged in one or another kind of collective activity, their behavior
hardly went unnoticed.

The difficulties small-town iron manufacturers faced especially beset
Alexander Swift, owner of the Swift Iron and Steel Works in Newport,
Kentucky. Although his workers suffered from almost indescribable poverty after the factory closed, they would not surrender. When Swift
reopened the mill, he hired armed "special policemen." Some of the new
workers left town after they learned of the conflict, and the "police"
accompanied the rest to and from their work. The old workers made
Newport uncomfortable for new hands. There was no violence at first,
but many strikers and their wives, especially the English and Welsh
workers, gathered near the mill and in the streets to howl at the "black
sheep" going to and from work. The Newport workers exerted pressure
on them in "the hundred ways peculiar to workingmen's demonstrations."
Swift was embittered, for by the end of January only a few men worked
in his mill.

He was not alone. Mill owners in Covington, Ironton, and Portsmouth faced similar difficulty. Early in February, therefore, the Ohio
Valley Iron Association announced that unless the men returned to work

---

48 See Herbert G. Gutman, "An Iron Workers' Strike in the Ohio Valley, 1873–
  1874," *Ohio Historical Quarterly*, 68 (Oct., 1959), 353–70.

on or before February 20 they would lose their jobs and never again be hired in the valley iron mills. When most of the workers refused to return, they were fired. New workers were quickly brought to the towns, and Swift demanded special police protection for them from the Newport City Council, but it assigned only regular police. Crowds jeered the new men, and there were several fights. A large number of new workers again left Newport. "We never went any further with those fellows," a striker explained, "than calling them 'black sheep' and 'little lambs.' " Swift vainly appealed to the police to ban street demonstrations by the workers and their families, then armed the new men with pistols. When the strikers and their supporters gathered to jeer them, one of the imported laborers shot wildly into the crowd and killed a young butcher's helper. The enraged crowd chased Swift's men out of the city. After blaming the shooting on the failure of the Newport authorities to guard his men properly, Swift closed the mill.

These events did not go unnoticed in the Ohio Valley. The *Portsmouth Times* leveled a barrage of criticism at Swift and the other manufacturers. It asked whether or not they had a "right" to circulate the names of strikers in the same manner as "the name of a thief is sent from one police station to another." Such action was "cowardly . . . intimidation," and the *Times* asked: "Does not continued and faithful service deserve better treatment at the hands of men whose fortunes have been made by these workmen they would brand with the mark of CAIN? . . . Is this to be the reward for men who have grown gray in the service of these velvet-lined aristocrats? . . . Out on such hypocrisy!" After the shooting in Newport, the *Times* turned on Swift and called him a "blood-letter." Violence was wrong, the *Times* admitted, but "if the gathered-up assassins from the slums and alleys of the corrupt cities of the East are brought here to do deeds of lawlessness and violence, the stronger the opposition at the beginning the sooner they will be taught that the city of Portsmouth has no need of them."

Immune to such criticism, Swift continued to try to break down the strength of the Newport workers. In the end he succeeded. He realized that the only way to weaken the strikers was to suppress their power of public demonstration and therefore urged the Newport mayor to enforce local ordinances against dangerous and "riotous" crowds, asked the Kentucky governor to send state militia, and even demanded federal troops. Although the mayor banned "all unusual and unnecessary assemblages" in the streets, Swift still asked for state troops, and on March 5, the Kentucky governor ordered twenty-five members of the Lexington division of the state militia to Newport. Their arrival weakened the strikers and created a favorable environment for Swift. Street demonstrations were banned. The police were ordered to arrest "all persons using threatening or provoking language." When a number of unskilled strikers offered to return at the lower wage, Swift turned them away. He also rejected efforts by a member of the city council to effect a compromise with the old workers. A week after the troops arrived and three and a half months after the start of the lockout, Swift was in full control of the situation. New men worked in his factory, and the strikers admitted defeat.

The use of troops, however, was bitterly condemned in the Ohio Valley. A reporter for the *Cincinnati Enquirer* found that the "general opinion" in Newport was that Swift's maneuver was "little else than a clever piece of acting intended to kindle public sentiment against the strikers and . . . gain the assistance of the law in breaking up a strike." A Newport judge assailed the Kentucky governor, and a local poet sang of the abuse of public power:

> Sing a song of sixpence
>   Stomachs full of rye,
> Five-and-twenty volunteers,
>   With fingers in one pie;
>
> When the pie is opened
>   For money they will sing,
> Isn't that a pretty dish
>   For the City Council Ring?

There was less drama in the other Ohio Valley iron towns than in Newport, but the manufacturers in Portsmouth, Ironton, and Covington faced similar trouble. The old workers persuaded many new hands to leave the region. When fourteen men from Philadelphia arrived in Ironton and learned of the troubles for the first time, they left the city. Strikers paid their return rail fare. The same happened in Portsmouth, and the departing workers declared: "A nobler, truer, better class of men never lived than the Portsmouth boys . . . standing out for their rights." Nonstrikers in these towns also acted contrary to the manufacturers' interests. Each week the *Portsmouth Times* attacked the mill owners. "We are not living under a monarchy," the *Times* insisted, and the "arbitrary actions" of the employers were not as "unalterable as the edicts of the Medes and Persians."

A Covington justice of the peace illustrated something of the hostility felt toward the companies. Three strikers were arrested for molesting new hands, but he freed one and fined the others a dollar each and court costs. A new worker, however, was fined twenty dollars for disorderly conduct and for carrying a deadly weapon. He also had to post a five-hundred-dollar bond as a guarantee that he would keep the peace.

In the end, except in Newport, where Swift had successfully neutralized the power of the workers, a compromise wage settlement was finally worked out. Certain mills brought in new men, but some manufacturers withdrew the blacklist and rehired striking workers. A friend of the Ohio Valley iron manufacturers bitterly complained: "Things of this sort make one ask whether we are really as free a people as we pretend to be." This devotee of classical laissez-faire doctrine sadly concluded: "If any individual cannot dispose of his labor when and at what price he pleases, he is living under a despotism, no matter what form the government assumes."

Although hardly any Negroes worked in coal mines before 1873, soon after the depression started mine operators in the Ohio Hocking Valley recruited hundreds from border and southern cities. Some had been sparingly employed in certain Indiana and Ohio mines, but attracted little attention. It was different in the Hocking Valley in 1874. A large number of white miners struck and showed an unusual degree of unanimity and staying power. They found support from members of the local middle class, and the operators, unable to wear down the strikers, brought in Negroes. Although the miners were defeated, the problems they raised for their employers indicated much the same social environment as that in Braidwood and the Ohio Valley iron towns.

The railroad opened new markets for bituminous coal, and the years between 1869 and 1873 were a time of great prosperity. In 1870, 105,000 tons left the valley, and in 1873 just over 1,000,000 tons were shipped. Two years later, more than 20 percent of the coal mined in Ohio came from the Hocking Valley. Although entry costs were low, the ten largest firms in 1874 employed nearly two-thirds of the valley's miners.[49]

The miners fell into two social groupings. Those born in and near the valley had spent most of their lives in the mines and often held local positions of public trust and esteem. A Cincinnati reporter found that miners held "a good position in society . . . as a class" and filled "a fair number of municipal, church, and school offices." These men had seen their status depersonalized as they quickly became part of a larger labor force, dependent on a distant and uncontrollable market. They unavailingly complained when operators brought in many more miners than needed for full-time work. A perceptive observer found that many of the older miners "have worked in these mines since they were boys and feel they have an actual property right to their places." Most of the new men who flocked to the valley after 1869 came from distant areas, and a good number were from England, Wales, and Ireland. The rapid growth of the industry made it difficult to support trade unions in the valley.[50]

Economic crisis in 1873 suddenly punctured the region's prosperity. At best, miners found only part-time employment, and cash wages were less common than usual, for working miners were paid mostly in ninety-day notes and store credit. The operators complained that labor costs were too high and made the selling price of coal in a competitive but depressed market prohibitive. Talk of wage cuts, however, turned the miners toward trade unionism, and in December, 1873, they founded several branches of the newly established Miners' National Association. The operators in turn formed a region-wide trade association, and each of them posted a $5,000 bond as proof he would follow its directives. They also announced a sharp wage cut effective April 1, 1874, and entirely proscribed the new union.

[49] See Herbert G. Gutman, "Reconstruction in Ohio: Negroes in the Hocking Valley Coal Mines in 1873 and 1874," *Labor History*, 3 (Fall, 1962), 243–64.

[50] *Cincinnati Commercial*, May 23, June 4, 1874; Edward Wieck, *The American Miners' Association* (New York: Russell Sage Foundation, 1940), p. 141.

Prominent union leaders lost their jobs. One operator closed his supply store "for repairs," and another locked his men in a room and insisted that they sign the new wage agreement. But the union thrived. Only nine "regular" miners favored the new contract, and no more than twenty-five or thirty regulars refused to join the union. The union men agreed to the lower wage but refused to abandon their organization. The operators remained adamant and insisted that the "progress or decay" of the region hinged on the destruction of the new union—"a hydra too dangerous to be warmed at our hearth." A strike over the right of labor organization started on April 1.[51]

The strike brought trouble for the operators. Except for the *Logan Republican,* the weekly valley newspapers either supported the strikers or stood between them and the operators.[52] No more than thirty regular miners accepted the new contract on April 1, and only seventy men entered the mines that day. Local public officials declined to do the bidding of prominent operators. The New Straitsville police deputized strikers, and after Governor William Allen sent the state inspector of mines to investigate reported miner violence, country and town officials assured him there was no trouble and a committee of merchants and "other property owners" visited Allen "to give him the facts."

New Straitsville town officials joined the miners to check the effort of operator W. B. McClung to bring in from Columbus "a posse" of nine special police armed with Colt revolvers and Spencer rifles. The miners felt it "unnecessary" for armed police to come to "their quiet town," and men, women, and children paraded the streets in protest. They made it uncomfortable for McClung's police, and he promised to close his mine and return the men to Columbus. But the mayor, on the complaint of a miner, issued a warrant for their arrest for entering the town armed, "disturbing the peace and quiet." Ordered to stand trial, the nine left town after McClung's superintendent posted their bond.

Except for the Nelsonville operators, other owners closed their mines on April 1 for two months and waited out the strikers. Toward the end of May, the operators divided among themselves. A few settled with strikers, but the largest rejected arbitration and rebuked the union.[53] Compromise was out of the question, insisted the more powerful operators, and they attacked the governor for not sending militia. The triumph of the union would soon lead to the "overthrow" of "our Government and bring upon us anarchy and bloodshed that would approach, if not equal, the Communism of Paris."[54]

Unable to exert authority from within, the owners brought in between 400 and 500 Negroes in mid-June. Most came from Memphis, Louisville, and Richmond; few were experienced coal miners. They were offered high wages, told nothing of the dispute, and were generally misinformed about conditions. One employer admitted that "the motive for

---

51 *Cincinnati Commercial,* May 23, 1874; *Hocking Sentinel,* Dec. 25, 1873, Jan. 8, 22, Feb. 12, 26, March 5, 1874.
52 *Logan Republican,* April 4, 1874.
53 *Cincinnati Commercial,* May 23, 1874; *Workingman's Advocate,* May 23, 1874.
54 *Athens Messenger,* May 7, 1874.

introducing the Negro was to break down the white miners' strike."
Another boasted of his "great triumph over Trades-Unions" and called
the use of Negroes "the greatest revolution ever attempted by operators
to take over their own property." Gathered together in Columbus, the
Negroes then were sped by rail to one of the mines, which was turned
into a military camp. The county sheriff, twenty-five deputies, and the
governor's private secretary were also there. Apparently with the approval
of these officials, the operators armed the Negroes with "Government
muskets," bayonets, and revolvers, and placed them on "military duty"
around the property. No one could enter the area unless endorsed "by
the operators or police." In the meantime, state militia were mobilized in
nearby Athens, in Chillicothe, and in Cincinnati.[55]

Anger swept the Hocking Valley when the strikers learned of this.
The first day 1,000 miners and their families stood or paraded near the
Negro encampment. No violence occurred, but the men called across
picket lines of armed Negroes and urged them to desert the operators.
The second day even more miners paraded near the encampment and
urged the Negroes to leave. The miners succeeded in "raiding" the operators with an "artillery of words," and around 120 Negroes went back
on the operators. Two of the defectors admitted they had been "led by
misrepresentations to come North" and "wouldn't interfere with white
folks' work." They defended unions as "a good thing" and advocated
"plenty of good things" for everyone. The strikers housed the Negroes
in union lodge rooms, and with the help of local citizens raised about
five-hundred dollars to help them return South. But this was only a small
victory for the strikers. Enough Negroes remained to strengthen the
hand of the operators and to demoralize the union men. Negroes went
to other mines, even though strikers begged them not to work and
"mothers held their children in their arms pointing out the negroes to
them as those who came to rob them of their bread."[56]

Outside the Hocking Valley, the press applauded the operators. The
Cleveland Leader thought the strikers were "aliens"; the *Cincinnati Commercial* called them drunkards, thieves, and assassins. In the Hocking
Valley, however, some residents complained of the "mercenary newspaper men and their hired pimps." The valley newspapers especially
criticized the owners for using Negroes. Some merchants and other business folk also attacked the operators. Certain Nelsonville businessmen
offered aid to the strikers and unsuccessfully pleaded with the operators
to rehire all the miners. The police also were friendly, and the New
Straitsville mayor prevented the sending of militia to his town.[57]

Destruction of the union and the introduction of Negro workers did
not bring industrial harmony. There were strikes over wage cuts in 1875
and 1877, and conflict between Negro and white miners. In 1875, when
the men resisted a wage cut, the employers tacitly admitted that their

[55] *Hocking Sentinel*, April 1, 1874; *Chicago Tribune*, June 30, 1874.
[56] *Cincinnati Commercial*, June 13, 14, 15, 1874; *New Lexington Democratic Herald*,
    June 18, 1874.
[57] *Cleveland Leader*, July 7, 1874.

power in the valley still was inadequate. Two of them, W. F. Brooks and T. Longstreth, visited Governor Allen and pleaded that he "restore order" in the valley towns. The governor was cautious, however, and sent no troops. But their pleas revealed the employers' anxieties and need for outside power.[58]

Nothing better illustrated the differences between the small town and large city than attitudes toward public works for the unemployed. Urban newspapers frowned upon the idea, and relief and welfare agents often felt that the unemployed were "looking for a handout." The jobless, one official insisted, belonged to "the degraded class . . . who have the vague idea that 'the world owes them a living.'" Unemployed workers were lazy, many said, and trifling.[59]

Native-born radicals and reformers, a few welfare officers, ambitious politicians, responsible theorists, socialists, and "relics" from the pre–Civil War era all agitated for public works during the great economic crisis of 1873–74. The earliest advocates urged construction of city streets, parks and playgrounds, rapid transit systems, and other projects to relieve unemployment. These schemes usually depended on borrowed money or fiat currency, or issuance of low-interest-rate bonds on both local and national levels. The government had aided wealthy classes in the past; it was time to "legislate for the good of all not the few." Street demonstrations and meetings by the unemployed occurred in November and December of 1873 in Boston, Cincinnati, Chicago, Detroit, Indianapolis, Louisville, Newark, New York, Paterson, Pittsburgh, and Philadelphia. The dominant theme at all these gatherings was the same: unemployment was widespread, countless persons were without means, charity and philanthropy were poor substitutes for work, and public aid and employment were necessary and just.[60]

The reaction to the demand for public works contained elements of surprise, ridicule, contempt, and genuine fear. The Board of Aldermen refused to meet with committees of jobless Philadelphia workers. Irate Paterson taxpayers put an end to a limited program of street repairs the city government had started. Chicago public officials and charity leaders told the unemployed to join them "in God's work" and rescue "the poor and suffering" through philanthropy, not public employment.[61]

The urban press rejected the plea for public works and responsibility for the unemployed. Men demanding such aid were "disgusting," "crazy," "loud-mouthed gasometers," "impudent vagabonds," and even "ineffable asses." They were ready "to chop off the heads of every man addicted to clean linen." They wanted to make "Government an institution to pillage

[58] *Cincinnati Commercial*, Oct. 3, 1874, March 22, 1875; *New Lexington Democratic Herald*, March 25, 1875; *Hocking Sentinel*, March 4, 25, 1875; *Ohio State Journal*, April 1, 1875.

[59] *New York Graphic*, Nov. 10, 1873; *Chicago Tribune*, Dec. 23, 1873; New York Association for Improving the Condition of the Poor, *Thirtieth Annual Report, 1873* (New York: 1873), pp. 41 ff.

[60] *New York Sun*, Oct. 22, Nov. 4, Nov. 20–Dec. 20, 1873; *Chicago Times*, Dec. 1–31, 1873.

[61] *New York World*, Dec. 27, 1873; see sources in note 60.

the individual for the benefit of the mass." Hopefully, "yellow fever, cholera, or any other blessing" would sweep these persons from the earth. Depressions, after all, were normal and necessary adjustments, and workers should only "quietly bide their time till the natural laws of trade" brought renewed prosperity. Private charity and alms, as well as "free land," were adequate answers to unemployment. "The United States," said the *New York Times*, "is the only 'socialistic,' or more correctly 'agrarian,' government in the world in that it offers good land at nominal prices to every settler" and thereby takes "the sting from Communism." If the unemployed "prefer to cling to the great cities to oversupply labor," added the *Chicago Times*, "the fault is theirs."[62]

None of the proposals of the jobless workers met with favor, but the demand by New York workers that personal wealth be limited to $100,000 was criticized most severely. To restrict the "ambition of building up colossal fortunes" meant an end to all "progress," wrote the *Chicago Times*. The *New York Tribune* insisted that any limitation on personal wealth was really an effort "to have employment without employers," and that was "almost as impossible . . . as to get into the world without ancestors."[63]

Another argument against public responsibility for the unemployed identified this notion with immigrants, socialists, and "alien" doctrine. The agitation by the socialists compounded the anxieties of the more comfortable classes. Remembering that force had put down the Paris Communards, the *Chicago Times* asked: "Are we to be required to face a like alternative?" New York's police superintendent urged his men to spy on labor meetings and warned that German and French revolutionaries were "doing their utmost to inflame the workingman's mind." The *Chicago Tribune* menacingly concluded, "The coalition of foreign nationalities must be for a foreign, non-American object. The principles of these men are wild and subversive of society itself."[64]

Hemmed in by such ideological blinders, devoted to "natural laws" of economics, and committed to a conspiracy theory of social change so often attributed only to the lower classes, the literate nonindustrial residents of large cities could not identify with the urban poor and the unemployed. Most well-to-do metropolitan residents in 1873 and 1874 believed that whether men rose or fell depended on individual effort. They viewed the worker as little more than a factor of production. They were sufficiently alienated from the urban poor to join the *New York Graphic* in jubilantly celebrating a country in which republican equality, free public schools, and cheap western lands allowed "intelligent working people" to "have anything they all want."[65]

The attitude displayed toward the unemployed reflected a broader

---

[62] *New York Tribune*, Dec. 12, 1873.

[63] *Ibid.*

[64] *Chicago Times*, Dec. 23, 30, 1873; *Chicago Tribune*, Dec. 23–30, 1873.

[65] See *Chicago Tribune*, Dec. 29, 1873; Thurlow Weed to the Editor, *New York Tribune*, Dec. 20, 1873; *Cumberland Civilian and Times* (Maryland), Feb. 12, 1874.

and more encompassing view of labor. Unlike similar groups in small towns, the urban middle- and upper-income groups generally frowned upon labor disputes and automatically sided with employers. Contact between these persons and the worker was casual and indirect. Labor unions violated certain immutable "natural and moral laws" and deterred economic development and capital accumulation.[66] The *Chicago Times* put it another way in its discussion of workers who challenged the status quo: "The man who lays up not for the morrow, perishes on the morrow. It is the inexorable law of God, which neither legislatures nor communistic blatherskites can repeal. The fittest alone survive, and those are the fittest, as the result always proves, who provide for their own survival."[67]

Unions and all forms of labor protest, particularly strikes, were condemned. The *New York Times* described the strike as "a combination against long-established laws," especially "the law of supply and demand." The *New York Tribune* wrote of "the general viciousness of the trades-union system," and the *Cleveland Leader* called "the labor union kings . . . the most absolute tyrants of our day." Strikes, insisted the *Chicago Tribune*, "implant in many men habits of indolence that are fatal to their efficiency thereafter." Cleveland sailors who protested conditions on the Great Lakes ships were "a motley throng and a wicked one," and when Cuban cigar makers struck in New York, the *New York Herald* insisted that "madness rules the hour."

City officials joined in attacking and weakening trade unions. The mayor forbade the leader of striking Philadelphia weavers from speaking in the streets. New York police barred striking German cigar workers from gathering in front of a factory whose owners had discharged six trade unionists, including four women. Plain-clothes detectives trailed striking Brooklyn plasterers. When Peter Smith, a nonunion barrel maker, shot and wounded four union men—killing one of them—during a bitter lockout, a New York judge freed him on $1,000 bail supplied by his employers and said his employers did "perfectly right in giving Smith a revolver to defend himself from strikers."[68]

Brief review of three important labor crises in Pittsburgh, Cleveland, and New York points out different aspects of the underlying attitude toward labor in the large cities. The owners of Pittsburgh's five daily newspapers cut printers' wages in November, 1873, and formed an association to break the printers' union. After the printers rejected the wage cut and agreed to strike if nonunion men were taken on, two newspapers fired the union printers. The others quit in protest. The *Pittsburgh Dispatch* said the strikers "owe no allegiance to society," and the other publishers condemned the union as an "unreasoning tyranny." Three publishers started a court suit against more than seventy union members charg-

[66] *New York Tribune*, June 22, 1874.
[67] *Chicago Times*, Aug. 26, 1874.
[68] *New York Herald*, Nov. 2, 1873; *New York Times*, June 3, 1874; *Cleveland Leader*, June 18, 1874; *Chicago Tribune*, April 15, 1874.

ing them with "conspiracy." The printers were held in $700 bail, and
the strike was lost. Pittsburgh was soon "swarming with 'rats' from all
parts of the country," and the union went under. Though the cases were
not pressed after the union collapsed, the indictments were not dropped.
In 1876, the *Pittsburgh National Labor Tribune* charged, "All of these
men are kept under bail *to this day* to intimidate them from forming a
Union, or asking for just wages." A weekly organ of the anthracite
miners' union attacked the indictment and complained that it reiterated
"the prejudice against workingmen's unions that seems to exist universally
among officeholders."[69]

In May, 1874, Cleveland coal dealers cut the wages of their coal
heavers more than 25 percent, and between four- and five-hundred men
struck. Some new hands were hired. A foreman drew a pistol on the
strikers and was beaten. He and several strikers were arrested, and the
coal docks remained quiet as the strikers, who had started a union, paraded
up and down and neither spoke nor gestured to the new men. Police
guarded the area, and a light artillery battery of the Ohio National Guard
was mobilized. Lumber heavers joined the striking workers, and the two
groups paraded quietly on May 8. Although the strikers were orderly,
the police jailed several leaders. The strikers did not resist and dispersed
when so ordered by the law. In their complaint to the public, they captured the flavor of urban-industrial conflict:

> The whole thing is a calumny, based upon the assumption that if
> a man be poor he must necessarily be a blackguard. Honest poverty
> can have no merit here, as the rich, together with all their other
> monopolies, must also monopolize all the virtues. We say now . . .
> we entertain a much more devout respect and reverence for our
> public law than the men who are thus seeking to degrade it into a
> tool of grinding oppression. We ask from the generosity of our fel-
> low citizens . . . to dispute [*sic*] a commission of honest men to
> come and examine our claims. . . . We feel confident they will be
> convinced that the authorities of Cleveland, its police force, and
> particularly the formidable artillery are all made partisans to a
> very dirty and mean transaction.

The impartial inquiry proved unnecessary; a few days later several firms
rescinded the wage cut, and the strikers thanked these employers.[70]

Italian laborers were used on a large scale in the New York building
trades for the first time in the spring of 1874. They lived "piled together
like sardines in a box" and worked mainly as ragpickers and street
cleaners. They were men of "passionate dispositions" and, "as a rule, filthy
beyond the power of one to imagine." Irish street laborers and unskilled
workers were especially hard on Italians, and numerous scuffles between

[69] *Pittsburgh Post,* Nov. 21–30, 1873.
[70] *Cleveland Plain Dealer,* May 7–11, 1874.

the two groups occurred in the spring of 1874. In spite of the revulsion toward the Italians as a people, the *New York Tribune* advised employers that their "mode of life" allowed them to work for low wages.[71]

Two non-Italians, civil engineers and contractors, founded the New York Italian Labor Company in April, 1874. It claimed 2,700 members, and its superintendent, an Italian named Frederick Guscetti, announced: "As peaceable and industrious men, we claim the right to put such price upon our labor as may seem to us best." The firm held power of attorney over members, contracted particular jobs, provided transportation, supplied work gangs with "simple food," and retained a commission of a day's wages from each monthly paycheck. The company was started to protect the Italians from Irish "adversaries," and Guscetti said the men were willing to work "at panic prices." The non-Italian managers announced the men would work for 20 percent less in the building trades. Employers were urged to hire them "and do away with strikes."[72]

Protected by the city police and encouraged by the most powerful newspapers, the New York Italian Labor Company first attracted attention when it broke a strike of union hod carriers. Irish workers hooted and stoned the Italians, but the police provided them with ample protection. The *Cooper's New Monthly* complained that "poor strangers, unacquainted with the laws and customs and language of the country," had been made "the dupes of unprincipled money sharks" and were being "used as tools to victimize and oppress other workingmen." This was just the start. The firm advertised its services in *Iron Age*. By the end of July, 1874, it had branched out with work gangs in New York, Massachusetts, and Pennsylvania.[73]

There is much yet to learn about the attitude toward labor that existed in large cities, but over all opinion lay a popular belief that "laws" governed the economy and life itself. He who tampered with them through social experiments or reforms imperiled the whole structure. The *Chicago Times* was honest, if callous, in saying: "Whatever cheapens production, whatever will lessen the cost of growing wheat, digging gold, washing dishes, building steam engines, is of value. . . . The age is not one which enquires when looking at a piece of lace whether the woman who wove it is a saint or a courtesan." It came at last almost to a kind of inhumanity, as one manufacturer who used dogs and men in his operation discovered. The employer liked the dogs. "They never go on strike for higher wages, have no labor unions, never get intoxicated and disorderly, never absent themselves from work without good cause, obey orders without growling, and are very reliable."[74]

The contrast between urban and rural views of labor and its fullest

---

[71] *New York Toiler*, Aug. 22, 1874; *New York Sun*, July 6, 1874; Board of Health of the City of New York, *Fourth Annual Report, May 1, 1873 to April 30, 1874* (New York, 1874), pp. 96–97.

[72] *New York Times*, June 25–30, 1874; *New York Tribune*, June 2–14, 1874.

[73] *New York Sun*, June 2, 10, 1874; *New York World*, July 23–24, 1874.

[74] *Chicago Times*, May 22, 1876; *Iron Age*, April 27, 1876, 24.

role in society and life is clear.[75] In recent years, many have stressed "entrepreneurship" in nineteenth-century America[76] without distinguishing between entrepreneurs in commerce and trade and those in industrial manufacturing. Reflecting the stresses and strains in the thought and social attitudes of a generation passing from the old pre-industrial way of life to the new industrial America, many men could justify the business ethic in its own sphere without sustaining it in operation in society at large or in human relationships. It was one thing to apply brute force in the marketplace, and quite another to talk blithely of "iron laws" when men's lives and well-being were at stake.

Not all men had such second thoughts about the social fabric which industrial capitalism was weaving, but in the older areas of the country the spirits of free enterprise and free action were neither dead nor mutually exclusive. Many labor elements kept their freedom of action and bargaining even during strikes. And the worker was shrewd in appealing to public opinion. There is a certain irony in realizing that small-town America, supposedly alien and antagonistic toward city ways, remained a stronghold of freedom for the worker seeking economic and social rights.

But perhaps this is not so strange after all, for pre-industrial America, whatever its narrowness and faults, had always preached personal freedom. The city, whose very impersonality would make it a kind of frontier of anonymity, often practiced personal restriction and the law of the economic and social jungle. As industrialism triumphed, the businessman's powers increased, yet he was often hindered—and always suspect—in vast areas of the nation which cheered his efforts toward wealth even while condemning his methods.[77]

Facile generalizations are easy to make and not always sound, but surely the evidence warrants a new view of labor in the Gilded Age. The standard stereotypes and textbook clichés about its impotence and division before the iron hand of oppressive capitalism do not quite fit the facts. Its story is far different when surveyed in depth, carrying in it overtones of great complexity. And even in an age often marked by lust for power, men did not abandon old and honored concepts of human dignity and worth.

---

[75] See Gutman, "Two Lockouts in Pennsylvania, 1873–1874," and Gutman, "Trouble on the Railroads in 1873–1874: Prelude to the 1877 Crisis."

[76] Louis Hartz, *The Liberal Tradition in America* (New York: Harcourt, Brace, 1955), pp. 110–13, 189–227; Richard Hofstadter, *The American Political Tradition and the Men Who Made It* (New York: Knopf, 1948), pp. v–ix; John Higham, ed., *The Reconstruction of American History* (New York: Humanities Press, 1962), pp. 21–24, 119–56.

[77] Cochran, *Railroad Leaders,* p. 181.

The Lower
East Side

MOSES RISCHIN

The period between 1820 and 1930 saw one of the greatest migrations of human beings in all recorded history. Over sixty-two million
people moved from one country to another, seeking better lives for
themselves and their families. The Western Hemisphere received a
large proportion of these immigrants, the United States getting two-
thirds of the sixty-two million.

People of many varied nationalities entered the United States
after 1880. These newcomers, often called the "new immigration,"
came from areas that had previously sent few settlers to the New
World—eastern and southern Europe. Between 1891 and 1920,
these countries sent over ten million settlers, while the northern
European countries, which had previously dominated the immigration
figures, sent less than three million.

Jews from eastern Europe—the area controlled by Russia and
the Austro-Hungarian Empire—made up a large portion of the new
immigration. Many of these Jews had lived in Poland before it was
dismembered. While the Polish rulers had been relatively tolerant of
the Jews' separateness, the Russians widely persecuted them and
sought either to destroy them as a people or brutally circumscribe
their lives. By the 1870s eastern Jews had begun to slip quietly
away from their homes and migrate to the United States. Because
the Jews were not given civil rights but were required to fight in the
Czar's armies, every time Russia engaged in a war, thousands of
Jewish army reservists would disappear from their homes and join
the river of emigrants to the West. In all, about two million Jews, one-
third of the Jews in eastern Europe, left for homes elsewhere, many
of them ending up on New York's Lower East Side.

Many Jews were already living in New York City, most of them
of German origin. The Jews of the new immigration were seen by
their German coreligionists as strange, in both religion and culture.
They practiced a religious orthodoxy that had grown up separate from
world Jewry, and they spoke Yiddish, a hybrid Germanic language
written in Hebrew script. Among these eastern immigrants were also

a number of political and social radicals who had participated in the
left-wing labor politics of the late nineteenth century.

Well over half of the Jewish immigrants who came at the turn
of the century possessed industrial skills, many of which were readily
transferable, although low paying. Others, possessing mercantile experience, set up the myriad pushcarts that provided the necessities of
life for those dwelling in the area.

In his book on New York City Jews, Moses Rischin, of San Francisco State University, includes a chapter that describes the conditions
of life on the Lower East Side at the turn of the century. Out of this
teeming tenement district came many of the most powerful influences
to shape American commercial and intellectual life.

From their homes they come rosy-cheeked and with health and
Spring. They have had little fish, little meat, little bread, and it is
to get more that they come hither. But they have had air and light.
. . . Air and light, and water have been from all time the heritage
of man and even of the animals.

Evening Journal (1903)

B y the first decade of the twentieth century, the Lower East Side had
become an immigrant Jewish cosmopolis. Five major varieties of Jews
lived there, "a seething human sea, fed by streams, streamlets, and rills of
immigration flowing from all the Yiddish-speaking centers of Europe."
Clustered in their separate Jewries, they were set side by side in a pattern
suggesting the cultural, if not the physical, geography of the Old World.
Hungarians were settled in the northernmost portion above Houston
Street, along the numbered streets between Avenue B and the East River,
once indisputably *Kleindeutschland*. Galacians lived to the south, between
Houston and Broome, east of Clinton, on Attorney, Ridge, Pitt, Willett,
and the cross streets. To the west lay the most congested Rumanian quarter,
"in the very thick of the battle for breath," on Chrystie, Forsyth, Eldridge,
and Allen streets, flanked by Houston Street to the north and Grand
Street to the south, with the Bowery gridironed by the overhead elevated
to the west. After 1907 Levantines, last on the scene and even stranger
than the rest, for they were alien to Yiddish, settled between Allen and

"The Lower East Side." Reprinted by permission of the publishers from *The
Promised City: New York's Jews, 1870–1914* by Moses Rischin, Cambridge, Mass.:
Harvard University Press. Copyright © 1962 by the President and Fellows of Harvard
College. Pp. 76–94.

Chrystie streets among the Rumanians with whom they seemed to have the closest affinity. The remainder of the great Jewish quarter, from Grand Street reaching south to Monroe, was the preserve of the Russians —those from Russian Poland, Lithuania, Byelorussia, and the Ukraine—the most numerous and heterogeneous of the Jewries of Eastern Europe.[1]

The leading streets of the Lower East Side reflected this immigrant transformation. Its most fashionable thoroughfare, East Broadway, bisected the district. To the north lay crammed tenements, business, and industry. To the south lay less crowded quarters where private dwellings, front courtyards, and a scattering of shade trees recalled a time when Henry, Madison, Rutgers, and Jefferson street addresses were stylish.

The Russian intelligentsia, for whom the Lower East Side was New York, fancied East Broadway as New York's Nevsky Prospect, St. Petersburg's grand boulevard. In addition to the physicians and dentists who occupied the comfortable brownstone fronts that lined its shaded curbs, an ever-growing number of public and communal buildings came to endow it with a magisterial air. By the second decade of the twentieth century, the ten-story edifice of the *Jewish Daily Forward*, set off by Seward Park on Yiddish Newspaper Row, loomed commandingly over the two Carnegie-built libraries, the Educational Alliance, the Home for the Aged, the Jewish Maternity Hospital, the Machzike Talmud Torah, the Hebrew Sheltering House, the Young Men's Benevolent Association, and a host of lesser institutions.

Only second to East Broadway was Grand Street. Long a leading traffic artery and a major retail shopping center of lower New York, Grand Street fell into eclipse after the turn of the century with the widening of the Delancey Street approach to the Williamsburg Bridge and the comparative decline in ferry traffic. Grand Street's popular department stores, Lord and Taylor's, Lichtenstein's, and O'Neill's, moved uptown, and Ridley's closed, leaving the way open for conquest by the newcomers. Bustling Delancey Street, lined with naphtha-lit stalls crammed with tubs of fish; Hester Street, with its agents on their way to becoming bankers after the example of Jarmulowsky's passage and exchange office; and the Bowery, with the largest savings bank in the world, symbolized the district's new retail character.[2]

Only after 1870 did the Lower East Side begin to acquire an immigrant Jewish cast. In the early years of the century a small colony of

---

[1] Abraham Cahan, *Yekl, A Tale of the Ghetto* (New York, 1896), p. 28; United States Immigration Commission, *Reports* (Washington, 1907–1910), XXVI, 167; *Seventeenth Annual Report, University Settlement Society* (1903), p. 8; *Arbeiter Zeitung*, June 20, 1890; *Forward*, March 23, 24, 1904; February 20, 1906, February 8, 1911; *Volksblatt*, February 18, May 27, 1910; I. L. Nascher, *The Wretches of Povertyville* (Chicago, 1909), p. 10 ff.; Miriam Blaustein, ed., *Memoirs of David Blaustein* (New York, 1913), pp. 123–24.

[2] Gregory Weinstein, *The Ardent Eighties* (New York, 1928), p. 79; *Yiddishes Tageblatt*, March 20, 1910; *Forward*, February 14, 1912; *Report, Committee on Manufactures on the Sweating System*, 52nd Congress, 2nd Session, H. R. Report no. 2309, 1893, p. 182; *Wegweiser in der Amerikaner bizness velt*, February 8, 1892; Nascher, *The Wretches*, p. 12.

Jewish immigrants had lived there. Dutch, German, and Polish Jews had
settled on Bayard, Baxter, Mott, and Chatham streets in the 1830s and
1840s. Shortly thereafter, German and Bohemian Jews took up quarters
in the Grand Street area to the northeast and subsequently Jews of the
great German migration augmented their numbers. Except for highly
visible store fronts, Jews made little impress on the dominantly German
and Irish neighborhood. But practically all East European immigrants
arriving after 1870 initially found their way to the Lower East Side. Virtually penniless upon their arrival in the city, they were directed to the
Jewish districts by representatives of the immigrant aid societies, or came
at the behest of friends, relatives, or employers.[3]

The changes brought about by the great Jewish migration forced the
district's middle-class Germans and Irish, living in predominantly two-
and two-and-one-half-story dwellings, to retreat to less crowded quarters.
By 1890 the Lower East Side bristled with Jews. The tenth ward (loosely
coinciding with the Eighth Assembly District), closest to the central factory area, was the most crowded with 523.6 inhabitants per acre; the
adjacent wards, the thirteenth and seventh, numbered 428.6 and 289.7
persons per acre respectively. Exceeding 700 persons per acre by 1900,
the tenth ward was the most densely settled spot in the city; residential
block density was even more appalling as factories and shops crowded
tenements. In 1896 a private census counted 60 cigar shops, 172 garment
shops, 65 factories, and 34 laundries in the tenth ward. In 1906, of fifty-
one blocks in the city with over 3000 inhabitants each, thirty-seven were
on the Lower East Side. On Rivington Street, Arnold Bennett remarked,
"the architecture seemed to sweat humanity at every window and door."
Hardy, older, or improvident remnants of the region's earlier Irish residents and a floating seafaring population still clung to the river edges
along Cherry and Water streets; at the turn of the century, Italian immigrants crossed the Bowery on Stanton and East Houston streets and
crowded into the low reaches of East Broadway. But in the second decade
of the new century, the Lower East Side, from the Bowery to within a
stone's throw of the East River, and from Market Street to 14th Street,
had become a mass settlement of Jews, the most densely packed quarter in
the city. In 1914 one sixth of the city's population was domiciled below
14th Street upon one eighty-second of the city's land area; most of New
York's office buildings, and factories that employed over one half of the
city's industrial workers were located in this district.[4]

[3] H. B. Grinstein, *The Rise of the Jewish Community of New York, 1654–1860*
(New York, 1945), p. 31 ff.; United States Industrial Commission, *Reports* (Washington, 1900–1902), XV, 476, 478; P. Cowen, *Memories of An American Jew* (New
York, 1932), p. 103; B. Weinstein, *Fertsig yor in di idishe arbeter bavegung in
amerika* (New York, 1924), pp. 21–22.
[4] *New York Labor Bulletin*, 10:314–315, 322 (September 1908); E. E. Pratt, *The Industrial Causes of Congestion in New York City* (New York: 1911), pp. 19–20;
Report of the University Settlement Society (1897), p. 3; Arnold Bennett, *Your
United States* (New York, 1912), p. 187; Harold M. Finley, "New York's Populous
and Densest Blocks," *Federation*, 4:8 (November 1906); H. C. Brearley, *The Prob-*

Once the immigrants had come to rest on the Lower East Side, there was little incentive to venture further. Knowing no English and with few resources, they were dependent upon the apparel industries, the tobacco and cigar trades, and other light industrial employments that sprang up in the area or that were located in the adjacent factory district. Long hours, small wages, seasonal employment, and the complexity of their religious and social needs rooted them to the spot. It was essential to husband energies, earnings, and time. Lodgings of a sort, coffee morning and evening, and laundry service were available to single men for three dollars a month. Bread at two and three cents a pound, milk at four cents a quart, a herring for a penny or two, and apples at from one to five for a cent, depending on quality, were to be had. Accustomed to a slim diet, an immigrant could save much even with meager earnings and still treat himself to a bracing three-course Sabbath dinner (for fifteen cents). Thrift and hard work would, he hoped, enable him in time to search out more congenial and independent employment. Until new sections of the city were developed at the turn of the century only country peddlers were to stray permanently beyond the familiar immigrant quarters.[5]

There was a compelling purpose to the pinched living. Virtually all immigrants saved to purchase steamship tickets for loved ones and many regularly mailed clothing and food parcels to dependent parents, wives, and children overseas. The power of home ties buoyed up the spirits of immigrants wedded to the sweatshop and peddler's pack, whose precious pennies mounted to sums that would unite divided families. Among the early comers women were relatively few, but the imbalance between the sexes soon was remedied. In 1890 an investigation by the Baron de Hirsch Society into the condition of 111,690 of an estimated 135,000 Jews on the Lower East Side counted 60,313 children and 22,647 wage-earners, with 28,730 unspecified, mostly women. Undoubtedly, the proportion of women and children in New York was far greater than it was elsewhere. In 1910 women exceeded men among Hungarians and Rumanians, were equal among Austrians, and made up 47 percent of the Russians. As non-Jews from these countries were heavily male, Jewish women clearly outnumbered men, accentuating the group's domesticity. Among the major ethnic groups of New York, only the Irish, 58 percent female, exceeded the Jewish ratio.[6]

lem of Greater New York and Its Solution (New York, 1914), p. 28; *Report of the University Settlement Society* (1896), p. 10.

[5] G. M. Price, *Di yuden in amerika* (Odessa, 1891), p. 13; *New York Herald*, November 25, 1892; Louis Waldman, *Labor Lawyer* (New York, 1944), pp. 23, 28; *Autobiography 45* (MS, YIVO Institute of Jewish Research), p. 153.

[6] Z. Szjaikowski, "The Attitude of American Jews to East European Jewish Immigrants, 1881–1893," *Publ. Amer. Jew. Hist. Soc.*, 40:272–73 (March 1951); *Report, Select Committee, H. R. Importation of Contract Laborers, Paupers, Convicts and Other Classes* (Washington, 1889), p. 289 ff.; W. T. Elsing, *The Poor in Great Cities* (New York, 1898), p. 103.

The following are the 1910 population figures for East Europeans in New York City:

A nondescript colony of Jews in the 1870s swelled into a center of Jewish life by the turn of the century, the drama of whose fortunes and passions was closely followed by fellow immigrants throughout the country as well as by those in the lands they left behind. A highly visible knot of Jews "huddled up together" around Baxter and Chatham streets had been engulfed by an influx that saturated the whole region with its flavor and institutions.[7]

THE TENEMENT BOOM

Ever since the 1830s New York's housing problem had been acute. Manhattan's space limitations exacerbated all the evils inherent in overcrowding, and refinements in the use of precious ground only emphasized the triumph in material necessities over human considerations. New York's division of city lots into standard rectangular plots, 25 feet wide by 100 feet deep, made decent human accommodations impossible. In order to secure proper light and ventilation for tenement dwellers twice the space was needed, a prohibitive sacrifice considering real estate values. No opportunity was overlooked to facilitate the most economical and compact housing of the immigrant population. To the improvised tenements that had been carved out of private dwellings were added the front and rear tenements and, finally, the dumbbell-style tenement of 1879.

With the heavy Jewish migration of the early 1890s, the Lower East Side, still relatively underdeveloped compared to the Lower West Side, became the special domain of the new dumbbell tenements, so called be-

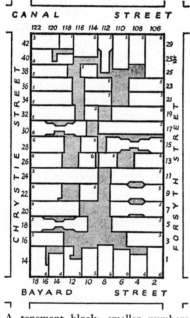

A tenement block: smaller numbers indicate number of stories.

	Total	Male	Female
Rumania	33,584	16,461	17,123
Hungary	76,625	35,224	41,401
Austria	190,237	95,941	94,296
Russia	484,189	257,418	226,771

Walter Laidlaw, *Statistical Sources for Demographic Studies of New York, 1910* (New York, 1912), I, i.

[7] W. M. R., "A Sabbath Among Orthodox Jews," *Galaxy*, 14:379 ff. (September 1872); *Report, Committee of the Senate, Relations between Capital and Labor* (Washington, 1885), I, 94.

cause of their shape. The six- to seven-story dumbbell usually included four apartments to the floor, two on either side of the separating corridor. The front apartments generally contained four rooms each, the rear apartments three. Only one room in each apartment received direct light and air from the street or from the ten feet of required yard space in the rear. On the ground floor two stores generally were to be found; the living quarters behind each had windows only on the air shaft. The air shaft, less than five feet in width and from fifty to sixty feet in length, separated the tenement buildings. In the narrow hallways were located that special improvement, common water closets. In 1880 a leading magazine described typical dumbbell tenements on Ridge, Eldridge, and Allen streets.

> They are great prison-like structures of brick, with narrow doors and windows, cramped passages and steep rickety stairs. They are built through from one street to the other with a somewhat narrower building connecting them. . . . The narrow courtyard . . . in the middle is a damp foul-smelling place, supposed to do duty as an airshaft; had the foul fiend designed these great barracks they could not have been more villainously arranged to avoid any chance of ventilation. . . . In case of fire they would be perfect death-traps, for it would be impossible for the occupants of the crowded rooms to escape by the narrow stairways, and the flimsy fire-escapes which the owners of the tenements were compelled to put up a few years ago are so laden with broken furniture, bales and boxes that they would be worse than useless. In the hot summer months . . . these fire-escape balconies are used as sleeping-rooms by the poor wretches who are fortunate enough to have windows opening upon them. The drainage is horrible, and even the Croton as it flows from the tap in the noisome courtyard, seemed to be contaminated by its surroundings and have a fetid smell.

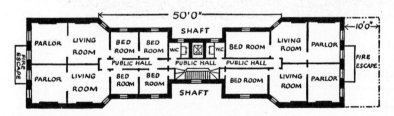

A typical dumbbell tenement

As if the tenement abuses were not degrading enough, the absence of public toilet facilities in so crowded a district added to the wretched sanitation. It was reported that "in the evening every dray or wagon becomes a private and public lavatory, and the odor and stench . . . is perfectly horrible."[8]

[8] C. D. Wright, *The Housing of the Working People* (Washington, 1895), p. 196;

Conditions became almost unendurable in the summer months. Bred in colder and dryer climates, tenement inhabitants writhed in the dull heat. Added to the relentless sun were the emanations from coal stoves, the flat flame gas jets in lamps, and the power-producing steam boilers. Inevitably, roofs, fire escapes, and sidewalks were converted into sleeping quarters, while the grassed enclosure dividing Delancey Street and Seward Park supplied additional dormitory space. Late July and early August of 1896 were especially savage. Between August 5 and 13, 420 New Yorkers perished from the continuous heat, "the absolute stagnation of the air, and the oppressive humidity," noted Daniel Van Pelt, although the temperature averaged 90.7 degrees and never reached 100.

Fire and the possibilities of fire brought added terror to the inhabitants of overcrowded tenements. "Remember that you live in a tenement house," warned insurance agents. In 1903, 15 percent of the tenements in the district still were without fire escapes. Of 257 fatalities in Manhattan fires between 1902 and 1909, 99 or 38 percent were on the Lower East Side, all victims of old-law tenements.[9]

Few families could afford the privacy of a three- or four-room flat. Only with the aid of lodgers or boarders could the $10 to $20 monthly rental be sustained. The extent of overcrowding in the tenements, reported a witness before the United States Immigration Commission, was never fully known.

> At the hour of retiring, cots or folded beds and in many instances simply mattresses are spread about the floor, resembling very much a lot of bunks in the steerage of an ocean steamer . . . The only way to properly determine the census of one of these tenements, would be by a midnight visit, and should this take place between the months of June and September, the roof of the building should not be omitted.

However trying tenement living proved to be for adults, for children it was stultifying, concluded a settlement worker. "The earlier years of the child are spent in an atmosphere which . . . is best described by a little girl, 'a place so dark it seemed as if there weren't no sky.' "

Evictions for nonpayment of rent and rent strikes were perennial. Uncertainty of employment, nonpayment of wages, unexpected obligations, dependents, and adversities contributed to the high incidence of evictions. In the year 1891–1892 alone, in two judicial districts of the Lower East Side, 11,550 dispossess warrants were issued by the presiding

---

Forty-third Annual Report, New York Association for the Improvement of the Condition of the Poor, 1886, p. 43 ff.; Allen Forman, "Some Adopted Americans," *The American Magazine*, 9:51–52 (November 1888): *Report of the Tenement House Committee of 1894*, New York (1895), pp. 8, 12, 104.

[9] Daniel Van Pelt, *Leslie's History of Greater New York* (New York, 1898), I, 544; *21st Annual Report, University Settlement Society*, 1907, pp. 27–28; *Abendblatt der Arbeiter Zeitung*, January 11, 1896; *Idisher Zhurnal*, July 14, 1899; *Fifth Report, Tenement House Department, City of New York, 1909*, pp. 106–07, 112–113.

magistrates. In 1900 the absence of mass evictions was regarded as a mark of unexampled well-being.[10]

Earlier residents of the Lower East Side and hereditary property owners profited from the overcrowding. The rise in real estate values, exorbitant rents, and the low upkeep provided tenement owners with ample returns upon their investments. Even allowing for losses due to nonpayment of rent and an average occupancy of ten months in the year, landlords earned ten percent. By more studied neglect, a resourceful agent might reap even higher returns. The Lower East Side tenements soon came to be recognized as the most lucrative investment in the city. Nowhere else did the speculator's market in tenement properties flourish as luxuriantly as it did here, where earlier immigrants had learned to exploit the misery of later comers.

In 1901 the further construction of dumbbell tenements was prohibited. The Tenement House Law of that year set new standards for future housing and attempted to correct the worst abuses in the existing buildings. All new tenements were to have windows that opened at least twelve feet away from those opposite. Toilets and running water in each apartment, unobstructed fire escapes, and solid staircases were required. In the old buildings modern water closets were to be installed in place of the outside privies. Finally, a Tenement House Department was established to supervise and enforce the provisions of the law. While the law never was effectively enforced, its initial achievements proved encouraging.

Many new tenements were quickly built according to the new specifications. In the fiscal year ending July 1, 1903, 43 percent of New York's new tenements were located on the Lower East Side. Its inhabitants eagerly welcomed the brightly lighted rooms, bathtubs, and other improvements. At first, landlords on the Lower East Side were more prompt to make alterations in old-law tenements than landlords elsewhere in the city, for the heavy pressure of population made even remodeled properties attractive. The years 1905 to 1909 saw an unparalleled boom throughout the city with houses to fit every taste, from tenements to palatial mansions for chance customers, at unprecedented prices ranging up to $500,000. "It is doubtful if New York City, or in fact any other city of the world, ever before witnessed the expenditure of so many millions of dollars in the construction of tenement houses during a similar period."[11]

While new housing was on the rise, the fast developing clothing

---

[10] *Report of the Year's Work, University Settlement Society, 1900*, p. 34; William P. McLoughlin, "Evictions in New York's Tenement Houses," *Arena*, 7:50–52 (December 1892); *Hebrew Standard*, August 25, 1893; Samuel Gompers to Henry Goldfogle, September 14, 1893 (Gompers Papers), *Yiddishes Tageblatt*, January 1, 1901.

[11] United States Industrial Commission, *Reports*, XIV, 87; Frank Moss, *The American Metropolis* (New York, 1897), III, 205; Joseph Barondess to Charles D. Spivak, June 11, 1908 (Barondess Papers); *Report, Tenement House Department, 1902–1903*, I, 141; *Fifth Report, Tenement House Department*, New York, 1909, pp. 19, 103; Ralph D. Paine, "Are Riches Demoralizing American Life?" *World's Work*, 6:3917 ff. (September 1903).

trades also were relocating and building. As the heavy settlement of East Europeans decisively affected the housing of the city's earlier residents, so the new growth of the apparel industry, manned by Lower East Side Jews, helped to transform the city's business districts. Once legislation and the advent of electric power combined to reduce Lower East Side sweatshops, thousands of garment shops and factories pushed up the axial thoroughfares of Lower Manhattan. By 1910 the continued march uptown found the garment industry intruding upon once fashionable Madison Square, the site of New York's tallest skyscrapers. Brownstones and brick residences were razed to be displaced by 16- to 20-story steel-girdered loft buildings trimmed with granite and marble and housing scores of clothing shops. In the course of this displacement, the city's central retailing district and its theater and hotel district were forced northward. The main retailing center, at 14th Street in 1880 and at 23rd Street in 1900, became anchored at 34th Street by 1910.[12]

DISEASE AND CRIME

Superficially, East European Jews seemed ill-prepared to contend with the demands that tenement living thrust upon them. "Their average stature is from five feet one inch to five feet three inches, which means that they are the most stunted of the Europeans, with the exception of the Hungarian Magyars." Shortest were the Galacians, tallest and sturdiest the Rumanians. Undersized and narrow-chested, a high proportion were described as "physical wrecks." Centuries of confinement, habituation to mental occupations, chronic undernourishment, and a deprecation of the physical virtues ill-fitted them for heavy labor. Between 1887 and 1890 nearly five thousand immigrants were returned to Europe labeled physically "unfit for work." Seemingly helpless and emaciated, they were to exhibit exceptional capacity for regeneration; traditional moral and religious disciplines were to serve them in good stead.

Despite the trying conditions under which the immigrants lived, they showed a remarkable resistance to disease. With the highest average density of tenants per house in the city, the tenth ward had one of the lowest death rates. Indeed only a business ward and a suburban ward surpassed it in healthfulness. Dr. Annie Daniel, a pioneer in public health, volunteered her interpretation of this before the Tenement House Committee:

> The rules of life which orthodox Hebrews so unflinchingly
> obey as laid down in the Mosaic code . . . are designed to main-

---

[12] Stephen Jenkins, *The Greatest Street in the World* (New York, 1911), p. 191; B. J. Hendrick, "The Jewish Invasion of America," *McClure's Magazine*, 40:134 (March 1913); M. Feinstone and H. Lang, eds., *Geverkshaftn* (New York, 1938), pp. 100–02; Donald H. Davenport, et al., *The Retail Shopping and Financial Districts in New York* (New York, 1927), p. 23; George Filipetti, *The Wholesale Markets in New York* (New York, 1925), p. 46.

tain health. These rules are applied to the daily life of the individuals as no other sanitary laws can be . . . Food must be cooked properly, and hence the avenues through which the germs of disease may enter are destroyed. Meat must be "kosher," and this means that it must be perfectly healthy. Personal cleanliness is at times strictly compelled, and at least one day in the week the habitation must be thoroughly cleaned.

True, only some 8 percent of Russian Jewish families had baths, according to a study of 1902, and these often without hot water. Yet the proliferation of privately owned bathhouses in the city was attributable largely to the Jewish tenement population. "I cannot get along without a 'sweat' (Russian bath) at least once a week," insisted a newcomer. In 1880, one or two of New York's twenty-two bathhouses were Jewish; by 1897, over half of the city's sixty-two bathhouses (including Russian, Turkish, swimming, vapor, and medicated bathhouses) were Jewish. If standards of cleanliness were not as faithfully maintained as precept required, the strict regimen of orthodoxy, even when weakened, contributed to the immigrant's general well-being.[13]

Nevertheless, close crowding and unsanitary conditions made all communicable diseases potentially contagious. Despite great apprehension between 1892 and 1894, Jewish immigrants did not carry to New York the cholera and typhus epidemics raging at the European ports of embarkation. But in 1899 the United Hebrew Charities became alarmed by the Board of Health's report of the mounting incidence of tuberculosis in the city. That Jewish immigrants might become easy victims of the "White Plague" was hardly to be doubted. "As many as 119 Jewish families have lived in one tenement house on Lewis Street within the past five years." Hundreds of flats had been occupied by fifteen successive families within a brief period. "Many of these houses are known to be hotbeds of the disease, the very walls reeking with it." Increasingly, the dread disease with its cough and crimson spittle took its toll. Ernest Poole, an investigator, frequently heard the plea of the afflicted. "Luft, gibt mir luft—Air, give me air." Especially susceptible were the intellectuals, whose often shattered spirits, overwrought minds, and undernourished bodies fell prey to the killer. Yet so great was the immigrant's concern for health that the mortality rate from tuberculosis was lower on the East Side than in the city's prosperous districts. Venereal diseases, previously almost unknown among Jews in Eastern Europe, became progres-

---

[13] M. Fishberg, "Health and Sanitation of the Immigrant Jewish Population of New York," *Menorah*, August-September 1902, pp. 4, 14; M. Fishberg, "Materials for the Physical Anthropology of the Eastern European Jews," *Memoirs of the American Anthropological and Ethnological Societies* (June 1905), vol. I, pt. 1, pp. 36–37, 41–42; Szjaikowski, "The Attitude of American Jews," p. 243; *Report of the Tenement House Committee of 1894*, pp. 21–22, 47–48; United States Immigration Commission, *Reports*, XXVI, 165; Joseph Barondess to Mrs. M. A. Davis, March 22, 1902 (Barondess Papers); cf. *Wilson's Business Directory of New York City, 1880–1881*, p. 45; *The Trow Business Directory of New York City, 1897*, pp. 86–87; *Trow Business Directory of Greater New York, 1907*, pp. 102–03.

sively more common among young men, as restraints were weakened by exposure to new temptations.[14]

Alcoholism, a prime contributor to poverty, ill-health, and mortality among other national groups, was unusual among Jewish immigrants. As Jews replaced the earlier inhabitants, the many saloons of the Lower East Side, trimmed with shields that proclaimed them "the workman's friend," declined. Those that survived drew few clients from a neighborhood addicted to soda water, "the life-giving drink"; they depended on the throng of transients that passed through the district. Jews did not abstain from drink. Yet only upon religious festivals and during the Sabbath ritual when the Kiddush cup was emptied did alcohol appear in the diet of most immigrants. In 1908, $1.50 a year for holiday and ritual wine seemed adequate for a family of six. "The Day of Rejoicing of the Law and the Day of Purim are the only two days in the year when an orthodox Jew may be intoxicated. It is virtuous on these days to drink too much, but the sobriety of the Jew is so great that he sometimes cheats his friends and himself by shamming drunkenness," Hutchins Hapgood noted. Jews habitually imbibed milder beverages. Russians were notorious tea drinkers. Hungarians were addicted to coffee. The less austere Galacians and Rumanians tippled mead and wine respectively. But in the New World all fell victim to the craze for seltzer or soda water with its purported health-giving powers. In his long experience, reported the president of the United Hebrew Charities in 1892, he had known only three chronic Jewish drunkards.[15]

Neurasthenia and hysteria, however, took a heavy toll of victims. Their sickness was the result of a history of continual persecution and insecurity, intensified by the strains of settlement in unfamiliar surroundings. Diabetes, associated with perpetual nervous strain, was common. Suicide, rarely recorded among the small-town Jews of Eastern Europe, also found its victims in the tenements of New York. Despair, poverty, and the fears generated in the imagination led some immigrants to take their own lives. "Genumen di gez" (took gas) was not an uncommon headline in the Yiddish press. Yet in the late 1880s only the city's Irish showed a lower suicide rate than did Russian Jews.

[14] C. E. A. Winslow, *The Life of Hermann M. Biggs* (Philadelphia, 1929), pp. 80, 95–96; *Eighteenth Annual Report, United Hebrew Charities, 1892–1893*, p. 21; United States Industrial Commission, *Reports*, XIV, 87; *Twenty-fifth Annual Report, United Hebrew Charities, 1899*, p. 35; Ernest Poole, *The Plague In Its Stronghold* (New York, 1903), p. 3 ff.; Joseph Barondess to Dr. J. S. Billings, September 9, 1908 (Barondess Papers); M. Fishberg, "Tuberculosis Among Jews," *American Israelite*, October 18, 1908; A. J. Rongy, "Half a Century of Jewish Medical Activities in New York City," *Medical Leaves*, 1:159 (1937). Cf. advertisements by specialists in "men's diseases" like "Old Dr. Grey," *Yiddishes Tageblatt*, January 16, 1899; *Forward*, March 2, 1901.

[15] *Abendblatt der Arbeiter Zeitung*, January 13, 1896; *Forward*, February 14, 1912; Ida Van Etten, "Russian Jews as Desirable Immigrants," *Forum*, 15:178 (April 1893); S. Foster, "The Workingman and the Synagogue," *Yearbook, Central Conference of American Rabbis*, 20:482 (1909); Hutchins Hapgood, *The Spirit of the Ghetto* (New York, 1902), p. 14; *Forward*, March 23, 1904; *Report of the Tenement House Committee of 1894*, p. 431.

However desperate the straits in which Jewish immigrants found themselves, confirmed paupers among them were few. The rarity of alcoholism, the pervasiveness of the charitable impulse, the strength of ties to family and *lanslite*, and a deep current of optimism preserved the individual from such degradation.[16]

Prior to the 1880s only the Rubenstein murder case spotted the record of New York's Jews. Upon the testimony of doubtful witnesses, Rubenstein was sentenced to death for the slaying of his girl cousin, but cheated the hangman by taking his own life. The first crime of violence attributed to a Jew in the city's annals, its very novelty gave rise to the popular street song, "My name is Pesach Rubinstein." So unassailable was the peaceful reputation of the Jewish districts that it was a matter for continual commendation. In 1878 Jews numbered 7 in a workhouse population of 1178; 8 among 485 prison inmates; and 12 among 1110 house-of-correction inmates.

The obloquy attached to the strident Jews of Baxter and Chatham Streets; to the Canal Street clothing shop puller-in and the Division Street millinery shop pulleress; to Michael Kurtz, better known as "Sheeney Mike," reputedly the "champion burglar of America"; and to "Marm" Mandelbaum, unmatched receiver of stolen goods, did not detract from the high repute of the city's Jews. The two dozen Bowery pawnshops were owned by Americans or earlier immigrants who catered to the needs of a heterogeneous population and were not part of the immigrant community.

The major crime and violence in the area did not stem from the immigrants. They were its victims. The Lower East Side had always attracted much of the city's criminal element to its margins. By the last decades of the nineteenth century, it had shed the ferocity of earlier years when the "Bowery B'hoys" and the "Dead Rabbits" terrorized the area. But Mayor Hewitt's reform drive in 1887 inadvertently reinforced the district's frailties by forcing criminals and prostitutes from their accustomed uptown resorts into the less conspicuous tenements of the tenth ward, where they remained, undisturbed even by the Parkhurst crusade. The Raines Law, which provided that only hotels could serve liquor on Sundays, worsened the situation. In 1896, of 236 saloons in the tenth ward, 118 were Raines Law hotels, while 18 were outright houses of prostitution. In the first decade of the twentieth century, crusading District Attorney William Travers Jerome kept open house in his special office on Rutgers Street, at the hub of the Lower East Side, and the most salient features of criminality were forced underground. By 1905 the "peripatetic sisterhood" had been driven from the Bowery, and Captain Godard's

[16] M. Fishberg, *The Jews* (London, 1911), pp. 367, 530–31; *Arbeiter Zeitung*, June 20, 1890; *Forward*, July 26, August 13, 1897, March 25, 1908; M. Osherowitch, "Di geshikhte fun forverts, 1897–1947" (MS, New York Public Library); 17; *Nayer Gayst* (December 1897), p. 133; L. K. Frankel, "Jewish Charities," *The Making of America*, ed. R. M. LaFollette (Chicago, 1906), X, 64; United States Industrial Commission, *Reports*, XIV, 119, 121; K. H. Claghorn, "Jewish Immigration and Pauperism," *Jewish Charity*, 3:31–32 (November 1903); L. K. Frankel to Herbert Parsons, January 12, 1905 (Parsons Papers).

Anti-Policy Society's campaign banished gambling from the thoroughfare. But the criminal elements soon returned.[17]

Crime was endemic to the Lower East Side. The close collaboration between police officers, politicians, and criminals, revealed in detail in the Lexow and Mazet investigations of the 1890s, had turned the district into a Klondike that replaced the uptown Tenderloin as a center of graft and illicit business. Invariably the culprits in these activities were not immigrants, but Americanized Jews learned in street-corner ways and shorn of the restraints of the immigrant generation. "It is not until they have become Americanized, have adapted themselves to the environment of the district and adopted its ways and vices, that they become full-fledged wretches," commented Dr. I. L. Nascher. In the early years of the twentieth century the effect of such conditions upon the young deeply disturbed those anxious for the public weal. In 1909 some 3000 Jewish children were brought before Juvenile Court and in the next few years Jewish criminals regularly made newspaper headlines. The appearance of an ungovernable youth after the turn of the century was undeniable and excited apprehension.[18]

The violations of the law that characterized the immigrant community differed from the crimes of the sons of the immigrants. The former were an outgrowth of occupational overcrowding, poverty, and religious habits. Straitened circumstances contributed to the large number of cases of family desertion and nonsupport. Concentrated in marginal commerce and industry, Jews were prone to transgress the codes of commercial law. "The prevalence of a spirit of enterprise out of proportion to the capital of the community" gave rise to a high incidence of felonious larceny, forgery, and failure to pay wages. Peddlers and petty shopkeepers were especially vulnerable to police oppression for evading informal levies as well as formal licensing requirements. Legislation controlling business on Sunday found Jewish immigrants natural victims. In so congested a district, the breaking of corporation ordinances was unavoidable and the

[17] Grinstein, *The Rise of the Jewish Community*, p. 16; *Trial of Pesach Rubinstein for the Murder of Sarah Alexander in the Town of New Lots* (New York, 1876), *passim;* Frank Weitenkampf, *Manhattan Kaleidoscope* (New York, 1947), p. 82; prison statistics are cited in Allen Tarshish, "The Rise of American Judaism; A History of American Jewish Life from 1848–1881" (doctoral dissertation, Hebrew Union College, 1938), p. 433; George Walling, *Recollections of a New York Chief of Police* (New York, 1887), pp. 19, 280 ff.; A. E. Costello, *Our Police Protectors* (New York, 1885), p. 324; I. Markens, *Hebrews in America* (New York, 1888), p. 24; Nascher, *The Wretches*, pp. 12, 40, 63, 129–30; Jacob Riis, *How The Other Half Lives*, p. 109; Moss, *The American Metropolis*, II, 366, III, 55, 154; Rupert Hughes, *The Real New York* (New York, 1904), pp. 333–34; *Report, University Settlement Society, 1896*, p. 10; C. C. Regier, *The Era of the Muckrakers* (Chapel Hill, 1932), p. 80.

[18] *Arbeiter Zeitung*, January 26, October 12, 1894; *Yearbook, University Settlement Society, 1899*, p. 89; Nascher, *The Wretches*, pp. 10–12, 40; *Forward*, May 15, 1908; United States Industrial Commission, *Reports*, XIV, 124; David Blaustein to Paul Abelson, January 29, 1907 (Abelson Papers); *American Hebrew*, December 17, 1909.

slaughtering of chickens in tenements in violation of the sanitary code proved to be a distinctly Jewish infraction.[19]

The Bowery, way-station of derelicts, transients, and unsuspecting immigrants, attracted the less stable and wary of the immigrant girls. The dancing academies that sprang to popularity in the first decade of the twentieth century snared impetuous, friendless young women. Lured by promises of marriage, they soon were trapped by procurers for the notorious Max Hochstim Association and other white slavers who preyed upon the innocent and the unsuspecting. The appearance of prostitution, previously rare among Jewesses, alarmed the East Side.[20]

The Lower East Side, girded by the Bowery with its unsavory establishments and Water Street with its resorts of ill-fame that catered to the seafaring trade, was surrounded by violence. Bearded Jews often were viciously assaulted by young hoodlums, both non-Jews and Jews, the area adjacent to the waterfront being especially dangerous. In 1898 and 1899, the newly organized American Hebrew League of Brooklyn protested a rash of outrages in the wake of the Dreyfus affair. Nevertheless there was only one instance of mass violence: the riot of July 30, 1902 at the funeral of Rabbi Jacob Joseph. This incident, the only one of its kind, can be attributed to the stored-up resentment of the Irish who were being forced out of the area by the incursion of Jews.[21]

SIGNS OF CHANGE

Gradually the miseries and trials of adjustment were left behind. For those who had inhabited the hungry villages of Eastern Europe, the hovels of Berditchev, and the crammed purlieus of Vilna and Kovno, the factories and sweatshops of New York provided a livelihood and possible stepping-stone. Despite unsteady and underpaid employment, tenement overcrowding and filth, immigrants felt themselves ineluctably being transformed. The Lower East Side, with its purposeful vitality, found no

---

[19] *Twenty-Sixth Annual Report, President, Treasurer, and Attorneys, Legal Aid Society, 1901,* p. 18; Joseph Barondess to Desertion Bureau, United Hebrew Charities, May 27, 1908 (Barondess Papers); S. Lowenstein, "Jewish Desertions," *Jewish Charity,* 5:143 (February 1905); *Yearbook, University Settlement Society, 1900,* pp. 28–29; J. B. Reynolds to Henry C. Potter, October 1, 1900 (Reynolds Papers); *Hebrew Standard,* August 25, 1893; *Twenty-Third Annual Report, United Hebrew Charities, 1896,* p. 45; *Twenty-Eighth Annual Report, Legal Aid Society, 1903,* p. 31.

[20] *American Hebrew,* December 17, 1909; *Report of the Tenement House Committee of 1894,* p. 81 ff.; *Importing Women for Immoral Purposes* (New York Senate, Doc. 196, 1909), p. 14; *Jewish International Conference on the Suppression of Traffic in Girls and Women* (London, 1910), *passim; Forward,* January 10, 1901, January 1, 1902.

[21] Morris D. Waldman, *Nor By Power* (New York, 1953), p. 298; J. D. Eisenstein, *Otser Zikhronotsay* (New York, 1929), pp. 79, 98, 112; S. Sheinfeld, *Zikhroines fun a shriftzetser* (New York, 1946), p. 33; Rose A. Halpern, "The American Reaction to the Dreyfus Case" (M.A. thesis, Columbia University, 1941), pp. 85–86.

analogue in the "leprous-looking ghetto familiar in Europe," commented the visiting Abbé Félix Klein. Physical surroundings, however sordid, could be transcended. Optimism and hope engulfed every aspect of immigrant life. For a people who had risen superior to the oppressions of medieval proscriptions, the New York slums acted as a new-found challenge. Each passing year brought improvements that could be measured and appraised. Cramped quarters did not constrict aspirations. "In a large proportion of the tenements of the East Side . . . pianos are to be seen in dingy rooms." And soon the phonograph was everywhere. "Excepting among the recent arrivals, most of the Jewish tenement dwellers have fair and even good furniture in their homes."[22]

The East Europeans began to venture beyond the boundaries of the Lower East Side into other areas where employment was available on terms compatible with religious habits. Brooklyn's German Williamsburg district, directly across the East River, where Central European Jews had been established for some decades, was settled early. In the late 1880s a few clothing contractors set up sweatshops in the languid Scottish settlement of Brownsville, south and east of Williamsburg. The depression delayed further expansion for a decade despite the extension of the Fulton Street El in 1889. Then the tide could not be stemmed. Between 1899 and 1904 Brownsville's population rose from ten thousand to sixty thousand. Land values soared as immigrants came at the rate of one thousand per week. Lots selling for two hundred dollars in 1899 brought five to ten thousand dollars five years later. As the real estate boom revolutionized land values, many a former tailor was suddenly transformed into a substantial landlord or realtor who disdained all contact with shears and needles of bitter memory.[23]

The mass dispersion of Jews from the Lower East Side to other parts of the city was in full swing in the early 1890s, as the more prosperous pioneers hastened to settle among their German coreligionists in Yorkville between 72nd and 100th streets, east of Lexington Avenue. For many a rising immigrant family in this period of swift change, it was judged to be a ten-year trek from Hester Street to Lexington Avenue.

The unprecedented flow of immigrants into the old central quarter, exorbitant rents, and the demolition of old tenements incidental to the building of parks, schools, and bridge approaches drastically reduced the area's absorptive capacity and spurred the search for new quarters. The construction of the Delancey Street approach to the Williamsburg Bridge in 1903 displaced 10,000 persons alone. The consolidation of the city and

---

[22] Anatole Leroy-Beaulieu, *Les Immigrants Juifs et le Judaisme aux Etats-Unis* (Paris, 1905), pp. 11–12; Felix Klein, *In the Land of the Strenuous Life* (Chicago, 1905), p. 3; Peter Wiernik, *History of the Jews in America* (New York, 1912), pp. 270–72; Fishberg, *The Jews*, p. 368; C. S. Bernheimer, *The Russian Jew in the United States* (Philadelphia, 1905), p. 112. Cf. ads for Schleicher and Weser pianos; *Abendblatt der Arbeiter Zeitung*, January 11, 1896; *Yiddishes Tageblatt*, January 16, 1899.

[23] *New York City Guide* (WPA: New York, 1939), p. 498; *The Menorah*, 27:298 (November 1904); *Weekly Bulletin of the Clothing Trades* 3:11 (April 29, 1904); H. C. Syrett, *The City of Brooklyn, 1865–1898* (New York, 1944), p. 237.

the growth and extension of rapid transit facilities connected what were once remote districts with the central downtown business quarters. In the new developments, cheaper land made possible lower rents that compensated for the time and expense of commuting. On Manhattan Island, the construction of underground transit opened to mass settlement the Dyckman tract in Washington Heights and the Harlem flats. The new subway also opened the East Bronx to extensive housing development. In Brooklyn, in addition to the heavy concentrations in Brownsville, Williamsburg, and South Brooklyn, Boro Park with "tropical gardens" and "parks" became increasingly accessible. Even distant Coney Island was brought into range by improved transit facilities.[24]

With 542,061 inhabitants in 1910, the Lower East Side reached peak congestion. Thereafter, a decline set in. By 1916 only 23 percent of the city's Jews lived in the once primary area of Jewish settlement, compared to 50 percent in 1903 and 75 percent in 1892. By the close of the first decade of the twentieth century the Lower East Side had lost much of its picturesqueness. In tone and color, the ghetto was perceptibly merging with the surrounding city. East European Jews had scattered to many sections of the city and were swiftly becoming an integral, if not as yet a fully accepted, element in the life of the community.[25]

In 1870 the Jews of New York were estimated at 80,000, or less than 9 percent of the city's inhabitants. By 1915 they totaled close to 1,400,000 persons (nearly 28 percent), a number larger than the city's total population in 1870. Before 1880 the Jews of the city were hardly more than a subject for idle curiosity. But thereafter, the flow of East European Jews quickened the city's industrial life, helped to transform its physical shape, and contributed a varied and malleable people to the metropolis. Despite poverty and great numbers, these immigrants created no new problems. But their presence accentuated New York's shortcomings in the face of unprecedented demands upon its imagination and resources. In the early years of the new century, their voice would be heard. The problems of industrial relations and urban living accentuated on the Lower East Side were to become the focus for major reforms.[26]

[24] Eisenstein, *Otser*, pp. 70, 124; United States Industrial Commission, *Reports*, XIV, 477; United States Immigration Commission, *Reports*, XLI, 198; *Weekly Bulletin of the Clothing Trades* 3:14 (April 29, 1904); Joseph Barondess to Thompson, November 12, 1907 (Barondess Papers).

[25] W. Laidlaw, *Population of the City of New York, 1890–1930* (New York, 1932), pp. 52, 53; Regional Survey, *Population, Land Values, and Government* (New York, 1929), p. 63.

[26] W. M. Rosenblatt, "The Jews, What They Are Coming To." *Galaxy*, 13:47 (January 1872), estimated their number at from 60,000 to 100,000; *The New York Times*, December 18, 1870, estimated 70,000; Z. H. Bernstein, "Dvorim achadim al dvar hayehudim lifnay shloshim v'arba shonim b'New York," *Yalkut Maarabi*, 1:4 (1904), estimated 80,000; Wiernik, *History*, p. 256. The religious census conducted by the Board of Delegates of American Israelites in 1878, by the nature of its method, appeared to err on the side of conservatism. 60,000 Jews for New York City, where the religiously unaffiliated were numerous indeed, seems low. *Statistics of the Jews of the United States* (Philadelphia, 1880), p. 9. In 1885, Carl Schurz

estimated that New York's German Jews alone numbered 85,000. Rudolf Glanz, *Jews in Relation to the Cultural Milieu of the Germans* (New York, 1947), p. 27; the figure 1,400,000 for 1914 is based on estimates for the years 1913 to 1917, *Jewish Communal Register of New York City, 1917–1918* (New York, 1918), p. 89. For a discussion of the problems of Jewish demography see *Jewish Communal Directory* (New York, 1912), p. 1 ff., and Henry Chalmers, "The Number of Jews in New York City," *Publications of American Statistical Association*, 14:68 ff. (March 1914).

Suggestions for Further Reading

Kenneth M. Stampp, *The Era of Reconstruction, 1865–1877** (Knopf, 1965), provides the best introduction to the new approach to the period. Other general works are R. W. Patrick, *The Reconstruction of the Nation** (Oxford University Press, 1967) and R. Cruden, *The Negro in Reconstruction** (Prentice-Hall, 1969). Examples of the new historiography are found in *Reconstruction: An Anthology of Revisionist Writings** (Louisiana State University Press, 1969), edited by Kenneth M. Stampp and Leon Litwack. W. E. B. DuBois, *Black Reconstruction in America, 1860–1880** (Harcourt Brace and World, 1935) was a pioneering effort, largely ignored at the time. Recent studies of individual states include Peter Kolchin, *First Freedom: The Responses of Alabama's Blacks to Emancipation and Reconstruction* (Greenwood Press, 1972) and Joe Gray Taylor, *Louisiana Reconstructed, 1863–1877* (Louisiana State University Press, 1974). Albion Tourgee's contemporaneous novels, *A Fool's Errand** (Fords, Howard and Hulbert, 1879) and *Bricks Without Straw** (Fords, Howard and Hulbert, 1880), depict Reconstruction life in the South from the point of view of a radical carpetbagger. Novels dealing with black life in the South during this period are Margaret Walker, *Jubilee** (Houghton-Mifflin, 1966) and Alex Haley, *Roots** (Doubleday, 1976). For a detailed historical presentation of the black family, see Herbert G. Gutman, *The Black Family in Slavery and Freedom, 1750–1925* (Pantheon Books, 1976). Nell Irwin Painter, *Exodusters: Black Migration to Kansas after Reconstruction* (Knopf, 1977), provides a fascinating study of the reactions of some blacks to the failures of Reconstruction.

For a general introduction to the Gilded Age, see Ray Ginger, *Age of Excess** (Macmillan, 1965), and Fred A. Shannon, *The Centennial Years: A Political and Economic History of America from the Late 1870s to the Early 1890s** (Doubleday, 1967). Perhaps the best introduction to the period, but a study that continues into the twentieth century, is Robert Wiebe, *The Search for Order, 1887–1920** (Hill and Wang, 1967). T. C. Cochran and William Miller deal with the economic development of the United States during the postwar years in *The Age of Enterprise** (Macmillan, 1942).

The impact of certain social and political theories that appeared late in the nineteenth century and the conflicts they engendered are discussed in Richard Hofstadter, *Social Darwinism in American Thought** (University of Pennsylvania Press, 1944); Sidney Fine, *Laissez Faire and the General Welfare State: A Study of Conflict in American Thought, 1865–1901** (University of Michigan Press, 1956); and Henry F. May, *Protestant Churches and Industrial America** (Harper & Row, 1949).

* Available in paperback edition.

The industrialists of the postwar years are viewed harshly in Matthew Josephson, *The Robber Barons: The Great American Capitalists, 1861–1901** (Harcourt Brace Jovanovich, 1934). Useful biographies of leading industrial figures are Allan Nevins, *John D. Rockefeller* (2 vols.; Scribner, 1940), and Joseph Frazier Wall, *Andrew Carnegie* (Oxford University Press, 1970). For a penetrating fictional treatment of a businessman by a contemporary author, see William Dean Howells, *The Rise of Silas Lapham** (Houghton Mifflin, 1885).

Two contemporary works that provide valuable insight into life in the late nineteenth century are Edward Bellamy's utopian novel, *Looking Backward, 2000–1887** (Ticknor, 1888), and Jacob Riis's *How the Other Half Lives: Studies Among the Tenements of New York** (Scribner, 1890).

For an intriguing look at the problems of children throughout American history, see Robert H. Bremner, et al. (eds.), *Children and Youth in America: A Documentary History**(3 vols.; Harvard University Press, 1970–74). On attempts to influence institutional policy for children see Walter I. Trattner, *Crusade for the Children: A History of the National Child Labor Committee and Child Labor Reform in America* (Quadrangle, 1970); Grace Abbott (ed.), *The Child and the State: Select Documents* (2 vols.; Greenwood, 1938; reprinted 1968); and Norman K. Denzin (ed.), *Children and Their Caretakers** (Transaction Books, 1972). A study of one aspect of juvenile reform, the George Junior Republic, is found in Jack M. Holl, *Juvenile Reform in the Progressive Era* (Cornell University Press, 1971).

The standard history of the American workingman is John R. Commons et al., *History of Labour in the United States* (4 vols.; Macmillan, 1918–35). A specialized survey of labor during the Gilded Age is Norman J. Ware, *The Labor Movement in the United States, 1860–1895** (Appleton-Century-Crofts, 1929). For the philosophy behind the labor movement, see Gerald N. Grob, *Workers and Utopia: A Study of Ideological Conflict in the American Labor Movement, 1865–1900** (Northwestern University Press, 1961). Herbert G. Gutman has written many articles describing the lives of the ordinary working man. They have been collected and published as Herbert G. Gutman, *Work, Culture and Society in Industrializing America** (Knopf, 1976). For another view of the influence of immigrants on the labor movement, see Gerard Rosenblum, *Immigrant Workers: Their Impact on American Labor Radicalism* (Basic Books, 1973).

Important labor conflicts are treated in Leon Wolff, *Lockout: The Story of the Homestead Strike of 1892** (Harper & Row, 1965); Almont Lindsey, *The Pullman Strike: The Story of a Unique Experiment and of a Great Labor Upheaval** (University of Chicago Press, 1942); D. L. McMurray, *Coxey's Army: A Study of the Industrial Army Movement of 1894** (Little, Brown, 1929); and R. V. Bruce, *1877: Year of Violence** (Bobbs-Merrill, 1959).

The standard treatments of European immigration in the United States are M. A. Jones, *American Immigration** (University of Chicago Press, 1960), and Oscar Handlin, *The Uprooted** (rev. ed.; Little, Brown, 1973). Special problems of the new immigration in the period after the Civil War are dealt with in Barbara Miller Solomon, *Ancestors and Immigrants** (Harvard University Press, 1956), and John Higham, *Strangers in the Land: Patterns of American Nativism, 1860–1925** (Rutgers University Press, 1955). Further studies of Jewish immigrants are found in Arthur A. Cohen, *New York Jews and the Quest for Community: The Kehillah Experiment, 1908–1922* (Columbia University Press, 1970); Leonard Dinnerstein and Mary Daly Palsson (eds.), *Jews in the South* (Louisiana State University Press, 1973); Thomas Kessner, *The Golden Door: Italian and Jewish Immigrant Mobility in New York City, 1880–1915* (Oxford University Press, 1977); and the best-selling *World of Our Fathers** (Harcourt Brace Jovanovich, 1976) by Irving Howe. Italian immigrants are described in Alexander De Conde, *Half Bitter, Half Sweet: An Excursion into Italian-American History* (Scribner, 1971), and Humbert S. Nelli, *The Italian in Chicago, 1880–1930: A Study in Ethnic Mobility** (Oxford University Press, 1970). See also Charlotte Erickson, *Invisible Immigrants: The Adaptation of English and Scottish Immigrants in Nineteenth Century America* (University of Miami Press, 1972). The leading journal of immigration studies is *The International Migration Review*.

2

The Early Twentieth Century

The American Woman
from 1900 to
the First World War:
A Profile

LOIS BANNER

Many standard narrative histories of the United States give the impression that the only occasions when women were important enough to be dealt with in American history were during the crusade for women's suffrage and the temperance movement. While it may be true that in terms of visible political activity these received the widest publicity, an overconcentration on overt political behavior leads to a misrepresentation of life as it is lived by ordinary women. In fact, when the feminist movement of the late nineteenth and early twentieth centuries lost sight of larger goals in its concentration on suffrage, both women and the nation suffered as a consequence.

At the time of the 1848 convention on women's rights in Seneca Falls, N.Y.—the event from which the women's rights movement usually dates itself—women saw disfranchisement as only one of a whole array of serious legal and social disabilities faced by women. Women were generally not allowed to own property—in many cases, not even the clothes they wore. A working wife was not allowed to keep her wages but was required to turn them over to her husband. In the case of separation or divorce, a woman had no legal claims on her husband and was not allowed to keep the children. She had no legal status, which meant that she was not permitted to bring suit or to give testimony in court. Often, she was not permitted to inherit property or to make a will. She was barred from public office and excluded from public life generally. For the most part, women lacked opportunities for education, vocational training, and professional employment. The national consensus was that women belonged in the home, and determined efforts were made to see that they stayed there.

In the beginning, there was a good deal of confusion and disagreement among the women as to the best method for improving their situation. Some women instituted petition campaigns and direct lobbying in their respective states. Others sought the help of friendly legislators, hoping to bring informal influence to bear. Eventually, most of the efforts of the women's movement were focused on secur-

ing the right to vote, for it seemed that only the use of the franchise
could generate the pressure necessary to eliminate legal discrimination
against women.

In retrospect, it may be difficult to understand why the idea of
female suffrage was so furiously opposed by the American public,
both male and female, in the closing years of the nineteenth century.
The opponents often used the argument that women were too frail,
too pure, too noble, to participate in the political arena. Indeed, the
Gilded Age was one of the most corrupt periods in American political
life, and men may actually have seen the extension of the franchise
as a step toward the corruption of a new segment of society. Or, believing their own rhetoric, they may have feared that women voters
would force overly rigorous reforms on the existing political and social structures. In the South, the vote of black women was viewed as
an even more unthinkable threat to the status quo than the vote of
white women. Generally, the opposition to the women's movement
can be understood as part of a wide ranging defensive reaction to
the apparent breakdown of the traditional family system.

In the selection printed below, Lois Banner, of Princeton University, describes the activities and attitudes of a variety of types of
women during the period when agitation for suffrage was growing.
She notes the conditions under which women lived that led them to
struggle to change their social, political, and economic status. Unfortunately, when women's suffrage came in 1920, it had virtually no
impact on the problems that had concerned women or the conditions
that had oppressed them.

"At the opening of the twentieth century," wrote suffragist Ida Husted
Harper, women's status "had been completely transformed in most respects."[1] Her judgment, however hopeful, was only partially correct. For
example, in most states by 1900 the common law doctrine of *femme*

[1] Elizabeth Cady Stanton et al., *History of Woman Suffrage*, 6 vols., vol. 5, ed., Ida
Husted Harper (New York, 1881–1922), p. xvii. Throughout this essay I have
relied particularly on William L. O'Neill, *Everyone Was Brave: A History of
Feminism in America* (Chicago, 1971), and William H. Chafe, *The American
Woman: Her Changing Social, Economic, and Political Roles, 1920–1970* (New
York, 1972).

"The American Woman from 1900 to the First World War: A Profile." From
Women in Modern America: A Brief History by Lois Banner © 1974 by Harcourt
Brace Jovanovich, Inc.

couverte, under which the wife, much like the Negro slave, had been the chattel of her husband, with no legal control over her children, her earnings, or her property, had been modified. But in most states women could not vote in general elections, hold office, or sit on juries, and in all states legal codes contained discriminatory laws against women in areas like property holding, divorce, and making contracts.

In the field of education, by the beginning of the twentieth century, most professional schools, albeit grudgingly, admitted women, and the majority of high schools and colleges throughout the nation were coeducational. This did represent a major step toward equality for women. Yet the 21 percent of the nation's women who were at work in 1900 occupied the lowest-paying, lowest-status positions in the work force, serving in large numbers as domestic servants and unskilled factory laborers. Even as professionals, women were primarily elementary school teachers. Although women's organizations were a mainstay of the Progressive movement, and women like Jane Addams were numbered among its leaders, women played little role in politics. Most church members were women, but few women were ministers.

Americans tolerated such discrimination because they believed that the woman's proper role in the social order was as wife and mother. It has been an article of American faith that women, "gentle and understanding," are to nurture their children and to provide a refuge from the competitive and exhausting world of work outside the home. The family has always been the most sacrosanct institution of American culture, and women have always been viewed as its lynchpin. Such notions have been well suited to a society in which some area of security has been needed to offset the unsettling experiences of industrialization and urbanization, violent labor conflict, declining religious faith, increasing crime, and periodic economic depression. And, in part, this belief that woman's place is in the home has mirrored reality: no less than 90 percent of American women—in the past as in the present—have married at some time during their lives. In the 1900s and 1910s only about 5 percent of married women took jobs outside their homes. The balance of working women was then drawn from the young and unmarried.

Even though marriage was a common experience for almost all American women, there was still a wide variety in life style and substance among women before, during, and after marriage. After all, the American population was made up of a variety of ages, classes, and ethnic groups. Many women were undoubtedly content with the expectation and fulfillment of the role of marriage. The happy housewife and the adolescent girl yearning for marriage, both of whom have dominated popular media from early women's magazines to the television serials of the 1970s, have always been based on real types. Yet, for others in the middle class as well as in the working class the role was not so easily played, especially since the mythic view of American woman as wife and mother made it difficult for American culture to take seriously any discrimination against women or any discontent women may have felt with their role.

I

Even women of the middle class whose financial positions were secure faced a conflict between their expectations and the reality of marriage by the early twentieth century. Victorian strictures had been difficult on the middle-class woman, but at least nineteenth-century America had clearly defined her role. She was to marry, have numerous children, and obey her husband. It was characteristic of Victorian times that "women cultivated submission to their husbands as a matter of conscience, and those who defied such authority brought scandal on themselves and dishonor on their husbands." But by the 1900s attitudes had changed. Well-to-do women in particular no longer universally cultivated submissiveness. The impact of feminist writings, their own experience in school or at work before marriage, and the example of professional women made them demand some independence in marriage. No longer was the word "obey" included in civil marriages, and many churches also had dropped it from their marriage ceremonies. Observers commented that "companionship" was the new standard in marriage.[2]

But companionship was difficult to attain in a culture that expected men to work hard and to excel. In pursuit of success many men were rarely at home. "The habit and fury of work, . . ." wrote one critic, "is a masculine disease in this country." Left to their own devices, middle-class women were drawn to shopping as sublimation or to social climbing as a way of status advance, and, according to sociologists Helen and Robert Lynd, "the coinage in this social market is much more subtle than that with which their husbands deal." More middle-class women began to limit their number of children. They, not their husbands, resorted to the divorce courts with increasing frequency. According to one conservative critic, fashionable young matrons were drinking, smoking, using makeup, playing bridge for money and demanding an "absolute independence of any power in heaven or in earth." As a general comment on middle-class behavior for the 1900s it was an overstatement, but it identified an important trend in style that by the 1920s would become dominant.[3]

The discontent of middle-class women is particularly evident in the way they treated their servants (and in the decades before the First World War status considerations plus the still demanding nature of housework dictated that every family of means have a servant). In the 1900s and 1910s there was an outpouring of writings on the so-called "servant problem"—the vast shortage of women willing to work as maids and cooks. This literature made it clear that female employers, and not just working conditions, were driving servants away. It was not simply that servants were expected to work long hours for little pay, it was also that

[2] Lydia Commander, *The American Idea* (New York, 1907), pp. 144–45.

[3] Anna A. Rogers, *Why American Marriages Fail and Other Papers* (Boston, 1909), pp. 62, 174–75; Robert S. Lynd and Helen Merrell Lynd, *Middletown in Transition: A Study in Cultural Conflicts* (New York, 1937), p. 95. On divorce, see William L. O'Neill, *Divorce in the Progressive Era* (New Haven, 1967).

they were subject to the whims and status anxieties of their mistresses. One analyst of domestic service concluded that middle-class women did not want intelligent, responsible servants. Rather they wanted inferiors before whom they could display superior airs and whose lives they could control. When well-to-do women met for tea and talk, problems with servants were a perennial subject of conversation. So empty were their lives, chided one observer, that the " '3 Ds' occupied their time: dress, disease, and domestics."[4]

Surely there were happy marriages among middle-class women in the 1900s and 1910s. And there were unhappy marriages before those years. It is not unique to the twentieth century that frustrated women turn their drive for power inward on their families in societies that permit them limited outlets outside of it. The results have often been destructive. The wealthy and pampered Mrs. Hurstwood in Theodore Dreiser's *Sister Carrie*, who waits for her husband's first pecadillo that she may destroy him, could exist in any age and any time. The shrews and the matriarchs created by twentieth-century novelists and critics have long been stock characters of fiction and fact. Moreover, nineteenth-century medical journals are full of reports of neurotic women who took out their anxiety indirectly against the patriarchal family by retreating into hysterical outbursts or other neurotic symptoms. So common was this problem among women patients that the term "hysteria" was coined to describe it, and it was long considered an illness peculiar to women.[5]

The rigid structure of Victorian marriage failed to ensure happiness, but at least the role of the wife was carefully spelled out, and there were limited external challenges to it. By the 1900s that was no longer true. On the question of sexuality, for example, confusing signals were coming from all sides. Experts like Havelock Ellis cast doubt on the Victorian beliefs that masturbation would result in insanity, that women physiologically were incapable of enjoying sex, that overindulgence in sex was dangerous for men, and that sex in marriage ought to be only for procreation. Popular publicists of birth control, like Margaret Sanger, and purveyors of household medical advice, like Edward Bliss Foote, whose *Plain Home Talk on Love, Marriage, and Parentage* went through numerous editions in the 1900s, argued that women could and ought to enjoy sex. Yet birth control devices were still illegal, and studies as late as the 1920s showed that douching (hardly foolproof) was the most common method of birth control. Child-rearing techniques still stressed the repression of sexuality among the young, and there was confusion among doctors and the general public as to what the normal fertility cycle of a woman was. Even if the "modern" woman of the 1900s wanted to experience sexual pleasure, she still ran the risk of pregnancy. And there were few sex manuals available with explicit instructions; even Foote's work

---

[4] Lucy Maynard Salmon, *Progress in the Household* (Boston, 1906); Mary R. Smith, "Domestic Service: The Responsibility of Employers," *Forum*, XXVII (Aug., 1899), 678–89.

[5] See Carroll Smith-Rosenberg, "The Hysterical Woman: Sex Roles and Role Conflict in Nineteenth-Century America," *Social Research*, IX (Winter, 1972), 652–78.

was nearly banned under the obscenity laws of the period, despite his brief and less-than-explicit discussions of female sexuality.[6]

The opening of colleges and the professions to women created a similar potential for conflict in the lives of middle-class women. With the appearance after the Civil War of coeducational colleges in the Midwest and of private women's colleges in the East, more and more women were taking their B.A.'s, and some college graduates were entering status professions, like law and medicine, from which women had been barred before the 1860s and 1870s. The number of women within these professions would remain small. In 1910 the 558 women lawyers in the nation represented one-half of one percent of the profession, and the 9,015 women doctors constituted about 7 percent of all doctors.[7] Moreover, most women doctors were pediatricians and gynecologists, while most women lawyers were relegated to office work—collecting claims, redressing minor grievances, preparing probate papers. Still they were an example to housewives of a world outside the home. And the occasional emergence of a woman lawyer or doctor to public prominence—like doctor Alice Hamilton who did pathbreaking work on industrial pollution, or lawyer Inez Milholland who led suffrage marches and wrote popular articles on feminism—could not help but arouse the envy of capable and ambitious women bound to husbands and families.

This is not to argue that women before the Civil War found it impossible to combine marriage and a career. Many women doctors and lawyers were married to men in the same field, and preliminary observations show that their husbands were often supportive of their careers. But other studies indicate that a significant number of career women did not marry. By the second decade of the twentieth century, nearly half the alumnae of the major eastern women's colleges were unmarried.[8] By then the spinster was no longer regarded with such derision: unmarried women in the settlement houses, in the suffrage movement, and in feminist writings were showing that alternatives to marriage could be not only possible, but exciting. In the nineteenth century, the small band of suffragists led by Susan Anthony had been effectively caricatured as ugly, shrewish, and above all "strong-minded" (a term of considerable oppro-

---

[6] Edward B. Foote, *Dr. Foote's New Plain Home Talk on Love, Marriage, and Parentage* . . . , rev. ed. (New York, 1904); Martha Wolfenstein, "Fun Morality: An Analysis of Recent American Child-Training Literature," in Margaret Mead and Martha Wolfenstein, eds., *Childhood in Contemporary Cultures* (Chicago, 1955), pp. 168–78; and Norman Himes, *Medical History of Contraception* (New York, 1963).

[7] For information on women at work, see the reports of the United States Bureau of the Census; National Manpower Council, *Womanpower* (New York, 1959); and Robert Smuts, *Women and Work in America*, 2d ed. (New York, 1971). Throughout the twentieth century, no more than 10 percent of the doctors and lawyers in the United States have been women. And except during wars, women have never constituted more than 10 percent of the skilled laborers in any industry.

[8] See Karen Meyer Willcox, "Women Lawyers in the United States, 1870–1900," Senior Honors Thesis, Douglass College, 1973; and Willystine Goodsell, *A History of Marriage and the Family*, rev. ed. (New York, 1945), p. 502.

brium when applied to women). But the number of strong-minded women had become sizable in the early twentieth century. And it was no longer possible to see career women as eccentric, particularly when so many of them, like Jane Addams and Lillian Wald, were involved in social welfare causes that humanitarian Americans were unlikely to condemn. Indeed, by 1900 the term "new woman" had come into widespread use to apply to women professionals and volunteers, and it was most often used as a term of admiration, not of criticism.

In the 1900s the experiences of many women gave them a taste of freedom before marriage. For in the first decades of the twentieth century most women married in their early twenties, not their late teens, as became popular by 1950. Among the middle class, marriage was being postponed to enhance the economic prospects of the newly married, but what it meant for women was that there was a period after physical maturity and before marriage when they experienced an independence that could not help but influence their later attitudes about their own role in marriage.

Because of the age at which they married, because of the increased opportunity for education, because of feminist writings and the example of the "new woman," many women looked for new roles within their marriages. Traditional associations like sewing circles and church sodalities were open to them, but by 1900 more wide-reaching activities were also available. Women's clubs, for example, were immensely popular in this period, and the women in them—including professionals as well as housewives—did not universally spend their time socializing or listening to lectures. They worked for conservation, civic improvements, better schools, kindergartens, better conditions for working women and children, and pure food and drug acts. Indeed, the Progressive movement itself depended on the women who joined women's clubs and other reform groups. As has often been true of reform movements in America, women were a key factor within the Progressive coalition.[9]

In addition to women's clubs and suffrage organizations, women's ethnic and religious sodalities, often drawing their clientele from among immigrant communities, also flourished. Jewish and Catholic women, for example, were not slow to organize, although due to the patriarchialism of Catholicism and Judaism, their women's organizations were often auxiliary to men's groups. Such, however was not the case among black women. Often excluded from white women's organizations, black women formed their own autonomous groups, where they directed their energies toward improvements within the black community. Their women's clubs, which functioned as social welfare agencies, were the forerunners of the NAACP and the Urban League. The General Federation of Colored Women was founded in 1895, nearly fifteen years before the two better-known black organizations appeared. Still by the 1880s and 1890s black women, like white women, had begun to move into the professions. Although most black women professionals were teachers, the percentages of black women

---

[9] See David P. Thelen, *The New Citizenship: Origins of Progressivism in Wisconsin, 1885–1900* (Columbia, Mo., 1972).

doctors and lawyers to black men doctors and lawyers was actually higher than the percentages for whites. In 1910 about 3 percent of black lawyers were women (one-half of one percent for whites) and 13 percent of black doctors were women (7 percent for whites). These professional women often formed a leadership cadre for the black women's clubs.[10]

Yet as similar in structure and function as the black and the white women's organizations were in this period, there were important variations between them in rhetoric and goals—variations that indicate the differing experiences of women of the various middle-class ethnic, racial, and religious subcultures. Both white and black organizations focused on social service, but beyond this, the black groups worked for racial identity while the white groups worked for a female identity. Reacting to the common charge that all black women were promiscuous, the black women's clubs took it as their special cause in the 1900s to prove to white America that black women were as virtuous as white women, that white middle-class norms of marital fidelity were their own. They were aware that black women had been "the center and source of the social life of the race," but in their common concern with male leaders to advance the interests of the race, they did not see their own needs for independence as uppermost.[11]

Such was not the case for white Progressive women's organizations. The opinion of many of their leaders was that men had made egregious errors in their use of power, and that women, because of their greater sensitivity and generosity, could rectify these mistakes. It was woman's job, as one representative figure felt, to organize as the "consumer and preserver" of humanity, to "correct the defects of man's activities." Jane Croly, who as "Jennie June" was a well-known newspaper columnist and clubwoman, exulted that women's clubs were providing "the fellowship and fraternity among women that is to bring us closer and closer to the millennium." At women's meetings, men were often portrayed as antagonists. One observer wrote that women's rights meetings in particular were pervaded with "bitterness, contempt, and positive enmity against men." Such rhetoric could only serve to put great pressure on the woman member who chafed within her marriage.[12]

[10] For black women, on whom little secondary literature is available, see Gerda Lerner, *Black Women in White America: A Documentary History* (New York, 1972), and Eleanor Flexner, *Century of Struggle: The Woman's Rights Movement in the United States* (Cambridge, Mass., 1959). United States Bureau of the Census, *Negro Population: 1790–1915* (Washington, D.C., 1918), is also useful. On the black women's clubs, see Fannie Barrier Williams, "The Colored Woman and Her Part in Race Regeneration," in Booker T. Washington, et al., eds., *A New Negro for a New Century* (Chicago, 1900); W. E. B. Du Bois, *Efforts for Social Betterment Among Negro Americans*, The Atlanta University Publications, no. 14 (Atlanta, 1909); and Allan H. Spear, *Black Chicago: The Making of a Negro Ghetto, 1890–1920* (Chicago, 1967), pp. 100–05.

[11] Williams, "Colored Woman," p. 379.

[12] Mary I. Wood, *The History of the General Federation of Women's Clubs . . .* (New York, 1912), p. 65; Women's Press Club of New York City, *Memoirs of Jane Cunningham Croly, "Jenny June"* (New York, 1904), p. 17; Annie Nathan

How did these pressures work themselves out in the lives of individual women? For exceptional women—women who emerged as leaders—the answer is fairly easily gathered from biographies and autobiographies. Some, like Lillian Wald and Jane Addams, did not marry at all. Some, like Margaret Dreier Robins of the Women's Trade Union League and Carrie Chapman Catt of the National American Women's Suffrage Association, were able to combine marriage and a career. Many women doctors and lawyers, married to men in the same field, were successful at home and on the job. For others it was not so easy. Margaret Sanger, whose advocacy of birth control ultimately brought women an essential freedom, suffered a nervous breakdown because she felt stultified in a seemingly happy marriage. She had to leave her husband and children and embark on her own career before she completely recovered. Charlotte Perkins Gilman, the foremost feminist ideologue of that age, had the same experience. Among blacks, journalist Ida Wells Barnett successfully combined marriage with a career of social service and agitation against lynching, while the husband of Mary McLeod Bethune, college founder and government administrator, left her early in their marriage because he could not tolerate her success. But it took an exceptional man to reconcile himself to a working wife in a era that regarded that arrangement as a sign of a husband's inability to provide or of his lack of masculinity.

For an understanding of the frustrations and satisfactions of the average middle-class woman in those years, perhaps the best portraits available—at least for the white middle-class—are of the women that Sinclair Lewis depicts in his novel, *Main Street*, which is set in a small town in the years before the First World War. Many types are represented here: the spinsterish schoolmarm; the embittered widow; and the prim, proper, sexually-starved matron, doting on doctors and on Christian Science. All are influenced by the new currents of their age—the automobile, the movies. But only Carol Kennicott, the heroine of the novel, is profoundly moved. She is inclined towards radicalism, skepticism, and feminism. Yet as discontented as she is with her marriage, she cannot find the strength to end it, give up her beliefs, or flee with the passionately romantic man, so different from her stolid husband, who might give her a more fulfilling life. She becomes a dilettante, continually embarking on one unsuccessful crusade after another, and her one lengthy attempt at independence ends with her return to her husband and the subsequent birth of a child. She, like many other women, finds the new ideas she learned in college, from books, or from friends, profoundly disturbing, but is able to work them out in her own life only with difficulty.

II

Middle-class women were not alone in finding it difficult to assume traditional female roles in a modernizing society. The difficulties for

Meyer, "Woman's Assumption of Sex Superiority," *North American Review*, CLXXVIII (Jan., 1904), 108.

working-class women were no less profound. For them, poverty was the first problem. Many of them were immigrants, recently peasants who had fled economic upheaval and political tyranny in Europe, and who flooded American shores from the 1880s on. Without funds and without experience in an industrial, urban society, they and their families were prey to industry's need for cheap labor. They jammed into the decaying city districts of cheap rents and tenement flats and crowded the company towns of the New England mills and the Pennsylvania mining fields. Their behavior varied according to their religious and ethnic backgrounds, but there were important similarities as well. For example, few married women of the working class worked away from their homes; middle-class women and working-class women alike in this period respected the dictate that wives ought not to take on remunerative labor in the same way as their husbands. Therefore, the typical married woman of the working class worked at home, taking in washing, boarders, or piecework from a factory, while her middle-class peers took on volunteer labor that was unpaid.

Among the working class, however, black women were an exception. Among them, 25 percent of married women worked in 1900. All working women were subject to the charge that they were not ladies, and each ethnic group was subject to specific nativist slurs, but such allegations were heightened when it came to black women. The descendants of slaves of southern plantation owners, they were still identified in the white mind either as "mammies"—the simple-minded, carefree domestics happy to do the whites' menial work—or as naturally promiscuous temptresses. Such mythology about their nature was used as a rationalization for exploitation. Thus, at a time when 25 percent of laboring women worked in factories, only 3 percent of black laboring women did so. And when 5 percent of married women in general were employed outside the home, 25 percent of black married women were so employed. For the most part they worked as laundresses or as domestic servants—the form of labor lowest in status—and often they had to take such jobs because their husbands, who faced similar discrimination, could not find work.

Among the working class as a whole, however, it was primarily widows, spinsters, and unmarried daughters who worked. For those women classified by the census as immigrants, the percentages were high: in 1900 66 percent of unmarried immigrant women worked, as did nearly all unmarried black women. From census data we can glean what kinds of work they did. In 1910, for example, 25 percent worked as farm laborers (a figure that indicated the continued—although decreasing—importance of farming in the economy). Another 25 percent were in manufacturing; 31 percent were in domestic service; 8 percent were in the professions, mostly as teachers and nurses; 4 percent were in clerical occupations; 4 percent were in trade, mostly as clerks and saleswomen; and a small number were classified in transportation and in public service, mostly as telephone and telegraph operators. Yet, whatever work women did, their jobs were distinct from men's, and often directly related to women's traditional roles in the home.

For example, women in manufacturing clustered in industries with a high percentage of unskilled workers, which did not involve heavy labor, and which were related to traditional household tasks. Those occupations in which more than 100,000 women were employed in 1910 included dressmaking and hand sewing at home or in shops, operating sewing machines, and working in textile factories or millinery shops. The cigar and tobacco industry, the printing industry, and the shoemaking industry each employed between 50,000 and 100,000 women. The commercial foods industry and the clothing industry each employed slightly under 50,000 women.

For the most part such distribution had historic roots. Women themselves had taken jobs in these industries during the nineteenth century as the work they had formerly done at home, like weaving, canning, or even rolling tobacco, moved into factory production. But in few industries did women advance to skilled labor or managerial positions in any great numbers: in 1910, for example, there were 93 women machinists in the nation and approximately 500,000 male machinists, 92 female electricians and approximately 135,000 male electricians. In most factories women were the assemblers, not the skilled operatives. On the average, women's salaries were one-half those of men, even when their jobs were similar, although the fact that 11 percent of factory foremen were women in 1910 indicates some possibility of promotion for them.

A graphic illustration of discrimination by sex and race is provided by the situation in southern tobacco factories, which had employed both black and white men and women since before the Civil War. In these factories white males held the supervisory and skilled-labor positions, white women did the weighing and counting, black men made containers and did the sweeping and cleaning, and black women did the hand work of shredding and blending. Each category of worker was segregated in a special building, and each had a separate pay scale—with black women at the bottom.[13]

The conditions of work, in addition to wages, were also exploitative for women in these years—as they were for male workers, too. An example is the women's garment industry, which was by the 1910s the nation's largest single employer of women. Centered in the cities, it was organized around a system that included both factory and home labor. Major firms often sent finishing work to individual subcontractors who set up small workshops in tenement apartments, where they could hire laborers—particularly women close to their homes—for a pittance. It was a cheap method of production, but the "sweatshops," as these workrooms came to be known, became a national scandal because of their unsafe and unsanitary conditions.[14]

---

[13] Lerner, *Black Women*, pp. 265–66.

[14] The most comprehensive survey of the conditions of work for women in this period is United States Bureau of Labor, *Report on the Condition of Woman and Child Wage Earners in the United States*, 19 vols. (Washington, 1910). See also Edith Abbott, *Women in Industry: A Study in American Economic History* (New York, 1915), and Elizabeth Faulkner Baker, *Technology and Woman's Work* (New York, 1964). On the ladies' garment industry, see Louis Levine, *The Women's Garment Workers: A History of the International Ladies' Garment*

Yet even women garment workers in a regular factory could expect to labor at least a ten-hour day and a half day on Saturdays, to be paid little, to be required to buy their own equipment, and to be relegated to tasks less prestigious and less well-paying than those the male factory workers were assigned. Men were the cutters and tailors; women operated the sewing machines. At the Triangle Shirtwaist Company in New York City (to become notorious in 1911 as the scene of a major industrial disaster), doors were regularly locked so that employees could not abscond with company merchandise, and a guard at the one open door searched each woman's pocketbook as she left the factory. Yet, given the conditions of work for these women it is not surprising that pilferage became a form of protest.

In the field of domestic labor, in which the largest percentage of women were employed, conditions were little better. Women working as cooks and housekeepers, even in private homes, were required to be available at all hours of the day and night, and their wages, although sometimes better than factory rates, were still minimal. Domestic workers, drawn substantially from among black and immigrant women, complained about the loneliness of their occupation and the irrationality of their employers. Waitresses, too, were subject to the whims of customers and managers. They often worked under unsanitary conditions, and they were dependent on tips for a living. Even in the relatively high-status position (within the working class) of department store clerk, there were often no vacations, no rest breaks, and no chairs on which to sit (store owners wanted saleswomen to appear busy even when the store was empty). Moreover, workers were required to work evenings and Saturdays during the shopping rush before Christmas.

Given such conditions, why did working-class women work? At the time, most Americans, blinded by the belief that women's place was in the home, were convinced that they did so for "pin money"—to accumulate a dowry and to buy clothes and frivolities. Native daughters of Anglo-Saxon parentage may have worked for this reason; indeed, less than 50 percent of this group were employed in 1900. Yet, study after study by private foundation and government agency alike proved that the pin money theory was a myth. Daughters of the working class worked because they had to, because their fathers and brothers did not earn sufficient money to support their families. And the large number of working women who lived with their families did so, not to save money to spend on themselves, as the pin money theorists argued, but because there was insufficient housing in American cities for unmarried working women; because in many immigrant cultures it was considered a disgrace if an unmarried daughter lived separately from her family; and, finally and most important, because many working women were not paid enough money to be able to support themselves in private apartments or boarding houses. A 1910 Women's Trade Union League census of Chicago

---

Worker's Union (New York, 1924); Benjamin Stolberg, *Tailor's Progress: The Story of a Famous Union and the Men Who Made It* (New York, 1944); and Leon Stein, *The Triangle Fire* (Philadelphia, 1962).

department store saleswomen showed that as many as 30 percent of even these workers did not make enough money on which to live.[15]

Why, then, did working women not rebel against their lot? More than occasionally they did. The leadership of the labor movement included women as well as men: heroines like the nonagenarian Mary "Mother" Jones, who devoted her long life to organizing laborers among the most oppressive industries in the nation—coal, western mining, and southern cotton mills—and Elizabeth Gurley Flynn, whose fiery oratory brought her to public prominence at the age of seventeen, were reproduced in local strikes and local organizations. Layoffs or cuts in wages could arouse the anger of women workers as well as men workers. In 1898 Chicago glovemakers went on strike when new assembly line techniques were introduced. They had tolerated piecework wages, tyrannical male foremen, and having to buy their own equipment, but an increase in the monotony of their work and a probable decline in wages were more than they could bear. In 1905, in Troy, New York, 8,000 women laundry workers went on strike because of the introduction of fines for talking and lateness, irregular work assignments, and a new machine, all of which substantially cut wages. In 1909 20,000 women shirtwaist workers in New York and Philadelphia took to the streets on their own behalf in the most famous strike of women workers of the century. And in 1912 the determination of striking women textile workers in Lawrence, Massachusetts, was central to the success of one of the decade's most violent confrontations between industry and labor.[16]

The evidence of the strikes in Chicago, Troy, New York and Philadelphia, and Lawrence amply demonstrates that it is incorrect to assume that working women in the early twentieth century did not have the capacity for labor militancy or for organization. Some observers at the time were convinced that women made better strikers than men—whether because of a "characteristic feminine tenacity," as one contemporary put it, or because, without husbands and children dependent on them, they felt freer in their response.[17] Yet, it was difficult for their strikes to succeed, for employers had the power to use the courts, the police, and the organs of public opinion to break such protests. For example, the success of the 1909 shirtwaist workers' strike was due, more than anything else, to the fact that a number of well-to-do female philanthropists joined the pickets and provided bail money. Their participation brought public

---

[15] State of Illinois, *Report of the Senate Vice Committee* (Chicago, 1911), p. 203.

[16] On women in the labor movement, see John B. Andrews and W. D. P. Bliss, *Report on Condition of Woman and Child Wage-Earners, History of Women in Trade Unions*, vol. 10; Helen Marot, *American Labor Unions, by a Member* (New York, 1914), pp. 65–77; and Theresa Wolfson, *The Woman Worker and the Trade Unions* (New York, 1926). For the Chicago strike, see Agnes Nestor, *Woman's Labor Leader: Autobiography of Agnes Nestor* (Rockford, Ill., 1954). For the Troy strike, see Alice Henry, *Women and the Labor Movement* (New York, 1923), pp. 74–75. On the shirtwaist strike, see Stolberg, *Tailor's Progress*. On the Lawrence strike, see Donald B. Cole, *Immigrant City: Lawrence, Massachusetts, 1845–1921* (Chapel Hill, N.C., 1963).

[17] Marot, *Labor Unions*, p. 74.

sympathy to the strikers and forced the owners to settle. Yet, not all the workers even in this strike were successful. Women at the Triangle Shirtwaist Company, who had been among the initiators of the strike, gained no concessions from their employers. Instead, many of them were killed in the disastrous fire that swept through the Triangle Company building in 1911 and that could have been prevented had the owners installed proper safety equipment.

Yet despite their capacity for organization during strikes, women workers were reluctant to unionize. Labor leader Mary Anderson, whose first act on coming to America from Scandinavia was to seek out a union for comradeship and the Chicago scrubwoman who found that unionization brought job security, regular pay, and a sense of comradeship with fellow workers whom she previously had feared as rivals, were the exceptions, not the rule. Dorothy Richardson, who wrote an insightful account of working women in New York City in the 1900s, provides the simplest explanation of the lack of unionization among women workers: "The lot of the working girl is hard, but she has grown used to it; for, being a woman, she is patient and long suffering."[18] Moreover, because the majority of working women were young, many looked on work as a temporary situation before marriage. Nor did all respond negatively to difficult labor. Girls of peasant background were used to long hours of labor on farms. Rose Schneiderman, reminiscing after some forty years as a labor leader, was proud of her years as shirtwaist worker, proud of her honest toil.[19] Theodore Dreiser in *Sister Carrie* sketched a brilliant portrait of a sensitive and selfish woman who could not tolerate factory labor, but he also described her co-workers in the factory who were not discontented with their lot. After all, the factory did provide a world outside the sometimes stifling immigrant culture at home, a world of young men and women with whom they could associate, just as the school or college provided a similar experience for young middle-class men and women.

Besides, working-class women had their pride and their own aspirations towards status. "The conventions of the working class," wrote one analyst, "are more rigid than any other class. They are the last to be affected by changing psychology or institutions."[20] Within the working class, as among the middle class, there was a hierarchy of respect—a hierarchy that was reflected in the scorn with which working-class women viewed domestic service and in their sensitive response to the common allegation that women who participated in strikes, in labor unions, or even in work outside the home were nothing more than prostitutes. In response to the vast immigration of the early twentieth century, nativism was rampant in the United States, and the nativist and antifemin-

---

[18] Alice Henry, *Memoirs of Alice Henry*, ed., Nettie Palmer (Melbourne, Australia, 1944, typescript), p. 71; Jane Addams, *Twenty Years at Hull House* (New York, 1960), p. 166; Dorothy Richardson, *The Long Day: The Story of a New York Working Girl* (New York, 1905), p. 303.

[19] Rose Schneiderman (with Lucy Goldthwaite), *All for One* (New York, 1967).

[20] Wolfson, *Woman Worker*, p. 43.

ist points of view easily merged into the argument that, since studies showed that the majority of prostitutes came from working-class and immigrant families, all female members of these groups were potential recruits to prostitution. Only white Anglo-Saxon women, who did not yet work in large numbers, so it went, had high moral standards.

Working women, themselves anxious for improved status, were sensitive to such allegations: in Perry, New York, a typical mill town, women who failed to keep a strict moral standard were called "bums," and their fellow workers forced them to quit. Lillian Wald at the Henry Street settlement recounted that neighborhood working women solicited her aid in unionizing because her status would lend respectability to a venture that might otherwise have been regarded as disreputable, while the 1909 New York shirtwaist strikers were particularly pleased to have upper-class allies for the same reason.[21]

Moreover, working women were often divided along ethnic lines, and this, too, made it difficult for them to unite. In Pittsburgh, for example, clerical work and sales jobs, the high-status positions, were reserved for white women of native birth, as was semiskilled work in the garment factories, although Jewish women had to some extent moved into the latter occupation. Immigrant women of Polish and Slavic background found their place in menial factory labor and in domestic work. Italian women were to be found in most of these occupations, but in Pittsburgh, as elsewhere, only a limited number worked outside the home because of the extreme patriarchal nature of the Italian family. In some areas employers apparently respected such status divisions; in others they employed women from a variety of immigrant backgrounds to create a "babel of tongues" and thereby make organization difficult.[22]

Above and beyond whatever inclinations toward conservatism kept working women from complaining, and however employers kept them apart, women also failed to protest their lot because labor unions were hesitant to organize them. The Knights of Labor, which flourished in the 1880s, welcomed women as members, supported their strikes, and helped them organize. But the American Federation of Labor, founded in 1886, came to dominate organized labor after violence and economic depression had destroyed the Knights of Labor. The AFL was a narrower organization, composed almost exclusively of skilled craftsmen. Intent on bettering their own position in an industrial world where the owners of industry had the support of the police, the courts, and the public, they displayed limited interest in extending their organization to the unskilled trades, in which women clustered. Nor were they interested in raising the specter that working women, always a cheap labor supply, might legitimately compete with them for their own jobs. And, for men the union was much more than a labor organization. It was a club, a refuge from

[21] Mrs. John Van Vorst and Marie Van Vorst, *The Woman Who Toils: Being the Experiences of Two Gentlewomen as Factory Girls* (New York, 1904), p. 92; Lillian Wald, *The House on Henry Street* (New York, 1915), p. 203; Wolfson, *Woman Worker*, p. 130.

[22] See Elizabeth Butler, *Women and the Trades: Pittsburgh, 1907–1908* (New York, 1909), pp. 22–26.

the family, a place where men could get together and create a world free from the difficulties of everyday life. Unions frequently met in saloons, the bastion of male group esprit. To allow women into those sanctums would be to destroy this spirit.

The AFL charter outlawed sex discrimination among member unions, and most unions, at least nominally, complied. But since in most industries women were not employed in the same jobs as men, it was easy to so define a craft organization as to exclude women. Traditional prejudices toward women and stereotypical notions of women's work augmented the argument. One official of the International Association of Machinists told a labor investigator, "There are few real machinists. A machinist is born and not made. One must have a feeling for machines and women haven't got that."[23] Such hostility toward women dominated many skilled crafts. Even in those few AFL unions, like the International Ladies Garment Workers Union, in which women predominated in membership, the officers were invariably men. Consistent with the sex stereotype, the secretary was frequently a woman.

The antifeminism of the AFL was not so true of the more radical unions. Like the Knights of Labor, the Industrial Workers of the World, for example, welcomed women into positions of leadership and made organizing mass production industries, without regard to sex, their primary goal. Yet, even the radicals were not entirely free of sex bias. Women members of the IWW local in Lawrence, Massachusetts, scene of the 1912 strike of textile workers, charged that the men in their union would no more elect them to office than would men in the AFL.[24]

When women workers decided to protest against the conditions of their employment, they often turned not to the radical unions nor to the AFL but rather to well-to-do female reformers. From this alliance grew two major organizations of the Progressive years: the Consumer's League and the Women's Trade Union League. Always small and primarily middle class in membership, the Consumer's League directed its attention to securing special legislation for women. The WTUL was more catholic in membership and goals. With strong financial and administrative ties to the AFL, the WTUL always considered itself a part of the labor movement. Its organizers worked in a variety of industries; its chapters were located in numerous cities throughout the nation. It consistently tried to remain an amalgam of the worker and the well-to-do. Among its early state and national presidents were Alice Henrotin, a former president of the General Federation of Women's Clubs, and Mary Anderson, a Swedish immigrant who began her career as a worker in a shoe factory. Indeed, the WTUL has been almost the only women's organization in the twentieth century in which women have been able to cross class barriers in a common cause, and its very existence illustrates the difficulty that the male worker and his labor organizations have had in dealing with women.[25]

[23] Wolfson, *Woman Worker*, p. 110.
[24] Marot, *Labor Unions*, p. 68.
[25] On the Women's Trade Union League, see Gladys Boone, *The Women's Trade Union Leagues in Great Britain and the United States of America* (New York, 1942).

Yet, even the WTUL, like the AFL, often drew back when it came to the hard task of organizing women workers on a permanent basis. Some critics complained that in local chapters its middle-class members stressed cultural uplift rather than union organization, while its supporters contended that its failures stemmed from the fact that the AFL did not consider it very important and limited its funding accordingly. Whatever the reason, local and state chapters of the WTUL often worked harder for special legislation for working women than they did for unionization among them, even though the special legislation campaign was based on the reasoning that women were weaker than men and that their reproductive systems, which were crucial to their eventual role as mothers of the nation, needed special protection by the state. The courts had previously invalidated special legislation for men on the grounds that it violated the doctrine of "freedom of contract" between worker and employer, and thus antifeminist arguments were used to justify an exception for women. Women's Trade Union League officials often justified their support of special legislation as a pragmatic measure, one they could more easily attain than unionization. But special legislation often became, even to them, a way of providing protection for women workers, who they themselves saw as the dependent sex. And it implied that male workers did not need such legislation—at a time when the conditions of labor were deplorable for both sexes.[26]

Most women at the time, and not just middle-class reformers, probably supported the idea of special legislation. Factory labor was hard. Moreover, current medical knowledge indicated, however erroneously, that women who worked strained their nerves and their physiques, did permanent damage to reproductive organs, and bore unhealthy children. Even socialist Elizabeth Gurley Flynn thought that working women needed special legislation and that an equal rights amendment would be against their best interests.[27] And even had union leaders been more militant, it is debatable that working-class women would have been willing to follow them. Their preponderant immigrant origins, if nothing else, cast a divisive wedge among them, and many of them came from peasant cultures that viewed women's work in the fields with equanimity while holding that a woman's proper role was to be subordinate to men. One of the reasons for the militancy of women shirtwaist workers, for example, was the origin of some of them in Russian and Polish Jewish im-

---

[26] The special legislation campaign itself was relatively successful. Between 1909 and 1917, thirty-nine states passed maximum hour laws for women. Minimum wage legislation, however, was outlawed by the Supreme Court in 1923. Enactment of the general concept of legislation for workers awaited the labor legislation of the New Deal. Special legislation was the exact opposite of the Equal Rights Amendment that feminists in the 1970s favor.

[27] Elizabeth Gurley Flynn, *I Speak My Own Piece* (New York, 1955), p. 269. Mother Jones went even further. Although she had organized wives of workers with buckets, mops, and brooms to fight scabs and police lines, she emphasized that she was not a suffragist and did not believe that women should have careers. "Women should raise children," she declared. Mary Jones, *Autobiography of Mother Jones,* ed., Mary Field Parton (Chicago, 1925), p. 237.

migrant families with revolutionary leanings. Most immigrant families
were not so inclined. In the late nineteenth century in Cohoes, New York,
for example, predominantly French-Canadian and Irish immigrant workers feared more than anything the loss of the modest economic advance
they had achieved, and they directed their anger not against their employer, but against the unemployed who might take over their jobs.[28]

Even those daughters whose contacts with the new culture had
prompted them to eschew some of the old ways found traditional attitudes about marriage reinforced in the new world. The open attitude
toward premarital sexual relations characteristic of some peasant societies
was reinforced by the free-and-easy society of the factory and the dance
hall, and both forces may have made some working women less protective
of their purity. But casual attitudes toward sex made them no less desirous
of finding the security and romance that marriage was said to promise.
Movies, plays, and novels hammered the theme home to them. The message of popular culture reinforced both the traditionalism of parents
anxious to make good matches for their daughters and the rebelliousness
of those daughters for whom marriage seemed the only way of ending
their status as perpetual dependants, supplementing their elders' incomes.

Yet, marriage among the working class had as many stresses on it
as marriage among the middle class. To generalize about working-class
marriage is difficult, for it varied from immigrant culture to immigrant
culture, from region to region within the country, between income sub-
categories, and between the generations of working-class families. Still,
some general conclusions can be drawn. For those families with small
incomes, who had not risen to the artisan class, whose wives worked at
home, and whose daughters worked outside the home (which constituted
the majority of this class), subsistence presented substantial problems. Information about birth control was hard to come by, husbands left the
responsibility for contraception up to their wives, and women were supposed to be sexually available at their husband's behest. According to one
commentator, many women tried to prolong nursing their infants as long
as possible in the mistaken belief that lactating mothers could not conceive.[29]

In this situation, many marriages became strained, with husbands and
wives living, according to one observer, with "little affection" and "little
spiritual comradeship." The husband generally gave his wages to his wife
to distribute—so much was she able to realize her own need for power
within the family. But then each too often retreated to his or her own
territory: the husband to the newspaper, saloon, or sporting event; the
wife to housework or children.[30] Divorce was especially difficult; it was
expensive, it required knowing how to find a lawyer, and in many Catho-

---

[28] Daniel Walkowitz, "Working-Class Women in the Gilded Age: Factory, Community, and Family Life Among Cohoes, New York Cotton Workers," *Journal
of Social History* (Summer, 1972), 464–90.

[29] Frank Hatch Streightoff, *The Standard of Living Among the Industrial People of
America* (Boston, 1911), p. 138.

[30] *Ibid.*, pp. 138–64.

lic and Jewish communities it was considered a disgrace. Poverty, ignorance, the shock of American culture and the city, and traditional views
about the nature of male-female relationships made marriage at least as
difficult among the working class as among the well-to-do.

Yet, there were compensating factors. Studies showed that knowledge and use of contraception grew as income rose and as length of stay
in America increased.[31] All immigrant groups quickly founded churches
and ethnic societies, which as nurturers of traditional values in a group setting helped draw off insecurity and hostility that might have focused inward on the family. Local chapters of the AFL formed women's auxil-
iaries, where wives could gain a sense of comradeship with their husband's
work.

Moreover, they could hope for the future of their children: that was
the promise of American life. And for women, as for men, it was a hope
not without realization. There was always the possibility that the young
factory worker might become a secretary or a nurse, with the promise
of greater status, a higher salary, and, above all, the hope of marrying a
businessman or a doctor. For society in general such mobility—and, more
important, the belief in its possibility—was an important safety valve.
And that women took advantage of its opportunities is apparent from
some significant statistics on women and work. In 1900 almost all women
who worked were domestics, farm laborers, unskilled factory workers, or
teachers. By 1910, however, stenography and typing had taken their place
as the eighth largest field of employment for women. By 1920 the proportions had risen even higher, and by 1930 these two occupations constituted the third largest field of women's employment. The transition from
domestic to factory to office work was rarely made in the same generation. But for the immigrant mother whose sons became lawyers and doctors and whose daughters became secretaries, nurses, and the wives of
lawyers and doctors, life held out the promise of some fulfillment.

III

Not all women in America in the early twentieth century—whether
black or white, immigrant or native—played the accustomed female role
of wife and mother or of volunteer worker or paid employee that society
officially approved. Some instead turned to prostitution—the role that
particularly challenged Victorian notions of female purity and propriety.
It is almost impossible to estimate the number of prostitutes in the United
States in the early 1900s. Since the occupation was illegal, few women
would have been willing to reveal their participation; thus, most statistics
must be based on arrest records or on whatever data sensitive investigators
can amass. In any event, prostitution seems to have been on the increase
in the late nineteenth and early twentieth centuries.[32]

[31] Commander, *American Idea;* Himes, *Medical History.*
[32] On prostitution, I have utilized the vice commission reports of the following
cities and states: Chicago, 1911; Minneapolis, 1911; Syracuse, 1913; Newark, N.J.,

Its expansion was largely due to the explosive growth of cities during that period. For among the floating and anonymous urban population, prostitution could flourish as it never had in rural, tradition-bound areas. For sailors in port, for unmarried young men living away from home, for businessmen on trips, for husbands bored at home, the prostitute had become a real or imagined necessity, readily available, knowledgeable about sex techniques, and willing to join in practices that would horrify Victorian wives. Moreover, polite society's unwillingness to recognize that prostitution existed only furthered the vacuum of public opinion within which it flourished.

During the late nineteenth century, public officials were aware of the existence of prostitution, but with a common Victorian attitude, they looked on it as a "necessary evil" to protect the virtue of pure women and to preserve the stability of marriage. Indeed, in most cities the police had driven prostitution, at least as practiced in brothels, into so-called "red light" districts, far from middle-class areas, which might be offended by it. Thus gathered together, prostitutes provided considerable revenue to the city and to individual policemen who threatened arrest unless regular payments were made. In many cities, something approaching the European system of licensing, under which prostitutes paid fees to the state and were required to have regular medical examinations for venereal disease, had come into being. Among the red light districts, which also functioned as havens for criminals, the French Quarter in New Orleans and the Barbary Coast of San Francisco were best known, but they were reproduced in cities large and small throughout the nation. Even in Muncie, Indiana, there were twenty to twenty-five brothels in the 1890s, with four to eight women per house. This in a town with a population of about 11,000.[33]

Why did women become prostitutes? Some observers at that time were convinced that all prostitutes were forced into a "life of vice" by male procurers who were employed by national and international syndicates. Indeed, for a time around 1910 concern about the so-called "white slave" trade reached the level of national hysteria, with rumors that men with drugged hypodermic needles traveled crowded streetcars and haunted amusement parks seeking likely victims to inject and abduct. Given the new feminism and the concerted efforts by reformers to force Americans to discuss taboo subjects like prostitution and venereal disease, it is no wonder that the nation indulged in one of its periodic outbreaks of paranoia. For reasons of health and social welfare, Americans could accept the creation of vice commissions in most American cities after 1900, but it was difficult for a society still shot through with repressive

---

1913–14; Massachusetts, 1914; Illinois, 1916. See also George Kneeland, *Commercialized Prostitution in New York City* (New York, 1913); Joseph Mayer, *The Regulation of Commercialized Vice . . .* (New York, 1922); Willoughby Waterman, *Prostitution and Its Repression in New York City, 1900–1931* (New York, 1932); and Walter Reckless, *Vice in Chicago* (Chicago, 1933).

[33] Helen Merrell Lynd and Robert S. Lynd, *Middletown: A Study in Contemporary American Culture* (New York, 1929), p. 113.

attitudes about sex to digest thoroughly the reports these commissions wrote. The white slave story was more shocking, more thrilling, and easier to "understand."

This paranoia was encouraged by some well-documented cases of women who were indeed drugged and who awakened in brothels. There were men who hung around dance halls, trying to strike up an acquaintance that might turn into a seduction. American society had still not rid itself entirely of the venerable notion that once an unmarried woman had lost her virginity, she might just as well take to the streets. Among some immigrant groups—the Italians and orthodox Jews, for example—a fall from virtue, if discovered, could result in family ostracism. But contrary to the popular myth, there was little evidence that national or state-wide syndicates lurked behind the recruitment to prostitution.

Most surveys of prostitution played down the white slave story and looked elsewhere to explain the reasons that women became prostitutes. Here economic need was the most common factor they found. Most prostitutes came from lower socioeconomic groups. Many reported that they turned to the streets as a last resort, either because they had a family to support or because they could earn much more as a prostitute than as a seamstress or even a salesclerk. "Poverty causes prostitution," concluded the writers of the Illinois Vice Commission Report of 1916, and the authors of other vice commission reports invariably agreed.[34] Again, all studies showed that many prostitutes were drawn from among domestic workers—those women who were not only poorly paid but who were also scorned by working women.

To argue that poverty caused prostitution, however satisfying to a society that still could not tolerate fully the idea of female sexuality, was to give only a partial explanation. Sensitive observers, despite their middle-class orientation, could not fail to note that many prostitutes contended that "personal inclination" had led them into prostitution. As early as 1858, in the first detailed investigation of prostitution conducted in the United States, Dr. William Sanger of New York's Bellevue Hospital found that about 25 percent of his sample of 2,000 women said that they had become prostitutes simply because they wanted to.[35] Sanger himself, despite his medical background, could not accept this explanation. It was beyond his Victorian comprehension that these women might be trying to shock him as a form of protest against their hospitalization or that they came from a world in which sexuality was open and in which a woman might consider prostitution as just another kind of work. "Personal inclination" to him indicated "an innate depravity, a want of true womanly feeling, which is actually incredible." He reasoned that these respondents were simply unaware that something exterior to themselves—probably liquor—had aroused the sexual feeling that they erroneously thought their own bodies had produced.

Yet few investigators could overlook the fact that many prostitutes

[34] Illinois Senate Vice Committee.
[35] William Sanger, *The History of Prostitution: Its Extent, Causes and Effects Throughout the World* (New York, 1927), p. 488.

had adjusted to their life and were not interested in being rehabilitated. Writing some fifty years after Sanger, Jane Addams, in her 1913 study of prostitution, *A New Conscience and an Ancient Evil,* was convinced that entrapment was the main road to prostitution, that pure women were defiled and then "degraded morally" by "horrible devices" so that they would willingly take to the profession. Exactly what Addams meant is difficult to say; one assumes that, like Sanger, she had to admit that women had some sensuality, but she could not admit that they might willingly become promiscuous.[36]

Other investigators were more sensitive to the causes and conditions of prostitution. From their observations and hints (for few individuals in that age wanted to imply that they condoned free sexuality) a fascinating picture, not only of prostitution but of the culture out of which it grew, can be constructed.

In the first place, many prostitutes (although probably not the majority) worked in brothels. Here the madam took responsibility for protection, solicitation, and rooming space. Street-walking could be dangerous, and there is an indication that in some cities it was mainly older women, having been edged out of brothels by younger competitors, who took to the streets as a final resort. Madams, too, were often resourceful and innovative businesswomen. Since the vice commissions and police drives of the early twentieth century often centered on their easily visible houses, they devised new methods of carrying on their operations. They reopened their houses under the guise of private dance studios and massage parlors, and they also invented clever call girl systems. Here the madam simply had a list of women, whom she could contact by telephone to arrange a meeting with a client at a convenient hotel whose location could be shifted if police surveillance was suspected.

Nevertheless, there were disadvantages to working in a brothel. Madams generally demanded sizable percentages of their employee's fees, and the prostitutes found it difficult to conceal their occupation from family, friends, and the police. Alternatively, in the 1910s assignations could be made relatively safely in dance halls and saloons, while there were aways hotels that catered to the prostitute and her clientele. Such conditions made prostitution attractive to some women unable to find work or anxious to supplement inadequate wages. There was, as one observer described it, a good deal of "semi-prostitution" among certain working women.[37]

The incidence of women holding regular jobs who were prostitutes on the side indicated the complex moral standards among the working class. To trace the morphology of popular attitudes is always difficult; in this case it seems that several opposite developments were occurring at the same time. To many working-class women who aspired to higher status it was clear that virtue was a valued possession of middle-class women, and they enforced on themselves and their daughters the Puritanical standards that seemed at the heart of the American way. Others, how-

---

[36] Jane Addams, *A New Conscience and an Ancient Evil* (New York, 1914), p. 22.
[37] Frances Donovan, *The Woman Who Waits* (Boston, 1920), p. 224.

ever, took the opposite direction. Polly Adler's exploits as the madam of a New York house of prostitution in the 1920s and 1930s became legendary. She lost her virtue (and subsequently underwent an abortion) to a handsome foreman in the glove factory where she worked. Under the pretext of taking her for an outing to Coney Island, he lured her to a deserted spot where he assaulted her.[38]

The point of the story is that Adler did not feel herself disgraced by what had happened to her. Nor, one suspects, would a certain proportion of working-class women in her position. For work had brought those women into contact with young men, while responsibility had given some the nerve to scorn parental restraints. They expected to go to dance halls and to meet young men. For some, sex was the next step. The investigators for the Massachusetts Vice Commission reported in 1914 that in every Massachusetts city sizable numbers of young women loitered around cafes and dance halls, waiting to be picked up by men. "To total strangers," the investigators reported, "they talk willingly about themselves, their desire to 'see life,' to 'get out of this dead hole,' to go to Boston, or to New York." Many, the investigators found, were willing to have sexual relations with them. Assuredly, this was sexual license, but it was not prostitution, as the Massachusetts investigators were quick to point out. For most of these women were incensed by the offer of direct payment for an assignation. They still drew a fine line between their own definitions of virtue and vice: payment meant prostitution, and they were not prostitutes.[39]

It seems clear that prostitutes themselves were for the most part recruited from the sexually experienced, probably from the very group of women that the Massachusetts investigators described. What was it that made one woman from this group marry and remain content with home and children while another became a prostitute? The most reasonable explanation is that for most it was an unthinking decision, that prostitution became a plausible option at the end of a series of experiences that pointed in that direction. All studies showed that the average prostitute had had her first sexual experience before she became a full-fledged prostitute, and that her first partner was generally someone she knew well. From there she drifted into casual relations with other men, until finally it came to seem reasonable that she accept money, especially when it was obvious that a successful prostitute could make double or triple what a factory worker or a servant could earn.

Yet the culture of prostitution itself indicates that for some women deeper psychological motivations may have come into play. For, then as now, many of the prostitutes sampled did not work entirely for their own benefit. Many reported to pimps—or "cadets," as they were then called—the males to whom they gave most of their earnings and from whom they received some spending money and affection. The relationship between the

[38] Polly Adler, *A House Is Not a Home* (New York, 1953).

[39] Massachusetts Commission for the Investigation of the White Slave Traffic, *Report of the Commission for the Investigation of the White Slave Traffic, so-called* (Boston, 1914), p. 43.

prostitute and the pimp has always fascinated and baffled psychologists. For it has seemed that, while giving much, the prostitute received little from the pimp. In the early twentieth century, he often functioned as her procurer: the Kneeland investigation of 1916 suggested that in New York City the pimp-prostitute relationship had grown out of youthful friendships among boys and girls in street gangs, and that in this case the pimps solicited for their women. Frequently, however, the pimp lived a life of leisure, supported by his woman. Often a pimp would have more than one prostitute working for him, and the women would vie for his affection.

The pimp obviously filled some psychological need for the prostitute, but what that need was is difficult to say. Playing a role that may have cut her off from previous relationships, the prostitute probably had to find some sort of stable relationship, someone with whom she could play out a desire to love and be loved. She may have chosen such a degrading relationship simply because it was normative in the culture of prostitution. Or in psychological terms, the relationship may have indicated either a masochistic need to be the slave of men or to have the power over men that the commercialization of sex implies. One study of prostitution in New York City in 1916 found that the largest group interviewed were daughters of first generation immigrants. Here generational conflict and the clash between traditionalist and modern culture may have lain behind the daughters' entering prostitution.

The actual category of prostitution was an ambiguous one. All investigators were aware that beyond those women actually committed to prostitution, who formed the core of their samples, lay a shadowy world in which some women worked as prostitutes part-time, while others took up the trade for a time between jobs or between husbands. These women successfully avoided both the law and the vice commission investigators. Sometimes, almost by accident, reporters stumbled into this world. Despite its ubiquitousness, only an unusually sensitive observer could analyze it without allowing middle-class blinders to get in the way.

One such observer was Frances Donovan, a reporter who for several months donned a uniform to study the occupation of waitress. There were many such studies of working women in the early twentieth century; many educated women eager to advance themselves and the cause of women found it challenging to enter the world of the working class and record what they saw. There were few, however, who investigated their subject with as much candor as Donovan, and who were so chastened and challenged by it.

At first Donovan was shocked as she plumbed the world of the waitress. For here sexuality was ever present. In their spare time her acquaintances boasted of their affairs and openly discussed their abortions. Her sheltered upbringing had not prepared her for their constant use of obscenities and profanities in speaking. Nor could she reconcile herself to their penchant for collecting off-color jokes from patrons and retelling them among themselves or their habit of pointing out to each other men who supposedly were sexual perverts.

But slowly Donovan came to respect the women among whom she worked. Gradually she came to see that their way of life represented a critique of middle-class culture. It was not simply that they were open about sexual relations, it went much beyond that. They had lived, Donovan saw, in a way that the middle-class woman, bound to convention, still could not. Many of them were divorced and that fact, plus their economic independence, lay at the heart of the matter. They were free of the dominance of men. "With economic independence the waitress has achieved a man's independence in her relations with men; she doesn't have to get married and she doesn't have to stay married very long. . . . She is a free soul,"[40] wrote Donovan.

Without doubt Donovan romanticized the life of the waitress, with its constant round of toil and its constant reminders of inferior status. Like many feminists she allowed her own suspicion of men to color her interpretation. Yet there was more than a grain of truth in what she had to say. Were not these waitresses, despite their condition of "semi-prostitution" (to use Donovan's phrase), more honest than their middle-class peers? "To go out into the world and grab from it the right to live in spite of the competition of youth is vastly more interesting than to make weekly pilgrimages to the beauty parlor in the vain attempt to get rid of the symbols of old age that bear witness to the fact that you have never lived. . . . Here," Donovan concluded, "we have the feminist movement and ideals embodied in a class."[41]

To a certain extent, Donovan was correct. Without sexual liberation, women could never be free. But was sexual liberation enough? And did women not have other responsibilities—to themselves, to their families, to society? For the next decades, such questions would form the core of the feminist debate.

[40] Donovan, *Woman Who Waits*.
[41] *Ibid.*, pp. 226–27.

The IWW Fight
for Free Speech
on the West Coast

MELVYN DUBOFSKY

For the most part, organized labor in America has been content to seek economic advantage for itself. On a few rare occasions, however, labor unions have participated in movements to restructure American society as a whole in order to bring about a more equitable distribution of wealth and more humane conditions of life. The Knights of Labor, organized in 1869, was such an organization. A radical utopian union, it opened its membership to all workers, regardless of race, sex, age, nationality, or type of work. Its program included not only the typical labor demands, such as the eight-hour day and the abolition of child labor, but also demands for equal pay for both sexes, an income tax, and prohibition of the sale of alcoholic beverages. At the peak of its strength, the Knights had over 700,000 members. But a reputation for violence and radicalism caused it to decline rapidly after about 1885, and by the middle of the 1890s it had virtually disappeared.

The next significant radical labor organization was the Industrial Workers of the World (the IWW), better known as the Wobblies. The IWW was founded in 1905 as an outgrowth of the Western Federation of Miners. The purpose of the new organization, according to its chairman and guiding spirit, William D. ("Big Bill") Haywood, was to reorganize American government and economic life. The Wobblies advocated what has been called anarcho-syndicalism—that is, the organization of society into cooperative labor groups that would control the means of production, distribution, and exchange. In other words, they believed in socialism without the state. The IWW avoided political action, however, and concentrated on trying to organize the bottom strata of the American labor force, particularly the unskilled migrant workers of the Western mining, lumber, and agricultural industries. Like the Knights, the IWW was open to workers of all races, sexes, ages, nationalities, and types of work.

The Wobblies were perhaps the most colorful labor organization in American history, partly because of their leadership. One of the most renowned of the Wobbly leaders was Joe Hillstrom, also known as Joe Hill, who composed many of the marching songs used by future industrial workers in organization drives. Hill is perhaps best known for a statement he made just before his execution on a contrived murder charge in Utah: "Don't mourn for me. Organize." It was this spirit that captured the imagination of thousands of wandering workingmen in the West and that later spread to the East, where the IWW organized several successful strikes in northern mill cities.

Almost from the inception of the IWW, the United States government as well as local governments and industries made every effort to destroy it. Although the Wobblies did not advocate violence, they stressed direct action in their organizing campaigns, and the violent reactions they sometimes evoked on the part of the authorities earned them the charge of fomenting violence. In 1917, with the approval of President Wilson, the Justice Department attacked the IWW headquarters, confiscated all records, and arrested the leaders on charges of sedition, espionage, and interference with the war effort. Though the case against them was nonexistent, the Wobbly leaders were found guilty and imprisoned. The movement was thus effectively suppressed. Subsequently, many of the Wobbly leaders joined the Communist party to continue their work for social change.

Melvyn Dubofsky, of the State University of New York at Binghamton, has written a richly textured and exhaustive study of the IWW entitled **We Shall Be All: A History of the Industrial Workers of the World**, a chapter of which is reprinted here. This selection, dealing with the Wobblies' doctrine that the streets belong to the people and that all people have the right to free speech, gives an indication of the spirit that activated the movement as well as of the vicious response it drew from the dominant forces in American society.

Quit your job. Go to Missoula. Fight with the Lumber Jacks for Free Speech," the *Industrial Worker* encouraged its readers on September 30, 1909. "Are you game? Are you afraid? Do you love the police? Have you been robbed, skinned, grafted on? If so, then go to Missoula, and defy the police, the courts and the people who live off the wages of prostitution." Thus did the IWW proclaim the first of its many fights for free speech.

"The Fight for Free Speech 1909–1912" (Editor's title: "The IWW Fight for Free Speech on the West Coast") reprinted by permission of Quadrangle/The New York Times Book Co. from *We Shall Be All: A History of the Industrial Workers of the World* by Melvyn Dubofsky, pages 173–79, copyright © 1969 by Melvyn Dubofsky.

Many years after the IWW's free-speech fights had faded from public memory, Roger Baldwin, founding father of the American Civil Liberties Union, recalled that the Wobblies

> wrote a chapter in the history of American liberties like that of the struggle of the Quakers for freedom to meet and worship, of the militant suffragists to carry their propaganda to the seats of government, and of the Abolitionists to be heard. . . . The little minority of the working class represented in the I.W.W. blazed the trail in those ten years of fighting for free speech [1908–1918] which the entire American working class must in some fashion follow.[1]

For Wobblies free-speech fights involved nothing so abstract as defending the Constitution, preserving the Bill of Rights, or protecting the civil liberties of American citizens. They were instigated primarily to overcome resistance to IWW organizing tactics and also to demonstrate that America's dispossessed could, through direct action, challenge established authority. To workers dubious about the results achieved by legal action and the reforms won through political action, the IWW taught the effectiveness of victories gained through a strategy of open, yet nonviolent confrontations with public officials. Roger Baldwin perceived as much when, writing long before the post-1954 civil rights movement had made the strategy of confrontation a commonplace of American protest movements, he commented about the IWW's approach: "Far more effective is this direct action of open conflict than all the legal maneuvers in the courts to get rights that no government willingly grants. Power wins rights—the power of determination, backed by willingness to suffer jail or violence, to get them."[2]

The IWW and its members did challenge the law and endure violence and imprisonment to win free speech—that is, the right for their soapboxers to stand on street corners, or in front of employment offices, and harangue working-class crowds about the iniquities of capitalism and the decay of American society. But behind the right to speak freely lay more important IWW goals. Many Wobblies considered street speaking the most effective means of carrying their gospel to Western workers. They had solid evidence for this belief. Experience had demonstrated that it was almost impossible for organizers to reach timber workers, construction hands, and harvesters out on the job where watchful employers harassed "labor agitators" and where workers were scattered over a vast geographical area. Only in the city did Western workers concentrate in sufficiently large numbers to be reached effectively by the handful of organizers proselytizing for the IWW, and only in the city did the "agitator" have a measure of freedom to recruit without interference by employers. Many an IWW recruit—among them, Richard Brazier, who

---

[1] IWW, *Twenty Five Years of Industrial Unionism* (Chicago, 1930), p. 20.
[2] *Ibid.*

later became a leader in the Northwest and also a member of the general
executive board—testified to how urban soapboxers such as Joe Ettor
aroused his initial interest in the IWW. The IWW and the Western
workers also had a common enemy in the city: the employment agent or
"shark." These "sharks," against whom the IWW directed most of its
street-corner harangues, controlled employment in agriculture and lumber. With anti-union employers they maintained the heavy labor turnover among the unskilled workers—one on the way, one on the job, one
leaving—that kept labor organization out of the fields and forests, wages
low, and working conditions primitive. The heavy labor turnover guaranteed substantial commissions to the employment agencies that located jobs
for the unemployed, as well as large payoffs to cooperating managers and
foremen. If the IWW could break the links connecting the "shark," the
employer, and the transient laborer, it could loosen the heavy chain of
economic circumstances that kept the Western worker in semi-bondage.

Breaking the hold of the employment agencies on the job market
would be the initial step in improving working conditions and raising
wages, results which would themselves insure a sharp rise in IWW membership. With this in mind, IWW organizers, conceding that industrial
conflict belonged in the *shop*, not on the street, stressed: ". . . To carry
the war into the shop we must first get into the shop—in this case the
camp. To control the source of supply in the industrial cities by forcing
the employers to hire men through the I.W.W. is a great step in the
direction of industrial control."[3] Put differently, this meant that Western
migratories had to be organized before going out on the job, which might
last only a few days; and this, in turn, could be accomplished only by
controlling the employment agencies, or abolishing them and replacing
them with IWW hiring halls. Here is the primary reason the IWW demanded free speech in Spokane, Fresno, Missoula, Aberdeen, Minot,
Kansas City, and scores of other Western cities where migratories laid
over between jobs, or patronized employment agencies to find new jobs.
Three of these many free-speech struggles reveal the pattern of IWW
confrontations and their role in the history and development of the organization: Spokane, 1909–1910; Fresno, 1910–1911; and San Diego, 1912.

The first significant IWW struggle for free speech erupted in Spokane, Washington, the hub of the Inland Empire's agricultural, mining,
and lumber industries and the central metropolis for all of western Washington, western Oregon, and northern Idaho. Here employers came to
locate labor for the mines of the Coeur d'Alenes, the woods of the interior, and the farms of the Palouse and other inland valleys. Migratory
workers came to rest up in Spokane during the winter after a long hard
harvest summer or an equally arduous season of railroad construction
work. In Spokane workers discovered cheap skid-row hotels and cheaper
whisky and women to spend their skimpy savings on. When spring approached and savings dwindled, the migratories could turn to the "sharks,"

[3] *Industrial Worker*, June 3, 1909, p. 2; August 5, 1909, p. 3.

who for a price offered another season of employment out in the country-side or forest.

What the IWW accomplished in Spokane was in some respects truly remarkable. Recruiting largely among workers whose lives were often bru-tal and violent and who had a view of masculinity somewhat akin to the Latin idea of *machismo*, the IWW channeled working-class hostility to-ward employment agencies into constructive courses. Soapboxers warned angry workers that broken heads and shattered windows would not put the "sharks out of business." No! they thundered. "There is only one way you can get out of their hold. That is by joining the I.W.W. and refusing to go to them for jobs."[4]

The IWW's message was heard. Overalls Brigade "General" J. H. Walsh had come to Spokane after the 1908 convention, and within six months rejuvenated a previously moribund IWW local. The revitalized union leased expensive new headquarters which included a large library and reading room, ample office space, and an assembly hall seating several hundred. It held inside propaganda meetings four nights a week, operated its own cigar and newsstand, and even featured regular movies: from conventional one-reelers to illustrated rebel songs and dry economic lec-tures. When local authorities restricted street speaking, the Spokane local published its own newspaper, the *Industrial Worker*, which reached a wide local working-class audience. Walsh's local even retained a Spokane law firm on a yearly retainer, as well as maintaining a voluntary hospital plan for members. All this was supported from March to April 1909 by the dues of twelve hundred to fifteen hundred members in good standing and double that number on the local's books.[5] For the first time, or so it now seemed, a labor organization had succeeded in reaching the Inland Empire's migratory workers.

IWW growth brought an immediate and inevitable reaction from Spokane's employers, "sharks," and officials. In March 1909 the city coun-cil, acting on complaints from the chamber of commerce, prohibited street-corner orations by closing Spokane's streets to Wobblies and all other "revolutionists." It did so partly because the soapboxers castigated organized religion and partly because IWW oratory had a greater effect than "respectable" citizens realized upon "the army of the unemployed and poorly paid workers." Spokane's city council's action was in accord with the observation made by a later federal investigator that the IWW's right to speak should be restricted when the organization denounced "everything we have been taught to respect from our earliest days . . . all kinds of religions and religious sects. . . ."[6] Christianity and patriotism thus became the employment agents' first line of defense against the IWW

---

[4] *Industrial Union Bulletin*, February 27, 1909, p. 1; J. H. Walsh in *ibid.*, February 21, 1909, p. 1.

[5] *Industrial Worker*, April 29, 1909, p. 5.

[6] Daniel O'Regan to Dr. Charles McCarthy, November 10, 1914, United States Com-mission on Industrial Relations Papers, Department of Labor, Record Group 174, National Archives (hereafter cited as CIR Papers); Charles Grant, "Law and Order in Spokane," *Industrial Worker*, March 18, 1909, p. 3.

onslaught. Thus, Spokane's initial street-speaking ordinance allowed religious groups, most notably the Salvation Army, the IWW's major competitor, the right to speak on the city's streets.

The IWW maintained that its organizers would continue speaking until the ordinance was repealed or made binding upon all organizations. On March 4 the city council placed religious groups under the ban, but the IWW remained unsatisfied. That very day J. H. Walsh himself mounted a soapbox and addressed his "fellow workers and friends," only to be hauled off to jail by local police. Later he was tried, convicted, and fined for violating the local street-speaking ordinance. For the next several days, as Walsh's legal appeals moved through the various courts, Wobblies spoke on Spokane's streets—and were promptly arrested and jailed. As the number of those arrested rose, so did the fines and the length of imprisonment. In March 1909 Spokane's jail filled with Wobblies, ten to twelve men crammed in cells built to accommodate only four. The free-speech prisoners, fed a diet of bread and water twice daily, could neither lie nor sit down. One Wobbly later recalled: "The misery in those cells was something never to be forgotten. . . ."[7]

But the Wobblies refused to give up the struggle. Instead, they sang revolutionary songs, refused to work on the jail rock pile, held daily business meetings, made speeches, and preserved their militancy even within the prison walls. Those who passed by Spokane's jail during those March days must have thought it an odd prison, when they heard the words of the "Red Flag" or the "Marseillaise" filtering out from behind the bars.

As spring approached, the migratories began to leave Spokane for the countryside. Under these circumstances, city authorities released the imprisoned Wobblies, while state courts considered the constitutionality of Spokane's street-speaking ordinance. Spring and summer were not the time for the IWW to contend for free speech: it had to wait for its members to return for another winter in the city.

With the bulk of the migratories temporarily away, Spokane's officials acted to avert another winter of discontent and tumult. On August 10 the city council enacted a revised law that allowed religious groups to hold street meetings but required all other organizations to obtain permits before doing so. The *Industrial Worker* promptly warned the city fathers that the IWW would not ask permission to speak on streets its members had built. "The toad-eaters who make up the Spokane city council are afraid of the I.W.W.," a Wobbly rhetorician noted in an editorial. "Even the devil is not afraid of the Starvation Army."[8] Thus a renewed clash between Wobblies and public authorities awaited summer's end.

Summer ended, the migratories returned to Spokane, and IWW soapboxers again took to the streets. The inevitable followed. On Monday, October 25, the police arrested Jim Thompson for street speaking without a permit. The IWW promptly demanded the inalienable right of free

[7] Grant, "Law and Order," p. 3.
[8] *Industrial Worker,* August 12, 1909, p. 1.

speech and also declared that it would send as many men to Spokane as were needed to win its struggle. Despite the IWW's threat and a legal ruling declaring the revised street-speaking ordinance discriminatory and unconstitutional, the battle continued to rage. On November 1, the day of the legal decision ruling the ban on speaking unconstitutional, the IWW initiated round-the-clock street meetings. Spokane's police promptly arrested each speaker who mounted a soapbox. Before long the city jail held every local IWW leader: Walter Nef, Jim Thompson, James Wilson, C. L. Filigno, and A. C. Cousins. Those not hauled off a soapbox were picked up in a police raid on IWW headquarters, which also netted three female sympathizers. The arrested Wobblies went to jail peaceably, for, as the *Industrial Worker* advised its readers, "it must be understood that any person, at any time, who would try to incite disorder or 'rioting' is an enemy of the I.W.W. Nothing of the kind will be tolerated at this time."[9] Passive resistance and confrontation tactics as a form of direct action were being put to the test in Spokane.

The city fathers used every instrument of power they controlled to thwart the IWW. Before the battle ended almost four hundred Wobblies had been jailed. For a time, public officials reasoned that if they could incapacitate the IWW's leaders, the fight would dissipate. Such reasoning lay behind the city's decision to raid IWW headquarters on November 3, and to arrest local Wobblies on criminal conspiracy charges; it was also behind the move to arrest the editors of the *Industrial Worker*. None of this decisively stifled the Wobblies, however, for as one policeman remarked: "Hell! we got the leaders, but damned if it don't look like they are all leaders."[10]

After their arrest Wobblies received a further taste of Spokane justice. When Frank Little appeared in court, the presiding magistrate asked him what he had been doing at the time of his arrest. "Reading the Declaration of Independence," Little answered. "Thirty days," said the magistrate. The prosecuting attorney demanded that the IWW "feel the mailed fist of the law," which for those leaders charged with criminal conspiracy meant four to six months in jail. For most Wobblies arrested for disorderly conduct the sentence was thirty days, then release, followed by further street speaking and another thirty-day sentence. This legal treatment, most Wobblies thought, justified their definition of government "as the slugging committee of the capitalist class."[11]

In Spokane, indeed, slugging soon became more than merely rhetorical. Arresting police officers used their clubs liberally. Jail life proved even worse: twenty-eight to thirty Wobblies would be tossed into an

---

[9] *Ibid.*, October 27, 1909, p. 1; November 3, 1909, pp. 1–2.

[10] *Ibid.*, November 10, 1909, p. 1.

[11] These descriptions of Spokane justice come from Elizabeth Gurley Flynn, "The Fight for Free Speech at Spokane," *International Socialist Review*, X (December 1909), 483–89; Flynn, "The Shame of Spokane," *ibid.* (January 1910), pp. 610–19; S. Sorenson to V. St. John, n.d., CIR Papers.

eight-by-six-foot sweatbox, where they would steam for a full day while staring at bloodstained walls.[12] After that they would be moved into an ice-cold cell without cots or blankets. Those who did not weaken from the heat of the first cell often collapsed from the chill of the second. Because Spokane's regular jails could not accommodate the hordes of IWW prisoners, the city converted an unheated, abandoned schoolhouse into a temporary prison. There in mid-winter jailers offered scantily clad prisoners two ounces of bread daily, soft pine for a pillow, and hardwood for a bed. Inside the schoolhouse guards woke the inmates at all hours of the night and then chased them from room to room. Under these conditions some Wobblies fell ill; others, no longer able to stand the strain, collapsed in the middle of the floor; still others maintained their spirits by walking around in a circle singing the "Red Flag." Once a week the school's jailers marched the prisoners out in order to have them bathe for allegedly sanitary reasons. Taken to the city jail, the Wobblies were stripped, thrust under an ice-cold shower, and then, frequently in frigid weather, marched back to their unheated prison.

The IWW estimated that, as a result of this treatment, 334 of the 400 men in prison for 110 days (from November through March) were treated in the emergency hospital a total of 1,600 times. Many left prison with permanent scars and missing teeth; the more fortunate walked away with weakened constitutions.

When police repression and prison brutality failed to weaken the Wobblies' resistance, the authorities resorted to different tactics. After raiding and closing IWW headquarters, they denied every hall in Spokane, except Turner Hall, to the Wobblies. Police seized copies of the *Industrial Worker* and arrested the men—even the boys—who peddled the paper. Unable to function in Spokane, the IWW moved its headquarters and all its defense activities to Coeur d'Alene City under the direction of Fred Heslewood, and published the *Industrial Worker* in Seattle. In the face of relentless repression, the IWW resisted.

The IWW ultimately triumphed because of the spirit and determination of its members. When IWW headquarters pleaded for volunteers to fight for free speech, scores of Wobblies descended upon Spokane. One Wobbly left Minneapolis on November 10, traveling across North Dakota and Montana atop a Pullman car despite sub-zero temperatures. Arriving in Spokane on November 21, somewhat chilled but ready to fight, he was arrested by police two days later. He was not alone: hundreds like him came to Spokane, and hundreds more were ready to come. All intended

[12] This account is drawn from Sorenson to St. John, CIR Papers; Robert Ross to CIR, September 19, 1914, CIR Papers; Spokane Free Speech Committee to United Brotherhood of Carpenters and Joiners of America, January 9, 1910, Department of Justice Files, Record Group 60, National Archives (hereafter cited as D/J 60); Flynn, "Shame of Spokane," pp. 610–19; Fred Heslewood, "Barbarous Spokane," *International Socialist Review*, X (February 1910), 705–13; *Industrial Worker*, November 1909–March 1910.

to make the free-speech fight an expensive and difficult proposition for Spokane's taxpayers. "Let them cry quits to their Mayor and police force if they do not relish it," threatened the Wobblies. "We can keep up the fight all winter."[13]

No one better exemplified this IWW spirit than the "Rebel Girl," Elizabeth Gurley Flynn.[14] Only nineteen years old and recently released from a Missoula jail (where another free-speech battle had ended), she was several months pregnant when she arrived in Spokane in November 1909. Local papers described her at that time as a "frail, slender girl, pretty and graceful, with a resonant voice and a fiery eloquence that attracted huge crowds." Another observer pictured her as a little woman, Irish all over, with "the Celt in her grey-blue eyes and almost black hair and in the way she clenches her small hands into fists when she's speaking." To Woodrow Wilson, she described herself in 1918 as

> an humble and obscure citizen who has struggled for democracy as her vision glimpsed it and who has suffered for espousing an unpopular and much misrepresented point of view. . . . For seven years I have supported my child, and helped to educate two sisters . . . and a brother. . . . This . . . has been a labor of love, but it is rather incompatible with the popular conception of a "labor agitator."[15]

Elizabeth Gurley Flynn, however, was all agitator. Daughter of immigrant Irish parents, at fifteen or sixteen she made her first speech as a "materialistic socialist" before her father's radical club in Harlem; at seventeen she had been arrested for street speaking in New York; and at nineteen she was jailed, first in Missoula, then in Spokane. So adept an agitator was she that the Spokane authorities considered her the most dangerous and effective of Wobbly soapboxers. When a young attorney suggested to the city fathers that she not be tried along with the men on charges of criminal conspiracy, the local officials responded: "Hell, no! You just don't understand. She's the one we are after. She makes all the trouble. She puts fight into the men, gets them the publicity they enjoy. As it is, they're having the time of their lives."[16]

Spokane brought Elizabeth Gurley Flynn to trial on charges of criminal conspiracy with a young Italian Wobbly named Charley Filigno. Not unexpectedly, the jury declared on February 24, 1910: "Filigno, guilty. Elizabeth Gurley Flynn, not guilty." An enraged prosecutor demanded of the jury foreman, "What in hell do you fellows mean by

[13] Sorenson to St. John, CIR Papers; Flynn, "Free Speech Fight," p. 488.
[14] The following sketch is based on Elizabeth Gurley Flynn, *I Speak My Own Piece* (New York, 1955); B. H. Kizer, "Elizabeth Gurley Flynn," *Pacific Northwest Quarterly*, LVII (July 1966), 110–12; "E. G. Flynn: Labor Leader," *Outlook*, CXI (December 15, 1915), 905.
[15] Quotations are from Kizer, "Flynn," p. 111; *Outlook*, p. 905; E. G. Flynn to Woodrow Wilson, January 10, 1918, File 188032–146, D/J 60.
[16] Kizer, "Flynn," pp. 111–12.

acquitting the most guilty, and convicting the man, far less guilty." To which the foreman calmly replied: "She ain't a criminal, Fred, an' you know it! If you think this jury, or any jury, is goin' to send that pretty Irish girl to jail merely for bein' bighearted and idealistic, to mix with all those whores and crooks down at the pen, you've got another guess comin'."[17]

But looks can be deceiving, and in Elizabeth Gurley Flynn's case they certainly were. After the fight in Spokane she proceeded to bigger and better battles. She was with the IWW at Lawrence, Paterson, and Everett. Still later, with Roger Baldwin, she helped found the American Civil Liberties Union, and fought to defend the rights of the poor and the exploited. Her vision of democracy as she glimpsed it took her from the Socialist party to the IWW to the ACLU and ultimately in the 1930's to the Communist party. During the forties and fifties she became American communism's leading female advocate as well as the only woman ever sentenced to a prison term under the Smith Act. While in Moscow attending a Soviet party congress in her capacity as chairman of the American Communist party, she died on September 5, 1964, at the age of seventy-four. From her first speech before the Harlem Socialist Club as a teen-ager to her last talk as a Communist, Elizabeth Gurley Flynn remained true to what she allegedly told theatrical producer David Belasco, upon turning down a part in a Broadway play: "I don't want to be an actress! I'm in the labor movement and I speak my own piece."[18]

The piece she spoke in Spokane in the winter of 1909–1910 aided the IWW immeasurably. She won national attention and sympathy that no male agitator could. Her clash with local authorities, her arrest, and the despicable treatment she received in jail made nationwide headlines. She exemplified the IWW's determination to win free speech in Spokane. If repression could not break the spirit of a pregnant, slightly built, teen-age girl, how could it crush the Wobblies' free-speech fighters flooding into Spokane in an unending stream?

Yet the Spokane struggle continued through the winter of 1910, as public officials resorted to further repressive measures. On February 22 Spokane officials crossed the state line into Idaho, raided IWW defense headquarters in Coeur d'Alene City, and arrested Fred Heslewood on a fugitive warrant. In response the IWW advised its members: "Let us go to Spokane, fill their jails and overthrow the whole tottering edifice of corruption misnamed the Spokane City Government." Five thousand volunteers were asked to demonstrate their contempt for the "slugging committee of the capitalist class."[19]

Faced with this unrelenting nonviolent resistance, city officials finally weakened. From the IWW's point of view, Spokane's authorities chose

[17] Quoted in *ibid.*, p. 112.
[18] Flynn, *I Speak My Own Piece*, p. 53.
[19] *Industrial Worker*, March 5, 1910, p. 1; February 26, 1910, p. 2.

a propitious moment for compromise, for by the end of February the Wobblies also were weakening in their resolve. St. John and other IWW officials found it harder and harder to recruit volunteers for the Spokane fight. When spring came it would be even more difficult. Acting the part of realists, not visionary revolutionaries, a three-man IWW committee, including William Z. Foster, a new member, approached Spokane's mayor to discuss peace terms. The mayor at first proved unresponsive. He approved the IWW's defense of free speech, yet stressed that street speaking would not be tolerated when it interfered with the normal flow of traffic or the business of citizens—a decision that would be made by responsible public officials. The mayor further reminded the IWW committee that only the city council and the courts could determine the constitutionality of city restrictions on street speaking. Somewhat ominously, he warned that continued IWW free-speech activities would be more stringently repressed. The Wobblies, in turn, threatened that the "IWW is going to use the streets of Spokane or go down fighting." In truth, neither side had much stomach for continued warfare. For one thing, the city could not stand the expense of several hundred individual legal trials, including the ensuing appeals; for another, the IWW had exhausted campaigners and it lacked new recruits to take up the slack. Thus, on March 3, 1910, after a series of conferences between IWW representatives and various city officials, peace came to Spokane.[20]

The IWW won its major demands. Indoor meeting places would no longer be denied to the organization, and it could also hold peaceful outdoor meetings without police interference. Spokane agreed to respect the IWW's right to publish the *Industrial Worker* and to sell it on the city's streets. Complicated terms were also devised to secure the release of those Wobblies still in prison. Significantly, the authorities assured the IWW that free speech would be allowed on city streets in the near future. Until the council enacted new speaking ordinances, it barred street corners to religious groups: the Salvation Army as well as the IWW would have to await the passage of a free-speech statute later that year.

Wobblies also won the secondary demands which had undergirded their fight for free speech. In the midst of the battle, Spokane officials had initiated reforms in the employment agency system, rescinding the licenses of the worst of the "sharks." After the battle, public officials throughout the Northwest attempted to regulate private employment agencies more closely.[21]

As viewed by the Wobblies, the Spokane free-speech fight had been an impressive triumph for the twin principles of direct action and passive resistance. The discipline maintained by the free-speech fighters and the

---

[20] *Ibid.*, March 5, 1910, p. 1; March 12, 1910, p. 1; William Z. Foster, *Pages from a Worker's Life* (New York, 1939), pp. 143–45; Foster, *From Bryan to Stalin* (New York, 1937), pp. 41–42.

[21] E. G. Flynn, "Latest News from Spokane," *International Socialist Review*, X (March 1910), 828–34; *Industrial Worker*, March 12, 1910, p. 1; March 19, 1910, p. 1.

passivity with which they endured brutalities won the respect of many parties usually critical of or hostile to the IWW. During the struggle local socialists, Spokane's AFL members, and WFM miners in the Coeur d'Alenes, as well as "respectable" townspeople, contributed money, food, or just plain sympathy to the Wobbly cause. Passive resistance also showed what migratory workers who lacked the franchise might accomplish by more direct means. *Solidarity* grasped the lesson of Spokane when it observed: "By use of its weakest weapon—passive resistance— labor forced civic authorities to recognize a power equal to the state." If labor can gain so much through its crudest weapon, it asked, "what will the result be when an industrially organized working class stands forth prepared to seize, operate, and control the machinery of production and distribution?"[22]

But free speech on the streets of Spokane did not guarantee successful labor organization among the workers of the fields, woods, and construction camps of the Inland Empire. In 1910 the IWW had only learned how to attract migratory workers during their winter layovers in town; it had not yet hit upon the secret of maintaining an everyday, effective labor organization out on the job among workers who moved freely. It had not yet discovered how to survive when employers set armed gunmen upon "labor agitators" and summarily discharged union members. Victory in Spokane did, however, inspire the soapboxers and organizer-agitators so prominent within the IWW to carry their campaigns for free speech to other Western cities where migratories gathered to rest or to seek employment.

One such city was Fresno, California, where ranchers from the lush San Joaquin Valley came to acquire labor for their vegetable and fruit farms. In Fresno, as in Spokane, lonely men recently returned from a season of fruit picking or construction work spent their hard-earned funds on whisky and women. Here Wobbly soapboxers found an audience ready for the IWW's gospel.

Fresno had become the most active IWW center in California, and no other local in the state could compare to Fresno Local 66 in size of membership or in militancy of spirit. Late in 1909 and early the following year, Local 66 had unexpected success in organizing Mexican-American railroad laborers and migratory farm hands—a development not at all to the liking of city officials, the management of the Santa Fe Railroad, or the ranchers. As Wobblies continued to hold open street meetings and to win more recruits for their organization, minor skirmishes with the police rose in number—so much so that by May 1910 the local IWW forecast a full-scale free-speech fight. Fresno, indeed, was ready for the challenge. Its police chief had revoked the IWW's permit to hold street meetings and had threatened to jail on vagrancy charges any man without a job (serving as an IWW official was not considered employment). This led Frank Little, the leading local Wobbly, to predict that when the summer

[22] *Solidarity,* March 19, 1910, p. 2.

harvest ended, Wobblies would invade Fresno to battle for free speech.[23]

That fall a struggle similar in all basic respects to the one recently terminated in Spokane erupted in Fresno. In this case no money would be wasted on lawyers and defense funds; whatever funds the Fresno local obtained would be used to keep Wobblies on the streets, the local court docket crowded, and Fresno's pocketbook empty. "All aboard for Fresno," announced the *Industrial Worker* on September 10, "Free Speech Fight On."

Fresno's town fathers responded to the IWW invasion just as their civic neighbors to the north had done. First, they closed every hall in the city to the Wobblies, who were thus compelled to re-establish headquarters in a large rented tent outside the city limits. Fresno police followed up with a series of wholesale arrests which, by mid-November, temporarily broke IWW resistance. By the end of the month, though, the Wobblies were back on the streets in increasing numbers, and the more men Fresno arrested, the more Wobblies seemed to materialize. Fresno learned the hard way that arrests did not subdue militant Wobblies. Worse yet, the city discovered that it had no statute forbidding street speaking, thus invalidating the charges upon which the bulk of the arrests had been made. With the city thus deterred from legal action, mob action resulted. On the evening of December 9 a large mob gathered outside the city jail, where it severely beat a number of Wobblies who had come to visit imprisoned fellow workers. Its martial spirit duly aroused, the mob promptly marched out to the IWW's tent camp and put it to the torch. That evening, St. John wired Fresno's mayor: "Action of 'respectable mob' will not deter this organization. . . . Free speech will be established in Fresno if it takes twenty years."[24]

Met by mob violence, the IWW counseled passive resistance, advising its fighters: ". . . Remember despite police brutality, don't retaliate in kind." So disciplined did the Wobblies remain that the *Sacramento Bee*, itself a bitter and sometimes unrestrained critic of the IWW, commented: ". . . When the good citizens and the authorities of any city countenance such outrages as those committed by the Fresno mob, the I.W.W. may be said to shine by comparison."[25]

Despite legal and extra-legal repression (Fresno on December 20 had enacted an ordinance banning street speaking), Wobblies continued to arrive in town in increasing numbers. Moving in and out of Fresno, and also in and out of jail, they encountered repression and brutality. What kept them coming and going was the same spirit and determination that motivated their leader in Fresno—Frank H. Little.

[23] W. F. Little to *Industrial Worker*, May 21, 1910, p. 4; F. H. Little to Editor, May 27, 1910, *ibid.*, June 4, 1910, p. 1; F. Little to Editor, May 29, 1910, *ibid.*, June 11, 1910, p. 2; Daniel O'Regan to Charles McCarthy, November 10, 1914, CIR Papers.
[24] *Industrial Worker*, September 3, 1910, p. 1; October 1, 1910, p. 1; October 8, 1910, pp. 1, 4; October 5, 1910, p. 4; November 9, 1910, p. 3; November 17, 1910, pp. 1, 3; November 30, 1910, p. 4; December 6, 1910, p. 4; V. St. John to Mayor of Fresno, December 9, 1910, in *ibid.*, December 15, 1910, p. 1; cf. O'Regan to McCarthy, November 10, 1914, CIR Papers.
[25] Quoted in *Industrial Worker*, December 22, 1910, p. 1.

If Elizabeth Gurley Flynn was the "Rebel Girl," Frank Little was the "hobo agitator." More than any other individual he personified the IWW's rebelliousness and its strange compound of violent rhetoric, pride in physical courage (the *machismo* element), and its seemingly contradictory resort to nonviolent resistance. Part American Indian, part hard-rock miner, part hobo, he was all Wobbly. A tall, spare, muscular man with a weatherbeaten yet ruggedly handsome face, Little looked the complete proletarian rebel. As James P. Cannon, an old friend who fought with Little in Peoria and Duluth, remembered him: "He was always for the revolt, for the struggle, for the fight. Wherever he went he 'stirred up trouble' and organized the workers to rebel. . . . He was a blood brother to all insurgents . . . the world over."[26]

This one-eyed rebel[27] never occupied a comfortable union office or kept books like his close associates, St. John and Haywood; instead, he always went where the action was. From 1900 to 1905 he fought in the major WFM industrial conflicts, joining with that union's militants and following them into the IWW, where he remained when the WFM withdrew. In 1909 he was in Spokane, the following year in Fresno. In later years Little would turn up in San Diego, Duluth, Butte—anywhere Wobblies fought for a better world. Whenever miners, harvesters, or construction workers needed a leader, Little was available. When fear immobilized workers, he set an example for others to follow. His utter fearlessness brought him to Butte in 1917 to aid rebellious copper miners. By this time he was an ailing rheumatic, bearing the vestiges of too many beatings and too many jailings, and hobbling about on crutches as the result of a recently broken leg. Yet Little remained the active agitator—an agitator apparently so terrifying to the "respectable" that on August 1, 1917, Montana vigilantes lynched him and left his body dangling from a railroad trestle on Butte's outskirts.

In 1910–1911 he was still a reasonably healthy man. He demonstrated in Fresno how a man unafraid, a man whose life had already taken him, and would later take him again, from one violent incident to another, could also lead a struggle based entirely on the moral suasion of passive resistance. Little proved in Fresno, as the IWW proved in so many other places, that even the potentially violent, given a good cause and a compelling ideology, could set an example of peaceful direct action.

Frank Little instilled his own rebelliousness in those who fought for free speech with him in Fresno. Only dedication and courage approximating Little's can account for teen-age Herbert Minderman's ability to

[26] James P. Cannon, *Notebook of an Agitator* (New York, 1958), pp. 32–36.
[27] W. D. Haywood and Charles Lambert, who served with Little on the IWW's last pre-war general executive board, were also prominent one-eyed Wobblies.

withstand the tortures endured by Wobbly prisoners in Fresno's jail. Minderman kept a daily diary which described in some detail the course of the Fresno struggle and the punishments inflicted upon IWW prisoners.[28] As Minderman described it, imprisonment had no appreciable effect on the Wobbly spirit. In jail Wobblies sang rebel songs, held propaganda meetings, and transacted the somewhat irregular business of Local 66. They talked so cantankerously and sang so loudly that their jailers took unusual steps to silence the noisy ones. A guard gagged one Wobbly with his own sock, causing a government investigator to comment: "The severity of this punishment can be understood only by one who is familiar with the rank and file of I.W.W.'s and knows how rarely they bathe."[29] Wobblies responded to repression within the jail by mounting what they labeled a "battleship," which meant continuous yelling, jeering, and pounding on cell bars and floors until the guards felt compelled to use more forceful measures.

The sheriff thus denied his prisoners adequate sleeping gear, tobacco, reading materials, and decent food. When this failed to still the tumult, he resorted to physical force. Firemen appeared at the city jail with a 150-pound pressure hose, which was turned upon the cell holding the Wobblies. Prisoners tried to protect themselves by erecting a barricade of mattresses. But the pressure of the water swept the mattresses away and drove the Wobblies against the cell wall. Some Wobblies sought refuge by lying flat on the floor, but the hose was aimed down upon them, the stream of water then thrusting them up into the air like toothpicks. Even the most rebellious soon had enough of this treatment. Yet the firemen maintained the water pressure for fully a half-hour, and before they left almost every prisoner found his clothes in shreds and his body black and blue. The Wobblies spent the remainder of that chill December night up to their knees in water.

Some Wobblies broke under these tactics, promising to leave town if released. But most refused to compromise. They served out their time and then returned to Fresno's streets to soapbox.

The IWW's refusal to terminate its struggle had the same effect in Fresno as it had had earlier in Spokane. Each prisoner demanded a jury trial, managed his own defense, and challenged as many prospective jurors as possible. Wobblies used every delaying tactic their limited legal knowledge made available. On a good day Fresno's courts might try two or three men; however many Wobblies they sentenced, it seemed more were always on the docket. To make matters worse, still more Wobblies were always on the road to Fresno. Although the IWW found it harder to attract volunteers than it had been in Spokane, nevertheless many Wobblies shared the militancy of Little and young Herbert Minderman and set off to join their fellow workers

---

[28] The following account comes largely from Minderman's diary of the Fresno fight and O'Regan's verification of it in O'Regan to McCarthy, November 10, 1914, CIR Papers.

[29] O'Regan to McCarthy, CIR Papers.

in Fresno.[30] This eventually became too great a burden for the city's taxpayers, its judges, and its businessmen.

Fresno's officials finally weakened in their resolve to repress their antagonists. Again, IWW leaders proved realistic and able negotiators. Well aware that local authorities hated to compromise while under pressure, the Wobblies allowed secret and informal talks to proceed. These conferences began on February 25 when a local citizens' committee visited the Fresno jail in order to ascertain the IWW's truce terms. In less than two weeks the citizens' committee and city officials consented to the release of all IWW prisoners and to a guarantee of the organization's right to speak on Fresno's streets. Finally, on March 6 Local 66 wired IWW headquarters: "The Free Speech Fight is over, and won. . . . Complete victory."[31]

What the IWW won in Fresno was not precisely clear. No public settlement terms were announced, either by the local IWW or by Fresno's citizens' committee. Moreover, for the next several years Local 66 and Fresno disappeared from mention in the IWW press; Frank Little left the area to fight IWW wars elsewhere, and the San Joaquin Valley's fruit pickers remained unorganized, overworked, and underpaid. In brief, an inglorious and inconclusive climax. In Fresno as in Spokane, the IWW had learned how to contact the migratories in town but not how to organize them on the job. Local 66 had succeeded in making its headquarters a community center for the West's dispossessed, yet it failed to carry the organization into the surrounding countryside where it was most needed.

As propaganda, however, the IWW may have gained something from the Fresno struggle. In a conflict which lasted over six months but cost less than $1,000, the IWW received enormous national publicity. Although the Fresno conflict did not attract quite the nationwide attention that Elizabeth Gurley Flynn had focused on Spokane, it did reinforce the image of the IWW as an organization that used passive resistance to defend clear constitutional rights. It demonstrated once again that the most exploited and dependent groups in American society could act for themselves—and act peaceably at that—as well as that they also had the power—nonpolitical power, of course—to alter the prevailing arrangements of the local community. Yet the Fresno fight left behind no effective labor organization to capitalize upon the IWW's apparent "victory," and no immediate membership growth followed this new triumph for free speech.[32]

[30] Albert Tucker to Vincent St. John, September 21, 1914, CIR Papers; cf. Thomas Whitehead to Editor, *Solidarity*, March 4, 1911, p. 1; and E. M. Clyde to Editor, *ibid.*, April 8, 1911, p. 4; *Industrial Worker*, February 23, 1911, p. 1; March 2, 1911, p. 1.

[31] *Industrial Worker*, March 9, 1911, p. 1; *International Socialist Review*, XI (April 1911), 634–36.

[32] Hyman Weintraub, "The IWW in California," unpublished master's thesis, University of California, Los Angeles (1947), pp. 23–32.

The Spokane and Fresno victories led Wobblies to contend for free speech elsewhere, though with uneven success. Almost always these fights were associated with efforts to organize lumber workers and migratory harvesters. In one tragic case the IWW's campaign for free speech was entirely unrelated to the objectives of labor organization. In San Diego in 1912 the IWW learned the limits of passive resistance, as well as the folly of concentrating its limited power on tangential causes.

In 1912 San Diego was a comfortable city of fifty thousand, mostly well-to-do devotees of the area's ideal climate. It had a small and contented working class and no important or large industries threatened by labor difficulties. No migratories drifted into town *en masse* to spend the winter, and no ground seemed less fertile for IWW efforts. As IWW martyr-bard Joe Hill noted: "A town like San Diego for instance where the main 'industry' consists of 'catching suckers' [tourists] is not worth a whoop in Hell from a rebel's point of view."[33] Indeed, never did the number of Wobblies in San Diego exceed a few hundred. Yet those few, as a contemporary journalist commented, "goaded the authorities and the populace into a hysterical frenzy, into an epidemic of unreasoning fear and brutal rage, into a condition of lawlessness so pronounced that travelers fear to visit the city."[34]

For years E Street between Fifth and Sixth Avenues in the heart of downtown San Diego had served as a sort of Hyde Park Speakers' Corner. Every evening socialists and anarchists, savers and atheists, suffragists and Wobblies, harangued the faithful from their accustomed spots on the corner. But in December 1911 San Diego's city council, acting upon a grand-jury recommendation, closed the downtown area, the so-called "congested district," to street meetings. In response, Wobblies, socialists, single-taxers, and even the local AFL men created a broad coalition called the Free Speech League. From the day the anti-street-speaking ordinance took effect, February 8, 1912, police and League members clashed over the right of free speech. By February 12, ninety men and women had been arrested, and by February 15, 150 prisoners languished in city and county jails. Day and night for the next several weeks, the League held free-speech meetings and the police arrested speakers, until the county as well as the city jails were crowded beyond normal capacity.[35]

Before long, what began as a common struggle by a broad coalition of anti-establishment organizations became a largely IWW-led struggle. Although the non-Wobbly groups continued to participate in the San Diego struggle, the public, locally and nationally, associated the conflict with the IWW. The battle did, in fact, feature the tactics the IWW had

---

[33] Joe Hill to E. W. Vanderleith, n.d., Frank Walsh Papers, Box 7, New York Public Library, Manuscript Division.

[34] Walter V. Woehlke, "I.W.W.," *Outlook*, CI (July 6, 1912), 512.

[35] Mary A. Hill, "The Free Speech Fight at San Diego," *Survey*, XXVIII (May 4, 1912), 192–94.

tested successfully in Spokane and Fresno. Again Wobblies threatened to fill the jails and crowd the court dockets until a financially drained city surrendered. Again the Wobblies looked to passive resistance to accomplish their aims. One IWW bard, an early, perhaps premature version of Dr. Seuss, advised: "Come on the cushions; Ride up on top; Stick to the brakebeams; Let nothing stop. Come in great numbers; This we beseech; Help San Diego to win *Free Speech!*"[36]

Although San Diego had less to fear from the Wobblies than either Spokane or Fresno, it nevertheless acted more savagely to repress free speech. No brutality proved beyond the imagination of San Diego's "good" citizens. What the police could not accomplish by stretching the local law's elastic fabric, private citizens, acting as vigilantes, did. Even discounting the predictable exaggeration of the reports in the *Industrial Worker* and *Solidarity*, repression proved the rule in San Diego. The city's citizens learned from the mistakes previously revealed in Spokane and Fresno. San Diego would not be invaded by armies of Wobblies, nor bankrupted by scores of prisoners who resided in jail as beneficiaries of the public purse and who demanded costly individual trials. San Diego devised just the remedy for these IWW tactics. Several nights a week vigilantes visited the jails, seized a group of free-speech prisoners, and escorted them beyond the county line. To any Wobbly who dared to return, and to those who attempted to join the fight, the vigilantes promised worse treatment.[37]

San Diego's brand of viligante justice has been described best by some of the Wobblies who experienced it. On the night of either April 4 or 5,[38] 1912, Albert Tucker and 140 other men, half of whom were under twenty-one years of age, hopped a freight train out of Los Angeles bound for San Diego. About one o'clock that morning the train slowed down and Tucker noticed on either side of the freight cars about four hundred men armed with rifles, pistols, and clubs of every variety. Tucker has vividly portrayed what ensued.[39]

> The moon was shining dimly through the clouds and I could see pick handles, ax handles, wagon spokes and every kind of club imaginable swinging from the wrists of all of them while they also had their rifles leveled at us . . . the only sign of civilization was a cattle corral. . . . We were ordered to unload and we refused. Then they closed in around the flat car which we were on and began clubbing and knocking and pulling men off by their heels, so

[36] *Industrial Worker*, February 22, 1912, p. 4; February 29, 1912, p. 4; March 7, 1912, p. 4.

[37] Hill, "Free Speech Fight," pp. 193–94; Woelke, "I.W.W.," p. 531; among other non-IWW sources.

[38] Tucker was not certain of the precise date when he wrote his account of these events two years later.

[39] A. Tucker to Vincent St. John, September 21, 1914, CIR Papers.

inside of a half hour they had us all off the train and then bruised and bleeding we were lined up and marched into the cattle corral, where they made us hold our hands up and march around in the crowd for more than an hour. . . . They marched us several times, now and then picking out a man they thought was a leader and giving him an extra beating. Several men were carried out unconscious . . . afterwards there was a lot of our men unaccounted for and never have been heard from since. The vigilantes all wore constable badges and a white handkerchief around their left arms. They were drunk and hollering and cursing the rest of the night. In the morning they took us out four or five at a time and marched us up the track to the county line . . . where we were forced to kiss the flag and then run a gauntlet of 106 men, every one of which was striking at us as hard as they could with their pick ax handles. They broke one man's leg, and everyone was beaten black and blue, and was bleeding from a dozen wounds.

The man with the broken leg, Chris Hansen, himself a veteran of other IWW free-speech fights, also described what happened that night: "As I was lying there I saw other fellows running the gauntlet. Some were bleeding freely from cracked heads, others were knocked down to be made to get up and run again. Some tried to break the line only to be beaten back. It was the most cowardly and inhuman cracking of heads I ever witnessed. . . ."[40] "Thus did San Diego," in the words of anti-IWW journalist Walter Woehlke, "having given its money to mark the historic highway [El Camino Real] with the symbols of love and charity, teach patriotism and reverence for the law to the travelers thereon."[41]

That all of this vigilante violence had occurred with the connivance of local public officials soon became known to the entire nation. Governor Hiram Johnson, Progressive politician extraordinary, under pressure from the AFL, the Socialist party, the IWW, and many influential Californians, some of whom had played a prominent role in his election, dispatched special investigator Harris Weinstock to San Diego. Weinstock's investigation corroborated all the Free Speech League's charges of police and vigilante brutality. A thoroughly outraged Weinstock compared San Diego's behavior to the worst excesses of the tsarist Russian regime.[42]

This public condemnation notwithstanding, San Diego vigilantes continued their previous activities. Early in May 1912 police fatally wounded an IWW member. On May 15 anarchist Emma Goldman and her manager-lover, Ben Reitman, arrived in town to lend their voices to the struggle. When they debarked at the railroad station they found a howling mob, including many women, screaming: "Give us that anarchist; we will strip her naked; we will tear out her guts." That evening vigilantes abducted Reitman from his hotel room. Placing him in the back seat of a

[40] Chris Hansen to Vincent St. John, n.d., CIR Papers.
[41] Woehlke, "I.W.W.," p. 531.
[42] Harris Weinstock, *Report to the Governor of California on the Disturbance in the City and County of San Diego in 1912* (Sacramento, 1912).

speeding auto, they tortured him as they sped out of town. About twenty miles beyond San Diego's limits the vigilantes stopped the car, got out, and proceeded to a second round of torture. As later described by Reitman, this is what happened: "With tar taken from a can [they] traced I.W.W. on my back and a doctor burned the letters in with a lighted cigar. . . ." Afterward, Reitman ran the gauntlet, and then he kissed the American flag and sang the "Star Spangled Banner." Beaten, bruised, and degraded, he dragged himself away clad only in his underwear, "because the Christian gentlemen thought that I might meet some ladies and shock them."[43]

Despite their militancy and the sympathy they received as a result of the kind of treatment described above, Wobblies lacked the power to alter conditions in San Diego. The state had the power, but it used it to condemn, not to reform. The federal government also had the power, but in 1912, unlike a half-century later, its power was not at the disposal of peaceful protesters being abused by local or state authorities.

In 1912 it was San Diego's public officials, not the beaten and intimidated Wobblies, who turned to the federal Justice Department for support. Early in May city police superintendent John Sehon asked Attorney General George Wickersham for federal assistance in local efforts to repress the subversive, un-American IWW. Well before that date Sehon had been cooperating with the federal attorney for southern California (John McCormick) and with private detectives appointed by a citizens' committee controlled by sugar king John Spreckels and anti-union Los Angeles newspaper magnate Harrison Grey Otis. Sehon, the federal attorney, and the private detectives searched for evidence linking the IWW to an alleged plot to overthrow the constituted authorities in San Diego and Washington, D.C., and also to join the Mexican Revolution, the aim here being to capture Lower California for the IWW. Where these diligent investigators could not find evidence, they manufactured it. On May 4 Sehon informed the Justice Department that Wobblies were congregating across the nation—275 in Los Angeles, 140 outside San Diego, 1,060 at various points in the state, and other bands in Chicago, Kansas City, and Oklahoma City—preparing "to overthrow the Government and take possession of all things. . . ." Armed with guns and dynamite and led personally by St. John and Haywood, the Wobblies, according to Sehon and United States Attorney McCormick, had organized "a criminally treasonous" conspiracy which had to be nipped in the bud by federal authorities.[44]

---

[43] Emma Goldman, *Living My Life* (New York, 1934), pp. 495–501; Richard Drinnon, *Rebel in Paradise: A Biography of Emma Goldman* (Chicago, 1961), pp. 135–36.

[44] John L. Sehon to George Wickersham, May 2, 1912, File 150139–7; F. C. Spaulding to Wickersham, May 3, 1912, File 150139–8; code message, John McCormick to Wickersham, May 4, 1912, File 150139–6, and May 6, 1912, File 150139–13, all in D/J 60.

Fortunately, Attorney General Wickersham remained calm and collected. Despite strong pressure from one of California's senators and from San Diego's congressman, Wickersham realized that the IWW posed no threat to American stability or security. What little disorder had occurred in San Diego, local authorities could manage, and the Attorney General certainly knew that San Diego had not been hesitant in its use of repression. But as a Republican politician with a presidential election upcoming, Wickersham mollified southern California Republicans by allowing McCormick to continue his federal investigation for evidence of IWW subversion.[45]

Throughout the summer of 1912, San Diego officials tried unsuccessfully to involve the Justice Department in the local conflict. McCormick even impaneled a Los Angeles grand jury to take evidence in an attempt to indict Wobblies for criminal conspiracy. In the opinion of a Justice Department official in Washington, McCormick's grand jury proved no more than that Wobblies "are apparently self-confessed liars and lawbreakers, but there is nothing indicating a specific attack upon the Government of the United States." After having allowed McCormick and his Republican supporters to have their fun, Wickersham ordered federal proceedings against the IWW dropped.[46]

At this juncture southern California's "reactionary" Republicans went over the Attorney General's head, carrying their case for federal repression of the IWW directly to President William Howard Taft. F. W. Estabrook, a prominent member of the Republican National Committee and an industrialist whose own factory had earlier been struck by the IWW, compared the California labor situation to that in Chicago in 1894 when Cleveland dispatched troops to crush the Pullman strike. He suggested to the President "that this matter [the San Diego conflict] is of the greatest importance, not only in a political way . . . but . . . it is time that vigorous action, whenever opportunity occurs, should be taken to stamp out the revolutionary methods of this anarchistic organization." More to the point, Estabrook assured Charles Hilles, Taft's secretary, that vigorous anti-IWW action would guarantee California's votes for Taft in the November election; furthermore, he added, such action would weaken the cause of the Hiram Johnson Progressive Republicans, who supported Theodore Roosevelt and the Progressive party in the 1912 election.[47]

[45] Senator John D. Works to Wickersham, May 4, 1912, and Wickersham's reply of May 6, 1912, File 150139–10; Congressman J. C. Needham to Wickersham, May 4, 1912, and Wickersham's reply, May 6, 1912, File 150139–12; Mayor James W. Wedham to Wickersham, May 5, 1912, and Wickersham's reply, May 6, 1912, File 150139–11; Wickersham to McCormick, May 6, 1912, File 150139–13; Wickersham to Senator Works, May 9, 1912, File 150139–14, all in D/J 60.

[46] McCormick to Wickersham, June 28, 1912; William R. Haar to Wickersham, July 5, 1912, and Wickersham's reply, July 6, 1912, File 150139–20; Wickersham to Senator Works, August 27, 1912, File 150139–26, all in D/J 60.

[47] F. W. Estabrook to Charles D. Hilles, September 5, 1912 (with enclosure: Charles H. DeLacour to Estabrook, September 5, 1912), File 150139–28, D/J 60.

Taft was receptive to Estabrook's suggestions. Political intrigue and his desire to be re-elected apparently clouded his usually clear mind, for Taft wrote as follows to Wickersham on September 7:

> There is not any doubt that that corner of the country is a basis for most of the anarchists and the industrial world workers [*sic*], and for all the lawless flotsam and jetsam that proximity to the Mexican border thrusts into those two cities. . . . We ought to take decided action. The State of California is under an utterly unscrupulous boss [Hiram Johnson], who does not hesitate . . . to [have to] do with these people and cultivate their good will, and it is our business to go in and show the strong hand of the United States in a marked way so that they shall understand that we are on the job.[48]

In other words, Taft expected repression of the IWW to win California's electoral votes.

Lacking presidential ambitions himself, Wickersham remained calm. Acceding to Taft's desire to investigate IWW subversion, the Attorney General nevertheless discounted the overblown reports and rumors emanating from southern California. Indeed, he maintained at the very end of the San Diego affair just as he had at the beginning: "I know of no reason why the [Justice] Department should take any further action."[49]

Although the federal government refused to intervene in San Diego, and Taft won neither California's votes nor re-election, the IWW continued to suffer at the hands of police and also private citizens. No agency of government was prepared in 1912 to defend the civil liberties of citizens who flaunted the traditions and rules of America's dominant classes.

Still, the IWW and its free-speech allies fought on. Pleading for funds and volunteers, they obtained money but precious few men. Even with a diminishing supply of manpower and close to defeat, the Wobblies remained defiant. Upon being sentenced to prison, one Wobbly, Jack White, proclaimed: "To hell with your courts; I know what justice is."[50]

Courtroom defiance was no substitute for victory. By October 1912, nine months after the inauguration of the free-speech fight, downtown San Diego remained vacant and lonely at night. "The sacred spot where so many I.W.W.'s were clubbed and arrested last winter," wrote Laura Payne Emerson, "lies safe and secure from the unhallowed tread of the hated anarchist, and in fact, from all other human beings." And she la-

[48] Taft to Wickersham, September 7, 1912, File 150139–29, D/J 60.
[49] Wickersham to Taft, September 16, 1912, and to C. D. Hilles, September 16, 1912, File 150139–31; Charles DeLacour to Wickersham, November 22, 1912, with marginal note by W.R.H. (William R. Haar?), File 150139–35, all in D/J 60.
[50] *Solidarity*, August 24, 1912, p. 3.

mented: "They have the courts, the jails and funds. What are we going to do about it?"[51]

Some Wobblies still counseled passive resistance, "the trump card that we hold and the vigilantes cannot use." Other Wobblies had their doubts. A crippled Chris Hansen vowed from his hospital bed: "My lesson is passive resistance no more." Albert Tucker, another survivor of the vigilantes' gauntlet, declaimed: "If I ever take part in another [free-speech fight] it will be with machine guns and aerial bombs." There must be, Tucker reasoned, "a better way of fighting and better results. . . ."[52] Similar frustration with nonviolent tactics appeared in a warning the *Industrial Worker* delivered to San Diego's public officials on April 4, 1912. "Take warning! Sehon, Wilson, Utley, Keno—take heed members of the 'vigilance committee'—Your names will be spread, broadcast! Reparation will be exacted! He laughs best who laughs last!"

Yet IWW threats and violence always remained rhetorical; the beatings suffered by nonviolent Wobblies, on the other hand, were very real. They hardly seemed worth it when the object to be gained, free speech, of and by itself brought no improvement in working conditions and added few members to the IWW. It seemed worth even less when, as Joe Hill remarked, San Diego was "not worth a whoop in Hell from a rebel's point of view."

If the battles in Spokane and Fresno demonstrated the effectiveness of nonviolence, San Diego starkly revealed the weakness of passive resistance as a tactic when the opposition refused to respect common decency and when no higher authority would intervene on behalf of the oppressed. Well before their defeat in San Diego, however, many Wobblies had had second thoughts about their organization's involvement in free-speech fights. At the time of the Spokane conflict, W. I. Fisher wrote to the *Industrial Worker:* "If we are to have a strong union we have to go to the job where the workers are and begin our agitation. . . . It is only where we control or are seeking control of the job that we can build up a lasting economic power." In 1911, during the Fresno struggle, Pacific Coast IWW representatives meeting in Portland voiced their opposition to unnecessary free-speech campaigns when more effective work remained to be accomplished in organizing and educating "wage slaves" on the job.[53]

But the IWW could not avert further free-speech fights. In the Far West and in other regions where migratory workers congregated, street speaking continued to be the most effective means for spreading the IWW gospel and for winning new recruits to the organization. After all, the migratories attracted to the IWW as a result of the 1909–1912 free-speech fights would become the dedicated Wobblies who later spearheaded the IWW's successful penetration of the woods and the wheat fields during the World War I years. Other motives also kept Wobblies on their soap-

---

[51] Quoted in *Industrial Worker*, October 17, 1912, p. 4.

[52] *Ibid.*, August 18, 1912, p. 2; Tucker to St. John, September 21, 1914, and Hansen to St. John, n.d., CIR Papers.

[53] *Industrial Worker*, January 15, 1910; A. Tucker to Vincent St. John, September 21, 1914, CIR Papers.

boxes. They were, to be sure, as much agitators as organizers, as much propagandists as labor leaders, and they needed their street corners and soapboxes in order to denounce capitalist society and "bushwa" morality. Wobblies also felt compelled to compete with the Salvation Army's street-corner preachers, who counseled the oppressed to be humble and content while awaiting their reward in heaven. In response to this advice, the IWW gospelers preached "a little less hell on earth" for exploited workers.

Racial Violence in Chicago
and in the Nation

WILLIAM M. TUTTLE, JR.

The racial division of American society has produced untold misery in this country and has given rise to a pattern of urban racial violence that seems virtually endemic to the United States. Episodes of racially motivated violence have marked American history almost from its beginnings, ranging from lynchings by whites in the South to more recent black ghetto uprisings in the North. There is evidence that genuine "race riots"—a distinct form of racial violence in which members of two races enter into active conflict—took place in New York City as early as 1712.

During the period between the beginning of the First World War and the end of the Second World War, riots were the characteristic form of racial violence, reaching a peak in the year 1919. Indeed, James Weldon Johnson, the executive director of the National Association for the Advancement of Colored People (NAACP), called the summer of 1919 the "Red Summer" because of the blood that flowed in the streets. At least twenty-two race riots broke out that summer in American cities of both the North and the South.

Several factors helped to build up the racial hostilities that exploded in 1919. First, the war had spurred a large migration of blacks from rural areas of the South to Northern cities, where many new jobs in commerce and industry were open to them for the first time. In addition to opening up new industries, the wartime mobilization cut off the normal flow of immigrant labor to the North, requiring the active recruitment of black workers. Furthermore, many native whites who might have filled the new positions were drawn into military service, thus permitting blacks to get a foothold in the war industries. When the war ended, demobilization produced a wave of unemployment, and blacks were often the first to be fired. Competition for jobs became acute and led to bitter feeling. Racial tension was increased as returning whites sought to restore the racial patterns that had been altered by the war.

In the vanguard of increasingly militant Northern blacks were those who had served in the armed forces during the war. Although the armed forces were segregated, and although there had been many racial incidents both at home and abroad during the war, black soldiers felt they had earned a share of the benefits of American society, and they were not inclined to be pushed around without fighting back. Upon their return to this country, several black soldiers, some still in uniform, were lynched by angry mobs. Such atrocities added to the determination of blacks to struggle against their attackers and to hold on to the meager gains they had made during the war.

On May 10, 1919, a riot in Charleston, South Carolina, marked the beginning of the Red Summer, which lasted until the end of September. The major riots of the summer took place in Washington, D.C.; Chicago, Illinois; Longview, Texas; Knoxville, Tennessee; and Omaha, Nebraska. The Chicago riot was the most costly in terms of life, leaving twenty-three blacks and fifteen whites dead and many others wounded. But the Washington riot was particularly startling, because it took place in the nation's capitol and because it began, not in some remote sector of the city, but on Pennsylvania Avenue, midway between the Capitol and the White House.

William M. Tuttle, of the University of Kansas, has studied the background and events of the Chicago riot. In the conclusion of his book, reprinted below, he compares the Chicago situation and several other riots of 1919 with the ghetto uprisings of the 1960s. While he finds significant differences between the two periods, some of them the result of the somewhat improved situation of blacks in the later period, he sees no reason to assume that racial violence will soon fade from the American scene.

Thirty-eight dead, 537 wounded, hundreds homeless—this was the toll, and an awesome one it was. Walter Lippmann, writing in 1919, deplored the Chicago race riot as "an event infinitely more disgraceful than that . . . Red Terror about which we are all so virtuously indignant. . . ."[1] Black and white Chicagoans also deplored the city's racial bloodshed. Some white people expressed astonishment at the news of the violence. Why Chicago? the incredulous asked. Chicago was a dynamic city, they

[1] In the preface to Carl Sandburg, *The Chicago Race Riots* (N.Y.: Harcourt, Brace & Howe, 1919), iii.

"Racial Violence in Chicago and in the Nation." From *Race Riot: Chicago in the Red Summer of 1919* by William M. Tuttle, Jr. New York: Atheneum, 1960, pp. 242–68. Copyright © 1970 by William M. Tuttle, Jr. Reprinted by permission of Atheneum Publishers.

said, a little rough perhaps, but at least its diverse ethnic, religious, and racial groups had been able to coexist for years without resorting to such rioting. Amazement and disbelief did not strike the black community, just sadness and a reaffirmation of self-defense. The riot, a black man recalled many years later, brought Chicago's black people "closer together than they had ever been before," and it accelerated the trend toward arming for future danger.[2]

The riot in Chicago should have surprised few people, black or white, for it was well within the context of two modern historical phenomena: twentieth-century urban racial violence in America, and the frenzy of the year 1919. Added to these, of course, were the many peculiarities of Chicago's troubled history of race relations. In fact, the surprising thing to a historian studying the riot is not that it happened, but that it did not happen time and time again, especially in the tense and potentially explosive months after July 1919. For if the historian, working as a social scientist, were to have fed the facts of Chicago's post-riot racial unrest into a computer, that machine, having digested the pre-riot history of Chicago's race relations, would in all likelihood have predicted renewed eruptions of racial bloodshed.[3]

Not surprisingly, the Chicago race riot of 1919 marked no surcease to that period of transition between war and peace; it was just the midpoint in a year of unrest and violence that had several months yet to run.[4] Not only was the nation still in the throes of the Red Scare, but in the succeeding months it became even more haunted by the specter of radicalism, Bolshevism, and revolution. Worse yet in terms of deaths, racial warfare continued to erupt in America.

After Chicago, the next major riot of the Red Summer erupted in Omaha, Nebraska. A meat-packing center like Chicago, Omaha had also attracted thousands of Southern black men and women to its stockyards during the war, and by 1919 its black population had doubled to well over 10,000.[5] As in Chicago, too, racial tensions in Omaha had mounted with its rising black population. And when the fires of racial hatred had flared out of control in Chicago in July and August, their ugly glare had

---

[2] Interview with Chester A. Wilkins, Chicago, June 25, 1969.

[3] Regarding the following pages of this chapter, if the historical data in this study fit into any sociological construct, it would most closely resemble the framework of Neil J. Smelser's *Theory of Collective Behavior* (N.Y.: Free Press, 1962). Also helpful to the historian are H. O. Dahlke, "Race and Minority Riots—A Study in the Typology of Violence," *Social Forces*, XXX (May 1952), 419–25; and to a lesser degree, Stanley Lieberson and Arnold R. Silverman, "The Precipitants and Underlying Conditions of Race Riots," *American Sociological Review*, XXX (December 1965), 887–98.

[4] See Dahlke, "Race and Minority Riots," 423–25; Smelser, *Theory of Collective Behavior*, 12–21.

[5] Omaha's black population was slightly in excess of 5 percent of the total population. Along with Omaha, the other "jailhouse" riot in 1919 was in Knoxville, Tennessee, in late August and early September; see Arthur I. Waskow, *From Race Riot to Sit-In* (Garden City, N.Y.: Doubleday & Co., 1966), 105–10.

made Omaha's black people uncomfortable and fearful for their lives. Black workers in South Omaha's packing plants had congregated in small groups on July 29 to discuss arming themselves; and before the chief of police could issue an order the next day banning the sale of firearms, black people had purchased scores of weapons and ammunition. Also at the time of the Chicago bloodshed, Mayor Edward P. Smith, realizing the precarious state of race relations in his city, had ordered a local movie house to cease showing *The Birth of a Nation* or to remain closed until aroused racial feelings had subsided. Unlike Chicago, however, white Omaha believed it was suffering from an epidemic of black criminality and especially of sex crimes. And when on September 28 police arrested William Brown, a black man accused of molesting a young white girl, a mob of whites began to assemble at the courthouse, angrily demanding that the authorities release the alleged rapist to them for the execution of quick justice. When Mayor Smith mounted the courthouse steps in an effort to persuade the whites to disperse peacefully, he was taunted and heckled as a "nigger lover"; for to these people, the mayor, whose law firm was then in the employ of the NAACP to defend two black men accused of assaulting white women, represented the enemy. His appeal for calm unheeded and abused, Smith was then seized by the mob, which placed a rope around his neck, and had nearly succeeded in hanging him from a trolley pole when police cut the rope and rescued him. Still undeterred, and indeed even angrier, the mob lit a fire in the courthouse. Beginning on the first floor, the flames quickly lept up to the higher floors, but when the fire department arrived to extinguish the fire, the men in the mob cut the hoses. Still the flames rose, and, fleeing from them, the prisoners climbed to the roof, and there, to escape death themselves, several of them tried to throw Brown down to the mob. Finally, several men pushed past policemen and entered the building to capture Brown. Once the mob had him, Brown was shot, hanged from a lamppost, and his body burned, riddled with hundreds of bullets, and mutilated beyond recognition. Dreading another Chicago race riot, the state of Nebraska wired for federal assistance, and the War Department responded by dispatching troops from various forts in the region. Yet it was not just the Nebraska authorities who were apprehensive. In Springfield, Illinois, Mrs. Frank O. Lowden recorded in her diary that the governor had read the "sensational [newspaper] accounts of a mob in Omaha yesterday and of mob violence done. . . . Such actions," she noted, "stir up more trouble or are liable to elsewhere and Frank feels uneasy and so has decided to go to Chicago this evening." No race riot erupted in Chicago; and in Omaha, assisted by a downpour so torrential that the city's streetcars had to stop operations for a half hour, the soldiers were able to restore order. But by then four people were dead and fifty injured.[6]

6 *Chicago Defender*, July 12, 1919; *Chicago Daily Journal*, July 30, August 1, 1919; *Chicago Herald-Examiner*, August 3, 5, 1919; diary of Mrs. Frank O. Lowden, September 29, 1919, in possession of Mrs. C. Phillip Miller, Chicago; Waskow,

On October 1, while federal troops were patrolling the streets of Omaha, news came from east central Arkansas of an armed insurrection of blacks against whites. In Phillips County, Arkansas, as in many cotton producing regions of the South, black farmers were not landowners but tenants or sharecroppers, working for a percentage of the cotton crops they cultivated. Much injustice plagued these black farmers. They could purchase provisions only at the "plantation" or other specified stores; and being continually in debt, they purchased goods on credit and in anticipation of a percentage of the sale price of their crops. They not only paid more than the average retail prices, but they were unable to obtain from the stores itemized statements of their indebtedness. Nor was this all. When the landowner sold the cotton, he customarily would not show the bill of sale to his tenants and sharecroppers, so they, of course, could not know the dollar value of the portion to which they were entitled. But an incident in mid-June 1919 warned the local black citizens of the futility and danger of protesting against such a system. A black farmer in Star City, Arkansas, who objected by refusing to work, was lynched and "a sign reading 'this is how we treat lazy niggers' was tacked to his head."[7]

Yet black farmers in Phillips County, singing "Organize, oh organize!" established a union, the Progressive Farmers and Household Union of America, through which they intended to protest to the landowners. Sixty-eight sharecroppers at a plantation near Ratio commissioned a white law firm in Little Rock to plead a test case. If the landowner would not produce an itemized statement of account, they would prosecute; failing that, they would refuse to pick cotton then in the field or to sell cotton belonging to them for less than the market price. Realizing the potential impact of this demand for their rights, black farmers in the county armed themselves. Then, on October 1, a special agent of the Missouri Pacific Railroad was shot to death outside a black church in Hoop Spur, and a deputy sheriff with him was wounded. There were two versions of the shootings, one stating that the white detective fired "promiscuously" into the church, where a chapter of the Progressive Union was in session, and that the blacks returned the gunfire. The Little Rock _Arkansas Gazette_ reported the other version, which was that the white men had parked near the church at Hoop Spur "to repair a puncture, and while working on the car the party was fired upon by unidentified persons," presumably black.[8]

From _Race Riot to Sit-In_, 110–20; numerous newspaper clippings and much correspondence regarding the Omaha riot in Papers of the NAACP (NAACP-2), in the possession of the Middle Atlantic office of the Youth Division, Washington, D.C.; _New York Times_, September 29, 30, 1919; _Omaha Daily Bee_, September 30, October 1, 1919; Robert T. Kerlin, _The Voice of the Negro, 1919_ (N.Y.: E. P. Dutton, 1920), 87; U. S. House of Representatives, 66th Cong., 2nd Sess., Committee on the Judiciary, _Hearings on H.J. Res. 75; H.R. 259, 4123, and 11873_ [_Antilynching Hearings_] (Washington: Government Printing Office, 1920), 58.

[7] _Chicago Defender_, June 21, 1919; _Antilynching Hearings_, 58.

[8] Little Rock _Arkansas Gazette_, October 2, 1919.

News of the clash at Hoop Spur spread rapidly throughout the county and to towns across the Mississippi River. Armed white men sped to Helena, Arkansas, from Clarendon, Marianna, and Marvell on the Arkansas side of the river, and from Lula, Tunica, Friars Point, and Clarksdale on the Mississippi side. Emergency posses, totaling 500 men and including a detachment from the American Legion post at Helena, inundated Elaine, Arkansas. Frightened for their lives, black men fled into the woods and canebrakes; and white men, motivated in part by reports that the Progressive Union was advocating "social equality" and by rumors that the blacks had scheduled "a general slaughter of white people in the locality" for October 7, pursued them and massacred them. Martial law was declared on October 2, and the violence abated as soldiers of the regular Army were ordered from Camp Pike to Phillips County at the request of Governor Charles Brough.

"The white citizens of the county," Governor Brough declared on October 3, ". . . deserve unstinted praise for their action in preventing mob violence." It is scarcely possible to conceive of a statement so hideously ludicrous. For at least twenty-five black people, and probably many, many more, had been hunted down by white mobs and slaughtered like animals, and at least five white men had been killed as well.[9]

Other factors also make it difficult to explain why there was not a recurrence of race rioting in Chicago. In addition to the continuing presence of the year of transition, 1919, with its Red Scare and Red Summer, the fact of migration to Chicago was still abundantly evident. Not only did Southern blacks and demobilized soldiers continue to settle in Chicago, but efforts by recruiters to entice black people to the South after the riot were almost totally unsuccessful. Advertisements appeared

[9] A thorough study of the Elaine, Arkansas, riot is needed, one that would explore the relationship between the 1919 union and the Southern Tenant Farmers' Union of the 1930s, as well as the relationship between the Arkansas riot and the Longview riot and between labor conflict and racial violence in general. Beginning points for such a study would be Waskow, *From Race Riot to Sit-In*, 121–74; in NAACP-2, legal briefs re the riot; "Arkansas Riot," undated story; [U. S. Bratton?] to Senator Charles Curtis, November 8, 1919; Robert L. Hill to NAACP, November 26, 1919; [?], Marvell, Arkansas, to Emmett J. Scott, November 12, 1919; "The Story of a Southern White Man"; and undated statement of George Washington Davis, Pine City, Arkansas, in General Records of the Justice Department (RG 60), Glasser Files, Major Eugene E. Barton to Acting Intelligence Officer, Chicago, October 9, 1919; and report on riot from Captain Edward P. Passailaigue to Assistant Chief of Staff, G-2, 3rd Division, October 13, 1919; Little Rock *Arkansas Gazette*, September 27, October 2–4, 6, 1919; Walter F. White, "The Race Conflict in Arkansas," *Survey*, XLIII (December 13, 1919), 233–34; White, " 'Massacring Whites' in Arkansas," *Nation*, CIX (December 6, 1919), 715–16; Kerlin, *Voice of the Negro*, 88, 89; Mary White Ovington, *The Walls Came Tumbling Down* (N.Y.: Harcourt, Brace, 1947), 154–64; *Congressional Record*, LVIII, 8818–21; *Crisis*, XIX (December 1919), 56–62; O. A. Rogers, Jr., "The Elaine Race Riots of 1919," *Arkansas Historical Quarterly*, XIX (Summer 1960), 142–50; J. W. Butts and Dorothy James, "The Underlying Causes of the Elaine Riot of 1919," in *ibid.*, XX (Spring 1961), 95–104.

in Chicago's newspapers, both black and white, after the riot. "TO COLORED LABOR SEEKING HOMES," read the statement in the *Broad Ax* of the Coahoma, Mississippi, Chamber of Commerce. Its purpose was to inform Chicago's black people that Coahoma "offers a home and great opportunities to those who care to come. . . ." Kentucky advertised for coal miners and loaders, with its inducements being modern buildings, "commissary the best," steady work, and, perhaps above all, "NO LABOR TROUBLES." Recruiters also came to the city from Louisiana, Tennessee, and other parts of Mississippi, and they all seemed to be agreed on one thing. "I want the southern Negro, who is familiar with the South's general attitude on the race question," said a Mississippian who was looking for cotton pickers. A Louisianian added that he wanted 1,000 families, but not "colored people who have always lived in the north. . . ." They wanted the migrants to come back, but the recruiters found few takers. "The colored people in Chicago feel this is their last ditch," explained banker Jesse Binga. "Here is something to look forward to, [while] in the South they know there are Jim Crow cars, segregation, humiliation and degradation." "The colored people see that if they can't make it in Chicago," noted A. L. Jackson of the Wabash Avenue YMCA, "then it's no use to try somewhere else. Of all places they don't want to go back South."[10]

In addition, as the residents of Chicago's black community well knew, the hostility of the surrounding white ethnic groups had not diminished since the riot. Chicago's racial bloodshed had been the "ideal-type" or "type-case" of Northern urban racial violence, with the riot involving direct "ecological warfare" between the residents of white and black neighborhoods. After the riot, the stereotypes and generalized beliefs, which the nearby Irish- and Polish-Americans and various other ethnic groups held about black people, continued to be invariably deprecating and hostile. The black skin not only served as a symbol arousing distinctly unfavorable feelings toward black people, it also helped to redefine ambiguous and anxiety-producing situations; how easy it was to identify and condemn the despised black people as the source of one's anxiety and as the threat to one's economic security and social status. Moreover, Chicago's press did not cease reporting the news of black people in a disparaging manner, frequently indulging in minority baiting. And, finally, white people continued to disdain black men and women as undesirable competitors—in the labor market, in politics, in contested neighborhoods, and in public accommodations.[11]

---

[10] Report from Director, Division of Negro Economics, to Secretary of Labor, covering the period August 1–31, 1919, in General Records of the Labor Department (RG 174), 8/102-E; *Chicago Broad Ax*, August 16, 1919; *Chicago Herald-Examiner*, August 8, 1919; *Chicago Daily Tribune*, August 31, 1919; T. Arnold Hill, "Why Southern Negroes Don't Go South," *Survey*, XLIII (November 29, 1919), 183–85; and in NAACP Papers, Library of Congress (NAACP-1), numerous newspaper clippings, all in (C-373).

[11] Smelser, *Theory of Collective Behavior*, 8–9, 81–82, 101–09, 222 ff.; Allen D. Grimshaw, "A Study in Social Violence: Urban Race Riots in the United States"

With even greater frequency after the riot than before, bombs demolished windows, porches, vestibules, and other portions of the homes of black people residing in contested neighborhoods. Also damaged were the residences and offices of the realtors of both races who sold and rented to them. One in August and five in December 1919; and in 1920, six in February, one each in March, April, September, and December, and two in October—this was the toll of bombings.[12] Other realtors, politicians, and even the coroner's jury investigating the deaths of riot victims advocated the residential segregation of the races as the solution to unrest in the city.[13] The property owners' associations were more vocal than ever before. "EVERY WHITE PERSON" was the addressee of a poster which the Hyde Park–Kenwood Association had nailed on trees and poles in the district. There would be a meeting, "the most important meeting ever held in the history of Hyde Park," the poster announced, on the evening of October 20, 1919. "Protect your property. . . . Shall we sacrifice our property for one third of its value? And run like rats from a burning ship?" the poster asked. "Or shall we put up a united front and keep Hyde Park desirable for ourselves?" The meeting drew 2,000 people, who at the end rose "with one accord," and shouted their intention "to free the district of Negroes." Pamphlets circulated in contested neighborhoods after the riot. One of them, "An Appeal of White Women to American Humanity," told of the "horrible conduct of [black] French Colonials on the Rhine and the abuse of German white women."[14] Yet the police did little or nothing to protect black residents, despite the public threats of realtors and property owners' associations to rid certain areas of the "invaders." "Property is being destroyed and life endangered by bomb throwing," Francis W. Shepardson, a white member of the Chicago Commission on Race Relations, complained to Governor Lowden in February 1920. "The facts are known to all. They are reported in the papers. But," he added, "there seems to be no authority

(unpublished Ph.D. dissertation, University of Pennsylvania, 1959), 155, 209–12; Dahlke, "Race and Minority Riots," 423–25; Waskow, *From Race Riot to Sit-In*, 10, 58–59.

12 Minutes of the meeting of Executive Committee, February 20, 1920, in Papers of the Chicago Commission on Race Relations (CCRR), Illinois State Archives, Springfield; Waskow, *From Race Riot to Sit-In*, 51, 53–55, 74–75; *Real Estate News*, XV (August 1919, January, February 1920), 3; 3; 1, 4–6; *Crisis*, XXI (March 1921), 213–15; and in *ibid.*, XXII (August 1921), 158; Chicago Crime Commission, *Illinois Crime Survey*, part three (Chicago: Illinois Association for Criminal Justice, 1929), 958–59; *Chicago Daily News*, August 29, 1919; list of bombings in NAACP-2; Interchurch World Movement, *The Inter-Racial Situation in Chicago* (no imprint), *passim*.

13 *Chicago Daily Tribune*, August 7, 12, 1919; Chicago Commission on Race Relations, *The Negro in Chicago* (Chicago: University of Chicago Press, 1922), 51.

14 In NAACP-2, a typescript copy of poster distributed to Hyde Park–Kenwood districts; excerpts from a letter to Mayor Thompson from the association, undated; *Chicago Herald-Examiner*, October 21, 25, 1919; Herbert J. Seligmann, *The Negro Faces America* (N.Y.: Harper & Bros., 1920), 212–17; Waskow, *From Race Riot to Sit-In*, 51, 53–55, 74–75.

interested in the protection of Americans whose skins are black. The condition is a disgrace to American citizenship"; and, Shepardson predicted, "Unless something is done soon another riot is certain."[15]

In the labor market, too, race relations during the aftermath of the riot were bitter.[16] In the stockyards, for example, the unions and the packers angrily denounced each other as the instigators of the racial bloodshed.[17] Once again, the black worker was the man in the middle, for he could not align himself with one side without alienating the other; and by March 1921 it seemed that racial violence would once again erupt in the stockyards. A strike threatened; and if there were a strike, D. E. Northam, a newspaperman and former company official in the stockyards, notified the Labor Department, "it will immediately develop into a race war, blinding the real issue by appealing to race hatred." Union officials agreed; a strike would precipitate the "bloodiest and most disastrous race war this country has ever known."[18] There was no strike at that time, but it was evident that labor conflict and racial violence in Chicago were still inextricably bound up with each other.

Acrid recriminations also marked Chicago's post-riot politics; and the scapegoat of these shouting matches often proved to be the black voter. The chief cause of the recent bloodshed, contended Mayor Thompson's bitter foe, State's Attorney Maclay Hoyne, was "black belt politics." The culprits were "City Hall organization leaders, black and white, [who] have catered to the vicious elements of the negro race for the last six years, teaching them that law is a joke and [that] the police car can be ignored if they have political backing." Had it not been for black gamblers, panderers, and grafters, with their involvement with "Big Bill" Thompson's machine, there probably would have been no riot.[19] Like Hoyne, the supporters of Mayor Thompson also engaged in the cynical exploitation of the bloodshed for political profit. With hyperbole and distortion, they, too, indicted the opposition for responsibility for the riot. "The recent regrettable disorders in Chicago," asserted the Thompson organization's *The Republican*, "fortunately nipped in the bud by the firm and prompt action of Mayor William Hale Thompson, were largely the logical and inevitable outcome of the encouragement given to violence and mob rule by newspapers like the *Chicago Tribune*. . . ." In World War I, as during the pacifist rally which Thompson had permitted to convene in Chicago in 1917, "papers of the *Tribune* stamp boldly and

---

[15] Shepardson to Lowden, February 2, 1920, CCRR Papers.

[16] For racial tension in the Chicago area during the 1919 steel strike, see *Chicago Daily Tribune*, October 30, 1919; *Chicago Herald-Examiner*, October 4, 1919; Seligmann, *Negro Faces America*, 206–07.

[17] *New Majority*, August 2, 9, 1919.

[18] In Records of Federal Mediation and Conciliation Service (RG 280), Suitland, Maryland, D. E. Northam to Secretary of Labor James J. Davis, March 22, 1921, in 170/1365; telegram from Starick Epworth League, Chicago, to Secretary Davis, March 20, 1921, in 170/1365-A.

[19] In NAACP-2, Walter F. White to John R. Shillady, August 26, 1919; "Lull after the Storm," *Survey*, XLII (August 30, 1919), 782; in *ibid.* (September 6, 1919), 826; *Chicago Daily News*, August 25, 1919.

unblushingly encouraged lawlessness and disorder of every kind, in the sacred name of 'patriotism.' " *The Republican* also took issue with the *Tribune's* statement that Chicago had "had the most horrible race riots of American history." This was a "contemptible falsehood"; Chicago had not had the worst riot in American history, for "hundreds" had been murdered in East St. Louis. The statement was but one more example of the *Tribune's* eagerness, "in its insane desire to discredit Mayor Thompson . . . to blacken the reputation of Chicago and to start dissension among its people. . . ."[20]

Despite these massive threats to the accommodative structure of race relations in Chicago, and the possibility of renewed violence, the city's police department seemed to be no better prepared, and no more willing, to enforce justice equitably than before the riot. Perhaps the best example of this was the intensification of residential bombings, with the continued total absence of arrests and convictions. The attitudes of hostile white policemen had not measurably improved, either, if the statement of Officer Daniel Callahan is any example. One year after the riot, Callahan —who had been suspended for his negligent conduct at the 29th Street beach and subsequently reinstated—offered his opinion that "the black people have since history began despised the white people. . . . It wouldn't take much to start another riot, and most of the white people . . . are resolved to make a clean-up this time." If a black person should talk back to him, Callahan declared, "or should say a word to a white woman in the park, there is a crowd of young men of the district . . . who would procure arms and fight shoulder to shoulder with me if trouble should come. . . ."[21] Certainly Chicago's black people had as little faith as ever in the police.[22] The memory of the department's behavior during the bloodshed was a bitter one, and it rankled in the black community. The twenty-four jurors on the all-white grand jury also expressed their amazement at the partiality of law enforcement during the riot. After hearing over thirty consecutive cases involving black defendants, the grand jury not only denounced State's Attorney Hoyne, it even staged a strike, refusing to hear further cases until Hoyne came forth with evidence against white rioters. "What the — is the matter with the state's attorney?" the jurors grumbled. "Hasn't he got any white cases to present?"[23]

It was not the lack of a precipitating incident that saved Chicago

[20] *The Republican*, August 9, 1919; and "Memorandum Re Conference with James Minnick . . . Chicago," Arthur B. Spingarn Papers, Library of Congress.

[21] Chicago Commission, *Negro in Chicago*, 451.

[22] Regarding faith in the police and the importance of police control as perhaps "the crucial factor" in determining whether or not a riot erupted, see Allen D. Grimshaw, "Actions of Police and the Military in American Race Riots," *Phylon*, XXIV (Fall 1963), 271–89.

[23] Report of the grand jury, undated, in CCRR Papers; memorandum re "Action of Chicago Branch, N.A.A.C.P. in re Legal Defense Chicago Riots," October 4, 1919, Arthur Spingarn Papers; *Chicago Daily Journal*, July 30, August 4, 1919; *Chicago Defender*, August 9, 1919; in NAACP-2, "Summary of Chicago Riots Cases in Report Submitted by A. Clement MacNeal," December 31, 1919, plus much cor-

from another race war. For, indeed, there were enough incidents in 1919 and 1920 to have precipitated a half-dozen riots.[24] In late August 1919, for example, rumors swept the South Side of "a repetition of the recent riots, only much more serious." The violence would erupt on Labor Day; the "gangs of white hoodlums," Walter White notified the NAACP, "are planning to break out then."[25] No violence erupted on Labor Day, and, despite further rumors, the night of Halloween was also devoid of a race riot.[26] Rumors, however, can have a logic and reality of their own; often it is not fact that precipitates a riot, but what people perceive to be fact. Rumors, like stereotypes and generalized beliefs, can redefine ambiguous situations by predicting what will happen, and sometimes it does.[27]

"We are standing on the brink of another such disaster as occurred last July," Dr. George Cleveland Hall, a black member of the Chicago Commission on Race Relations, predicted in February 1920.[28] Two months later, Walter White echoed this prediction, adding specifically that the causes of the riot would be bombings and the black belt's lack of faith in the police. Black people feel "that they will have to depend upon themselves for proper defense," a "feeling" which, White added, had "developed to the point of martyrdom." It was "a dangerous and serious matter to have so large a percentage of Chicago's population in this frame of mind."[29] There were numerous other predictions of a riot that spring, many of them designating May 1 as the date. Then, on June 20, short-lived violence did erupt.

Sometime earlier in 1920, R. D. Jonas, a white man, and Grover Cleveland Redding, a black man who claimed to be a prophet and a native of Ethiopia, established Chicago's Star Order of Ethiopia and Ethiopian Missionaries to Abyssinia. Apparently the organization was an illegitimate offspring of Marcus Garvey's Universal Negro Improvement Association, and Jonas and Redding fostered the notion that their movement, like Garvey's, would facilitate the return of black people to Africa. On Sunday, June 20, Redding gathered a small group of "Abyssinians." Wearing

---

respondence, many reports, press releases, and memoranda re legal defense of riot victims and defendants; *Chicago Daily Tribune*, August 7–9, 1919; *Chicago Herald-Examiner*, August 9, 1919; Waskow, *From Race Riot to Sit-In*, 45 ff.; Allan H. Spear, *Black Chicago: The Making of a Negro Ghetto, 1890–1920* (Chicago: University of Chicago Press, 1967), 217–18; Chicago Commission, *Negro in Chicago*, 46–49.

[24] For the significance of precipitating incidents, see Smelser, *Theory of Collective Behavior*, 12–21, 247 ff.

[25] Walter White to John R. Shilladay, August 26, 1919, NAACP-2.

[26] Castle M. Brown to Military Intelligence Branch, October 28, 1919, in Glasser Files; and Major Thomas B. Crockett to Director of Military Intelligence, October 30, November 26, 1919, in *ibid.*; *New York Times*, December 21, 1919; Chicago Commission, *Negro in Chicago*, 572–73.

[27] Smelser, *Theory of Collective Behavior*, 81–82, 247–48; Gordon W. Allport and Leo Postman, *The Psychology of Rumor* (N.Y.: Henry Holt, 1947), 193–96.

[28] Minutes of the meeting of the CCRR, February 25, 1920, copies in both CCRR Papers and Julius Rosenwald Papers, University of Chicago.

[29] Statement prepared by Walter F. White, *ca.* April 15, 1920, NAACP-2.

the toga of an Abyssinian prince and sitting astride a white horse, Redding led the others in parade. An automobile filled with rifles was also in the procession. At 35th Street the parade stopped in front of a biracial café at 35th Street. Redding drew out of his robe an American flag, and, after dousing it with gasoline, he set it afire. Two white policemen argued with the Abyssinians, but fled after being intimidated with threats and loaded revolvers. A black patrolman arrived as a second American flag was being burned. He also remonstrated with the men, accusing them of disloyalty; and they shot him. A protesting white sailor was also shot; he staggered into the doorway of a cigar store and collapsed with fatal wounds. Before they escaped temporarily, the Abyssinians had fired twenty-five shots, injuring several people and killing two. Had the police not been vigilant and impartial, this conflagration could easily have escalated into unrestrained and generalized violence. The Chicago Commission on Race Relations praised the police and the press for their "careful handling of the matter."[30]

Further rumors cited Labor Day 1920 as the date of the race riot; yet there was none. And there was no riot in September of that year, when three black men stabbed a white man to death in the stockyards district, nearly severing his head from his body.[31] As late as August 1921 three members of the Chicago Commission on Race Relations sent an urgent telegram to Governor Lowden, warning him that "Chicago still faces possibility of another race riot . . . unless importance of spirit of cooperation is magnified."[32] Yet again there was no riot. It was not that the antagonists were not organized; if anything, they were more tightly organized than they had been before. The black people, as one of their number recalled, had had a new feeling of togetherness since the riot.[33] The same was true of the hostile white groups. In fact, one of the supreme ironies of 1921 was that the Ragen Colts were not only "mobilized for action," but that the gang's target at that time was not Chicago's black people, but rather the Ku Klux Klan, for its anti-Catholicism. In September, 3,000 people from the stockyards district watched as the Colts hanged in effigy "a white-sheeted Klansman."[34]

[30] In *ibid.*, "Defender of the Abyssinian Name and Mission: My Duty: Statement of R. D. Jonas," undated; and T. Arnold Hill to Walter White, June 24, 1920; material from Cook County coroner's jury investigating the incident in RG 60 (158260–2); interview with Mr. Wilkins; "Abyssinia and America," *Survey,* XLIV (July 3, 1920), 491; *Chicago Daily Tribune,* June 21, 23, July 24, 1920; Graham R. Taylor to Francis W. Shepardson, June 21, 1920, CCRR Papers; Chicago Commission, *Negro in Chicago,* 59–64, 480, 521, 537–38.

[31] Chicago Commission, *Negro in Chicago,* 64–67, 572–73.

[32] Telegram from Julius Rosenwald, Harry Eugene Kelly, and Francis W. Shepardson, Tuskegee, Alabama, to Frank O. Lowden, Chicago, [August?] 1921, Lowden Papers, University of Chicago.

[33] See A. Clement MacNeal to John R. Shilladay, March 10, 1920, NAACP-2; *Crisis,* XXII (August 1921), 158.

[34] Smelser, *Theory of Collective Behavior,* 253 ff., re mobilization for action; and Kenneth T. Jackson, *The Ku Klux Klan in the City, 1915–1930* (N.Y.: Oxford University Press, 1967), 95.

Why, then, was there no riot? Perhaps the answer lies in such rays of hope as the Chicago Commission on Race Relations, which Governor Lowden had appointed to survey the causes of racial violence in Chicago.[35] But few people in authority took its conclusions seriously. Perhaps the answer lies in a widespread but unexpressed revulsion, shared by black and white alike, at the excesses of the 1919 bloodshed. Perhaps the riot was a cathartic, purging people of some of their anger for a time. It is a fact that throughout American history major race riots have seldom recurred in the same city within a short period of time. Most probably, the answers lie in some such intangible factor, something that cannot be programmed, something that might forever escape detection by the historian or social scientist, but something that might be worth more than all the studies and surveys of riots and violence put together.

People used to think of "The Long Hot Summer" as the movie version of a William Faulkner novel. Beginning in 1964, with outbursts of racial violence in Harlem, Rochester, Jersey City, Paterson, Elizabeth, the Chicago suburb of Dixmoor, and Philadelphia, these words came to mean fear, hatred, bloodshed, death, even apprehension about America's ability to survive as a nation. "Will this be another long hot summer?" news commentators asked in 1965 and every year thereafter. The answer was always in the affirmative, and it took the form of a succession of place names—Watts in 1965, Chicago and Cleveland's Hough section in 1966, Tampa, Cincinnati, Atlanta, Newark and other New Jersey cities, and Detroit in 1967, and scores of cities in the spring of 1968, following the assassination of Dr. Martin Luther King, Jr. These names conjured up a plethora of disturbing scenes: wounded black men and women, their faces covered with blood, lying unconscious or sobbing with pain; helmeted firemen using tear gas, club-swinging policemen, phalanxes of marching soldiers, their rifles extended, their bayonets unsheathed; overturned and burning police cars; block after block of flaming buildings; looters climbing through smashed windows into grocery, liquor, clothing, and appliance stores and emerging with their arms filled.

By 1968 racial distrust and anger divided the nation as it had not been divided for 100 years. "Arming for Armageddon," as one writer observed, were countless people, including the white ladies in the suburbs who practiced assiduously with their pistols until they could hit the target every time; if there were to be a "second Civil War," they would be ready. White vigilantes and self-proclaimed black revolutionaries were also armed and prepared to shoot to kill. Patrolling certain communities in northern New Jersey, for example, were white members of an organization known as People's Rights Enforced Against Riots and Murders; its acronym was thus PRE-ARM, and its purpose was to guard against the "rising tide of [black] insurrection."

Governments, too, succumbed to the unrest and even to the hysteria. Jittery politicians, along with cynically ambitious ones, enacted state and

---

[35] For the operations of the CCRR, see CCRR Papers, and the extensive account in Waskow, *From Race Riot to Sit-In*, 60–104.

federal antiriot laws. While broadening police powers in New York State, legislators also debated authorizing policemen or private citizens to shoot suspected arsonists, even if the suspects were not trespassing on the property involved. "Law and order," with or without justice, became a political rallying cry in that presidential election year, and its appeal was not confined to the South. Police agencies in 1968 stockpiled tear gas grenades, shotguns and high-powered rifles, mace spray guns, and other antiriot equipment. They also bought armored cars and helicopters, weapons not designed to help apprehend the individual law violator, but lethal weapons with the potential for indiscriminate destruction. Moreover, the police enlisted white civilians for reserve duty in the event of race riots. In Cook County, Illinois, for example, the sheriff announced his intention to recruit a riot control unit of 1,000 volunteers to act with full authority as deputy sheriffs if mobilized. And that spring the U. S. Army announced that it would conduct weekly courses in riot control at Fort Gordon, Georgia, for any police departments and National Guard units that wished to enroll.

What had caused these eruptions of urban racial violence with their resultant outpouring of fear, distrust, and hostility? Why had the high hopes for racial equality and brotherhood of the earlier 1960s degenerated into bloodshed? These were questions to which various local, state, and federal commissions sought answers.[36] With more honesty than most of these commissions, the National Advisory Commission on Civil Disorders (the Kerner Commission) imputed the riots to "white racism," to a societal structure and to attitudes and mores premised on white superordination and black subordination. The legal proscription of slavery, disfranchisement, and segregation, the corruption of vagrancy and indebtedness laws to perpetuate bondage and debt peonage, lynchings and other deadly expressions of white people's animosity toward black people, white exclusiveness in residential neighborhoods, politics, the labor movement, schools, and recreational facilities, the urban race riots of the World War I era—all these, the Kerner Commission asserted, attested to the existence of America's caste society with its proclivity for violence. Moreover, the Commission added, racial separation, despite the enactment of civil rights laws, was growing, not decreasing. With the continuing migration of Southern blacks to the metropolises of the North, and with the accelerating flight of frightened whites to the suburbs, two worlds were ever emerging in the United States, one white, one black.

Because of the racial violence of the 1960s, scholars and other observers began to rediscover the fact of the World War I riots. Urban race riots were not new, they said; there was a history of such violence in America. But were these riots similar in origins, ecology, and partici-

---

[36] See especially the California Governor's [McCone] Commission on the Los Angeles Riots, *Violence in the City—An End or a Beginning?* (Los Angeles: n. pub., 1965); *Report of the National Advisory Commission on Civil Disorders* (Washington: Government Printing Office, 1968); National Commission on the Causes and Prevention of Violence, *To Establish Justice, To Insure Domestic Tranquility* (Washington: Government Printing Office, 1969).

pants to the more recent urban conflagrations? Was Chicago in 1919, for example, similar to Harlem, Rochester, Watts, Newark, and Detroit forty-five years later?

"Get whitey," cried out black men and women in the 1960s as they firebombed white-owned shops in black ghettos. Yet the objects of these angry attacks were symbols, not real people; they were whitey's property, not whitey himself. The white lady marksman in the suburbs could not point to actual examples of black assaults and invasions as justification for her fears. In Chicago in 1919, however, blacks actually assaulted whites, not just their property, and sometimes they killed them; and whites were even more violent in their attacks on blacks. Waged not primarily for psychic gratification, but waged over such gut-level issues as jobs and a place to live, the Chicago riot pitted people of one race against those of another. Many black people died in the disorders of the 1960s, but they did not die at the hands of white rioters; they usually fell as a result of bullets fired by the police. Whites also died in the riots of the 1960s, but these whites were not marauders who had invaded the black belt in search of victims; they were ordinarily policemen and firemen who had been dispatched to the scenes of violence to suppress mobs and extinguish fires. Self-defense was the byword in Chicago in 1919; but there were no invaders to defend against in the 1960s. Black people in the 1960s judged their actions to be "justifiable retaliation" against faceless white oppression. "I clean the white man's dirt all the time," recalled a cleaning lady during the 1964 Harlem riot. But when she got home Saturday night, during the apogee of the violence, "something happened to me." She went onto the roof, "but hearing the guns I felt like something was crawling in me, like the whole damn world was no good, and the little kids and the big ones and all of us was going to get killed because we don't know what to do. And I see the cops are white and I was crying. Dear God, I am crying! And I took this pop bottle and it was empty and I threw it down on the cops, and I was crying and laughing."[37]

But there are certain similarities between the riots of World War I and the outbursts of the 1960s. Both sets of riots occurred during periods of rising expectations on the part of black people. During World War I black men and women threatened the nation's accommodative race system of white supremacy and black inferiority as they had not done since the years of Reconstruction. Whites had long been hostile to the aspirations of black people, and this hostility deepened as a half-million Southern blacks migrated to the North. There, in overcrowded metropolises like Chicago, blacks met in bitter competition with whites over access to employment, housing, political power, and facilities for education,

---

[37] August Meier and Elliott Rudwick, *From Plantation to Ghetto* (N.Y.: Hill and Wang, 1966), 247–51; Meier and Rudwick, "Black Violence in the 20th Century: A Study in Rhetoric and Retaliation," in National Commission on the Causes and Prevention of Violence, *Violence in America*, prepared under the direction of Hugh Davis Graham and Ted Robert Gurr (N.Y.: Signet edition, 1969), 384–87; Joseph Boskin, "Violence in the Ghettos: A Consensus of Attitudes," *New Mexico Quarterly*, XXXVII (Winter 1968), 317–34; *Time*, LXXXIV (July 31, 1964), 11.

transportation, and recreation. Having migrated in anticipation of a better life for themselves and their children, and having fought in a war that purportedly would make the world safe for democracy, black people entered the year 1919 with aspirations for a more equitable share in both the nation's democracy and its wealth. But racial tension mounted, and eventually violence erupted, as these aspirations collided with the general white determination to reaffirm the black people's prewar status on the bottom rung of the nation's racial ladder.

In the 1960s, too, the expectations of black men and women reached heights unhoped for in recent years. The civil rights movement, the Freedom March on Washington in 1963, federal laws guaranteeing equal access to public accommodations and assuring the right to vote, Supreme Court decisions sympathetic to racial equality—these events seemed to offer hope of a better life, one that would make black people conscious agents of their own destinies. Integration was the promise of the civil rights movement, but it did not deliver on this promise, especially in the urban North. There, in the mid-1960s, the public schools were more segregated than they had been ten years before. The same was true of housing. The unemployment rate for blacks was still much higher than that for whites, while the rate for black teenagers was astronomical; and the increases in black wages in the 1960s, though notable, were far outstripped by the increases in white wages. "The Second Reconstruction," muttered disconsolate blacks, had been as dismal a failure as the first. "The Blackman in America," declared a black revolutionary, "must realize that integration of the Black and white races in the U.S. will never work. He must realize that he is not a citizen denied his rights but a colonized captive held in colonial bondage inside the U.S." Clearly, as one observer noted in the mid-1960s, "the revolution of rising expectations had become the revolution of rising frustrations."[38]

It was this frustration, augmented by the opportunism of looters to enrich themselves, that gave birth to the violent impulse to destroy the visible signs of white authority in urban black belt areas. Later, rioters and black militants justified the riots as insurrections and rebellions, as indeed they probably were to some. "We're men now," said one. "We won't take any more from Whitey." "We won," added another. "We won because we made the world pay attention to us."[39]

The riots of World War I resemble those of the 1960s in other ways as well. Both groups of riots erupted during periods of war and international unrest. Indeed, war, throughout American history, has provided a setting conducive to racial violence. Draft and labor riots between the races broke out frequently during the Civil War. In 1917 there were race riots in Houston and East St. Louis. The year of the Red Summer was 1919, the first year of peace after one of the most disruptive wars in

[38] John H. Bracey, Jr., August Meier, and Elliott Rudwick (eds.), *Black Nationalism in America* (Indianapolis: Bobbs-Merrill, 1970), 514; see also Victor H. Bernstein, "Why Negroes Are Still Angry," *Redbook Magazine*, CXXVII (July 1966), 54 ff.
[39] See Boskin, "Violence in the Ghettos," 330–32.

history and also a year of worldwide anxiety and disorder. Race riots engulfed Detroit and Harlem in 1943, during World War II. And most of the riots of the 1960s were contemporaneous with the military violence in Vietnam. Generative of rapid social and economic change, wars also seem to stimulate a generalized climate of violence, which, like the ghetto-based "subculture of violence," itself a promoter of riots, fosters an acceptance of violence as normal in everyday life.[40] It is significant, too, that in both eras the riots occurred in clusters, giving credence to the "contagion phenomenon" thesis held by certain students of violence.[41]

Also, virtually every riot erupted in the summer, when the weather was hot and uncomfortable, and when many people were restless and susceptible to the commission of acts of violence. In addition, the preponderance of the rioters of both races were teenagers and young adults, typically unattached males with fewer inhibitions and responsibilities than their elders. And in both periods of widespread rioting, blacks advocated retaliatory violence. Finally, an indispensable element in these riots was an attitude of derision and contempt for the police, and an almost utter disbelief in the willingness and ability of the police to deal justly with black people. Feeling thus, it was a short step for black people to rationalize the use of violence. Certainly this was true in Chicago in 1919, and it was also abundantly evident in the 1960s. White policemen in Harlem, James Baldwin wrote in 1960, cannot possibly understand "the lives led by the people they swagger about in two's and three's controlling. Their very presence is an insult, and it would be, even if they spent the entire day feeding gumdrops to children. They represent the force of the white world." A white judge and former police chief could do no less than concur with Baldwin. "The Negro citizen," stated George Edwards, "sees the police officer in blue coat, with white face, as the representative of the white man's law who for nearly 300 years enforced the laws—first of slavery and next of legally sanctioned segregation." The "historic function" of the police, he added, "has been 'keeping the Negro in his place.' . . ."[42]

When the Kerner Commission indicted white racism for being "essentially responsible for the explosive mixture which has been accumulating in our cities since the end of World War II," it alluded specifically to "pervasive discrimination and segregation" and to the "black migration and white exodus."[43] All these contributed to "the massive and growing concentration of impoverished Negroes in our major cities. . . ." In these "teeming racial ghettos," moreover, "segregation and poverty have in-

---

[40] Grimshaw, "Study in Social Violence," 180; Bernard F. Robinson, "War and Race Conflicts in the United States," *Phylon*, IV (4th Quarter 1943), 311–27; Marvin E. Wolfgang and Franco Ferracuti, *The Subculture of Violence: Towards an Integrated Theory in Criminology* (N.Y., London: Tavistock Publications, 1967), *passim.*

[41] Richard Maxwell Brown, "Historical Patterns of Violence in America," in *Violence in America*, 55, 76n.

[42] Both Baldwin and Edwards quoted in *Civil Rights Digest*, II (Fall 1969), 27, 31.

[43] *Report of the National Advisory Commission on Civil Disorders*, 91–93.

tersected to destroy opportunity and hope and to enforce failure." Most whites, on the other hand, "have prospered to a degree unparalleled in the history of civilization." Thus emerged the two worlds to which the Kerner Commission referred. The importance of this concept in understanding the Chicago race riot of 1919 is that these processes leading to the virtual physical isolation of blacks from whites in cities were just beginning to gain momentum in the World War I era. Racial segregation, of course, had always existed to some degree in Chicago. As Allan H. Spear has noted, Chicago had its black ghetto in 1915, even before the migration of tens of thousands of Southern blacks to the city. Thus "the period between 1915 and 1920 was more a time of continuity than of change"; and, indeed, Spear has added, "in many significant ways, remarkably little had changed since 1920 as well."[44] In terms of the essential character of the institutions serving the ghetto and of the fundamental nature of the white resistance to black expansion outside the ghetto, Spear's observation might be an accurate one. But can one doubt that the increase of Chicago's black population from 110,000 in 1920, itself an increase of 148 percent over 1910, to well over 800,000 in 1960 presented immense possibilities for change, some of it of the most profound nature? In 1920 Chicago had just one black ghetto, on the South Side. Now it has two, with a large concentration of blacks on the West Side as well as on the South. Furthermore, in 1920 the federal census listed 4.1 percent of Chicago's population as being of the Negro race; in 1960, the figure was over 23 percent.[45]

These statistics for Chicago, as well as population figures for the nation's other metropolises, provide insights vital to an understanding of the evolution of urban racial violence in the United States. The fact that Chicago's black belt abutted on neighborhoods of Irish- and Polish-Americans and other ethnic groups which were violently antiblack, and not just rhetorically so, was mirrored in the ecology of the 1919 riot. It was clear that the origins of the violence were imbedded deep in the competing social, economic, and political structures of the neighborhoods east and west of Wentworth Avenue. In Chicago in 1919 contacts between blacks and whites tended to be charged with animosity and hostility— but they were contacts nevertheless. By the 1930s and 1940s, however, interracial contacts had diminished, as black people were increasingly isolated in Chicago and other American cities. The racial violence of these years reflected this change. "New-style" riots like those of the 1960s erupted in Harlem in 1935 and again in 1943, with angry blacks demolishing symbols of white authority. Yet, as August Meier and Elliott Rudwick have demonstrated, it was the Detroit race riot of 1943 that marked a transition between the "old-style" and the "new." For while the retaliation of black people against white aggression precipitated the bloodshed,

---

[44] Spear, *Black Chicago*, 129–30, 223–29.

[45] U. S. Department of Commerce, Bureau of the Census, *14th Census of the United States, 1920* (Washington: Government Printing Office, 1922), III, 274; Bureau of the Census, *Statistical Abstract of the United States, 1967* (Washington: Government Printing Office, 1967), 22.

"the Negro mobs' major attention was directed toward destroying and looting white-owned business in the Negro ghetto, and . . . most of the Negroes who were killed were shot by white policemen. . . ."[46]

By the 1960s, with the emergence of America's two worlds of black and white, the new-style riot had definitely arrived. Unparalleled in American history had been the exodus of Southern blacks to Northern cities in the decades from 1910 to the advent of World War II; but this migration paled beside that of subsequent decades. Each decade since 1940 has matched or even exceeded the figure for the entire thirty-year period, 1910–1940. Millions of people poured into inner-city areas; and, aided by the demolition of slums through urban renewal and the Supreme Court's decision that restrictive covenants were legally unenforceable, the vast ghettos continued to expand. By the 1960s, urban black voters in the North were able to elect mayors from their own race, and it was evident that before long black people would constitute a majority in numerous cities. "Indeed," as Meier and Rudwick point out, "compared to the enormous ghettos of today, the Negro residential areas of the World War I period were mere enclaves." No white person with any sanity would invade such massive black belts to commit violence against black people; even in earlier riots hostile whites had been hesitant about entering any areas but isolated black neighborhoods and the peripheries of the ghetto. More important, though, as these scholars have also noted, the massive ghettos "provide a relatively safe place for the destruction and looting of white-owned property. . . ." In such hostile territory, police and soldiers find it difficult if not impossible to protect property from destruction.[47]

What the future holds regarding race relations in America nobody knows. With examples like the Chicago race riot of 1919, the nation's unhappy history of the relations between black and white people is frightening enough to survey. There have been predictions, of course, including the disturbing one made in the 1830s by the prescient Alexis de Tocqueville. "If ever America undergoes great revolutions," he wrote, "they will be brought about by the presence of the black race on the soil of the United States; that is to say, they will owe their origin, not to the equality, but to the inequality of condition."[48] Whether Tocqueville is correct only time can tell, but one thing is evident. The optimist cannot take solace in the past.

---

[46] Meier and Rudwick, "Black Violence in the 20th Century," 385–87; Meier and Rudwick, *From Plantation to Ghetto*, 247–51.

[47] Meier and Rudwick, "Black Violence in the 20th Century," 386–87.

[48] Alexis de Tocqueville, *Democracy in America* (N.Y.: Vintage edition, 1964), II, 270.

The Failure

of the

Melting Pot

STANLEY COBEN

The period just after the First World War saw a great wave of nativist sentiment in America. Nativism, or anti-foreign attitudes, first emerged in the late eighteenth century in reaction to the French republicans who were fleeing the excesses of the French Revolution. It emerged full blown in the period of Irish immigration just before the Civil War, when the Native American Party, or Know-Nothings, gained moderate success at the polls on the platform that only native-born Americans should be able to vote or hold office.

Nativism swelled with the beginning of the new immigration. This time the enemy was seen as the Jews and Catholics from eastern and southern Europe. And this time the nativists were bolstered by emerging theories of racial inferiority put forth by social scientists at the great universities.

However, whites needed no new racist theories to continue denying to nonwhite (primarily black, oriental, and Mexican) Americans their rightful place in society. The patterns of discrimination that were established prior to the Civil War continued, only slightly altered, up to the First World War when changing industrial needs gave blacks an opportunity to move into jobs in the North.

After the war the nativist, antiradical, and antiblack traditions came together to bring about one of the most repressive periods in American history. Actions by officials of the United States government and groups like the Ku Klux Klan led to a concerted campaign against all non-Protestant, nonwhite peoples in the 1920s. This campaign is described by Stanley Coben, of the University of California at Los Angeles, in the article reprinted below.

An interesting question raised by Professor Coben is whether or not the nativists and racists won their campaign. While it is true that "undesirable" immigration from countries outside the Americas was severely limited by legislation in 1924, those new immigrants who were here remained to play an important role in American society. Nonwhites have continued to struggle for their rights and the Anglo-Saxon elites who controlled almost all aspects of American life in the 1920s no longer have the same power that they had then. Members of oppressed groups, white and non-white alike, have adopted many of the cultural traits and attitudes of the formerly dominant elites, and although there has been a resurgence of various cultural movements among minorities, these movements have fed basically on resentment rather than a desire to re-establish former life styles, and the minorities tend to drift back to the dominant American culture.

During the late nineteenth and early twentieth centuries Americans and Western Europeans carried out an insidious type of conquest throughout the world; tearing apart established religious, economic, and political re-lationships, attempting to replace them with Western cultural forms. Minority ethnic groups in the United States were subjected to similar cul-tural assaults, usually more subtle, but in many respects more effective than attacks on cultures in foreign lands. Only the United States, among the Western powers, contained among its population large elements of many races generally believed in the West to be inferior. Nowhere else were nativist organizations and official policies directed against internal minor-ities which together formed such a substantial portion of the population. Only the United States, therefore, suffered massive counterattacks anal-ogous to the revolts of colonial races elsewhere. There was an element of reality, then, in the terror experienced by millions of Americans when revolution swept eastern and central Europe during 1919 to 1920, and propagandists among hitherto subservient races threatened similar rebel-lion in the United States.

I

A series of short-term, postwar dislocations further disturbed the psychological equilibrium of large numbers of Americans. Some of these events—runaway prices, a brief economic depression, and a stock market crash—could be connected to racial minorities only by the most preju-diced. But thousands of returning soldiers were disgruntled when they found their old jobs occupied by Negroes and recent immigrants. And other disturbances—race riots, labor strikes, formation of Communist

"The Failure of the Melting Pot," by Stanley Coben. From *The Great Fear: Race in the Mind of America*, edited by Gary B. Nash and Richard Weiss. Copyright © 1970 by Gary B. Nash and Richard Weiss. Reprinted by permission of Holt, Rine-hart and Winston, Inc.

parties, widespread bomb explosions and bombing attempts, and an out-pouring of arch-radical propaganda—were easily linked in the public mind with alien races and peoples. The formation of the Comintern in Moscow in 1919 and the revolutions then raging in eastern Europe seemed to give credence to the fear that a new revolutionary force was loose in the world that threatened to overwhelm American institutions. The result was an intensification of nativist patterns of thought. These found expression in a quasi-religious nativist movement aimed at unifying an apparently disintegrating culture against an onslaught by darker, in-ferior races. Americans who took part in this crusade for "100 percent Americanism," as it was popularly called, hoped to eliminate the intrusive influences felt to be the chief cause of contemporary anxieties, if they could not eliminate the intruders themselves.[1]

A similar movement, less frenzied, perhaps, but with the same objec-tives, probably would have taken place even without the stimulation pro-vided by postwar disturbances. The real foundation of the movement for 100 percent Americanism was a long-term crisis for the nation's dominant cultural groups: the urbanization of America and the peopling of its great cities by black migrants from the southern states, and by other dark immi-grants from Italy, eastern Europe, Mexico, and the Caribbean. These were regarded by white native-born Americans as dangerous, immoral people, easily associated with the immorality they read about and believed they saw all around them in the nation's urban centers.

The dimensions of the problem facing native-born white Americans can be indicated by a few demographic statistics. Of a total population of 106 million in 1920, 54 million lived in urban areas, the first time in the nation's history that the urban exceeded the rural populace. In 1860, only 20 percent of all Americans had lived in towns and cities. Of 106 million Americans in 1920, 23 million were immigrants or the children of immi-grants, and over 10 million of these had migrated in the fifteen years be-fore World War I, the height of the exodus from Italy and eastern Eu-rope. In the year before the war, immigrants from southern and eastern Europe outnumbered those from northwestern Europe by six to one. The majority of these "new" immigrants settled in the metropolitan centers.[2]

Even more alarming to white Americans was the concurrent move-ment of southern Negroes to the cities, especially the large northern cities. There they congregated, or were forced to concentrate, in huge ghettos. Of 11 million Negroes in the United States, 2 million lived in the North by 1920, and, like the influx of Europeans, the migration showed signs of continuing if not increasing its pace. Tired of low pay, mistreatment, and a losing battle against the boll weevil, at least 600,000 Negroes moved north during the 1920s, and tens of thousands more came from the Carib-

---

[1] These events are described and an attempt made to link them theoretically with similar movements at other times and places, in Stanley Coben, "A Study in Nativ-ism: The American Red Scare of 1919–1920," *Political Science Quarterly,* 79 (March 1964), pp. 52–75.

[2] U.S. Bureau of the Census, *Historical Statistics of the United States, Colonial Times to 1957* (Washington, D.C., 1960), chapter C.

bean Islands, especially Jamaica, after World War I. The 1930 census revealed that 273,000 Negroes lived in New York City alone, only 9000 of whom had been born in any of the North Atlantic states. Most had come from Virginia and the Carolinas. Harlem, a white, middle-class area in 1910, was inhabited almost entirely by 106,000 blacks in 1930. By that year, also, 232,000 Negroes were settled in Chicago, most of them from states of the Deep South. Another 118,000 Negroes lived in Detroit by 1930. The same kind of movement away from the tenant farms and rural villages took place within the South. According to the 1930 census, 96,000 Negroes lived in Memphis, 35,000 of whom had come from Mississippi alone; 99,000 Negroes lived in Birmingham; 90,000 in Atlanta; 63,000 in Houston, and 38,000 in Los Angeles, only 6700 of whom had been born anywhere in California.[3]

White leaders attempted to check the shift in Negro population both at its source and its destination. Mississippi employers, facing a labor shortage, formed an association and hired agents to woo blacks back to the pleasant land they had left. Advertisements promising jobs and transportation were placed in northern newspapers, agents made personal pleas, and even intimidation was tried. Some tactics closely resembled kidnapping. But nothing worked. Those Negroes who did return to the South often acted as labor agents for northern employers, and soon returned to northern cities accompanied by friends and relatives. The most common attitude was that periodic unemployment and freezing weather in the North was preferable to certain peonage and possible lynching in the South. A contemporary folk tale, frequently repeated in northern ghettos, describes an unemployed Negro migrant, cold, wet, and hungry, appealing to God for advice. "Go back to Mississippi," the Lord told him. "You don't mean it, Lord," the poor man replied, "You're jesting." The Lord repeated, "Go back to Mississippi!" Finally, the man relented: "Very well, Lord, if you insist, I'll go. But will you go with me?" The Lord answered: "As far as Cincinnati."

Most of the Negro migrants were young, and, at first, predominantly single men. The Department of Labor's Division of Negro Economics, established primarily to find the causes and probable duration of the black exodus, gave as a typical example of the process at work, this account by a rural Negro preacher:

> My father [said he] was born and brought up as a slave. He never knew anything else until after I was born. He was taught his place and was content to keep it. But when he brought me up he let some of the old customs slip by. But I know that there are certain things that I must do, and I do them, and it doesn't worry me. Yet in bringing up my own son, I let some more of the old customs slip by. He has been through the eighth grade; he reads easily.

[3] U.S. Department of Labor, Division of Negro Economics, *Negro Migration in 1916–17* (Washington, D.C., 1919); Louis V. Kennedy, *The Negro Peasant Turns Cityward* (New York, 1930); Bureau of Census, *Historical Statistics of the United States,* chapter C.

For a year I have been keeping him from going to Chicago; but he tells me that this is his last crop; that in the fall he's going. He says, "When a young white man talks rough to me, I can't talk rough to him. You can stand that; I can't. I have some education, and inside I has the feelins of a white man. I'm goin'."[4]

Most northerners were not pleased by their new black neighbors, and thousands organized either to keep Negroes out of their residential areas, or to ensure that the newcomers acted as Negroes were supposed to act—subserviently. A letter sent to a Lenox Avenue, New York City, realty company warned, "We have been informed of your intention to rent your house . . . to Negro tenants. This is wholly un-American, and is totally against our principles. We ask you in a gentlemanly way to rescind your order, or unpleasant things may happen." The note was signed: Ku Klux Klan, Realm 7, Chapter 3. In Chicago, twenty-four bombs were thrown at the houses of Negroes who moved into previously all-white neighborhoods, or at the offices of the real estate agents who sold or rented them the houses. No arrests were made as a result of these bombings.[5]

The extent of residential and school segregation varied widely from city to city. A study published in 1930 found the least segregation in Minneapolis, Buffalo, and New York City, where over 100,000 Negroes lived outside Harlem. In Chicago, the city administration held office by grace of Negro votes, so official racist policies were opposed at the highest level. Nevertheless Chicago's citizens proved adequate to the task of confining Negroes to certain slum areas, and keeping the better schools limited to white children. In Philadelphia, twelve schools had 100 percent Negro student bodies. Other schools in the city contained separate entrances for Negroes. Chester, Pennsylvania, operated parallel school systems for Negroes and whites through junior high school. Segregationists also enjoyed wide success in such midwestern cities as Gary, Dayton, and Indianapolis.[6]

Nevertheless, schools in all the northern cities were far superior to those operated for Negroes in the South. This was an important reason why the harrassment mentioned above, and even the race riots described below, tended to stimulate withdrawal into the Negro ghettos and into Black Nationalist organizations, rather than a mass return to the South.

The hostility these demographic shifts provoked among thousands of whites can be seen most vividly in the pattern of violent racial disturbances which shook a dozen northern urban centers following the end of World War I. Chicago was typical. A teen-aged Negro boy, Eugene Williams, swimming off a Lake Michigan beach on a hot Sunday afternoon, July 27, 1919, accidentally wandered over the traditional line separating white and black swimming areas. Whites on the shore began throwing rocks at him.

4 Department of Labor, *Negro Migration in 1916–17*, p. 33.
5 Clyde Vernon Kiser, *Sea Island to City* (New York, 1932), p. 22. Chicago Commission on Race Relations, *The Negro in Chicago* (Chicago, 1922; reprinted, New York, 1968), p. 3.
6 Kennedy, *The Negro Peasant Turns Cityward*, pp. 193–200.

Some apparently found their target for the boy sank and drowned. Blacks insisted that a policeman at the scene arrest one of the white rock-throwers, but the officer refused and tried to arrest a Negro instead. Groups of blacks then attacked the policeman; whites came to his rescue, and a wild battle began on the beach. Accounts of the fighting on the Lake Michigan shore quickly spread through the sweltering south side of Chicago.

That night, white teen-aged gangs captured Negroes who worked in white areas of the city, and beat, stabbed, or shot them. Two died and over fifty reported their injuries to hospitals or the police. For the next twelve days, law and order almost disappeared from Chicago as armed white gangs in automobiles invaded black districts, shooting from their cars into Negro homes and setting some of them on fire. Snipers fired from rooftops on these cars and on others driven by whites. Negroes working in white areas continued to be attacked on the streets and in buses and streetcars. Black gangs retaliated against whites who made the mistake of venturing into the Negro ghetto (where hundreds of them worked) on foot. Eventually the state militia restored relative peace; but by then 23 Negroes and 15 whites were known to have died in the fighting, at least 520 were seriously injured, and over 1000 were left homeless by fires set in the Negro district.

Perhaps the most significant statistics from the Chicago race riot were the number of whites killed and injured. These indicated that from the Lake Michigan beach to the south side ghetto Negroes were fighting back. In all, six major race riots and about twenty other racial conflicts erupted in American cities during the summer and fall of 1919. Some, like the battles in Washington, D.C., and Knoxville, Tennesee, were only slightly less violent than the conflict in Chicago. A race war in and around Elaine, Arkansas, was the bloodiest of all. In every case, whites were the aggressors in the large-scale fighting; but blacks fought back, which helps account for the ferocity of the riots. Negroes shed most of the blood everywhere, and black spokesmen termed the months of race riots the "Red Summer" of 1919.[7]

II

Although the major riots took place in the eastern and central sections of the nation, Americans in the southwest also were gripped with severe racial fears, though they could hardly have been alarmed by the comparatively small number of Negroes and "inferior breeds" of European immigrants in their section. The role that these groups played in the East and Midwest was filled instead by Orientals and Mexicans. With their yellow and brown skin color, their tendency to speak languages other

[7] The best account of the Chicago riot can be found in Chicago Commission on Race Relations, *The Negro in Chicago*. The other riots of the period are described in Arthur I. Waskow, *From Race Riot to Sit In* (Garden City, N.Y., 1966), chapters 1–9. As indicated in earlier chapters, race riots were not a new phenomenon in United States history. But never had riots been even remotely as widespread or as violent on *both* sides as in 1919.

than English, and their willingness to work hard for low wages, these peoples clearly established their cultures as inferior in the view of the white majority.

Chinese immigration to the United States was negligible after passage of the Exclusion Act of 1882; but Japanese entrants increased sharply at the turn of the century, setting off demands for further exclusion legislation aimed at this new source of Oriental immigration. "The Japanese are starting the same tide of immigration which we thought we had checked twenty years ago," complained San Francisco's Mayor James Duval Phelan in 1900. "They are not the stuff of which American citizens can be made. . . . Let them keep at a respectful distance." Phelan would continue to inveigh against the presence of Japanese in America for the next thirty years, including a period when he served as United States senator.[8]

Japanese armed forces annihilated the Russian fleet and mangled the Russian army in 1905. Californians, alarmed by this powerful "yellow peril" in the Pacific, joined labor representatives fearful of economic competition and nativists from all classes terrified of "racial mongrelization," to form the influential Asiatic Exclusion League. Under pressure from the league, the San Francisco Board of Education barred Japanese-American children from all but special "Oriental" schools in 1906, creating a major diplomatic issue. To avoid further strife, President Theodore Roosevelt and Secretary of State Elihu Root negotiated the Gentlemen's Agreement with the Japanese government, ending the migration of Japanese laborers to America.

Nonlaborers, especially wives of Japanese men already resident in the United States, continued to enter the country, however. As Japanese families bought land, mostly in the fertile California valleys, demands for anti-Japanese legislation spread from San Francisco throughout the state. An Alien Land Law, passed in 1913, limited Japanese ownership of farms; but in most cases it was evaded easily.

In conformity with the national pattern, the most virulent phase of the agitation against Japanese began in 1919. In September of that year leading California politicians of both parties responded to public clamor for action by meeting "to consider the Japanese question." After the conference, the politicians issued a report stating: "All agreed that their [Japanese-American] loyalty was first to Japan and second, if at all, to America; that they were here in large part in pursuance of a plan to populate the Pacific Slope of America and that they were a peril, economically, politically, and socially."[9]

The California American Legion fought the "peril" by producing a movie, *Shadows of the West*, circulated in 1920. Japanese-American characters in the film were revealed as spies and sex fiends. At the tale's climax, two innocent white girls were rescued from the Oriental fiends by brave Legionnaires—just in time.

The political highlight of this California campaign was an initiative measure placed on the state ballot in 1920, forbidding further purchase of

[8] In Roger Daniels, *The Politics of Prejudice,* University of California Publications in History, Volume 71 (Berkeley and Los Angeles, 1962), p. 21.

[9] In Daniels, *The Politics of Prejudice,* p. 84.

California land by Japanese or their agents. The measure passed by a vote of 668,483 to 222,086. National endorsement of the California position came with the passage of the Immigration Act of 1924, which excluded all Japanese immigration to the United States. California nativists, working for a Constitutional amendment which would deprive American-born Orientals of their citizenship, continued to warn about the menace posed by the "little brown men." But until World War II they were unable to convince even southern congressmen that such drastic action was necessary.

The great fear in the Southwest after the mid-1920s was occasioned by the movement of more than a million Mexicans into that area—at least one-tenth of Mexico's total population. The basis for this migration was the federally financed irrigation of vast stretches of desert land in the area from California to Texas. A series of laws, beginning with the Reclamation Act of 1902, made possible this government action. Then, during the 1920s, Americans drastically shifted their eating habits, consuming a much greater quantity of fruits and vegetables. New canning methods and refrigeration cars made it possible to carry perishable crops long distances and to store them for lengthy periods. The irrigated southwestern lands were ideally suited for production of fruits and vegetables; but these required enormous numbers of laborers with special characteristics to prepare the land and harvest the crops.

Growth and harvest of an acre of wheat during the 1920s required 13 man hours; an acre of lettuce, however, took 125 man hours; and an acre of strawberries took 500 man hours. Very cheap labor, therefore, was a necessity in the Southwest. Furthermore, these low-paid workers would have to farm a reclaimed desert, where temperatures frequently rose above 100 degrees, clearing and planting a terrain that few white Americans understood.

By 1925, the southwestern states produced 40 percent of the nation's fruits, vegetables, and truck crops, almost all on farms developed during the twentieth century. Only an enormous influx of Mexican labor made this production possible. The Mexicans, who could withstand the heat, who knew how to clear the many varieties of desert brush, and who would work for infinitesimal wages at a time when American farm help was scarce, provided about 75 percent of the labor that cultivated the new southwestern crops. They also contributed most of the labor that created cotton fields on irrigated land in Arizona, Texas, and California; as well as 60 percent of the mine workers and approximately 80 percent of the railroad laborers employed in the western states between 1910 and 1930.[10]

Immigration from Mexico, and other Western Hemisphere countries, was not limited by the 1921 and 1924 Immigration Acts, which set quotas for other nations. In 1923 and 1924, Mexican entrants comprised over 12 percent of total immigration to the United States, and in 1927 and 1928 about 20 percent. Almost half a million Mexicans entered the country during the ten-year period from 1920 to 1929, according to official records. However, Labor Department officials estimated illegal entries from Mexico

[10] Carey McWilliams, *North from Mexico* (New York, 1948, 1968), chapter 9.

at two to five times the number who passed through immigration stations. Most of these immigrants crossed the border into Texas and the majority remained there; but at least 200,000 moved to California during the 1920s alone.[11]

Until the late 1920s, the Mexicans were almost universally welcome. They seemed content to live in their own communities, and to exist in squalor, while earning the contempt of native Americans by working at the most menial labor for wages which seldom rose above an average of $100 a month for an entire family.[12] But the passivity of the Mexican laborers was coming to an end.

A suggestion of what was to come occurred in Arizona during 1920 when 4000 cotton field workers—all migrants from Mexico—struck for higher wages. Scores of workers were arrested, the leaders deported, and the strike broken. Mexican-American farm laborers in Texas and California began organizing on a large scale in 1927. To some observers it seemed that they were protesting against social subordination and humiliation as much as they were attempting to improve their economic condition. The *Confederación de Uniones Obreras Mexicanas*, established in southern California in 1927, was able to call out on strike as many as 5000 Mexican-American field workers in the Imperial Valley. Mexicans also comprised three-quarters of the farm workers' union in the lower San Joaquin Valley.

From Texas to California, the pattern was the same. Strikes were broken with large-scale violence, including the use of tear gas, clubs, and guns. Strikers were arrested by legal authorities or kidnapped and beaten by growers' private armies. The leaders were deported. Starting in 1931, California officials resorted to mass deportations. During 1932, over 11,000 Mexicans were "repatriated" from Los Angeles alone.[13]

This series of events, beginning in the 1920s changed for decades to come the dominant attitude of western Americans toward the Mexicans who had built the foundations of their agricultural economy. Creation of labor organizations and consequent strikes ended the myth of the docile

[11] Bureau of the Census, *Historical Statistics of the United States*, chapter C.

[12] McWilliams estimated the average wage at $600 annually per family; but outside of the beet sugar industry the majority of Mexican-American families seem to have earned slightly over $1000 a year. In any case, the average was well below that set by the Bureau of Labor Statistics as the minimum for subsistence. For incomes of large samples of Mexicans in a variety of California agricultural and nonagricultural industries, see *Mexicans in California, Report of Governor C. C. Young's Mexican Fact-Finding Committee* (San Francisco, 1930), chapters 4–5.

[13] The report compiled for the Mexican Fact-Finding Committee on the formation of the chief California unions and their treatment by growers and local officials was both detailed and fair. When the committee's chief investigator showed a copy of his account of the cantaloupe pickers' strike to the district attorney of Imperial County, the official complained that "while the report was on the whole correct and accurate as to details, it gave the erroneous impression that the district attorney's office was unreasonable in its conduct during the labor troubles." Actually the report indicated that the county sheriff, not the district attorney, was arresting strikers indiscriminately. *Mexicans in California*, chapters 6, 7; also McWilliams, *North from Mexico*, chapter 10.

Mexican laborer. Machinery invented late in the 1920s began to replace human labor in fruit and vegetable harvesting. Then the depression halted the steady rise in demand for those crops.

In response to the unrest among agricultural laborers, the governor of California appointed a "Mexican Fact-Finding Committee" which reported in October 1930. The committee employed as investigators social scientists sympathetic with the Mexicans. Nevertheless, as often happens, the group's final report reflected the prejudices of the government officials named to head the project. Its conclusions provided a rationale for the treatment accorded Mexican-Americans during the following decades. The committee estimated that whites comprised less than 10 percent of Mexico's population. It quoted George P. Clements, Director of the Agricultural Department of the Los Angeles Chamber of Commerce, who stated that 13 of the 15 million inhabitants of Mexico were Indians, "as primitive as our own Indians were when the first colonists arrived in America." These barely civilized Indians, the committee concluded, now were inundating California. Forty percent of all alien immigrants entering the state came from Mexico; and the proportion of Mexican migrants who gave California as their eventual destination when they crossed the border increased annually. The committee reported also that Los Angeles police department records "indicate an increasing proportion of arrests of Mexicans in the city." About 40 percent of the Mexican-Americans in California already lived in Los Angeles.[14]

As in the case of Oriental-Americans, California's treatment of Mexican immigrants and their descendents is among the more dismal chapters in the national history. Mobilized by newspapers, politicians, and official publications like the Mexican Fact-Finding Committee report, Californians resorted to violent means of ridding their state of racial minorities. Almost immediately after Japanese-Americans had been dispatched to "relocation" camps in March 1942, police, servicemen, and other citizens in southern California started a campaign of terror against Americans of Mexican origin, especially Mexican-American youths. Beginning in August 1942, police dragnets in Mexican sections of Los Angeles periodically stopped all cars entering or leaving the districts. As many as 600 persons were arrested in one night for possession of dangerous weapons that included jackknives and equipment for changing automobile tires.

In June 1943, young Mexican-Americans and some Negroes were the victims of what California newspapers and police called "zoot-suit riots." Less prejudiced observers termed these events mob violence, and even mass lynching. For almost a week, mobs of hundreds and even one of several thousand roamed those areas of Los Angeles and nearby cities that were inhabited or frequented by Mexicans, savagely beating and stabbing Mexican-Americans and Negroes. Los Angeles police sometimes followed the mobs, arresting the bleeding or unconscious victims on charges ranging from assault to inciting a riot. In no reported cases did the police intervene, except to help beat Mexicans.[15]

---

[14] *Mexicans in California*, pp. 20, 25, 43, 49, 59.
[15] McWilliams, *North from Mexico*, chapters 12, 13. McWilliams led efforts first to prevent, then to end, these events.

The anxiety generated in native Americans by migrant Negroes, Orientals, and Mexicans closely resembled the panic created at the same time by the vast flow of Italian and Slavic immigrants. Some of the country's politicians, editors, and polemicists made the association explicit. Speaking in favor of immigration restriction legislation, Oscar W. Underwood of Alabama, the most influential Democrat in the House of Representatives, contrasted the pure white blood of those who had made America great with the mixture of African and Asian blood that fixed the character of southern European immigrants. In the Senate, while debating the same issue, Fernifold M. Simmons of North Carolina warned that Anglo-Saxon civilization in America was in danger of destruction from immigrants who "are nothing more than the degenerate progeny of the Asiatic hordes which, long centuries ago, overran the shores of the Mediterranean . . . [and] the spawn of the Phoenician curse." Thomas Abercrombie of Alabama also pointed to *prima facie* evidence of the new immigrants' inferiority: "The color of thousands of them differs materially from that of the Anglo-Saxon."[16]

A torrent of literature expressing this sense of white racial superiority flowed from the presses in the 1920s. The most popular polemic on the subject was Theodore Lothrop Stoddard's *The Rising Tide of Color Against White World Supremacy*, which appeared in 1920. In this and a score of other books, Stoddard parroted the theme developed in prewar racist literature, that progress and civilization were products of "Nordic" blood. This magnificent breed had "clean, virile, genius-bearing blood, streaming down the ages through the unerring action of heredity, which, in anything like a favorable environment, will multiply itself, solve our problems, and sweep us on to higher and nobler destinies." Stoddard warned of the danger to Nordic supremacy from less civilized eastern and southern European, as well as Oriental and other "colored," peoples. Another popular author on the same topic, Henry Pratt Fairchild, a former president of the American Sociological Society, wrote in 1926 that "if America is to remain a stable nation it must continue a white man's country for an indefinite period to come." Fairchild's statement was part of a plea, not for Jim Crow laws in the South, but for immigration restriction directed largely against "inferior" European races.[17]

The alleged relationship between darker peoples and urban problems was made to seem even more menacing during 1919–1920 by those who attempted to associate these groups with the specter of international com-

[16] John Higham, *Strangers in the Land: Patterns of American Nativism 1860–1925* (New Brunswick, N.J., 1955), pp. 164–65, 168.
[17] Theodore Lothrop Stoddard, *The Rising Tide of Color Against White World Supremacy* (New York, 1920), p. 89; Thomas F. Gossett, *Race: The History of an Idea in America* (Dallas, 1963), pp. 387, 395–96. A recent survey of anti-Negro literature in the United States concluded that "By 1925 a marked change was occurring in the attitude of scientific circles toward the subject of race . . . By 1930 the amount of scientific literature purporting to prove the Negro's alleged inferiority had precipitously declined." A conspicuous reduction in the amount of popular anti-Negro writing followed immediately afterward. I. A. Newby, *Jim Crow's Defense: Anti-Negro Thought in America 1900–1930* (Baton Rouge, La., 1965), pp. 50–51.

munism. By mid-1919 almost every nation in eastern and central Europe had undergone a communist revolution, several of them successful, although only the Bolshevik government in Russia retained power. Russian and Baltic language organizations in the United States moved—or were moved by their leaders—into the new American communist parties, partly out of pride in the Bolshevik achievements. Probably 90 percent of the parties' members in 1919 were eastern European immigrants. Several men who became Bolshevik leaders in Russia during the Revolution, including Leon Trotsky, sat out most of World War I in New York City. Therefore, there was some slight basis in fact for Attorney-General A. Mitchell Palmer's assertion in 1920 that the Bolshevik triumph was led by "a small clique of outcasts from the East Side of New York. . . . Because a disreputable alien—Leon Bronstein, the man who now calls himself Trotsky—can inaugurate a reign of terror from his throne room in the Kremlin; because this lowest of all types known to New York can sleep in the Czar's bed . . . should America be swayed by such doctrines?"[18]

Palmer's alert antiradical division, directed by J. Edgar Hoover, discovered that American Negroes were deeply involved in the communist conspiracy. Hoover, an avid reader of dissident books, journals, and newspapers, hardly missed an expression of seditious propaganda. Although there is no evidence that Negroes took part in founding the communist parties in September 1919, or that any joined soon afterward, dozens of black propagandists sounded enough like revolutionists to convince the Justice Department experts that they constituted an authentic menace. The antiradical division's collection of this inflammatory literature was published in the fall of 1919 in a pamphlet entitled "Radicalism and Sedition among the Negroes as Reflected in Their Publications." Among the black radicals cited were A. Philip Randolph, a moderate socialist best known as president of the Pullman Car Porters; and Marcus Garvey, one of the country's more enthusiastic champions of capitalism. Both men had written powerful diatribes against contemporary American white culture, especially its racist aspects, which sounded to Hoover like calls to revolution.[19]

Theodore Lothrop Stoddard also warned his fellow countrymen that the world-wide movement to undermine the Nordic's natural superiority was being encouraged if not directed from Moscow: "In every quarter of the globe . . . the Bolshevik agitators whisper in the ears of discontented colored men their gospel of hatred and revenge. Every nationalist aspiration, every political grievance, every social discrimination, is fuel for Bolshevism's hellish incitement to racial as well as to class war."[20]

[18] Palmer is quoted more fully on this subject in Stanley Coben, *A. Mitchell Palmer: Politician* (New York, 1963), p. 198, and chapters 11 and 12, *passim*.

[19] A. Mitchell Palmer, "Radicalism and Sedition among the Negroes as Reflected in Their Publications," Exhibit 10, *Investigation Activities of the Department of Justice*, Volume XII, Senate Document 153, 66 Cong. 1 Sess. (Washington, D.C., 1919), pp. 161–87. By far the best account of Negroes' role in the American communist movement after World War I can be found in Theodore Draper, *American Communism and Soviet Russia* (New York, 1960), chapter 15.

[20] Stoddard, *The Rising Tide of Color Against White World Supremacy*, p. 220.

Almost all the racial fears felt by white Americans after World War
I were distilled and promulgated by one organization: the Ku Klux Klan.
The Klan gave voice also to the traditional culture—such as the dangers
carried by new ideas and moral standards. The KKK of that period was
started by a small group in Atlanta during 1915. The time and place were
chosen to coincide with excitement generated by the showing of the motion picture "The Birth of a Nation." In that tremendously popular epic,
white-hooded Klansmen of the post-Civil War era were depicted redeeming the South and its most cherished values from the clutches of black
Reconstruction.

Until the cultural crisis of 1919–1920, however, the twentieth-century Klan remained a small, southern organization. When it expanded, the
professional publicists who managed the membership drive discovered that
the largest potential source of Klan dues lay not in Georgia or South
Carolina, nor even in Alabama and Mississippi, those traditional strong-
holds of vigilante justice for Negroes. The greatest response to the Klan's
brand of racism appeared in growing cities of the Southwest and Midwest: Shreveport, Dallas, Youngstown, Indianapolis, Dayton, and Detroit;
and in smaller cities like Joliet, Illinois; Hammond, Indiana; Oklahoma
City; San Antonio; Babylon, New York; Camden, New Jersey; and Anaheim, California.

In areas where Klan organizers—or Kleagles, as the invisible empire
called them—were most successful in recruiting, they entered towns instructed to discover the prejudices of prospective members, then to exploit
these peoples' complaints. At first it was assumed that the Klan once again
would be chiefly a device for keeping southern Negroes and their white
friends in place. When he called together the first small group of Klansmen in 1915, William J. Simmons explained that Negroes were getting
"uppity." Klan recruiting efforts played cleverly on the Reconstruction
Klan's reputation for punishing ambitious Negroes and for protecting
white women against threats to their purity. A Klan recruiting lecturer
promised: "The Negro, in whose blood flows the mad desire for race
amalgamation, is more dangerous than a maddened wild beast and he must
and will be controlled."[21]

However, when questions and applications from all over the country
poured into Atlanta headquarters during 1920, Imperial Wizard Simmons
readily conceded that Negroes were not the only enemies of 100 percent
Americans. Furthermore, he announced: "Any real man, any native-born
white American citizen who is not affiliated with any foreign institution
(that is, not a Catholic) and who loves his country and his flag may become a member of the Ku Klux Klan, whether he lives north, south, east,
or west."[22] The only other requirement for membership was a man's will-

---

[21] In Kenneth T. Jackson, *The Ku Klux Klan in the City, 1915–1930* (New York,
1967), p. 22.

[22] In Charles C. Alexander, *The Ku Klux Klan in the Southwest* (Lexington, Ky.,
1966), p. 9. The prejudice of Klan leaders against women, who were segregated
in separate organizations, deserves more exploration by historians than it has received.

ingness to part with a $10 initiation fee, of which $4 went to the Kleagle, $2 to Simmons, $2.50 to the publicists in Atlanta, and the rest to the local Grand Goblin. Further payments were extracted later for membership dues and for uniforms (sheets), which were supplied from Atlanta.

Throughout the nation, Kleagles discovered a fear of Catholics, Jews, and recent immigrants, as well as Negroes. They also found native Americans worried about the erosion of moral standards, and angry about widespread lawlessness. Frequently this laxity was associated with foreign or colored races. Violation of prohibition statutes especially was blamed on urban minorities. Established governmental institutions seemed incapable of handling these elements—incapable of protecting white, Anglo-Saxon Victorian civilization. So Kleagles received a warm welcome when they came to town and gave native Americans an opportunity to fight back. One of the most effective pieces of Klan recruiting literature read:

> Every criminal, every gambler, every thug, every libertine, every girl ruiner, every home wrecker, every wife beater, every dope peddler, every moonshiner, every crooked politician, every pagan Papist priest, every shyster lawyer, every K. of C., every white slaver, every Rome-controlled newspaper, every black spider —is fighting the Klan. Think it over, which side are you on?[23]

Local chapters took action against what they considered indecent motion pictures and books. They destroyed stills, and attacked prostitutes and gamblers. Groups of hooded men even invaded lovers' lanes and beat up the occupants of cars, in one case beating a young couple to death. This work was considered no less important than political efforts to destroy parochial schools, to enforce Bible reading in classrooms, and to defeat Catholic and Jewish candidates for public office.

Although membership figures remain largely shrouded in secrecy, available records indicate that the hooded empire probably enrolled over 5 million members during the 1920s, with a peak membership of about 2 million in 1924. Because members were concentrated so heavily in certain northern and western areas, the Klan won considerable political power in at least six states, and in large sections of about ten others.

In the great cities, however, and eventually in the country as a whole, the Klan discovered that the time had passed when an organization devoted to the supremacy of white Anglo-Saxon Protestants could operate both violently and safely. In some respects the whole movement for 100 percent Americanism was an anachronism in the post World War I era; but the Klan especially depended upon a widespread delusion that this was still the world of Wade Hampton and the young Rudyard Kipling.

The Klan's fate in New York City was pathetic—and illustrative. In the world's wealthiest city, the nation's largest by far, with a million native-born white Protestants among its inhabitants, the KKK was treated like a band of shabby criminals. The great majority of New York's population of 6 million were Catholics and Jews; and the Irish Catholics who dominated the city's politics and police force were especially offended

[23] Jackson, *The Ku Klux Klan in the City*, p. 19.

when the Klan dared organize in New York. The city seethed with bigotry against Negroes, Catholics, and Jews, including considerable distaste
within these groups directed at members of the others. But even among
white Protestant New Yorkers eligible for Klan membership, few were so
foolhardy during the 1920s as to identify themselves publicly with an organization so clearly marked for disaster. It was not an absence of racial
prejudice that doomed the Klan in New York, but rather the fact that in
most respects the city already was controlled by the "minority" groups
which the Klan aimed to suppress.

A year after Kleagles entered the city, two grand juries commenced
investigations of the secret order. Special legislation, directed at the KKK,
forced all unincorporated associations to file annual membership lists. New
York Mayor John F. Hylan denounced Klan members as "anarchists,"
and the city police force was ordered to "ferret out these despicable disloyal persons who are attempting to organize a society, the aims and purposes of which are of such a character that were they to prevail, the
foundations of our country would be destroyed."[24]

In most of New York City, the customary march of hooded Klansmen, carrying banners with messages that were so popular in Kokomo and
Anaheim, would have been a feat of amazing courage. In certain sections
—the lower east side and Harlem, for example—such a march would have
been the most foolhardy event since General Custer's seventh cavalry left
a day early for the Little Bighorn. New York's borough of Queens, however, remained predominantly suburban and Protestant in the 1920s. Although subject to hostile laws and unsympathetic policies there as in the
rest of New York City, a Klan chapter continued to operate in Queens.
In 1927, it received permission to take part in the Queens County Memorial Day Parade to the local Soldier's Monument.

Both the Boy Scouts and the Knights of Columbus withdrew from
the patriotic celebration rather than march in the same line as the KKK.
The New York police did their best to stop or divert the Klan members,
but something less than their best to hold back angry crowds determined to halt the hooded patriots. After 1500 Klansmen and Klanswomen
—including a 100-man paramilitary unit—broke through several police
barricades, the police simply left the KKK to the parade audience. According to the *New York Times:* "Women fought women and spectators
fought the policemen and the Klansmen, as their desire dictated. Com-
batants were knocked down. Klan banners were shredded. . . ." Five
Klansmen were arrested during the melée. Finally the police ceased holding back traffic as the remnant of the Klan cavalcade passed, and motorists
tried to run the white-robed marchers down. The Klan parade disintegrated, although three Klansmen in an automobile managed to reach the
war memorial monument and placed a wreath with the KKK signature
upon it. The wreath promptly was stolen.[25]

Throughout the Northeast, the Klan found only mild support, and
even that sometimes aroused the kind of mob violence for which the Klan

---

[24] Jackson, *The Ku Klux Klan in the City,* p. 177.
[25] *New York Times,* May 31, 1927, pp. 1, 7.

itself was so well known in the South. In Boston, Mayor James Michael Curley incited crowds by speaking before flaming crosses—the Klan's favorite symbol—and pointing to the cross while he shouted to his predominantly Irish Catholic audiences: "There it burns, the cross of hatred upon which Our Lord, Jesus Christ, was crucified—the cross of human avarice, and not the cross of love and charity. . . ." Curley declared Klan meetings illegal even in private homes, and in Boston he obtained support in his crusade not only from the City Council, but also from city's Catholic and Jewish leaders. It was just as well for the Klan that they did not meet in Boston; houses of people only suspected of being Klan members were attacked with bricks and stones.[26]

In Pittsburgh, another center of Catholic population, Kleagles enjoyed great success in recruiting members. Ten thousand Klansmen from the area, led by the national Imperial Wizard, Hiram Wesley Evans, gathered outside the nearby town of Carnegie for an initiation rally in August 1923. When they marched into town, however, they were met not with cheers, but with angry shouts and a hail of rocks and bottles. The Klansmen continued until a citizen started shooting and a Klan member fell dead. There were no further Klan parades in the Pittsburgh area. The Klan chapter in Perth Amboy, New Jersey, obtained substantial police protection for its meetings; but guards availed little in that heavily Catholic and Jewish industrial and resort area. The entire city police and fire department, protecting a meeting of 500 Knights of the Secret Order, were overwhelmed by a mob of 6000 on the evening of August 30, 1923, and the Ku Kluxers were beaten, kicked, and stoned as they fled.

When the Klan reached its peak strength in 1924, less than 4 percent of its members lived in the Northeast—the entire area from Portland, Maine, through Baltimore, Maryland—despite strenuous organizational efforts. The Klan itself claimed that over 40 percent of its membership lived in the three midwestern states of Indiana, Illinois, and Ohio. Even in that hospitable area, however, the Klan's brand of racism was not welcome everywhere.

For a while it appeared that white Protestants in Chicago, disturbed by a rapid influx of Negroes and immigrants, and by the city's infamous lawlessness during the 1920s, might make it the hub of the Klan empire. By 1922, Chicago had more Klan members than any other city, and initiation fees continued to flow from the midwestern metropolis into Atlanta. When Imperial Kleagle Edward Young Clarke visited the city in June 1922, he announced that 30,000 Chicagoans already belonged to the Klan, and implied that the branch soon would be large enough to help enforce the law in Chicago, thus reducing the city's alarming crime rate. In smaller communities, where violators of Klan mores were easier to intimidate, bootleggers were forced to obey Prohibition laws, and gamblers and other sinners were punished by the secret order. When a major civic association started investigating crime in Chicago, however, the group's leader—a prominent clergyman—was found shot to death in Cicero, Illinois,

---

[26] Jackson, *The Ku Klux Klan in the City*, p. 182. The Klan's activities in northern cities like Boston, Pittsburgh, and Chicago are described in Jackson's volume.

then the center of Al Capone's operations. After Clarke returned to Atlanta, the Chicago Klan wisely continued to leave the war against crime to the police, the FBI, and the Treasury Department, even though these organizations were overwhelmed by the task.

As soon as the Klan's strength in Chicago became known, powerful enemies sprang up to protect the threatened minority groups. Mayor "Big Bill" Thompson, elected with crucial aid from Negro votes, denounced the Klan. The City Council opened an investigation of the society, and made its findings available to other state and local political bodies. One consequence was a bill prohibiting the wearing of masks in public, that passed the Illinois House of Representatives by a vote of 100 to 2, and the State Senate by 26 to 1. The City Council itself resolved by a vote of 56 to 2 to rid the city's payroll of Kluxers. Within a week, two firemen were suspended and the Klan's attorney had to be rushed from Atlanta to take legal steps halting the purge. Meanwhile the American Unity League, dominated by Catholics, started publishing the names of Klan members, concentrating on those in business and the professions. Salesmen, milkmen, and even a bank president were forced out of their jobs when their customers refused to deal with Klan members. The disheartened bank president, complying with his board of directors' request that he resign, explained, "I signed a petition for membership in the Klan several months ago, but did not know it was anything else than an ordinary fraternal order."[27] He may not have realized either how many Jewish, Irish, and Negro depositors had placed their money in his bank.

A counterattack was also launched in the press. In a front-page editorial headlined "To Hell with the Ku Klux Klan!" the Chicago *Defender*, the nation's leading Negro newspaper, advised readers to get ready to fight against "those who now try to win by signs and robes what their fathers lost by fire and sword." A prominent rabbi warned that "Protestantism is on trial. Protestantism must destroy Ku Kluxism or Ku Kluxism will destroy Protestantism."[28]

Political candidates backed publicly by the Klan fared badly in Chicago. Enough excitement was generated during the city election of 1924 to bring forth a series of threatening letters from the Klan. Some of these went to Chicago's largest Negro church, which was completely destroyed one night by fire. On the other hand, bombs demolished a shop just vacated by the Klan journal, *Dawn*, and other bombs were exploded against offices of Klan members and of advertisers in Klan periodicals.

The accumulation of outside pressures on the Klan in Chicago—political, economic, and physical—served to increase internal dissension in the order. Although the Klan enrolled well over 50,000 members in Chicago by 1924, at the end of that year the organization was practically dormant in the city. For similar reasons it already was on the way to destruction as a major political and social force throughout the United States. The failure of the KKK, after temporary success in the immediate postwar years, should not be interpreted as a sign that racism was waning. The Klan simply had tried to take on too many enemies. The "minorities"

---

[27] Jackson, *The Ku Klux Klan in the City*, p. 104.
[28] Jackson, *The Ku Klux Klan in the City*, p. 102.

which the Klan was organized to suppress possessed far more members, votes, wealth, and almost every other kind of power than the Klan itself. The order's fate should have served as a warning to the American people of the changes taking place in a world in which white Protestants were far outnumbered; but it did not.

III

Another ominous development for the future of "Nordic" supremacy in America was the creation after World War I of an impressive movement for black nationalism and black power. Although dozens of organizations devoted to those ends were formed during the postwar period, by far the largest was the Universal Negro Improvement Association, sometimes called the Garvey movement after its founder Marcus Garvey. The history of the UNIA, and of black as well as white reaction to it, illuminates many qualities of the ferment that arose forty years later when Negro protest again tended to move in the direction of black separatism.

The societal dislocations which gave rise to the movement for 100 percent Americanism, affected Negro Americans also. The shift from the rural South to densely populated northern cities, despite the obvious compensations, left even the most adaptable migrants somewhat disoriented. Not only were familiar and loved friends and relatives left behind, but so were southern customs, games, climate, landmarks, and to some extent even language. For those who made the move directly from the farm, all these difficulties were magnified. Certain aspects of the white nativist response—the great increase in lynchings and Klan membership beginning in 1919, the ferocious race riots, the organized hostility of white property owners—also helped make black Americans susceptible to a movement similar, in some respects, to that of the Klansmen. They differed drastically, however, in one crucially important respect: Garvey's movement attempted to uplift a long-exploited people; whereas the Klan intended to continue suppression of racial minorities.

Marcus Garvey repeatedly stated: "I believe in a pure black race, just as all self-respecting whites believe in a pure white race."[29] He scorned attempts at integration and ridiculed Negro leaders who worked in any way toward that objective. Whites respected nothing but power, he insisted, and Negro equality could come only from black unity in America combined with a strong black nation in Africa.

Garvey, a stocky, intense, black-skinned man, born on the West Indian island of Jamaica, was a dynamic orator with all the charismatic qualities of the successful visionary, including an inability to handle administrative details. His speeches, and to a lesser degree his essays in his newspaper, *Negro World*, awakened a pride in their race and color among millions of Negroes throughout the world. Garvey delighted in telling his audiences: "I am the equal of any white man." A black skin, he declared repeatedly, far from being a badge of shame, was a glorious symbol of

[29] Amy Jacques Garvey, ed., *Philosophy and Opinions of Marcus Garvey* (New York, 1923), p. 37.

racial greatness, even superiority; a reminder of the African past when, he claimed, black civilizations were the most advanced in the world. These could be thrilling words to Negroes born and raised in the North as well as the South, who had been trained never to think such thoughts, much less express them publicly.

The 1920 UNIA convention, held in New York, was a memorable event for American Negroes, and a disturbing experience for whites accustomed to Negro subservience. Black delegates attended from almost every nation in the Western Hemisphere, as well as from several African states. The convention opened with a silent march by thousands of delegates through the streets of Harlem. The parade, and all subsequent activities connected with the convention, were pervaded by a fervent spirit of black nationalism.

At the convention's climax, Garvey addressed an overcapacity crowd of 25,000 jammed into Madison Square Garden: "We are the descendants of a suffering people. We are the descendants of a people determined to suffer no longer." In another speech during the convention he warned that Negroes never again would fight in the service of whites, as they had during World War I: "The first dying that is to be done by the black man in the future will be done to make himself free."[30]

Black Americans were far from unanimous in accepting Garvey's leadership. Among New York's Negro intellectuals—vitally involved in creating their own image of the "new Negro"—hostility to Garvey's style if not the content of his message, was common. Garvey's disdain for the intellectuals, and for all light-skinned Negroes, his enthusiasm for capitalism, and his emphasis on action in Africa rather than in the United States, displeased the men who led the Harlem literary and artistic renaissance of the 1920s. Established Negro politicians in major cities also criticized Garvey and his program, although some important Negro dissident political organizations in Chicago and New York were more sympathetic. This criticism became more intense when Garvey's plans for a steamship line, and then for an industrial corporation, failed.

As Garvey and his lieutenants spoke increasingly of violence, they further antagonized the Negro intellectuals and worried the politicians. The UNIA leader even appeared willing to reach some agreement with the Ku Klux Klan, defending this attempt by explaining: "I regard the Klan, the Anglo-Saxon Clubs and White American Societies as better friends of the race than all other groups of hypocritical whites put together." Garvey's ambassador to the League of Nations, William Sherrill, unsettled some Americans by stating in 1922: "Black folk as well as white who tamper with the Universal Negro Improvement Association are going to die."[31] Not long afterward, one of Garvey's most vociferous critics, James W. H. Eason, was shot and murdered in New Orleans where he had gone to address an anti-Garvey rally. Two of Garvey's henchmen had arrived in New Orleans about the same time as Eason; however, the men were acquitted of complicity in the crime. Nevertheless, the

---

[30] In Edmund David Cronon, *Black Moses, the Story of Marcus Garvey and the Universal Negro Improvement Association* (Madison, Wis., 1955), p. 65.

[31] In Cronon, *Black Moses*, pp. 109, 190.

murder, and the growing paramilitary element in Garvey's organization, turned Negro intellectuals increasingly toward open opposition.

A week after Eason's murder, eight of the most highly respected Negro leaders in the country protested to the Justice Department that Garvey's trial for mail fraud already had been postponed for a year and a half. They asked why this "unscrupulous demagogue" was being treated differently than ordinary citizens. Garvey responded by charging that the "Committee of Eight" were almost all octoroons or quadroons, or married to quadroons, and were enemies of the black race. Nevertheless, Garvey soon was tried, convicted, sentenced to prison, and a few years later deported to the West Indies.

Garvey's organization disintegrated after his removal from the scene. By the mid-1920s, however, Garvey's was not the only movement unable to sustain the high promise of 1919–1920. Dozens of smaller black nationalist groups also were fading, including W. E. B. Du Bois's Pan African movement. The African Blood Brotherhood, a propagandistic society whose members included some of the most intelligent and able black leaders in the country, merged and practically disappeared into the Communist Party during this period. A meeting in 1924 of representatives from sixty-four Negro organizations—ranging in the political spectrum from the NAACP to the Blood Brotherhood—seemed to foreshadow unified action on some issues, at least; but the movement toward unity soon faltered.[32]

At about the same time, membership in the Ku Klux Klan began falling rapidly, despite a temporary recovery during the crusade against Al Smith's presidential candidacy in 1928. The massive "Americanization" campaign directed at recent immigrants lost its urgency after passage of immigration restriction legislation in 1924. A marked decline in the publication of pseudo-scientific racist literature was noted about 1925. Even efforts to enforce prohibition, and to spread and protect the doctrines of fundamentalist religion, were reduced in fervor after the mid-1920s.

It would be an exaggeration to state that "normalcy" had returned; that the movement for 100 percent Americanism was successful enough to obviate the need for organizations like the Klan; that dissident groups like Garvey's and the communists were doomed by that success. Too many other factors were involved; such simple statements provide only partial explanations. However, they *are* partial explanations. The movement to protect the established culture, which included the maintenance of attitudes and institutions based on the concept of white racial superiority, did accomplish many of its objectives. Nevertheless, it left the major problems facing modern American society basically unsolved, especially those involving racial and cultural differences within the society. The holding action conducted by 100 percent Americans from 1915 to 1930 handed these problems to future generations, who would have to deal with them in even more acute forms, at a time when temporary expedients would not suffice.

[32] Alain Locke, "The Negro Speaks for Himself," *The Survey* (April 15, 1924), pp. 71–72; Draper, *American Communism and Soviet Russia*, chapter 15.

Suggestions for Further Reading

Works that survey various portions of the early twentieth century are Robert Wiebe, *The Search for Order, 1877–1920** (Hill and Wang, 1967); Henry F. May, *The End of American Innocence** (Knopf, 1959); William E. Leuchtenberg, *The Perils of Prosperity, 1914–32** (University of Chicago Press, 1958); and Frederick Lewis Allen, *Only Yesterday** (Harper & Row, 1931). Perhaps the best description of the conflicts engendered in American life during this period is given in novelist John Dos Passos' monumental trilogy, *U.S.A.** (Houghton Mifflin, 1937).

Studies of the Progressive period include Richard Hofstadter, *The Age of Reform: From Bryan to F.D.R.** (Knopf, 1965); John Chamberlain, *Farewell to Reform: The Rise, Life and Decay of the Progressive Mind in America** (Day, 1932); Gabriel Kolko, *The Triumph of Conservatism** (Free Press, 1963); and James Weinstein, *The Corporate Ideal in the Liberal State, 1900–1918** (Beacon, 1968). Contemporaneous works of interest are Lincoln Steffens, *The Shame of the Cities** (McClure, Phillips, 1904); John Spargo, *The Bitter Cry of Children** (Macmillan, 1904); Robert Hunter, *Poverty** (Macmillan, 1904); and Herbert Croly, *The Promise of American Life** (Macmillan, 1909).

William L. O'Neill has written an interpretive history of feminism published under the title *Everyone Was Brave: The Rise and Fall of Feminism in America** (Quadrangle, 1969). Other histories of feminism include Eleanor Flexner, *Century of Struggle: The Woman's Rights Movement in the United States** (Harvard University Press, 1959), and Aileen Kraditor, *The Ideas of the Woman Suffrage Movement** (Columbia University Press, 1965). To be used with care but valuable nevertheless are Andrew Sinclair, *The Emancipation of the American Woman** (Harper & Row, 1965), originally published under the title *The Better Half;* Robert E. Riegel, *American Feminists** (University of Kansas Press, 1963); and David Morgan, *Suffragists and Democrats: The Politics of Woman Suffrage in America* (Michigan State University Press, 1972). A history of the movement written by the leaders themselves is Elizabeth Cady Stanton et al., *The History of Woman Suffrage* (6 vols.; Fowler and Wells, 1881–1922). Aileen Kraditor has edited a valuable collection of documents from the movement entitled *Up from the Pedestal: Selected Writings in the History of American Feminism** (Quadrangle, 1968). Two important publications by leading feminists are Charlotte Perkins Gilman, *Women and Economics** (Small-Maynard, 1898), and Carrie Chapman Catt and Nettie Rogers Shuler, *Women Suffrage and Politics** (Scribner, 1923). Good biographies of feminist leaders are Mary Gray Peck's *Carrie Chapman Catt* (Wilson, 1944), and Alma Lutz's *Created Equal: A Biography of Elizabeth Cady*

---

* Available in paperback edition.

197

Stanton (Day, 1940) and *Susan B. Anthony: Rebel, Crusader, Humanitarian* (Beacon, 1959). Important works on special problems include Anne Firor Scott, *The Southern Lady: From Pedestal to Politics, 1830–1936** (University of Chicago Press, 1970); Gerda Lerner (ed.), *Black Women in White America** (Pantheon, 1972); and Barbara Mayer Wertheimer, *We Were There: The Story of Working Women in America* (Pantheon Books, 1977). Changing sexual mores are reflected in June Sochen, *The New Woman: Feminism in Greenwich Village, 1910–1920** (Quadrangle, 1972); William L. O'Neill, *Divorce in the Progressive Era** (Yale University Press, 1967); and David J. Pivar, *Purity Crusade: Sexual Morality and Social Control, 1868–1900** (Greenwood, 1973).

Patrick Renshaw has written a short history of the IWW entitled *The Wobblies** (Doubleday, 1967). Apart from Melvyn Dubofsky's work, *We Shall Be All: A History of the Industrial Workers of the World* (Quadrangle, 1969), the best available source of information on the Wobblies is the collection of documents from the movement edited by Joyce L. Kornbluh, *Rebel Voices: An I.W.W. Anthology** (University of Michigan Press, 1964). On the history of labor in the early twentieth century, see John Laslett, *Labor and the Left: A Study of Socialist and Radical Influences in the American Labor Movement, 1881–1924* (Basic Books, 1970); Irving Bernstein, *The Lean Years: A History of the American Worker, 1920–1933** (Houghton Mifflin, 1960); and David Brody, *Labor in Crisis: The Steel Strike of 1919** (Lippincott, 1965).

Arna Bontemps and Jack Conroy consider the migration of blacks to urban areas early in the new century in *They Seek a City* (Doubleday, 1945), expanded and published in paperback under the title *Anyplace But Here.** Also of interest is the contemporaneous work by Emmett J. Scott, *Negro Migration During the War** (Oxford University Press, 1920). An excellent new study is Florette Henri, *Black Migration: Movement North, 1900–1920** (Anchor Books/Doubleday, 1975). Studies of the black migration that focus on specific cities include Gilbert Osofsky, *Harlem: The Making of a Ghetto** (Harper & Row, 1966); Allan H. Spear, *Black Chicago: The Making of a Negro Ghetto, 1890–1920** (University of Chicago Press, 1967); and Constance M. Green, *The Secret City: A History of Race Relations in the Nation's Capital** (Princeton University Press, 1967).

Racial strife is the subject of Allen Grimshaw (ed.), *Racial Violence in the United States* (Aldine, 1969). For studies of specific race riots, see the report of the Chicago Commission on Race Relations, *The Negro in Chicago: A Study of Race Relations and a Race Riot* (University of Chicago Press, 1922); William Ivy Hair, *Carnival of Fury: Robert Charles and the New Orleans Race Riot of 1900* (Louisiana State University Press, 1976); Robert V.

Haynes, *A Night of Violence: The Houston Riot of 1917* (Louisiana State University Press, 1976); and Elliott M. Rudwick, *Race Riot at East St. Louis, July 2, 1917** (Southern Illinois University Press, 1964). Organized antiblack agitation is described in David Chalmers, *Hooded Americanism** (Doubleday, 1965), and in Kenneth Jackson, *The Ku Klux Klan in the City, 1915–1930** (Oxford University Press, 1968).

The best studies of the ghetto revolts of the 1960s are found in David Boesel and Peter H. Rossi (eds.), *Cities Under Siege: An Anatomy of the Ghetto Riots* (Basic Books, 1971), and *The Report of the National Advisory Commission on Civil Disorders** (U.S. Government Printing Office, 1968), published also by Bantam Books. For descriptions of the changing mood of the black community that led to the eruptions, see Allen J. Matusow, "From Civil Rights to Black Power: The Case of SNCC, 1960–1966," in Barton J. Bernstein and Allen J. Matusow (eds.), *Twentieth-Century America: Recent Interpretations** (Harcourt Brace Jovanovich, 1969), pp. 531–57, and Vincent Harding, "Black Radicalism: The Road from Montgomery," in Alfred F. Young (ed.), *Dissent: Explorations in the History of American Radicalism** (Northern Illinois University Press, 1968), pp. 321–54.

Charles E. Silberman, in *Crisis in Black and White** (Random House, 1964), provides an excellent study of the background to the racial explosions that took place in Northern cities in the mid-1960s. In *Dark Ghetto: Dilemmas of Social Power** (Harper & Row, 1965), Kenneth B. Clark explores the psychological aspects of life in a black ghetto. Claude Brown is concerned with many of the same themes in his autobiographical *Manchild in the Promised Land** (Macmillan, 1965). Robert Conot's excellent *Rivers of Blood, Years of Darkness** (Bantam, 1967) describes the background and foreground of the Watts rebellion of 1965.

Attempts to suppress radicals at the conclusion of the First World War are described in R. K. Murray, *The Red Scare: A Study in National Hysteria, 1919–1920** (University of Minnesota Press, 1955); in two works by Stanley Coben, *A. Mitchell Palmer: Politician* (Columbia University Press, 1963) and "A Study in Nativism: The American Red Scare of 1919–20," *Political Science Quarterly*, Vol. 79 (March, 1964), 52–75; and Julian F. Jaffee, *Crusade Against Radicalism: New York During the Red Scare, 1914–1924* (Kennikat Press, 1972). For a more general study, see William Preston, Jr., *Aliens and Dissenters: Federal Suppression of Radicals, 1903–1933** (Harvard University Press, 1963). The most significant anarchist trial of the twentieth century is closely examined in G. L. Joughin and E. S. Morgan (eds.), *The Legacy of Sacco and Vanzetti** (Harcourt Brace Jovanovich, 1948).

3

Depression
and War

The Okie Impact

WALTER J. STEIN

Migrant farm workers have been and remain perhaps the most consistently depressed segment of the American labor force. Wandering from harvest to harvest, up and down both coasts, these low-paid agricultural laborers never have enough steady work to maintain even a passable standard of living. Their children rarely stay in one community long enough to have successful school experiences; instead, they tend to pass the school years in the fields, while local truant officers look the other way. Because they have no home base, the migrant workers seldom have a chance to exercise their political rights; and because they are relatively few in number, they have little economic or social influence in the areas they traverse. Their labor serves primarily to put money in the pockets of those engaged in large-scale agriculture—the current "agribusiness."

An important factor in the success of large-scale agriculture in this country has been the cooperation of local, state, and national political and law enforcement authorities with landowners. In industrial labor disputes, government forces have generally supported the factory owners and managers against the workers. They have demonstrated an even more negative attitude toward agricultural workers, as witnessed by the persistence of chattel slavery as a source of agricultural labor until the second half of the nineteenth century. In the late nineteenth century the convict-lease system, vagrancy laws, and other laws drastically limiting the freedom of the individual working person turned the South into a near-feudal state.

In the South the emphasis was on making the labor force stay put, but in the West the important thing was to keep the labor force in motion—up through California, into Oregon and Washington, and back again, following the harvests of the fruits and vegetables for which the West Coast is justly famous.

Through the years of this century, much of the migrant labor population in California has been of non-European ancestry. Mexican-Americans, in particular, have often found that the only work available to them was at harvest time. Frequently, the structures of society have been marshalled against these minority populations in a manner suggestive of Jim Crow in the South. Segregated schools, segregated housing, and clearly discriminatory social and political practices have severely restricted the freedom of minorities all along the West Coast. Not only non-whites but whites as well have borne the terror of vigilante justice and lynch law in the West—practices in which California has taken second place only to the South. Indeed, the lawlessness of the western mining camps and of San Francisco's Barbary Coast in the nineteenth century is legendary. Today, although agribusiness has replaced mining as the state's leading industry, the patterns of coalitions against agricultural workers' groups on the part of public officials, law-enforcement authorities, and leaders of business and industry remain much as they were in the nineteenth century.

Throughout most of the history of California, its farm laborers were not European in ancestry, but during the great depression this situation was altered for a time. Drought on the Great Plains created a vast dust bowl where the topsoil had literally blown away. Generally depressed agricultural prices led to the foreclosure of many small farms and the subsequent homelessness of many farm families. Increasing mechanization made it difficult for those small farmers who still owned their land to compete with large-scale operations. All these factors led to a vast migration of white farm families from the Great Plains to the West Coast. Celebrated, if that is the word, in song and story, these migrants moved into California looking for work and a new home.

In his study of this migration, Walter J. Stein, of the University of Winnipeg, Canada, describes the peculiar problems faced both by the migrants and by the receiving society. In the selection reprinted below, the author points out the unique quality of these migratory workers. Although they were migrants when they entered California, they intended to stay, migrants no more. This presented the state and local authorities with a set of problems they had not been required to face in dealing with the traditional non-white migrant stream. California society ultimately absorbed many of the "Okies" into defense plants during the Second World War, and the migrant farm labor population returned to its traditional complexion.

8

"Every where I go I hear nothing but the migrant problem," a concerned Californian wrote in 1940.[1] But, in one sense, there was no migrant problem; there were, rather, California problems made visible by the coming of the Okies. By displacing the Mexican labor force on California's farms, the Okies exposed an agricultural system that had existed for three-quarters of a century, but had lain hidden because its victims were alien, nonwhite, and thus unseen. The migrant problem rose and fell, not only because the Okies dislocated the economy, but because, for a brief few years, they provided a superb foil for political conflicts tearing at the state.

California's industrialized agriculture, born in the years immediately following the Civil War, was, for its time, both anomalous and a foretaste of things to come for American agriculture. From the beginning, no family-sized farms worked by an extra hand or two at harvest time dominated California's agricultural landscape. Nor were California's farms fashioned after the Southern postbellum model; they were not plantations broken into cropper units or worked by resident laborers. They were, rather, factories in the fields,[2] cultivated by migratory laborers who miraculously turned up for the harvest and disappeared once the crops were laid by. This agricultural pattern was produced by a combination of land monopolization, the necessity for expensive irrigation, and the availability of a floating supply of cheap migratory labor.

When the United States took possession of California in 1846, its decision to respect previously existing land grants determined the future of land tenure in the state. The Spaniards had been niggardly, issuing only thirty grants in the region; but the Mexican authorities, during the months just prior to transfer to the United States, connived with American speculators in a fantastic land boondoggle, issuing many fraudulent grants. The critical aspect of this fraud was "not that settlers were swindled and huge profits made, but that the grants were not broken up."[3] Intensive crops, cultivated and irrigated upon the immense ranches which evolved from these grants, became the model for the state's growing agricultural regions.

---

[1] *Bakersfield Californian*, April 2, 1940.
[2] The term is Carey McWilliams'. Since 1940, however, the phrase has passed into general use. McWilliams' remains the best treatment of the rise of California's industrialized agriculture, and is relied upon heavily in this study for historical perspective. Carey McWilliams, *Factories in the Field* (Boston, 1939), passim.
[3] Ibid., p. 15. See also, La Follette Committee, *Reports*, 77th Cong., 2d sess., No. 1150, pp. 220–32 passim.

"The Okie Impact," pages 205 to 234, taken from *California and the Dust Bowl Migration* by Walter J. Stein, Westport, Conn.: Greenwood Press, 1973, pp. 32–64. Reprinted with the permission of the publisher, Greenwood Press, Inc.

Three lush and fertile inland valleys dominate California's agriculture. Virtually two-thirds of the state's interior, from Chico in the north to Bakersfield in the south, comprises the great Central Valley, divided into the valleys of the Sacramento and the San Joaquin. The Sacramento Valley is humid and can sustain crops naturally; the San Joaquin Valley, however, requires expensive irrigation—a good deal of it supplied at public expense—for cultivating its year-round crops. Even the San Joaquin's fertility pales before that of the state's southernmost tip, the Imperial Valley, one huge garden, reclaimed from desert by water imported from other states, so hot that even its residents shun it most of the year. Turn off the Imperial's water supply, and her crops would die overnight. So long as the canals flow, she supplies harvests unparalleled elsewhere. These three valleys, and smaller growing regions—east and north of Los Angeles, around Monterey-Salinas, the tiny Napa and Livermore valleys famed for their wines—have yielded rich profits since the Civil War. In the wheat bonanzas of the 1870s (one wheat farm consisted of 57,000 acres), then in fruit, followed at the turn of the century by sugar beets and finally, beginning in the 1920s, in cotton, the state flourished. By 1930, over 180 different farm products grew in California, maturing throughout the year in the state's croplands.

There had been small family homestead farms in California for nearly a hundred years but they could not, and never did, dominate the state's agriculture. Corporate farms drew the bulk of profit and wielded the political and economic power inherent in the state's major industry. The costs of irrigation, coupled with the preexistent pattern of land tenure, demanded large-scale corporation farming. And—what concerns us here—intensive crops cultivated upon corporation farms required armies of migratory labor.

In the 1870s, wheat, the first of California's bonanza crops, collapsed in the wake of drought and depression. Growers sought and found a new, more profitable cash crop in fruit orchards. Fruit, however, could not be harvested by a few men operating machinery. The crop must be handpicked quickly, before it falls from the trees or dies on the vine, individually packed, and shipped. Without a plentiful supply of labor to perform these tasks, fruit, and later vegetables, would not be feasible crops. The conversion from wheat to fruit was a critical moment in California's agricultural history, begetting a pattern of labor relations that persists today. Except during harvest or thinning-time, the crops require little labor, and the agricultural regions seem deserted; an occasional outcropping of farm buildings is visible along the rural roads but the familiar American agricultural landscape of frequent homes, fences, and rusting machinery is nonexistent in, say, the San Joaquin Valley. But during harvests, the fields come alive with the thousands of migrants who pick the crops and then move on. Indeed, chroniclers of California's agricultural history have suggested that the continuation of the pattern of land tenure in the state has been "a direct response to the volume and the supply of agricultural labor."[4] Further, they maintain, intensive agricul-

---

[4] Lloyd Fisher, *The Harvest Labor Market in California* (Cambridge, 1953), p. 4.

ture, coupled with irrigation and requiring large numbers of hand laborers, has been responsible for the growth in California of a "semi-indus-
trialized rural Proletariat."[5]

Hundreds of volumes have explored the history of the urban
industrial worker from 1870 to 1930. Few, however, have investigated
the history of agricultural labor during the same epoch. Yet the system
of migratory labor that developed in California harbored for these sixty
years nearly every problem to which urban labor was subject, with the
sole qualification that work and housing conditions, market instability,
and exploitation of labor were even worse in California's fields than in
many of the nation's cities.

Even more than in urban mass-production industries, intensive agriculture found in wages a flexible cost which, in hard times, could be
manipulated to insure continued profit. Irrigation, land, and machinery
costs, on the other hand, were relatively inflexible. Squeezed, like other
American farmers, by the competitive advantages of industry during the
postbellum years, California's growers kept agricultural wages low. Were
wages occasionally to rise, surpluses of field labor nonetheless kept annual
earnings of farm migrants below subsistence. Demand requirements for
perishable crops can fluctuate on a day-to-day basis. A favorable market
for California lettuce meant high lettuce-picking wages. It also meant,
however, that growers must immediately harvest the crop with every
available laborer. Growers, therefore, preferred that a large number of
unemployed migrants be concentrated in the agricultural regions during
harvest periods. The total cost of picking the crop was divided among
the workers, and wages fluctuated inversely with the size of the total
labor force. Low wages and labor surpluses in California were the rule,
and the ethnic composition of the labor force enhanced the ability of
growers to continue the exploitation of agricultural migrants.

The immigrants who supplied cheap labor surpluses in America's
cities were not, to be sure, Anglo-Saxon Protestant stock. But they were
mostly white and European. From the beginning, California's farm labor
force was neither white nor European nor "American." Until the 1930s,
two streams of migratory agricultural labor comprised California's harvest
force. On the one hand was a sprinkling of single men, white American
professional agricultural labor known as tramps and noted in the 1870s by
Henry George and in the 1890s by Frank Norris. These were men who,
after 1906, would help swell the ranks of the IWW, following the crops
via freight, their red cards supplying free rides. Of far greater numerical
importance than these bindle stiffs, however, were the nonwhite battalions
who had picked California's lush harvests since the 1870s.

Had a plentiful supply of labor not been available, growers could
not have converted their wheat fields into fruit orchards and vegetable

---

See also Varden Fuller, "The Supply of Agricultural Labor as a Factor in the
Evolution of Farm Organization in California" (Ph.D. diss., University of California, Berkeley, 1940).

[5] Paul S. Taylor and Tom Vasey, *California Farm Labor*, Social Security Board,
Bureau of Research and Statistics, Reprint Series No. 2 (n.p., 1937), p. 2.

gardens in the 1870s. Fortuitously for them, such a supply was ready and willing in the Chinese, who, by pouring into the rural regions, began a fifty-year flirtation between California's growers and aliens. The docile Chinese in the fields were cherished by growers; they were all one could ask of agricultural migrant labor. But not all Californians had the same attitude. Years of anti-Chinese agitation in the state ended in 1893 and 1894 when violence and social pressures from rioting urban workers forced growers to end their reliance upon "John Chinaman." With the coming of beet sugar during the same decade, however, Japanese laborers obviated the need for their Chinese predecessors and, by 1909, 300,000 of them were cultivating California's beet sugar crops.[6] The Japanese were accepted by the Californians because, unlike the Chinese, they did not immediately settle in large aggregations and were less visible than the latter. But the Japanese desired, and soon obtained, land of their own and in turn became prey to a new wave of anti-Oriental hysteria.

In the 1910s, hoping to replace the now-hated Japanese, growers experimented with Hindus and with European immigrants, notably Portuguese and Italian. Their numbers were minimal, however, and, in the 1920s, as cotton was developing into a major crop, Mexican labor, augmented by gangs of Filipinos, became the mainstay of the state's agricultural army. At least 150,000 Mexicans—the Okies' immediate predecessors in the fields—were following California's crops in the Normalcy years.[7]

Growers found in the Mexicans a splendid labor supply. The *bracero*, whether Mexican or Mexican-American, knew the state's diverse crops, and handled cotton, fruit, sugar beets, and vegetables with great skill. While the Midwest's farmers suffered a depression in the grain market, California's reaped profit from the changing eating habits of the American people. Fruits, vegetables, and other perishables picked by Mexicans and shipped east brought profit to the growers and revenue to the state. Required only during harvest time, the Mexicans during off-season slipped away to Mexican towns on the outskirts of major cities like Fresno, Bakersfield, and especially Los Angeles, and went on relief.[8] During the 1920s, Los Angeles' Mexicans were studied, analyzed, and "Americanized" by social workers as few other groups in the state's history, and agriculturists favorable to Mexican labor became concerned over the "habit" of relief and what some noted as an unfamiliar "surliness" developing among them.[9] But the Mexicans were, for all that, bringing wealth to the

---

[6] McWilliams, *Factories in the Fields*, pp. 79–106.

[7] Ibid., p. 125. The precise number of Mexican workers is uncertain. Migrants, by virtue of their occupation, do not "stay put" long enough to be counted. Other estimates run to a figure as low as 80,000 workers, plus their families. See William T. Cross and Dorothy Cross, *Newcomers and Nomads in California* (Palo Alto, California, 1937), pp. 50–51.

[8] A good résumé of the subject is Carey McWilliams, "Getting Rid of the Mexican," *American Mercury* 28 (March 1933): 322–24.

[9] Dr. George P. Clements, Los Angeles' prime authority on Mexican labor during the era, predicted trouble as early as 1926. "The Mexican on relief is being unionized and used to foment strikes among the still few loyal Mexican workers. The

state, and, for the prosperity decade, that was sufficient justification for retaining the Mexican-dominated agricultural labor system.

The onset of depression intervened and rapidly transformed the situation. In tight economic times, California's cities could not tolerate the relief-harvest labor-relief cycle that developed in prosperous times among the Mexicans. In 1930, urban relief authorities, especially in Los Angeles, embarked upon a program of voluntary repatriation for Mexicans and Mexican-Americans who chose to accept a free ride to Mexico City. At $14.70 per capita, repatriation was a bargain for the state. For the Mexicans, spurred by rumors of agrarian reforms by Mexico's perennial revolution, a free ride home seemed a welcome respite from hard times. From February 1931 to early 1933, the repatriation of Mexicans removed between 50,000 and 75,000 of the now-unwelcome group. By 1937, an estimated 150,000 Mexicans had returned home.[10] Simultaneously, the depression restricted the flow of new Mexican migrants into the United States: the first half of 1930 saw only one-fifteenth the normal annual Mexico–United States immigration of the 1920s.[11]

Neither the decline of Mexican immigration nor the repatriation decimated California's Mexican population; the majority remained. But for California's growers, the decline in total numbers brought concern. No sooner had the repatriation begun than agricultural journals noted "anxiety in numerous sections of the state. . . . It is reported that Mexican laborers are returning to Mexico at the rate of 10,000 per month, one of the greatest migrations ever witnessed. . . . It is feared that severe labor shortages will prevail in the cotton, fruit, and field crop districts this summer." Anticipated labor shortages did not develop in 1930 and 1931: there remained in the state many more Mexican laborers than growers required even at peak harvest times.[12] By mid-1933 and early 1934, however, both production in the fields and the supply of labor were diminishing. From a peak in 1933 of 186 workers for every 100 available agricultural jobs, the harvest labor force declined by a quarter in 1934 to 142 men per 100 jobs, many of whom preferred to remain on relief rather than pick the 1934 crop at low wages.[13] These combined effects of repatriation and depression wage cuts persuaded the farmer that he was faced with an actual under-supply.[14]

Mexican casual labor is lost to the California farmer unless immediate action is taken to get him off relief." La Follette Committee, *Hearings*, Part 53, Exhibit 8743, pp. 19,673–675. "A Brief History of California's Agricultural Labor" originally published by the Los Angeles Chamber of Commerce.

[10] *San Francisco News*, February 14, 1938. McWilliams, "Getting Rid of the Mexican," 323; Cross and Cross, *Newcomers and Nomads*, pp. 50–51.

[11] *San Francisco Examiner*, August 5, 1930. Average annual rate, 1925–1929: 56,747; January–June 1930: 3,674 or (doubled) 7,348 for the entire year.

[12] *Pacific Rural Press*, April 25, 1931; Cross and Cross, *Newcomers and Nomads*, pp. 50–51. In 1928, growers insisted that they required 80,000 field workers for peak periods in September.

[13] California State Relief Administration, "Migratory Labor in California," mimeographed (San Francisco, 1936), p. 48.

[14] W. V. Allen and A. J. Norton, "Agriculture and Its Employment Problems in

Coming as it did, at precisely the moment when Mexican field workers had organized themselves into unions and gone on strike in the fields, bringing great anxiety to the growers, this contraction of the labor force might have had far-reaching results for California agriculture. As even a committee of the state chamber of commerce admitted, the increased planting of cotton during the 1930s, in view of a declining labor supply, might have accorded the migrant workers a "substantial increase in their annual earnings."[15] Or California's growers, conversely, might have turned more rapidly to mechanization in crops requiring less intensive manual labor, thus ending by quick, if unintentional surgery, the desperate social problem of migratory labor. These alternatives were cut short by the migration of the Okies, which so affected the labor market that liberal writers were, at first, hostile to the new migrants. "The growers were in desperate straits," one wrote, "until drought and depression intervened to turn the tide in their favor by started [sic] the great trek of the Dust Bowlers."[16] The migration foreclosed the possibility of higher wages suggested by the chamber of commerce. It was in agriculture, therefore, that, by preventing potential change, the Okies wrought their first major effect upon the state.

The Okies left their home states and followed Route 66 through New Mexico and into Arizona, where they often stopped for a short season in the cotton fields. Then they drove on into California, armed only with the name of one of a hundred valley towns—Delano, Shafter, Wasco, Arvin—where friends or relatives had already "lit." Sometimes they lacked even a destination other than the "cotton fields." For these, the highway pointed the route. From its desert entry into the state, Route 66 climbed northwest into the southern half of the San Joaquin Valley, where the cotton grew, and there the new arrivals stopped, swelling the population of earlier migrants already camped on ditch banks or on vacant lots outside the towns, in grower-owned shacks or, after 1936, in the federal migratory camps. Settled for the moment, they sought out the local growers' employment service or showed up early at the fields for anticipated work. The cotton picked, they drove their jalopies north to the Sacramento Valley or south to the Imperial, learning along the way how to pick the unfamiliar citrus, peach, grape, potato, or sugar beet crops. In this manner, they quickly supplanted the Mexican agricultural workers.

Wherever the Okies went within the state, their increasing dominance in the agricultural labor force was quickly noted. In late 1935, for example, the San Joaquin Valley bore the main brunt of the Okies. "North

---

California," mimeographed, n.d., Paul S. Taylor Collection, Bancroft Library, University of California, Berkeley, Carton 2.

[15] Subcommittee of Factfinding to the Statewide Migrant Committee of the California Chamber of Commerce, *Report*, April 9, 1940, George P. Clements Papers, University of California, Los Angeles.

[16] George H. Britton, "Parade of Races," manuscript, p. 1, Federal Writers Project Collection, Bancroft Library, University of California, Berkeley, Folder 709.

of the Tehachapi," Paul Taylor testified at the time, "I have never seen so many whites in California agriculture in my life as this year from Kern County up."[17] Not only the San Joaquin, but also the Sacramento Valley to the north received a flood of migrants so great that one of the first two federal migrant camps would be built near Marysville–Yuba City, the hub of that growing region. Even in the Imperial Valley, where whites were always considered unsuitable for "squat labor as in general they are too tall . . . clumsier and do much damage," the Okies moved in, supplanting Mexican and Filipino vegetable workers.[18]

Almost from the beginning, California's growers knew that major changes were taking place in their labor force. They were, after all, the group that first came into contact with the migrants. A Modesto farmer, for example, who had used only local labor in past years noted a sudden change: "about one hundred workers are employed on our farm. . . . However, recently the population has changed—new-comers from the Midwest and South constitute most of our labor supply."[19] Asked in 1937 to describe the "most significant factors affecting the quantity and quality of the agricultural labor supply," 75 percent of growers in the San Joaquin Valley, 70 percent in the Sacramento, and 52 percent in southern California placed "migration from other states" at the head of the list.[20]

Of immediate significance for growers was the question whether the Okies would meet the needs for an adequate labor supply: would they enter the fields in sufficiently large numbers to keep agricultural wages low? And, as importantly, could they be relied upon, like the Mexicans, to turn up when required and then disappear? Officials of the FSA found strong fears among Imperial Valley growers that the new migratory workers were "agricultural workers in the sense that they are only trying to work their way westward."[21] Bemused, FSA sought advice from State Senator John Phillips from the Imperial Valley. Phillips' response merely echoed the growers' concern: "When you speak of the changing migratory labor, that is changing from Mexican to white . . . much of the

---

[17] "Conference on Housing of Migratory Agricultural Laborers, Marysville, October 12, 1935." La Follette Committee, *Hearings*, Part 62, p. 22,599. See also Lillian Creisler, "Little Oklahoma, or, the Airport Community" (Master's thesis, University of California, Berkeley, 1939), p. 67.

[18] "Miss Brace, January 25 [no year]," typed interview, Taylor Collection, Carton 2; author's interview with Mrs. Eleanor Engstrand, September 7, 1965, Berkeley, California; James Rorty, "Lettuce—With American Dressing," *Nation* 140 (May 15, 1935): 575; Carey McWilliams, "Memorandum on Housing Conditions Among Migratory Workers in California," California State Division of Immigration and Housing, March 20, 1939, pp. 3–4, Taylor Collection, Carton 2.

[19] Creisler, "Little Oklahoma," p. 67.

[20] California State Relief Administration, *Agricultural Laborers in the San Joaquin Valley, July, August 1937*, reprinted in La Follette Committee, *Hearings*, Part 62, p. 22,660.

[21] Jonathan Garst to John Phillips, February 12, 1937, in Brawley Camp Reports, Simon J. Lubin Papers, Bancroft Library, University of California, Berkeley, Carton 13.

labor . . . is not what we could call genuine labor. It is merely a transitory group coming in from the east into the state which would seem destined to become the poorhouse of America."[22]

Nonetheless, from 1935 to 1937, the Okie labor supply exceeded the hopes and calmed the fears of California agriculture. Slowly recovering from production lows in 1933 and 1934, crops increased in value and volume. The available labor supply rose, however, at a far more rapid rate, each year exceeding the demand for labor by a larger proportion.[23] Growers admitted only backhandedly that the Okies were supplying their labor needs, while simultaneously denying that the influx of migrants was creating an oversupply. Prior to the 1937 cotton harvest, when a Los Angeles relief official warned that 70,000 destitute Okies were camped in the San Joaquin, the manager of the grower-controlled San Joaquin Valley Agricultural Labor Bureau scoffed at the claim and announced that "there will be little surplus labor when cotton and grapes are in full swing."[24] Despite such assertions, especially during the 1935 harvest when growers claimed there had been an actual labor shortage, the ever-increasing migrant stream clearly satisfied the growers, especially in the San Joaquin. In their yearly reports, the San Joaquin Valley Agricultural Labor Bureau's directors gave clear indication that the Okies were indeed fulfilling the state's requirements. In 1935, for example, they claimed that "local labor" (i.e., Mexicans) was inadequate and only "outside labor," brought in from other portions of the state, ended the undersupply. The harvests of 1936, 1937, and 1938, however, saw "adequate" supplies. In 1936 "it was extremely difficult to expedite local labor from labor centers and the labor that came voluntarily from the drought area came at the opportune time." In 1937 "we were . . . especially fortunate in having sufficient for all our agricultural operations exception [sic] during the peak of the cotton harvest. . . . However, a large influx of cotton pickers from the drought area in Oklahoma and Arkansas, helped the situation at the opportune time." And, in 1938, when—as will be seen—an immense oversupply of migrants brought misery to the Okies and national attention to the problem, the bureau was still alleging local shortages, but grudgingly admitted the value of the Okie to California agriculture: "Acute shortages of labor have been experienced up to within the last two years, however, there appears now to have been *some reversal* [my italics] of the situation due to the migration of the white laborer from the Southern Great Plains."[25]

In claiming labor shortages despite the Okie influx, the bureau and

22 John Phillips to Jonathan Garst, February 19, 1937, U.S. Department of Agriculture, Agricultural Stabilization and Conservation Commission Papers, Federal Records Center, San Francisco, 36,881.
23 National Resources Planning Board, Field Office, Region VIII, *Some Effects of Recent Migration on California's Population and Economy*, June 25, 1940, p. 8, copy in Farm Security Administration Papers, Bancroft Library, University of California, Berkeley.
24 *Berkeley Gazette*, July 27, 1937.
25 Agricultural Labor Bureau of the San Joaquin Valley, *Annual Report*, 1936, 1937, 1938, 1939, in La Follette Committee, *Hearings*, Part 72, pp. 26,536–538.

farmers who echoed its sentiments were not wholly disingenuous. Agriculture had become so accustomed to the "fluid Mexican workers who miraculously appeared on harvest day" that an efficient method of recruiting and transporting labor to the exact point where and when it was needed had never developed.[26] The San Joaquin Valley Agricultural Labor Bureau had, in fact, consistently maintained that such a system was desperately needed and long overdue. In each of its annual reports, the bureau's manager recommended that "proper steps be taken to prepare a program of labor reports for different crops where seasonal labor will be employed, so that when demands for labor are made, it may be possible to supply our growers without loss of time."[27]

In another way, however, users of harvest labor were being disingenuous. In justifying their use of Okie labor when local labor was unavailable, they blamed relief distributed to the locals, Mexican or white, for keeping them from the fields.[28] What they neglected to admit was the critical role the Okie influx played in keeping wages so low that local residents actually lost money if they went off relief in order to pick the crops. Had there been no Okie influx, wages in California agriculture likely would have risen. As events turned out, the size of the Okie influx allowed growers to hold farm wages down. Kern County's Health Department frankly admitted, for example, that 1937's Okie influx had provided "only enough surplus labor to maintain prevailing wage structure."[29]

A widespread assumption that Okies would not accept "Mexican wages" was but a strand in the fabric of California's unconscious racism. As one angry Democrat had written to Philip Bancroft, grower and Republican senatorial candidate in 1938: "The only reason you do not want farm labor organized is that you will probably have to pay WHITE AMERICAN CITIZENS decent wages, instead of hiring Orientals. SHAME."[30] This assumption was incorrect. The Okies did accept lower wages—wages that Mexicans, in fact, had refused. The new arrivals, dis-

[26] Kern County, Department of Public Health, Sanitary Division, "Survey of Kern County Migratory Labor Problems, Supplementary Report as of July 1, 1939," mimeographed, n.p. copy in Carey McWilliams Collection, University of California, Los Angeles. See also Emily Huntington, *Doors to Jobs* (Berkeley, 1942), pp. 203–04.

[27] Agricultural Labor Bureau of the San Joaquin Valley, *Annual Reports*, 1937, 1938, 1939, pp. 26,536–538.

[28] Roy Pike to Commonwealth Club, in "California Farm Labor Problems," *Commonwealth Club Transactions* 30 (April 7, 1936): passim; Lewis Kuplan, "The Problems of Relief and Agriculture in California," manuscript, December 1937, McWilliams Collection; Commonwealth Club, Minutes of Section on Agriculture, April 14, 1936, copy in Harry Drobish Papers, Bancroft Library, University of California, Berkeley.

[29] Kern County Health Department, Sanitary Division, "Survey of Kern County Migratory Labor Problem," Supplementary Report as of July 1, 1938, mimeographed, p. 6, copy in vertical file, Public Health Library, University of California, Berkeley.

[30] Torn title page of *California Commonwealth* with handwritten notation, n.d., Philip Bancroft Collection, Bancroft Library, University of California, Berkeley.

oriented, penniless, and unable to receive state relief for a year, accepted any wage in the cotton fields. In early 1936, when Mexicans in the upper San Joaquin Valley were threatening a strike for wages higher than the twenty-five cents an hour being paid there, migrants in the federal camp at Arvin were satisfied with the prevailing wage, and only a "few groups" would have refused twenty cents an hour.[31] In the same year, Oklahomans and Texans "anxious to work" replaced Mexicans in San Bernardino County who "after a taste of relief . . . were neither so efficient nor so anxious to work."[32] A rumor spread that the Hoover Ranch (owned by the family of the ex-President) had corralled on its property a group of new migrants from the southern Great Plains who, the informant feared, would work for anything.[33] In 1938, when the Okie oversupply of labor had brought concern to the state and the nation, growers used low agricultural wages as evidence of their desire for public service. In that year wages were cut from thirty cents to twenty cents per hour on the grounds that there were too many migratory workers from the Midwest and South who must be discouraged by forcing them to work at poor wages.

It was not wholly true that the Okies would "work for anything." The irony of their situation was that California's pittance seemed munificent in contrast with wages or tenant shares in their home states. The Associated Farmers continually emphasized this theme in their publications, as in the following, drawn from an anti-union pamphlet: "Once inside her Cabin, she whispered to me: 'Us folks don't dare talk. We were afraid of what might happen to us. We're glad to get eighty cents a hundred. Cotton picking here ain't like it was down in Texas. You can pick a sackful of California cotton in half the time it takes back home.' " Neutral sources reported similar comments, as did the *New York Times* correspondent who asked an Okie if he intended returning home. "Ahm agoin back to Oklahomy? I should say not mistah. Why this yere country is the promised land . . . we've made more money in the spud season than we made in three years back home. . . . Believe it or not, last yeah I made $240 cash money."[34] Another Oklahoman, Mr. Higgenbottom, told the Tolan Committee that he was glad he'd come to California. "You see, probably the cheaper wages there drives people out. . . . You see, the wages in Oklahoma—they are so scarce and there is so little, you know."[35]

Even the argument that California's wages were higher was not unimpeachable. Unquestionably, hourly or piece-rate wages were higher in California than in Texas or Oklahoma, and it was to this fact that the Okies honestly—and the growers sometimes guilefully—testified. But wages had to be amortized over the year, and California supplied fewer day's

---

[31] Arvin Camp Reports, May 2, 1936, USDA ASCC Collection, 36,879.

[32] Commonwealth Club, *Minutes of Section on Agriculture*, n.p.

[33] Arvin Camp Reports, August 15, 1936, USDA ASCC Collection, 36,879.

[34] Sue Sanders, *The Real Causes of Our Migrant Problem* (n.p., 1940); *New York Times*, July 18, 1937.

[35] Tolan Committee, *Hearings*, Part 7, p. 2,823.

work for each Okie. The cost of living was higher, and transportation from job to job took still another bite from the paycheck.[36] Finally, growers well understood that the swollen labor supply furnished considerable room for maneuver in the area of wages. When the manager of the immense DiGiorgio farms refused to pay the prevailing wage of thirty cents an hour in the Arvin area of Kern County, he utilized popular fears of a grower conspiracy to strengthen his point. He "reminded his hearers that an advertising campaign in the Oklahoma and Arkansas press would bring out, on short notice, hundreds and probably thousands of workers from those states and that these workers would be very willing and quite happy to work for the 25 cents per hour scale."[37]

For the depression decade from 1929 to 1939, the migrant influx retarded the recovery of wage levels that should have accompanied the reviving farm income of the same period. California's agricultural income had suffered considerably during the initial stages of the depression. In 1932, the index of agricultural income, using 1924–1929 averages as a base figure of 100, stood at 60.[38] Beginning in 1933, however, farm income slowly began to increase. In 1937, a high-yield year, the index was 112, and by 1939, in spite of the 1937 recession and its effects, the index was 94.4. Farm wages did not, however, keep pace with farm income. In the bumper year 1937, for example, farm wages, using the same base period, were only 65 percent of what they had been in the years 1924–1929; and in 1939, they declined to 59 percent. Even making allowance for a 25 percent increase in productivity per worker that developed during the decade, it is clear that in relation to his employer, the agricultural laborer was earning far less in the late 1930s than in the late 1920s. His employer's income, on the other hand, was usually near, and sometimes above, that of the Normalcy years. In effect, California's growers recovered at the expense of the Okie migrants who picked the increasingly profitable crops.

As the above figures indicate, productivity per worker had increased during the decade, even while the Okies were supplying a growing excess of labor. Each year, more disinherited southern Great Plains migrants showed up in rural California to fill a declining number of paid jobs. Growers were satisfied with the labor oversupply and took advantage of it. In late 1936, for example, the Associated Farmers officially replied to charges that they had "met" the Okies "with hatred." The organization countered with an assertion that farmers "liked" the new "citizenry" from Oklahoma: "They have come here hopefully. They have brought their families. They want work. They will prove to be good citizens."[39]

[36] For an extended discussion of wages and costs for California migrant workers, see the following: La Follette Committee, *Hearings*, Part 62, pp. 22,529–530; *Wage Rates and Expenditures for Labor, California Agriculture, 1909–1935*, copy in Giannini Foundation Library, University of California, Berkeley.

[37] Arvin Camp Reports, July 11, 1936. USDA ASCC Collection, 36,879.

[38] These figures and the following statistical data are drawn from La Follette Committee, *Reports*, 77th Cong., 2d sess., No. 1150, pp. 384–85.

[39] *San Francisco News,* October 23, 1936.

The seemingly beneficient influx of Okies nonetheless contained a hidden liability that, in 1938, would undermine the growers' satisfaction with this new wave of migrants, forcing them to take a leading role in political and social action to stem the influx from the Great Plains.

In order to understand fully California's migrant problem, one must realize that this was really two overlapping problems. On the one hand, the migrant problem was the response of California to the agricultural labor system that had developed, unnoticed save by a few, during the sixty years since 1870. There was, however, another migrant problem attendant upon the Okies' influx. The Okies were not bindle stiffs or single men. They were families, and they wanted to relocate permanently in California. They had never intended to become migratory agricultural laborers, carrying their few belongings from place to place, incessantly following the crops in a never-ending cycle of grinding harvest labor. Drawn by the promise of a new start in California's fertile valleys, they settled in the state's farming areas. As their numbers increased, they threatened to become a serious social and political dislocation in counties that could not possibly absorb a new population of such magnitude within sufficient time to avoid misery for the newcomers and expense for the older residents.

Unlike the Mexicans or the Filipinos, they did not disappear after harvest; they stayed. Unlike the Mexicans, they were not swarthy, not unseen; their poverty in the shacktown or ditch-bank settlements could not be ignored. By 1937, the Okies had become a local embarrassment, by 1938 a state concern, and by 1939, with the publication of *The Grapes of Wrath*, a national scandal. This was California's other migrant problem. Had the Okie been simply an agricultural laborer, his coming would not have convulsed the state as it did. That he was both agricultural laborer *and* new, poverty-stricken resident of the rural regions was the cause of the panic that gripped the "older" Californians, and threatened to drive a wedge between the growers and the valley towns that had, heretofore, coexisted in a tight symbiosis.

It has been demonstrated that the Okie influx, in absolute numerical terms, was not extraordinary. The net increase of some 300,000 or 400,000 erstwhile southern Great Plains people over the course of a decade was not, in itself, cause for alarm. Had they been distributed proportionally throughout the state's urban centers, even during the depression's dislocation, their coming would probably have gone unnoticed. Indeed, some Okies did move into Los Angeles and the Bay Area, and these metropolitan centers absorbed them in silence.[40] Even if inflated border counts of "persons entering the state in need of manual employment," or the fearful guesses of some that the influx was approaching 500,000 or 600,000 had been more accurate than the census returns, the total migration would still have fallen far short of the easily absorbed

[40] During the course of research for this study, I have turned up no studies viewing the coming of Okies to the major coastal cities with alarm, nor viewing them as a specific group.

population increases of the 1920s and 1940s. One could conclude, therefore, that the Okie influx was unworthy of note; that it was a chimera, a myth fostered by radicals to discredit the growers or, conversely, by growers to discredit the Olson or Roosevelt administrations. Growers, the argument might continue, blamed the influx of Okies upon high relief payments, and radicals saw grower conspiracies to advertise for cheap labor, both for purely political reasons.

Such a conclusion would be incorrect. The Okies did not distribute themselves proportionally within the state, nor was their trek spread evenly across the decade. The majority of the refugees came to California between 1935 and 1937. This three-year period accounted for nearly half the entire influx for the decade and, consequently, the migration seemed larger than it actually was.[41] Further, since they had come to pick cotton, or to get a farm of their own, the great majority of them descended upon the state's agricultural counties, bringing with them poverty, and political and social habits different from those of the residents.

The Okies who left the Great Plains during the depression and who resided in California in 1940 were but a third of the total number of migrants to California during the decade.[42] One hundred eighty thousand of them, however, had taken up residence in agricultural regions of the state, and most of these, in turn, in the San Joaquin Valley. Small in absolute terms, the number was nonetheless large in relative terms, and herein lay the basis for the San Joaquin's, and to a lesser extent, the Sacramento Valley's anxiety. As Table 2 indicates, the agricultural counties received relative population increases far larger than the more diverse urban regions. During the 1920s, the cities, notably Los Angeles, had been the fastest growing areas in the state. The Okie migration reversed that trend. From 1935 to 1940, only one San Joaquin Valley county—Fresno—received smaller proportional population gains than Los Angeles; and Yuba County in the Sacramento Valley, and heart of the north's growing regions, gained fully half again the population it had in 1930. In all, the Okie migration demanded that the San Joaquin and the Sacramento valleys absorb, during the depression years, twice as many migrants as had settled in them during the prior decade.[43]

For a variety of reasons the figures above, compiled from the Census of 1940, were probably conservative. For one, the defense boom had already begun in the major urban centers of the state, and Okies who had swollen the agricultural labor supply in 1937 or 1938 were beginning the trek that would assimilate them into the cities in the war years. Further, it was not inconceivable that census takers might have missed large numbers of Okies camped in squalor on the ditch banks in the more remote sections of the agricultural valleys. In any case, other estimates, taken earlier than 1940, supplied even larger rates of population growth, es-

[41] Seymour Janow and William Gilmartin, "Labor and Agricultural Migration to California, 1935–40," *Monthly Labor Review* 53 (July 1941): 21.

[42] Commonwealth Club of California, *The Population of California* (San Francisco, 1946), p. 19.

[43] Commonwealth Club, *Population of California*, p. 57.

TABLE 2

POPULATION INCREASES, SELECTED COUNTIES, 1935–1940

County	Population change	Percent Increase
Kern (SJV)	52,554	63.6
Yuba (Sacto V)	5,703	50.3
Madera (SJV)	6,150	35.8
Kings (SJV)	9,783	38.5
Tulare (SJV)	29,710	38.4
San Diego	79,689	38.0
Monterey	19,327	36.0
Stanislas (SJV)	18,225	32.2
San Joaquin (SJV)	31,267	30.4
Merced (SJV)	10,240	27.9
Los Angeles	577,151	26.1
Fresno (SJV)	34,186	23.7
San Bernardino	27,208	20.3
Sacramento	28,334	20.0
Santa Barbara	5,388	8.3
Alameda	38,128	8.0
San Francisco	142	0.8

Source: Commonwealth Club of California, *The Population of California* (San Francisco, 1946), pp. 19–20.

pecially for the five upper (southern) counties of the San Joaquin Valley, which were the center of cotton cultivation in California. One compilation presented to the La Follette Committee estimated that Tulare, Madera, and Kern counties had each experienced 50 percent population increases; another survey added Kings to the counties undergoing 50 percent increases and estimated a 70 percent growth for Kern.[44] It was, in all, virtually impossible to assess accurately the migrants' numbers. A local census taken at the height of harvest season could, for example, count authentic migratory workers, as well as resident Okies, and come up with horrendous statistics, as when one writer terrified Madera's population with the following: "In 1930 the population of Madera County was 17,164; today it is around 35,000. Most of this increase has come since 1935 and most of the new residents are migrants. In other words Madera now has a footloose population approximately equal to its resident population."[45]

It would have been difficult for the state's undiversified agricultural counties to accommodate population increases of this magnitude even had

---

[44] Testimony of James Musatti, La Follette Committee, *Hearings*, Part 59, pp. 21,864, 21,866–870.

[45] Ben Hibbs, "Footloose Army," *Country Gentleman* 110 (February 1940): 7.

the migrants been financially solvent. Their poverty, however, forced the migrants to settle temporarily under conditions inferior even to those they had left in Oklahoma or Arkansas. For those migrants who were fortunate enough to find work in the fields quickly, grower-maintained living quarters, squalid as most were, provided a measure of shelter at least during the working season. Some of the others found decent, if plain, housing in the federal government's rapidly expanding migratory labor camps. But the great majority of the newcomers found shelter where they could. These migrants pitched their tents along the irrigation ditches, in empty fields near the large ranches, and in private trailer camps. As the migration reached its peak in 1936 and 1937, the ditch bank settlements grew in size, number, and squalor, and finally became a menace to the Okies themselves and to the resident populations nearby.

The ditch bank settlements are not easily described. Journalists visiting them sought adjectives commensurate with the misery, ultimately falling back upon the photographs of Dorothea Lange whose camera captured with documentary ruthlessness the poverty sprouting in California's fertile valleys.[46] A journalist traveling through the state in 1937, for example, discovered "the haven of the fruit tramps in California's 'peach bowl' [in] the willow and cottonwood groves along the Yuba and Feather Rivers near the twin cities of Marysville and Yuba City." Disturbed by the poverty he had witnessed in the Sacramento Valley, he moved south to the San Joaquin and found that the northern region's camps were "clean and respectable" compared to conditions in Kern County. "There," he continued, "in the dry Kern Lake bottom, Tuckerton, Buttonwillow and Buena Park—migrants live in almost unimagineable [*sic*] filth—festering sores of miserable humanity."[47]

Journalists, growers and their opponents, liberals and conservatives, all who visited the ditch banks agreed at least that living conditions were loathsome. "Hungry 'Dust Bowl' refugees . . . are reportedly living in the fields and woods 'like animals,'" reported the *Berkeley Gazette* in 1937. Actress Helen Gahagan, later to be elected congresswoman from California, told relief investigators after visiting the Sacramento Valley camps: "I went around in a sick daze for hours after witnessing unimaginable suffering."[48]

Filth and squalor among the Okies was upsetting, for some even nauseating, but for the farmers who struck in anger at those who laid the blame for these conditions upon them, it was explainable. "The conditions," Lee A. Stone, Madera's controversial health director affirmed, "are not to be blamed on the growers, but on the people themselves."[49] The Okies had lived in squalor for generations, he continued, and were a de-

---

[46] A large collection of Miss Lange's photographs of migrant Okies may be found in the Bancroft Library, University of California, Berkeley.

[47] *San Francisco Chronicle*, March 8, 1937.

[48] *National Ham and Eggs*, August 26, 1939. *Berkeley Gazette*, July 10, 1937.

[49] Lee Alexander Stone, "What Is the Solution to California's Transient Labor Problem?" mimeographed (June 22, 1938), p. 6, copy in vertical file, Public Health Library, University of California, Berkeley.

graded American stock. One of John Steinbeck's critics admitted that the Okie children in the camps were "probably hungry" and frequently developed high fever and dysentery. But, after all, these were simply the results of eating fresh fruit among people whose traditional fare was beans and fried dough. When visiting these camps, he continued, one should "keep his feet on the ground and remain clear in the brainpan," or he might "go off raving mad, write another 'Grapes of Wrath,' and thus falsely indict the whole California system of Agriculture."[50]

These explanations, even had they been accurate, did not remove the problem. In any event, the camps menaced the Californians as well as the migrants. Typhoid was not uncommon along the ditch banks where pure water was unavailable and the barest sanitary facilities nonexistent. Smallpox epidemics broke out in camps in Madera, Tulare, and Imperial; tuberculosis, malaria, and pneumonia were endemic.[51] None of these diseases asked of their victims whether they were Okies or "old Californians," and the possibility that contagion would spread from the ditch banks into the towns and cities brought prompt action by county health departments. As early as 1934, local officials had recognized the potential health hazard inherent in the ditch bank settlement, and had begun a systematic campaign of evicting migrants and destroying their camps.[52] Kern County's medical officials led the state in programs for eliminating the unsanitary camps, and Madera's Lee Stone, armed with a violent prejudice against the Okies, followed suit. By 1937, both counties had vacated large numbers of Okies from unsanitary camps.[53] Well-intentioned as these programs were, they could not solve the problem. Evicted Okies with no funds simply moved down the road, or into another, less concerned county, where they pitched new camps. And, of course, the constant influx of new migrants in 1936 and 1937 made a Hydra of the ditch banks: "Old" Okies, evicted, might move into the towns; newcomer Okies would take their place. The efforts of harried public health officials prevented the outbreak of serious epidemics. The final solution to the ditch bank camp problem was, however, supplied by the Okies themselves.

The ditch banks were dramatic evidence of the Okies' distress, but they were not the most significant form of settlement among the migrants. They were, rather, way stations along the Okies' road to permanent residence in the agricultural regions, especially in the San Joaquin Valley. The single, fundamental, irreducible fact about the Okies was that

50 George Thomas Miron, *The Truth About John Steinbeck and the Migrants* (Los Angeles, 1939), p. 20.
51 Stone, "What Is the Solution?" p. 2; Testimony of Lawrence Hewes, U.S., Congress, House, Select Committee of House Committee on Agriculture to Investigate the Activities of the Farm Security Administration, *Hearings*, 78th Cong., 1st sess., 1943, Part 2, pp. 624–25 (hereafter *Cooley Committee*); *Oakland Tribune*, February 1, 1938.
52 *Bakersfield Californian*, November 26, 1934, April 8, 1937.
53 Kern County, Health Department, *Supplementary Report as of July 1, 1938*, passim; Stone, "What Is the Solution?" passim; *Madera Express*, June 30, 1938; Testimony of Walter M. Dickie, La Follette Committee, *Hearings*, Part 62, p. 22,730.

they successfully resisted the inherent tendency of California's agricultural system to force them into permanent intrastate wandering, following the state's crops. Back in the southern Great Plains, the Okies had been permanent residents of agricultural counties. Even those who were agricultural laborers had a place to "light," and they retained that pattern in California. The dual meaning of the word "migrant"—it can mean "endlessly wandering agricultural laborer" or "person relocating from one state to another"—confused California for a time when it confronted the migrant Okies. The Okies were persons moving from one state to another; they were also agricultural laborers. For the most part, however, they were not "*migratory* agricultural laborers" in the traditional sense of the word. They did follow crops, they toured the length and breadth of the great Central Valley during harvest seasons. But—and here lies the key to California's "other migrant problem"—they retained a permanent residence in one of the towns in the agricultural regions. "Few have joined the ranks of the 'fruit tramp' and toted their family broods in rattletrap cars," noted one reporter, and Kern's health department explained the novelty of the Okies quite clearly when it reported to the county's board of supervisors: "Growers have lost their fluid Mexican workers who miraculously appeared on harvest day and silently slipped away after their work was done . . . the large family of the Southwesterner harvests the cotton of the Kern Valley; when the cotton harvest is over, the family hangs on."[54]

Because the Okies came permanently to relocate in California, they came in families; and, because they came in families, it was inevitable that they would ultimately establish residence in or near the rural cities. The breadwinner might migrate during the harvest season, returning home weeks or months later, but a residential base for these forays was necessary. Wives, after all, became pregnant; there were children to tend; and, even more important, the children went to school.

The Okies resented being called "migratory workers" even when they did migrate within the valleys during harvests.[55] When John Steinbeck, before writing *The Grapes of Wrath*, produced a series of articles about the new migrants, the *San Francisco News* published the reports under the title "California's Harvest Gypsies." At the Farm Security camp in Arvin, the camp manager was forced to obliterate the title when he distributed the articles to the campers, so furious were they at the implication that they were bindle stiffs no better than the Mexicans or Filipinos.[56] "Plunking down" at first where they could, the Okies soon reasserted their traditional desire to retain a permanent place to live by converting those squatters' camps that were located just outside towns into permanent suburban slums. No longer simply ditch bank collections of tents or lean-tos, the Little Oklahomas that dotted the rural landscapes of the San Joaquin Valley and, to a lesser extent, the Sacramento Valley,

[54] *San Francisco News*, February 15, 1938; Kern County, Health Department, *Supplementary Report as of July 1, 1939*, p. 1.

[55] Creisler, "Little Oklahoma," p. 35.

[56] Arvin Camp Reports, October 10, 1936, USDA ASCC Collection, 36,879.

were themselves towns, their populations steadily increasing as Okies moved to them from the less-permanent ditch bank settlements farther from town, or from the Farm Security or privately owned agricultural labor camps.

By July 1939, Kern County could announce the total elimination of squatters' camps, but only in part was this the result of a two-year campaign by the county's health officers. A more important reason for the disappearance of the camps was the fact that the "Southwesterner [was] by instinct a home lover and poor fluid laborer."[57] The Okie had not departed Kern. The county had not lost undesirable squatters; it had gained new citizens. The squatters' camps had been replaced by permanent settlements populated almost entirely by recent migrants from the southern Great Plains. Southeast of Bakersfield, two virtually brand-new towns—Lamont and Weedpatch—supplied the DiGiorgio farms with labor. Older cities found new settlements on their outskirts. Delano, Wasco, McFarland, Shafter, Arvin, and the county's metropolis, Bakersfield, each had its Little Oklahoma.[58]

Nor was Kern the sole inheritor of such new settlements. Wherever the large farms attracted labor, there the Okies built new communities. To the north of Kern, Tulare County discovered that the small community of Earlimart had become an Okie town, and that Visalia and Farmersville were gaining new residents in direct proportion to the increase in cotton planting. Madera, Kings, and Fresno counties experienced similar growth in their towns. Outside Stanislaus County's major city, Modesto, an immense Little Oklahoma sprang up. What had been swampland encircling the town's airport now became a community of permanently settled farm laborers. Six miles north of Little Oklahoma, Salida's old residents found themselves far outnumbered by the new Okies.[59]

The development of Okie towns was not confined to the San Joaquin Valley. Other agricultural regions acquired similar but smaller suburban slums. Sacramento, capital of the state and the gateway to the rich northern valley, had given birth early in the depression to Hooverville, populated by unemployed single men. By 1939 Hooverville was well on

[57] Kern County, Health Department, *Supplementary Report as of July 1, 1939*, p. 2.
[58] Mary Helen Williamson, "Unemployment Relief Administration in Kern County, 1935–1940" (Master's thesis, University of California, Berkeley, 1941), pp. 25–26; testimony of Carey McWilliams, La Follette Committee, *Hearings*, Part 59, p. 21,891; Kern County, Health Department, *Supplementary Report as of July 1, 1939*, p. 7; Walter R. Goldschmidt, *As You Sow* (Glencoe, 1947), passim; "Interview with Mr. Thayer, Arvin," Bureau Agricultural Economics Collection, Federal Records Center, San Francisco, 306,068.
[59] California State Relief Administration, "A Social Survey of Housing Conditions Among Tulare County Relief Clients," mimeographed (Visalia, 1939), p. 23; testimony of George Gleason, Tolan Committee, *Hearings*, Part 7, p. 3,005; Work Projects Administration, Division of Social Research and California State Relief Administration, *The Economic Problem of Rural Relief in California with Special Reference to Selected Counties*, Bulletin No. 7, Madera County (September 1936), pp. 10–11; Creisler, "Little Oklahoma," passim; *San Francisco Chronicle*, February 12, 1940.

its way to becoming an Okie town.[60] Marysville–Yuba City had two such Okie settlements, Bull Tract and Live Oak, the latter an entire Pentecostal community, which had migrated en masse from the Southwest.[61]

And, finally, the Okies established communities outside the two major valleys. Salinas had Hebron Heights, otherwise known as Little Oklahoma. Even the garden farms on the outskirts of Los Angeles attracted Okies, and migrant towns could be found at Sawtelle and Bell Gardens. Only in the Imperial Valley did the pattern fail to reproduce itself. There, the Mexican settlement, impermanent and unseen, remained the rule. But the Imperial, after all, had a climate so inhospitable that not even the grower lived there except when it was absolutely necessary, and Okies who had ended their California trek at Brawley generally moved north to settle in the San Joaquin after harvest.[62]

These Okie settlements, and uncounted others in the rural regions, all shared one characteristic with undeviating and almost uncanny similarity. With a rhythm produced by the ability of the migrants to find cash, the ditch banks became communities, integrated, poverty-ridden, and permanent. The journalist Ernie Pyle expressed in a singular manner what many other reporters and social scientists had observed in the Okie towns when he mused in mid-1941 about the question "whatever became of the Okies?"

> They say you can go into a big settlement . . . and you can judge by a man's place to the very month how long he has been here. . . . If he's living in a tent or trailer, he's been here less than six months. If a family is in a garage on the back of a lot, they've been here more than six months. If the garage now houses the car, and the family is in a two room shack in the front of the lot, they've been here more than a year. And if the house has expanded and living is fairly decent, they've been here more than two years.[63]

What Pyle described in 1941 was true of earlier Okie settlements, with one difference: before the coming of the defense boom, Okies had less money and the transitions noted by Pyle took longer. Nonetheless, the conversion from ditch-bank impermanence to residential permanence was inevitable.

The development of the Okie settlements brought a major change in California's relationship to the migrants. "What was once the problem of squatters camps along ditchbanks has now become the problem of the

60 Testimony of Carey McWilliams, La Follette Committee, *Hearings*, Part 59, p. 21,892.

61 Stuart M. Jamieson, "A Settlement of Rural Migrant Families in the Sacramento Valley," *Rural Sociology*, 7 (March 1942): 51, 57.

62 Federal Writers Project, "A Report on the Background and Problems Affecting Farm Labor in California," manuscript, Oakland, California, n.d., Bancroft Library, University of California, Berkeley, Testimony of George Gleason, p. 2,997.

63 *San Francisco News*, May 13, 1941.

growth of rural and suburban slums."[64] This was the simple manner in which one sociologist put the fact that, after sixty years of disregarding a transient mass of alien male laborers, California's valley cities discovered that profits in agriculture did not always compensate for the human and financial losses that attended the labor system.

There was, paradoxically, no room for the migrants in the immense valleys. The possibilities for small-scale farming were negligible; agriculture required immense expenditures for land and irrigation. Industrial employment opportunities were limited, confined for the most part to canning, processing, and packing the crops grown on the outlying ranches. Depression conditions multiplied the difficulty of assimilating newcomers. What made the problem most pressing, however, was the fact that the Okies were not a typical group of California migrants: they were broke and they were chronically unemployed.[65] It cost public money to provide for them and their contribution to the state's taxable income was, by virtue of the low wages they could earn in the fields, very small. These new settlements affected the older towns in three ways, each of which increased the hostility and the concern of local residents toward the newcomers who now resided on the outskirts of town. The Okies required health services; they sent their children to school, thus increasing taxes required for educational services; and they collected relief.

Frequent raids upon the ditch bank settlements in the San Joaquin Valley counties had eliminated the dangers of epidemics. Communicable disease, however, was but a small part of the migrants' medical problems, and the removal of the ditch banks did little to end malnutrition or to limit costs of medical care for healthy migrants. Public health officers frequently despaired at the inherited dietary habits of the Okies, habits bred of generations of rural poverty in their home states. At the Brawley FSA camp, for example, a twenty-eight-year-old man died of pellagra while government nurses endeavored with little effect to persuade migrant mothers that a steady diet of soda pop was less valuable than milk for their children.[66] Poverty, as well as habit, prevented the migrants from eating meals adequate to provide resistance against minor illness, and the only recourse for sick migrants was to seek aid at county-supported public hospitals.

Illness was not the only physical condition that took Okies to the county hospital. Although they were not more prolific than the resident population, and, indeed, had fewer children per family than the national average, pregnant migrant women had little money for private physicians. In Kern County, in June 1937, 42 percent of the infants born had fathers

[64] Williamson, "Unemployment Relief in Kern County," pp. 25–26.

[65] See, for example, the analysis in Davis McEntire et al, "Migration and Resettlement Problems in Pacific Coast States," p. 16, June 20, 1938, Taylor Collection, Carton 18.

[66] Engstrand interview; Stone, "What Is the Solution?" pp. 1–6; S. F. Farnsworth, "Health of the Migratory Worker," address before the Health Officers' Section, League of California Municipalities, San Jose, September 15, 1937, in Taylor Collection, Carton 18.

from the four Okie states. In 1939, Kern's health directors pronounced the migrant use of county medical service "amazing." During the latter year, 75 percent of Okie newborns were delivered, at county expense, at the Kern General Hospital.[67]

Kern had the most enlightened county health department in California's agricultural regions, supplying medical care to anyone in need of prompt treatment, resident and nonresident alike; therefore, it was the most affected in the area of public health. Other counties, too, felt the influx. Madera, whose health director, Lee Stone, spent considerable time complaining about Okie degenerates, took its public-health problems as seriously as did Kern. Because these two counties supplied more inclusive health services to residents as well as Okies than any other county, their health and sanitation budgets doubled from 1935 to 1940. Tulare County's part-time medical staff did creditable work within its limitations. Each of the other San Joaquin Valley counties increased their public health budgets during this five-year period between 30 percent and 50 percent, as did Yuba County in the Sacramento.[68]

Increased public-health costs was not the most burdensome of the problems raised by the coming of the Okies. Of far greater significance, both in terms of county finances and friction between migrants and local populations, was the manner in which the migration affected educational systems in the rural counties. The Okies maintained smaller families than the national average. But, the migration also attracted a higher proportion of young people than the national population contained. Put another way, it might be said that while the Okies had fewer children in each family, there were many more families with children of school age than might be found in a more typical area of the country. Therefore, the Okie impact upon educational facilities was proportionately larger than their impact upon other public services such as hospitals and prisons.

The migrant problem in the schools was exacerbated by the condition of the Okie children, who could not, for a variety of reasons, appear well-scrubbed, apple-in-hand, and smiling with anticipation in traditional Becky Thatcher fashion on the first day of school. The Okie family tended to settle down in one place, but not without some delay and considerable hardship. Their last months in the Great Plains and their first year in California were unsettled, transient, and characterized by restless scrambling for sufficient funds. Child labor, a matter of necessity rather than habit, was common during this initial stage of resettlement, and California's child-labor laws did not prevent it completely. Observers frequently saw small children dragging cotton sacks through the rows, their average ninety-eight-cents-a-day income contributing "substantially to

[67] U.S., Department of Agriculture, Farm Security Administration, *A Study of 6,655 Migrant Households in California* (San Francisco, 1939), pp. 48–51; Kern County, Health Department, "Relation of the Migratory Problem to Health and Hospitalization in Kern County," mimeographed (July 1, 1937), p. 2; testimony of Gleason, p. 3,003.

[68] *San Francisco News*, February 15, 1938; La Follette Committee, *Hearings*, Part 59, pp. 21,866–870; Tyr V. Johnson and Frederick Arpke, *Interstate Migration and County Finance in California* (n.d., n.p.), passim.

family earnings." The desperation of the Okie migrants was probably nowhere more evident than in the fact that child labor in some cases "undoubtedly meant the difference between a living wage and relief status."[69] Some Okies reportedly left California to return to Arizona because county authorities in the former were "too strict," keeping children from the fields during the harvest season.[70]

Once settled, the Okies doggedly sought education for their offspring. Their move to California was designed to better their conditions, and schooling for the children was part of that design. Parents in Modesto's Little Oklahoma were "extremely apprehensive lest their children suffer from the same limitations of education that hampered them" and intended to use California's "splendid" educational system.[71] Okie parents at the FSA camps occasionally left their children in the government's care while themselves migrating in search of ripe crops so that the children could attend school. "My mother and father has gone to Idaho to pick spuds" one Okie child wrote to a camp newspaper. "I did not cry the morning they left," she added, and a friend explained, "I will be glad when school starts again. . . . I like to go to school."[72]

From 1935 to 1940, Okie children swelled the school populations in each of the agricultural counties to which their parents had migrated. They brought with them the necessity for increases in county disbursements for education, and, because of their deprivation during the first year or two of migration, they tended to be scholastically retarded by at least one full year. By nearly all measurements, the Okie children were not inferior to California children except that their absence from school had impeded their education; but their greater age at any grade level, coupled with the patterns of prejudice developing against the migrants, led a number of counties to attempt to segregate the Okie children in separate classrooms or in mobile schools, either of which increased still further the costs of education.[73]

County school district supervisors felt themselves harassed, overburdened, and encroached upon by the Okie influx. The case of Porterville's high school was typical. This Tulare County school had boasted for years of its high rating with the state's college system, and many of its students had received scholarships at Stanford and the University of California.

---

[69] James E. Sidel, *Pick for Your Supper* (National Guild Labor Committee, June 1939), pp. 3–5.

[70] La Follette Committee, *Hearings*, Part 62, p. 22,743.

[71] Creisler, "Little Oklahoma," p. 51.

[72] *Voice of the Agricultural Worker* (hereafter *VOTAW*), September 10, 1940.

[73] California State Relief Administration, *Agricultural Laborers in the San Joaquin Valley*, p. 22,650: Two-thirds of migrant children were scholastically retarded at least one year; 40 percent, at least two years; 20 percent, at least three years; 10 percent, at least four years; Testimony of Gleason, p. 2,999; Theodore T. Dawe, *A Study of the Migratory Children in Kern County for the School Year, 1936–1937* (n.d., n.p.), copy in Federal Writers' Project Collection, Carton 703; La Follette Committee, *Hearings*, Part 62, pp. 22,742–744; *Bakersfield Californian*, September 11, 1937; *People's World*, February 21, 1940; *San Francisco News*, February 16, 1938.

"But," the district noted in late 1939, "the situation is rapidly changing. In the school year 1937–38, there were 88 Oklahoma-born students in the high school." The next year, 128 Oklahomans, 48 Arkansans, and 42 Texans swelled the school's Okie population to over 200. Further increases were predicted for the coming year. Teachers were "frantic, trying to teach these incoming migrant children," while simultaneously attempting to retain the earlier standards. Many of the Okie students, they discovered, required extra-curricular tutoring. The Porterville school was "always in trouble with its budget." Nonetheless, local folk counted themselves lucky. Porterville was in the county's citrus belt, where fewer Okies settled. They recognized that schools in the neighboring cotton belt were faring worse.[74]

Amid a chorus of complaints from local school trustees, state legislators, and, finally, from the state superintendant of public instruction who dubbed the Okie influx a "calamity" for education in many districts, school taxes rose at a more rapid rate than population in the five counties of the upper San Joaquin. Fresno County's tax bill for schools increased 134 percent; Kings', 282 percent; Madera, Kern, and Tulare counties' school expenses varied between these two extremes.[75] Expense alone did not account for the anxiety raised by the coming of the Okies to the valley's schools. Local residents recognized that the migrants desired to send their children to the schools and feared that improved facilities would attract more migrants to their districts. Since, however, local residents also wanted *their* own children to benefit from superior educational facilities, they were confronted with a dilemma.[76] This dilemma, in turn, increased the irritation that communities in the rural regions experienced when the Okies arrived.

The higher tax rates that greeted rural Californians each year in the San Joaquin and Sacramento valleys were blamed almost totally upon the migrant influx. The state chamber of commerce asserted that "not all of the increases [in school costs, social welfare aids, hospitals, health, and sanitation] can be attributed to migrants, but most of them were caused by migration," and the valley's inhabitants accepted the argument.[77] Despite frequent complaints about the relationship between the migrants and increasing tax assessments, there existed considerable evidence that the migrants' effect upon local taxes was overemphasized in the public mind. One obvious explanation, neglected by valley residents, linked rising tax rates to returning prosperity during the years of slow recovery from depression lows. Tax rolls, assessments, and revenues all reached a nadir in

[74] *Pacific Rural Press*, December 30, 1939.
[75] *Bakersfield Californian*, August 27, 1938; La Follette Committee, *Hearings*, Part 59, pp. 21,866–870.
[76] *Los Angeles Times*, July 26, 1937; California League of Women Voters, Educational Facilities for the Children of Migratory Workers ("Penny Sheet No. 4," September 1939), p. 1, copy in Giannini Foundation Library, University of California, Berkeley.
[77] California State Chamber of Commerce, *Migrants: A National Problem* (1940), p. 12.

1933. By 1938 and 1939, however, county residents were capable of bearing higher assessments, and improved services purchased with taxes were now available to residents. These accounted for a great deal of the increased tax load. More subtle arguments demonstrated that, in one sense, the coming of the distressed migrants proved a bargain, possibly an asset, to allegedly harassed agricultural counties. Property taxes, for example, did not rise in proportion to increased expenditures: state and federal relief grants and subventions migrated to these counties with the Okies. Each dollar of federal or state relief entering the rural regions was a redistribution in their favor. Further, relief funds spent by the migrants on food or lodging contributed to business recovery in the valleys.[78]

Finally, while it was undoubtedly the case that local school requirements expanded to mammoth proportions in direct relation to the Okie influx, even here the issue was more complex than it appeared on the surface. The state assumed a large measure of education costs financed through the sales tax, and the PWA supplied many new school buildings at the nation's expense. In short, older residents in California's agricultural communities, faced with the demand for expansion of public facilities, made two errors: they overlooked the more favorable aspects of the Okie migration, and, rather than searching for more basic causes of increased taxation, they refused to go beyond the visible and convenient scapegoat supplied by the migrants.[79] Ex post facto and rational arguments proving the Okies an asset allayed few fears. The presence of masses of dust bowlers along the approaches to the inland towns was upsetting and frightening. Taxpayers in Bakersfield, Tulare, Yuba City, and other towns could not avoid viewing with alarm the steadily increasing property taxes to which, they believed, the migrants had subjected them. In testimony before Senator La Follette, the president of the State Chamber of Commerce accurately assessed the frustration of rural Californians: "In the California counties of Fresno, Kern, Kings, Madera, and Tulare particularly, a strong feeling of injustice exists. People do not bear others' burdens if they feel those burdens are alien and unfair."[80] This phase of the migrant problem was certainly difficult for local people who became hysterical and for Okies who found it hard to accept with calm stoicism the life on the ditch bank, the low wages, and the sick children in the tent or shack.[81] Mutual hostility of local for migrant, migrant for local, led to prejudice from the residents and segregation and humiliation for the migrants.

The migrant problem in the inland valleys was not confined to the physical dislocation wrought by the Okie influx. Beneath the rational, conscious anxieties voiced by residents facing the "migrant hordes" lay a deeper, irrational pattern of prejudice and hatred directed at the migrant. This darker side of the California migrant problem colored, confused,

---

[78] Arpke and Johnson, *Interstate Migration and County Finance*, passim.
[79] Ibid., pp. 3, 25–27.
[80] Testimony of Harrison S. Robinson, La Follette Committee, *Hearings*, Part 59, pp. 21,737–738.
[81] Testimony of Helen G. Douglas, Tolan Committee, *Hearings*, Part 6, p. 2,404.

and complicated an already serious situation and rendered attempts to solve the problem even more difficult.

The anti-Okie prejudice grew from the fertile soil of social stratification that had developed in response to the needs of industrialized agriculture.[82] The half century from 1870 to 1930, which saw the growth of California's factories in the fields, also witnessed the evolution of a distinctive social structure in the inland towns dependent upon the great farms. In many respects, rural communities in California resembled those in the cotton belt of the deep South. Both contained classes and castes defined by race and employment.

California's valley towns were not like the rural communities in the Midwest or East where slavery had never supplied an agricultural labor force. Farming in the Midwest had produced a relatively fluid social structure in which white farmhands achieved status simply by purchasing or renting a farm, marrying the boss' daughter, or opening a store. No racial prejudice was directed at field hands, nor was their occupation considered an inferior one, unfit for white Americans.

Until the coming of the Okies, race had differentiated California's Mexican, Filipino, or Oriental field hand from the white populations of the inland towns. In the value systems of the white population, race combined with field work to produce a pattern of caste relationships between the racial minorities and the "Californians." Contacts between the two groups were stylized by racial prejudice and confined to employer-employee, vendor-consumer roles. In all other respects, minority races were separate from the dominant white community. Social advancement of a Negro, Mexican, Filipino, or Oriental was only "within his own group; he did not enter the social sphere of the white community."[83]

In the 1930s, the intricate system of social relationships that had developed around race and field labor was forced to attempt to accommodate itself to conditions changed by the coming of the Okies. The migrant population camped on the outskirts of town or ensconced within the FSA camps was rapidly becoming the mainstay of the harvest army. The Okies posed a problem that the social system had to resolve: they were white, old-stock Americans, but they were also field labor. California's towns faced the choice of responding to the Okies in racial or economic terms. The future unfolding of the migrant problem hinged upon whether the Okie's whiteness or his role as field worker took priority in the perception of the Californians.

The coming of an individual stranger, or of a small group of them, into a complex and highly organized social structure presents no great difficulty either for the stranger or for the resident. The "number of categories in which the stranger may be placed is large, and the personal characteristics of the individual are more fully evaluated" than they

[82] I am indebted, except where otherwise noted, for material regarding the rural community in California, to Goldschmidt, *As You Sow.*

[83] Ibid., p. 67; see also Davis McEntire, Tyr V. Johnson, and W. W. Troxell, "Migration and Resettlement Problems in Pacific Coast States," manuscript, June 20, 1938, Taylor Collection.

would be in a primitive society. "Personality . . . counts for more and the distinctions are finer."[84] If a few Okie families had migrated to each of California's small towns, their presence as Okies probably would have been totally unnoticed. Many of the towns' residents were transplanted midwesterners themselves, and the new migrants would have found status in the community upon the basis of their individual characteristics.

The Okies, however, did not come singly or in small groups. They came in droves, and their numbers precluded the possibility that the Californians in the affected areas would respond to them as individuals. Where large groups of strangers enter a community, residents strive to discover characteristics common to the intruders in order to relate to them more easily. In the search for an accommodation to the strange group, "the tendency [is] to follow lines suggested by the nature of the relationships which comprise the existing social order."[85] Despite their whiteness, the Okies rapidly became identified in the minds of rural Californians as field workers. Field workers had always been viewed as racial inferiors in the social order. In spite of their white skins, the Okies inherited the racial prejudice that Californians had hitherto applied to the minority groups.

Californians found in "Okie," "Arkie," and "Texie" convenient derogatory epithets by which to identify the newcomers. As one sociologist observed during the height of the influx: "The new migration elicits reactions of a somewhat ethnocentric nature, which attribute distinct physical and moral characteristics to the new native whites. These formerly were made to apply only to races. 'Okies,' 'Arkies' and 'Texies' have taken the place of 'Chinks,' and 'Dagos' in rural terminology."[86]

The content of anti-Okie prejudice was a composite of the most negative characteristics attributed by rural Californians to Negroes, Filipinos, Mexicans, and Orientals. The malnourished physique of the migrants, the deplorable settlements along the ditch banks, even the slightly nasal drawl which had come with them from the southern Plains were the touchstones for a stereotype of the Okie as a naturally slovenly, degraded, primitive subspecies of white American. Lee A. Stone, Madera's health director, maintained an almost Darwinian view of the Okie as a racial type, and many Californians echoed his analysis. In an instructional pamphlet directed to California farmers interested in improving the living accommodations for their field workers, Stone cautioned "sob sisters" against building cabins with more than one room. The Okies, he warned, would tear down the partitions:

> It is recognized that such a condition is not ideal and far from being what it should be, but on the other hand . . . one has to deal with a people whose cultural and environmental background is so bad that for a period of more than three hundred years no

[84] Margaret Mary Wood, *The Stranger* (New York, 1934), p. 283.
[85] Ibid., p. 34.
[86] Stuart M. Jamieson, "A Settlement of Rural Migrant Families in the Sacramento Valley," *Rural Sociology* 7 (March 1942): 50n. See also Goldschmidt, *As You Sow*, p. 47.

advances have been made in living conditions among them and
ethically they are as far removed from a desire to attain the privileges which present day culture and environment offers, than they
were in the days before the revolutionary war. To many this indictment may seem too severe, but to me it is not severe enough.
The poor white of the United States has lived in close proximity
to an advancing civilization and culture for several hundred years
and yet outwardly has made little or no advance.[87]

Stone's comments were public and official. Compared with private
sentiments expressed by many Californians, they were also extremely
mild. At taverns in the Sacramento Valley, one journalist encountered
less analysis and more vituperation among the old-timers at the bar:
"Damned Okies. No damned good. Don't do a damned thing for the
town. Damned shiftless nogoods. Damned Okies. Damned bums clutter
up the roadside."[88] FSA officials contemplating new camp locations were
forced frequently to deal with virulent anti-Okie prejudice. One private
letter, painfully handwritten to President Roosevelt and relayed by his
staff to the FSA offices, summed up in microcosm the tendency of rural
Californians to generalize from specifics when viewing the Okie:

> A Federal migratory camp is being established adjacent to my
> property at Porterville, Tulare County, California.
> Knowing the character of migrants from my experience in
> dealing with them, I object to these hordes of degenerates being
> located at my very door.
>
> These "share croppers" are not a noble people looking for a
> home and seeking an education for their children. They are un-
> principled degenerates looking for something for nothing.
> The fact that they are leaving their native land unfit for
> human habitation is not surprising. Their ignorance and malicious-
> ness in caring for trees, crops, vines, and the land is such that Cali-
> fornia will be ruined if farming is left to them.
>
> Please do not put these vile people at my door to depreciate
> my property and to loot my ranch.[89]

In addition to the charge that they were a degraded people, the Okies
were indicted for other, often contradictory, offensive characteristics. On
the one hand, they were accused of moral degeneracy, of incest, of
"loose morals," and of "oversexedness." On the other hand, organizers
attempting to lure the migrants into unions, as well as ministers of valley
churches, found in the Okie a distasteful holier-than-thou rigidity. The

---

[87] Stone, "What Is the Solution?" pp. 6–7.
[88] *San Francisco Chronicle*, March 11, 1937.
[89] Mrs. Effie Ball Magurn to FDR, April 17, 1940, USDA ASCC Collection, 36,890.

Okie was simultaneously accused of "shiftlessness" and lack of ambition and of "stealing jobs" from native Californians.[90]

It is difficult to measure accurately the extent to which anti-Okie prejudice developed naturally, since a good deal of it was artificially induced by a propaganda campaign launched against the migrants in 1938. Whatever its origins, it penetrated deeply into the popular consciousness. In 1939, Lillian Creisler, a graduate student in economics at the University of California, investigated Modesto's attitude to the "Little Oklahoma" that had sprung up near the airport on the outskirts of town. Miss Creisler asked students at the city's junior college to write short essays about the migrants. The results indicated that the students either hated or were "tolerant to" the migrants in roughly equal proportions.[91] Both groups, nonetheless, shared common anti-Okie attitudes. Even students who sympathized with the plight of the migrants considered them inferior and degraded. They sympathized principally because they felt that California had attracted the migrants and must assume the responsibility for their poverty. Modesto's response to the Okies was typical of California's inland cities. Sociologists, economists, and journalists in other valley towns found similar anti-Okie sentiments to be widespread.[92]

One outgrowth of California's reliance upon minority racial groups to harvest its crops was the segregation of Mexican migrant workers into "Jim towns."[93] Since rural California had displaced onto the Okie the prejudices that had been applied to the Mexicans, it was natural that the migrants would be subjected to segregation and other external signs of their supposed inferiority. The most obvious manifestation of this phenomenon was the Little Oklahomas, the ghettos in which the migrants congregated. In part, these segregated settlements were the natural result of the migrants' poverty and, of course, their numbers; the valley towns had no place to put the new migrants, so the migrants built their own communities. The resident communities accepted the Little Oklahomas as normal for it was proper that migrant workers should be separate from the dominant white community.

The segregation of Okies into separate residential areas was not fostered by the Californians. It developed naturally. In other areas of community life that necessitated contact between the resident and the mi-

[90] John Steinbeck in *The American Guardian*, April 29, 1938, copy in Federal Writers' Project Collection, Carton 2; *Camp Herald*, December 19, 1941; Interview with Mrs. Caroline Decker Gladstein, San Francisco, October 5, 1965; "Interview with Pastor Dwight Brown," USDA BAE Collection, 306,068; Goldschmidt, *As You Sow*, p. 84; Creisler, "Little Oklahoma," p. 63; "Migratory Labor: A Social Problem," *Fortune* 19 (April 1939): 116; Douglas W. Churchill, "Exiles from the Dust Bowl," *The New York Times Magazine* (March 13, 1938): 20.

[91] Creisler, "Little Oklahoma," p. 68.

[92] Goldschmidt, *As You Sow*, passim; Gladstein interview; Jamieson, "A Settlement of Rural Migrant Families," passim; California State Relief Administration, "Agricultural Laborers in the San Joaquin Valley, July, August, 1937," in La Follette Committee, *Hearings*, Part 62, pp. 22,642–666.

[93] Testimony of McWilliams, Part 59, p. 21,777.

grant, segregation and/or exclusion of the Okie was conscious community policy. Even when migrant children were not segregated in the classroom, their relations with the young Californians were strained by the prevailing anti-Okie attitudes. Friendliness might develop between Okie and Californian in the classrooms, but deep friendships were discouraged by the Californian's parents "as they feel it would cut down their social prestige."[94] Teachers, frustrated by the educational backwardness of their Okie pupils, spoke slightingly of them, and sometimes commented upon their alleged willingness to accept charity in the form of free school lunches.[95] Migrant parents could do little to undo the stigmatizing of their school-age offspring. The parents were Okies, too, and rarely made the mistake of attending Parents-Teachers Association meetings more than once. A couple of Okie mothers from Arvin once "came and sat near the edge [of a PTA meeting] but these two recognized that they were out of place and they never came again . . . they were dressed very sloppily and looked very shabbily and did not mingle with the others."[96]

Although the migrants were an intensely religious group, they were no more welcome at the local churches than their children were at the schools. Pastors of the established community churches avoided contact with the migrants, and missionary groups were shocked that ministers "utterly neglected" the FSA camps.[97] The migrants, in turn, avoided the resident congregations. As with the PTA, so with the churches: "The migrants don't come into our churches because they don't feel comfortable . . . they don't have the clothes. . . . They are more at home in the Church of Christ and the Nazarenes. These churches are more like their homes. They can live in a tent and feel comfortable there."[98]

Okies were excluded from clubs and service organizations in many valley towns and were thus deprived of any voice in these organizations. Migrants seeking to extricate themselves from the harvest labor market by entering the nonagricultural job market sometimes found that prospective employers were initially courteous. When the applicant's Oklahoma or Texas origin came up, courtesy became; "Sorry, but we cannot do a thing for you now."[99] Finally, in the summer of 1939, an event reported from the San Joaquin Valley summed up with ruthless precision the social role that Okies were expected to play: a sign appeared in the foyer of a local theater that read "Negroes and Okies upstairs."[100]

The migrants were aware of the manner in which they were viewed by the Californians and resented it. Many had expected hospitality "such

94 *VOTAW*, April 30, 1940.

95 Shafter Camp Reports, October 20, 1939, USDA ASCC Collection, 36,886.

96 *Camp Herald*, November 14, 1941; Interviews with "Pederson" and Frank Stockton, USDA BAE Collection, 306,068.

97 Lloyd B. Thomas, "The Argonauts of Agriculture," *The Witness* 21 (July 22, 1937).

98 Goldschmidt, *As You Sow*, pp. 135–36; Interviews with Rev. John Woolett and Rev. Friesen, USDA BAE Collection, 306,068; Jamieson, "A Settlement of Rural Migrant Familes," 58.

99 *Fresno Bee*, April 8, 1940.

100 Carey McWilliams, "California Pastoral," *Antioch Review* 2 (March 1921): 116.

as they knew in their homes to prevail in California," and were "cruelly shocked, very shortly, by the rude hospitality of the employers and country folk in California."[101] Some, frustrated, went home to Texas, Oklahoma, Arkansas. "We're going back to 'Big D' . . . where the gen'ral sto' keeper treats yo' all lak humans, and where hospitality reigns," one family announced when it left the Marysville FSA camp "A fellow don't appreciate home until he comes to California."[102] Most migrants, however, knew that "home" had been blown into the Atlantic Ocean, been leveled by tractors, or been padlocked by banks. They were determined to stick it out in California, and they lashed out in bitter humor or anger at the prejudice directed against them.[103] The joke columns in the camp newspapers, the songs of Woody Guthrie, the fugitive comments of migrants interviewed by "big city reporters"—these were a catalog of the social tensions developing in the Golden State's valleys:

> . . . when they came over the mountains in 1849, they were called "pioneers," now when we come over the same mountains, in 1939, we are called migrants. Where in Hell did they get that word "Migrant"?[104]

> A tourist and his small son were traveling in California through the cotton belt. The son upon seeing a cotton picker stand up asked his father what it was. His father replied, "That's a cotton picker, son." The son boy after some thought said, "Daddy, them things look almost like people when they stand on their hind legs, don't they?"[105]

> Kaint see how cum folks kinda hate us migrants. The Good Book says as how Jesus went from place to place when he wuz on erf. Aint it so Jesus wuz a migrant?[106]

> Rather drink muddy water
> An sleep in a hollow log

> Rather drink muddy water
> An sleep in a hollow log

> Than to be in California
> Treated like a dirty dog.[107]

---

[101] Unsigned, untitled, undated manuscript, Drobisch Papers, Bancroft Library, University of California, Berkeley.

[102] *VOTAW*, January 26, 1940. Also see *Covered Wagon News*, February 4, 1940: *Tow Sack Tatler*, November 11, 1939.

[103] Creisler, "Little Oklahoma," p. 63.

[104] *VOTAW*, January 26, 1940.

[105] Ibid., December 8, 1939.

[106] Arvin Camp Reports, February 22, 1936, USDA ASCC Collection, 36,879.

[107] Margaret Valiant, *Migrant Camp Recordings* (n.p., n.d.), record no. 5059, "California Blues," copy in Giannini Foundation Library, University of California, Berkeley.

The Year of the
Old Folks' Revolt

DAVID H. BENNETT

Among the many Americans who felt the deprivation of the great depression in a particularly harsh way were the increasing number of aged and retired persons. Until the twentieth century most people died before they reached "the golden years." Improvements in diet, hygiene, and public health began to bring about a drastic decrease in the death rate, however, leading to an increased life expectancy for ordinary Americans. Approximately 90 percent of the Americans born in 1960 could expect to reach the age of sixty, compared to 60 percent of those born in 1860 and only 25 to 40 percent of those born anytime in the seventeenth century. This remarkable demographic shift should require the society to consider seriously the needs of the aged population and to attempt to develop the kinds of resources it requires.

At the time of the depression there were few such services. Retirement and pension plans were rudimentary in the few areas in which they existed, and many older persons found their life savings wiped out by the widespread failure of banking institutions in the early years of the depression. Many of these were people who had worked hard all their lives, and saved carefully for their retirement years. Believers in and practitioners of the protestant ethic, which had held out success or at least comfort for those who followed it, old people in the depression found their futures blighted and their resources depleted. They were a constituency looking for relief from their plight. It is remarkable that for the first time in American history, this growing group with quite specific interests and needs found itself a movement.

The individual who drew the old people of America together briefly during the depression was one of them himself. Dr. Francis Townsend, founder, in spite of himself, of The Old Age Revolving Pensions, Ltd., better known as the Townsend Plan, lost his job in 1933 and came up with an idea that he felt could save both the old people and the nation as a whole. In the selection reprinted below,

David H. Bennett, of Syracuse University, describes the origin, growth, and final disintegration of the Townsend movement. It is a sad story because the noble dream of Dr. Townsend ended the victim of divisiveness brought about by the involvement in the movement of two of the most despicable demogogues in recent American history—the anti-Semitic and red-baiting Gerald L. K. Smith and Father Coughlin.

One positive result of the Townsend Plan and the movement supporting it was the passage of the Social Security Act early in the administration of Franklin Roosevelt. (As so often happens in American politics, the major political parties grudgingly passed legislation sought by special interest groups; these groups might have otherwise developed into political parties that threatened the hegemony of the two old parties. While this legislation provided some immediate benefit for those seeking it, it tended to prevent the formation of a genuinely radical political movement that sees its own programs adopted, albeit in a half-hearted and often piecemeal fashion, by those in power.)

In recent years we have seen an increasing interest in the problems of aging and the life situation of older people. The growing field of gerontology is an example of this development. The scandals surrounding the programs of medical care for the aged and nursing homes have brought to the attention of many the plight of some of the elderly unfortunates. Changes in life style and work style that seem to be coming about slowly may have a greater impact on retired persons than other, more obvious, programs. As people begin to see themselves as other than merely workers and/or consumers, the sharp shift from employed to retired will cease to take such a psychic toll on those going through the next to last rite of passage in industrial society.

For Cleveland, Ohio, the summer of 1936 was a time to remember. In the steaming month of July, during which a twelve-day heat wave in the Midwest and East cost 3,000 lives, there came to the great lake-front city a procession of people—gray, simple, sixtyish, and poor—from all across the nation. They came in buses and railroad coaches and broken-down Fords. Carrying their battered suitcases, they found dollar-a-night lodgings on the city's outskirts and travelled to the downtown convention hall in trolleys, eating bananas and oranges out of bags to save lunch money. They had calloused hands and wore clean but threadbare Sears, Roebuck clothing. They were the delegates to the second annual convention of Old Age Revolving Pensions, Ltd.—disciples of Dr. Francis E. Townsend, whom they fervently believed had been sent by God to save the old people of America in their time of deepest need.

The year before, at Chicago, the first national meeting of the organization had attracted 7,000 delegates. The Cleveland convention drew 11,000. Banners proclaimed "The Three Emancipators: Washington, Lincoln, Townsend." One speaker suggested that "God almighty placed this great idea in the mind of one of His servants." Another announced that "the Doctor is the leader of a greater army than any known to history." Yet another wondered why no star had hung over Dr. Townsend's birthplace to "guide Wise Men of that generation to his side."

If the Townsend Plan was an idea so explosive as to merit this kind of response, then in the presidential election year of 1936 it could prove to be political dynamite. Of this the organizers of the meeting were very much aware. Indeed, the Townsendites were assembling in the very hall where, only a month earlier, the Republican party had met to nominate Alfred M. Landon. As one journalist pointed out, Townsend's convention had at least two advantages over Landon's: it was bigger and it was livelier.

The Cleveland gathering of Townsendites marked the high point of one of the most curious and potentially formidable mass movements in modern American history. The road which led to Cleveland began some three years before in Long Beach, California, where Francis Everett Townsend had his great vision. In 1933 Townsend was almost sixty-seven—a country-bred physician who had come to the retirement community of Long Beach in 1919 to recover his health and seek a livelihood. Educated in rural Illinois schools, he was successively a ranch hand and farm laborer in the West; a mucker in Colorado mines; a homesteader, teacher, and salesman in Kansas. Finally, at the age of thirty-one, he entered medical school in Omaha and after graduation practiced medicine in South Dakota, where he was driven out of Belle Fourche for fighting local political corruption. In 1927–28 he was a real-estate promoter in Long Beach. When the Depression struck, most of his savings were wiped out, and he had to accept an appointment as assistant director of the City Health Office. There he could see just how cruelly the economic crisis was ravaging the old people of America. Years later he recalled that "I stepped into such distress, pain and horror as to shake me even today with its memory. . . . They were good men and women, they had done all they could, had played the game as they had been taught to play it, and suddenly, when there was no chance to start over again, they were let down."

In 1933 the Doctor lost his job when the City Health Office ran out of funds; his own crisis seemed only to intensify a growing feeling that something had to be done to help the old people of America.

For most men the years after age sixty-five are the twilight of their careers, but for Dr. Townsend, all the years that went before seemed to serve only as a prelude for the great work he was now to undertake.

For Townsend had a vision of America's elderly people permanently freed from economic privation by means of a substantial pension, disbursed monthly by the federal government to every citizen aged sixty and over. The government was to raise this money through a small "transaction tax," a multiple sales tax, levied not just at the point of ultimate sale but at each point that a commodity changed hands along the way from raw material to finished product.

The Doctor had read somewhere that in 1929 the gross business done in the United States amounted to $935 billion. He deduced that it would be possible, by tapping this enormous business transaction with a sales tax, to produce twenty to twenty-four billion dollars per year, enough to give $150 a month—later he raised it to $200—to everyone over sixty.

As the months rolled by, Townsend began to advertise his program as a solution to the economic woes of not only the aged but the rest of the population as well. He decided that spending the $200 within thirty days should be made mandatory, and thus began to stress the revolving aspect of his proposal—that twenty to twenty-four billion dollars paid to the elderly every year would tend to stimulate the entire economy as the old people spent their pensions on all manner of consumer goods. He now spoke in terms of the "velocity of money," pointing out, for example, that the dollar spent by an old man for food would be used by his grocer to pay the wholesaler, and so on down the line. In this way, the pension money would "revolve" and would multiply: the pension checks coursing through the economy would stimulate every aspect of American enterprise and finally would end the Depression.

Townsend began to make even more sweeping claims for his plan. Millions of new jobs, he promised, would be made available to younger men by withdrawing the aged from the employment rolls. State and local governments would save the billions of dollars consumed yearly by crime and crime prevention as his plan eliminated poverty and privation; even more billions would be saved which were now spent on charity.

When Townsend described his dream to the aged, it did not seem too far-fetched. To them, the economy of abundance of the 1920s had come to be the normal thing; the Depression, a grotesquely atypical phenomenon. When Townsend drew upon these memories of prosperity and added to them his own thesis, few old people challenged his arguments.

Indeed, there were few who would have wanted to doubt the plan's validity, so bleak were the prospects for the elderly during the Depression. In 1934, only twenty-eight of the forty-eight states had any pension plan at all; three of those were bankrupt and the others were woefully inadequate. Almost three-quarters of a million Americans aged sixty-five and over were on some form of federal relief, and the situation appeared to be getting worse. For, while the elderly were relentlessly being displaced in the job market, they were steadily increasing both in absolute numbers and in percentage of the total population. In 1930 the aged comprised 6.6 million, or 5.4 percent of all the people in the United States; by 1935 these figures had grown to 7.5 million and 6 percent.

Thus it was not surprising that when Dr. Townsend first proposed his plan in late 1933, almost immediately support for it sprang up across America.

The plan grew out of a letter Townsend wrote to the "People's Forum" column of a Long Beach newspaper in late September. At the time, he planned no program of action. But within days of the letter's appearance, replies flooded the paper, which soon devoted a daily page to discussion of Townsend's ideas. At the same time he was approached directly by people who wanted concrete proposals for putting his ideas into action. By November, Townsend had decided to devote his life to realizing his plan. When the Doctor advertised for canvassers to obtain signatures on petitions for congressional action, he was overwhelmed by replies. Within a matter of days he had received completed petitions containing the names of 2,000 supporters.

The Doctor now searched about for a promoter, a person to help him set up the organization that would push the Townsend Plan into law. He turned to Robert Earl Clements, a young, driving real-estate broker.

The two men began collecting names and sending out Old Age Revolving Pensions literature. After five weeks, they were getting an average of one hundred replies a day. Physicians and ministers in the Long Beach area became spokesmen for the plan, and a newspaper, *The Townsend Weekly*, was started. As the movement continued to grow, local Townsend clubs began to spring up, and by January, 1935, five months after the first of these had been founded, the leaders proudly announced that more than 3,000, with a total membership approaching one-half million, were operating—actually there were only 1,200 clubs, but even that figure was impressive. Organizers were soon at work across the nation setting up more clubs, and the Doctor had to hire a staff of ninety-five to handle his mounting flow of mail. Almost overnight, the Townsend movement had become a force to be reckoned with.

The fanaticism with which Townsend's growing thousands of followers promoted his plan astounded and finally frightened journalists and politicians throughout the nation. There were ugly rumors that newly organized Townsend clubs in the Pacific Northwest were threatening merchants and newspaper publishers with economic boycotts if they refused to support the plan. "This thing's become a religion," one alarmed editor said. "It holds the whole town in its grasp."

Clearly, Dr. Townsend had struck into a subsoil of fear and discontent which went far deeper than the immediate material privations of the Depression. Most Townsendites had grown to adulthood believing that they were heirs to a tradition of self-reliance and rugged individualism. The America of their youth was a land in which opportunity abounded, in which a man's failure was seen generally as the result of his own inadequacy, in which the thrifty could count on security in their old age. It was also a land of close family ties, where age was respected.

But in the 1930s, these ideas were becoming only memories. Industrialization and urbanization were destroying the nation's traditional rural and small-town way of life. A man was less independent and less secure in the new America: the factory assembly line robbed him of his individualism and the economics of industrial capitalism subjected him to the vagaries of the business cycle. Family ties were all too often broken as children moved far from their parental homes. Even old age seemed to lose its dignity: the highest premium in the land now seemed to be on youth.

Dr. Townsend appeared on the scene to soothe and comfort the aged. By arguing that a comfortable pension was fully deserved after a lifetime of sacrifice and devotion, he appealed to their hurt pride. He appealed also to their self-esteem, asserting that "people over sixty were selected to be the circulators of large sums of money because they have more buying experience than those of fewer years." He called old people "Civil Veterans of the Republic" and told them that they could become a "research, educational, and corrective force in both a material and spiritual way in the United States."

Thus were the aged offered the best of all possible worlds. They might live in comfort, but they need not feel idle or useless, for as "circulators of money" or, as Townsend preferred to call them, "distributor custodians," they would be serving a vital function.

Furthermore, Townsend did not force his followers to choose between his plan and basic American values. One could be a Townsendite without the risk of being called a foreigner, a "red," or an atheist. The leaders proclaimed their faith in the political and economic system of the nation, and although their solution was clearly a radical one, it was presented in conservative terms. It offered to preserve the "American way of life." It became for its followers, in the words of a contemporary observer, "simply the means of redeeming the promises of the little red school house."

Along with this wholesomely patriotic tone, the movement had a definite religious content. The aura of the evangelist's camp meeting surrounded Townsendism. The leadership included many clergymen; the spokesmen described their cause as being "God-given" and "ordained by the Lord"; well-known religious songs became anthems of the movement; and Bible reading was a part of most of its gatherings.

Aided by this combination of religiosity and patriotism, the Townsend organization, by the start of the election year of 1936, claimed a membership of some 2.2 million in 7,000 local clubs operating across the nation. Dr. Townsend liked to tell his followers that "the movement is all yours, my friends; it belongs to you." In reality, it was very much the property of Francis E. Townsend and the few leaders who surrounded him. Moreover, the old physician began to be affected by his meteoric rise to fame. The speechmaking, the plane trips, the cheering throngs, made him feel, as he confessed to one interviewer, that he "had been chosen by God to accomplish this mission." The movement's newspaper began to compare him to the great men of the past—to Washington and Lincoln, to Columbus and Copernicus, to Franklin and Luther, and even to Christ.

Townsend revelled in the praise, but he did not change his speaking style. His soft, warm voice was not fitted for oratory, and even after delivering dozens of addresses, the old man still seemed ill at ease on the speaker's platform. This very ineptitude proved to be an asset, for the old folks in the Townsend crusade did not want their leader to be too articulate and dynamic; they wanted him to be like themselves. And this the Doctor knew. His conversation was punctuated with homely phrases such as "dang" and "by gum." His publicists pictured him as the folksy older American who had triumphed over adversity and who was now helping all America overcome its troubles.

But Dr. Townsend was not an organizer. He needed a covey of sleek and efficient proselyters, men who were accustomed to talking for their living, men who were willing to serve as the salesmen of Utopia—men, in short, like Robert E. Clements.

Clements, who insisted on calling himself the "co-founder" of the movement, was its manager and fund-raiser. It was he who devised its authoritarian system of centralized control, which Townsend eventually employed to dispose of those dissidents who rebelled against official policy. Clements made the promotion of the Townsend Plan a big business. He marketed Townsend emblems and stickers for automobiles, pictures, pamphlets, songs, buttons, badges, and banners, all sold at a handsome profit. But of all his lucrative schemes, none was so profitable as the *Townsend Weekly*. Its circulation rose steadily to over 300,000; this and other publications of their Prosperity Publishing Company were soon grossing Townsend and Clements $200,000 a year. The bulk of the income from the *Weekly* came from advertisements, many of which preyed on the fears and anxieties of old people, filling the newspaper with testimonials to the magical qualities of bladder tablets, gland stimulants, and kidney pills.

The intensive campaign to build the organization was paying rich dividends by late 1935. Townsend headquarters announced that in the first fifteen months of its existence, total receipts approached three-quarters of a million dollars. In order to justify this growth the Townsend leaders had to exert political pressure for legislative adoption of the plan. But this presented no problem, for Dr. Townsend eagerly awaited the hour when the whole nation would hail his idea.

The Townsendites entered the national political arena when John Steven McGroarty was elected to Congress from southern California. A seventy-two-year-old dramatist and official poet laureate of his state, McGroarty, though a Democrat, was an ardent anti–New Dealer and a confirmed believer in the Townsend Plan, and his election was due in large part to a strong campaign waged in his behalf by local O.A.R.P. organizers. In 1935, McGroarty introduced a bill to implement the pension plan, and within three months the movement's leaders claimed they had twenty million signatures urging its passage.

But this massive pressure was not sufficient. When the revised McGroarty bill came to a vote, it lost by almost four to one. Yet Dr. Townsend and his followers were not discouraged. The loss was considered merely a tactical setback; the war was still to be won. When

Verner W. Main, a Republican from Michigan, won both a primary and a by-election in the spring of 1935 and attributed his victory to strong backing from the O.A.R.P. organization, the Townsendites were elated. "As Main goes, so goes the nation" became the battle cry as the movement assembled for its first national convention in Chicago. In a remarkable address Francis E. Townsend told cheering thousands:

> We dare not fail. Our plan is the sole and only hope of a confused and distracted nation. . . . We have become an avalanche of political power that no derision, no ridicule, no conspiracy of silence can stem. . . . Where Christianity numbered its hundreds in its beginning years, our cause numbers its millions. And without sacrilege we can say that we believe that the effects of our movement will make as deep and mighty changes in civilization as did Christianity itself.

Now Dr. Townsend was sure that he had power as well as purpose. By late 1935 he was ready to use all of this power to turn his plan into law.

Early in December, the Townsend Plan high command wrote to all 531 congressmen, asking whether they would vote for a Townsend bill in the next session. Only sixty answered, and only thirty-nine said yes. The old doctor was angry. He could not understand the rebuff when all across the country there was new evidence of the movement's strength.

Townsend decided that there must be a congressional "conspiracy" against his plan, and that the New Deal was behind it. Although President Roosevelt himself had carefully avoided making a public statement on the pension proposal, his lieutenants—Labor Secretary Frances Perkins, Harry Hopkins, and Senate Majority Leader Joseph Robinson among them—had clearly indicated the administration's opposition.

A major cause of Townsend's irritation with the New Deal was that F. D. R. had once refused to see him. Another and more important reason was the Social Security bill. The Doctor considered its provision of $30 a month for people age seventy and over to be "a miserable dole," an "insult to elderly Americans," and "a mere bid for political support." There may have been some grain of truth in Townsend's charge that Social Security was an attempt to take the spotlight off his plan. The Social Security bill would probably have become law even if Townsend had never come on the scene, but there is little doubt that the existence of the O.A.R.P. organization did speed its adoption. As F. D. R. said to Secretary Perkins: "We have to have it. . . . The Congress can't stand the pressure . . . unless we have a real old-age insurance system. . . ."

A final reason why Dr. Townsend was displeased with the administration was the humiliating experience he had undergone in testifying before the House Ways and Means and the Senate Finance committees during the February, 1935, hearings on the first McGroarty bill. In attempting to explain the intricacies of his plan to the highly critical congressmen, he had become confused and befuddled. For example, asked by the Senate committee to define his transactions tax, Townsend grew un-

certain. The following dialogue took place between Townsend and
Senator Alben W. Barkley of Kentucky.

Senator Barkley: It is a percentage tax based on the amount involved in each transaction?

Dr. Townsend: Yes.

Senator Barkley: So it is really a sales tax.

Dr. Townsend: There is a distinction, but there is very little difference. A sales tax has to necessarily be a tax on
a transaction. All taxes on transactions of a financial nature are sales taxes.

Senator Barkley: So it is a distinction without a difference?

Barkley, a key New Deal spokesman in the Senate, was one of the
Doctor's most derisive critics. When told that all recipients must spend
the money, Barkley asked Townsend for what.

Dr. Townsend: For commodities or for services.

Senator Barkley: Would shooting craps with about six fellows
be services?

Dr. Townsend: No, no, that is not services. . . . We propose
that this shall be spent for commodities.

Senator Barkley: That part of it that went to purchase the craps
be for commodites?

Dr. Townsend: Certainly.

The Roosevelt administration never seriously considered adopting
even a modified version of the Townsend Plan. The President had been
advised by professional economists that if put into practice, it would not
only be unworkable but might well destroy the nation.

Merely reviewing the price of implementing the plan stunned economists; they estimated that its yearly cost would be one and one-half times
the amount spent by all government—federal, state, and local—in 1932,
and almost one-half the total national income for 1934.

The transaction tax, they decided, would almost certainly fail to produce the requisite income, for while the Townsendites based their estimates of income on the gross national product of the last of the
pre-Depression years, 1929, their taxing program would operate in a far
less prosperous America. Moreover, the argument concerning the velocity
of money, the economists said, was mythical—a dollar would not "turn
over" ten times within a month, for even in the boom years of the 1920s
the average turnover amounted to less than three times monthly. And although Townsend looked for economic wonders through money distribution, the promised goods and services simply could not be produced
because of the limitations of existing plant capacity. But the transaction
tax had still another defect. It was essentially a sales tax, and as such, it
was ungraduated. The burden would have fallen on those least able to
afford it. Paul Douglas, professor of economics at the University of Chicago (now U.S. Senator from Illinois), estimated that if this tax had be-

come law, the real income of most workers would have been reduced by about one-half.

Economists of the day asked another question: How would the government make sure the elderly spent their monthly payments promptly? Frugal oldsters, unaccustomed to such a sizable income, might well have attempted to save part of their monthly checks in case the golden faucet should ever be turned off.

When all of its deficiencies had been uncovered, the plan became the butt of economists' jokes. Dr. Louis Haney of New York University wryly suggested that Townsend had not gone far enough, that $200 should be given to everyone every week. If the government can afford $24 billion, Haney said, it can afford $2,400 billion. In Battle Creek, Michigan, a "rival" to the O.A.R.P. was announced. The "Retire at Birth Plan" proposed that every newborn child receive $20,000, payable with interest at age twenty.

Townsend's supporters tried to counterattack. "The politicians should stop listening to these academics," one urged, "for they are but husk-dry pedants, who rely upon books, formal rules, and abstract theories." And a leading publicist for the plan even asserted that "the physician, understanding physiology, may be especially qualified to feel, by the process of intuitive analogy, the most fundamental economic principles."

Convinced of the absurdity of the Townsend Plan, F. D. R. moved to meet the political threat it represented by encouraging, in early 1936, a new series of attacks on it by Democratic congressmen.

Senator Kenneth McKellar of Tennessee opened the assault by stating that the plan was nothing more than a "fantastic . . . devastating . . . wild-eyed scheme for looting the treasury of the United States." Representative Phillip Ferguson of Oklahoma termed it "a racket," and Representative Maury Maverick of Texas argued that it was "a way of avoiding discussion of the real issues."

Dr. Townsend, now certain that "the politicians" were his enemies, was ready to fight back. He accused the New Deal of being "a misdeal . . . where political appointees experiment in human misery." He termed certain actions of the administration "nothing more than Mussolini Fascism." And he even hinted at the formation of a new political party.

Townsend had declared war on Congress and on the White House; retaliation was inevitable. The weapon was a new congressional subcommittee, headed by Missouri Democrat C. Jasper Bell.

The Bell committee's formally stated purpose was to investigate old-age pension plans in order to propose legislation to prevent frauds, but its unstated purpose was to undermine the Townsend organization's effectiveness as a political force in the 1936 elections. The thrust of the attack came in the committee's careful scrutiny of the financial aspects of the Townsend operation. It was revealed that Townsend and Clements took profits far greater than the small salaries they listed on the O.A.R.P. books. Clements' income in 1935 was shown to be $5,200, plus $7,385 from Prosperity Publishing (the *Townsend Weekly*), for a total of $12,585. O.A.R.P. also paid for his Washington, D.C., apartment, and for his transportation, tips, and meals. Clements testified that Townsend made $68,000 in two years with O.A.R.P.; while Townsend did not deny this, he claimed he had "given many dollars to the O.A.R.P. to every one that I received from it."

Midway in its weeks of hearings, the committee called Townsend himself to the witness stand. The Doctor, sensitive to the harsh questions, began to crack under the pressure. His economic naïveté was revealed time and time again. As E. B. White put it, "When forced to deal with the fundamental problems, he quietly came apart, like an inexpensive toy."

For Townsend, the Bell committee hearings represented a disaster. Not only was he publicly humiliated, but key members of his movement began to desert. In April the Doctor had a sudden and bitter quarrel with Representative McGroarty, and the Congressman dissociated himself from the O.A.R.P. organization. But more serious was the defection of Robert Earl Clements. Relations between Clements and Townsend had cooled perceptibly in the weeks before the investigation. The younger man objected particularly to Townsend's occasional threats to start a third political party.

Clements resigned from the movement the day after he was called to appear at the Bell hearings. And once he faced the congressional investigators, he proved willing to give damaging anti-Townsend testimony.

Dr. Townsend was now in trouble. But his followers rallied to their leader. Angry letters poured into the White House, and many Townsendites travelled to Washington to provide moral support for the Doctor, some bearing petitions with hundreds of thousands of signatures attesting that members had "donated the money to be used as the leader saw fit."

Heartened by the evidence of widespread support, Dr. Townsend decided to defy the committee and the New Deal. He lashed out at the hearing, calling it an "inquisition," and he shrewdly played the part of the innocent victim of slander, while his newspaper headlined MOSES BEFORE PHARAOH. Then, after several days of particularly gruelling questioning, Townsend finally had had enough. Suddenly saying, "Good day, gentlemen," the Doctor stood up and walked toward the exit. The congressmen were flabbergasted. The frail old physician had trouble pushing through the crowd, but a large, powerful man leaped to his feet, seized Townsend's arm, and helped him through the throng to the corridor and safety.

The Doctor's savior was the Reverend Gerald L. K. Smith, an experienced and ambitious leader of mass movements, who had his eye on the O.A.R.P. After several years as a successful minister in Indiana and Louisiana, Smith had joined forces with Senator Huey Long and had become the organizer of the national Share-Our-Wealth movement, the vehicle which Long hoped to ride to the Presidency. Spreading rapidly across the South, the Share-Our-Wealth clubs appealed to poor white farmers and small-town merchants, men who wanted to believe that money and power could be wrenched from the leaders of southern society and the captains of eastern industry and be redistributed. Like Long, Smith was a master of the art of crossroads oratory upon which demagogues in the South had for generations built a following among the poverty-stricken "redneck" farmers. Shrewdly exploiting the wealth-sharing theme in the depths of the Depression, the minister was making political headway when, in 1935, the assassination of the "Kingfish" robbed him of his chance for glory. The heirs to Long's Louisiana machine quickly thrust Smith out of his seat of influence, leaving him desperately hungry for power.

Smith's career to that date had been short but spectacular. The roster of organizations he had flirted with included William Dudley Pelley's fascistic Silver Shirt Legion of America and Georgia Governor Eugene Talmadge's violently anti–New Deal Grass Roots Convention. But in the spring of 1936 Smith was without an organization, and he saw Dr. Townsend as the answer to his prayer.

After his rescue in the hearing room, the Doctor took Smith to the Baltimore office of the O.A.R.P., spoke briefly to reporters, and then saw his impromptu press conference taken over by Smith. The following day Smith grandly told newsmen that "we here and now join hands in what shall result in a nation-wide protest against this Communistic dictatorship in Washington."

Townsend seemed dazzled by the powerful personality of his new ally, and Smith persuaded the Doctor to join him on a speechmaking tour of eastern Pennsylvania. In a dramatic climax to that trip, he took the old man to Valley Forge, where, as he told the press, "the Doctor and I stood under the historic arch and vowed to take over the government." By this time Townsend was parroting his younger companion: "We are presenting a common front against the dictatorship in Washington."

Townsend's other subordinates were greatly disturbed: they felt that the Doctor might soon find himself playing Trilby to Gerald Smith's Svengali. But even before meeting Smith, Townsend had become convinced that radical action was necessary if his pension scheme was to become a reality. He had told his followers:

> The only way for us to lick the stuffing out of the old parties is to become militant and go after them hammer and tongs for being totally incompetent . . . We should begin to talk about the Townsend Party and not wait in the foolish hope that one of the old groups will adopt us. If they do, they will treat us like poor adopted trash. To hell with them.

Aware of newspaper reports which indicated that Townsendites were in practical control of at least eight and probably ten states, he began to boast that "we have strength enough to elect a candidate. We have at least thirty million votes."

Now Smith heightened the old man's anger and channeled his thinking along more radical lines. And Smith was anxious to play a role in the formation of the new third party. He told an interviewer at this time, "You know what my ambition is? I think chaos is inevitable. I want to get as many people as I can now, so that when chaos comes, I'll be a leader."

Townsend had been rather hazy about the political nature of the new Townsend party of which he had talked, and he acquiesced when Smith proclaimed himself "director in charge of political policy." The Doctor was naïve enough to believe in Smith's simple but startling arithmetic: six million Townsend Planners plus four million Share-Our-Wealth members equals ten million votes "to start with." Smith could thus convince the unsophisticated old pension promoter that the Share-Our-Wealth movement was a formidable political force, but he himself knew that this was only a dream. In fact, Gerald L. K. Smith had lost control of the Share-Our-Wealth mailing lists after Long's assassination and his organization was now defunct. He knew that he and Dr. Townsend would need allies if they were to achieve a political revolution.

Such allies were readily available. The Reverend Charles E. Coughlin, a Catholic priest with a parish in a Detroit suburb, had experienced a meteoric rise to fame and power during the Depression years by effectively utilizing that new tool of mass communication, the radio. The "radio priest" advocated a strong central bank and the distribution of large amounts of unbacked currency as a means of bringing the United States out of the Depression. He accused international bankers and the Roosevelt brain trusters alike of being part of a conspiracy to undermine America's position at home and abroad.

His audience was composed mainly of lower and lower-middle class Irish and German Catholics living in large cities. For these people Coughlin offered both an explanation of their Depression-born woes and an emotional outlet for their frustration. By identifying their oppressors as rich eastern bankers, white Anglo-Saxon Protestant aristocrats, and Ivy League intellectuals, he appealed both to a hidden ethnic and religious bias and to the insecurity of his listeners as relative newcomers still not fully assimilated into the American melting pot. In accusing these "oppressors" of being somehow un-American—that is, both communistic and capitalistic in an evil "international" sense—he gave his followers at once more security in their own Americanization and a scapegoat for their anger.

The priest had organized his followers into a huge, active movement, the National Union for Social Justice, and by the spring of the presidential election year, he, like Townsend, was talking in terms of a new political party. His candidate was to be William Lemke, a Republican congressman from North Dakota, a veteran of third-party organizing efforts in his home state, and a man who commanded a wide following among the dissatisfied farmers of the northern Plains.

The Coughlin and Lemke forces soon became the prime object of Gerald Smith's plans. At first Townsend balked. He had, in the past, made derogatory statements about both the Congressman and the priest. But Smith slowly built a bridge between Father Coughlin and the Doctor. Coughlin's strong support for Townsend after the Bell committee hearings softened the pension leader's attitude, and Lemke's defense of the plan made him more palatable to Townsend.

In May, Smith told the press that he, Coughlin, and Townsend were about to "congeal under a leadership with guts." By June 16 he was as-

serting that "more than twenty million votes" could be controlled by a
"Smith-Townsend-Coughlin-Lemke Axis." A working agreement was developing among the four.

On June 19, Lemke announced the formation of the new Union
party, with himself as the presidential candidate. Lemke told newsmen
that "we are assured that all these groups—the Coughlin followers, the
supporters of Dr. Townsend and the members of the Share-Our-Wealth
movement—welcome the opportunity to unite under the banner of this
party." Smith moved quickly to win Townsend's cooperation. He escorted
the Doctor to Washington, D.C., where they conferred with a Coughlin
spokesman and with candidate Lemke himself. Townsend was impressed,
and his desire to advertise himself and his plan increased with the rising
fervor of political activity around the country as the 1936 presidential
election approached. The old doctor decided to cast his lot with the
Union party. But although he would give it his personal backing, he
decided it would be a tactical error to have his organization formally endorse Lemke; he wished to avoid the risk of officially backing a losing
horse.

The new third party, then, came into the world as the product of a
curious coalition, bound together by somewhat similar inflationist programs and a unifying hatred of Franklin D. Roosevelt. But there were
significant divisive factors: the rival personal ambitions of the leaders and
the strikingly different groups of supporters to which each appealed. If
the Union party was to be successful, its disparate elements would have to
work together.

One of these elements was already facing an internal test. In July, the
Townsend National Recovery Plan, as it was now called, prepared to hold
its second annual convention in Cleveland. As thousands of aged Americans trekked to the Lake Erie city for the event, the road that had begun
in Long Beach, California, two years earlier reached its most important
turning point.

On the first day of the convention, good fellowship overflowed. A
man on the rostrum instructed each member of the audience to shake
hands with the neighbor sitting at each side. Another told everybody to
shout, "God bless you." But the warm glow experienced that first day
was cooled by the proceedings of the next, when Representative Gomer
Smith—a Democrat from Oklahoma, a famous lawyer of Indian blood,
and a stirring orator—stood up to speak. Gomer Smith was a power in
the movement, and he was angry at recent developments. Now he blasted
Father Coughlin and Gerald L. K. Smith, accusing them of trying to use
Townsend for their own purposes. He praised F.D.R. and spoke against
endorsement of the Union party.

The crowd gave Gomer Smith a rousing ovation. An angry Dr.
Townsend hurried to the microphone to say that "poor Gomer" was a
"troublemaker" and should not be applauded. The permanent chairman
of the convention then stated that "there will be no more free speech at
these meetings." But the trouble was not over. The whole question of the
Townsend movement's role in the coming campaign had been opened,

and by the end of the day some fifteen state delegations had caucused and voted against backing Lemke.

Townsend and Gerald L. K. Smith were prepared for this revolt. They had already decided that they would follow the course which the dissenters were now demanding: no "official" endorsement of the new party by the organization. Townsend now pushed on with the remainder of the convention program: speeches by the four key men of the Union party.

Gerald L. K. Smith was first. He had been having a fine time at the convention. He roamed the floor of the auditorium, shaking hands with the delegates and looking the part, as one newsman put it, of "the irrepressible young man smashing his way into the leadership of the movement."

Smith's speech was perhaps the best of his career. An astounded H. L. Mencken wrote:

> His speech was a magnificent amalgam of each and every American species of rabble-rousing, with embellishments borrowed from the Algonquin Indians and the Cossacks of the Don. It ran the keyboard from the softest sobs and gurgles to the most ear-splitting whoops and howls, and when it was over the thousands of delegates simply lay back in their pews and yelled. Never in my life, in truth, have I heard a more effective speech.

Smith spoke clutching a Bible. Coatless, sweat plastering his shirt to his broad shoulders and barrel chest, he roared hatred of Wall Street bankers, millionaire steel magnates, Chicago wheat speculators, and New Deal social engineers who "sneezed at the Doctor's great vision." He issued his call to arms and bellowed:

> We must make our choice in the presence of atheistic Communistic influences! It is Tammany or Independence Hall! It is the Russian primer or the Holy Bible! It is the Red Flag or the Stars and Stripes! It is Lenin or Lincoln! Stalin or Jefferson! James A. Farley or Francis E. Townsend!

As the crowd gave Smith a standing, screaming ovation, the next speaker fidgeted nervously. Jealous of his new ally's platform delivery, Father Coughlin had sulked at the back of the auditorium through most of Smith's address. And as Smith concluded, the priest decided to make a dramatic gesture.

Midway through his address, Coughlin halted for an electric pause. He stepped back from the microphone and, peeling off his black coat and his Roman collar, literally unfrocked himself before the audience of 10,000 people. Striding back to the rostrum, he roared: "As far as the National Union is concerned, no candidate who is endorsed for Congress can campaign, go electioneering for, or support the great betrayer and liar, Franklin D. Roosevelt." And then he concluded: "I ask you to purge the man who claims to be a democrat from the Democratic Party—I mean Franklin Double-Crossing Roosevelt."

After a moment of stunned silence, the delegates stamped and shouted their approval of this vicious assault upon the nation's President. And they kept on shouting as Coughlin proclaimed Townsend, Smith, and himself as the "trinity of hope" against the "unholy trinity of Roosevelt, Landon, and Browder."

Now, Charles E. Coughlin made his bid:

> . . . there is Dr. Townsend and there is the Reverend Gerald L. K. Smith. By those two leaders I stand foursquare. Ladies and gentlemen, you haven't come here to endorse any political party. [Their principles] have been incorporated in the new Union party. You are not asked to endorse it. Your beloved leader endorses them and how many of you will follow Dr. Townsend?

The Townsendites, almost to a man, rose in response to Coughlin's question.

After such oratorical pyrotechnics, Dr. Townsend's speech seemed tepid stuff. But his adoring followers did not care. Making his position in the coming election clear, he affirmed that he "could not do otherwise" than to support William Lemke for President.

It was Lemke who was the featured speaker on the last day of the convention. The meeting's organizers, hoping for a large crowd, had hired the 85,000-seat Cleveland Municipal Stadium. But many Townsendites decided to head home early, and Lemke addressed a disappointing gathering of 5,000 people. The audience response to the Union party candidate was listless. Townsendites had amply demonstrated in the past that they would do almost anything for their beloved leader, but it became clear that they might refuse to back the man Dr. Townsend had endorsed for the Presidency. The Townsendites, as one member explained, were "just folks . . . just Methodist picnic people." Most of them were Protestants of Anglo-Saxon origin and could trace their genealogy far back into American history. They were farmers, small-businessmen, clerks, or skilled independent workers. They were political conservatives, and despite their fanatical commitment to Townsend's proposals, despite their cheering of the demagogues at the Cleveland convention, they were reluctant to support an extremist political organization such as the new Union party. And yet if Lemke lost badly, the Townsend Plan, now so heavily tied to his candidacy, stood to lose as well. This was the dilemma facing Francis E. Townsend as the Cleveland convention came to a close and the presidential campaign got under way.

Throughout July and August, Townsend relentlessly toured the nation for the Union ticket, and when Coughlin's National Union for Social Justice held its own convention in mid-August, the old doctor was on hand to make a speech along with Lemke, Smith, and the radio priest. It seemed as if the strange coalition of radical leaders was indeed going to hold together.

This proved to be an illusion. Except for the curious hold that Gerald Smith had over Townsend, relations among the four key men of the Union party were never cordial. Each was primarily concerned with promoting his own program and/or personality. Coughlin, for example, withheld full backing of Townsend's plan even after the Cleveland convention. Moreover, when asked by reporters if he intended to make a joint speaking tour with his allies, he snapped: "Why must they be tagging around after me all the time?"

Candidate Lemke was inept at personal relations with his major supporters. He conducted his own campaign, and his contacts with the other three party leaders were incredibly infrequent.

As the weeks went by and autumn approached, the strains in the alliance began to show. Dr. Townsend's wavering enthusiasm soon became a critical factor in the weakening of the party's drive. After his exertions at the two conventions and his strenuous speaking tour, the sixty-nine-year-old physician fell ill. He did make a few appearances, but he could not contribute as much to the Union cause as his fellow party leaders.

Even when his health improved sufficiently to allow him to resume active campaigning, the Doctor proved to be an inconsistent champion of Lemke's candidacy. On some occasions he would wholeheartedly praise the North Dakotan, but at other times he would qualify his endorsement. He refused, for instance, to insist that local Townsend clubs play any role in the grass-roots organization of the Union party.

By late August, pressures began building up within the Townsend movement which were to cause the Doctor to lose heart for the Union crusade. Several of his important subordinates had been complaining about the influence of Gerald L. K. Smith and had been opposing the founder's endorsement of Lemke. When Townsend fired these men, they brought suit against the Townsend National Recovery Plan, Ltd., asking that Townsend be ousted as president. The Doctor survived this attack only after lengthy court action.

Townsend's troubles were compounded by the poor showing of candidates endorsed by his movement in various primary elections held in the late summer. And in September and October, the pension promoter began to receive disturbing reports about the reaction of his large California following to the Lemke candidacy. A presidential preference poll of 50,000 California Townsendites showed 28 percent for Roosevelt, 52 for Landon, 4 neutral and only 6 percent for Lemke.

At this point, Gerald L. K. Smith might have been expected to step in to convince the Doctor to stay with the new political party. But Smith had been undergoing his own metamorphosis. After his performances at the Townsend and Coughlin conventions, he had left his political allies and embarked alone on a speech-making tour of the South. As the Union party campaign progressed, Smith's statements to the press began to take on a somewhat paranoid tone. He talked of a Communist plot to kill him and revealed that he had "definite information" that F.D.R. was planning to seize dictatorial power. In October, he shouted at reporters, "Politics is prostitution . . . The democratic method is a lot of baloney, it doesn't mean anything. We can tell what they're thinking without taking a vote." Late in the month, Smith announced that he was proceeding immediately with the formation of an organization aimed at "ultimately seizing the government of the United States." He then began a speaking tour of the East to raise money for this new venture. When asked if this tour were not part of the Union party campaign, Smith's reply was, "I joined the Union party only for a forum. . . . What I am really interested in is forming this new force . . ."

Townsend's reaction was quick and sharp. "If the press reports concerning the fascist action of Gerald L. K. Smith are true," said the old man, who felt betrayed by one he had befriended, "then I hereby disavow any connection that I may have had with Mr. Smith." Thus ended Gerald L. K. Smith's adventure in third-party politics and his connection with the Townsend Plan. But in leaving the pension organization, he left Dr. Townsend alone and confused as to his participation in the Union party.

In the weeks before the election Townsend began moving toward Landon, telling the press, "I shall cast my vote for an untried man in hope that he may prove of greater value to the nation than the incumbent. . . . I do this because I will not be permitted to vote for Mr. Lemke, my choice for the office." He referred to the fact that in his own state of California—and in thirteen others as well—Lemke's name would not be on the ballot. In these areas, as the days passed, Townsend widened his appeal for Landon support. "Lemke has my endorsement," he proclaimed, "but remember, Roosevelt is our sworn enemy. . . . He must be beaten!" This last-minute switch confused his supporters and seriously weakened the Union party.

When the returns came in on November 3, the dream of power that the radical leaders had shared when they had made their summer alliance was blasted. William Lemke received less than 900,000 votes as Franklin D. Roosevelt, the hated foe, rolled up the most one-sided Electoral College victory in American history; he received more than 27 million popular votes, to Alfred Landon's 16 million.

All of the leaders of the new political organization were to pay a severe price for the horrendous defeat. And after the election their careers curved downhill.

Father Coughlin returned to the spotlight in December, 1937, when he formed the Christian Front Against Communism, a movement which reflected his increasingly totalitarian ideology. In a series of radio broadcasts Coughlin initiated an anti-Semitic crusade, accusing the Jews of originating Communism and excusing Nazism as an understandable attempt to block Jewish-Communist plans for subjugating Germany. The priest spoke at German-American Bund rallies, and when hostilities broke out in Europe, he actively supported Hitler's "sacred war . . . against the Jews." After Pearl Harbor, when Coughlin's newspaper was barred from the mails under the Espionage Act and his church insisted that he discontinue his political activities, the golden radio voice was finally silenced. [. . .] Never again was Father Coughlin to be active in the political arena.

Gerald Smith also crusaded against Communists and Jews in the late thirties and early forties. But unlike Coughlin, he persisted throughout the war years and after. Smith's anti-Semitism was particularly vile; he led what he called the "Stop-Ike-the-Kike" campaign before the 1948 primaries, and later vilified the United Nations as the "Jew-nited Nations." In the 1950s Gerald Smith became just another bitter old man lost in the radical crowd.

Townsend's course, never that of a true demagogue, was very different. He returned to diligent work for the group whose support had brought him into the limelight. But the 1936 election had exposed the pension organization to the nation as an ineffective political pressure group. It had no real power—it could not defeat a President or intimidate the major parties.

And the old doctor was now vulnerable as he had never been in the past. Shortly after the election, it was announced in Washington that Townsend would be prosecuted on the contempt citation voted against him when he had dramatically walked out of the Bell committee hearings in the spring. He was convicted in early 1937, and only a barrage of pleading letters from those who remained faithful moved the President to commute the thirty-day jail sentence, though he was required to pay a $100 fine.

Dr. Townsend remained a free man, but his organization was faltering. Membership fell off, and from the decay of the plan sprang other panaceas, such as the "Thirty Dollars Every Thursday" clubs in California. Although Dr. Townsend pushed on, continuing to lead his dwindling band of followers, publishing his newspaper, and maintaining a national headquarters throughout the war and postwar years, nothing could reverse the growing tide of unconcern among the elderly toward the movement and its founder. The end of the Depression and the prosperity of the 1940s and 1950s eliminated the fear and privation upon which the plan had fed. Yet Francis E. Townsend carried on until 1960, when, still speaking hopefully of the future, the man who had found a career when most men think of retirement died in Los Angeles at ninety-three.

Dr. Townsend did not achieve his long-sought goal. But in the Depression decade this dedicated, sincere man, despite his ignorance of economics and naïveté about politics, carved out an important place for himself in American life. "It is dissatisfaction with the attainable," Raymond Gram Swing has written, "which leads to fanaticism and at last to social fury. . . . When great masses are ready to believe the impossible, that is an ominous political fact." In the 1930s, when the great Depression created a crisis in which messianic leaders could flourish, millions of pathetically eager, infinitely hopeful, and dangerously credulous people trooped blindly after Dr. Francis E. Townsend. The old Doctor pushed his followers too far and too fast in the election campaign of 1936, but for many hectic months his movement was a force to be reckoned with in the United States. Winston Churchill, then sixty-two years old, came to this country during those months and dismissed the Townsend Plan as "an attempt to mint the moonlight into silver and coin the sunshine into gold." Perhaps it was. But for a time millions of Americans fervently believed in it. The year was 1936—the year of the old folks' revolt.

Pearl Harbor

and the

Yellow Peril

ROGER DANIELS

In 1882, when Congress passed the Chinese Exclusion Act, which virtually ended Chinese immigration to the United States, there were fewer than two hundred Japanese in this country. The exclusion of the Chinese, however, produced a drastic shortage of labor on the West Coast, thus stimulating immigration from Japan. Although the rulers of Japan had long been opposed to emigration (in fact, prior to 1854 it was a crime punishable by death), in the late nineteenth century they were persuaded to change their policy, and there was a large movement of Japanese citizens into the Western Hemisphere. In the first ten years of the twentieth century, over ninety thousand Japanese entered the United States.

The immigrants were at first welcomed because they filled necessary slots in the expanding economy, but quickly antagonisms began to mount. Since the turn of the century, Japan had been rising to prominence as a world power, and many Californians saw the influx of Japanese laborers as a prelude to invasion by the Japanese state. Labor groups, fearing competition from foreign workers, joined an inflammatory press and opportunistic politicians to have the Japanese excluded from the United States along with the Chinese under the act of 1882. In 1900, the Japanese government consented to curb the emigration of labor to the United States by denying passports to would-be emigrants. Then, in 1907, when the Japanese government protested the increasing racial discrimination faced by the Japanese in California, President Theodore Roosevelt arrived at what was called the "Gentlemen's Agreement" with the rulers of Japan, under which both the United States and Japan were to take measures to stop migration between the two countries. Finally, virtually all immigration from East Asia was permanently halted by the Immigration Act of 1924.

Because the Naturalization Act of 1790 had limited the privilege of naturalization to "free white persons," East Asian migrants to this country legally remained "aliens." This condition was used against them when California passed the Alien Land Act of 1913, barring "aliens ineligible for citizenship" from owning land in the state. Meanwhile, other discriminatory practices were spreading in the West. Many of the stereotypes that white Americans had developed with regard to the Chinese were transferred to the Japanese. They were accused of being devious, unreliable, and dishonest. They were seen as a threat to Christian civilization, to the democratic way of life, to the virtue of white women. Because of the fear of "moral contamination," the San Francisco School Board barred Japanese children from public schools in 1906. The racism inherent in the attitudes of the dominant whites of the West was demonstrated in increased agitation against the "yellow peril."

In the 1930s, Japanese incursions into China built up increasing hostility toward the Japanese-Americans living on the West Coast. Then, on December 7, 1941, when the Japanese navy bombed Pearl Harbor, shock and outrage swept through the American people. Much of this was to be vented on the West Coast Japanese. On the eve of the war, there were 126,947 persons of Japanese ancestry living in the United States, 112,935 of whom were concentrated in the states of California, Oregon, Washington, and Arizona. Of the latter group, 41,089 were foreign born, or Issei, the remainder were Nisei, citizens of the United States who were born in this country to foreign-born parents.

In the early months of 1942, the war went well for the Japanese army and navy but badly for the Japanese residents of the United States. Racist feelings were intensified by wild rumors of sabotage and espionage, and a variety of groups demanded the expulsion of Japanese-Americans from the West Coast. Then, under the direction of the United States Army and the War Relocation Authority, set up by President Franklin Roosevelt, the Japanese living along the coast were urged to move from their homes to "resettlement centers" in the nation's interior. When voluntary relocation failed, the army forcibly moved over one hundred thousand persons to the centers and held them there under armed guard.

The selection reprinted below from a book by Roger Daniels, of the University of Cincinnati, describes the growing antagonism of the Californians to the Japanese both before and after Pearl Harbor that led to their internment.

After a year or two, the "security" of the camps relaxed, and many of the prisoners—none of whom had been proven guilty of disloyalty —were allowed to work and to move around outside the so-called critical areas. In 1944, some Japanese-Americans were allowed to return to the coast, and in 1946, the last of the shameful internment camps was closed.

If the attack on Pearl Harbor came as a devastating shock to most Americans, for those of Japanese ancestry it was like a nightmare come true. Throughout the 1930s the Nisei generation dreaded the possibility of a war between the United States and Japan; although some in both the Japanese and American communities fostered the illusion that the emerging Nisei generation could help bridge the gap between the rival Pacific powers, most Nisei, at least, understood that this was a chimera. As early as 1937 Nisei gloom about the future predominated. One Nisei spoke prophetically about what might happen to Japanese Americans in a Pacific war. Rhetorically he asked his fellow Nisei students at the University of California:

> . . . what are we going to do if war does break out between United States and Japan? . . . In common language we can say "we're sunk." Even if the Nisei wanted to fight for America, what chances? Not a chance! . . . our properties would be confiscated and most likely [we would be] herded into prison camps—perhaps we would be slaughtered on the spot.[1]

As tensions increased, so did Nisei anxieties; and in their anxiety some Nisei tried to accentuate their loyalty and Americanism by disparaging the generation of their fathers. Newspaper editor Togo Tanaka, for example, speaking to a college group in early 1941, insisted that the Nisei must face what he called "the question of loyalty" and assumed that since the Issei were "more or less tumbleweeds with one foot in America and one foot in Japan," real loyalty to America could be found only in his own generation. A Los Angeles Nisei jeweler expressed similar doubts later the same year. After explaining to a Los Angeles *Times* columnist that many if not most of the older generation were pro-Japanese rather than pro-American, he expressed his own generation's fears. "We talk of almost nothing but this great crisis. We don't know what's going to happen. Sometimes we only look for a concentration camp."[2]

While the attention of Japanese Americans was focused on the Pacific, most other Americans gave primary consideration to Europe, where in September 1939 World War II had broken out. Hitler's amazing blitzkrieg against the west in the spring of 1940—which overran, in quick succession, Denmark and Norway and then Holland, Belgium, Luxembourg, and France—caused the United States to accelerate its defense pro-

[1] *Campanile Review* (Berkeley), Fall, 1937.
[2] Tom Treanor, "The Home Front," Los Angeles *Times*, August 6, 1941.

gram and institute the first peacetime draft in its history. Stories, now known to be wildly exaggerated, told of so-called fifth column and espionage activities, created much concern about the loyalty of aliens, particularly German-born aliens, some 40,000 of whom were organized into the overtly pro-Nazi German-American Bund. As a component part of the defense program, Congress passed, in 1940, an Alien Registration Act, which required the registration and fingerprinting of all aliens over fourteen years of age. In addition, as we now know, the Department of Justice, working through the Federal Bureau of Investigation, was compiling a relatively modest list of dangerous or subversive aliens—Germans, Italians, and Japanese—who were to be arrested or interned at the outbreak of war with their country. The commendable restraint of the Department of Justice's plans was due, first of all, to the liberal nature of the New Deal. The Attorney General, Francis Biddle, was clearly a civil libertarian, as befitted a former law clerk of Oliver Wendell Holmes, Jr.

Elsewhere in the government however, misgivings about possible fifth column and sabotage activity, particularly by Japanese, were strongly felt. For example, one congressman, John D. Dingell (D-Mich.), wrote the President to suggest that Japanese in the United States and Hawaii be used as hostages to ensure good behavior by Japan. In August 1941, shortly after Japanese assets in the United States were frozen and the Japanese made it difficult for some one hundred Americans to leave Japan, Dingell suggested that as a reprisal the United States should "cause the forceful detention or imprisonment in a concentration camp of ten thousand alien Japanese in Hawaii. . . . It would be well to remind Japan," he continued, "that there are perhaps one hundred fifty thousand additional alien Japanese in the United States who [can] be held in a reprisal reserve."[3]

And, in the White House itself, concern was evidenced. Franklin Roosevelt, highly distrustful of official reports and always anxious to have independent checks on the bureaucracy, set up an independent "intelligence" operation, run by John Franklin Carter. Carter, who as the "Unofficial Observer" and "Jay Franklin" had written some of the most brilliant New Deal journalism and would later serve as an adviser to President Harry S Truman and Governor Thomas E. Dewey, used newspapermen and personal friends to make special reports. In early November he received a report on the West Coast Japanese from Curtis B. Munson. His report stressed the loyalty of the overwhelming majority, and he understood that even most of the disloyal Japanese Americans hoped that "by remaining quiet they [could] avoid concentration camps or irresponsible mobs." Munson was, however, "horrified" to observe that

> dams, bridges, harbors, power stations etc., are wholly unguarded. The harbor of San Pedro [Los Angeles' port] could be razed by fire completely by four men with hand grenades and a little study in one night. Dams could be blown and half of lower California

[3] Dingell to FDR, August 18, 1941, Franklin D. Roosevelt Library, Hyde Park, Official File 197.

> could actually die of thirst. . . . One railway bridge at the exit
> from the mountains in some cases could tie up three or four main
> railroads.[4]

Munson felt that despite the loyalty or quiescence of the majority, this situation represented a real threat because "there are still Japanese in the United States who will tie dynamite around their waist and make a human bomb out of themselves."[5] This imaginary threat apparently worried the President too, for he immediately sent the memo on to Secretary of War Henry L. Stimson, specifically calling his attention to Munson's warnings about sabotage. In early December, Army Intelligence drafted a reply (which in the confusion following Pearl Harbor was never sent) arguing, quite correctly as it turned out, that "widespread sabotage by Japanese is not expected . . . identification of dangerous Japanese on the West Coast is reasonably complete."[6] Although neither of these nor other similar proposals and warnings was acted upon before the attack on Pearl Harbor, the mere fact that they were suggested and received consideration in the very highest governmental circles indicates the degree to which Americans were willing to believe almost anything about the Japanese. This belief, in turn, can be understood only if one takes into account the half century of agitation and prophecy about the coming American-Japanese war and the dangers of the United States being overwhelmed by waves of yellow soldiers aided by alien enemies within the gates.

This irrational fear of Oriental conquest, with its racist and sex-fantasy overtones, can be most conveniently described as the "yellow peril," a term probably first used by German Kaiser Wilhelm II about 1895. As is so often the case, the phenomenon existed long before the name. Between 1880 and 1882 three obscure California publicists produced works describing the successful invasion and conquest of the United States by hordes of Chinese. These works were undoubtedly concocted to stimulate and profit from the initial campaign for Chinese exclusion, successfully consummated in 1882. There is no evidence that they were taken seriously by any significant number of people; in that period, after all, China was a victim, not a predator. But, by the end of the century, a potential predator had appeared; in 1894 formerly isolated and backward Japan won its first modern naval battle, defeating the Chinese off the Yalu River. The very next year, that prince of Jingoes, Henry Cabot Lodge, then a Republican congressman from Massachusetts, warned Congress that the Japanese "understand the future . . . they have just whipped somebody, and they are in a state of mind when they think that they can whip anybody." In 1898, during the discussion of the American annexation of Hawaii, Senator Cushman K. Davis (R-Minn.), chairman of

---

[4] Munson's Report enclosed in Memo, FDR-Stimson, November 8, 1941, Franklin D. Roosevelt Library, Hyde Park, "Stimson Folder."

[5] *Ibid.*

[6] Stetson Conn, "Notes," Office, Chief of Military History, U.S. Army. Illuminating but fragmentary details of the Carter intelligence operations may be found in the Carter Mss., University of Wyoming.

the Senate Foreign Relations Committee, warned his colleagues that the mild controversy with Japan over Hawaii was merely "the preliminary skirmish in the great coming struggle between" East and West.

These still nascent fears about Japan were greatly stimulated when the Japanese badly defeated Russia in the war of 1904–1905, the first triumph of Asians over Europeans in modern times. The shots fired at Mukden and in the Straits of Tushima were truly shots heard round the world. Throughout Asia the Japanese victory undoubtedly stimulated nationalism and resistance to colonialism; in Europe, and particularly in the United States, it greatly stimulated fears of conquest by Asia. Shortly after the end of that war the "yellow peril" was adopted by its most significant American disseminator, newspaper mogul William Randolph Hearst. Although the theme of possible Japanese attack had been initiated by a rival paper, the San Francisco *Chronicle,* it was Hearst's San Francisco *Examiner,* as well as the rest of his chain, which made the theme of danger from Asia uniquely its own. Although there are earlier scattered references to the external Japanese threat, the real opening salvo of what the chain later called its thirty-five-year war with Japan began in the *Examiner* on December 20, 1906. Its front page that day proclaimed

JAPAN SOUNDS OUR COASTS
Brown Men Have
Maps and Could
Land Easily

The next year the Hearst papers printed the first full-scale account of a Pacific war between the United States and Japan. Richmond Pearson Hobson, who had translated an inept but heroic exploit in the Spanish-American War into a seat in Congress (he was an Alabama Democrat), was the author of the two-part Sunday Supplement fantasy. Under the headline JAPAN MAY SEIZE THE PACIFIC COAST, Hobson wrote, "The Yellow Peril is here." Unless a really big navy were built, Hobson calculated, an army of "1,207,700 men could conquer the Pacific Coast." He predicted that Japan would soon conquer China and thus "command the military resources of the whole yellow race."

An even more elaborate military fantasy—or rather a series of fantasies—was concocted by "General" Homer Lea. Lea was a Sinophile who served as a military adviser to Sun Yat Sen. There is no evidence, despite the claims of naïve publicists, that he ever commanded troops in battle. His most important literary work, *The Valor of Ignorance,* was published in 1909 and reissued, with an effusive introduction by Clare Booth Luce, shortly after Pearl Harbor. It foretold, in great detail, a Japanese conquest of the Philippine Islands, quickly followed by a landing on the Pacific Coast and the occupation of California, Oregon, and Washington. Lea, who felt that only professional armies could fight, insisted that the small American army would be no match for the Japanese. In florid prose, he described the results of this conquest.

Not months, but years, must elapse before armies equal to the Japanese are able to pass in parade. These must then make their way over deserts such as no armies have ever heretofore crossed; scale the entrenched and stupendous heights that form the redoubts of the desert moats; attempting, in the valor of their ignorance, the militarily impossible; turning mountain gorges into the ossuaries of their dead, and burdening the desert winds with the spirits of their slain. The repulsed and distracted forces to scatter, as heretofore, dissension throughout the Union, breed rebellions, class and sectional insurrections, until this heterogenous Republic, in its principles, shall disintegrate, and again into the palm of re-established monarchy pay the toll of its vanity and its scorn.

Hearst, Hobson, and Lea were all essentially conservative, social Darwinistic racists. But the yellow peril was popular on the left as well. The English Fabian Socialist H. G. Wells, perhaps the greatest English-speaking science fiction writer, is best known for his fantasy about a Martian invasion. But in his *War in the Air* (1908) Orientals rather than Martians were the bogeymen. In the novel Wells rather accurately predicts World War I, and has the United States, France, and Great Britain locked in a death struggle with Germany. Then, without warning, Japan and China indiscriminately attack the white powers almost destroying civilization in the process. A character comments, "the Yellow Peril was a peril after all."

Even during World War I, when Japan fought Germany, anti-Japanese military propaganda did not cease; the publications of the infamous Zimmermann telegram of early 1917 which proposed a German-Mexican-Japanese alliance against the United States further inflamed American, and particularly Pacific Coast, feeling, even though Japan, interested in annexations in the Pacific and on the East Asian Mainland, clearly wanted to have nothing to do with it. During and after the war a number of anti-Japanese movies, which often showed the Japanese actually invading or planning to invade the United States, were produced and shown in theaters throughout the country; some of the most noxious were made by the motion picture arm of the Hearst communications empire. Sunday supplements and cheap pulp magazines featured the "yellow peril" theme throughout the 1920s and 1930s and a mere inventory of "yellow peril" titles would cover many pages. It is impossible, of course, to judge with any accuracy the impact or influence of this propaganda, but it seems clear that well before the actual coming of war a considerable proportion of the American public had been conditioned not only to the probability of a Pacific war with Japan—that was, after all, a geopolitical fact of twentieth-century civilization—but also to the proposition that this war would involve an invasion of the continental United States in which Japanese residents and secret agents would provide the spearhead of the attack. After war came at Pearl Harbor and for years thereafter many Japanophobes insisted that, to use Wells's phrase, "the Yellow Peril was a peril after all," but this is to misunderstand completely Japan's intentions and capabilities during the Great Pacific War. The Japanese military planners never contemplated an invasion of the continental United States, and, even had they done so, the logistical problems were obviously beyond Japan's capacity as a nation. But, often in history, what men believe to be true is more important than the truth itself because the mistaken belief becomes a basis for action. These two factors—the long racist and anti-Oriental tradition plus the widely believed "yellow peril" fantasy—when triggered by the traumatic mechanism provided by the attack on Pearl Harbor, were the necessary preconditions for America's concentration camps. But beliefs, even widely held beliefs, are not always translated into action. We must now discover how this particular set of beliefs—the inherent and genetic disloyalty of individual Japanese plus the threat of an imminent Japanese invasion—produced public policy and action, the mass removal and incarceration of the West Coast Japanese Americans.[7]

.   .   .

As is well known, despite decades of propaganda and apprehension about a Pacific war, the reality, the dawn attack at Pearl Harbor on Sunday, December 7, 1941, came as a stunning surprise to most Americans. Throughout the nation the typical reaction was disbelief, followed by a determination to close ranks and avenge a disastrous defeat. Faced with the fact of attack, the American people entered the war with perhaps more unity than has existed before or since. But if a calm determination to get on with the job typified the national mood, the mood of the Pacific Coast was nervous and trigger-happy, if not hysterical. A thousand movies and stories and reminiscences have recorded the solemnity with which the nation reacted to that "day of infamy" in 1941. Yet, at Gilmore Field, in Los Angeles, 18,000 spectators at a minor league professional football game between the Hollywood Bears and the Columbus Bulldogs "jumped to their feet and cheered wildly when the public address system announced that a state of war existed between Japan and the United States."

The state's leading paper, the Los Angeles *Times* (Dec. 8, 1941), quickly announced that California was "a zone of danger" and invoked the ancient vigilante tradition of the West by calling for

> alert, keen-eyed civilians [who could be] of yeoman service in co-operating with the military authorities against spies, saboteurs and fifth columnists. We have thousands of Japanese here. . . . Some, perhaps many, are . . . good Americans. What the rest may be we do not know, nor can we take a chance in the light of yesterday's demonstration that treachery and double-dealing are major Japanese weapons.

Day after day, throughout December, January, February, and March, almost the entire Pacific Coast press (of which the *Times* was a relatively restrained example) spewed forth racial venom against all Japanese. The term Jap, of course, was standard usage. Japanese, alien and native-born,

---

[7] For a fuller treatment of the "yellow peril," see Roger Daniels, *The Politics of Prejudice* (Berkeley and Los Angeles: University of California Press, 1962), pp. 65–78.

were also "Nips," "yellow men," "Mad dogs," and "yellow vermin," to name only a few of the choicer epithets. *Times* columnist Ed Ainsworth cautioned his readers "to be careful to differentiate between races. The Chinese and Koreans both hate the Japs more than we do. . . . Be sure of nationality before you are rude to anybody." (*Life* Magazine soon rang some changes on this theme for a national audience with an article—illustrated by comic strip artist Milton Caniff, creator of *Terry and the Pirates* and, later, *Steve Canyon*—which purported to explain how to tell "Japs" from other Asian nationalities.) The sports pages, too, furnished their share of abuse. Just after a series of murderous and sometimes fatal attacks on Japanese residents by Filipinos, one sports page feature was headlined FILIPINO BOXERS NOTED FOR COURAGE, VALOR.

Newspaper columnists, as always, were quick to suggest what public policy should be. Lee Shippey, a Los Angeles writer who often stressed that *some* Japanese were all right, prophetically suggested a solution to California's Japanese problem. He proposed the establishment of "a number of big, closely guarded, closely watched truck farms on which Japanese-Americans could earn a living and assure us a steady supply of vegetables." If a Nazi had suggested doing this with Poles, Shippey, a liberal, undoubtedly would have called it a slave labor camp. But the palm for *shrecklichkeit* must go to Westbrook Pegler, a major outlet of what Oswald Garrison Villard once called "the sewer system of American journalism." Taking time off from his vendettas with Eleanor Roosevelt and the American labor movement, Pegler proposed, on December 9, that every time the Axis murdered hostages, the United States should retaliate by raising them "100 victims selected out of [our] concentration camps," which Pegler assumed would be set up for subversive Germans and Italians and "alien Japanese."

Examples of newspaper incitement to racial violence appeared daily (some radio commentators were even worse). In addition, during the period that the Japanese Americans were still at large, the press literally abounded with stories and, above all, headlines, which made the already nervous general public believe that military or paramilitary Japanese activists were all around them. None of these stories had any basis in fact; amazingly, there was not one demonstrable incident of sabotage committed by a Japanese American, alien or native-born, during the entire war. Here are a few representative headlines.

JAP BOAT FLASHES MESSAGE ASHORE

ENEMY PLANES SIGHTED OVER CALIFORNIA COAST

TWO JAPANESE WITH MAPS AND ALIEN LITERATURE SEIZED

JAP AND CAMERA HELD IN BAY CITY

VEGETABLES FOUND FREE OF POISON

CAPS ON JAPANESE TOMATO PLANTS POINT TO AIR BASE

JAPANESE HERE SENT VITAL DATA TO TOKYO

CHINESE ABLE TO SPOT JAP
MAP REVEALS JAP MENACE
Network of Alien Farms Covers
Strategic Defense Areas over Southland

JAPS PLAN COAST ATTACK IN APRIL WARNS CHIEF OF KOREAN SPY BAND[8]

In short, any reading of the wartime Pacific Coast press—or for that matter viewing the wartime movies that still pollute our television channels—shows clearly that, although a distinction was continually being made between "good" and "bad" Germans (a welcome change from World War I), few distinctions were ever made between Japanese. The evil deeds of Hitler's Germany were the deeds of bad men; the evil deeds of Tojo and Hirohito's Japan were the deeds of a bad race. While the press was throwing fuel on the fires of racial animosity, other faggots were contributed by politicians, federal officials, and, above all, the military. The governor of California, Culbert L. Olson, a liberal Democrat, had insisted, before Pearl Harbor, that Japanese Americans should enjoy all their rights and privileges even if war with Japan came, and correctly pointed out that equal protection under the law was a "basic tenet" of American government. But Olson's constitutional scruples were a casualty of Pearl Harbor: on December 8, the governor told the press that he was thinking of ordering all Japanese, alien and citizen, to observe house arrest "to avoid riot and disturbance."[9]

The Department of Justice, working through the FBI and calling on local law enforcement officials for assistance and detention, began roundups of what it considered "dangerous" enemy aliens. Throughout the nation this initial roundup involved about 3000 persons, half of whom were Japanese. (All but a handful of these lived on the Pacific Coast.) In other words the federal officials responsible for counterespionage thought that some 1500 persons of Japanese ancestry, slightly more than 1 percent of the nation's Japanese population, constituted some kind of threat to the nation. Those arrested, often in the dead of night, were almost universally of the immigrant, or Issei, generation, and thus, no matter how long they had lived here, "enemy aliens" in law. (It must be kept in mind that American law prohibited the naturalization of Asians.) Those arrested were community leaders, since the government, acting as it so often does on the theory of guilt by association, automatically hauled in the officers and leading lights of a number of Japanese organizations and religious groups. Many of these people were surely "rooting" for the Emperor rather than the President and thus technically subversive, but most of them were rather elderly and inoffensive gentlemen and not a threat to anything. This limited internment, however, was a not too discreditable perform-

---

[8] Headlines and quotations from the Los Angeles *Times*, December 8, 1941–February 23, 1942, *passim;* similar material may be found in almost any West Coast paper for the period.

[9] Robert E. Burke, *Olson's New Deal for California* (Berkeley and Los Angeles: University of California Press, 1953), p. 201.

ance for a government security agency, but it must be noted that even at this restrained level the government acted much more harshly, in terms of numbers interned, toward Japanese nationals than toward German nationals (most known members of the German-American Bund were left at liberty), and more harshly toward Germans than to Italians. It should also be noted, however, that more than a few young Nisei leaders applauded this early roundup and contrasted their own loyalty to the presumed disloyalty of many of the leaders of the older generation.

In addition to the selective roundup of enemy aliens, the Justice Department almost immediately announced the sealing off of the Mexican and Canadian borders to "all persons of Japanese ancestry, whether citizen or alien." Thus, by December 8, that branch of the federal government particularly charged with protecting the rights of citizens was willing to single out one ethnic group for invidious treatment. Other national civilian officials discriminated in other ways. Fiorello La Guardia, an outstanding liberal who was for a time director of the Office of Civilian Defense as well as mayor of New York, pointedly omitted mention of the Japanese in two public statements calling for decent treatment for enemy aliens and suggesting that alien Germans and Italians be presumed loyal until proved otherwise. By implication, at least, Japanese were to be presumed disloyal. Seventeen years earlier La Guardia had been one of three congressmen who dared to speak in favor of continuing Japanese immigration, but in December 1941 he could find nothing good to say about any Japanese.

Even more damaging were the mendacious statements of Frank Knox, Roosevelt's Republican Secretary of the Navy. On December 15 Secretary Knox held a press conference in Los Angeles on his return from a quick inspection of the damage at Pearl Harbor. As this was the first detailed report of the damage there, his remarks were front-page news all across the nation. Knox spoke of "treachery" in Hawaii and insisted that much of the disaster was caused by "the most effective fifth column work that's come out of this war, except in Norway."[10] The disaster at Pearl Harbor, as is now generally acknowledged, was caused largely by the unpreparedness and incompetence of the local military commanders, as Knox already knew. (The orders for the relief of Admiral Kimmel were already being drawn up.) But the secretary, who, as we shall see, harbored deep-felt anti-Japanese prejudices, probably did not want the people to lose faith in their Navy, so the Japanese population of Hawaii—and indirectly all Japanese Americans—was made the scapegoat on which to hang the big lie. (Knox, it should be remarked, as a Chicago newspaper publisher in civilian life, had a professional understanding of these matters.)

But the truly crucial role was played by the other service, the United States Army. The key individual, initially, at least, was John L. De Witt, in 1941 a lieutenant general and commander of the Western Defense Command and the 4th Army, both headquartered at San Francisco's Presidio. Despite these warlike titles, De Witt, who was sixty-one years old and

---

[10] Knox Press Conference transcript, December 15, 1941, Knox Collection, Office of Naval History, Washington Navy Yard.

would be retired before the war's end, was essentially an administrator in uniform, a staff officer who had specialized in supply and had practically nothing to do with combat during his whole Army career. Even before Pearl Harbor, De Witt had shown himself to be prejudiced against Japanese Americans. In March 1941, for example, he found it necessary to complain to Major General William G. Bryden, the Army's Deputy Chief of Staff, that "a couple of Japs" who had been drafted into the Army, were "going around taking pictures." He and Bryden agreed to "just have it happen naturally that Japs are sent to Infantry units," rather than to sensitive headquarters or coast defense installations. De Witt's prejudices, in fact, extended all along the color line. When he discovered that some of the troops being sent to him as reinforcements after Pearl Harbor were Negro, he protested to the Army's chief of classification and assignment that

> you're filling too many colored troops up on the West Coast. . . . there will be a great deal of public reaction out here due to the Jap situation. They feel they've got enough black skinned people around them as it is. Filipinos and Japanese. . . . I'd rather have a white regiment. . . .[11]

Serving under De Witt, in December 1941, as the corps commander in charge of the defense of Southern California, was a real fighting man, the then Major General Joseph W. Stilwell, the famed "Vinegar Joe" of the heartbreaking Burma campaigns. His diary of those days, kept in pencil in a shirt-pocket notebook, gives an accurate and pungent picture of the hysteria and indecisiveness that prevailed at De Witt's headquarters and on the Coast generally.

> *Dec. 8*
> Sunday night "air raid" at San Francisco . . . Fourth Army kind of jittery.
> *Dec. 9*
> . . . Fleet of thirty-four [Japanese] ships between San Francisco and Los Angeles. Later—not authentic.
> *Dec. 11*
> [Phone call from 4th Army] "The main Japanese fleet is 164 miles off San Francisco." I believed it, like a damn fool. . . .
>   Of course [4th Army] passed the buck on this report. They had it from a "usually reliable source," but they should never have put it out without check.
> *Dec. 13*
> Not content with the above blah, [4th] Army pulled another at ten-thirty today. "Reliable information that attack on Los Angeles is imminent. A general alarm being considered. . . ." What jackass

---

[11] Telephone conversations: De Witt to Bryden, March 13, 1941, Office, Chief of Staff Binder #11; De Witt and General Green, January 31, 1942, Office, Chief of Staff Binder #2, both from Stetson Conn, "Notes."

would send a general alarm [which would have meant warning all civilians to leave the area including the workers in the vital Southern California aircraft industry] under the circumstances. The [4th] Army G-2 [Intelligence] is just another amateur, like all the rest of the staff. Rule: the higher the headquarters, the more important is *calm*.[12]

Stilwell's low opinion of General De Witt was apparently shared by others within the Army; shortly after Vinegar Joe's transfer to Washington just before Christmas, he noted that Lieutenant General Lesley J. McNair, Deputy Commander, Army Ground Forces, had told him that "De Witt has gone crazy and requires ten refusals before he realizes it is 'No.' "[13] De Witt, it must be understood, was a cautious, conservative officer in the twilight of his career. He saw, throughout the Army, younger men being promoted into key posts; his contemporary, Lieutenant General Walter C. Short, the Army commander in Hawaii, was in disgrace. With misplaced concreteness De Witt apparently decided that there would be no Pearl Harbors on the West Coast. It is interesting to note that the cautious De Witt, in safe San Francisco, was more alarmed by the famous "war warning" telegram of November 27 than was Short in exposed Honolulu, and had the former been the Hawaiian commander, the Army at least, might have been in a more advanced state of readiness. But after Pearl Harbor, caution turned into funk; no one who reads the transcripts of De Witt's telephone conversations with Washington or examines his staff correspondence can avoid the conclusion that his was a headquarters at which confusion rather than calm reigned, and that the confusion was greatest at the very top.

It was in this panic-ridden, amateurish Western Defense Command atmosphere that some of the most crucial decisions about the evacuation of the Japanese Americans were made. Before examining them, however, it should be made clear that the nearest Japanese aircraft during most of December were attacking Wake Island, more than 5000 miles west of San Francisco, and any major Japanese surface vessels or troops were even farther away. In fact, elements of the Luftwaffe over the North Atlantic were actually closer to California than any Japanese planes. California and the West Coast of the continental United States were in no way seriously threatened by the Japanese military. This finding does not represent just the hindsight of the military historian; the high command of the American army realized it at the time. Official estimates of Japanese capabilities made late in December concluded correctly that a large-scale invasion was beyond the capacity of the Japanese military but that a hit-and-run raid somewhere along the West Coast was possible.

In the days just after Pearl Harbor there was no concerted plan for mass incarceration. As evidence of this, on December 9 General Brehon Somervell, the Army's G-4 (Supply), ordered the construction of "fa-

[12] Theodore H. White, ed., *The Stilwell Papers* (New York: William Sloane Associates, 1948), pp. 3–23; and Stilwell Diaries, The Hoover Institution.
[13] *Ibid.*

cilities for the internment of alien enemies and other prisoners of war";
the three facilities authorized within De Witt's Western Defense Command had a total capacity of less than 2000, a figure consistent with the
number of enemy aliens the FBI was in the process of rounding up.[14] But
De Witt and his nervous headquarters staff, ready to believe anything,
soon began to pressure Washington for more drastic action against the
presumbably dangerous enemies in their midst.

The first proposal by the Army for any kind of mass evacuation of
Japanese Americans was brought forward at a De Witt staff conference
in San Francisco on the evening of December 10. In the language of a staff
memo, the meeting considered "certain questions relative to the problem
of apprehension, segregation and detention of Japanese in the San Francisco Bay Area." The initial cause of the meeting seems to have been a
report from an unidentified Treasury Department official asserting that
20,000 Japanese in the Bay Area were ready for organized action. Apparently plans for a mass roundup were drawn up locally, and approved
by General Benedict, the commander of the area, but the whole thing was
squelched by Nat Pieper, head of the San Francisco office of the FBI, who
laughed it off as "the wild imaginings" of a former FBI man whom he
had fired. The imaginings were pretty wild; the figure of 20,000 slightly
exceeded the total number of Japanese men, women, and children in the
Bay Area. But wild or not, De Witt's subordinate reported the matter to
Washington with the recommendation that "plans be made for large-scale
internment." Then on December 19 General De Witt officially recommended "that action be initiated at the earliest practicable date to collect
all alien subjects fourteen years of age and over, of enemy nations and
remove them" to the interior of the United States and hold them "under
restraint after removal" to prevent their surreptitious return.[15] (The age
limit was apparently derived from the federal statutes on wartime internment, but those statutes, it should be noted, specified males only.)

De Witt was soon in touch with the Army's Provost Marshal General,
Allen W. Gullion, who would prove to be a key figure in the decision to
relocate the Japanese Americans. Gullion, the Army's top cop, had previously served as Judge Advocate General, the highest legal office within
the Army. He was a service intellectual who had once read a paper to an
International Congress of Judicial Experts on the "present state of international law regarding the protection of civilians from the new war technics." But, since at least mid-1940, he had been concerned with the problem of legally exercising military control over civilians in wartime. Shortly
after the fall of France, Army Intelligence took the position that fifth
column activities had been so successful in the European war in creating

[14] General Somervell, Memo for the Adjutant General, "Construction of Facilities
for the Internment of Alien Enemies . . . ," December 9, 1941, Adjutant General's
Office 14.311, National Archives.

[15] Stetson Conn, "Japanese Evacuation from the West Coast," pp. 116–18, in Stetson
Conn, Rose C. Engleman, and Byron Fairchild, *United States Army in World War
II: The Western Hemisphere: Guarding the United States and Its Outposts* (Washington: Government Printing Office, 1964).

an internal as well as an external military front that the military "will actually have to control, through their Provost Marshal Generals, local forces, largely police" and that "the Military would certainly have to provide for the arrest and temporary holding of a large number of suspects," alien and citizen.

Gullion, as Judge Advocate General, gave his official opinion that within the United States, outside any zone of actual combat and where the civil courts were functioning, the "Military . . . does not have jurisdiction to participate in the arrest and temporary holding of civilians who are citizens of the United States." He did indicate, however, that if federal troops were in actual control (he had martial law in mind), jurisdiction over citizen civilians might be exercised.[16] Although martial law was never declared on the Pacific Coast, Chief of Staff George C. Marshall did declare the region a "Theater of Operations" on December 11. This declaration, which was not made with the Japanese Americans in mind, created the legal fiction that the Coast was a war zone and would provide first the Army and then the courts with an excuse for placing entirely blameless civilian citizens under military control.

By December 22 Provost Marshal General Gullion, like any good bureaucrat, began a campaign to enlarge the scope of his own activities, an activity usually known as empire building. He formally requested the Secretary of War to press for the transfer of responsibility for conduct of the enemy alien program from the Department of Justice to the War Department. This recommendation found no positive response in Stimson's office, and four days later Gullion was on the telephone trying to get General De Witt to recommend a mass roundup of all Japanese, alien and citizen. Gullion told the Western Defense commander that he had just been visited by a representative of the Los Angeles Chamber of Commerce urging that all Japanese in the Los Angeles area be incarcerated. De Witt, who would blow hot and cold, was, on December 26, opposed. He told Gullion that

> I'm very doubtful that it would be common sense procedure to try
> and intern 117,000 Japanese in this theater. . . . An American citi-
> zen, after all, is an American citizen. And while they all may not
> be loyal, I think we can weed the disloyal out of the loyal and lock
> them up if necessary.[17]

De Witt was also opposed, on December 26, to military, as opposed to civilian, control over enemy aliens. "It would be better," he told Gullion, if "this thing worked through the civil channels."[18]

While these discussions and speculations were going on all about them, the West Coast Japanese in general and the citizen Nisei in particular were desperately trying to establish their loyalty. Many Japanese com-

---

[16] Memo, Gullion to Assistant Chief of Staff (G–1), "Internment of Enemy Aliens," August 12, 1940, JAG 383.01, National Archives.

[17] Stetson Conn et al., *United States Army in World War II . . .* , *loc. cit.*

[18] *Ibid.*

munities on the Coast were so demoralized by the coming of war that little collective action was taken, especially in the first weeks after Pearl Harbor. But in Los Angeles, the major mainland center of Japanese population, frantic and often pitiful activity took place. Most of this activity revolved around the Japanese American Citizens League, an organization, by definition, closed to Issei, except for the handful who achieved citizenship because of their service in the United States armed forces during World War I. Immediately following Pearl Harbor the Japanese American Citizens League (JACL) wired the President, affirming their loyalty; the White House had the State Department, the arm of government usually used to communicate with foreigners, coolly respond by letter that "your desire to cooperate has been carefully noted." On December 9 the JACL Anti-Axis Committee decided to take no contributions, in either time or money, from noncitizens, and later, when special travel regulations inhibited the movement of aliens, it decided not to help Issei "in securing travel permits or [giving] information in that regard." In addition, Nisei leaders repeatedly called on one generation to inform on the other.

On the very evening of Pearl Harbor, editor Togo Tanaka went on station KHTR, Los Angeles, and told his fellow Nisei:

> As Americans we now function as counterespionage. Any act or word prejudicial to the United States committed by any Japanese must be warned and reported to the F.B.I., Naval Intelligence, Sheriff's Office, and local police. . . .

Before the end of the week the Los Angeles Nisei had set up a formal Committee on Intelligence and had regular liaison established with the FBI.[19] These patriotic activities never uncovered any real sabotage or espionage, because there was none to uncover. Nor did it provide the protective coloration that the Nisei hoped it would; race, not loyalty or citizenship, was the criterion for evacuation. It did, however, widen the gap between the generations, and would be a major cause of bitterness and violence after the evacuation took place.

[19] Minutes of the Japanese American Citizens League Anti-Axis Committee, John Anson Ford Mss., Box 64, Huntington Library.

Suggestions for Further Reading

For a survey of the Depression, see Dixon Wecter, *The Age of the Great Depression, 1929–1941** (Macmillan, 1949); Frederick Lewis Allen, *Since Yesterday** (Harper & Row, 1940); and Carolyn Bird, *The Invisible Scar** (McKay, 1966). Several excellent documentary collections dealing with the Depression years are available, including David A. Shannon (ed.), *The Great Depression** (Prentice-Hall, 1960); Daniel Aaron and Robert Bendiner (eds.), *The Strenuous Decade: A Social and Intellectual Record of the Nineteen-Thirties** (Doubleday, 1970); and Louis Filler (ed.), *The Anxious Years: America in the 1930's** (Putnam, 1963). Bernard Sternsher has edited two volumes of studies related to specific aspects of the Depression: *The Negro in Depression and War: Prelude to Revolution** (Quadrangle, 1969) and *Hitting Home: The Great Depression in Town and Country** (Quadrangle, 1970). An interesting oral approach to the history of the era is taken in Studs Terkel (ed.), *Hard Times: An Oral History of the Great Depression** (Pantheon, 1970).

For the history of the labor movement during the Depression, see Irving Bernstein, *Turbulent Years: A History of the American Worker, 1933–1941** (Houghton Mifflin, 1970). An important labor dispute of the period is described in Sidney Fine, *Sit-Down: The General Motors Strike of 1936–37* (University of Michigan Press, 1969). In *Middletown in Transition** (Harcourt Brace Jovanovich, 1937), Robert and Helen Lynd describe the impact of the Depression on Muncie, Indiana.

The position of blacks in the rural South during the Depression is the subject of Charles S. Johnson, *Shadow of the Plantation** (University of Chicago Press, 1934). On the general economic condition of American blacks in this period, see Raymond Wolters, *Negroes and the Great Depression: The Problem of Economic Recovery** (Greenwood, 1970). For the condition of tenant farmers during the same period, see Arthur F. Raper, *Preface to Peasantry** (University of North Carolina Press, 1934). David Conrad is concerned with the small farmer and the New Deal in *The Forgotten Farmer: The Story of Share Croppers and the New Deal* (University of Illinois Press, 1965). In *Scottsboro: A Tragedy of the American South** (Louisiana State University Press, 1969), Dan T. Carter examines the complex events that surrounded the most famous race trial of the 1930s. For a firsthand view of the same case, see the autobiographical *Scottsboro Boy** (Doubleday, 1950), by Haywood Patterson and Earl Conrad. Agrarian socialism is described in Jerold Auerbach, "Southern Tenant Farmers: Socialist Critics of the New Deal," *Labor History*, Vol. 7 (Winter, 1966), 3–18, and Donald H. Grubbs, *Cry from the Cotton: The Southern*

* Available in paperback edition.

Tenant Farmers' Union and the New Deal (University of North Carolina Press, 1971).

Carey McWilliams treats the problems of migrant labor in *Factories in the Field: The Story of Migratory Farm Labor in California** (Little, Brown, 1939) and in *Ill Fares the Land: Migrants and Migratory Labor in the United States* (Little, Brown, 1942). A powerful fictional treatment of attempts to organize farm workers in California is John Steinbeck's *In Dubious Battle** (Viking, 1938). The classic statement on the westward movement of poor migrants is John Steinbeck's monumental novel *Grapes of Wrath** (Viking, 1939). Walter J. Stein has studied the migration west in *California and the Dust Bowl Migration* (Greenwood, 1973). For a general study of the homeless wanderers who proliferated during the Depression, see Henry Hill Collins, *America's Own Refugees: Our 4,000,000 Homeless Migrants* (Princeton University Press, 1941). The continuing problems of migrant workers are considered in Dale Wright, *They Harvest Despair: The Migrant Farm Worker* (Beacon, 1965); T. E. Moore, *The Slaves We Rent* (Random House, 1965); and Ronald B. Taylor, *Sweatshops in the Sun**(Beacon, 1973).

David Hackett Fischer has tried to survey the problems of America's aged in *Growing Old in America* (Oxford University Press, 1977). The work of Dr. Townsend and others is described in Abraham Holtzman, *The Townsend Movement* (Twayne, 1963) and David H. Bennett, *Demagogues in the Depression: American Radicals and the Union Party, 1932–1936* (Rutgers University Press, 1963). The organization of the aged from the twenties until today is the subject of *The Gray Lobby* (University of Chicago Press, 1976) by Henry J. Pratt. Books dealing with the life of old people in America today include Zena Smith Blau, *Old Age in a Changing Society** (New Viewpoints, 1973) and Robert N. Butler, *Why Survive: Being Old in America** (Harper & Row, 1975).

For the background to anti-Japanese sentiment at the outbreak of the Second World War, see Roger Daniels, *The Politics of Prejudice: The Anti-Japanese Movement in California and the Struggle for Japanese Exclusion** (University of California Press, 1962), and Carey McWilliams, *Prejudice: Japanese Americans, Symbol of Racial Intolerance* (Little, Brown, 1944). Two pertinent works published under the auspices of the University of California Education and Resettlement Study are Dorothy Swaine Thomas and Richard Nishimoto, *The Spoilage: Japanese American Evacuation and Resettlement** (University of California Press, 1946), and Dorothy Swaine Thomas, Charles Kikuchi, and James Sakoda, *The Salvage* (University of California Press, 1952). The political aspects of the Japanese-American internment are analyzed by Morton Grodzins in *Americans Betrayed: Politics and the Japanese Evacuation* (University of Chicago Press, 1949). Recent studies of the events surrounding the evacuation include Bill

Hosokawa, *Nisei: The Quiet Americans** (Morrow, 1969); Andrie Girdner and Anne Loftis, *The Great Betrayal* (Macmillan, 1969); and Michi Nishiura Weglyn, *Years of Infamy: The Untold Story of America's Concentration Camps* (Morrow, 1976). Dillon S. Myer, the director of the War Relocation Authority, has told his story in *Uprooted Americans: The Japanese Americans and the War Relocation Authority During World War II* (University of Arizona Press, 1971).

4 Postwar America

Chavez, the Farm Workers, and the Boycott

RONALD B. TAYLOR

In 1848, when the Treaty of Guadalupe Hidalgo was signed ending the Mexican War, about half the territory of Mexico was incorporated into the United States. With the land came its inhabitants, of whom many were Mexican citizens of Spanish or Spanish-Indian descent, but the majority were Indians. Under the terms of the treaty, former Mexican citizens were granted American citizenship. But the Indians were treated in the traditional American fashion, and the subsequent history of the Mexican-American has been one of dispossession and discrimination.

In the 1960s, however, a widespread revolt began among the Spanish-speaking citizens of the United States. This segment of the American population is divided into three major groups: the Chicanos, or Mexican-Americans; the Latinos, immigrants from other Latin American countries; and Puerto Ricans. In the past there had been little cooperation among these various groups, who have different historical and cultural backgrounds and are concentrated in different areas of the country. Under Chicano leadership, however, an attempt has been made to unify the Spanish-speaking people of the country, and several national meetings have been held for the express purpose of binding together the various elements of **La Raza** (the race), a term used in reference to all Hispanic-Americans.

Among the issues that concern the leaders of La Raza are the use of Spanish as the primary language of instruction in schools in Spanish-speaking communities; land reform, including the restoration to Chicanos of land taken from them after the Mexican War; economic protection for migrant farm workers, many of whom are Chicano, Latino, or Puerto Rican; and the development of cooperative economic institutions that will allow the communities themselves to benefit from their labor.

The most startling program of land reform to emerge from the revolt of the 1960s was that proposed by Reies Lopez Tijerina in New Mexico. His movement, known as the **Alianza**, attempted to make the United States government honor the terms of the Treaty of

Guadalupe Hidalgo and restore to the Chicanos of that state the land guaranteed to them in perpetuity by the treaty.

On the local level, one of the most effective attempts at Chicano organization took place in Crystal City, Texas—the "Spinach Capitol of the World." Here, 85 percent of the population is Chicano, but only 5 percent of the farms are Chicano-owned. For decades, the town was run by the Anglos, largely for their own benefit. In the late 1960s, as a result of political organization, the Chicanos were able to take over the town government, an event which promised that subsequently attention would have to be focused on the needs of the majority of the town's inhabitants.

Perhaps the most dramatic and certainly the most widely known of the episodes in the growing Chicano revolt was the successful organization, led by Cesar Chavez and the United Farm Workers Organizing Committee, of migrant workers in California. This campaign was conducted largely in the Spanish language, and its rallying cries of **huelga** (strike) and **La Causa** (the cause) echoed throughout the vineyards and fields of California, doing much to unify members of **La Raza**. Fittingly, the symbol of the farm workers' union was the Mexican eagle, and organizers made frequent use of appeals to the Mexican heritage and religious tradition.

The move to organize farm workers might not have been successful, however, had not national attention been focused on the issue for a time by a widespread boycott of certain of California's agricultural products. Ronald B. Taylor, a reporter for the Fresno **Bee**, who has written widely about farm labor, tells the story of the boycott in the chapter from his book on **La Causa** reprinted below. The successful signing of labor contracts with which the selection ends does not complete the story, however. The struggle has continued, with both gains and losses for the farm workers along the way. Unless the national government intervenes vigorously to protect migratory workers, they will continue to remain vulnerable to the aggression of agribusiness and the usual unconcern of those of us who feast on the products of their labor.

The farmers made ideal adversaries. Their tactics were predictable, their public relations efforts dull and unimaginative. None of their moribund maneuvers worked . . . for long. Agribusiness was entrenched and defensive, the Chavez forces were mobile and aggressive; time and again the

"Chavez, the Farm Workers, and the Boycott," pp. 208–249 in *Chavez and the Farm Workers*, by Ronald B. Taylor. Copyright © 1975 by Ronald B. Taylor. Reprinted by permission of Beacon Press.

issues created by the farmers were turned by Chavez to the advantage of the farm workers.

The farmers controlled most of the local press, and in the past that—and their rough tactics—had been enough. The small daily and weekly newspapers told the farmers' side of the conflict without reservation, and the small-town editors had offered their opinions about what should be done with "outside agitators" and old-style communists and the newer variety of long-haired radicals. But Chavez sidestepped the small-town media and took *La Causa* out into the national arena, where the big influential metropolitan newspapers and network news departments were attracted to the farm workers' struggle. Agribusiness had no economic leverage over the big-city press, and farm spokesmen were soon complaining that the metropolitan labor writers, network news crews, and magazine journalists were biased, that they reported with a left-leaning tilt that obscured the truth about Delano. Despite what the liberal journalists reported, the farmers insisted *there was no strike.*

Never before had a strike been worked to the lasting advantage of the farm laborers. In the past they had been kept voiceless and powerless because they had no access to a public forum, and they were unable to shut off the growers' inexhaustible supplies of cheap labor imported from China, Japan, the Philippines, Puerto Rico, Yemen, and Mexico, always Mexico. As Chavez studied the lessons of farm labor history it became obvious the UFWOC's only route to power had to come through alternative tactics, tactics that developed from a power base outside agribusiness's sphere of influence.

Over the years, Chavez had assiduously developed an ever-increasing number of contacts with men and women who were sympathetic to the causes of the CSO (Community Services Organization) and then the farm workers. These contacts formed a constituency that could be developed into a power base within the urban churches, labor unions, civic organizations, and political bodies. The national press was the conduit through which this power base could be energized and expanded. The Chavez plan was to develop and harness the power of public opinion; once stimulated, such power could make itself felt either politically or economically. Because economic pressure appeared to be the fastest and the most direct route to agribusiness collective bargaining agreements, Chavez launched the consumer boycotts. By using both the primary boycott—informational picketing urging customers to shun specific products within a market—and the secondary boycott—the picketing of a whole store, urging customers to boycott the entire market because it carried the offensive product—the farm workers increased their pressures.

In 1965 the farmers had underestimated Chavez and the NFWA. They had economic control over Delano, and the power that went with it; and they forsaw no problems they could not handle in the traditional ways. When the grape pickers walked out of the vineyards, the farmers declared there was no strike and shouted their warnings about communist agitators stirring up trouble within the work force.

The red-hunting California State Senate Subcommittee on Un-American Activities responded. Its investigators snooped around the grape strike, followed up John Birch Society innuendoes, pored over the 5,000 photos and background dossiers in the sheriff's office files, and came away frustrated. When the 1967 subcommittee report was finally issued it didn't even make good reading. The report writers waltzed all the way around Farmer Brown's red barn, poked under the haystacks, recounted the communist horror stories of the 1930s, dropped in the names of kids from SDS, SNCC, CORE, and the W. E. B. Du Bois Club, mentioned three or four real live communists seen in Delano, and after all of the stalling and padding, the staff reported on page 77:

> We are certain that the 500 members of the AWOC and a large majority of the members of the NFWA were in no way connected with any of the New Left or subversive organizations that swarmed into Delano. The concern of the membership unions, and after they merged of the resulting union, was and is to obtain better wages and working conditions.

The farmers were angry. They hadn't expected the report to say the Chavez-led movement was a legitimate union bent on normal union business. But that was the case; the UFWOC was a union, albeit a new one just taking permanent shape and form. As contracts were signed, its operations were becoming structured into hiring halls, social service centers, medical clinics, and administrative offices. More and more, the striking of ranches and the conflict with lawmen over restrictive court injunctions limiting picket activities became the instruments of confrontation. Rather than exerting economic pressure on the growers by depriving them of workers, the strikers were using the confrontations to provoke issues that could be exploited by boycotters in the metropolitan areas.

Magazines like *Saturday Evening Post, Look, The New Yorker,* and *Business Week* joined with the metropolitan dailies and television news programs in recording the strike and boycott. *Time* devoted its July 4th cover story to the "Grapes of Wrath, 1969: Mexican Americans on the March." According to *Time*:

> The welfare of agricultural workers has rarely captured US attention in the past, but the grape strike—la huelga—and the boycott accompanying it have clearly engaged a large part of the nation. . . . As if on a holy crusade, the strikers stage marches that resemble religious pilgrimages, bearing aloft their own stylized black Aztec eagle on a red field along with the images of the Virgin of Guadalupe, patroness of Mexicans and particularly those who work the soil. . . . La Causa's magnetic champion and the country's most prominent Mexican American leader is Cesar Estrada Chavez, 42, a one-time grape picker who combines a mystical mien with peasant earthiness. La Causa is Chavez's whole life; for it he has impoverished himself and endangered his health fasting. In soft, slow speech, he urges his people—nearly 5,000,000 in the US—

to rescue themselves from society's cellar. As he sees it, the first step is to win the battle of the grapes.

Conservative columnists William Buckley and James Kilpatrick were attracted to the subject. After a trip to Delano, Kilpatrick wrote about, "Hippies, yippies, priests, professors, political figures, and housewives with time on their hands—all of them whooping it up for the downtrodden grape pickers of Kern County, California . . ." Kilpatrick called the farm worker movement "a hoax, a fantasy, a charade, a tissue of half truths and whole fabrications. . . . [To] swallow the Chavez line you must believe grape workers in the Delano area are miserably paid, wretchedly housed, and cruely treated . . ."

While the total media exposure was invaluable to the boycott of California table grapes, Chavez did not—and still does not—enjoy the public role. When asked about his notoriety, Chavez physically winced and turned away, shaking his head. He acknowledged such things had to be endured, because they were necessary to build the union, but he added, "There is a tremendous price you pay for this notoriety. It has an effect on your family, and on you, yourself. It is very sad that it should happen this way, but it does. We are in a society where people want to know who is the head of a movement, there is a tremendous demand for that identification. I am talking about the outside public now. But there is also a demand within the movement to have someone who can tell the grower, who can tell the judge, who can speak out on TV. You know when some of the workers see me on TV they come up later and say '*We* were on TV last night and I heard you . . .' They use the word 'we' just like they were there with me . . ."

As Cesar talks about the union, and its demands on his time, it is obvious he is actually operating on four separate levels: He is the figurehead who must keep a high public profile; a tough administrator who can be something of a tyrant; an able organizer who relates to the field workers on a personal level; and a family man, a husband, and father of eight. For most men there is not enough time in the day to take on all four of these roles. Chavez manages by working incredibly long hours, and by focusing his entire attention on one subject at a time.

Chris Hartmire, after watching Chavez for a dozen years, observed: "The public does not see Cesar as a hard-nosed leader, but he is. He has a rare combination of organizational skill and toughness and a deep religious conviction, coupled with a healthy personality. He takes this healthy personality with this organizational experience and toughness and religious conviction and pours it 100 percent into the struggle. At some point in history he and Helen decided this is what he had to do and that he would be with her and the kids when the struggle allowed that to happen."

Commenting on the Chavez family, Dolores Huerta said, "Helen is the strength that holds the family together; she and Cesar agreed in the beginning that if he was working with the people, the people had the priority, and the family must understand."

But Helen Chavez and the children have played a far more important role than just understanding. They are the great levelers; they bring a sense of reality to Chavez's life. Chavez explained, "Don't let the public part fool you. Me, here, I am just a plain human being, and I get reminded of this constantly at home. My wife sees me just as the same old guy, you know. She has the advantage, she is removed from the public part and she lets me know very definitely who I am. I think that sometimes, although I don't enjoy being taken down, it is a good thing, that reminder at home . . .

"My kids don't like the public stuff either. I don't think the kids resent my being away. Maybe some but not much. Generally they don't go to public functions with me. If they saw what happens there, I think they might resent it. I remember taking them to a performance of the Ballet Folklorico, and they let me know they didn't want to go again because the people, the reporters, and photographers wouldn't let us alone and the kids said they felt like freaks. They didn't like it and I didn't like it either. I still don't like it, when they point a camera at me I have this tremendous battle inside. I want to say, 'Don't take my picture!' but I have had to decide that the best thing to do is just submit, and try to act normal, to forget it."

As a public figure, on tour, campaigning for the boycott, for a political ally or against a farmer-sponsored legislative proposal, Chavez has learned to submit to those around him who plan the meetings, speeches, and tours each day. As an administrator, he runs the union; and, frequently he will dominate the union's board of directors. It is the board that is supposed to set the policies for Cesar and the staff to follow, but his feelings are so strong in some subject areas, Chavez frequently rides over objections and overwhelms any arguments.

Bill Kircher gave an example: "In 1967 the UFWOC had won contracts with Schenley, DiGiorgio, Perelli-Minetti, Christian Brothers, Almadén, Paul Masson, and a few other wineries. We had a meeting in Delano, ten or twelve of us. I wanted to go after the rest of the winery operations because they were the most vulnerable to boycotts; I wanted to go after everything that was in a bottle until we had 100 percent of that part of the grape industry.

"Cesar wanted to go after the table-grape guys. . . . [He] saw them as the dirty sons-of-bitches that had shit on the workers for so many years. Cesar said the farm workers would never be men until they could prove themselves by taking on that segment of the grape industry. He was so aggressive on his side of the argument, I found myself alone, and that's when they set out after the table grapes . . ." Kircher, a big, forceful man, used to dominating the scene, laughed a bit as he told the story, but it was obvious he was still awed by the strength of Chavez's determination.

Chavez has very strong ideas, based in part on his own experiences and prejudices, and in part on his feel for what "the people" want. He likes to be close to the farm workers, to keep in touch with their feelings, but as the union began to grow, he found the NFWA and then the UFWOC bureaucracy insulating him. On several occasions as we talked about the union's bureaucratic problems he would stop, sigh, and say he wished he was back, in the beginning, back with the house meetings and the close contact with the people.

Pablo Espinosa, a migrant farm worker from the Rio Grande Valley of Texas and now a union organizer, explained: "Cesar gave me attention that I had never had before; I don't know how to describe it. I wanted somebody to listen to me. You know, you never shake hands with the labor contractor, you never shake hands with a foreman, you never shake hands with your boss. I wanted somebody to pay attention to me, as a man, as a person.

"Cesar had the direct attention for us, not like the politician that shakes your hand, says 'how are you?' and pats you on the back and is gone . . . Cesar gave his attention to me. We didn't have much to say, you know. He asked about the strike. What I thought. What did I want to do? He asked about my interest in the union." As Espinosa talked it became apparent he was not talking about a personal meeting with Chavez, but a group meeting. Espinosa had been one of a dozen workers from Woodville who had come to Delano one evening to meet with Chavez.

Espinosa said, "Cesar made me feel like nobody made me feel. Manuel and Jim and Gilbert used to tell us about Cesar this and Cesar that, and I really didn't pay all that much attention, not until I met him."

But there was more to Espinosa's feelings than just the meeting with Chavez. Even in the middle of a strike, the union was paying attention to the tiny problems that are important to a worker's life. Espinosa and his family were living in a 10-by-16 tin shack in the Woodville farm labor camp, and he was interested in learning to repair his own car to save money. A door-to-door magazine salesman talked him into making a down payment on an $80 set of books that he thought would be instruction manuals. Instead he began receiving do-it-yourself magazines on boating and other hobbies. There had been a language confusion and the salesman had used a lot of flimflam, so one of the UFWOC's volunteer lawyers had little trouble in breaking the contract and frightening the salesman off.

It is this kind of service that is one of the founding stones in the Chavez movement. Within weeks after the first union contracts were signed, Chavez asked Leroy Chatfield to establish a network of service centers throughout the farming areas of California and Arizona. Chatfield, a former Christian Brother who gave up his vows to join *La Causa*, raised $25,000 from a foundation, AFL-CIO's Industrial Union Department contributed $50,000 more to the project.

The union purchased 40 acres of alkali land west of Delano, near the city dump, and began to construct its service center–union headquarters complex. Under Chatfield's direction the service center became the organizational umbrella under which the union developed its medical clinics and its cooperative auto supply and service station. Richard Chavez constructed an adobe gasoline station, complete with lubrication racks and shops for mechanical repairs on the 40-acre site. The credit union—still managed by Helen Chavez—was brought into the service center jurisdiction, and Chatfield later developed the health and welfare programs that were to give the farm workers their first medical insurance.

The union's land was named "The Forty Acres," and it became something special to Chavez; he had trees planted and talked of a cooperative farm; an irrigation system was built and pasture was planted for a few head of cattle to graze. The United Auto Workers donated $50,000 for the construction of an administrative building, and it was dedicated by the UFWOC to the memory of Roy Reuther. The union staff moved from the two old houses and the storefront at 102 Albany out to the Forty Acres. The new building had offices, a reception area, and a big meeting room that doubled as the hiring hall for the dispatch of workers to ranches under contract.

Chavez had an office in the northeast corner of the building; Larry Itliong moved his old AWOC operations from the Filipino Community Hall to the Forty Acres, and he took up offices just down the hall from Chavez. Administratively the UFWOC was run by a board of directors weighted four to three between the old NFWA and AWOC; the board members were Chavez, Huerta, Padilla, and Julio Hernandez on the Mexican side, and Itliong, Phil Vera Cruz, and Andy Imutan on the Filipino side.

From 1967 through 1968 the union not only was fighting its guerrilla warfare against the table-grape growers, but it was also feinting toward the wine grapes. Kircher had been right, the vintners were very susceptible to boycott pressures; even the threat of a boycott produced results, and, one by one, Almadén, Paul Masson, Gallo, Novitiate, and Franzia recognized that the UFWOC did represent the vineyard workers and began negotiating labor contracts. Chavez left the negotiations up to Dolores Huerta.

She explained, "Our first contract language came right out of the ILWU (Longshoremen) pineapple-worker contracts in Hawaii. I met with our workers to see what they wanted, and I put their ideas into contract language. If the grower wanted to negotiate, things moved pretty fast, but if they didn't want to negotiate, then the talks dragged out like Christian Brothers. They were very difficult, and this is where persistence pays off, you just have to keep hammering away. You may have to have five meetings to change two words . . . this is where Cesar gets uptight. He never really quite trusted what I did until he started to negotiate himself; then he found it was pretty hard to get the kind of language that I had gotten, and he started respecting what I had done.

"When I am negotiating, I go by my instincts, and I guess that is what is hard for people to understand. I think my instincts are really good, and I know what we want. Where Cesar is the head of the union and is forced into compromising, I'm not, and he can always override me, if I go too far."

The wine-grape victories were heady stuff, but the primary fight was with the table-grape industry in general and the Giumarra Vineyards particularly. Six thousand of the Giumarra's 11,000 acres were in vines, the payroll fluctuated from 200 permanent workers up to 2,000 at the peak of harvest.

The Giumarras were tough, aggressive opponents; they were well financed, and they had solid political connections. Giumarra lawyers went into court frequently and argued successfully that they needed protection for their workers; understanding judges issued injunctions restricting the number of pickets the UFWOC could place around the various ranches; the judges also banned, or severely limited, the use of portable voice amplifiers called "bullhorns." No matter that higher courts later were to find such injunctions were an abridgment of free assembly and free speech; the court orders had their intended effect, to restrict and inhibit union activities.

With the strike line activity limited, the growers could continue to import strikebreaking labor without major confrontations. Secretary of Labor Willard Wirtz had ordered the flow of Mexican aliens north, across the border to the struck ranches, shut off, but the order had little effect. The farmers continued to use alien labor, legal and illegal. The workers with entry documents artfully dodged Wirtz's orders, and those without documents sought out a coyote—a smuggler. These operators charged the alien $250 to $300 to bring him across and find him a job.

Through the early spring of 1968 the union focused its attention on fighting the flow of strikebreakers. UFWOC members sought out the farms using illegal alien workers and reported them to the U.S. Border Patrol. Patrol apprehension rates soared, but not as fast as the flow of illegal aliens coming through the border; and the alien returned to Mexico frequently slipped back across and returned to work within a few days.

On May 30th, U.S. Attorney General Ramsey Clark flew into San Francisco to address a convention; as he drove up to the hotel he was confronted by 200 UFWOC pickets protesting that the Justice Department's Immigration and Naturalization Service was not doing enough to enforce the laws. Six days later Clark issued orders to crack down on the flow of illegal strikebreakers. The order was dramatic, and it put the administration on record in opposition to the use of illegal aliens, but it had little practical effect, so Chavez switched tactics. He ordered Manuel Chavez to the border area, to begin a concerted drive to organize the thousands of alien workers living in Mexicali and Calexico. He asked the Mexican government for permission to establish a medical clinic in Mexicali's *Colonia Nueva*. Permission was granted. The clinic, in addition to providing medical care, was an attractive organizing tool.

Simultaneously with the fight over the green-card and illegal alien strikebreakers, the union cranked up its boycott efforts against Giumarra. But the decision to single out just one table-grape grower was causing too many problems. There was no practical way to boycott just one grower. The table grapes on the supermarket counters were seldom identified by producer, and, when they were, labels could be switched. Chavez changed tactics, ordering an all-out effort against all table grapes not carrying the union's black Aztec eagle imprint. The UFWOC had been depending a great deal upon volunteers from the Civil Rights Movement to staff the boycott efforts in the major cities. These volunteers complained their efforts were hampered by the fact that they were obviously not farm workers. They asked that some farm workers be sent out on the boycott. Chavez agreed and asked for farm workers to volunteer. The AFL-CIO unions were asked to help supply transportation, food, and shelter for these farm worker boycotters. An alliance of Colorado unions donated enough money to buy a new sixty-passenger bus that was given to the UFWOC to transport boycotters across the country. The group of farm workers was dispatched to New York City, where the central labor council endorsed the boycott and offered the help of its member unions. Paul Hall's Seafarers' Union housed and fed the boycotters while they were in New York City.

But the boycott wasn't going anywhere; there was no emotional steam in it, no dramatic issues to exploit. The whole UFWOC effort was turning dull—there was no spark, no new confrontation. A restlessness was setting in among the young Chicanos, they wanted action. They had watched the civil rights protest grow, they had seen the Watts riots in Los Angeles on television, they had heard the cry of Black Nationalism from Malcolm X, and watched as the ghettos of Newark and Detroit were burned and sacked by rioting blacks. In Denver, tough-talking Rodolfo (Corky) Gonzales was leading a move toward Brown Nationalism and Chicano Power; in Crystal City, Texas, José Angel Gutierrez led Chicano activists in verbal and political attacks on the *gringo* establishment; in northern New Mexico, Reies Tijerina and his followers gained notoriety when they seized a federal forest campground, took rangers hostage, then raided the Rio Arriba County Courthouse in a violent shootout. Tijerina proclaimed the land belonged to the Indian and Mexican populations, not to the *gabachos* who had stolen it.

For some within the farm worker movement, the nonviolence of Cesar Chavez was a tactic that had been tried, and found wanting; these young men and women felt it was time to return to the tactics of Pancho Villa and Emiliano Zapata. The Mexican revolution had been violent and romantic, and they wanted the struggle of the farm workers to follow the same course. Older people began to listen to the talk, and to nod their heads. Such undercurrents worried Chavez, and, in late February of 1968, he called an unexpected meeting of the membership to announce that he had started on a personal fast February 15th. The fast was an act of penance, because the union was moving toward violence; but the fast was also an act of militancy on Chavez's part, started in the hope that it would counter the violent rhetoric.

Chavez said, "You reap what you sow; if we become violent with others, then we will become violent among ourselves. Social justice for the dignity of man cannot be won at the price of human life. You cannot justify what you want for *La Raza*, for the people, and in the same breath destroy one life. . . . I will not compromise. Racism is wrong, racism is not the way, nationalism is not the way."

For his fast, Chavez walked to the Forty Acres. He had a cot installed in a small storage room within the adobe service station building. The room became a monastic cell; just outside, and across a narrow breezeway, there was a larger room that was turned into a combination chapel and administrative office. From this room Chatfield directed the logistics of the fast; he created a tent city outside the service station to house the hundreds of farm worker families that came to spend a day or two to meet with Chavez and show their solidarity.

In the second week of the fast, news of what was happening was leaked to reporters from the Los Angeles *Times, Time* magazine, and TV newsmen. Overnight the fast became a national news event. For twenty-five days Chavez drank only water. As word of the fast spread through the farm worker communities of California and Arizona, the people started coming to Delano. They stood in line for hours waiting for their turn to meet and talk to this man who, by the act of religious fasting, became a symbol of their suffering. The fast became a powerful organizing tool. Chatfield explained, "Cesar would talk about the workers' home area, he would ask about the conditions there, and then he'd suggest they should try to help themselves, to help form a coordinated effort among the workers, and they would agree. It was like the march [to Sacramento] only different, instead of his going to the people as he did on the march, they came to him."

Jerry Cohen said, "The fast meant a lot of different things to different people. I could see the fast really molded the union for the first time. We had nine different contracts at the time, but we had nine separate ranch committees, working separately. That fast gave us an opportunity to bring all the ranch committees together on a project, and it was Giumarra that gave us the project we needed."

Giumarra had court injunctions against mass picketing, and the union had refused to obey these court-imposed restrictions. Giumarra had gone back into court and argued the union had violated the injunction on twelve occasions and asked for contempt citations. The judge ordered Chavez to appear in court to determine if the farm labor leader and his union were in contempt of the court. A media event within a media event was in the making. On February 26th, Chavez appeared, weak and disheveled; assisted by Chatfield and Cohen, he walked to the courthouse between lines of kneeling farm workers. The workers—their numbers were estimated between 800 and 1,000—were absolutely silent. The line of silent, kneeling workers extended from the courthouse steps, through the main doors, into the hallways, up the stairs to the courtroom itself.

Cohen explained, "The ranch committees organized the protest, they led the workers to the courthouse, and ordered them to kneel and pray. It was the first time they had worked together. It shook everybody. Johnny Giumarra, Jr., and about four others walked into the judge's chambers. They wanted to kick all the farm workers out of the courthouse. I had some cases about peaceful demonstrations near public buildings that I was going to argue . . . but the judge looked at Giumarra and said, 'Kick the workers out of here? If I did that it would be just another example of *gringo* justice.' To hear that coming from a Kern County judge was something . . ."

It was obvious the fasting Chavez was in no shape for a protracted court appearance, so the judge postponed the hearing until April 22nd. (A few weeks later the Giumarra attorneys quietly asked the judge to dismiss the case; the kind of mileage Chavez worked out of the initial court appearance gave the boycotters something they could use for months and the Giumarras weren't about to repeat the performance.) Much of the strategy for this particular demonstration was developed by Cohen; while he was without experience when he came to the union, he was bright and aggressive and he soon developed the kind of law practice that might be described as legal karate. He learned to use the law—and lawsuits—to expose grower tactics and enhance worker power positions.

Chavez allowed him the room to try and fail and try again. Cohen said, "Cesar has a really good ability to instill confidence in people. You go and get the shit kicked out of you, say in court, and you tell him and he says 'That's great' and turns whatever happened into something good. You soon learn that there isn't a hell of a lot that can happen that can't be turned around into some good. He has a lot of guts, and you can sense his guts and people get a lot of strength from the positions he takes or the things he does."

I asked Cohen why he thought Chavez had fasted. He answered, "Cesar was mad. There had been a lot of loose talk about violence. He had told them the life of one man or woman was worth more than the success of the cause, but they were not listening, so he decided he had to teach them a lesson. They had to find out who had the balls, and he showed them. *He scared the hell out of them.* He didn't say, 'I'm not going to eat until you guys shut your mouths about violence,' he just said the union was committed to nonviolence, then started fasting. The people responded like 'God, what is this guy doing?' The people were scared and frustrated, they didn't know what the hell to do with him.

"Then, too, it was the third year of the strike and there wasn't much happening. So Cesar gave them something, he sort of spent himself. He talked to them privately and attended the Mass each night. What I liked about the Masses was the spirit of the farm workers. People came from all over the valley. I know that Cesar could feel it too; he saw what a fantastic cement that fast was . . . it was an amazing organizing tool."

The twenty-five-day fast came to an end on March 11, 1968, in the public park in Delano. Senator Robert Kennedy was there to break bread with Chavez, and to lend his support to the farm worker cause. No man in American politics had so stirred the poor people in this nation, no one had responded to the white poverty in Appalachia, the black poverty of the south and the urban ghettos and now the brown poverty of the farm worker like "Bobby." There were 4,000 farm workers in the Delano park that day, and when Kennedy arrived he found them on both sides of a mile-long processional path, waiting for him. He walked through the entire group, flanked by three aides. Every farm worker there tried to touch him, to kiss him, to shake his hand. In the press of the mob, Kennedy staff men and Dolores Huerta tried to form a human shield around him. The crowds, the photographers, and TV crews were swept up in the turmoil.

All the newsmen were up close, moving, backing along in front of Kennedy. I was blocking for Fresno *Bee* photographer Carl Crawford, trying to force enough room for him to get his pictures. He would get swept away in the ebb and flow and have to fight his way back.

Dolores spotted me and yelled, "Ron, help us."

She held her hand out, and I grabbed it and was pulled into the shielding circle around Kennedy. It was hard to keep your feet as the crowds pushed hard to look, to touch. Kennedy, reaching over our arms, smiling, moved hand over hand, left then right, touching, shaking hands. Finally, we were before the truck trailer platform and someone got Kennedy into a small roped-off area in front that was reserved for Chavez, Helen, Cesar's mother and father, Librado and Juana Chavez. Kennedy sat next to Cesar.

There was an ecumenical Mass—ministers, rabbis, and priests participated—then speeches and the ceremonial breaking of the bread ended the fast. After Chavez and Kennedy had broken bread the senator mounted the platform and talked to the workers. He advocated inclusion of farm labor under the NLRA, he urged a crackdown on the use of green-card aliens and illegal aliens as strikebreaking workers, and he brought cheers when he said, "Farm workers need equal rights under the laws."

Several times Kennedy attempted to speak in Spanish, but his Boston Irish accent was too strong. Dolores Huerta, peering over his shoulder to see his text, translated his Boston Irish Spanish into the much softer Mexican version, and everyone laughed. Kennedy, obviously enjoying the moment, looked down at Cesar, and asked: "Am I destroying the Spanish language?"

Chavez had prepared a statement, but was too weak to read it himself. An aide read:

> Our lives are really all that belong to us . . . only by giving our lives do we find life. I am convinced that the truest act of courage, the strongest act of manliness, is to sacrifice ourselves for others in a totally nonviolent struggle for justice. To be a man is to suffer for others. God help us be men.

Months later, in an open letter to an agribusiness association, Chavez tried to explain the fast and the movement's nonviolent philosophies:

> Knowing of Gandhi's admonition that fasting is the last resort in place of the sword, during a most critical time in our movement last February, I undertook a 25-day fast. I repeat to you the principle enunciated to the membership at the start of the fast: "If to build our union required the deliberate taking of life, either the life of a grower or his child or the life of a farm worker or his child then I would choose not to see the union built."
>
> We advocate militant nonviolence as our means for social revolution and to achieve justice for our people, but we are not blind or deaf to the desperate and moody winds of human frustration, impatience, and rage that blow among us. Gandhi himself admitted that if his only choices were cowardice or violence, he would choose violence. Men are not angels and the time and tides wait for no man. Precisely because of these powerful human emotions, we have tried to involve the masses of people in their own struggle. Participation and self-determination remain the best experience of freedom; and free men instinctively prefer democratic change . . . only the enslaved in despair have need of violent overthrow. . . . We hate the agribusiness system that seeks to keep us

enslaved, and we shall overcome and change it not by retaliation or bloodshed, but by a determined nonviolent struggle carried on by those masses of farm workers who intend to be free and human.

The union's primary nonviolent tactic is the boycott. Dolores Huerta explained, "The whole thrust of our boycott is to get as many supporters involved as you can. You have to get organizers who can go out to the unions, to the churches, to the students and get that support. You divide an area up—in New York we split it up into eight sections—and each organizer is responsible for an area. We get supporters to help us picket and leaflet; we go after one chain at a time, telling the shoppers where they can find other stores."

From 1968 through 1969 the UFWOC maintained boycott structures in forty to fifty cities. One or two farm worker families were assigned to each city to work with the Anglo staff volunteers. It had been decided the union could not support salaried people, and everyone—brown, black, or white, from Chavez on down—was paid $5 a week and expenses. Even so the cost of the strikes, the boycotts, and setting up the union administration was running from $30,000 to $40,000 a month. The boycotters were supposed to find room and board wherever they could and to seek out financial support. In New York and Los Angeles they got good support from liberal entertainers, like Pete Seeger and Peter, Paul, and Mary. Their concerts brought in from $5,000 to $15,000 each. Dolores Huerta traveled the liberal cocktail circuit speaking and lobbying.

For each volunteer the boycott is a trial-and-error learning process. Nick Jones, who has coordinated the boycotts in eight metropolitan areas in eight years, explained, "At first, you don't have any idea what the hell you are doing, but after a while you get a feeling for how it's done. It takes six months to crank up a boycott in any city; it takes time to get the churches and the unions and students organized into workable units."

As he talked we were driving back to Boston from a small upper New England town where an interfaith committee had been meeting to discuss the boycott. Two of the liberal Protestant ministers—both outfitted in corduroy sport coats and turtleneck sweaters and puffing on smelly pipes—were concerned about the "moral implications of taking sides in a labor issue," and there was a practical problem: if they became involved they might lose a $500 movie projector donated to a church youth project by local Kiwanians. They and their parishioners were concerned Christians who wanted to help, but was the boycott the way to do it? Was it fair to picket a store, asking customers to turn away just because grapes were being sold?

The interfaith meeting was not a failure. Nick pointed out: "We go to a meeting like this for several reasons. First, did you notice there was a nun and a priest who looked like they might become strong supporters? And one or two of the others, especially the rabbi, may turn out to help us. You can pick out individuals in these meetings. Then I wanted to see how our volunteers were going to handle it, that's why I let them run the meeting, even though they let it get out of hand. They're learning."

The interfaith meeting had taken place in late afternoon of what turned out to be an incredibly long day. I had started out with Nick Jones and a half dozen volunteers picketing the vegetable and fruit produce terminal market in the Chelsea district before dawn. Long lines of trucks rumbled and bounced through the industrial back streets, past crumbling, dingy warehouses, their drivers cranking the big steering wheels around tight corners, as they came in with loads of fresh vegetables and fruit from as far away as California. As they neared the produce market the trucks queued up, starting, stopping, starting again, they crawled along the narrow, rutted roadways leading into the market's front gate. All you could hear was the clashing gears, the honking horns, roaring diesel engines, swearing drivers, and the shouting UFWOC pickets as they waved their homemade boycott signs and pushed leaflets at the passing drivers.

It was late fall and the weather was cold; the air stank, and the mood was bustling foul. When the sun was up far enough to turn the smog to iodine yellow, the pickets called it quits, gathered up their picket signs, and climbed into the UFWOC van. After taxiing his passengers home, Nick drove to a morning meeting with a state AFL-CIO official, drove to another meeting with the director of the Massachusetts Council of Churches; after a quick bite at a donut shop, he was off to look at a picket line, then to another meeting. In between meetings he made a half dozen phone calls, borrowing the use of a phone here, another there. He kept up the pace all day. By 10:30 P.M. we ended up in a tavern off Harvard Square, meeting with law professor Gary Bellow, who was helping the UFWOC with boycott legal problems. At the time, supermarkets had filed suit to prevent UFWOC boycott pickets from entering the public parking lots maintained by the markets. As we sipped beer, Bellow explained his legal theories on the case to Nick and a young lawyer who was donating his time to the union. By midnight we were driving back through the dark streets, headed home to the boycott house. Nick was proud of the fact the Boston boycott was raising $3,000 a month more than it spent, and this was being sent to the union's general fund.

The Boston boycott house was a big, old, gray three-story rectory that once served a Catholic church next door. It is in the heart of a black ghetto, and the building has had little care since it was abandoned by the church and donated to the union cause. The house has seven bedrooms and three bathrooms, in various states of disrepair. What formerly was the front sitting room has been converted into a workroom and print shop, while the large dining room and kitchen have retained their original functions. The ten to fifteen boycott people living in the house rotate the cooking and housekeeping chores. Because of the racial tension in Boston everyone who was white was warned about walking the streets alone at night. Two of the volunteers had been robbed at knife point a few days before I arrived.

The boycott house in Jersey City is almost a duplicate of the one in Boston, except it is located on the dividing line between the Puerto Rican and black neighborhoods. Violence and burglary are common occurrences; the Jersey City boycotters have lost duplicating machines, movie projectors, and tape recorders in a series of thefts. The burglars come in over the rooftops, and drop down the fire escapes to gain entry.

In New York City and Washington, D.C., the boycott houses are in comfortable, older neighborhoods; and in sprawling Los Angeles the boycott people live in a number of rented, single-family tract houses scattered over a wide area.

Over the years, the boycott tactics have jelled into recognizable patterns. As the grape season starts with the Coachella harvest in late May or early June, the union sets up its intelligence operations to track the fruit from the farm to the eastern supermarkets. Experience has shown that if pickets can be on hand when a railcar or truckload of grapes arrives in the big terminal market-produce dock in Boston or New York or Chicago, all kinds of things can happen. An intimidated broker may simply refuse the shipment, a sympathetic Teamster working on the loading dock may accidentally mess up the delivery orders, a warehouseman may misplace the non-union fruit.

The picketing of terminal markets ends by midmorning, and the boycott crews head back to their house, or to a nearby cafe for some breakfast and a planning session. Some of the volunteers will picket supermarkets, some of the farm workers will give talks to civic groups or women's clubs, urging support for the boycott. In addition to the boycotters living in the boycott houses, there are local volunteers who agree to come out and form the picket lines when they are called.

In Baldwin, on Long Island, three housewife pickets were working Hill's Market. Ann, the most outspoken of the trio, explained, "We belong to a Christian-family movement and my husband and I are leaders in the group. We had about six couples and we decided to take the farm worker boycott on as a project. At least we've informed a lot of people, we've written letters to the market presidents, we've gone from store to store and asked the managers not to sell grapes, we've asked them to support the farm workers."

Whenever the farm workers themselves appear on the picket lines the morale of the volunteers soars, and the effect on the customers flowing in and out of the supermarkets is noticeable. In Toronto, Mrs. Ophelia Diaz, one of the workers fired by DiGiorgio for her UFWOC sympathies, explained why she and her husband closed up their Earlimart home and brought their family out into the boycott: "We've got to fight until we win. If we stayed home we couldn't picket anymore without looking down the gun barrels, so we came over here to ask the people not to buy the grape."

In New York City, Mrs. Maria Colon swore she would live in this city until the boycott was won, until the contracts were signed, even if it took two or three years. Speaking rapidly in Spanish, she said, "Cesar Chavez is a miracle for the workers, he has taken the blindfold off our eyes so we can see what needs to be done. We see the people in the union must work to bring about change in the fields and that is why we are here in this big city."

The volunteer housewives and farm workers were having negative effects on the grape markets. Some supermarket chains and independent stores did withdraw grapes from the shelves; market managers complained that boycotters were telling shoppers the grapes were poisoned with pesticide, that boycotters staged sit-ins and shop-ins in the stores, harassing the customers. While the boycott caused the shippers to divert truck and train carloads of grapes from one terminal to another in search of open markets, California agribusiness spokesmen were not admitting the union tactics were having any effect.

Allan Grant, president of the California Farm Bureau Federation and former Governor Reagan's appointee to chair the state board of agriculture, categorically stated, "The boycott has been unsuccessful." But in almost the next breath, Grant said the boycott was "the most serious crisis that California agriculture has ever faced. It has developed into the ultimate confrontation. . . . [It is] immoral, unethical, and reprehensible. . . . [The UFWOC] is trying to blackmail California."

The boycott was an indiscriminate weapon; it shut some markets off to everyone, including the small grape growers of Fresno County who were then outside the strike area. Although the UFWOC attempted to coordinate boycotts, the efforts in each city were quite autonomous and were frequently chaotic. The boycott staff people were shifted from city to city; men like Eliseo Madina and Nick Jones became experts at applying the boycott pressures effectively, but some of the volunteers who were put in charge could never get things together. In some places individuals used the farm worker cause to work out their own hostilities toward society.

Through 1968 and 1969, the boycott stirred the farmers as nothing else had for years; the American Farm Bureau Federation and its state affiliates began to push union-busting legislation that would outlaw boycotts and strikes at harvest time and place control of all farm labor relations securely in the hands of agribusiness. U.S. Senator George Murphy agreed to carry the legislation in Congress. A coalition of California agribusiness organizations joined in the hiring of a high-priced, San Francisco-based public relations firm, Whitaker and Baxter, to help Murphy push his bill and to generally polish the farmers' sagging image. While no figures were ever released, the cost of such a move must have totaled more than $1 million.

Whitaker and Baxter had a solid, conservative reputation; the firm had been hired by the American Medical Association in the late 1940s to defeat President Harry Truman's National Health Insurance legislation. W and B coined the phrase "socialized medicine" and built a successful campaign around slogans using those two words. Year by year, the firm built its reputation, using the same sloganeering techniques. For the agribusiness anti-boycott effort, W and B came up with "consumer rights" and established Consumer Rights Committee offices across the country to protest the withholding of grapes from the marketplace. Supermarkets had no right to withhold grapes; the public had the right to choose what it would and would not purchase.

Whether by coincidence or not, Richard M. Nixon began his 1968 presidential campaign in San Francisco that fall, and one of his first concerns was for the farmers who he felt were being unfairly used by the

Chavez forces. Nixon ate some grapes to show his support, then he made a surprising statement that was clearly out of touch with legal reality. He said, "We have laws on the books to protect workers who wish to organize. We have a National Labor Relations Board to impartially supervise the elections of collective bargaining agents. . . . The secondary boycott of California grapes is clearly illegal. . . . [It] is to be condemned . . . with the same firmness we condemn any other form of law breaking."

Somebody on the Nixon staff had goofed. Politicians like Nixon, acting on behalf of their agribusiness constituents, had opposed the inclusion of farm labor under the NLRA for thirty-three years. At the time Nixon made the San Francisco statement the National Labor Relations Board had no jurisdiction over farm workers. The UFWOC's secondary boycott actions were clearly legal.

In the San Joaquin Valley, some Delano grape growers and Californians For Right to Work were attempting to come up with a public relations campaign of their own based on a new variation of their old company union routine; the new "worker" organization was called the Agriculture Workers Freedom to Work Association (AWFWA). Among its officers were some of the same labor contractor–crew boss names that had appeared in the old TKIFW group. The AWFWA was headed by a general secretary named José Mendoza, a former shoe salesman, who once worked as an OEO poverty fighter in Kern County. He was a man who carried a passionate hatred for Cesar Chavez and the UFWOC. This hatred was never explained. Investigation revealed the AWFWA was financed in part by Californians For Right to Work. One member of CRW's board of directors was Delano grape grower Jack Pandol. A suit brought by UFWOC attorney Jerry Cohen alleged AWFWA was a company union. The suit alleged Pandol and the Giumarras were among those farmers who supported the AWFWA financially.

A firm called Public Research Institute also supported AWFWA. Officials of PRI, a private Southern California publishing company, acknowledged Mendoza had been paid for some investigative work in connection with a booklet it was producing on the grape strike. The editor of the booklet, Donald Gazzaniga, wrote in the foreword: "What he [Chavez] espouses is as Un-American as Karl Marx. . . . The Cesar Chavez stories are lies . . . the Chavez movement is a fraud."

The UFWOC suit brought the AWFWA to the attention of the U.S. Department of Labor, and, after an investigation, the labor department declared the Mendoza organization was required by law to file a Form LM-20, an annual report disclosing its internal structure and financial resources. The LM-20, dated February 22, 1969, revealed a list of 14 growers who had either contributed funds or worked for the AWFWA cause. Pandol, John Giumarra, Jr., and John Giumarra, Sr., were named as principal organizers of the AWFWA. Gazzaniga and PRI were an integral part of the AWFWA operation.

The LM-20, signed by both the AWFWA president and secretary, contained a statement that explained that AWFWA was the outgrowth of an untitled group led by growers and its function was "to tell workers not to be afraid of Chavez, to be united and we [AWFWA] as an organization would support and protect the workers; we were to oppose the UFWOC efforts to organize and to boycott. . . . [we were to] try to enlist workers and to obtain information on UFWOC's plans . . ."

Cono Macias's name appeared on the AWFWA forms filed with the labor department. Macias, the Bianco Ranch foreman who opposed the Chavez movement, said he had been unaware of the grower influence on the AWFWA until Mendoza started traveling and giving speeches. "I didn't like that, because he was being paid by the right-to-work people, and then a [Department of] Labor investigator came around and asked me some questions and showed me some canceled checks from the growers. After that I didn't want anything more to do with the AWFWA."

One of Mendoza's primary functions was to travel—at CRW expense—across the country denouncing Chavez and telling the audiences that the vineyard workers were not on strike, and that the farm workers did not support the UFWOC boycott. In December 1968, Mendoza appeared before the 50th annual American Farm Bureau Federation Convention in Kansas City. A writer for the *California Farm Bureau Monthly* reported Mendoza was "the spokesman for the bona fide farm workers" and as such he received "a standing ovation at the conclusion of his talk."

Mendoza's words were just what Farm Bureau wanted to hear and read. Allan Grant—writing in *Presbyterian Life* (December 1968) and his own *California Farm Bureau Monthly* (January 1969)—used Mendoza and the AWFWA as proof of the farmers' story, contending the AWFWA "has the greatest following among farm workers and their families." But all was not going well within the AWFWA. It had little or no membership, its farmer-oriented constituency had been exposed, and José Mendoza had disassociated himself from the organization sometime during the fall of 1968, weeks before he spoke to the Farm Bureau convention and weeks before he had been the subject of Grant's articles. Mendoza continued to travel and speak out against Chavez.

During much of 1968 Cesar Chavez was confined to a hospital bed at home. The fast had left him weak, and he began to suffer severe back pains. Doctors suggested these muscle spasms may have been caused by the fact that one of Chavez's legs was shorter than the other, resulting in a twist in the spinal alignment; or the problem might have been muscle deterioration, or a degenerating spinal disc. Helen was worried because her husband refused to stop work. She called Bill Kircher to help get proper care for him. Dolores Huerta flew in from New York and refused to go back out on boycott assignment until Chavez paid attention to what the doctors said and began to take care of himself. Chavez continued working from his hospital bed, or from the rocking chair beside it.

During this time I used to drop in, to visit, to ask a few questions, and to listen to Cesar talk about his childhood. One afternoon he began to talk about the 1935 National Labor Relations Act and the Taft-Hartley amendment made in 1947. I paid little attention at first, because I knew he favored passage of a Senator Harrison Williams proposed amendment that would place farm workers under the act's jurisdiction. But then it dawned on me he was saying just the opposite. He had changed his mind; the NLRA—as amended—was no good for farm workers: it would take away the right to the secondary boycott and would provide farmers with the legal machinery to stall strikes at harvest. Chavez pointed out that the original Wagner Act was pro-union and allowed workers to build strong organizations; but the Taft-Hartley amendment, passed over President Truman's veto, was anti-union.

Chavez had never made such statements publicly, and I asked if I could quote him directly. He said that I should not quote him directly, but I could attribute the story to an unnamed source. The story caught the growers and the AFL-CIO by surprise. No one in the federation, with the exception of Bill Kircher, really understood farm workers or Chavez, and for him to switch positions without informing federation leaders was a breech of protocol. Top AFL-CIO leaders were angry. Kircher, acting as a go-between, managed to smooth George Meany's ruffled feathers and patch together a workable agreement: the AFL-CIO would maintain its position that farm workers should be brought in under the NLRA, but it would do so quietly, without confronting the new Chavez position.

The years from 1967 through 1968 were slow for the UFWOC. The death of Robert Kennedy and Martin Luther King, Jr., cast a pall over the whole movement; the Murphy bill, the Whitaker and Baxter consumer-rights campaign, the continued marketing of grapes, despite the increasing boycott pressures, all had a deadening effect. The Chavez fast had buoyed the campaigns, but Cesar's back troubles, the fact that he was bedridden and not able to move among the union people, had its effect.

By 1969 the union's fortunes began to improve. Chavez's back began to mend, the boycott structures began to build the kinds of pressures they were designed to produce, and the tempo quickened once more.

The consumer-boycott aspects of the grape hassle almost obscured the more important aspects of the pesticide controversy, from a union point of view. Chavez testified: "The real issue is the danger that pesticides present to farm workers. We have come to realize in the union that the issue of pesticide poisoning is more important today than even wages." Chavez told the Senate Subcommittee that a state public health survey among 774 Tulare County farm workers revealed only 121 of them were free of symptoms that indicate pesticide poisoning may be taking place.

Workers are seldom sprayed directly; instead, most pick up the pesticide residues from the plant foliage as they work. Most of the poisoning takes place when the weather is hot and the workers are sweating; the residues are absorbed through the skin or inhaled as the dust flies from the leaves. The results are flu-like symptoms: dizziness, split vision, nausea, respiratory problems like those associated with colds. These symptoms are insidious. As the worker exposure is prolonged, the symptomatic results are cumulative. Continued exposure can result in serious illness and death. If exposure ceases, the symptoms slowly disappear. Skin rashes are common; eye irritation goes with most farm jobs.

As Chavez learned more about pesticide problems, he ordered Cohen and Huerta to write strong worker protections into the contracts.

During the winter of 1969–70 little progress was being made in the effort to get the Coachella growers back to the negotiating table. Chavez turned to the National Conference of Catholic Bishops, asking for their support of the boycott. Rather than endorse the boycott, the bishops decided to establish an ad hoc committee to attempt to bring the growers and union representatives together for talks. Bishop Joseph Donnelly was named chairman of the committee, Bishops Timothy Manning and Hugh Donohoe of California were also members, Monsignor George Higgins, of the National Catholic Conference in Washington, D.C., was made the farm labor committee chief of staff. He was assisted by Monsignor Roger Mahoney, of the Fresno diocese.

Donnelly and Higgins invited all grape growers and the union to a meeting in Fresno. Some growers did attend, but the affair did not come off well, so later in the spring of 1970 a second meeting was called. The dozen growers who had already expressed an interest in talks were invited, and so were the leaders of the Delano growers, including the Giumarras. During this second meeting the bishops talked first with growers, then with the union, and then suggested both sides join in informal exploratory talks. This was done. In the week following, Higgins and Donnelly traveled the state, talking privately to farmers, preparing the way for negotiations.

Higgins recalled: "Steinberg said he was ready to go into talks, the boycott was hurting him badly but that he would not move unless the bishops' committee sat in on the meetings. All the growers took this position; they felt they had been burned badly the year before, and that was why those talks had broken down. They didn't want to go through what they called 'that circus' again; they said the union had twenty or thirty people in the room, workers and what not. They said the union didn't negotiate, it made demands. Steinberg and the others said if we would sit in on the meetings it would insure some kind of order."

The bishops agreed, and Steinberg began negotiations with the UFWOC once more. By April a contract was worked out, and the Coachella Valley's largest table-grape farming operation was signed. A small grape ranch next to Steinberg was owned by K. K. Larson. Larson had been a farm manager and he had purchased twenty acres then, year by year, had added to his operations until he farmed 148 acres of bearing vines. He cooperated with Steinberg in the use of labor—when the Steinberg crews were finished with a job, some would move over to the Larson farm—and when Steinberg signed a contract Larson decided he would ask his workers—through a secret ballot election—if they wanted the UFWOC to represent them.

Larson, a big Scandinavian who is deeply suntanned, works with his crews, personally supervising every phase of the operation. He works for a quality product and he says of the workers and himself, "We all live off the vines, so what we do is important." Commenting on the economics of 1969 he said, "The boycott had been so devastating that we could not make mortgage payments and the banks will go along with that for a year but not two. We had to do something, but I wasn't about to make the workers go into the union."

Larson asked his local Presbyterian minister, the Rev. Lloyd Saatjian, to supervise the elections, and Monsignor Roger Mahoney was brought in as an observer. The vote on Larson's ranch was 78 favoring the UFWOC and only 2 opposing. Larson said later, "I did have an honest, secret-ballot election on my ranch, prior to the signing of the contract. I was the only one who did that; that was a legitimate election won by Chavez." He added, "Had the workers voted 'no' and the boycott been continued, we'd have been out of business and I think the workers knew that. I think that influenced their vote."

After Steinberg and Larson signed, the other Coachella growers came to the negotiating table; one by one they signed contracts. Almost without exception, the bishops' committee was in the midst of the negotiations, arranging to bring both sides together. While the bishops worked with the union and the grape growers, Dolores Huerta went underground briefly, then surfaced in Fresno county, where Cal-Mission orchard workers were striking. This 1,800-acre peach, plum, and vineyard operation was part of a 43,000-acre farming empire put together by Hollis Roberts, a big, cigar-chewing farmer who had been blown out of the Dust Bowl and who had come into California "dirt poor." Roberts was a self-made man, an arch conservative, who idolized H. L. Hunt and considered Cesar Chavez a communist threat. Yet, when the strike—and the specter of a boycott—threatened his ripe fruit crop, Roberts agreed to meet with Huerta. They began negotiations, and, just before final agreement was reached, Roberts did another surprising thing. He is a Protestant fundamentalist, yet he asked for the Bishops' Farm Labor Committee to come into the last stages of the talks.

Higgins said, "When we arrived for the final sessions it was obvious Cesar and his people had been meeting with Roberts. We were brought in as observers. There was Cesar with his bodyguards, with their feet up on the rich furniture, and everyone was relaxed and having a drink. After everything was settled, Hollis went around to meet everyone and we were curious. He had been calling Cesar a communist, and all that, yet he had signed. Why? He explained it to us, 'Well, Reverend, I had Cesar all wrong. I discovered in dealing with him he's a God-fearing Christian. Besides, I couldn't get anybody to pick my peaches.'"

As Higgins watched Dolores Huerta negotiating contract after contract, getting them into final form before Chavez stepped in to take over the last sessions, he commented, "She's tough. Relentless. Tireless. Generally Dolores would bring in an entourage of ten to fifteen workers, and this distressed the growers. In theory the negotiations were open and these workers were ranch representatives. They nit-picked every damn word in those contracts. Dolores would aggravate the growers by calling a recess right in the room and then turn to the workers and talk to them in Spanish, filling them in, getting their counter-proposals.

"I never knew if it was an act or not, but she wouldn't answer some questions without turning first to the workers to hear their answers. On such things as the hiring hall and pesticide regulations, they would not budge. One company brought in a pesticide expert and he would try to tell Dolores what she was saying was not scientific, but she would just bluff him, drive him crazy, tell him, 'That's not what our experts tell us,' and then go right on with her demands. The growers tried to be adamant, the control of the work force and the application of pesticides were man-

agerial prerogatives to them, but in the end they gave in . . . they had
no other choice, the boycott was too much for them."

The domino theory worked. From the Steinberg and Larson contracts in April through mid-July almost all of the grape growers, except
the twenty-six in Delano, had signed contracts with the UFWOC. Then in
the second week of July the Delano growers sent word, through labor
relations consultant Phillip Feick, they wanted to start talks. Chavez
called Bill Kircher in Washington and asked that he help out in the talks.
The grower committee, headed by consultant Feick, Bishop Donnelly,
and Monsignor Higgins, and the union, represented by Chavez, Kircher,
Huerta, Itliong, and Cohen, started talks on July 17 in a Bakersfield
motel. Kircher led off with the union's proposals, the growers countered,
and negotiations were underway. During the two-day talks there were
recesses and delays, but progress was made.

Kircher said, "We had it down to where we thought we had a basis
for settlement. But there were two encumbrances Chavez had placed on
me. The first had to do with a Chicano student walkout at the Delano
High School. Some of the kids had been expelled and, because one of the
school board members was a farmer negotiating with us, Cesar wanted
him to order the kids back in school. I couldn't see a chance for anything
so far from the purview of the negotiations.

"The other condition was that the farmers had to come to the union's
new hiring hall—it was located in the new administration building at the
Forty Acres—to sign the contracts. When I told them this, well they just
about shit. They said 'No. No way.' But I got it, I finally got them to
agree. But you know, before we could reach any overall kind of agreement, Dolores started raising issues, and the talks almost blew up. So we
recessed."

Kircher was convinced Chavez had used him as a stalking horse, to
feel the growers out so that when Chavez, Huerta, and Cohen finally sat
down to hard negotiating they would know what to expect. Kircher had
not been told this was his role, he said, adding, "I'm not bitter, but the
point is they didn't tell me. If that is a negative judgment, then, so be it.
That man Cesar is a great game player . . ."

Cohen disagreed that Cesar was using Kircher as a stalking horse.
Cohen explained, "Cesar was trying to get the best contract possible. I
think it was Feick who caused the meeting to blow up; he was very
negative."

Whatever the cause, the talks were broken off, with no date set to
reconvene. Chavez took off for the Filmore–Santa Paula area, in Southern
California, to be with striking citrus workers who had called and asked
for help. He met with the strike leaders, listened to their tactics and
plans, counseled them. In the meantime Manuel Chavez, who had been
down in the Calexico-Mexicali area with the lettuce and melon workers,
leading strikes, had moved north with the season. He was organizing
those families that travel with the strawberries and vegetable crops into
the Santa Maria–Salinas areas. Gil Padilla was already up in these coastal
valleys, rekindling the house meetings, getting local workers organized.

A week after the talks with the Delano growers had blown up, John

Giumarra, Jr., called Jerry Cohen late one Saturday night and said he had to talk with the union representatives right then, that if the talks could not be put back together, the whole issue would take a "drastic turn."

Cohen said, "I never did learn what the drastic turn would be, but I got ahold of Cesar—he was somewhere down south near Santa Paula—and we got everyone together early Sunday morning."

The final agreement was worked out in the pre-dawn, in a Delano motel, by Chavez, Cohen, and Huerta on one side and by the Giumarras—father and son—on the other. The rest of the growers were called into a special meeting in the St. Mary's school building and the details of the agreement were spelled out for their approval. Kircher had been notified and was flying out from Washington, D.C. He arrived as the final meeting was taking place. After the growers and the union set the time and place for the official contract-signing ceremonies, Cesar and Kircher took off for the Filmore–Santa Paula–Santa Maria area to continue Cesar's series of meetings with farm workers.

Kircher recalled, "These farm workers had been making plans for organizing in the lettuce. They were getting ready for something big. There was a rally in Santa Maria, a massive meeting in the high school gymnasium. Everyone was there, must have been 1,000 people inside. Each group of people came forward and said they supported a strike. We finished up there about 10:40 and went back to the motel.

"Manuel Chavez had been running the organizational work—he was staying at one of those Motel 6s and we went there to sleep. When we got there, about 11 P.M., we turned the TV on to see the news and goddamn there came the announcement that the Western Conference of Teamsters had signed agreements with all of the lettuce growers in the Salinas Valley. . . . I thought it was a joke, or the goddamn announcer had things balled up . . . but Cesar had this funny look on his face. . . . [We] called a guy on the Salinas paper that we knew and we asked him if it was true. He said it was, he'd gotten the press release and checked it with the Teamsters. He said the Teamsters claimed to have signed thirty lettuce growers, and the contracts covered 5,000 workers.

"So we didn't go to bed after all; we took off for Salinas. We'd stop along the way, at a pay phone, call our people, get press releases started, schedule a press conference. We got to Salinas, got about two hours' sleep, and then held the press conference to declare a strike in the lettuce. We set up a few battle stations and then took off back to Delano for the signing of the table-grape contracts."

The historic pact, ending the five-year-long Delano grape strike, was signed by all twenty-six of the Delano grape growers on July 29, 1970. When the strike was started, in the fall of 1965, the workers had asked for $1.40 an hour and 25 cents a field-packed box. The contract set the wage at $1.80 an hour, with 20 cents for the field-packed box. The growers also agreed to pay 10 cents an hour into the Robert Kennedy Health and Welfare Fund and 2 cents an hour into a social service fund. The workers would be dispatched from the Delano hiring hall, and they would be protected by special pesticide safety language.

The Delano contracts brought 50 percent of the table-grape harvest under the control of the UFWOC, the Coachella and Arvin contracts added 35 percent more. The remaining 15 percent that was unorganized lay in tiny 10- and 20- and 40-acre farming parcels belonging to the notoriously independent small family farmers of Fresno and Madera counties. But these growers would have to be forgotten for a while, as Chavez moved his headquarters to Salinas and prepared for the lettuce strikes and the battle to drive the Teamsters out of the fields again.

The Red Man's Burden

PETER COLLIER

After the defeat and subjugation of the Plains Indians late in the nineteenth century, the United States government undertook a program of breaking up the Indian reservations that remained in out-of-the-way corners of the West and thus forcing the nation's Indians to disperse and to adapt to white ways of life. For the purpose of dismantling the reservations, the government revived the policy of land allotment developed during the presidency of Andrew Jackson to remove the Five Civilized Tribes from the Southeast. Under the Jacksonian removal program, land that had been granted by treaty to the entire Indian nation was divided among individual Indians, who were subsequently persuaded—often fraudulently—to sell to white speculators. Theoretically, individual land holdings would lead the Indians to work harder and would thus help them to conform to the white American ideal of individual achievement. But economic individualism is foreign to Indian culture, and the land-allotment program only worked to divest the Indians of the little land that still belonged to them.

In the late nineteenth century, government policies struck hard at the Indian way of life, forbidding the practice of Indian religions and seeking to undermine tribal organization. Typical of the Indian legislation passed during this period was the Dawes Severalty Act of 1887, which empowered the President to allot one hundred and sixty acres of reservation land to individual Indian families and lesser amounts to single Indians. The leftover reservation land—often the choice portions—was then sold by the government. Under this program, the Indians lost about 86,000,000 acres from a total of 138,000,000 between 1887 and 1934.

With the New Deal and President Roosevelt's appointment of John Collier as Commissioner of Indian Affairs, the government's devastating Indian policy was temporarily reversed. Collier was a scholarly and sensitive friend of the Indians and recognized the destruction wrought by the severalty process. He recommended not only that the allotment program be ended but also that previously distributed lands be returned to the Indian nations for communal use. At Collier's urging, Congress passed the Wheeler-Howard Act (known as the Indian Reorganization Act) in 1934, which ended the allotment process and called for the use of public funds to purchase new lands for certain Indian nations victimized by the old policy. Under Collier's leadership, the New Deal government also gave a boost to Indian culture. The constitutional right of the Indians to practice their own religions was asserted despite complaints from various missionary organizations, and Indian crafts were revived even though the Indians had forgotten many of the traditional skills. Government relief policies and public health measures contributed to a slight improvement in the standard of living and a decrease in the death rate among Indians. For the first time since their conquest by white America, the Indian population began to increase.

Unfortunately, the beneficial effects of the Indian Reorganization Act began to be undone in the 1950s when the Eisenhower administration adopted the policy of "terminating" all Indian reservations in order to "get the government out of the Indian business." Recently, the outlook for the Indian has been somewhat brighter. Various Indian groups are working hard to develop a viable movement for the preservation of a distinctive Indian life and culture, and the Nixon administration went on record as opposing the policy of termination and advocating Indian control of Indian affairs. Even so, progress is halting, and in 1973 the frustration of the Indians living off reservations led them to occupy the Bureau of Indian Affairs in Washington, D.C., and then to seize Wounded Knee, S.D., to publicize their grievances.

In the following article, Peter Collier discusses the plight of the Indians today as a result of past and present federal action. In particular, he is concerned with the problems of health, employment, and education and with the adverse cultural effects of the policies pursued in recent years by the United States Bureau of Indian Affairs.

When fourteen Indian college students invaded Alcatraz on a cold, foggy morning in the first part of November—claiming ownership "by right of discovery," and citing an 1868 treaty allowing the Sioux possession of unused federal lands—they seemed in a light-hearted mood. After establishing their beachhead, they told the press that they had come there because Alcatraz already had all the necessary features of a reservation: dangerously uninhabitable buildings; no fresh water; inadequate sanita-

"The Red Man's Burden," by Peter Collier. From *Ramparts*, VIII (February 1970), 27–38. Copyright 1970 by Ramparts Magazine. By permission of the author.

tion; and the certainty of total unemployment. They said they were planning to make the five full-time caretakers wards of a Bureau of Caucasian Affairs, and offered to take this troublesome real estate off the white man's hands for $24, payment to be made in glass beads. The newspapers played it up big, calling the Indians a "raiding party." When, after a 19-hour stay, the Indians were persuaded to leave the island, everyone agreed that it had been a good publicity stunt.

If the Indians had ever been joking about Alcatraz, however, it was with the bitter irony that fills colonial subjects' discourse with the mother-country. When they returned to the mainland, they didn't fall back into the cigar-store stoicism that is supposedly the red man's prime virtue. In fact, their first invasion ignited a series of meetings and strategy-sessions; two weeks later they returned to the Rock, this time with a force of nearly 100 persons, a supply network, and the clear intention of staying. What had begun as a way of drawing attention to the position of the contemporary Indian developed into a plan for doing something about it. And when the government, acting through the General Services Administration, gave them a deadline for leaving, the Indians replied with demands of their own: Alcatraz was theirs, they said, and it would take U.S. Marshals to remove them and their families; they planned to turn the island into a major cultural center and research facility; they would negotiate only the mechanics of deeding over the land, and that only with Interior Secretary Walter Hickel during a face to face meeting. The Secretary never showed up, but the government's deadlines were withdrawn.

> *On this island, I saw not whether the people had personal property, for it seemed to me that whatever one had, they all took share of, especially of eatable things.*
>
> CHRISTOPHER COLUMBUS

Alcatraz is Indian territory: The old warning to "Keep Off U.S. Property" now reads "Keep off Indian Property"; security guards with red armbands stand near the docks to make sure it is obeyed. Women tend fires beneath huge iron cauldrons filled with food, while their kids play frisbee in what was once a convicts' exercise yard. Some of the men work on the prison's wiring system or try to get more cellblocks cleared out for the Indian people who are arriving daily from all over the country; others sit fishing on the wharf with hand-lines, watching quietly as the rip-tides churn in the Bay. During the day, rock music plays over portable radios and a series of soap operas flit across a TV; at night, the prison is filled with the soft sounds of ceremonial drums and eerie songs in Sioux, Kiowa and Navajo.

In the few weeks of its occupation, Alcatraz has become a mecca, a sort of red man's Selma. Indian people come, stay a few days, and then leave, taking with them a sense of wonderment that it has happened. Middle-aged "establishment" Indians are there. They mix with younger insurgents like Lehman Brightman (the militant Sioux who heads a red

power organization called the United Native Americans), Mad-Bear
Anderson (the Iroquois traditionalist from upstate New York who fought
to get the United Nations to stop the U.S. Army Corps of Engineers'
flooding of precious Seneca Indian lands), Sid Mills (the young Yakima
who demanded a discharge from the Army after returning from Viet-
Nam so that he could fight his real war—against the state of Washington's
denial of his people's fishing rights), and Al Bridges (one of the leaders
of the first Washington fish-ins in 1964, who now faces a possible ten-
year prison sentence for defying the state Fish and Game Commission). The
composition of the ad hoc Indian community changes constantly, but the
purpose remains the same: to make Alcatraz a powerful symbol of liberation springing out of the long American imprisonment.

The people enjoy themselves, spending a lot of time sitting around
the campfire talking and gossiping. But there is a sense of urgency beneath the apparent lassitude. Richard Oakes, a 27-year-old Mohawk who
worked in high steel construction before coming West to go to college,
is one of the elected spokesmen. Sitting at a desk in the old Warden's
Office, he talks about the hope of beginning a new organization, the
Confederacy of American Indian Nations, to weld Indian groups all over
the country into one body capable of taking power away from the white
bureaucracy. He acknowledges that the pan-Indian movements which
have sprung up before have always been crushed. "But time is running
out for us," he says. "We have everything at stake. And if we don't
make it now, then we'll get trapped at the bottom of that white world
out there, and wind up as some kind of Jack Jones with a social security
number and that's all. Not just on Alcatraz, but every place else, the
Indian is in his last stand for cultural survival."

This sentiment is reflected in the slogans lettered on walls all over
the prison, the red paint bleeding down onto the concrete. One of them
declares: "Better Red than Dead."

> *I also heard of numerous instances in which our men had cut out
> the private parts of females and wore them in their hats while
> riding in the ranks.*
>
> A U.S. ARMY LIEUTENANT, TESTIFYING
> ABOUT THE SAND CREEK MASSACRE OF 1864

The Alcatraz occupation is still popularly regarded as the engaging
fun and games of Indian college kids. In its news coverage of the U.S.
Coast Guard's feeble attempt to blockade ships running supplies to the
island, one local television station found amusement in showing their films
to the musical accompaniment of U.S. cavalry bugle calls. It was not so
amusing to the occupiers, however. The California Indians now on the
Rock know that their people were decimated from a population of
100,000 in 1850 when the gold rush settlers arrived, to about 15,000 thirty
years later, and that whole tribes, languages and cultures were erased
from the face of the earth. There are South Dakota Indians there whose
grandparents were alive in 1890 when several hundred Sioux, mostly

women and children leaving the reservation to find food, were caught at Wounded Knee, killed, and buried in a common grave—the old daguerreotypes still showing heavily-mustachioed soldiers standing stiffly over the frozen bodies like hunters with their trophies. Cowboys and Indians is not a pleasant game for the Alcatraz Indians and some must wonder whether, in another 150 years, German children will be gaily playing Nazis and Jews.

But the past is not really at issue. What is at stake today, as Richard Oakes says, is cultural survival. Some of the occupiers have known Indian culture all their lives; some have been partially assimilated away from it and are now trying to return. All understand that it is in jeopardy, and they want some assurance that Indian-ness will be available to their children. It sounds like a fair request, but fairness has never ruled the destiny of the Indian in America. In fighting for survival, the Indians of Alcatraz are challenging the lies perpetuated by anthropologists and bureaucrats alike, who insist that the red man is two things: an incompetent "ward" addicted to the paternalism of government, and an anachronism whose past is imprisoned in white history and whose only future is as an invisible swimmer in the American mainstream. The people on Alcatraz have entered a struggle on a large scale that parallels the smaller, individual struggles for survival that many of them have known themselves; it is the will to exist as individuals that brought them together in determination to exist as a people.

When Robert Kennedy came, that was the only day they ever showed any respect for the Indian, just on that one day, and after that, they could care less.

A FRESHMAN STUDENT AT BLACKFOOT, IDAHO, HIGH SCHOOL

One of the original 14 on Alcatraz was a pretty 22-year-old Shoshone-Bannock girl named La Nada Means. Her hair is long and reddish-black; her nose arches slightly and prominent cheekbones square out her face. Her walk is slightly pigeon-toed, the result of a childhood disease for which she never received treatment. If you tell her that she looks very Indian, she will thank you, but with a searching look that suggests she has heard the same comment before, and not as a compliment.

"When I was little," she says, "I remember my family as being very poor. There were 12 of us kids, and we were always hungry. I remember sometimes getting to the point where I'd eat anything I could get my hands on—leaves, small pieces of wood, anything. The other thing I remember is the meanness of the small towns around the reservation. Blackfoot, Pocatello—they all had signs in the store windows to keep Indians out. One of them I'll never forget; it said, 'No Indians or Dogs Allowed.' There were Indian stalls in the public bathrooms; Indians weren't served in a lot of the restaurants; and we just naturally all sat in the balcony of the theaters. You learn early what all that means. It becomes part of the way you look at yourself."

She grew up on the Fort Hall reservation in Southern Idaho. The

Jim Crow atmosphere of the surrounding small towns has lessened somewhat with the passage of time and the coming of the civil-rights bills, but it is still very much present in the attitude of white townsfolk towards Indians. And while there are no longer the small outbreaks of famine that occurred on the reservation when La Nada was growing up in the '50's, Fort Hall is still one of the bleakest areas in the country, and the people there are among the poorest.

Like most Indian children of her generation (and like a great many today), La Nada Means was sent away to school. Her youth became a series of separations from home and family, each more traumatic than the one before. The first school she attended was St. Mary's School for Indian Girls in Springfield, South Dakota. "I took a lot of classes in subjects like 'Laundry,' " she remembers, "where the classwork was washing the headmaster's clothes. All Indian people are supposed to be good with their hands, you know, and also hard workers, so we didn't do too much regular schoolwork at St. Mary's. They also had what they called a Summer Home Program where you're sent out during the summer break to live with a white family. It was supposed to teach you white etiquette and things like that, and make you forget your savage Indian ways. When I was 13, I was sent up to Minnesota, where I became a sort of housekeeper for the summer. I don't remember too much about it, except that the wages I got, about $5 a week, were sent back to St. Mary's and I never saw them. After being at that school a little while, I got all upset. They said I was 'too outspoken,' and expelled me. After I got back to Fort Hall, I had my first breakdown."

For awhile she attended public school in Blackfoot, the small town bordering the reservation. She was suspended because she objected to the racial slurs against Indians which were built into the curriculum. She was 15 when the Bureau of Indian Affairs (BIA) sent her to its boarding school in Chilocco, Oklahoma. On her first day there, the matrons ordered her to lower the hems on the two dresses she owned. She refused and was immediately classified as a troublemaker. "At Chilocco, you're either a 'good girl' or a 'bad girl,' " she says. "They put me in the bad girls' dormitory right away with Indians mainly from the Northwest. The Oklahoma Indians were in the good girls' dorm, and the matrons constantly tried to keep us agitated by setting the tribes to fighting with each other. Everything was like the Army. There were bells, drills and set hours for everything. The food was called 'GI Chow.' There was a lot of brutality, but it was used mainly on the boys, who lived in another wing. Occasionally they'd let the boys and girls get together. You all stood in this big square; you could hold hands, but if the matrons saw you getting too close, they'd blow a whistle and then you'd have to march back to the dorm."

La Nada made the honor roll, but was expelled from Chilocco after a two-month stay for being involved in a fight. "The matrons just had it in for me, I guess. They got about 100 other Indian girls against me and a few other 'bad girls.' They put us in a small room and when the fight was ready to begin, they turned out the lights and walked out, locking the doors behind them. We had a 'riot,' and I got beat up. The next day, the head of the school called me into his office and said that I didn't fit in."

She was sent off with one dollar, a sack lunch, and a one-way bus ticket from Chilocco back to Idaho. She lived with her family for a few months, helping her father collect data about conditions at Fort Hall, and then was sent by the BIA to another of its boarding schools, Stewart Institute, in Carson City, Nevada. Her reputation as a "difficult Indian" followed her, and she was again sent home after being at Stewart for less than a day. The BIA threatened to send her to "reform" school; then it forgot about her. "I stayed around the reservation for awhile," she says, "and when I got to be 17, I took GED [high school equivalent] exams. I only had about nine real years of schooling, but I scored pretty well and got into Idaho State College. I lasted there for a semester, and then quit. I didn't really know what to do. At Fort Hall, you either work in some kind of menial job with the BIA agency there, or you go off the reservation to find a job in one of the towns. If you choose the BIA, you know that they'll try to drill a subservient mentality into you; and in the towns, the discrimination is pretty bad."

La Nada again spent time working with her father, a former tribal chairman. They sent out letters to congressmen and senators describing conditions on the reservations, and tried to get the Bureau of Indian Affairs office to respond. As a result, her father was harassed by local law enforcement officials. La Nada drifted for a time and then asked the BIA for "relocation" off the reservation. Many of the Fort Hall Indians have taken this route and 80 per cent of them return to the reservation, because as La Nada says, "things in the slums where you wind up are even worse than on the reservation, and you don't have your people to support you."

The BIA gave her a one-way ticket to San Francisco, one of eight major relocation centers in the country. When she first arrived, she sat in the local BIA office from 8 to 5 for a few days, waiting for them to help her find a job. They didn't, and she found a series of temporary clerk jobs by herself. As soon as she found work, the BIA cut off her $140 a month relocation payment. She wound up spending a lot of time in the "Indian bars" which are found in San Francisco and every other relocation town. She worked as a housekeeper in the private home for Indian girls where the BIA had first sent her, and as a barmaid in a beer parlor. She was "drunk most of the time," and she became pregnant. She was 17 years old.

"After I had the baby," she says, "my mother came out from the reservation and got him. She said they'd take care of him back home until I got on my feet. I really didn't know what to do. The only programs the BIA has are vocational training for menial jobs, and I didn't especially want to be a beautician. Actually, I wanted to try college again, but when I told this to a BIA counselor, he said they didn't have any money for that and told me I was being 'irrational and unrealistic.'

"All types of problems develop when you're on relocation. The Indian who has come to the city is like a man without a country. Whose jurisdiction are you under, the BIA's or the state's? You go to a county hospital when you're sick and they say, 'Aren't you taken care of by the Indian Affairs people?' It's very confusing. You hang around with other Indians, but they are as bad off as you are. Anyway, I started sinking lower and lower. I married this Sioux and lived with his family awhile. I got pregnant again. But things didn't work out in the marriage, and I left. After I had the baby, I ended up in the San Francisco General psychiatric ward for a few weeks. I was at the bottom, really at the bottom. Indian people get to this point all the time, especially when they're relocated into the big city and are living in the slums. At that point, you've got two choices: either kill yourself and get it all over with —a lot of Indians do this—or try to go all the way up, and this is almost impossible."

As she looks at it now, La Nada feels she was "lucky." She tried to get admitted to the local colleges, but was refused because of her school record. Finally, because the University of California "needed a token Indian in its Economic Opportunity Program for minority students," she was admitted in the fall of 1968. She did well in her classes and became increasingly active, helping to found the United Native Americans organization and working to get more Indian students admitted into the EOP program. "After my first year there," she says, "everything was going along all right. I liked school and everything, and I felt I was doing some good. But I felt myself getting swallowed up by something that was bigger than me. The thing was that I didn't want to stop being an Indian, and there were all these pressures, very hidden ones, that were trying to make me white." At the summer break she went back to the reservation and spent some time with her family. The next quarter she became involved in the Third World Liberation Front strike at Berkeley, fighting for a School of Ethnic Studies, including a Native American program. She was suspended by the University.

La Nada's experiences, far from being extreme cases, are like those of most young Indians. If she is unique at all, it is because she learned the value of fighting back.

> We need fewer and fewer "experts" on Indians. What we need
> is a cultural leave-us-alone agreement, in spirit and in fact.
>
> VINE DELORIA, JR.

Each generation of Americans rediscovers for itself what is fashionably called the "plight" of the Indian. The American Indian today has a life expectancy of approximately 44 years, more than 25 years below the national average. He has the highest infant mortality rate in the country (among the more than 50,000 Alaskan natives, one of every four babies dies before reaching his first birthday). He suffers from epidemics of diseases which were supposed to have disappeared from America long ago.

A recent Department of Public Health report states that among California Indians, "water from contaminated sources is used in 38 to 42 per cent of the homes, and water must be hauled under unsanitary conditions by 40 to 50 per cent of all Indian families." Conditions are similar in other states. A high proportion of reservation housing throughout the country is officially classified as "substandard," an antiseptic term which fails to conjure up a tiny, two-room log cabin holding a family of 13 at Fort Hall; a crumbling Navajo hogan surrounded by broken plumbing fixtures hauled in to serve as woodbins; or a gutted automobile body in which a Pine Ridge Sioux family huddles against the South Dakota winter.

On most reservations, a 50 per cent unemployment rate is not considered high. Income per family among Indian people is just over $1,500 per year—the lowest of any group in the country. But this, like the other figures, is deceptive. It does not suggest, for instance, the quality of the daily life of families on the Navajo reservation who live on $600 per year (exchanging sheep's wool and hand-woven rugs with white traders for beans and flour), who never have real money and who are perpetually sinking a little further into credit debt.

To most Americans, the conditions under which the Indian is forced to live are a perennial revelation. On one level, the symptoms are always being tinkered with half-heartedly and the causes ignored; on another level, the whole thrust of the government's Indian policy appears calculated to perpetuate the Indians' "plight." This is why La Nada Means and the other Indians have joined what Janet McCloud, a leader of the Washington fishing protests, calls "the last, continuing Indian War." The enemies are legion, and they press in from every side: the studiously ignorant politicians, the continuously negligent Department of the Interior, and the white business interests who are allowed to prey upon the reservations' manpower and resources. But as the Indian has struggled to free himself from the suffocating embrace of white history, no enemy has held the death grip more tightly than has his supposed guardian, in effect his "keeper": the Bureau of Indian Affairs.

The Bureau came into being in 1834 as a division of the War Department. Fifteen years later it was shifted to the Department of the Interior, the transition symbolizing the fact that the Indian was beginning to be seen not as a member of a sovereign, independent nation, but as a "ward," his land and life requiring constant management. This is the view that has informed the BIA for over a century. With its 16,000 employees and its outposts all over the country, the Bureau has become what Cherokee anthropologist Robert Thomas calls "the most complete colonial system in the world."

It is also a classic bureaucratic miasma. A recent book on Indian Affairs, *Our Brother's Keeper*, notes that on the large Pine Ridge reservation, "$8,040 a year is spent per family to help the Oglala Sioux Indians out of poverty. Yet median income among these Indians is $1,910 per family. At last count there was nearly one bureaucrat for each and every family on the reservation."

The paternalism of the BIA, endless and debilitating, is calculated to keep the Indian in a state of perpetual juvenilization, without rights, dependent upon the meager and capricious beneficence of power. The

Bureau's power over its "wards," whom it defines and treats as children, seems limitless. The BIA takes care of the Indian's money, doling it out to him when it considers his requests worthy; it determines the use of the Indian's land; it is in charge of the development of his natural resources; it relocates him from the reservation to the big city ghetto; it educates his children. It relinquishes its hold over him only reluctantly, even deciding whether or not his will is valid after he dies.

This bureaucratic paternalism hems the Indian in with an incomprehensible maze of procedures and regulations, never allowing him to know quite where he stands or what he can demand and how. Over 5,000 laws, statutes and court decisions apply to the Indians alone. As one Indian student says, "Our people have to go to law school just to live a daily life."

The BIA is the Indian's point of contact with the white world, the concrete expression of this society's attitude towards him. The BIA manifests both stupidity and malice; but it is purely neither. It is guided by something more elusive, a whole world view regarding the Indian and what is good for him. Thus the BIA's overseership of human devastation begins by teaching bright-eyed youngsters the first formative lessons in what it is to be an Indian.

> *It is unnecessary to mention the power which schools would have over the rising generation of Indians. Next to teaching them to work, the most important thing is to teach them the English language. Into their own language there is woven so much mythology and sorcery that a new one is needed in order to aid them in advancing beyond their baneful superstitions.*
>
> JOHN WESLEY POWELL

The Darwinian educational system which La Nada Means endured is not a thing of the past. Last spring, for instance, the BIA's own Educational Division studied Chilocco and came to the following conclusions: "There is evidence of criminal malpractice, not to mention physical and mental perversion, by certain staff members." The report went on to outline the disastrous conditions at the school, noting among other things that "youngsters reported they were handcuffed for as long as 18 hours in the dormitory . . . or chained to a basement pillar or from a suspended pipe. One team member . . . verified a youngster's hurt arms, the deformed hands of another boy, and an obviously broken rib of another. . . ."

The BIA responded to this report by suppressing it and transferring the investigators who submitted it. The principal of Chilocco was fired, but more as punishment for letting such things be discovered than for the conditions themselves. The same story is repeated at other BIA boarding schools. At the Intermountain Indian School in Utah, Indian children suspected of drinking have their heads ducked into filthy toilets by school disciplinarians. At Sherman Institute in Riverside, California, students of high school age are fed on a budget of 76 cents a day.

But there is a far more damaging and subtle kind of violence at work in the school as well. It is, in the jargon of educational psychology, the initiation of a "failure-orientation," and it derives from the fact that the children and their culture are held in such obviously low regard. Twenty-five per cent of all BIA teachers admit that they would rather be teaching whites; up to 70 per cent leave the BIA schools after one year. If a teacher has any knowledge at all of his students' needs and backgrounds, he gets it from a two-week non-compulsory course offered at the beginning of the year. One teacher, a former Peace Corps volunteer who returned to teach at the Navajo reservation, told the Senate Subcommittee on Indian Education that the principal of her BIA school habitually made statements such as "All Navajos are brain-damaged," and "Navajo culture belongs in a museum."

The results of the Indian's education, whether it be supervised by the BIA or by the public school system, indicate how greatly the system fails him. Twenty per cent of all Indian men have less than five years of schooling. According to a recent report to the Carnegie Foundation, there is a 60 per cent drop-out rate among Indian children as a whole, and those who do manage to stay in school fall further behind the longer they attend. A study of the Stewart Institute in Carson City, Nevada, for instance, shows that Indian sixth graders score 5.2 on the California Achievement Test. Six years later, at graduation, their achievement level is 8.4.

In a strange sense, the Indian student's education does prepare him for what lies ahead. What it teaches him is that he is powerless and inferior, and that he was destined to be so when he was born an Indian. Having spent his youth being managed and manhandled, the Indian is accustomed to the notion that his business must be taken care of for him. He is thus ideally equipped to stand by and watch the BIA collect mortgages on his future.

> *We should test our thinking against the thinking of the wisest Indians and their friends, [but] this does not mean that we are going to let, as someone put it, Indian people themselves decide what the policy should be.*
>
> STUART UDALL

The Indians of California have more than their share of troubles—in part because they never received an adequate land base by government treaty. They are scattered up and down the state on reservations which are rarely larger than 10,000 acres and on rancherias as small as one acre. It takes a special determination to find these Indians, for most of them live in backwoods shacks, hidden from view as well as from water and electricity.

They have to struggle for every bit of federal service they get; disservice, however, comes easy. In 1969 the only irrigation money the BIA spent in all of Southern California, where water is an especially precious commodity to the Indians, was not for an Indian at all, but for a white farmer who had bought an Indian's land on the Pala reservation. The BIA spent $2,500—of money appropriated by Congress for the Indians—to run a 900-foot pipeline to this white man's land. The Indians at Pala have been asking for irrigation lines for years, but less than one-half of their lands have them.

At the Resighini rancheria, a 228-acre reservation in Northern California, the Simpson Timber Company had been paying the Indians 25 cents per 1,000 feet for the lumber it transported across their land. The total paid to the Indians in 1964 was $4,725, and the right of way was increasing in value every year. Then the BIA, acting without warning, sold the right of way outright to Simpson Timber Company for $2,500, or something less than one-half its yearly value.

The tiny Agua Caliente band of Indians sits on top of some of the most valuable land in the country: over 600 acres in the heart of Palm Springs. In the late '50's, the BIA, reacting to pressure from developers, obligingly transferred its jurisdiction over the Agua Caliente to a judge of the State Superior Court in the Palm Springs area who appointed "conservators" and "guardians" to make sure that the Indians would not be swindled as development took place. Ten years later, in 1967, a Riverside Press Enterprise reporter wrote a devastating series of articles showing the incredible fees collected for "protecting" the Agua Calientes. One conservator collected a fee of $9,000 from his Indian's $9,170 bank account; an Indian minor wound up with $3,000 out of a $23,000 income, his guardian taking the rest. The "abdication of responsibility" with which the BIA was charged is surely a mild description of what happened to the Agua Calientes, who are supposedly the "richest Indians in the world" living on what is regarded as "an ermine-lined reservation."

The Indian Claims Commission was set up in the 1940's to compensate tribes for the lands stolen during the period of white conquest. In the California claims award of 1964, the Indians were given 47 cents an acre, based on the land's fair market value in 1851. The total sum, $29 million, less "offsets" for the BIA's services over the years, still has not been distributed. When it is, the per capita payout will come to about $600, and the poorest Indians in the state will have to go off welfare to spend it. The BIA opposed an amendment to the Claims Award which would have exempted this money in determining welfare eligibility. The BIA testified that such an amendment constituted preferential treatment, and that it had been struggling for years to get *equal* treatment for the Indian. The amendment failed, and California's Indians will have to pay for a few months' bread and rent with the money they are getting in return for the land that was taken from them.

Cases such as these exist in every state where Indian people live. If the Indian is the Vanishing American, it is the BIA's magic which makes him so. California Indians are fortunate only in one respect: they have an OEO-funded legal rights organization, the California Indian Legal Services, which attempts to minimize the depredations. Most Indians have no one to protect them from the agency which is supposed to be their advocate.

Once we were happy in our own country and we were seldom hungry, for then the two-leggeds and the four-leggeds lived to-

gether like relatives, and there was plenty for them and for us. But the Wasichus [white men] came, and they have made little islands for us . . . and always these islands are becoming smaller, for around them surges the gnawing flood of the Wasichu; and it is dirty with lies and greed. . . .

BLACK ELK, AN OGLALA HOLY MAN

At the entrance to the Fort Hall reservation, where La Nada Means grew up, there is a plaque which commemorates the appearance in 1834 of the first white traders and indicates that the Hudson Bay Company later acquired the Fort and made it into an important stopover on the Oregon Trail. But other aspects of the history of Fort Hall are left unmentioned. It is not noted, for instance, that by the time a formal treaty was signed with the Bannock and Northern Shoshone in 1868, the whites who settled this part of Southern Idaho were paying between $25 and $100 for a good Indian scalp.

Today, the approximately 2,800 Shoshone-Bannocks live on the 520,000-acre reservation, all that remains of the 1.8 million acres of their land which the treaty originally set aside for their ancestors to keep. The largest single reduction came in 1900, when the government took over 416,000 acres, paying the Indians a little more than $1 an acre for the land. As late as the beginning of World War II, the government took over another 3,000 acres to make an airfield. It paid the Indians $10 an acre; after the war, it deeded the land to the city of Pocatello for $1 an acre, for use as a municipal airport. Each acre is now worth $500.

But the big problem on the Fort Hall reservation today is not the loss of large sections of land; rather it is the slow and steady attrition of Indian holdings and their absolute powerlessness to do anything about it. In 1887, the Dawes Allotment Act was passed as a major piece of "progressive" Indian legislation, providing for the break-up of community-held reservation land so that each individual Indian would receive his plot of irrigable farming land and some grazing land. The federal government would still hold the land in trust, so it could be sold only with BIA approval, the assumption being that an individual holding would give the Indian incentive to be a farmer and thus ease him into American agricultural patterns. Fort Hall shows that the law had quite different effects.

Today, some of these original allotments are owned by anywhere from two to 40 heirs. Because of the complexity of kinship relationships, some Indian people own fractional interests in several of these "heirship lands" but have no ground that is all their own. These lands are one of the symbols of the ambiguity and inertia that rule at Fort Hall. As Edward Boyer, a former chairman of the tribal council, says, "Some of the people, they might want to exchange interests in the land or buy some of the other heirs out so they can have a piece of ground to build a house on and do some farming. Also, a lot of us would like the tribe to buy these lands up and then assign them to the young people who don't have any place of their own. But the BIA has this policy of leasing out these lands to the white farmers. A lot of the time the owners don't even know about it."

The BIA at Fort Hall doesn't like the idea of any Indian lands laying idle. And the land is rich, some of the best potato-growing land there is. Its value and its yield are increasing every year. Driving through the reservation, you can't avoid being struck by the green symmetry of the long cultivated rows and by the efficiency of the army of men and machinery working them. The only trouble is that the men are white, and the profits from Fort Hall's rich land all flow out of the Indian community. The BIA is like any technocracy: it is more interested in "efficient" use than in proper use. The most "efficient" way for Fort Hall's lands to be used is by white industrialist-farmers with capital. Thus the pattern has been established: white lessees using Indian land, irrigating with Indian water, and then harvesting with bracero workers.

All leases must be approved by the BIA superintendent's office; they may be and are given without the consent of the Indians who own the land. The BIA has also allowed white lessees to seek "consents" from the Indians, which in effect provide for blank leases, the specific terms to be filled in later on. The BIA authorizes extremely long leases of the land. This leads to what a recent field study of Fort Hall, conducted by the Senate Subcommittee on Indian Education, calls "small fortunes" for white developers:

> One non-Indian in 1964 leased a large tract of Indian land for 13 years at $.30–$.50/acre/year. While the lease did stipulate that once the lessee installed sprinkler irrigation the annual rent would rise to $1.50–$2.00/acre, Indians in 1968 could have demanded $20–$30 for such land. Meanwhile, the independent University Agriculture Extension Service estimates that such potato operations bring the non-Indian lessee an annual *net* profit of $200 per acre.

In addition, these leases are usually given by the BIA on a non-competitive, non-bidding basis to assure "the good will of the surrounding community." Fort Hall has rich and loamy land, but Indian people now work less than 17 per cent of it themselves and the figure is declining.

The power of white farmer-developers and businessmen within the local Bureau of Indian Affairs office is a sore point with most people at Fort Hall. They have rich lands, but theirs is one of the poorest reservations. They are told that much revenue comes both to the tribe and to individuals as a result of the BIA farm and mine leasing program, yet they know that if all the revenues were divided up the yield would be about $300 per capita a year. But for some of them, men like Joseph "Frank" Thorpe, Jr., the question of farming and mining leases is academic. Thorpe was a successful cattleman until BIA policies cut down the herds; now he is in the business of letting other people's cattle graze on his land.

Livestock are something of a fixation with Thorpe. He comes from a people who were proud horsemen, and he owns an Apaloosa mare and a couple of other horses. As he drives over the reservation, he often stops to look at others' cattle. In the basement of his home are several scrap-books filled with documents tracing the destruction of the cattle business at Fort Hall. There is a yellowing clipping from the Salt Lake City *Tribune* of November 4, 1950, which says: "Fort Hall Indians have been more successful in cattle raising than any other activity. Theirs is the oldest Indian Cattleman's Association in the country. Association members raise more than 10,000 head of purebred herefords, and plan gradually to increase the herd. . . ." That was how it was 20 years ago. Thorpe, just back from war-time duty with the Marines, worked his herd and provided jobs for many of his kinsmen; the future was promising. Yet by 1958, there were only 3,000 head of Indian-owned cattle left, and today there are only ten families still involved in full-time cattle operation.

"Around the early '50's," Thorpe says, "the BIA decided that the Indians who'd been using tribal grazing lands without paying a grazing fee were going to be charged. The BIA also made us cattle people set up a sinking fund to pay grazing fees in advance. The bills just got higher and higher, and pretty soon we found we had to start selling off our seed stock to pay them."

Less than 30 per cent of all Fort Hall Indians are permanently em-ployed today. Men like Frank Thorpe once had a going business that harked back to the old times and also provided jobs on the reservation. The BIA had decided that the best use for Fort Hall land was farming; it removed the Indians' cattle from trust status, which meant they could be sold, and began the accelerated program of leasing Indian lands to whites that is still in effect today.

Thorpe spends a good deal of time driving his dust-covered station wagon along the reservation's unpaved roads. A former tribal chairman, he spends much time checking up on the BIA and trying to function as a sort of ombudsman. He drives slowly down the dirt highways where magpies pick at the remains of rabbits slaughtered by cars. He points out where white farmers have begun to crop-dust their leased fields from air-planes. "The game, rabbits and pheasants and all, is disappearing," he says. "Our Indian people here rely on them for food, but the animals are dying out because of the sprays. And sometimes our kids get real sick. These sprays, they drift over and get in the swimming holes. The kids get real bad coughs and sometimes rashes all over their bodies."

Near the BIA agency office on the reservation sits a squat, weathered concrete building. "That's the old blouse factory," he says. "The BIA cooked up this deal where some outfit from Salt Lake City came in here to start a garment plant. The tribe put up the money for the factory, about $30,000, and in return the Salt Lake people were going to hire Indians and train them to sew. It lasted for about a year, and now we've still got the building. The last few years, they've used it to store the government surplus food that a lot of Indians get."

The old blouse factory is one symbol of the despair that has seized Fort Hall. Thorpe points out another one nearby. It is known as a "hold-ing center," and it is a place for Fort Hall Indians who are suspected of being suicidal. The reservation has one of the highest suicide rates in the nation. Last year there were 35 attempts mostly among the 18–25 age group. Many of them occurred in the nearby Blackfoot City Jail.

Blackfoot town authorities, embarrassed by the number of Indian suicides which have occurred in their jail, now use the holding facility at Fort Hall. It is headed by John Bopp, a former Navy man who is the public health officer on the reservation. "I guess kids here just feel that their future is cut off," he says. "A lot of them are dropouts and rejects from schools. They look around and see their elders pretty downtrodden. They get angry, but the only thing they can do is take it out on themselves. From reading some of their suicide notes, I'd say that they see it as an honorable way out of a bad situation."

"The young people," says Thorpe, "they're our only hope. They've got to clean things up here. But a lot of our young guys, they've just given up." The human resources at Fort Hall, like the land, seem to be slipping away. The best interpretation that could be placed on the BIA's role in it all is to use the words of a teacher at nearby Idaho State College who says that they are "guardians of the poorhouse."

There are other reservations that seem to be in better shape. One is the mammoth Navajo reservation, whose 25,000 square miles reach into portions of Arizona, New Mexico, Utah and Colorado. On the one hand, it too is a place of despair: many of the 120,000 Navajos live in shocking poverty, doing a little subsistence farming and sheep-raising, suffering severe discrimination when they go outside the reservation for a job, and being preyed upon by the white traders and the exotic diseases which infest the reservation. But it is also a place of hope: Navajo land is rich in resources—coal, oil, uranium and other minerals—and the tribe gets about $30 million a year from rents and royalties. While this would come to less than $1,000 a year if distributed to each family, the Navajos have tried, and to some extent succeeded, in using it as seed money to begin a small but growing series of tribal industries—a sawmill, a handcrafts center, a tourist motel—which provide valuable jobs and income organized around the tribal community.

Private enterprise has also come onto the reservation, epitomized by the large Fairchild Industries plant. There has been much discussion of giving tax incentives to get industry to locate on reservations all over the country, but in general little has come of it. Of an estimated 10,000 jobs opened up by industries on Indian lands, more than half of them have been filled by whites. On the Navajo reservation, however, the tribe has seen to it that practically all the employees hired are Indian, and it seems like a good beginning. Everything there, in fact, appears to be on the upswing; the Navajos seem to be the one tribe that is beginning to solve its problems. This, however, is an oversimplification.

As far as private enterprise is concerned, the plants are mainly defense-oriented: they use federal money for job training and then work on a cost-plus basis. In effect, the government is underwriting private profit, when the same money could have gone into setting up community businesses. The Navajos do get about 1,000 jobs, but they are generally low-paying and are given to women, thus destroying the ecology of the Indian family.

Roughly the same thing applies to the rapid development of their natural resources. The way in which these resources are exploited —be it strip-mining or otherwise—depends on the desires of the businesses exploiting them, not on what the Navajos want or need. One result is that the Navajos have no way of planning the development of resources for their own future needs as a community. Navajos get royalties, but private concerns off the reservation get the profits (as well as the depletion allowances, though it is Navajo resources which are being depleted). Indian people have often brought up the possibility of joint economic development of their reservation with the help of private firms. This is always rejected by the BIA, which has an age-old bias against "socialistic" tribal enterprise as well as a very contemporary regard for big business.

The Navajos are seemingly doing well, but their environment is in the hands of others who are interested only in revenue, and not in the Indians' future. The Navajos are thankful, however, for short-term gains, which most tribes don't have; and they have no choice but to leave tomorrow up to the BIA. As anthropologist David Aberle has pointed out,

> Let us suppose that we cut a cross-section through the reservation territory . . . and make a rapid-motion picture of the flow of population, money and resources. . . . We would see oil, helium, coal, uranium, and vanadium draining off into the surrounding economy; we would see rents and royalties flowing into the tribal treasury, but, of course, major profits accruing to the corporations exploiting the reservation. We would see the slow development of roads, water for stock and drinking, government facilities, and so forth, and a flow of welfare funds coming in, to go out again via the trader. The net flow of many physical resources would be outward; the flow of profits would be outward; and the only major increases to be seen would be population, with a minor increment in physical facilities and consumer goods. This is the picture of a colony.

The BIA is an easy organization to whip. Its abuses are flagrant, and the Indians it is charged with protecting are in great jeopardy. But if places like the Navajo reservation resemble a colony, the BIA is no more than a corps of colonial officers whose role is not to make policy but rather to carry it out. It is impossible not to feel that the Bureau itself has, over the years, taken on the most outstanding feature of the Indians it administers: their utter lack of power. It could make life on the reservation less complicated and cruel and establish some provisions for the Indians' cultural future, but it could never solve the larger issues that lie behind federal Indian policy. The BIA is only a unit within the Department of Interior, and not a very important one at that—certainly nothing like the powerful Bureaus of Land Management and Reclamation. It is the Department of Interior itself which is involved in the big power moves in Indian affairs. As trustees both for the Indians' private trust lands and for public trust lands, it is involved in an irremediable conflict of interest which it solves by taking from the red man's vanishing domains.

> *It can be said without overstatement that when the Indians were put on these reservations they were not considered to be located in the most desirable area of the Nation. It is impossible to believe that when Congress created the great Colorado River Indian reservation . . . they were unaware that most of the lands were of the desert kind—hot, scorching sands—and that water from the river would be essential to the life of the Indian people. . . .*

CALIFORNIA VS. ARIZONA

The Navajo reservation is mainly arid, and alkaline deposits gather at the foot of the small hills like snowdrifts. Here, as on other reservations, water is a precious asset, and groundwater is minimal. And when the tribal council recently almost gave away the Navajos' rights to the Colorado River, it didn't do so willingly or with forethought; it was conned.

The population of the Colorado River Basin has exploded during this century, and there has been much feuding among the various states over water. The 1922 Colorado River Compact apportioned the Colorado River water between the Upper Basin states (Colorado, Utah, Wyoming, New Mexico and Arizona) and those of the Lower Basin (California, Nevada and, again, Arizona). After the Supreme Court water decision of 1963, Arizona conceived an ingenious plan to use the water it had been allotted: the annual 50,000 acre-feet of Upper Basin it had been awarded would be used for power to pump its Lower Basin water (2.8 million acre-feet per year) into the gigantic Central Arizona Project, thus irrigating much of the state and providing for its industrial development. The only thing standing in the way of this plan was the Navajos.

Water rights are one of the few Indian prerogatives laid out in clear judicial terms. They are considered an intrinsic part of the reservation the Indians occupy, and the so-called Winters Doctrine, most recently validated in *California vs. Arizona*, specifies that Indians have priority in the use of waters adjacent to, surrounding or underneath their land, and that upstream and downstream non-Indian users can have only that which is left over after Indian needs are fulfilled. These rights are guaranteed, and not subject to some "use it or lose it" free for all.

The Navajos have never yet asserted a claim to the Colorado River because their underdevelopment has not required it. But if and when they do, most water lawyers feel that their award could be very large, especially since a much smaller group of Indian tribes on the lower Colorado was awarded one million annual acre-feet in 1963 in *California vs. Arizona*. The Navajos could, in fact, probably get enough of the Colorado to turn their reservation into an oasis. For this reason, and because their potential rights could destroy Arizona's plan for using the water it had been awarded (not to mention the whole basis for the apportionment of water among the Upper and Lower Basin states), the Navajo tribal council was persuaded, in December 1968, to waive virtually all rights to the river "for the lifetime of the [pumping] plant, or for the next 50 years, whichever occurs first." In return for passing this resolution, the council received some minor considerations, including a $125,000 grant for its new Navajo Community College. The deal was presented casually as an administrative courtesy with adequate compensation, and the tribe was not aware of what lay behind it.

Actually, the Navajos were caught in the middle of some high-level maneuvers. Wayne Aspinal, congressman from Colorado and chairman of the House Subcommittee on Interior and Insular Affairs, had made it clear to the Department of Interior that he would kill legislation funding the Central Arizona Project unless this waiver of the Navajos' Upper Basin Claim—which could affect his own state—was obtained. By the same token, then Secretary of the Interior Stuart Udall was committed to the Central Arizona Project, which, among other things, would benefit his own home state. Thus it was he who had the resolution drafted and sent to the tribal council via the local BIA superintendent's office.

All of this would probably have gone unchallenged, perhaps to be discovered several years later, if it hadn't been for the OEO-funded legal rights organization on the reservation. This group, the DNA (the acronym derived from the Navajo phrase meaning "economic revitalization of the people"), has been a constant irritation to those who are accustomed to raiding Navajo resources, and it has earned both a large grassroots following and the enmity of the BIA-influenced tribal hierarchy. The DNA found out about the politics behind the waiver last spring, documented its implication for the Navajos' future, and by early summer was able to persuade the tribal council to rescind its resolution.

The Fort Mojaves of California are currently involved in another fight related to the Colorado River. They have learned, over the last few months, the truth of the maxim widely quoted in California parapolitics: "Water is the name of the game." The Fort Mojaves woke up one morning to find that the state of California, working in concert with the Interior Department's Bureau of Land Management, had swindled them out of 1,500 acres of invaluable river frontage.

The state had had its eyes on this acreage for many years. It first tried to grab it in 1910, using provisions of the Swamp and Overflow Act of 1850 (which allows swampland created by a river to be placed under state jurisdiction). This initial attempt failed, as did others over the years. Then, early in 1967, the state, supported by the Bureau of Land Management, finally succeeded in obtaining the land, again citing the Swamp and Overflow Act because its regular powers of eminent domain did not apply to tribal land. The Mojaves didn't even know that hearings on the matter were taking place; they found out that their land had been confiscated only several months afterward, and then it was by accident.

The acreage claimed by California is clearly too high to have ever been a swamp. Moreover, in 1850, when the Swamp and Overflow Act applied, the wild Colorado River's course ran nowhere near the 1,500 supposedly swampy acres, having been "channelized" into its present regular course only in the early 1940's. Independent hydrologists' studies have proven conclusively that the contested area was never part of the river bed.

The state is driven to assert fraudulent claims to land in this apparently low-value desert area, just as Interior is bound to back them up, because of their fear that the Mojaves will develop the area. Private developers are eager to come in: they feel that the Colorado River area will become invaluable, especially as Southern California's population spills outward in search of recreation space. Indian water rights are the prime water rights and developers know that even if there is a water shortage, the Indians will get their allotment first because of the Winters Doctrine, spelled out in *California vs. Arizona.*

The state of California and the Bureau of Land Management, reacting to pressure from the powerful Metropolitan Water District of Southern California, do not want this development to take place, even though it is a key to the Indians' future survival. They fear a water shortage and they are fighting it in the easiest way—by confiscating the prior water rights attached to Indian land out of the Indians' hands.

> *The Earth is our Mother, and we cannot sell our Mother.*
>
> IROQUOIS SAYING

Behind the machinations of the BIA and the grander larcenies of the Department of Interior stands the Indians' final enemy, that vague sense of doom called federal policy. It has always been sinister, and no less so today than in the days when Indian tribes were nearly annihilated by the white man's gifts of blankets saturated in smallpox. The current mode of attack began in the 1950's, with by far the most ominous title in the lexicon of Indian affairs: termination. Its objectives were stated innocuously in a 1953 act of Congress:

> It is the policy of Congress, as rapidly as possible to make the Indians within the United States subject to the same privileges and responsibilities as are applicable to other citizens of the United States, to end their status as wards of the United States, and to grant them all of the rights and prerogatives pertaining to American citizenship. . . .

Cultural assassination always comes cloaked in such altruisms, and the crucial phrase, "to end their status as wards of the United States," was neatly circumscribed by florid rhetoric. But that phrase was the heart of the resolution, and its impact was disastrous.

Over the last two decades, the Indian has learned that he must fear most those who want to eliminate the Bureau of Indian Affairs and who make pompous statements about it being time "for this country to get out of the Indian business." A hundred and fifty years ago, perhaps, attaining such equilibrium with the red man would have been laudable; but America got into the Indian business for good when it stole a continent and put its inhabitants in land-locked jails. While the Indian knows that the BIA works against him most of the time, he also realizes its symbolic value as the embodiment of promises made in the treaties which secure his land and culture. Indian people and lands have been, and continue to be, terribly damaged by their relationship to the federal government. But their federal trust status guarantees their Indian-ness. And if it is terminated, they know there will be nothing left to mismanage.

The reservations which were actually terminated as a result of this sudden shift in federal policy in the '50's provide ample warning. The Minominees of Wisconsin, for instance, whose termination began in 1854 and was completed in 1961, had a stable pattern of life which was destroyed. They owned a thriving tribally run sawmill. They had a hospital and other community services; they had a fairly large tribal bank account. Then came termination, which made the Minominees citizens of Wisconsin and nothing more. The hospital had to close down because it didn't meet state standards; the tribal bank account was doled out to the tribesmen in per capita payments, which were quickly dissipated. The sawmill became a corporation and floundered because of mismanagement, thereby no longer providing the Minominees with jobs. The Indians were supposed to become just like everyone else in Wisconsin, but today they still stand apart as among the poorest people in the state. Much of their land, which was not taxable when held in trust, has been sold at forced auctions to make up defaulted state property taxes.

Another classic case of termination is that of the Klamaths of Oregon. As part of the proceedings in 1954, their richly forested reservation was sold off and the receipts distributed equally among enrolled members of the tribe. The payout came to over $40,000 per person, and even before it was made the predators began to descend, offering high-interest loans and a treasure house of consumer goods. A few years after termination was accomplished, many of the Klamaths were destitute and on welfare; they had no land left, no money and no future. As one member of the tribe said, "My grandchildren won't have anything, not even the right to call themselves Indian."

Because of the disasters it caused, termination is now "voluntary," although the Congressional resolution which authorized it has yet to be rescinded. Temporarily, at least, it has taken a backseat to the New Frontierish strategies like luring private enterprise onto the reservation and allocating meager OEO funds. However, today there are still tribes in the process of termination—several small ones in California and the Colvilles of Washington—and no attempt is made to stop the misinformation given Indians about the benefits that will result from such an option. Nor will termination ever disappear for good until Indians hold in their own hands the life and death powers over their communities which others now wield. Every time an Indian is "successfully" relocated in a city far from his people, it is a kind of termination, as it is when a plot of ground or the rights to water slip out of his hands. It is not necessary for Indian people to have Secretary of Interior Hickel tell them that they should "cut the cord" that binds them to their reservation to know that termination exists as the final solution to the Indian Problem.

> *He is dispossessed in life, and unforgiving. He doesn't believe in us and our civilization, and so he is our mystic enemy, for we push him off the face of the earth.*
>
> D. H. LAWRENCE

Strangled in bureaucracy, swindled out of lands, forcibly alienated from his own culture, the Indian continues to be victimized by the white man's symbolism: he has been both loved and hated to death. On the one hand, the white looked out at him from his own constricted universe of acquisition and grasping egocentrism and saw a Noble Savage, an innocent at peace with his world. Here was a relic of a better time, to be protected and preserved. But on the other hand the white saw an uncivilized creature possessing, but not exploiting, great riches; the vision was conjured up of the Murdering Redskin whose bestiality provided the justification for wiping him out and taking his land. The Indian's "plight" has always inspired recurrent orgies of remorse, but never has it forced us to digest the implications of a nation and culture conceived in genocide. We act as if the blood-debt of the past cannot be canceled until the Indian has no future; the guiltier he has made us, the more frantic have been the attempts to make him disappear.

Yet, having paid out almost everything he has, the Indian has survived the long exercise in white schizophrenia. And there are some, like Hopi mystic Thomas Banyaka, who give out prophecies that the red man will still be here long after whites have been destroyed in a holocaust of their own making.

American Women
in the 1970s

MARY P. RYAN

In an age of revolt and general questioning of traditional authority, it came as no surprise that the largest oppressed segment of society should try to free itself from the restraints that have bound it over the years. Thus, in the 1960s, a new women's liberation movement was born.

This movement can be traced to a variety of sources. For many middle-class women, the issues behind the women's revolt were defined in 1963 by Betty Friedan in **The Feminine Mystique,** a book in which she discusses the profound discontent of the college-educated housewife who finds herself tied to a house in the suburbs and is expected to find personal fulfillment through her husband and her children. Other women joined the movement as a result of disillusioning experiences in the radical student movement of the middle 1960s. Many young women activists working in the civil rights drive and in a variety of college-based organizations found themselves relegated by male associates to the stereotyped female chores, such as typing, cooking, housekeeping, and providing sexual companionship. In the later sixties, still another source of support for the women's movement was a group composed predominately of poor black women, the militant National Welfare Rights Organization, which fought to improve welfare programs.

On occasion, the different strands of the women's liberation movement cooperated to bring their case against male supremacy dramatically before the public eye. For instance, a broad-based coalition of groups participated in the Women's Strike for Equality on August 26, 1970, the fiftieth anniversary of the ratification of the Nineteenth Amendment giving women the right to vote. As a rule, however, the various women's groups function independently, seeking different, specific goals related to their own perception of the nature of their oppression.

The middle-class, professional associates of Betty Friedan, who founded the National Organization for Women (NOW) in 1966, have been primarily interested in securing equal opportunity for women

in education and employment. Although there are federal laws designed to protect women in these areas, they have frequently been
neglected or ignored. Thus the women of NOW have been in the
leadership of the campaign to enact the equal rights amendment
(ERA) to the Constitution first proposed to Congress by Alice Paul
of the Women's Rights Party in 1923. This amendment, which would
prohibit sex-based discrimination by state or federal governments,
has been opposed by some women's labor organizations on the
grounds that it would abolish certain protective legislation that works
to the advantage of women in commerce and industry. Advocates of
the amendment argue that, to the contrary, the laws that are truly
protective can be extended to males in the work force as well. Aspects of the NOW program that have more general support from the
nation's women include the establishment of free, twenty-four-hour
day-care centers for the children of working women and the provision
of free abortion on demand.

Another segment of the women's liberation movement stresses
what it calls "consciousness raising"—a process in which women
come together regularly in small groups to explore their common
problems and ways in which society might be changed to permit more
freedom for women. This process is based on the belief that it is
necessary for women to reach a heightened awareness of the discrimination inherent in the traditional sex roles before they can
realize the possibilities of true liberation. In an effort to raise the
general consicousness, radical women's groups published several
journals with titles such as **Up From Under** and **No More Fun and
Games,** which contained intensely personal and probing analyses of
sex roles in the present society and analyses of continued male attempts to keep women in inferior and submissive positions. For the
most part, the women of the movement are seeking neither female
supremacy nor isolation from men. Rather, they are seeking to define their social roles for themselves. If they are successful, their
struggle may free men also from the burden of stereotyped sex roles.

In the concluding pages of her book on the history of women
in America, reprinted below, Mary P. Ryan, of the State University of
New York at Binghampton, provides a critique of the women's liberation movement at the mid-point of the 1970s. Among the items
dealt with are the changing employment patterns among women, the
attempt to develop alternate styles of family living, and the controversy over the nature of female sexuality. In concluding she issues an
eloquent warning against an overemphasis on the meritocracy so
favored by middle-class feminists which reinforces the structure of
American capitalism. An appropriate movement for female liberation,
on the other hand, would seek to remove the burden of discrimination, oppression, and onerous work from the backs of all.

When the census takers made their rounds in 1972, 43 percent of all American women were in the job market. In the course of that year 52 percent of America's females would spend at least some time in the work force. Women continued to be the major source of labor force expansion; fully two-thirds of the new employees of the 1960s were females. Furthermore, the typical female worker was no longer marking time before and after her career as a mother. By 1969, 48.6 percent of the women with children ages six to seventeen were in the work force, and 28.5 percent of the mothers of preschoolers were employed outside the home. As more young wives and mothers went to work, the age scale of female employment began to resemble the male pattern. Women were more solidly integrated into the work force than ever before.[1]

There were also some signs that the women of the 1960s and '70s were securing jobs outside the female sector of the labor force. In 1970 the census bureau had some sticky problems in categorizing jobs by sex— the anomalies of 756 female telephone "linemen" and 138 male "midwives." Women had assaulted some male domains in force. They accounted for one-half of the new reporters and editors, 75 percent of the novice bus drivers, and swamped the market for bartenders. Simultaneously, a few men timidly approached female occupations, particularly elementary-school teaching, and librarianship, while a handful of brave souls entered the field of nursing as well.[2]

These occasional renegades from the sex segregated labor force, however, accounted for only a tiny proportion of the job corps. The mammoth gains in female employment occurred in the most familiar place, as 3.8 million women took up clerical jobs, thus raising the proportion of women so employed from 30 to 35 percent in the space of a decade. On the other hand, the increase of women in the professions amounted only to 2 percent, despite the rapid growth in the number of college-educated women over the decade. Overall, the line of demarcation between the male and female work spheres grew slightly sharper in the 1960s.[3]

Consequently, the wage differential between male and female workers also grew larger. The millions of women entering the clerical and sales occupation with wages under $2 an hour counter-balanced any advances of more experienced and highly qualified female workers. In 1955 the

---

[1] Elizabeth Waldman, "Changes in the Labor Force Activity of Women," in *Women in a Man-Made World*, N. Glazer-Malbin and H. Y. Waehrer, eds. (Chicago, 1972), pp. 30–38.

[2] *The New York Times*, February 11, 1973, p. 1.

[3] *Ibid.*

earnings of full-time female workers amounted to 64 percent of the income of male workers; in 1970 women were making a paltry 57 percent of what men were. Even after the enactment of legislation prohibiting sexual discrimination in wages, in the period between 1968 and 1971 there was no appreciable increase in women's wages relative to men's. Female income was actually highest among professional people, but even here women's earnings were less than half of men's, a scandalous 48 percent. A large part of this inequity stemmed from the low level positions women obtained within the professions: public defenders rather than corporate lawyers, public health doctors rather than private physicians, elementary-school teachers rather than principals. Still, an estimated 20 percent of the income imbalance between male and female professionals was outright discrimination, unequal pay for equal work.[4]

By the 1970s the systematic discrimination against women clearly belied the trumpeted ideal of technological society, the meritocracy. By the arbitrary dictates of sex, women were removed to a secondary status system, a very squat pyramid in which only 1.1 percent of female workers earned more than $15,000 a year, while 45 percent of them made less than $5,000 annually.[5] Sexual discrimination also cut across the racial hierarchy of economic rewards. The median income of white and nonwhite men amounted to $9,373 and $6,598 respectively. Women of all races were amassed at the bottom of the economic ladder, with white women earning about $900 more than nonwhite females annually.[6] The aspiration of black women to achieve economic equity with white females was hardly an extravagant ambition.

Typically, however, a woman's economic status was still determined by her husband. Her wages usually accounted for less than one-fourth of the income in most two-worker households. For increasing numbers of families, nevertheless, the wife's income had become the measure of affluence in the 1960s. The highest level of female employment occurred in families with incomes between $12,000 and $15,000 a year. Highly educated women, who could command relatively large wages, for females, were particularly prone to reenter the work force in later life. By age forty-five, more than 80 percent of all women with five or more years of college education were gainfully employed and providing an ample increment of luxury for their families.[7] Most female participation in the labor force, however, was not the result of a desire for an extra fillip of affluence among these select segments of the population. Sixty-five percent of all working women and 80 percent of nonwhite women joined the labor force because they were either the sole support of themselves and their children or because their spouses made less than $7,000 a year.[8]

Still, the female labor market seemed to operate on the assumption that women worked only for pin money, perpetuating blanket sex dis-

---

[4] *Ibid.,* December 27, 1972, p. 34.
[5] *Ibid.,* January 7, 1973, p. 52.
[6] *Ibid.,* December 27, 1972, p. 34.
[7] Glazer-Malbin and Waehrer, *op. cit.,* pp. 34, 194–97.
[8] *The New York Times,* January 18, 1973, p. 35.

crimination and causing special hardships for poor families as well as countless widows, divorcées, and single women. This consequence of the sex segregated wage scale was dramatically illustrated in the plight of black women in the 1960s. While the number of male-headed black families living beneath the poverty level was cut in half in that decade, female-headed families, which grew in number over the decade, remained mired in poverty. Forty-seven percent of all poverty families were female-headed in 1969, an increase of almost 26 percent over the last ten years.[9] The specter of becoming the sole provider for one's self and children haunted women of all races as the divorce rate continued to skyrocket. The promise of alimony was a very weak reed for the divorced woman to lean upon. The typical child-support payments awarded by the courts were not only insubstantial, but also very difficult to collect.[10] By 1970, one in every ten American families was headed by a female, and nearly half of these were poor.[11] Protest against sex discrimination in the labor force was not trivial reformism for the middle class; it assailed a major source of poverty in America.

The typical employed woman, furthermore, worked overtime in the home with no pay whatsoever. Researchers in the 1970s calculated that a working mother with two small children devoted forty-two hours a week to housework. The overall domestic labor of women, evaluated at $8,600 annually, would increase the gross national product by 38 percent if they were remunerated. Working women could expect only eleven hours of assistance from their husbands in a typical week. Thus, it becomes clear why 1/3 to 1/2 of America's working women were employed outside the home only part-time. The unemployed wife and mother was hardly a laggard either. According to a conservative estimate, the typical mother of two spent sixty-seven hours per week engaged in household chores. The more liberal calculations of Chase Manhattan Bank estimated this workweek at 99.6 hours. Whether a woman worked in the home or outside of it, and most likely she did both, her labors were seldom evaluated according to male standards.

Woman's work was still rewarded with the honorific rhetoric of the feminine mystique. The advertisers of the late '60s alluded to the multiple burdens of the working wife in the usual glamorous and evasive manner. Pond's advertisements played on the theme "She's busy yet she's beautiful." This image was projected by such personages as a dress designer, who simultaneously mothered three children and served as a hostess for her famous husband. An actress, wife, and mother proclaimed in another ad, "I'm often tired but I never show it."[12] The *Ladies' Home Journal*, unable to ignore female participation in the labor force in the 1970s, nestled a regular column on the working woman in between its customarily elaborate advice on housekeeping, maternal care, and sexual ac-

[9] Juanita Kreps, *Sex in the Marketplace* (Baltimore and London, 1971), p. 10.

[10] Kirsten Amundsen, *The Silenced Majority* (Englewood Cliffs, N.J., 1971), pp. 26–28.

[11] Kreps, *op. cit.*, p. 10.

[12] *Ladies' Home Journal*, March 1960.

complishment. The women who shouldered the double burdens of homemaker and worker and struggled to live up to this multi-faceted ideal were indeed likely to be tired, and a quaff of Geritol and a bit of male flattery were hardly adequate supplements to their low salaries.

One might expect that by 1970 women recognized this double bind and determined to escape it by remaining single and applying themselves whole-heartedly to work. Highly trained single women, it turned out, did secure a level of economic success that rivaled men.[13] It was clear that the single state had acquired unprecedented stature and significance in the 1960s and '70s. As of 1970 there were thirty-seven million single adults in the United States, more than a twofold increase in fifteen years. In addition, the majority of single persons lived in independent households, apart from their parents, another sharp break with tradition.[14] Market researchers and magazine tycoons were among the first to comprehend the significance of this demographic phenomenon. In 1973 a group of shrewd entrepreneurs announced the forthcoming publication of *Single*, a magazine addressed to "one out of every three adults—the *largest undetected* market in America." Ladies' magazines had also begun to court the market of singles—*Cosmopolitan* in its racy style and the *Ladies' Home Journal* in its wholesome fashion with articles on such themes as "Saucepans and the Single Girl." Single women had at least achieved notice and fashionable status as an important category in the consumer market.

The expansion of the single population, however, was not the result of a widespread repudiation of marriage. It was, first of all, a delayed consequence of the postwar baby boom, which had deposited a heavy concentration of population in the traditionally single age group, eighteen to twenty. A slight tendency to delay marriage, raising the median age at which women married to twenty-one, also replenished the ranks of the single. By their early thirties, however, only 6 percent of the female population remained unmarried. The skyrocketing divorce rate also provided only a temporary increase in the ranks of the single. Ninety percent of the women who divorced before age thirty would remarry, most of them within a few short years. Thus, despite the swelling ranks of the single population, marriage was as popular as ever. In fact, the marriage rate increased a few percentage points each year through 1973.[15]

The single state, for all the glamour, sexiness, and hedonism surrounding it in the media, did not waylay women from matrimony for very long. Apparently the social life of the single bar and the swinger's apartment was not enduringly satisfying, and the typical job in the female labor force did not inspire lifelong dedication. The most congenial environment for the single person was the college community. Yet if college attendance declines, as is expected, in the '70s, the marriage rate may climb even higher. So women rushed to the altar as enthusiastically as

[13] Larry E. Suter and Herman P. Miller, "Income Differences Between Men and Career Women," in Glazer-Malbin and Waehrer, *op. cit.*, p. 297.

[14] *The New York Times*, October 15, 1972, p. 58.

[15] *Monthly Vital Statistics Report*, Vol. 21, March 1973, p. 1. See also, Oppenheimer in *American Journal of Sociology*, January 1973, *passim*.

ever, only a bit tardily, and in so doing turned away from all the daring values of singles culture, reverting to nineteenth-century feminine fantasies. More than 80 percent of the brides of 1971 donned the frills and lace of a wedding gown and embraced the ritual of a traditional ceremoney. The pragmatic agents of the consumer economy welcomed the bride as well as the single women: The wedding business added $7,000,000,000 to the economy annually.[16]

The young married women of the '70s did, however, flaunt one central ideal of the feminine tradition. For the first time in history young women surveyed by the Census Bureau in 1971 aspired, on the average, to bear fewer than three children. The plummeting birth rate of the 1960s seemed destined to reach an all-time low. The dramatic confirmation came in 1972 when, based on the current birth rate, demographers projected that the mothers of the '70s would bear on the average 2.08 children, a jot below the replacement rate. If such a level of fertility could be sustained for seventy years, the American population would stabilize.[17] The achievement of zero population growth was still a precarious goal, but more probable than ever before. The predilections of women and economic expertise concurred in the opinion that unchecked fertility was profligacy. In 1972 the presidential commission on population growth, headed by John D. Rockefeller 3rd, carefully pointed out that per capita income would be 15 percent higher in the year 2000 if the typical woman bore two rather than three children.[18] The *Ladies' Home Journal* set Sylvia Porter to calculating the prohibitive cost of having a baby, a fact made patently obvious by soaring inflation. Such convincing arguments against the large family combined with the availability of oral contraceptives and the Supreme Court decision on abortion to provide women with both the incentive and the power to moderate their fertility. They acted decisively: In New York State in 1971 abortions actually exceeded live births.

With her maternity in check, woman's role was no longer so starkly different from man's. She could complete childbearing by her mid-twenties and enter the work force soon thereafter, putting in almost as much time as her husband over a lifetime. Simple clichés about woman's unique place could no longer justify discrimination between the sexes. The combination of woman's role in the work force with her residual home responsibilities, however, was still hopelessly cumbersome. Her dual performance entailed an excessive burden in the home and commanded an inferior wage in the job market. The mediation between these two roles functioned as an economic expedient, the best arrangement whereby to maximize income and at the same time provide domestic comfort for the prudently smaller family. Woman's place was being swallowed up by the voracious forces of advanced capitalism as the economic man was paired with the economic woman. The latter remained an unperfected economic creature, however, still dependent on a husband for much of

---

[16] Marcia Seligson, *The Eternal Bliss Machine* (New York, 1973), pp. 1–2.

[17] *The New York Times,* December 5, 1972.

[18] *Report of the Commission on Population Growth and the American Future* (New York, 1972), p. 46.

her status and support, still handicapped by femininity in the job market. The discomforts of this position were heightened in the 1960s by an 80 percent increase in the divorce rate. A woman faced about a fifty-fifty chance that her marriage would be dissolved, leaving her an economic cripple. The status of women in the 1970s was built not only on an exhausting collection of conflicting roles, but on a precarious economic foundation as well.

This complicated arrangement of sex roles provoked a great deal of thought about alternative family styles. The '70s gave rise to proposals for revised marital contracts, communal households, even polyandry and group marriage.[19] A program for "open marriage" sold hundreds of thousands of copies in short order. All these schemes promised to grant women a more equitable marital role; all repudiated the prescriptions for femininity that pervaded the 1950s. The general malaise among domesticated women, which Betty Friedan originally called "the problem that has no name," was now confirmed by statistics on mental illness. Devoted mothers whose children had left home flooded psychiatrists' offices and mental institutions. While the incidence of psychic disorder was highest among single men, the married woman was almost as prone to mental illness, at a rate far above the single woman. Put another way, the healthiest and happiest wedded Americans seemed to be husbands married to discontented and neurotic wives.[20] Obviously, the marital relationships that provided such lopsided benefits to the two sexes needed reform. The favored remedy of the critics of the '60s and '70s was by one minor modification of the family or another to enlarge the wife's opportunities for self-fulfillment outside the home.

This new ethic was most apparent in the aspirations of educated women, as illustrated by a comparison of attitude surveys conducted by Mirra Komarovsky in 1943 and 1971. Fifty percent of the women attending a prestigious eastern college in 1943 indicated that they intended to retire permanently from the labor force after they became mothers. In 1971 only 18 percent of the women attending the same college planned to do the same. The majority of the women of the '70s looked forward to returning to work after their children were grown: 62 percent of them chose an option preferred by only 30 percent of the alumnae of the '40s. These highly educated women of the 1970s were prepared to assume dual roles and an interrupted career pattern, apparently oblivious to or unconcerned about the likelihood that they would receive considerably lower salaries than their husbands who remained continuously in the work force. Only 20 percent of the respondents intended to devote themselves wholeheartedly to a career, exactly the same percentage as in the 1943 survey.[21]

Komarovsky also discovered that the college women of the 1970s had, by and large, discarded that demeaning practice of their counter-

[19] Herbert A. Otto, ed., *The Family in Search of a Future* (New York, 1970).

[20] Walter Grove and Jeanette F. Tudor, "Adult Sex Roles and Mental Illness," *American Journal of Sociology* (January 1973), p. 828.

[21] Mirra Komarovsky, "Cultural Contradictions and Sex Roles," *American Journal of Sociology* (January 1973), p. 883.

parts in the '50s, that of "playing dumb" to please potential mates. While intellectual equality was now regarded as a valuable aspect of the hetero-sexual relationship, college women were still reluctant, however, to apply their intelligence to career goals. Few of even the self-acknowledged liberated women were contemplating a precise program of professional or intellectual achievement. A survey of the career plans of 1971 college graduates revealed that despite a slight elevation in the ambitions of fe-males (whose grades as a group were superior to males), men still out-reached women in professional and academic aspirations by a margin of three to one.[22] A suggestive and partial explanation for this poor showing of women has been offered by psychologist Matina Horner.

During the late 1960s, Horner had uncovered a deep-seated resistance to wordly achievement on the part of women, which she called "fear of success." More than 80 percent of the college women Horner studied exhibited this disturbing symptom, which at times took on horrifying manifestations. For example, when one young woman was asked to com-plete a narrative about the subsequent career of a medical student named Anne who found herself at the top of the class, she responded as follows: "Anne starts proclaiming her surprise and joy. Her fellow classmates are so disgusted with her behavior that they jump on her in a body and beat her. She is maimed for life." Most of the women whom Horner sub-jected to this test, in dramatic contrast to the men, reacted negatively, if not with such a vehement sense of self-destrucion. Overall, these women felt that career achievement jeopardized their femininity and marital prospects.[23] Whatever the flaws in Horner's experiments she had touched upon a sore spot in the career development of woman, and one that was a logical outgrowth of feminine conditioning, from her maternal role model as an infant to the retiring heroines of children's literature, and the adult images of the languid sexy female. This systematic stereotyping re-mains largely undisturbed today and continues to seduce the girl children of America into their dual and secondary adult roles.

Husbands continue to show a vested interest in the feminine stereo-type as well. Men polled at an ivy league college in the '70s overwhelm-ingly endorsed the inferior and peripheral economic role of women. While only 24 percent of the sample expected their prospective wives to remain permanently stationed in the home, 48 percent preferred that they remain there until the children were grown. Only 16 percent of them would recommend that wives remain at work for their entire married life, and a paltry 7 percent of this intellectual and social elite had any intention of sharing home as well as work roles with their wives. One up-to-date ivy leaguer provided a complete scenario for the convoluted inequality of the wife of the near future:

> I believe that it is a good thing for mothers to return to full time work when the children are grown, provided the work is impor-tant and worthwhile. Otherwise housewives get hung up with

[22] Leonard L. Baird et al., *The Graduates, 1971* (Princeton, N.J., 1973), Chapter 6.

[23] Vivian Gornick, "Why Radcliffe Women Are Afraid of Sex," *The New York Times Magazine*, January 14, 1973, p. 54.

tranquilizers because they have no outlet for their abilities. A woman should want her husband's success more than he should want hers. Her work shouldn't interfere with or hurt his in any way.

While the beatification of homemaking and motherhood gave way to nasty condescension toward the housewife, the roles she was offered outside the home were not invested with dignity or significance comparable to a man's work. The unfortunate wives of men like this would be expected to do double duty for half the honors, in the shadow of a self-important mate. Such revised but hardly liberating presumptions about woman's place undoubtedly lurk in the minds of many men in the 1970s.[24]

Yet the demand for egalitarian intimacy between husbands and wives was made more imperative than ever. Deep communion between mates was the cause célèbre of the most popular volume on marital reform, *Open Marriage* by Nina O'Neill and George O'Neill. This program for absolute trust, uninhibited communication, and mutual personal growth came complete with instructions for practice sessions in marital openness, schemes to develop sensitivity to the other, and ritualistic steps toward perfect intimacy. Modern couples scampered to encounter groups and sensitivity sessions in pursuit of the same maximization of heterosexual intimacy. Advertisers endorsed this subordination of domestic routine to marital companionship in their own crude fashion: "A woman's place is next to her husband not by her sink."[25]

Ideally, open marriage allowed for the independent identities, interests, friendship, and love affairs of the husband and wife. Yet there was no doubt that the personal bond and emotional support of the married couple would transcend all other human ties and undermine their strength. The communes of the '60s and '70s provided a more sympathetic environment than did "open marriage" for those men and women who valued a wider circle of integral human contact. By most accounts, however, these collective living arrangements were fragile and incomplete alternatives to marriage. Disruptive vestiges of the nuclear family, and pernicious sex roles as well, accompanied the modern communards to their new homes, which rarely rested on an autonomous and self-supporting economic base. Wracked by internal tensions and external pressure, the typical collective had a very short life, provided salutary but brief relief for a few eccentrics from the linear, enclosed relationship of heterosexual coupling.[26] As long as the American workplace proved to be a ruthless and alienating environment and society remained amorphous and impersonal, men and women would turn to the private sphere in search of salve for their discomfort. The simplest recourse was to the family, which women entered with their age-old liabilities, the excessive demands and inferior rewards of their traditional sphere.

[24] Komarovsky, *op. cit.*, p. 881.

[25] *Ladies' Home Journal*, September 1970.

[26] Bennett Berger, Bruce M. Hackett, and R. Mervyn Millar, "Child-Rearing Practice in the Communal Family," *Family, Marriage and the Struggle of the Sexes,* Hans P. Dreitzel, ed. (New York, 1972), pp. 271–300.

Like the mystique of conjugal intimacy, the cult of maternity was in some disarray by the 1970s. The theoretical underpinnings of the maternal obsession encouraged by Dr. Spock were undercut by experiments in the institutional care of young children. The iconoclastic opinions of one such experimenter, child psychologist Bettye Caldwell, were emblazoned across the front page of the Los Angeles *Times* in 1971. Dr. Caldwell had concluded from her experience with day care that a child's mental growth was accelerated and his or her emotional development unharmed by removal from the mother. In fact, Caldwell dared to confess that she would accept a six-month-old infant into public group care without trepidation. Concurrently, sociologists and psychologists were reassessing the presumed connection between working mother and juvenile delinquency and found no direct correlation between the two.[27] Yet the old guard was not easily converted. President Richard Nixon vetoed day-care legislation with an invocation of the old saws: Institutional child care would "diminish both parental authority and parental involvement with children, particularly in the decisive early years when social attitudes and conscience and religious and moral principles are first inculcated."

Nixon's authority to speak on the origins of "moral principles" may have been diminished of late, but more legitimate experts also continue to buoy up the principle of maternal nurture. The women's page of *The New York Times* consulted four child psychologists on this issue and all concurred that children under three were better off at home with their mothers. Their cautionary refrain was familiar: "Day care can result in permanent damage to an infant's emotional development." The feasibility of day care for older children was also cause for controversy. Dr. Juliet Kestenberg discouraged it on the grounds that "a child can sense the tension in a working mother and it breeds anxiety. . . . A mother usually drops off her child at a day-care center on the way to work, often in a rush. That evening, very tired, she picks up the child and has to dash home for grocery shopping, dinner, and housework. What benefit can this pressure have for the child?" One might well ask what benefit this exhausting routine of multiple roles could have for a mother, but neither these child psychologists nor the editors of the women's page were concerned about reforming women's roles. The title of the article said it all, in the familiar guilt-inducing way: "Day Care: It's Fine for Mother, but What about the Child?"[28] Most of the debates about child-care were stymied between the poles of traditional motherhood and makeshift day care, incognizant of either paternal or societal responsibility for the rearing of America's young.

While the experts argued the relative benefits of maternal and institutional child care, however, both government and private industry were setting up a few day-care centers. Their motivation was rarely the welfare of either the mother or the child but rather sound economic policy. The KLH Corporation, for example, was at the vanguard of the

---

[27] F. Ivan Nye, ed., *The Employed Mother in America* (Chicago, 1963).
[28] *The New York Times*, March 24, 1973, p. 38.

day-care movement. Company literature was quite explicit about the goals of their child-care facilities. The availability of free child care enabled mothers to enter the labor force and to stay there for cheap wages; day care "helps prevent competition for workers that pushes up wage rates, promotes inflation and causes production bottlenecks."[29] Smaller firms relied on the government to provide these profit-enhancing facilities. For example, the garment manufacturers of New York's Chinatown gave their female employees (the direct descendants of the immigrant sweatshop operatives of the nineteenth century) time off to protest government cutbacks in day-care funds. When the benefits of public day care to the employers of poor, nonwhite women are kept in mind, the appearance of support for these measures in illiberal quarters becomes intelligible. Why else would conservative southern senators be such staunch supporters of federal day-care legislation? Public day-care regulations are calculated to secure female employees willing to work for low wages. A low ceiling on the maximum income a mother may make and still receive free day care insures that many women will remain in the ranks of the working poor. In addition, unemployed mothers are often allowed the use of day-care facilities only for a few months, until they have secured employment at the appropriate low wage. Middle-class women, on the other hand, are expected to boost the economy by the direct purchase of child care. *Barron's* magazine summoned the ambitious entrepreneurs to invest in private day-care services, tempting them with the promise of a $7,500,000,000 market.[30] A long and hazardous wait is in store for mothers, nonetheless, if they are to rely on the benevolence of government, employers, and businessmen for assistance; in 1970 only 6 percent of the children of working mothers were placed in day-care centers.[31] Thus the supple threads of sexism wove through all female roles, drawing women of all classes into their dual burdens and inferior status.

Since the roles of women in the home and in the work force had become so muddled, the creators of mass culture were at a loss as to how to construct a simple evocative image of femininity. An evasive tactic was in order: Rather than presenting the ideal woman as either a mother or a worker, or an unwieldy combination of the two, she was projected as transcendent sexiness. By the mid '60s the beatific mother and the wide-eyed housewife were taking a back seat to the sinewy, streamlined seductress. On the glossy pages of popular magazines, models of femininity were posed in sensuous array. In 1965 a perfume ad in the *Ladies' Home Journal* surrounded a woman with no less than seven men and was accompanied by the caption "dashingly different on every man in your life." Another torrid vamp warned "If you don't give him 007 . . . I will."[32] These paragons of sexiness made a sales pitch for an appropriate

[29] Katherine Ellis and Rosalind Petchesky, "Children of the Corporate Dream: An Analysis of Day Care as a Political Issue," *Socialist Revolution* (November–December 1972), p. 14.

[30] Ellis and Petchesky, *ibid.*, pp. 22–23.

[31] *Ladies' Home Journal*, December 1965.

[32] Kreps, *op. cit.*, p. 5.

series of products. The prime advertising spaces of the *Ladies' Home Journal,* once reserved for baby and homemaking products, were filled with full-page ads for cosmetics, perfumes, and explicitly sex-linked commodities such as the deodorizers of the female genitals. Eye makeup alone had become a $48,000,000 market by the 1970s. Not only was the female stereotype more aggressively sexual than ever before, but it also objectified men who were themselves embalmed in body enhancing products: cologne, deodorants, and hair sprays. Males and females doubled as pursuers and objects in the popular game and lucrative business of sexual voyeurism. *Playboy* "bunnies" met their match in the *Cosmopolitan* centerfold. *Playboy* magazine itself was mimicked by the publication of *Playgirl* in 1973, though the latter was a long way from achieving the circulation of fourteen million achieved by the master salesman of female sex objects, Hugh Hefner. Nonetheless, the boundaries between male and female seemed to be becoming more muted in matters of sex and work alike.

In fact, the sex researchers of the '60s and '70s were granting a special preeminence to woman. This at least was the implication of the laboratory investigations of William Masters and Virginia Johnson. Their work lent more authoritative and widely publicized support to the fact that all female orgasms center in the clitoris. Among the more novel findings of the Masters and Johnson research was the demonstration of the capacity of the female to experience more intense and more numerous orgasms than the male. This clinical evidence was frequently interpreted as a proclamation of the sexual insatiability of women. One daring psychologist, Mary Jane Sherfey, went so far as to suggest that the female animal was driven by an unquenchable sexual desire. Her lusts were so overpowering, in fact, that the development of human civilization was retarded five thousand years while her sexuality was painstakingly brought under control.[33] Those familiar with the long and ingenious history of feminine stereotypes might be suspicious that this reading of biology was yet another Trojan horse, an apparently generous gift to women in which was hidden an arsenal of prescriptions for sexual inequality. The theory of the sexual insatiability of women could be construed as yet another invidious focus on the biological differences between the sexes calculated to divert females into secondary and primitive pursuits, this time the single-minded pursuit of orgasms.

Such an interpretation of the sexual obsession of the 1970s may be a bit paranoid but it is not entirely unfounded. The pervasiveness and profitability of the sexy female imagery in American popular culture must be viewed with suspicion. Women's magazines were all too ready to present instructions in every issue on how to maximize sexual pleasure. The *Ladies' Home Journal's* enthusiasm for the sex craze of the '70s extended to establishing a regular column on the issue and even to the recounting of "Everything You Always Wanted to Know About Your Pet's Sex Life." Dr. David Reuben's similarly titled encyclopedia of

---

[33] Mary Jane Sherfey, "A Theory of Female Sexuality" in *Sisterhood is Powerful,* Robin Morgan, ed. (New York, 1970), pp. 220–29.

human sexuality sold eight million copies in the same year. Meanwhile, the most popular novels of the era were penned by Jacqueline Susann, an author whose ability to mold the sexual sensibilities of women into a fast-paced, all-absorbing vicarious experience recalls the sentimental finesse of Harriet Beecher Stowe. At the very least this cultural obsession with female sexuality distracted women from the contemplation of the practical contradictions of their condition in the 1970s.

The popular literature of the '70s honored as cultural heroines women renowned primarily for their erotic exploits. The sex crazed culture elevated the prostitute to a glamorous position, in the person of Xaviera Hollander. Her paean to the delights of a life devoted to selling the female body, *The Happy Hooker*, sold four million copies in the space of a year. A career in the same field but without pay was recommended by the best seller *The Sensuous Woman*. The author, who chose to remain anonymous, directed the reader to build her life around sex: to choose her place of employment according to the fringe benefits of sexual contacts it offered; to decorate and redecorate her bedroom to enhance her love life; to routinely spend countless hours arranging her appearance and setting up social situations for the conquest of lovers. The author of *The Sensuous Woman* assumed that her readers were in one of two vulnerable positions: the pit of the female labor force (i.e., secretaries) or the wasteland of the suburban home. Sexual adventure was calculated to enliven the monotony of these women's lives and served to deflect their consciousness from the concrete problems of their lowly social and economic position.[34] Barbara Seaman, on the other hand, addressed her treatise on female sexuality, *Free and Female*, to independent and successful professional women. Seamen was, in fact, something of a sexual snob, proclaiming that this class of women had the best and most frequent orgasms. The orgasm was a major source of woman's liberation in Seaman's view: "Once an individual has experienced transcendent sex, even once, it seems to change her (or him) for a lifetime, making her (or him) more spontaneous, more open, more confident, more loving, more purposeful and more peaceful." The orgasm, an "almost mystical experience of renewal . . . giving meaning and immortality," appeared as one of the proudest accomplishments of these emancipated women, and every act that could possibly engender it, including breast-feeding and childbirth, was a sacred event of womanhood.[35]

Despite the vigor of the cult of female orgasm, female sexuality was still clothed in mystery in many quarters in the 1970s. A woman's gynecologist was still apt to be the source of ignorance and misinformation. Two-thirds of the gynecological textbooks published after 1967 failed to mention the findings of Masters and Johnson and continued to assert that women's sexual desires were weaker than men's. Some of these "experts" still repeated the old clichés of sexual politics: "An important feature of the sex drive is the man's urge to dominate the woman and subjugate her

---

[34] "J", *Sensuous Woman* (New York, 1971), p. 11.
[35] Barbara Seaman, *Free and Female: The Sex Life of the Contemporary Woman* (New York, 1972), p. 191.

to his will. In the woman acquiescence to the masterful takes a high place."[36] The sexual revolution had not eliminated violent sexual attacks upon women. One study conducted at a midwestern college in 1967 disclosed that 23 percent of the males interviewed admitted to attempting to rape women they dated, while one-half of the women reported they had been the victims of sexual attacks by all-American college men.[37] In the 1970s a rising incidence of rape (perhaps attributable in part to the diminishing reluctance of women to report this crime) testified to the fact that female sexual experience often proved the occasion of painful degradation rather than "transcendent" joy. Furthermore, the actual increase in sexual behavior and freedom, as measured by statistics on premarital sexual experience, was hardly as dramatic as the cult of sexuality would suggest. The celebration of sexual liberation could, in fact, operate as another annoying and dehumanizing constriction on a young woman's behavior, now making virginity a cause for scorn and self-rebuke, prompting at times a grim submission to popular pressure and male desires. In summary, the cult of sexuality yielded an updated mystique of female fulfillment, an orgy of voyeurism, and pressure to conform to a new standard of womanhood. The actual resurrection of the body was often lost sight of, perhaps impeded, in the process.

The possible impact of the sexual standards of the '60s and '70s upon the quality of a woman's life is recounted in Ingrid Bengis' *Combat in the Erogenous Zone*. By her mid-twenties, the author had ricocheted from one feminine image to another and was emotionally exhausted: "I can't become the person each decade newly assumes I ought to be. I cannot be the completely feminine woman of the '50s, the emancipated sexually free woman of the '60s, and the militant, anti-sexist woman of the '70s." As Bengis recounted her personal history, however, it becomes clear that it was the pursuit of the ideal of sexual freedom that entrapped her and propelled her through "one experiment after another in alternative love-styles." She admitted that flight from affair to affair, with men and women both, had been an "ersatz progress," impelled by a force "over which we have no control." Yet, she remained enthralled by the false promises of fulfillment through romantic sexuality, committed to a continual quest for "authenticity in search of sex and love which reflects that authenticity, and reflects the kind of purity which is reserved for essentials, even when those essentials prove to be less than pleasant." *Combat in the Erogenous Zone* is more than anything else the biography of a sex life and, consequently, a one-dimensional personal statement.[38]

Exhausted by this feminine odyssey, convinced that divisive combat was innate to sexual relations, Ingrid Bengis took refuge in some of the most shopworn theories of sexual differences. "There are times when I

---

[36] Diana Scully and Pauline Bart, "A Funny Thing Happened on the Way to the Orifice: Women in Gynecology Textbooks," *American Journal of Sociology* (January 1973), p. 1048.

[37] Randal Collins, "A Conflict Theory of Sexual Stratification," in Dreitzel, *op cit.*, p. 73.

[38] Ingrid Bengis, *Combat in the Erogenous Zone* (New York, 1972), p. xvii.

wonder whether nature isn't really the one to hold responsible. It seems a lot easier to blame nature than to blame men (although blaming society runs a close second), and I conclude that the real trouble derives from the fact that man and woman are vitally different not in those ways that provide an interesting variety, but in ways that make of sexuality a veritable war zone." These "natural" differences between the sexes included the familiar elements of the soap-opera mentality, which decreed that men were poorly endowed with the capacity for lasting love and nurture. To explain the superior emotional needs and sensibilities of women, Bengis took refuge in the oldest catchall of the female stereotype, maternity: "The need for growth and gestation seems to be extremely powerful and perhaps even innate."[39]

Unlike the nineteenth-century cult of motherhood, however, Bengis' typology of feminine nature did not foster an expansive humanism. Mired in the private universe of sexuality, Bengis, and the class and generation of women she presumed to speak for, moved "ever inward" toward introspection and self-fulfillment. Political and social action was suspect. For example, Bengis chose to deplore the "combat in the erogenous zone" rather than the destruction of life in the Indochina War. "If bodies are being killed all over the world because of politics rather than love, spirits are being smashed right next door, in apartment houses and shacks and on the street because of love rather than politics . . . love that can't—no matter how hard we try—be reinterpreted to fit any political mold, not even the mold of female oppression."[40] Thus, Bengis shied away from politics even as an avenue of escape from the sexual combat that she so bitterly decried. This heightened sexual consciousness could privatize and isolate women like never before and leave them to wallow in the ruins of a personal war.

Fortunately, not all women were mired in the mystique of sexual romance as the contradictions of the multiple female role sharpened in the 1960s. The political reawakening of women began with a subdued rumbling of discontent among upper-middle-class women. President Kennedy's Commission on the Status of Women, set up in 1961, proved one focus of rising discontent. The original purpose of the commission, to determine why the talents of educated women were under-utilized in the economy, was by no means feminist. The women set to grapple with this narrow problem, however, soon uncovered problems of another order. First, the disclosure of blatant discrimination against women in the professions raised a question of sexual equality rather than simple economic utility. Second, the commission members discovered the peculiar professional handicaps of the married women, the difficulties of balancing their home and work roles. The problem of the dual roles for educated women was also central to the spring issue of *Daedalus* published in 1964, which was devoted to women's issues and included the path-breaking essay by Alice Rossi, "Equality of the Sexes: An Immodest Proposal."

[39] *Ibid.*, p. 82.
[40] *Ibid.*, p. 208.

It was at this conspicuous moment that murmurings of discontent were also heard in the cloisters of suburbia, later to be trumpeted in a best seller, Betty Friedan's *The Feminine Mystique*. Slowly the problems of women began to take on an autonomous significance, consequential enough to demand a revival of organized feminism. Women did not acquiesce in the discriminatory adjustment of their kaleidoscopic roles for very long and, once again, womanhood was under siege. All these concerns came together in a Washington, D.C., hotel where in 1966 concerned women were assembled for a meeting of the National Conference of Commissions on the Status of Women. In Betty Friedan's room the National Organization for Women was quietly founded.[41]

From the start, NOW displayed the strengths and the weaknesses of the habitat in which it had germinated. NOW's leaders were in an opportune position to exploit the American ethic of equality of opportunity. By the 1960s it was clear that contrary to the old sayings about woman's place, women were in the work force to stay and entitled to the same rights that men enjoyed there. Americans could not argue with the simple justice of equal pay for equal work. The governmental experience of NOW's founders in the Presidential Commission also placed them in an opportune situation to enact their forthright demands. They were there to see to it that a clause forbidding sexual discrimination was included in the Civil Rights Act of 1964, and NOW was intent upon enforcing it despite the congressmen who thought the sex clause was something of a joke. The energy and efficiency of the National Organization for Women has brought untold benefits to thousands of women who have taken advantage of their legal rights and won millions of dollars in equity payments.

NOW, whose membership exceeded thirty thousand in 1973, had considerably broadened its programs: championing the rights of the poor, the nonwhite, and the Lesbian, as well as the middle-class middle-American woman and demanding abortion, day care, and political power as well as equal pay for women. Yet the organization's chief goals remain the piece by piece legislative alleviation of the most glaring sexual contradictions to the American dream of equality of achievement. The climb to equality so-defined is a steep and treacherous one, which requires that a woman be placed beside a male equivalent at each position along the immensely complicated occupational hierarchy of America. Feminism as espoused by groups like NOW summons each and every woman to the rugged status-climbing long required of men by the rags to riches myth. Such an assault upon the pinnacle of American politics is a particularly gargantuan feat. Women have hardly scratched the surface of the American political elite, capturing in the half century since suffrage only two cabinet posts, four governorships, and 2 percent of the seats in the United States Congress. Feminists can contemplate another fearsome struggle to penetrate the corporate establishment, with women now constituting

[41] Jo Freeman, "The Origins of the Women's Liberation Movement," *American Journal of Sociology* (January 1973), pp. 798–99.

around 2 percent of the nation's executive elite. The media of communication, the labor unions, and the educational elite also are formidable bastions of male supremacy.[42]

With supreme dedication and stamina, some women undoubtedly will succeed in infiltrating the ruling class, but the possible casualties of the struggle bear consideration. The cost to individual women of scraping and grappling to reach the top and the high price of staying there, as well as the quality of the prize itself, demand careful assessment. What is the inherent value of power within a corporation that creates useless or pernicious products, or a political party that sacrifices the common good to garner votes and campaign funds, or a profession that merely breeds esoteric information, unnecessary services, or vested interests? To say that the mere presence of women will automatically humanize the power elite is naïvely to embrace the old stereotypes. This is not to say that women should disdain power, but only that they should reconsider both the purposes to which it is put and the justice of consolidating it in the hands of a few persons of either sex before they set out on the campaign to help rule America. As they rebound from the "feminine mystique," some feminists uncritically attach themselves to its polar opposite, the imperative of male "achievement."

A similar myopia lurks in the unqualified demand of equal pay for "equal" work. The NOW constituency fails to question the basic assumption of competitive capitalism and the contemporary meritocracy, that all human labor can be neatly classified, its value ranked, and a man or a woman's just share of the fruits of the economy thereby be determined. This principle has provoked and justified the subjugation of masses of women in the past and could easily continue to do so. There is no guarantee that the elevation of talented, ambitious, and privileged women to high income levels will erase the inequities that all women suffer. In fact, it could have an opposite effect. Black women, intimately aware of the limited number of lucrative jobs available in the American occupational system, are quick to see the possible economic gains of white women as their probable losses. The unassailed assumption that the wealth of America will be held in family units compounds the potential of inequality, within the female sex, allowing the successful woman to pool her salary with an affluent man, while unsuccessful women are subject to poverty compounded by broken marriages. This development was already apparent in statistics on family income in the 1960s. Over the decade the economic differential between the middle and lower classes grew dramatically larger, just as middle-class wives entered the work force and while increasing numbers of poor mothers were left husbandless.[43] The advantages of middle-class women within the American meritocracy may herald an exacerbation of the mal-distribution of wealth and the continuing oppression of lower-class women, unless the structural underpinnings of sexual inequality, the free labor market, and the family are somehow revised.

[42] Amundsen, *op. cit.*, pp. 68, 73, 76, 92.
[43] *Consumer Income*, July 1972, p. 1.

Fortunately the tide of feminism in the 1960s emanated from a number of sources, many of them less prone to these oversights than the National Organization for Women: the civil rights movement, the youth culture, the new left. The political and social environment in which the feminism of younger women was kindled highlighted the issues of race, class, and alternative life-styles. The women who lent their whole-hearted support to these movements, however, confronted some particularly grating exhibitions of misogyny. In the new left, women were routinely delegated the most menial tasks, like leafleting, mimeographing, and generally serving as the secretaries of the revolution. Simultaneously, they were expected to be sexually accommodating "chicks," "prone" in SNCC, saying "yes to men who say no" during the anti-draft offensive. When women raised the issue of sexual oppression before male-dominated groups or formed a women's caucus within them, they were often greeted with condescension toward their "trivial" "personal" demands. A woman who raised the issue of sex on the podium of the 1967 New Politics Convention in Chicago was patted on the head by a male leader and called a "little girl." That woman was Shulamith Firestone, whose political maturity would soon be demonstrated as a theorist for an autonomous movement for the holistic advancement of the female sex, women's liberation.[44]

The women's liberation movement grew up wherever small groups of women jointly identified and articulated the sexual barriers that blocked their paths. Once the long suppressed question of woman's place was raised, an avalanche of complaints, aggravations, demands, and programmatic manifestos spurted forth. Contagious, seemingly spontaneous combustions of women's protest erupted throughout America, especially in the supportive habitat of the college campus. Despite the decentralization of the younger phalanx of the new feminism, a characteristic ambience suffused the movement, one inextricably tied to its social-historical origins. In keeping with both the amorphousness of student culture and the new left's suspicion of elitism, women's liberation groups eschewed the rigid organizational structure of NOW, disdained hierarchy, and never erected an explicit national organizational network. Organized into small groups, which aimed to maximize and equalize the participation of all members, women's liberation proceeded to delve into the ubiquitous restraints and commonplace inhumanities visited upon the female sex. The consciousness-raising group was designed first to express the complaints of individual women, to articulate the sexual oppression that all women shared, and then to identify its broader social causes. Ideally this process would strengthen individual women and bind them together for an assault on their common problems. Both the participatory organizational structure and the politics of the personal bespoke the origins of women's liberation in the youth rebellion of the 1960s. The women's movement merged these techniques with the age-old channels of supportive female communication, and transformed "woman's talk" into a mode of resistance and liberation.

The movement had its peculiar weaknesses as well as its strengths.

[44] Freeman, *op. cit.*, p. 801.

The small group could detain its members in personal therapy and under-mine their political and social effectiveness. The consciousness-raising sessions could become obsessed with the narrow issue of male-female re-lations, dishearteningly reminiscent of woman's "expressive function" and catch women in the familiar trap of the personal. The women's liberation rap session and some of its propagators came dangerously close to being captured by the snare of sexual stereotyping, elevating the symptoms of female confinement to feminine virtues. Both Kate Millett and Germaine Greer encouraged the belief that women were, by historical accident if not by nature, morally superior to men, the agents of love and peace rather than violence and aggression. The women's liberation movement was not able to escape the wiles of contemporary culture, and conse-quently its spokesmen verged occasionally toward the tempting obsession with free sexuality as a cure-all for female oppression. Germaine Greer, for example, would wage revolution in the bedroom and stake women's liberation on the act of transforming the penis from a weapon into a piece of human flesh. Some Lesbians within the movement also climbed out on the vulnerable limb of a sexual panacea, construing sexual relations between women not merely as a liberation of sexual behavior and en-richment of women's experience, but as a new chapter in sexual romanti-cism, portending in and of itself a Utopian equality in sexual relations. Each of these seductive byways of the women's liberation movement sapped the energies required for a concerted attack upon the integral and formidable system of sexual inequality in America.

As long as women's liberation eschewed organizational precision and strategic assaults outside the sphere of personal relations as masculine, the formless spirit of the movement was also prey to cavalier treatment by the mass media. Women's liberation was given definition by unsympa-thetic and often mercenary agencies of popular culture, attuned to the spectacular and trivial manifestations of feminism, or prone to construct an artificial national leadership from the most photogenic and femininely captivating women they could associate with the cause. Until feminists exercised firmer control over popular channels of communication, they were subject to the whims of fad and fashion and in danger of becoming passé at any moment. Those feminists who mimicked the techniques of the established media were easily ensnared in its limitations and contra-dictions. *MS.* magazine, for example, not only catered to a mainstream, upper-middle-class audience, but adopted a pragmatic advertising policy that gave an honored status to the excessive consuming habits of its afflu-ent readers. *MS.* was so successful in this sphere that it has formed its own marketing corporation, which offers to advise manufacturers of the tastes of its readers, as well as the etiquette of nonsexist advertising. Such a smooth symbiosis with agencies that have so often manipulated and de-graded women suggests that the editorial offices of a mass circulation magazine may not be the most congenial forum in which to develop challenging feminist policy. In fact, while *MS.* serves as an efficient and relatively far-reaching communications network for feminist sympa-thizers, it seldom issues a proclamation that would startle a reader of the

Ladies' Home Journal and rarely questions the moderate feminism of NOW.

While one wing of women's liberation did battle with the American culture industry, another fought for autonomy and power within the American left. The bitter break of feminists from radical organizations was only one of the many setbacks and fragmentations that befell the student left in the late 1960s. As these splintered groups and interests attempt to rebuild American socialism in the 1970s, feminists stand uneasily to the side, clinging to their hard-won independence while deliberating about strategic alliances with other radicals or returning to organizations whose leadership is male. Left-wing feminism has been both enriched and complicated by the rejuvenation of Marxist theory, whose doctrines, which were not designed with the sexual division of labor clearly in mind, have occasioned the proposition that the women's movement is a petty bourgeois distraction from the struggles of the proletariat. Practice as well as theory was at stake in the feminist-socialist debates, as such programs as the Equal Rights Amendment, trade union organizing, and domestic reform all came under questioning. These debates pivot around one basic agreement, however: that sex roles must be related to larger social parameters and the hoped-for future of woman is irrevocably tied to the dialectics of history. By challenging the hegemony of capitalism as it encroaches from economic relations to social decisions and into private lives, the feminist-socialists secure a vantage point from which to assault all the serpentine snares of sexism.

Consequently, the feminist of the 1970s confronts American society with a substantially more sophisticated theory and broader programs than her foremothers. As early as 1966 the British new leftist Juliet Mitchell had assaulted the poverty of previous Marxist writing regarding the all-important social-historical category of sex. Mitchell's seminal article and subsequent book, *Woman's Estate,* dissected the structure and delineated the functions of womanhood and formulated a strategy for redistributing the onerous duties of the second sex. The publication in 1971 of Shulamith Firestone's *The Dialectic of Sex* molded social theory, history and psychology into a provocative treatise on sex and society. With a daring thrust, Firestone shattered a variety of icons, including romantic love, maternity, and childhood, and illuminated more Utopian goals for a socialist-feminist revolution. Both Mitchell and Firestone, whose writings served as a take-off point for further critical analysis of the feminist left, displayed acute awareness of the societal uses of sex roles and total freedom from the mystique of motherhood and domesticity.

This creative debate continued through 1974, infused with Marxist analysis, enlivened by provocative European feminists such as Mariarosa Dalla Costa and Selma James, and painstakingly elaborated in the American radical press. Prompted by feminists, socialist theorists began at last to seriously examine the basic dichotomy of modern society between public and private life, man's world and woman's place. Such clarity regarding the social roots of sexism is duplicated on the level of cultural analysis by the pristine feminist cry for an androgynous humanity. Caro-

lyn Heilbrun has devoted a volume to this ideal, which has been poign-
antly described by Barbara Deming: "I think the world has been split in
half for much too long—between masculine and feminine. . . . And I
would like to argue that perhaps our most crucial task at this point of
history—a task for women and men—is not to celebrate these so-called
differences between our natures but to question boldly, by word and act,
whether they properly exist at all, or whether they do not violently distort us, whether they do not split our common humanity."[45]

The stubborn, poisonous haze of sexual differences, the omnipresent
assumption that the soul of humankind must be divided into male and
female, showed most hopeful signs of clearing by the 1970s. But the task
of mediating between the enlightened consciousness of a few men and
women and the murky confusion of contemporary culture seemed more
arduous than ever. The anti-feminist backlash was under way in every
quarter, among fearful men and timid women. In 1973 the anti-feminists
took the offensive, represented by such audacious spokesmen as Stephen
Goldberg, whose *The Inevitability of Patriarchy* defended the sexual
status quo with extraordinary snideness and a minimum of the analytic
intelligence which he claimed was a feature of maleness. The reflex reaction to feminism was at times almost inane. Such was George Gilder's
jeremiad *Sexual Suicide*. Gilder invoked the old cliché that "the differences between the sexes are the single most important fact of human
society." Unabashedly, he lumped feminism, gay liberation, sexology, and
pornography together, and declared them suicidal on the grounds of a
hackneyed Freudian theory. To Gilder, the simple reform of equal pay
for equal work portended the annihilation of civilization. "Under such
conditions, the men will bolt and this development, an entirely feasible
one, would probably require the simultaneous emergence of a police state
to supervise the undisciplined men and a child care state to manage the
child. Thus would the costs of sexual equality be passed on to the public
in vastly increased taxes. The present sexual constitution is cheaper."[46]
This bizarre scenario, envisioning suicidal sexual warfare, a police state,
and increased taxes with equal fear and trembling, exposes American
sexism backed up against the wall and jibbering incoherently. Although
the likes of George Gilder do not represent a worthy opposition to feminism, they illustrate the obstinacy of the dogma of gender differences
and signal the fierceness of the continuing battle for sexual equality.

Today's and tomorrow's feminists must contend with more powerful
and less shadowy enemies than the anti-feminist ideologues. They will
face off against a whole economic and social system and a historical
course that may veer in entirely unexpected directions. The position of
woman at present, inhabiting two spheres and performing a dual role,

---

[45] See Juliet Mitchell, *Woman's Estate* (New York, 1972); Shulamith Firestone, *The
Dialectic of Sex* (New York, 1970); Sheila Rowbotham, *Woman's Consciousness
Man's World* (Great Britain, 1973); *Radical American* (July–October, 1973);
Barbara Deming, "Two Perspectives in the Women's Struggle," *Liberation*, June
1973, p. 33.

[46] George Gilder, "Sexual Suicide," *Harpers,* July 1972, pp. 48–49.

gives her a certain advantage. As women become more tightly integrated into all facets of American life, at the nexus of social order in the home and simultaneously central to the economy in the female labor force, their collective power to shape the future course of history expands dramatically. Yet this status remains uncertain and at any point may be jeopardized by the changing demands of the labor market and the precarious predicament of the entire economy. If such a crisis occurs, woman, still the second sex, will be especially vulnerable to the forces of retrenchment and reaction. In any event the strength of women can grow only out of persistent vigilance and solid organization. The fundamental test of feminism in the 1970s, a time that seems to be characterized by cynical capitulation to the blandishments of the status quo, will be to remain steadfast in the fight, to keep criticism alive, and to maintain constant pressure upon every word, act, and institution that conspires to construct a new cage for womankind. No class, race, or constituency can be neglected; every opportunity for alliances, every woman's issue must be utilized. Concerted demands by women for equal economic rewards, beyond what the present beleaguered structure of capitalism can accommodate, pose a particularly menacing threat to the American system at this point in time. Such pressure challenges the obstinate assumption of man's history since the days of Plymouth, that the status and comfort of each and every American is to be determined by a ferocious struggle to obtain a superior portion of the world's goods, then to be hoarded within the male-headed family. The Utopian possibility that a feminist challenge can overtax this system of distributing wealth, with its legacy of inequality and joyless labor, must be kept alive in a multi-faceted and organized battle against the tyranny of manhood and womanhood in America.

The Buffalo Creek Flood:
An Ecological Disaster

KAI T. ERIKSON

America, as a rule, has kept its poverty out of sight. Traditionally, the poor people in the countryside have been isolated in "pockets of poverty," and in cities and towns they have lived "across the tracks." By formal or informal zoning regulations, most American towns and cities have successfully walled off areas of affluent living, blocking the poor from entering the communities of the rich, except, of course, as domestic workers or service personnel.

One of the most powerful and persistent myths in American life has been that of social and economic mobility. The pattern of economic growth in nineteenth-century America, along with the traditional emphasis on hard work, sobriety, and thrift, suggested to most white Americans that any man who was willing to work hard and save his money could get ahead in this society. This idea found popular expression in the rags-to-riches tales of Horatio Alger, and it found powerful spokesmen in such industrialists as Andrew Carnegie and such clergymen as Henry Ward Beecher. In the last quarter of the nineteenth century, a veritable "Gospel of Wealth" was elaborated, taking its cues from the laissez-faire mood of the times and from the doctrine of social Darwinism. According to the new gospel, economic success would inevitably come to those who worked hard and were blessed by God's favor. Thus the rich were the natural aristocracy of the state and should be its leaders. The poor were lazy, dissolute, and clearly not in God's good graces. Though their plight was unfortunate, the deprivation of some individuals was natural within the total scheme of things and ought not to be meddled with by the state.

The historical evidence on the causes of poverty in America tells quite a different story. Indeed, even in periods of rapid economic growth and general prosperity, there have always been barriers to the achievement of economic success in this country. Ethnic, religious, and sex discrimination have undermined the efforts of large groups of Americans to attain a reasonable degree of economic security. Regressive taxation has favored the well-to-do and further op-

pressed the poor. Government aid and protection for certain industries have prevented masses of workers from gaining economic
independence. The rural poor have been consistently neglected by
the state. Yet the myth persists, sustained by rich and poor alike.

After a period of relative prosperity at the close of the Second
World War, poverty in America was "rediscovered," and for the first
time Americans registered alarm. While it was widely known that
many nonwhites were poor, the surprising discovery was that most
of the poor were whites, and many of these of Anglo-Saxon descent.
The white poor were concentrated in rural areas, and huge numbers
of them lived in the mountainous region of the Eastern states,
known as Appalachia. There, in the hollows and on the hillsides of
the mountains that stretch from Pennsylvania to Georgia, tens of
thousands of native-born whites of English, Scottish, and Scots-Irish
ancestry lived in poverty and despair, passed over and forgotten by
the larger society. The realization of the extent of poverty among
whites in this country shocked the mass media of the nation as well
as the federal government and led to a short-lived "war on poverty"
that died aborning in the turmoil of the shooting war in Indochina.

Ironically, the poverty in Appalachia began to be relieved somewhat by the growing energy crisis of the late 1960s and early 1970s.
After having been downgraded as an energy source for several decades, coal was again in demand. New methods of mining, however,
brought increased threats of ecological disaster. And the disaster
struck in the winter of 1972, when an earthen dam broke, and the
flood that followed destroyed an entire valley of settlements.

In the first chapter of his study of the impact of the flood on
the lives of the survivors, Kai T. Erikson, of Yale University, describes the events of the day the dam collapsed; this chapter is reprinted below. The psychological aftermath of the destruction has prevented the people of Buffalo Creek from making a concerted effort to
rebuild their communities. In addition, during the winter of 1976–77
torrential rains and flooding again threatened the hills and hollows of
Appalachia. In the process of removing the coal from the mountains
of Appalachia, much of the human life in the mountains may be lost
as well.

Logan County, West Virginia, lies on the western flank of the Appalachians. Most of its forty-five thousand inhabitants live in the watershed
area of the Guyandotte River, spread along the edges of the river itself

or wedged into the many coves and hollows that open on to it. Geologists call this region a "plateau" because once, when the surface of the earth was younger and the streams that trace through it like a network of veins had not yet done their work, the area formed an upland sloping away from the central crests of the Appalachians. With age, though, the plateau has become lined and wrinkled. The land is made up of sharp mountain ridges slicing high into the air and narrow creek bottoms in the spaces below, looking like creases in the folds of the earth. The slopes are covered with a thin growth of second-stand timber and a heavy mat of underbrush.

The ways of nature have done much to form the raw contours of this land, but men have made a contribution too. The warm greens of the surface world are now streaked with the blacks and grays and rusty reds of the underworld, for the debris from hundreds of mine operations spills down the slopes like ashes from long-dead fires and the walls of the hollows are slashed laterally with strip-mine benches, the oldest of them camouflaged by a layer of brush and the newest of them exposed like long gray scars.

Buffalo Creek is one of those mountain hollows, some seventeen miles in length. At the top of the hollow, where three small forks come together to form the creek itself, the valley floor varies in width from sixty to one hundred yards, barely enough room to accommodate the creek bed, the road, the rail line, and a row or two of houses crouched in the shadow of the slopes. As Buffalo Creek curls its way toward the Guyandotte, however, the flood plain broadens to a width of two hundred yards or more. Some five thousand persons lived on this narrow strip of land in the winter of 1972, stretched along the creek bed in what amounted to a continuous string of villages. The official state map gives names to sixteen of those villages and marks their location along the creek with crisp dots—Kistler, Crown, Accoville, Braeholm, Fanco, Becco, Amherstdale, Robinette, Latrobe, Crites, Stowe, Lundale, Craneco, Lorado, Pardee, and Three Forks or Saunders. But the people of the creek visualize their community as an almost unbroken line of settlement, with heavier clusters of houses here and there and an occasional church or store or post office to mark the center of recognizable towns.

Almost everyone on Buffalo Creek depends for a living on the mining of coal. More than a thousand men are employed in the mines themselves, and virtually everyone else in the hollow either lives off those wages, provides support services of one kind or another, or draws pensions as the result of disability, retirement, or death. The men work in underground mines cut into the mountains above the creek, and now that a certain prosperity has reached the coal fields they can earn wages of thirty or forty or even fifty dollars a shift—a far cry from the days, not so long ago, when men might work for twelve hours in the dim recesses of the ground for two or three dollars' worth of scrip.

Most of the houses on Buffalo Creek were built by the coal companies in the second and third decade of this century, beginning in 1912 when the first spur line was laid up the hollow by the Chesapeake and Ohio Railway. They were hammered together with efficiency and speed, each a duplicate of its neighbor and each as spare as the circumstances permitted. As was generally the case throughout the coal fields, these frame cabins were rented out to incoming miners for a decade or more, and then, when they had earned back their original cost at least once, they were sold off to the people living in them for a clear profit. Houses like these can be found all over the coal fields. Most of them disintegrate into weathered shacks as the boards begin to splinter and the roofs sag and the floors warp and sink on their concrete-block pillars; but some of them are converted into handsome homes as owners invest time and money and pride into the job of putting siding on the outside and paneling on the inside, of shoring up the foundations from underneath and fastening a serviceable roof on top, of adding rooms and installing plumbing and replacing floors and putting in new wiring—making change after change, in short, until a wholly new structure has been built around the shell of the old.

A large number of houses had been renovated in this manner on Buffalo Creek. The percentage of home ownership is difficult to establish reliably, but it compared favorably with far more prosperous areas in other parts of the country and was a source of continuing satisfaction to the people of the hollow.

Buffalo Creek changed measurably over the years. Coal booms came and went and the population fluctuated accordingly, but the grim trend underlying all those momentary shifts is that mechanization of the coal industry has cut deeply into the character of the region. Old residents estimate that the population of Buffalo Creek was once two or even three times larger than was the case in 1972. Many of the people who left the hollow to find employment in other parts of the country were transient to begin with; they had moved in during good times and were ready to leave when the tides of the market shifted elsewhere. Among those who departed, however, were a fair number of lifelong residents and an even more substantial number of young persons who had grown up in the area. Some left because they were reluctant to follow their fathers into the mines (or to marry men who did); others left because opportunities for employment were shrinking with every new piece of machinery brought into the valley. As a result, the people of Buffalo Creek have both lost and gained.

When their children moved away, the people who stayed lost some of the sense of family continuity that meant so much to them. At the same time, though, they took advantage of their gradually thinning ranks to transform the grimy old coal camps into comfortable new neighborhoods. As properties became vacant here and there along the creek, they were bought up by people who remained, the houses torn down "for the wood that was good in them" and the cleared lots used for yards and gardens and a general sense of space.

So the residents of Buffalo Creek were fairly well off in the early days of 1972. Most of the men were employed and earning good wages, and if the hollow did not quite reach the national mean on the conventional indices of wealth, the people nonetheless owned their own houses, paid modest taxes, enjoyed a certain measure of security, and were generally satisfied with their lot. They had survived the crisis of automation and were even beginning to profit from it, and to that extent, at least, they were one of the most affluent groups in an otherwise impoverished region. Most of them had worked their way out of the hardships their parents had known in the old coal camps and the poverty their grand-parents had known in the remote mountains of Appalachia. Looking back, the men and women of Buffalo Creek remember it as a secure, honest, comfortable life.

But all of this came to an abrupt end on February 26, 1972.

Buffalo Creek is formed by three narrow forks meeting at the top of the hollow, each contributing a thin trickle of drainage to the larger flow. The middle of these forks, reasonably enough, is called Middle Fork, and it has served for several years as the site of an enormous pile of mine waste, known by the local residents as a "dam" because it looks and acts like one, but known by spokesmen of the coal company as an "im-poundment" because they have very sound reasons for being embarrassed by the former designation. Whatever its title, the mound of refuse in Middle Fork was there because it solved two important disposal problems for the company.

The first problem is that every time one digs four tons of coal out of the ground, one also digs up a ton or so of "slag," or "gob"—a heavy mixture of mine dust, shale, clay, low-quality coal, and a vast assortment of other impurities. The coal companies of Appalachia have traditionally disposed of these wastes by depositing them wherever the law of gravity and the logic of convenience might suggest, spilling them down the sides of the mountains, piling them at the foot of the slopes, or hauling them away by truck or aerial tram and dumping them into the nearest hollow. The slag itself is as black as the coal from which it is separated. When dry, it is crumbly and crisp like cinders; when wet, it is viscous and slushy, looking like an oily batter of mud. Wet or dry, it contains all manner of combustible materials and may smolder quietly for years on end or even explode in a moment of chemical irritation.

Middle Fork was full of slag. The Buffalo Mining Company, owned by the Pittston Corporation, had begun to deposit its wastes there as early as 1957, and by the winter of 1972 it was dumping about one thousand tons every day, the refuse from five underground mines, two auger mines, and one strip mine. Slag simply clogged up Middle Fork, forming a steaming bank of waste more than two hundred feet deep at the mouth of the fork, averaging six hundred feet in width, and reaching some fifteen hundred feet upstream.[1]

The second disposal problem involves the huge quantities of water it takes to prepare a ton of coal for shipment. The Buffalo Mining Com-pany used more than a half million gallons of water a day to clean the

---

[1] For these and the following figures, see Hearings Before the Subcommittee on Labor of the Committee on Labor and Public Welfare, United States Senate, May 30 and 31, 1972 (Washington, D.C.: U.S. Government Printing Office, 1972); and Report of the Governor's Ad Hoc Commission of Inquiry into the Buffalo Creek Flood and Disaster (Charleston, W.Va.: State of West Virginia, 1972).

four thousand tons of coal it loaded onto railroad cars, and this water, when it had done its work, was black with coal dust and thick with solids. In the old days, the companies solved their disposal problem by pouring this mess into nearby streams, but by the 1960s the coal operators were under a good deal of pressure to retain this water until at least some of the impurities had settled out of it. The companies were beginning to see the virtues of having a regular supply of water on hand anyway, so they responded to these pressures by dumping new refuse on top of the old in such a way as to form barriers behind which the black water could be stored and reused. In theory, at any rate, the water held behind these rough impoundments would gradually become clarified as the solids drifted to the bottom, and the water that managed to seep through those thick walls of slag would be filtered a good deal cleaner in the process.

The first impoundment built by the Buffalo Mining Company was begun in 1960, just a few feet up from the mouth of Middle Fork. It was a modest structure, no more than twenty feet high, and it soon proved inadequate. In 1966, then, another impoundment was formed six hundred feet farther upstream. This structure, too, was scarcely twenty feet high, and by 1968 a third impoundment was under way still another six hundred feet upstream. This new effort soon towered above its predecessors. It was constructed (if that is the word) by the simple procedure of dumping tons of new mine wastes into the back of the settling pond formed by the impoundment below and grading it from time to time with a bulldozer. The only compaction the structure ever experienced was the weight of the bulldozers and the dump trucks that passed across its surface. The dam, then, such as it was, rested on a spongy base of silt and sludge, the deposits from the reservoir of water held by the impoundment below, and it was composed not only of slag but whatever fragments of metal or timber—mine posts, crib blocks, roof bolts, wedges— that had been thrown aside into the refuse pile. At the time of the disaster, the barrier varied from forty-five to sixty feet high as it stretched across the hollow. It was fashioned from nearly a million tons of waste, graded into a huge flat tier 465 feet from side to side and 480 feet from front to back, and it trapped 132 million gallons of black water—a lake some twenty acres in size and forty feet deep at the edge of the impoundment.

And it was still growing in size. Middle Fork had become an immense black trough of slag and silt and water, a steaming sink of waste rearranged in such a way as to create small reservoirs behind the first two impoundments and a gigantic lake behind the third—sitting there, as Harry Caudill put it, "like a pool of gravy in a mound of mashed potato."[2] Each year, 200,000 tons of additional refuse were being dumped onto the impoundment, and each year another 100,000 tons of silt were settling at the bottom of the lake.

The days preceding February 26 were wet days. It was the middle of winter and rain mixed with occasional flurries of snow was to be expected. According to experts, the volume of precipitation was altogether

---

[2] Harry M. Caudill, "Buffalo Creek Aftermath," *Saturday Review*, August 26, 1972, p. 16.

normal for the season, but company officials in charge of the dam were uneasy because the lake of water seemed to be rising dangerously close to the crest. During the night of the twenty-fifth, officials inspected the structure every hour or two, measuring the level of the water by means of a notched stick placed at the edge of the dam, and rumors began to circulate throughout the length of Buffalo Creek that something was very amiss. Residents of the upper half of the hollow, long apprehensive about the mountain of slag looming above their homes, began to move to higher ground. Toward dawn, company officials were concerned enough to order a spillway cut across the surface of the barrier to drain off excess water and relieve some of the pressure. As the level of the water rose, however, and the level of anxiety with it, the company issued no warnings. Indeed, the senior official on the site dismissed two deputy sheriffs who had been called to the scene to aid evacuation in the event of trouble.

A few minutes before 8:00 A.M., an experienced heavy-equipment operator named Denny Gibson inspected the surface of the dam again and was alarmed to find not only that the water was very close to the crest, a fact he already knew, but that the structure itself had suddenly turned soft. "It was real soggy," he told an investigatory commission later, "it was just mush. . . . I had a funny feeling. I just wanted to get off of it." He wheeled his car around, tore down the dirt haul road to the valley floor, and rushed off to his family, honking his horn and yelling warnings at whatever passers-by he happened to encounter on his run home.[3]

At one minute before 8:00, the dam simply collapsed. There is little evidence that water came over the top of the dam, although that remains one of the obvious possibilities. It is a good deal more likely that the whole structure became saturated with moisture, dissolved into something resembling wet paste, and just slumped over on its foundation of silt and sludge. In any event, the entire lake of black water, all 132 million gallons of it, roared through the breach in a matter of seconds. It was already more than water, full of coal dust and other solids, and as it broke through the dam and landed on the banks of refuse below, it scraped up thousands of tons of other materials, the whole being fused into a liquid substance that one engineer simply called a "mud wave" and one witness described as "rolling lava." The wave set off a series of explosions as it drove a channel through the smoldering trough of slag, raising mushroom-shaped clouds high into the air and throwing great spatters of mud three hundred feet up to the haul road where a few men were returning from the mines. The rock and debris dislodged by those explosions were absorbed into the mass too. By now, there were something like a million tons of solid waste caught up in the flow.

All of this took only a minute or two, and then the wave shot out of Middle Fork and landed on the town of Saunders. It was not really a flood, not a straight thrust of water, but a churning maelstrom of liquid and mud and debris, curling around its own center and grinding its way

[3] Testimony of Denny Gibson, Report of the Governor's Ad Hoc Commission, *op. cit.*, Vol. I, p. 189.

relentlessly into Buffalo Creek. As the mass hit the valley floor with a sound that could be heard miles away, it destroyed a power line. The one surviving clock served by that line stopped abruptly at 8:01.

At about that time, a woman who lived in Amherstdale, halfway down the hollow and out of earshot, looked out her window and thought the world seemed strangely quiet. "There was such a cold stillness. There was no words, no dogs, no nothing. It felt like you could reach out and slice the stillness."

But nine miles upstream the carnage had already begun.

I was about a hundred and fifty feet above where the water came out. It was burning there, and when the water hit the fire, it shot right through the air about two hundred feet high, right through the air. There was a lot of dust and black smoke. And when we looked back down there [toward Saunders] and the water was down and the smoke had cleared up, we couldn't see nary a thing, not a living thing, nothing standing.

The wave demolished Saunders entirely. It did not crush the village into mounds of rubble, but carried everything away with it—houses, cars, trailers, a church whose white spire had pointed to the slag pile for years—and scraped the ground as cleanly as if a thousand bulldozers had been at work. At this point, the wall of mud and water was fifteen or twenty feet high when measured from the flood plain and thirty or forty feet high when measured from the creek bed. But it was erratic in its course, pausing for a moment to develop into a great frothing pyramid before plunging ahead toward a new cluster of homes, lashing up one side of the valley and then the other as it turned the corners like a bob-sled in a chute, driving straight toward some helpless target only to change direction in a shower of black foam. The size of the wave, of course, changed a good deal as the mass churned its way toward the Guyandotte. It was a twenty-foot wall at Saunders; it was half that size by the time it reached such midway points as Amherstdale; it was hardly more than a conventional flood when it arrived at towns like Kistler, near the mouth of the creek. But this is to speak of averages, because the leading edge of the wave was renewed again and again as the mass became trapped momentarily behind a bridge clogged with the splintered remains of houses and telephone poles and sections of railroad track and then smashed through that barricade with new life and momentum. Moreover, the course of the water seemed a thing of almost uncanny whim. Clusters of homes on one side of the tracks were swept away altogether while clusters on the other side, lying at precisely the same elevation, were barely splashed.

This water, when it came down through here, it acted real funny. It would go this way on this side of the hill and take a house out, take one house out of all the rows, and then go back the other way. It would just go from one hillside to the other.

No wonder, then, that this writhing mass of water, driving houses before it and bouncing trucks on its crest "like beach balls," making a sound like thunder and belching smoke and sparks as it wrenched power lines apart—no wonder that people would remember it as a living creature.

I cannot explain that water as being water. It looked like a black ocean where the ground had opened up and it was coming in big waves and it was coming in a rolling position. If you had thrown a milk carton out in the river—that's the way the homes went out, like they were nothing. The water seemed like the demon itself. It came, destroyed, and left.

And another witness:

I can still see in my mind the houses floating on the water along with the cars and those gas tanks exploding in a big blast of fire. I'll never forget the loud awful sound of the big substation blowing up and shooting up in the air and crumbling down and over. Then the water hit another row of houses in that narrow valley and it started backing up Toney Fork. I felt as though the water was a thing alive and was coming after us to get us all. I still think of it as a live thing.

There are only a few eyewitness reports on the erratic behavior of the water as it passed through Saunders and upper Pardee for the good reason that most of the people who survived it were not there to see it and most of the people who saw it did not live to tell about it. One young but seasoned miner who ignored warnings to evacuate and barely scrambled up the side of the hill in time remembered:

Well, there was one explosion, and that's when all the water come, and then there was another big explosion and everything come out, just like them houses wasn't nothing, just like bowling pins when you roll a ball against them.

And his fourteen-year-old daughter, frightened and out of breath, described the same scene.

When we got up to the hill I saw all the camp just go, the water took the whole camp. And I saw our house—it just crushed up. And I saw the woman that lived down below us in a trailer, I saw her trailer split right down the middle and just fold back.

As the edge of the flood turned the corner into Pardee, armed now with the entire contents of the town of Saunders, it had lost none of its original ferocity. One eighteen-year-old man, the only survivor of a family of six, caught a brief glimpse of the wave before it carried him off in the bed of a pickup truck.

I looked back and I saw, just around the corner of the barn—nothing but water, that's all. It looked just like coal dirt. It was real black. It was way above the creek banks, I'd say about fifteen feet higher than the ground.

And an older veteran of the mines, alone in his home when the wave suddenly appeared a few feet upstream, could not remember anything that happened to him except that the water, as it struck, "was just as high as my house."

Farther down the hollow, though, the flood was witnessed by hundreds of people, some of whom were caught up in it and some of whom just managed to clamber up the nearby slopes and had to stand there helplessly as the torrent rushed by a few feet below them. Several miles below the site of the dam the water was still an awesome sight. It "towered high as telephone poles," said one witness, looking "like an ocean coming toward us." "To me it looked like it was tipping the sky," said another.

The view from the Lorado and Lundale area, about one-third of the way down the hollow:*

When I looked back, I saw the houses coming. They just looked like toy boats on the water, and they was abusting and hitting against each other and bringing the lines down there. But what scared me out of my mind was that debris up against the bridge going sky high. I went to screaming.

I jumped out of bed and I looked out the door and I couldn't believe it. It was a wall of water and debris. It looked like it was about twenty-five or thirty foot high coming running at us. And it was just black-looking. It was just rumbling and roaring and the houses was popping and snapping and they was breaking up.

I could see all the houses in Lorado just being kicked around like so many toys. I looked down at Lundale and it was completely gone, wiped out.

When I think about the flood, the first thing that hits my mind is the water. It just looked like a black mountain going down that hollow, and there was houses on top of it. A big tank blew up right on top of it, a gas tank from the trailers that was up there. It just blew completely. You could see fire in those houses and everything. There was a big transformer sitting down there close to where the old ball diamond used to be, and it just ripped out and crumbled those big steel beams just like you was twisting them around. And the wires! Electricity was shooting up the mountain, those wires were boing bzzz, bzzz. . . . One mass of ugliness was all it was to me, the water and houses and the gas exploding and the electricity lines buzzing and things like that. Crashing sounds. Everything

---

* Here, as throughout the report, each paragraph represents a different speaker.

was completely out of control, and the sound of it, you know, was just a roar, a heavy roar.

The view from Braeholm, about two-thirds of the way down the hollow:

I could see Amherst Camp up there at the crossing right above me. It looked like the whole town just raised up and started moving down the hollow, just like it was sitting. I seen the first house hit the bridge, then the second, then the third and fourth. And then a mobile home hit those houses where they had done jammed up against the bridge, and I guess the pressure and the impact was rolling under and that mobile home just vanished underneath. I never did see no more of it. There were three women in it. They were standing in a big picture window and their mouths were moving. I gathered they were hollering.

When I looked back, our house had picked up, went over and hit the neighbor's house, and then it came out of there flying. It came down past two houses and then the other houses picked up and followed it. It set down at the railroad trestle. Two more houses came in against it and splinters went everywhere. We had nothing left.

Suddenly I looked up to the bend in the creek. A railroad bridge crossed the creek there, and at the instant I focused my eyes on the bridge I could see the boards were piling up against it and shooting up in the air, as if they were exploding. I began to run home as hard as my body would allow, screaming for my wife to get the children on the hill to safety.

I don't remember getting out of the building, but I remember getting to a tree. I remember hollering for somebody to help me, throw me a rope. They couldn't throw me a rope because they were too far away and they had no rope anyway. There were trailers and cars and logs and ties and everything coming at me. I was knocked down several times, knocked under the water several times by logs and everything. A trailer was coming at me. That's what I was scared of most, afraid it was going to turn over on me. Beyond the tree was where the roughest water was. It was boiling and the waves were bigger than this table, just over and over and over, and I couldn't get across that. No one was going to help me and the water kept rising and I couldn't hardly hold on to that tree. There was so much debris there I seen no way to keep holding on to it, and the force of the water was pretty strong.

And, finally, the view from Kistler, near the mouth of the hollow:

We watched some houses down below there. I seen one house—It was kind of funny. The water hit it and it looked like it went down a little bit and it just—Have you ever pushed a rubber ball down in the

*water and turned it loose? It'll jump up out of the water. When that
house moved, it jumped plumb up like that, like a rubber ball, and down
the creek it went.*

*Well, after I had gotten up on the hill, the water had already cov-
ered most of the entire area. But shortly thereafter, where I was standing,
some of the houses looked as though they were lifted up. They looked
like pieces of a puzzle moving, you know, a little ant farm. This one
would float this way, that one that way. There was no wall of water
where I lived. It was a gradual rise.*

The front edge of the flood knifed out of Middle Fork around 8:00
A.M. and passed through the town of Man, where Buffalo Creek finally
empties into the Guyandotte River, at 10:00. An hour later, the last of
the water was gone. During its seventeen-mile plunge down the hollow,
the flood had moved slowly, almost deliberately, but its awesome forces
were turning and twisting and seething inside the advance wave so that it
pulverized everything caught in its path. The mass had come out of
Middle Fork armed with a million tons of solid wastes, but by the time it
had passed through places like Saunders and Pardee it had added buildings and railroad ties and vehicles and every conceivable kind of projec-
tile to its arsenal. The dark wave that landed on the villages below, then,
was more like a battering ram than a current of water. The edge of the
flood churned down the steeper grades of the upper valley at something
like twelve miles an hour and then slowed to half that velocity as it
reached the lower valley and fanned out over a wider and more even
plain.

During those hours, most of the homes on Buffalo Creek had been
touched in one way or another and a large number of them had been
wholly destroyed. Four thousand of the area's five thousand inhabitants
were homeless.

It is difficult to imagine what the hollow must have looked like in
the days that followed. Photographs offer only a hint. The wreckage of
hundreds of homes and other buildings was strewn all over the landscape,
much of it splintered into unrecognizable mounds of debris, and the entire valley was coated with a thick layer of sludge. Trees that still stood
despite the force of the flood had been stripped of their foliage and the
very contours of the land had been reshaped. Miles of railroad track had
been torn loose from the roadbed and were now twisted around trees or
bent into coils like barbed wire. And scattered somewhere in all this litter
were 125 bodies, hanging from tree limbs, pinned in wreckage, buried
under piles of silt, or washed up limp on the banks of the creek. It took
a long time to recover the bodies. To this day, seven have not been found
at all, and three—young children of identical size—lie in anonymous graves
because they were too badly battered to tell apart. The story is that they
were headless.

When the last of the black water finally melted into the Guyandotte,
an aching silence fell over the hollow. The survivors were huddled to-

gether all over the hillsides, numb with shock, afraid to move. "We were like a litter of puppies," said one, "wet and cold, with no place to go." No one could believe that the worst was really over, and when rumors of a second dam rupture spread up and down the hollow, people accepted the news as if it were somehow inevitable. And as they waited, soft flakes of snow curled into the valley, as if to accentuate the blackness below and to mock their misery.

But soon people began to drift around in slow dazed circles, looking for missing relatives, seeking shelter, picking through the damaged stores for food and blankets and shoes, and trying to comprehend the sheer enormity of what had happened. A man of seventy, himself spared the worst of the flood, tried to convey the futility of that afternoon: "Well, the day of the flood we just milled around to see what we could find. Just drifted around. Nobody knowed what to do or what they was looking for." And a girl of fifteen said afterward:

Everybody was wandering around and asking if you had seen so-and-so, and I never saw a time like it. People would just stop to go to the bathroom right beside the railroad because there wasn't anywhere to go, and dogs that had been washed down and weren't dead were running up to you and they were wet. We walked up to the bridge at Proctor [above Amherstdale] and a bulldozer was starting to clear the debris from the bridge there. The bulldozer picked a little girl up, and when he saw he had her on, he dropped her off because it cut her back and her back was still pink. Her face was tore up so bad they couldn't tell who it was. Then we saw a hand under her, sticking up through the debris.

Bit by bit, in whispers, people heard that a spouse or a child had been washed ashore some distance downstream or that a loved one feared dead was somehow alive and safe, although many of the living bore the marks of death. A combat veteran of Vietnam, having just heard that his wife's whole family had been washed away, was surprised to encounter his father-in-law on the edge of the hillside. "He was in a shape where I could not recognize him, you know. He had to speak before I could recognize the man. He had silt all over his body and he looked like he was half frozen to death, you know. He just looked like a walking piece of dirt."

In the lower part of the valley, where most of the houses were more or less intact, people came down off the hillsides to survey the damage and begin the exhausting job of restoring a little order to their lives. In the upper half of the valley, however, where the devastation had been almost complete, survivors had no choice but to remain on the hillsides, crowding around campfires or wandering disconsolately among the ruins. There were those who could scarcely recall what had happened to them or where they lived, those who muttered vaguely or stared off into the distance with vacant eyes, those who jumped to their feet and started off on desperate errands only to forget what the urgency had been. For the most part, though, it was quiet. As the morning turned to afternoon and the winter light faded early, most people did nothing at all.

There wasn't anything to do but just sit there. We looked out over that dark hollow down there and it just looked so lonesome. It just looked like it was God forsaken. Dark. That was the lonesomest, saddest place that anybody ever looked at.

Within hours a local National Guard unit had sealed off the Buffalo Creek area and begun the difficult job of opening up an access road. Mobile medical units from nearby hospitals moved into the hollow along with Civil Defense helicopters to evacuate the badly injured, while organizations like the Red Cross and the Salvation Army brought in needed supplies and began to prepare the first of what would become 200,000 meals and several million cups of coffee. Local schools were converted into temporary refugee centers, and a makeshift morgue was created in one of them. Bodies wrapped in black plastic bags were brought in on the back of Army trucks and were laid out in rows on the floor so that survivors could file by and claim their own. A number of volunteers from the surrounding countryside found a way through the roadblock into the area, most of them intent on the job of rescue, but some of them—or so the story goes on Buffalo Creek—to root among the wreckage for whatever valuables could be salvaged.

By Sunday, the pace of activity had picked up considerably. Details of the disaster were now being broadcast to the rest of the nation, and the roadblock at Man was crowded with survivors who wanted to get out, newsmen and relatives who wanted to get in, and a constant traffic of rescue teams passing back and forth. President Nixon was reached in Shanghai with brief reports of the disaster, and he responded with expressions of regret and a promise of Federal aid. The Office of Emergency Preparedness authorized $20 million for emergency relief and set up a field office to handle those funds, while the U.S. Army Corps of Engineers moved in with heavy equipment to clear away the mountains of debris. And, in the meantime, rescue teams continued the grim search for bodies, and public health nurses gave typhoid immunizations to everyone in sight.

Organized activity, however, was largely provided by outsiders. Most of the people of Buffalo Creek were still numbed by the savagery of the disaster, still trying to make sense of their shattered world. The first visitors to the hollow, aside from rescue workers called to the scene, were relatives who, made frantic by the early news broadcasts, hurried home to see for themselves. The following account by a twenty-three-year-old native of Buffalo Creek who was visiting in Florida and whose parents and brother lived halfway up the hollow is typical.

Well, it was Saturday morning. I was watching television and we got a flash that a twenty-foot wall of water ripped through Buffalo Creek hollow. I tried to get in touch with my family but the lines were all busy. I tried calling the State Police, but I couldn't get ahold of them. I tried the Red Cross and they did not know any details of it. I kept trying until about twelve or one o'clock. I finally got in touch with the State Police, you know, and I asked exactly where the flood hit. He told me everything in Buffalo Creek was either gone or destroyed. So I went home and packed a couple of shirts and pants and stuff and started coming home, hitchhiking. I arrived on Sunday morning, I don't remember exactly when, and I went over to the high school first. That's where all the people were at. I asked a couple of friends if they'd seen my parents, and they said no. I went over to the hospital and talked to some of the people over there where my mother used to work in the kitchen, and the lady over there thought my mother was in the morgue and my brother and dad were missing. I asked the lady where the morgue would be at and she told me in an old warehouse up there at Proctor. Then I started up Buffalo Creek, but they stopped me at Man and told me I could not go up the creek. I backtracked and went up the side of the mountain and went up the creek on my own. As I was going up through there I realized how bad it was then because I seen people taking bodies out of the creek and laying them beside the road. Right below where I live I seen a friend's house and they had three bodies in front of it. I went on up and finally got to the warehouse in Proctor and started in there and seen all them people there and I couldn't believe it. I turned back and went home to be sure, because I didn't want to go in there half messed up. I didn't really want to go in there and see what I thought I was going to see, I guess. I seen a neighbor of mine and asked him if he'd seen my mother and dad and asked him if they got out of the water. He said he seen them that morning and he said he was pretty sure they got out. So I just sat down and let it all out, you know. I started crying and stuff like that. After about an hour, just setting there, I met them in front of our house as they were coming up from Accoville. . . . We was walking around like everybody else, you know, looking for friends. We got to Amherstdale and they was just taking this young girl out of a bunch of debris. We seen her, and—well—we decided just to come back home. We went back home and went upstairs and stayed in our house. . . . The worst thing about the flood to me was walking across the mountain not knowing if I was going to find my mother in the morgue or find her home safe. And seeing that little girl being drug out of that pile of debris and her blond hair falling back on her shoulders. That's the two things I really think about. And when I dream, that's what I dream about.

Once the dead were lifted out of the wreckage and the injured were taken to hospitals, cleaning up became the big problem. In the upper half of the hollow this meant bulldozing the debris into great mounds so that it could be burned, while homes in precarious condition were marked with huge X's by the State Department of Health and were leveled by the Army Corps of Engineers. In the lower half of the hollow, however, where most of the houses were at least standing, cleaning up meant trying to dispose of an incredible mess.

The water was halfway up my curtains. Everything was full of mud and water. The mud was way up in the wardrobes, and the clothes, they wasn't no good. All the furniture was turned over except the sink and stove and stuff that was hooked up. My living-room floor had torn loose at the end and all my living-room furniture was hanging in the creek.

Everything was wet and black. I went into the bathroom and stepped on a body at the door, so I just got out of there.

Well, there was mud all over the house, no place to sleep. There was mud in the beds, about a foot and a half of it on the floors. And I had all that garbage. It was up over the windows. In the yard I had poles and trees and those big railroad ties from where they had washed out at Becco—furniture, garbage cans, anything that would float in the water. They was all around the house and caught in the fence.

Both of the above speakers were middle-aged women, the first married to a disabled miner and the second widowed and alone. The carnage they were surveying those first hours after the flood would turn out to be their lonely burden.

Eventually, of course, the debris was cleared away from houses like these, the muck hauled away, the sewerage restored, the walls scrubbed clean, the yards stripped of rubbish so that grass might one day try to force its way through a drying crust of sludge. But a smell still hung in the air more than a year later and the warped boards continued to emit streaks of oily black mud from the deposits that had caked under the floors and between the walls.

When the initial rescue and cleanup operations had been completed, the valley was little more than a long black gash, devastated almost beyond recognition. But most of its inhabitants were still there. A few had left the creek for a time to seek shelter with relatives elsewhere; others were gathering what possessions they had left in order to move away permanently. But the majority found a precarious niche somewhere in the hollow itself and hung on—staying with friends, camping out in the school gymnasium, or trying to make the most of scarred and twisted homes. The most serious recovery problem, then, was finding adequate quarters for the many refugees, scattered as they were all over the territory they had once called home, and it was in response to this emergency that the most important outside agency of all moved into Buffalo Creek.

This was the U.S. Department of Housing and Urban Development. HUD went to work providing mobile homes for everyone without accommodations of their own, placing most of them on vacant lots in the general vicinity of Buffalo Creek and permitting them to be occupied rent-free for a year. The idea itself was sound in principle and the agency did a remarkable job of administering it. Within a short span of time HUD had established thirteen trailer camps, supplied almost seven hundred mobile homes, and found shelter for close to twenty-five hundred persons, half the original population of Buffalo Creek. Yet the long-range costs of this program turned out to be a good deal higher than anyone had anticipated. HUD assigned applicants to vacant spaces on a first-come, first-served basis, the theory being that people should be moved under a secure roof as soon as possible. The net result of this procedure, however, was to take a community of people who were already scattered all over the hollow, already torn out of familiar neighborhoods, and make that condition virtually permanent. Most of the survivors found themselves living among relative strangers a good distance from their original homes, and although they continued to be within commuting range of old friends and churches and stores, they felt alien and alone. In effect, then, the camps served to stabilize one of the worst forms of disorganization resulting from the disaster by catching people in a moment of extreme dislocation and freezing them there in a kind of holding pattern.

There were other complications, too, and we'll come to them later. But for more than two years, Buffalo Creek lay in a kind of suspension, unable to forget the dark torments of the past and unable to plan a brighter future. "You know what it's like?" said one survivor. "It's like you were watching the best movie ever made and it stops for a commercial or something like that. And the commercial just goes on and on and on . . ."

So most of the survivors remained on or near Buffalo Creek. But they were a very long way from home.

Visible Man: Twenty Years after *Brown* v. *Board of Education*

RICHARD KLUGER

The American social upheaval of the past two decades began on a Monday in May, 1954, when the Supreme Court ruled unanimously that racial segregation in public schools was unconstitutional. To those who had been watching closely, the decision did not come as a complete surprise (though the unanimity of the Court did). As early as 1915 the Court, under the aggressive legal prodding of the National Association for the Advancement of Colored People (NAACP), had ruled against the continued use of the grandfather clause as a device to prevent blacks from voting. For the next four decades the NAACP, forcing issue after issue through the cumbersome judicial appeal system, had received from the Supreme Court a series of victories that extended the equal protection of the laws to Afro-Americans in increasingly significant ways. Only those who were blinded by bigotry were unable to see where the Court's decisions would inexorably lead. The only question was how soon.

Among most Americans the decisions of the Supreme Court had usually been seen as arcane and largely irrelevant legal maneuvers affecting only a few small special interest groups. The school desegregation decision, however, burst like a bombshell in the midst of time-honored tradition and threatened what portions of the nation saw as institutions necessary for cultural survival. Suddenly the Supreme Court, under the activist leadership of Chief Justice Earl Warren, began to affect the lives of millions of Americans who had previously been only marginally aware of its existence. For the first time in over seventy-five years, an agency of the federal government could be counted on to seek the extension of the rights of the Fourteenth Amendment to all Americans. What some have called the Second Reconstruction began.

But as shown during the first Reconstruction, establishing law is one thing; achieving enforcement is quite another. Increasing black militancy in the face of massive white resistance led to fifteen years of confrontation and violence. The intransigence of many white Southern politicians, the development of the nonviolent civil rights movement, the emergence of such dynamic black leaders as Martin Luther King, Jr. and Malcolm X (both later murdered under curious circumstances), and the violent eruptions of black ghettoes made the headlines and occupied the attention of the nation during these years. All during this time, however, the NAACP successfully continued its appeals to the Supreme Court for a broader establishment of racial justice.

With the election of Richard Nixon to the presidency, the Second Reconstruction began to slow down, and many have concluded that it is over. While this judgment may be accurate, at least as far as governmental activity is concerned, the aftermath is not likely to be as fatal to black ambitions and desires as was the period after 1877. Blacks have become too visible and their political strength potentially too powerful for them to simply fade away into the same kind of oppressive caste system that so blighted their existence between Reconstructions.

The history of the events leading up to the May 17, 1954 decision of the Supreme Court has been exhaustively chronicled by Richard Kluger in his book **Simple Justice.** The concluding pages of that work, reprinted below, attempt to assess the condition of black America two decades after the **Brown** decision. While noting the retrogressive impact of the Nixon appointees to the Supreme Court, Kluger indicates certain positive changes in the racial patterns in American life which seem securely established. He warns, however, of the mounting despair of increasing numbers of urban black youth —unemployed, undereducated, and hopeless. Without massive federal economic intervention and a concerted attempt to establish racial justice in the nation's troubled cities, the future is bleak indeed for those for whom justice delayed continues to be justice denied.

Whatever other crimes history may finally assign to Richard Nixon, he was hopelessly guilty of debasing the Queen's English. It was not that he was especially ungrammatical, but that he never uttered a memorable phrase, never rose above the most banal selection of words, and seemed to think the use of slang might somehow endear him to the masses. It was thus the height of eloquence for Nixon during his 1968 campaign for the presidency to assure black America that he thought it was entitled to "a piece of the action."

But it was hard to mistake Richard Nixon for a friend of the colored people. Nothing in his political past suggested that he was concerned with civil rights or the complex racial problems besetting the country. Indeed, he came to the White House on a platform bedecked with cryptic racism. He would end the internal strife in America by restoring "law and order" in the streets. He would name "strict-constructionists" to the Supreme Court to replace the criminal-coddling Justices who thought hoodlums deserved as much protection as their victims. He thought all the mismanaged giveaways of the Great Society had to be curbed and the long-neglected rights of the sovereign states had to be restored.

He meant what he said. His accession to power signaled a crackdown on rebelliousness in all forms. Black rioting fell off sharply. Peace demonstrations declined as well, the more so after bullets fired by National Guardsmen ended the student display at Kent State University in Ohio. But if violence ebbed, hope did, too, in the disadvantaged sectors of the population. Richard Nixon seemed inclined to roll back the gains scored by black America or, at the least, to check them; in the process, he would strengthen his standing in the more conservative cantons of Dixie. This "Southern strategy" worked too well; eventually, the rest of the nation would turn its back on him.

He began by phasing out the anti-poverty programs as rapidly as was feasible. Away with Model Cities and offices of economic opportunity and all such inflationary flotsam. He slashed federal spending for education and school lunches. He talked about a guaranteed annual wage and welfare reform but did not bother pushing Congress for his social legislation the way Lyndon Johnson had. He picked Warren Burger, a moderate conservative, as Chief Justice and then for a second vacancy on the Court nominated two Southern judges, neither of whom was destined to rival Robert E. Lee for flawless character. The first of his Southern choices, while judicially competent, was found to have committed several financial improprieties stemming from cases on which he had sat; the second was found both judicially incompetent and apparently sympathetic to white supremacy. The President settled for Harry Blackmun, a Midwestern judge who was a pale carbon of the Chief Justice. Two years later, he named Lewis Powell, a moderate, upright, and skilled Richmond lawyer,* and William Rehnquist, the bright, very conservative law-and-order Assistant Attorney General, to fill two more vacancies. Gone now were Earl Warren, Hugo Black, Abe Fortas, and John Marshall Harlan—three liberals and a constructive conservative, and four of the ablest men ever to sit on the Court. His four appointees by no means did all the President might have wished, but the spirit of the highly activist, humanitarian Warren Court had departed. The Nixon bloc, voting together more often than any foursome since Harry Truman's sodden appointees, commanded the Court.

It was in the quarter-hearted way the Nixon administration applied the anti-discrimination laws of the Johnson era that its indifference to the

---

* He was a member of the same firm as Justin Moore and Archibald Robertson, who handled the state's case in the original Virginia school-segregation suit, *Davis* v. *County School Board of Prince Edward County.*

claims of black America was perhaps most obviously measurable. A 1974 report by the U.S. Civil Rights Commission, for example, reviewed federal-government enforcement of the 1968 Fair Housing Act and concluded: "Present programs often are administered so as to continue rather than reduce racial segregation." State and local officials were, with impunity, using zoning regulations, building codes, and highway construction to keep out or remove poor and minority-group families from many suburban areas, the commission found. Private real-estate brokers were, with still less fear of federal intrusion, steering buyers to all-white or all-black neighborhoods, and white real-estate boards were widely refusing to admit black brokers, who as a result were denied access to lists of homes for sale.

In school desegregation, the administration's policy was more than Fabian; it became downright obstructionist, and those in the Justice Department and HEW who disagreed with it either left or were purged.

Just how this foot-dragging went on was documented by a report issued in September 1974 by the Center for National Policy Review, an outcropping of the law school at Catholic University of America in Washington. Titled "Justice Delayed and Denied," the 117-page report noted that HEW had begun reviewing cases in Northern and Western communities in earnest in 1968 to see if school-desegregation guidelines were being met; if not and the districts did not remedy the situation, federal funds were to be cut off. In 1968, HEW initiated 28 such community reviews. In 1969, the first Nixon year, the number dropped to 16; in 1970, to 15; in 1971, to 11; in 1972, to 9; in 1973, to one; in 1974, to zero—all at a time when the Office of Civil Rights staff was growing. The average length of an HEW investigation was thirty-two months—before a decision was made whether to advise a district it was in non-compliance. If a district under investigation became the target of private litigation, the HEW investigation was suspended, as if the district should therefore be immune from federal hectoring. HEW also had an odd sense of priorities; it preferred to review small or medium-sized cities involving relatively few Negroes rather than large cities with severe compliance problems affecting tens of thousands of black students.

When an HEW review finally did point to the need for a cutoff of federal funds, the department's Office of the General Counsel sat on the case, sometimes for years, insisting that the evidence be airtight before proceeding with a reprimand and possible punitive measures. So dilatory was Nixon's HEW that in February 1973 a federal District judge had to order the department to begin enforcement proceedings against seventy-four Southern school districts found in non-compliance in 1971 or which had reneged on their desegregation plans, and to commence proceedings against forty-two other Southern districts in probable non-compliance. The Center for National Policy Review concluded its report by declaring "there is little question that the Nixon Administration's negative policy declarations have impaired enforcement action and demoralized the HEW civil rights staff. . . . All of this means that minority citizens face continued disappointment of their legitimate expectations that the federal government will protect their children's rights. This situation could be altered—by a Congress prepared to exercise its oversight responsibilities to assure that its laws are obeyed by the executive branch, by new political leadership committed to the rule of law and ready to appeal to people's aspirations rather than their fears, by federal officials determined to be faithful to their oaths of office. . . ."

The HEW record in desegregation amply demonstrated what the Nixon people meant when they suggested in 1970—in the memorable words of the resident (and solitary) White House intellectual, Daniel Moynihan—that "the time may have come when the issue of race could benefit from a period of benign neglect . . . in which Negro progress continues and racial rhetoric fades." But it was not just neglect that Nixon offered the Negro; it was downright opposition, most notably in an effort to reverse the mandates of the Supreme Court by trying to push a constitutional amendment through Congress prohibiting bussing of schoolchildren to achieve desegregation.

"Bussing" replaced "law-and-order" as the white-backlash code word of the early Seventies. There was, to be sure, a good deal to be said on both sides of the question, though it cannot be said the President did anything to elevate the level of the public discussion; rather, he played to the galleries for all the emotion he could wring from the heated subject. Few whites had objected when, before *Brown*, black children were bussed all over the map to segregated schools far from their homes while white children were generally within easy walking distance of their neighborhood school. Topeka had been a classic example: black children were bussed to the four colored schools in town, usually passing one or more white schools en route; white youngsters attended eighteen schools scattered conveniently around the city and needed no buses. Thus, bussing to maintain segregation had been happily countenanced by white parents, but the prospect of bussing their own youngsters for the purpose of integration produced bared teeth. Why should any child have to forgo a nice white neighborhood school to take an exhausting bus ride to an older school with broken equipment and inexperienced teachers in a black neighborhood? It was well known, moreover, that Negro children had far lower educational standards than whites, who would therefore likely suffer both academic malnutrition and the constant threat of a shakedown at the point of a switchblade.

Blacks, for their part, were also finding fault with bussing; going to a white-majority school was no automatic ticket to paradise. Their white classmates often snubbed them and left them out of extracurricular activities. Their white teachers often assumed they could not handle the intellectual challenge and had them "tracked" into heavily black classes where low academic expectations prevailed. And their white principals were said to be far quicker to charge them with infractions of the rules and seek their expulsion than they were with wayward whites.

The President proclaimed his opposition to "forced integration" by bussing. It was a popular stand with both races. Unfortunately, it placed him in opposition to the Supreme Court, which sanctioned bussing as one of a number of ways that school districts could get on with the long-delayed business of desegregation.

In Earl Warren's last term as Chief Justice, the Court made clear that, whatever it had meant in *Brown II* by ordering the nation's school districts to desegregate "with all deliberate speed," the "deliberate" part of that phrase had about expired. In *Green* v. *County School Board of New Kent County, Virginia,* the Court punctured the "freedom of choice" scheme prevalent in much of the South as an evasive device. Though in theory the open-enrollment system allowed black parents to send their children to schools in white neighborhoods, only about 10 percent of black families exercised that option, even when free transportation was available. The system was flawed because it cast the black child in the role of interloper; almost no whites, moreover, exercised their "freedom of choice" by going to black schools, and so many all-black schools remained until the Court spoke in *Green.* The key to the acceptability of any school-district plan submitted in compliance with the original *Brown* decision was, quite simply, how effectively it was accomplishing desegregation. Freedom-of-choice plans had obviously functioned to perpetuate segregated schools. "The burden on a school board today," said the Court, "is to come forward with a plan that promises realistically to work . . . until it is clear that state-imposed segregation has been completely removed . . . root and branch." The time to come forward with such a plan, said the Justices, was now.

At its next term, the Court was presided over by Richard Nixon's choice to lead it, Warren Earl Burger. The new President was apparently not warm to the drift of the Warren Court's *Green* decision. Things would be different now under Burger. A temperate outlook would be most welcome at a time when the issue was being disputed by what Nixon on September 26, 1969, called "two extreme groups"—namely, "those who want instant integration and those who want segregation forever." A few weeks later, the President learned, to his distress, that his new Chief Justice was among the former group of extremists. Writing a short, blunt opinion for a unanimous Court in *Alexander* v. *Holmes County (Mississippi) Board of Education,* Burger asserted: "Under explicit holdings of this Court, the obligation of every school district is to terminate dual school systems at once and to operate now and hereafter only unitary schools." There was no confusing the timetable of the Court. Fifteen years of deliberate speed were more than enough. Compliance was now required "at once."

In rural areas of the South, where white and black lived interspersed, effective compliance could readily be attained simply by assigning children of both races to the nearest schoolhouse, no matter which color it had previously served. And indeed throughout much of the rural South, including the most virulent white-supremacist country in Mississippi, the process began to be accomplished, and without violence. The Justice Department, while maintaining a very low profile, spread word that it was not eager to press the crown of thorns upon Dixie but the Court's command was unmistakable and a beginning would have to be made everywhere. But in urban areas, where the races lived largely apart, going to the neighborhood school meant remaining in a racially unmixed setting because of *de facto* segregation. Had the Court intended to outlaw schools that were segregated by social conditions as well as by state and local laws? And if so, how could desegregation be accomplished if not by massive bussing, pairing of schools, use of non-contiguous zones, and similar devices that worked against the long-honored concept of the neighborhood school? The Court addressed itself to those questions in 1971.

Charlotte, the biggest city in North Carolina, and surrounding Mecklenburg County made up the most populous school district in the state. In June of 1969, when black litigants began to press for desegregation, only 29 percent of the district was Negro, but two-thirds of the 21,000 colored children in the Charlotte-Mecklenburg district attended schools that were either entirely black or nearly so. An expert appointed by the District Court—after the school district itself offered an inadequate plan—proposed a comprehensive desegregation plan that involved considerable reshuffling of students by pairing schools (e.g., transferring grades one to three at an all-black school to an all-white school and shifting grades four to six from the all-white school to the all-black school), drastic gerrymandering, carving school-attendance zones out of non-contiguous areas, clustering schools, and a considerable amount of bussing, though not a great deal more than the district itself was already practicing. In April of 1971, the Supreme Court, in an opinion again unanimous and again written by Chief Justice Burger, ruled in the case of *Swann* v. *Charlotte-Mecklenburg Board of Education* that, all things being equal, it was desirable to assign pupils to schools nearest their homes, but "all things are not equal in a system that has been deliberately constructed and maintained to enforce racial segregation." It was not enough now for such a community to come forward with a "racially neutral" assignment plan based on existing residential patterns that in themselves had developed around segregated schools in the past, because

> such plans may fail to counteract the continuing effects of past school segregation resulting from discriminatory location of school sites or distortion of school size in order to achieve or maintain an artificial racial separation.

Thus, while every school in every community did not have to reflect the racial composition of the school district as a whole, the district was obliged to undertake as much desegregation as possible; the preservation of neighborhood schools was not sacrosanct. Remedial steps, like some of those proposed in the plan the District Court had approved for Charlotte, might be "administratively awkward, inconvenient and even bizarre in some situations and may impose burdens on some," but that price had to be paid in the interest of eliminating dual school systems. Bussing specifically was approved as a constructive way to attain maximum desegregation, provided it did not place an undue hardship on pupils. Some 40 percent of all schoolchildren in the nation already traveled to school by bus each day, the Court remarked; it could not be said that to achieve desegregation by bussing necessitated a radical departure from custom.

The NAACP Legal Defense Fund, by then under the command of

Jack Greenberg for ten years, moved swiftly to follow up the *Swann* breakthrough by pushing similar cases elsewhere. President Nixon himself moved to circumvent *Swann*. He instructed Justice Department officials to start drafting a constitutional amendment against bussing to nullify the Court's decision. The South, by contrast, obeyed the Court. By the 1972–73 school year, 46.3 percent of the black children in the eleven Southern states were attending schools in which the majority of children were white. No other sector of the nation had achieved anything near that degree of desegregation.

Two years later, the laggard North and West were put on notice by the Court that they, too, had to comply. Outside the South and border states, in 1972–73 only 28.3 percent of Negro children were attending schools where the majority of students were white. Ghettoization in most cities was growing more severe; the largely unused Fair Housing Act of 1968 had made no dent in the pattern, and the white middle-class exodus to suburbia left more and more cities with a lopsided population composed of a slim economic elite, blue-collar whites too poor to move, and an inner core of blacks. In Denver, the situation was less severe than elsewhere, but local officials had plainly rigged the black Park Hill area to confine its residents to heavily black schools and blamed the result on *de facto* segregation. In the Legal Defense Fund-sponsored case of *Keyes* v. *Denver School District No. 1*, the Supreme Court ruled in June of 1973 by a seven-to-one vote (Justice Rehnquist dissenting) that the district could not disclaim responsibility for its policies that served, as effectively as any openly Jim Crow statute might have, to keep 38 percent of the city's Negro school population racially isolated. Among the policies cited were the building of a new school in the heart of the black area instead of on the fringe, gerrymandering student-attendance zones to include blacks and exclude whites from the Park Hill district, establishment of optional zones on the outer edge of the black area so that whites were free to choose their school (almost always the nearest white one), and excessive use of mobile classrooms so that children in crowded black schools would not have to be assigned to available classrooms in white schools. The Court held that "a finding of intentionally segregative school board actions in a meaningful portion of a school system, as in this case, creates a presumption that other segregated schooling within the system is not adventitious." Once partial segregation by design was shown, the burden was on the authorities to show that the entire system was not so infected. As in *Swann*, the Court said that past segregative practices obliged the school district to go well beyond providing a racially neutral assignment plan in the future.

Court-ordered desegregation had now reached beyond the South. The rest of the nation could no longer pretend that so long as it did not have segregation laws on its books, it was exempt from the *Brown* imperative. In 1954, the Court had spoken not against "segregation" but "racial discrimination" in any form that resulted in separate schools.

In his last eighteen months in office, the Nixon Court finally gave the President two school decisions that must have pleased him. In March of

1973, all four Nixon appointees voted together and were joined by Eisenhower holdover Potter Stewart in a five-to-four opinion that headed off a revolution in the funding of public schools in America.

Since the Court had held in *Brown* that state-ordered discrimination resulting in racially separate schools was a denial of equal protection, why wasn't a state-approved disparity in the per-pupil funds spent in that state a similar denial of equal protection? Why, in other words, should a child living in a poor school district be provided with a less costly public education than a child living in a wealthy one? Or to put it yet another way: once a state made school attendance compulsory and required each community within it to operate free public schools, wasn't that state obliged to assure every one of its schoolchildren a public education on equal terms with every other? What else did equal protection of the laws mean if not that? Just these troubling questions were raised in a case coming to the Court from San Antonio, Texas.

Edgewood, a poor section in the heart of San Antonio, had a population 90 percent Mexican-American, 6 percent Negro, and the rest white. Its property-tax rate of $1.05 per each $100 of assessed valuation yielded just $26 for the education of each pupil in the district; to this was added $108 in federal funds and $222 from the state of Texas's so-called Foundation Program (to provide the foundation for at least a minimal public education). That brought the total per-pupil outlay in the Edgewood area to $356. In the Alamo Heights section of San Antonio, the richest part of town, where the population was 18 percent Mexican-American, less than 1 percent black, and the rest white, the prevailing tax rate was 85 cents per $100 of assessed valuation, well under the rate in Edgewood. But the average family's property was worth so much more in Alamo Heights that the local school tax yielded $333 per pupil. To this, the federal government added $36 and the state Foundation Program $225 (slightly *more* than it gave in Edgewood), bringing the per-pupil outlay there to $594. That meant that for every dollar spent to educate a child living in the wealthiest section of San Antonio, only 60 cents was spent on a child living in the ghetto of the same city. Was that equal protection of the laws? Why shouldn't Texas either have supplemented Edgewood's meager property resources or added a good deal less to the Alamo Heights per-pupil kitty?

A sharply divided Court said, in *San Antonio Independent School District* v. *Rodriguez*, that the state was not discriminating in a suspect fashion against any identifiable class. The deprivation permitted by the Texas school-funding method was relative, not absolute. The whole thrust of the state-aid program, moreover, was "affirmative and reformatory" and part of a system that bore a rational relationship to a legitimate state purpose—namely, providing a basic education for every pupil in Texas while encouraging local community participation and control. Besides, asked Justice Powell's lengthy opinion, where would the Court draw the line? If local taxes for local schools were unconstitutional because they provided unequal benefits, would not the same hold true for local police and fire protection, hospitals, and other public health services? It was a good question. To raise it, though, was not to answer it. Lurking unspoken in the background was the profoundly unsettling question of how far government in a capitalist nation dared to venture toward wiping away the advantages of private wealth in order to provide truly equal public services.

Of the dissenting opinions, Justice Thurgood Marshall's was, not surprisingly, the most outspoken. He asserted that "the majority's holding can only be seen as a retreat from our historic commitment to equality of educational opportunity and as unsupportable acquiescence in a system which deprives children in their earliest years of the chance to reach their full potential as citizens." Once a state conferred any right upon its citizens, the Fourteenth Amendment required that "the right must be available to all on equal terms"—that was what *Brown* had said with regard to public education. The Texas system did not narrow the gap between the haves and the have-nots; indeed, it widened it.

Marshall's position failed to carry the Court by but a single vote. The issue, though, appeared almost certain to come before the Justices again. Just a month after the San Antonio case was decided, the New Jersey Supreme Court ruled, in essentially the same kind of case, that the state constitution's requirement of a "thorough and efficient system" of public education for all schoolchildren was not met by a financial system based on a widely varying property-tax base. Property taxes are regressive, said the highest court of New Jersey, and impose financial burdens on poor districts in inverse proportion to the residents' ability to pay them. The court instructed the New Jersey legislature to devise a new and more equitable method of funding public education in the state. By 1975, California and Connecticut were also under state-court orders to restructure their school-funding arrangements, and at least eleven states had passed reform measures aimed at reducing the disparity in per-capita pupil outlays between their wealthiest and poorest municipalities. Thus, the insistence in *Brown* on equal educational opportunity had begun to open up once undreamed-of routes to that goal outside the Fourteenth Amendment. The states themselves were redefining the meaning of equality in citizenship without being leaned upon by the Supreme Court.

Having declined to extend the reach of *Brown* in the San Antonio school-tax case, the Court predictably shrank from a no less revolutionary step in the last school case it was to consider during the Nixon administration. The decision came twenty years and sixty-nine days after *Brown I*—and just a month before Nixon was shamed out of office. It was, in a way, his final gesture of neglect of black America, for the Court's five-man majority again included all four Nixon appointees.

The Charlotte and Denver cases had involved school districts in which Negroes were in a distinct numerical minority. There were plenty of whites in those communities with whom to integrate. But what could or should be done in districts where blacks were in the majority? Detroit was a striking example. A city of broiling racial relations during much of the century, the motor capital was being abandoned by tens of thousands of whites. By 1973, the school population in Motown was 70 percent black. When legal action was launched in 1970 to force greater desegregation, 69 of the city's schools were 90 percent or more white and 133 schools were 90 percent or more black.

Lower courts found that the Detroit school board, like the one in Denver, had adopted or sanctioned policies that intensified segregation. It had not been a simple matter of letting human dynamics operate by themselves. The Detroit Board of Education had created and altered attendance zones and feeder patterns from the elementary to the secondary schools in a way "naturally and predictably perpetuating racial segregation of students." It had bussed Negroes to predominantly black schools "which were beyond or away from closer white schools with available space." It had constructed most new schools in either overwhelmingly all-Negro or all-white neighborhoods so that they opened as predominantly one-race institutions. And it had established optional-attendance areas in neighborhoods in which Negro families had recently begun to settle so that white students were permitted to transfer to predominantly white schools nearer the city limits. Because public education in Michigan was constitutionally defined as a function of the state and because the state board of education exercised superintendency over municipal officials, Detroit Negroes sued Governor William G. Milliken for relief.

In a sweeping opinion, the U.S. District Court for Eastern Michigan held that an adequate system of desegregated schools could not be established within the Detroit school district's geographic limits and that a multi-district metropolitan area plan, mixing 503,000 students, most of them white, in fifty-three suburban school districts(among them, deluxe Grosse Pointe) with Detroit's 276,000 students should be undertaken promptly. The Court of Appeals upheld the decision. Suburban whites, who had fled from the crime-infested city, stormed. They objected that municipal and school-district lines could not be so blithely disregarded and that massive bussing would destroy the basic American concept of neighborhood and community schools. A similar case in Richmond, Virginia, had reached the Supreme Court in 1973 but was left unresolved when the Justices split four-to-four, Justice Powell not participating because he had in the past served as counsel to the Richmond schools. The Detroit case, though, was even more typical of the urban regions across the nation succumbing to the bull's-eye population pattern—a black inner-city core surrounded by rings of mostly white suburbs; America was rushing headlong back to the segregated-school arrangement that had existed in the South before *Brown*. But now the scale was many times vaster: instead of rigidly separate black and white schools within the same community, racially separate whole communities were growing within a single metropolitan area. Was the segregative effect any different? Was the legal principle any different from that in *Brown*?

In *Milliken* v. *Bradley*, a closely divided Supreme Court decided on July 25, 1974, that the broad metropolitan plan integrating inner-city and suburban schoolchildren was not justified. Detroit would have to get as much integration as it could by scrambling, sincerely, its rapidly dwindling white pupil population among the city's blacks—a directive certain to speed the white flight to suburbia. The Court clearly implied that involving the suburban districts in Detroit's segregation problem was punitive to the outlying whites. More troubling, it denied the organic cohesiveness of metropolitan regions and the responsibility of satellites for the problems of the urban core around which they economically and often culturally revolved. Chief Justice Burger's majority opinion said that since no official acts by the suburban school districts had been responsible for or contributed to the discriminatory practices of the Detroit board, the courts were not free to reach across district boundaries to disrupt the deeply rooted tradition of local control of schools.

Such "talismanic invocation of the desirability of local control of education" did not address itself to the root problem, responded Justice White in the most biting and carefully reasoned of the three dissenting opinions.* The Court majority had declined to state why, in ordering remedies in a school-segregation case, courts were obliged to stop at the district line. Nothing in *Brown* or *Swann* imposed such a crippling condition. It was the state, after all, that was commanded by the Fourteenth Amendment not to deny equal protection to its citizens, and racially separate schools, the Court had settled in *Brown*, constituted such a denial. The courts, said White, "must be free to devise workable remedies against the political entity with the effective power to determine local choice"— in this case, the state of Michigan. Municipalities and school districts are not sovereign entities but merely creatures chartered by the state; thus, the state should have been ordered by the Court to fashion an interdistrict remedy that was well within both its power and its constitutional obligation.

Justice Douglas, in his thirty-fifth year on the Court, said sharply that the majority's opinion, coupled with *Rodriguez*, the San Antonio school-tax case decided the year before, "means that there is no violation of the Equal Protection Clause though the schools are segregated by race and though the Black schools are not only 'separate' but 'inferior.' So far as equal protection is concerned we are now in a dramatic retreat from the . . . decision in 1896 that Blacks could be segregated in public facilities provided they received equal treatment." *Rodriguez*, in other words, had approved unequal schools; now, in the Detroit case, the Court was accepting separate ones as well. Between the two decisions, the Negro was worse off than he had been under *Plessy*, Douglas was asserting. The interdistrict plan for desegregating metropolitan Detroit presented "no new principles of law," he added. "Metropolitan treatment of metropolitan problems is commonplace." He cited sewage, water, and energy problems, and might well have added transit (e.g., the Metropolitan Transit Authority of New York).

The man who had successfully led the plaintiffs' case in *Brown* twenty years earlier offered the most memorable words of dissent. In his seventh year on the Court, Justice Thurgood Marshall did not pull his punches. He said that the evidence in the Detroit case "showed that Negro children had been intentionally confined to an expanding core of virtually all-Negro schools immediately surrounded by a receding band

---

* The fourth dissenter, Justice William J. Brennan, did not file an opinion.

of all-white schools. . . . We deal here with the right of all of our children, whatever their race, to an equal start in life. . . . Those children who have been denied that right in the past deserve better than to see fences thrown up to deny them that right in the future. Our nation, I fear, will be ill-served by the Court's refusal to remedy separate and unequal education, for unless our children begin to learn together, there is little hope that our people will ever learn to live together." In his profound unhappiness with the decision, Marshall said that after "twenty years of small, often difficult steps" toward the constitutional ideal of equal justice under law, "the Court today takes a giant step backwards." He concluded:

> Desegregation is not and was never expected to be an easy task. Racial attitudes ingrained in our nation's childhood and adolescence are not quickly thrown aside in its middle years. But just as the inconvenience of some cannot be allowed to stand in the way of the rights of others, so public opposition, no matter how strident, cannot be permitted to divert this Court from the enforcement of the constitutional principles at issue in this case. Today's holding, I fear, is more a reflection of a perceived public mood that we have gone far enough in enforcing the Constitution's guarantee of equal justice than it is the product of neutral principles of law. In the short run, it may seem to be the easier course to allow our great metropolitan areas to be divided up each into two cities —one white, the other black—but it is a course, I predict, our people will ultimately regret. I dissent.

By the mid-Seventies, encouraged by the Court's liberating suburbia of any obligation to share its wealth and classrooms with nearby urban blacks, the white exodus from cities of every size was turning into a full and blatant gallop. The very concept of school integration was thus being severely imperiled by a new generation of massive residential segregation beyond apparent reach of the law.

Thurgood Marshall was at least somewhat justified, then, in his gloom over the Detroit case, but there was other evidence everywhere twenty years after *Brown* that the drive for black equality in America was not abating. Americans more than most people tend to believe that progress must be upward linear, steadily and unbrokenly upward, or it is not progress at all. The conduct of human affairs, though, does not move that way. It runs in cycles and must be viewed from a longer perspective than most of us are capable of—in terms of years and decades and lifetimes. Yet even in the relatively short span since May 17, 1954, a great deal has occurred to raise hope that history may yet judge the United States to have been a humane nation, not a continuously cruel one.

The years since *Brown* have established the federal government as an active participant in the effort to guarantee the equal rights of all citizens. The pace and enthusiasm of that participation have varied a good deal because for twelve of the twenty years since the Court acted, the executive branch of the government has been under the direction of Presidents who have been unsympathetic to the civil-rights cause. If Dwight Eisenhower and Richard Nixon had used the power of the White House to insist that the nation meet its moral obligations to black Americans, racism in the nation might long since have become a fugitive. It is nevertheless in retreat. And if black interests were surely not served by the Supreme Court's important decisions in the San Antonio and Detroit cases, the narrowness of those decisions must be kept in mind. The switch of a single vote would have produced a different and hugely promising result. Other men, appointed by Presidents perhaps more kindly disposed to the earnest petitions of social justice, will one day join the Court.

Black Americans, meanwhile, are no longer merely the wards of the courts. They are voting now in massive numbers everywhere, no less so than whites. If they have been ghettoized, they are at least benefiting by the concentration of elective might. More than 3,000 Negroes held public office across the nation in 1974—767 of them on local school boards, 108 of them as mayors (of, among other cities, Los Angeles, Detroit, and Newark), 17 as members of the United States Congress. In Mississippi, long regarded as the red-hot center of racial bigotry, black voter registration rose from 22,000 in 1964 to 300,000 ten years later—and no one seeking state office there hollers "nigger" any more.

Despite all the bends in the road, school desegregation overall has not retreated. Nearly half the black children in the South in 1974 were attending schools in which a majority of the students were white, and fewer than 10 percent still attended schools without any whites. A four-year study of Southern schools receiving federal desegregation-aid funds showed that by 1974 black male students in high schools had gained half a grade level in their academic standing. Added the U.S. Office of Education report: "Fears that white achievement has suffered because of Southern school desegregation appear to be unfounded." The University of Alabama, where the court-ordered admission of two blacks in 1963 brought the federal-state relationship to the flash point, was enrolling 600 Negroes in 1974, half its powerful football team was black, and Governor Wallace, whose racism had modulated, was on hand to crown the university's 1973 Homecoming Queen, a black woman. In once hatred-contorted Birmingham, instead of bombing black churches, they were listening to the local symphony orchestra inaugurate the city's new multi-million-dollar complex of 3,000-seat concert hall and 800-seat theater. In Jackson, Mississippi, public swimming pools were integrated in the summer of 1975. It was a new South. And across the nation, Negroes in the 25-to-29-year-old age category—those who began school at the time of the *Brown* decision and in its immediate wake—had attended school for 12.4 years on the median; whites in the same age category had attended for 12.7 years. In relative terms, the young black was taking giant steps in education.

Those cultural gains were slowly but steadily being translated into economic progress as well. In earning power, the Negro was still worth only three-fifths as much as a white man in America, but that proportional figure was not indicative of what was happening to individual blacks. Negroes with an education and skills were advancing briskly all along the line, moving into better and higher-paying positions in nearly all job categories. The situation was brightest for younger blacks; those in the 25-to-34-year-old category were earning 80 percent of what whites of the same age did, though they often had to moonlight to do it. Negroes without an education and skills useful to a technologically mature economy were falling farther and farther behind, with scant prospect of catching up. Still, the number of Negroes living at or below the poverty level had dropped from an appalling 56 percent in 1959 to a still intolerable 33 percent by the early Seventies—nothing to celebrate, but strong movement in the right direction. How far Negroes had to go before exerting real economic influence on America was told by another set of numbers. Blacks, comprising 11.3 percent of the American population, owned only 1.2 percent of the business equity and but one-tenth of one percent of the value of all stock holdings in the nation in 1974.

The civil-rights movement itself was fractured and seemingly spent as an identifiable crusade. Instead, individual blacks were stepping forward to claim their rights. A new kind of black leader, more poised and confident, was surfacing, stressing the Negro's economic needs. The NAACP seemed on the brink of being declared as superannuated as the term "colored people"; its high command, after devoted and durable service, was suddenly very old. Yet the fight waged by the NAACP's remarkable offspring, the Legal Defense Fund, moved ahead on all cylinders.

In the first half-dozen years after *Brown*, while the federal government lagged badly in its enforcement efforts, the Legal Defense Fund, Inc., had never faltered in pressing the desegregation drive in countless courtrooms throughout the South. In the Kennedy years and after, alumni of the Fund's *Brown* campaign moved to the federal benches—Robert Carter, Constance Motley, and Jack Weinstein were United States District Court judges in New York; Spottswood Robinson was on the U.S. Court of Appeals for the District of Columbia; William Hastie, though retired, still sat occasionally on the Third Circuit Court of Appeals, of which he had been the chief judge (a post in which he had been succeeded by Collins Seitz, the former chancellor of Delaware), and Thurgood Marshall, of course, sat on the nation's highest court. A new crop of lawyers at the Fund carried on with more energy and success than ever under Jack Greenberg, who in 1974 marked his twenty-fifth year in the organization. Dozens of Fund lawyers and affiliated attorneys were pushing several hundred cases across the nation to widen black rights. In New York, the Fund was charging the state legislature with gerrymandering political districts to deny blacks their fair representation. In Alabama, it was winning the right of black youngsters not to be expelled from schools for alleged misbehavior without a hearing by the board of education. In Washington, it was carrying on six employment-discrimination lawsuits in behalf of 13,000 black steelworkers and challenging the federal government for working out too soft a settlement with the nine big steel companies involved. It had appealed to the Supreme Court for injunctive relief and got turned down in behalf of an Arkansas Negro to whom a leading white real-estate developer refused to sell a home lot.

But it had just won a sweeping federal court order requiring the Georgia Power Company to double its black work force from 9 to 17 percent. In Mississippi, it was following up on a pathbreaking decision by the Fifth Circuit Court of Appeals that the 1,500 black residents of the little town of Shaw (total population: 2,500) were plainly being denied equal protection by the community's failure to provide them with certain municipal services (e.g., 98 percent of the homes fronting on unpaved roads belonged to Negroes, as did 97 percent of those not served by sanitary sewers). Greenberg was preparing to apply the decision to other communities where blacks were being denied public services. And in Philadelphia, William Coleman, then president of the Legal Defense Fund, won settlement of a four-year-old employment-discrimination case he brought in behalf of eighty-eight blacks against the General Electric Company, which agreed to hire one-third more Negro workers at its Philadelphia-area plants.*

Beyond the law, America was beginning to honor black culture and demonstrate genuine admiration for both its outward forms and its animating force. The "Afro" was no longer an outlandish hairdo or frizzy emblem of protest but was understood widely to be a source of pride and an object of beauty. Whites with curly hair were growing their own, and the "soul" handshake was not the exclusive greeting of black brothers. Negro performers and black casts were multiplying in television programming, though they were still placed mostly in comic or crime situations, and every group scene in a commercial had at least a token black. Black performers were dominating the sports world, and black music, language, and style were almost everywhere far more a source of joy and admiration than a target of scorn or denigration. The new Babe Ruth was black, and the nation applauded just the same.

There was, however, no sugarcoating the fearsomely high rate of crime, drug use, and joblessness that hung over the ghettos in unholy trinity. That the three were intimately linked and formed a paralyzing cycle of despair was beginning to be widely recognized in white America. But psychological explanation of black lawlessness was no more sufficient to excuse it than the generations of white oppression that had nurtured it. As black America's economic status improved, its respect for the law was now required to keep pace. Sympathetic liberals were fond of saying that those without rights of their own could hardly be expected to respect the rights of others. But once those rights were won, the black man's obligations as citizen were plain. Equal protection of the law is a two-way street.

The nation as a whole, though, still had a major piece of work in front of it before it could acclaim black equality a reality, whether Negroes chose to exercise it in the form of full membership in integrated communities—a goal reachable only by rigorous enforcement of civil-rights laws by federal, state, and local authorities—or of economically

* Early in 1975, Coleman, one of Thurgood Marshall's closest advisors during the *Brown* litigation, became the second Negro to serve in a presidential Cabinet. Gerald Ford named him Secretary of the Department of Transportation.

healthy black communities whose members prefer, but are not forced, to live apart from whites. Among the nation's most pressing social priorities as it looked toward its third century was the rebuilding of its slums and ghettos, ideally with the muscle and skills of their own underemployed inhabitants. There were signs, despite a depressed national economy, that the rehabilitation of battered black neighborhoods might in fact become America's next great public-works project. In New York late in 1974, as a prominent example, responsible planners unveiled a visionary ten-year blueprint to rebuild Harlem—with more than 50,000 apartments, thousands of new jobs, and two major commercial and retail arteries—at an estimated cost of $6.6 billion. The price of one year of the Vietnam war at its height could yet buy four or five such rebuilt Harlems.

Unless or until the nation decided to put its massive resources at the disposal of black Americans, they were still forced in too many places to cope with spiraling segregation in housing and, with it, education. In New York in the 1974–75 school year, more than half of the state's minority-group pupils were attending "grossly segregated" (more than 90 percent minority-group enrollment) schools, and the State Board of Regents had pointedly disavowed the use of racial enrollment quotas or ratios in judging a school district's compliance with the Supreme Court mandate to integrate as much as possible. In Chicago, twenty years after *Brown*, 259 out of 537 schools had enrollments 90 percent or more black (109 were 90 percent or more white); the number of all-black schools had risen from 128 in 1972 to 144. In Washington, the white abandonment of the city had nearly reached the terminal stage: 96 percent of the public-school children in the nation's capital, site of one of the five desegregation cases decided by the Supreme Court in 1954, were black. Yet black spirit was not broken. "You can have a beautiful lesson without integration," said one Negro principal. "It's just not true that you need whites to have a good school."

In the other four communities where the cases comprising *Brown* arose, the goal of thoroughly integrated schoolhouses had not yet been realized after twenty years. But it was not beyond reach and was no longer a hopeless dream.

In Topeka, Kansas, the former Linda Brown was a divorced working mother living in an integrated housing complex with her two children, who attended a public school that was 35 percent black. More than half of the 1,700 black grade-school students in the city were concentrated in just six of the thirty-four elementary schools in town, four of them 60 percent or more black. Parents of both races were balking at city-wide bussing that could readily accomplish far more thorough desegregation, and a new suit outside of NAACP auspices was in the courts to force the situation.

In Delaware, the residential pattern in the greater Wilmington area had heavily altered and become like that in Detroit. The white withdrawal, the coming of urban renewal, the upheaval wrought by thruways had all contributed to converting the city's population to nearly half black; the schools were about 90 percent black. Pressed by desegregationists, the Delaware legislature had passed a statewide school-redistricting program, but the Wilmington district boundaries had explicitly been retained, thereby locking the city's blacks into nearly all-Negro schools. Louis Redding, the veteran NAACP attorney, was leading a court fight to upset the sweet-and-sour state law and mingle Wilmington's black youngsters with suburban whites.

In Prince Edward County, Virginia, where white intransigence had been so strong that the public schools were closed entirely from 1959 to 1964, most white schoolchildren—about 1,000 of them—were attending the private white academy while 1,728 black youngsters went to the public schools. But the whites were drifting back to the public schools: in 1969, only two dozen of them enrolled in the overwhelmingly black public schools; five years later, the whites numbered 358 and the upward trend was expected to continue.

Only in School District No. 1 in Clarendon County, South Carolina, site of the first of the school-segregation cases to reach the Supreme Court of the United States, had nothing much changed. In August of 1974, twenty years and three months after the Court had crowned with glory the black agrarian revolt he had sparked in his hapless native county, the Reverend Joseph A. DeLaine died of cancer at the age of seventy-six in Charlotte, North Carolina, where he had lived out his old age in exile. In the area of Manning, the Clarendon county seat, where the reverend was born and the population was about evenly divided between black and white, about one out of every three white children in the area was attending one of the public schools, which were three-quarters black. But in the Summerton area, in the school district where Reverend DeLaine had organized the *Briggs* case and paid so dearly for it, the public school system twenty years later had an enrollment of more than 3,000 black youngsters—and just one white child.

Perhaps, as the school district's attorney, Emory Rogers, had intimated to the Supreme Court at the oral argument in 1955, integration would not come to that defiant, time-shrouded end of Clarendon County, South Carolina, until well into the twenty-first century. But to almost everywhere else in America it had already come, and more was due.

Suggestions for Further Reading

Few good surveys of the postwar period are available. But see Eric F. Goldman, *The Crucial Decade—And After: America, 1945–1960** (Knopf, 1960); Howard Zinn, *Postwar America, 1945–1971** (Bobbs-Merrill, 1973); and Godfrey Hodgson, *America in Our Time: From World War II to Nixon—What Happened and Why* (Doubleday, 1976).

For an introduction to some of the groups discussed in this section, see John R. Howard (ed.), *The Awakening Minorities: American Indians, Mexican-Americans, Black Americans and Puerto Ricans** (Aldine, 1970).

The story of the chicano is told in Carey McWilliams, *North from Mexico** (Lippincott, 1949); Manuel P. Servín (ed.), *The Mexican-Americans: An Awakening Minority** (Glencoe, 1970); Leo Grebler, et al., *The Mexican-American People: The Nation's Second Largest Minority* (Free Press, 1970); and Joan Moore with Alfredo Cuellar, *Mexican Americans** (Prentice-Hall, 1970). The contemporary situation of America's chicanos is explored in Julian Samora (ed.), *La Raza: Forgotten Americans** (University of Notre Dame Press, 1966), and in Stan Steiner, *La Raza: The Mexican Americans** (Harper & Row, 1970). Peter Nabokov tells the story of the Alianza in *Tijerina and the Courthouse Raid** (University of New Mexico Press, 1969). See also Richard Gardner, *Grito!: Reies Tijerina and the New Mexico Land Grant War of 1967** (Bobbs-Merrill, 1972). The California grape-pickers' strike led by Cesar Chavez is described in John Gregory Dunne, *Delano** (Farrar, Straus and Giroux, 1967), and in Peter Matthiessen, *Sal Si Puedes: Cesar Chavez and the New American Revolution** (Random House, 1969). On the history of organizing farm labor, see Dick Meister and Anne Loftis, *A Long Time Coming: The Struggle to Unionize America's Farm Workers* (Macmillan, 1977).

For the history of Indian-white relations in the United States, see William T. Hagan, *American Indians** (University of Chicago Press, 1961). Also useful are the collection of documents edited by Wilcomb E. Washburn, *The Indian and the White Man** (Doubleday, 1964) and his *Red Man's Land/White Man's Law: A Study in the Past and Present Status of the American Indian* (Scribner, 1971). Two good introductions to Indian life and culture are Alvin M. Josephy, Jr., *The Indian Heritage of America** (Knopf, 1968), and Peter Farb, *Man's Rise to Civilization as Shown by the Indians of North America from Primeval Times to the Coming of the Industrial State** (Dutton, 1968). The story of the white man's conquest of the Western Indians in the late nineteenth century is told by Dee Brown in *Bury My Heart at Wounded Knee: An Indian History of the American West** (Holt, Rinehart and Winston, 1971).

* Available in paperback edition.

The current revolt among young Indians is described by Stan Steiner in *The New Indians** (Harper & Row, 1968). Vine Deloria, Jr., a Standing Rock Sioux, has challenged American history in *Custer Died for Your Sins: An Indian Manifesto** (Macmillan, 1969). A stimulating symposium on the contemporary Indian is Stuart Levine and Nancy O. Lurie (eds.), *The American Indian Today** (Everett-Edwards, 1968), originally published in the fall 1965 issue of *Mid-Continent American Studies Journal*. See also Howard M. Bahr, et al., *Native Americans Today: Sociological Perspectives** (Harper & Row, 1971). For the background of recent pan-Indian movements, see Hazel Hertzberg, *The Search for an American Indian Identity: Modern Pan-Indian Movements* (Syracuse University Press, 1971). The American Indian Historical Society has published Jeannette Henry (ed.), *The American Indian Reader* (2 vols.; Indian Historian Press, 1972). Three novels that offer perhaps the best means of understanding the cultural conflict faced by American Indians today are Frank Waters, *The Man Who Killed the Deer** (Holt, Rinehart and Winston, 1942); Hal Borland, *When the Legends Die** (Lippincott, 1963); and N. Scott Momaday, *House Made of Dawn** (Harper & Row, 1968).

The current women's liberation movement began with the publication of *The Feminine Mystique** (Norton, 1963), by Betty Friedan. Two works that provide background for the current revival of interest in women's rights are William H. Chafe, *The American Woman: Her Changing Social, Economic and Political Roles, 1920–1970**(Oxford University Press, 1972), and J. Stanley Lemons, *The Woman Citizen: Social Feminism in the 1920's**(University of Illinois Press, 1972). A study that offers a good deal of insight into the problems of women in America is Robert J. Lifton (ed.), *The Woman in America** (Beacon, 1967), first published in the spring 1964 issue of *Daedalus*. Kate Millett's *Sexual Politics** (Doubleday, 1970) is a provocative analysis of the literary sources of male supremacy. Two important collections of essays on male-female relationships are Robin Morgan (ed.), *Sisterhood Is Powerful: An Anthology of Writings from the Women's Liberation Movement** (Random House, 1970), and Betty Roszak and Theodore Roszak (eds.), *Masculine/Feminine: Readings in Sexual Mythology and the Liberation of Women** (Harper & Row, 1969). In *Woman in Sexist Society: Studies in Power and Powerlessness** (Basic Books, 1971), Vivian Gornick and Barbara K. Moran have edited an excellent collection of analytical articles. The current movement for women's liberation is described in detail in Judith Hole and Ellen Levine, *Rebirth of Feminism** (Quadrangle, 1971). Writings from the radical wing of the movement are collected in Anne Koedt, Ellen Levine, and Anita Rapone (eds.), *Radical Feminism** (Quadrangle, 1973). Special problems of women and work are dealt with in Helen Z. Lopata, *Occupation: Housewife** (Oxford University Press, 1971); Louise Kapp Howe, *Pink Collar Workers: Inside the World of Women's Work* (Putnam's, 1977);

and Rosalyn Baxandall, Linda Gordon, and Susan Reverby (eds.), *America's Working Women: A Documentary History—1600 to the Present** (Vintage Books, 1976). A new collection of essays on women's history can be found in Carol Ruth Berkin and Mary Beth Norton (eds.), *The Women of America: Original Essays and Documents** (Houghton-Mifflin, 1978). Two works that provide perspective on the current movement are William H. Chafe, *Women and Equality: Changing Patterns in American Culture* (Oxford University Press, 1977), and Gayle Graham Yates, *What Women Want: The Ideas of the Movement* (Harvard University Press, 1975).

The rediscovery of poverty in postwar America is often attributed to the publication of *The Other America: Poverty in the United States** (Macmillan, 1963), by Michael Harrington. For a description of life in Appalachia, see Harry M. Caudill, *Night Comes to the Cumberlands: A Biography of a Depressed Area** (Little, Brown, 1963) and Jack E. Weller, *Yesterday's People: Life in Contemporary Appalachia** (University of Kentucky Press, 1965). Thomas N. Bethell describes a recent mine disaster in *The Hurricane Creek Massacre** (Harper & Row, 1972). Lauree Shackelford and Bill Weinberg have produced a fascinating oral history of the mountains in *Our Appalachia* (Hill and Wang, 1977). In *The Buffalo Creek Disaster** (Random House, 1977), Gerald M. Stern describes the lawsuit brought by the survivors of the flood against the mining companies.

For the legal background of the *Brown* decision of the Supreme Court, see Jack Greenberg, *Race Relations and American Law* (Columbia University Press, 1959). Anthony Lewis and the editors of the *New York Times* provide a survey of the first ten years of desegregation in *Portrait of a Decade: The Second American Revolution* (Random House, 1964). Opposition to the *Brown* decision is described in Numan V. Bartley, *The Rise of Massive Resistance: Race and Politics in the South during the 1950's* (Louisiana State University Press, 1969). The continuing struggle over school desegregation can be followed in the regular publications of the United States Commission on Civil Rights.

Illustration Credits *(Continued from page ii)*
8–9: The Bettmann Archive, Inc.
104: Culver Pictures, Inc.
105: Brown Brothers.
200–201: The Bettmann Archive, Inc.
274: (top) Roy Zalesky/Black Star. (bottom) Bob Fitch/Black Star.
275: Ginger Chih.

A 8
B 9
C 0
D 1
E 2
F 3
G 4
H 5
I 6
J 7